New Directions in Law and Literature

NEW DIRECTIONS
IN LAW AND LITERATURE

Edited by
Elizabeth S. Anker

and

Bernadette Meyler

UNIVERSITY PRESS

Oxford University Press is a department of the University of Oxford. It furthers
the University's objective of excellence in research, scholarship, and education
by publishing worldwide. Oxford is a registered trade mark of Oxford University
Press in the UK and certain other countries.

Published in the United States of America by Oxford University Press
198 Madison Avenue, New York, NY 10016, United States of America.

CIP data is on file at the Library of Congress
ISBN 978–0–19–045636–8 (hbk.); 978–0–19–045637–5 (pbk.)

9 8 7 6 5 4 3
Paperback printed by Webcom, Inc., Canada
Hardback printed by Bridgeport National Bindery, Inc., United States of America

CONTENTS

Introduction *1*
Elizabeth S. Anker and Bernadette Meyler

PART 1: Genealogies and Futures
1. Minding Previous Steps Taken *33*
   Brook Thomas
2. Who Wouldn't Want to Be a Person? Histories of the Present in Law and Literature *46*
   Caleb Smith
3. From Charisma to Routinization and Beyond: Speculations on the Future of the Study of Law and Literature *59*
   Austin Sarat

PART 2: Methods
4. There's No Such Thing as Interpreting a Text *69*
   Martin Jay Stone
5. Retrospective Prophecies: Legal Narrative Constructions *92*
   Peter Brooks
6. Law's Affective Thickets *109*
   Ravit Reichman
7. Paranoia, Feminism, Law: Reflections on the Possibilities for Queer Legal Studies *123*
   Janet Halley
8. Proof and Probability: Law, Imagination, and the Forms of Things Unknown *144*
   Lorna Hutson
9. Law, Literature, and History: The Love Triangle *160*
   Bernadette Meyler

10. Pictures as Precedents: The Visual Turn and the Status
of Figures in Judgments   *176*
Peter Goodrich

11. Law as Performance: Historical Interpretation, Objects, Lexicons, and
Other Methodological Problems   *193*
Julie Stone Peters

12. Globalizing Law and Literature   *210*
Elizabeth S. Anker

PART 3: Cases

13. Ornament and Law   *229*
Anne Anlin Cheng

14. The Flowers Are Vexed: Gender Justice, Black Literature, and the
Passionate Utterance   *252*
Imani Perry

15. Genocide by Other Means: US Federal Indian Law and Violence
against Native Women in Louise Erdrich's *The Round House*   *264*
Eric Cheyfitz and Shari M. Huhndorf

16. Pluralism, Religion, and Democratic Culture: Nadeem Aslam's *Maps for
Lost Lovers*   *279*
Elliott Visconsi

17. Regulatory Fictions: On Marriage and Countermarriage   *294*
Elizabeth F. Emens

18. Legal and Literary Fictions   *313*
Simon Stern

19. Copyright and Intellectual Property   *327*
Paul K. Saint-Amour

20. Replicant Being: Law and Strange Life in the
Age of Biotechnology   *344*
Priscilla Wald

21. Weak Reparation: Law and Literature Networked   *359*
Wai Chee Dimock

Acknowledgments   *379*
Bibliography   *381*
Contributors   *415*
Index   *423*

Introduction

ELIZABETH S. ANKER AND BERNADETTE MEYLER

The university today is abuzz with talk of interdisciplinarity, including discussion of its virtues and its limits. Law and literature represents one of the most enduring of the many interdisciplines that are now commonplace within the university. It claims a long and storied history, traceable at least to the work of John Wigmore, longtime dean of Northwestern Law School, at the beginning of the twentieth century.[1] In the approximately 100 years since, it has been taken up by some of the academy's most prominent literary critics as well as influential legal scholars and judges. Developments like the legal storytelling movement have shaped received views about both legal interpretation and the everyday operations of law, just as the status of legality and the juridical have frequently been at the forefront of questions within literary theory and criticism. For almost a century, the separate disciplines of law and literature have, in various ways, conspired, sparred, and joined forces.

By many accounts, the 1970s and '80s marked the heyday of law and literature, the era during which it evolved into a full-fledged movement engaging both law and literature faculties. Since law and literature's emergence, scholars have recurrently debated how best to explain and justify the interdisciplinary traffic between the two fields. Especially in its early guises, law and literature was often credited with endowing the study of literary texts with a much-needed real-world, practical focus, especially in the wake of the formalism that characterized the New Criticism. Conversely, the interdiscipline was seen as humanizing law, returning overly utilitarian or legal realist modes of legal study to their humanistic, ethically minded origins. Yet virtually since its institutional founding, law and literature has inspired contention and dissent. The discipline's death knell has often been sounded; indeed, almost as soon as it was born in its institutional form, law and literature was diagnosed as dead or dying.[2]

But the reality is far different, as this volume demonstrates: law and literature is currently thriving. In the past decade, the interdiscipline has experienced something of a renaissance. Despite cries of its lagging fortunes, new methodological questions, inquiries, and approaches proliferate. The field is expanding in new geographical and temporal directions, whether to previously understudied regions of the world or to the futuristic scene of science fiction. Just as climate change and spiraling geopolitical conflict tied to the war on terror have introduced unprecedented juridico-political challenges, the internationalization of law and literature has opened up an array of evolving issues, controversies, and debates. And while some critics gaze into the horizon of looming socio-environmental threats, historical approaches to law and literature have also flourished, demonstrating the deep connections among law, sovereignty, and early modern drama, as well as the imbrication of the Victorian novel with nineteenth-century legal culture and writing.

Meanwhile, innovations in literary criticism and theory have engendered fresh methodological grounds for conjoining literature with law. With those new methodologies have come new rationales for interdisciplinarity, as well as new accounts of the law and literature nexus. The time is therefore ripe for a reevaluation both of the nature of the interdisciplinary encounter and of what scholars and students alike can gain from it.

It is in the midst of an abundantly fertile, generative episode in the story of law and literature, then, that this Introduction and volume set out to assess recent developments within the field. We aim to make sense of where law and literature has been; where it is now; where it might be heading; and what we consider its most urgent challenges and questions, questions that the chapters in this volume take up.

THE INSTITUTIONAL SETTING

One might be tempted to cynically attribute recent enthusiasm for law and literature to troubling institutional, professional, and other factors. It is increasingly hard to dispute the view that the golden age of the modern university is ending, if not already over. Shrinking job markets, budget cuts, and other forms of belt tightening have placed heightened pressures on many academic fields, including practice-oriented disciplines like law. While the long-term consequences of these changes are impossible to predict, by some accounts they have rendered interdisciplinary expertise and other forms of "credential inflation" newly attractive, whether to hiring committees or exacting administrators. In this climate, there is furthermore little doubt that the humanities face the greatest threat, and humanists have not surprisingly voiced some of the loudest and most embittered complaints about what is often deemed the "corporate" or "neoliberal" university. As skeptics argue, calls for interdisciplinarity risk becoming instrumentalizing moves that forebode the obsolescence or marginalization of specialized knowledge and disciplinary autonomy.[3] Doomsaying over the future of the university has thus fanned mistrust of the very kinds of interdisciplinarity embodied in law and literature.

This volume, however, adopts a very different attitude toward the recent flowering of interdisciplinary activity. Regardless of the current institutional crisis, the present moment can also be characterized as a time of widespread methodological rethinking and rejuvenation. Precisely such a burgeoning of innovative ideas, theories, and approaches within law and literature is what this volume aims to tackle.

Within literary studies, established ways of "doing theory" and interpreting texts have come under reexamination in recent years. Many core intellectual positions and premises—whether the antinormativity bias, constructivist theses about the subject, the overriding value of negative critique, or the linguistic turn—are increasingly being displaced. As critics newly evaluate those orthodoxies, some have devised emergent theoretical paradigms and alternate frameworks for interpreting texts.[4] Those novel approaches—including, among others, actor-network theory, performance studies, affect theory, distant reading, and attention to the reparative aspects of theory—inform a number of the chapters in this volume. It is not accidental that many of those inventive perspectives within literary studies were catalyzed by interdisciplinary encounters, whether involving Bruno Latour's work on the history of science, theater and the visual arts, or anthropologies of law in the postcolony and global South. If anything, the current fashion of relatively new conjunctions like "science and literature" and "the digital humanities" risks eclipsing the longer, more complex history and influence of a longstanding interdiscipline like law and literature. Yet most importantly, what some decry as a mounting backlash against critical theory in language and literature departments not only has inspired pioneering new insights and analytics but also has been productively incited by interdisciplinarity from the beginning.

Meanwhile, the legal academy has experienced a rising tide of professors hired with joint degrees, which reached a highwater mark with 68 percent of entry-level hires at top schools from 2013 to 2015 holding JDs/PhDs. This trend heralds more than the prestige or influence of interdisciplinarity within law; it also marks a growing disciplinary specialization within legal scholarship, which had previously tended to conceive itself in more generalist terms.[5] In view of the contracting market for both academic and practice-based jobs in law, this narrowing of expertise might appear ironic. In addition, it stands in contrast to the increasing emphasis by the American Bar Association, state bars, and law schools themselves on experiential learning delivered through vehicles like law school clinics and externships with legal organizations.[6] In a saturated legal market, progressive job scarcity has also motivated repeated media attacks on the structure as well as the goals of legal education, with visible calls for law schools to justify the debt their students incur and to explain away aspects of their curricula that might appear tangentially related to actual legal practice.[7] Here, too, prioritizing multidisciplinary expertise in both hiring and scholarship might appear to contradict those demands.

Although this increasing specialization of the legal professoriate might suggest fertile ground for law and literature scholarship, very few of the PhDs hired in recent years hold degrees in fields related to literature.[8] For legal scholars working within the humanities, degrees in history and philosophy instead dominate, and the vast majority of JDs/PhDs entering the legal academy have been trained in the empirical social sciences.[9] Meanwhile, pressures within legal education have further sidelined law and literature, on both the pedagogical and scholarly fronts. While the growing onus of demonstrating the practical relevance of legal education has jeopardized the existence of law and literature courses, many law and literature scholars seem to have internalized the perceived need to devise skill-based rationales for that intellectual focus. Justifications for law and literature that foreground legal storytelling, rhetoric, or the value of literary analysis to legal writing and argumentation have consequently gained currency, arguably overshadowing and, by extension, demoting other bases for the interdiscipline.

The status of critical theory and continental thought within law schools has often been intertwined with that of law and literature, and that story, too, has largely been one of progressive marginalization. The critical legal studies (CLS) movement, one of law and literature's initial fellow travelers, had largely dissipated by the early 1990s, leaving behind more disparate strands of critical thought pursued by splinter groups or individual legal academics.[10] Although CLS fragmented into a range of subfields including critical race studies, feminist legal studies, and more recently work on settler colonialism, the influence of those approaches has likewise been circumscribed. But if CLS and its offspring receded into the background of legal education and scholarship, recent events promise to newly galvanize leftist, humanities-based forms of critique and to revitalize their role within the study of law. For instance, the rise of the Black Lives Matter movement and corresponding law students' activism have led to renewed calls to offer courses on critical theory and to include critical race studies across law school curricula.[11]

What the foregoing has at times meant is that those scholars with backgrounds in literary study have tended to mask or downplay their reliance on the tools of literary and theoretical analysis, even while they actively employ them. Hence, Jeannie Suk's book *At Home in the Law* reads the figure of the home as a trope to illuminate a range of Supreme Court cases, yet never mentions law and literature.[12] Likewise, Elizabeth Emens has drawn from literary, anthropological, and philosophical sources to envision alternatives to contemporary family arrangements but rarely explicitly invokes law and literature as informing her methodological approach.[13] Others, like Simon Stern, have enlisted varieties of historical analysis derived from literary studies in order to wrestle with the genesis and derivation of specifically legal concepts like copyright.[14] In this way, literary criticism and theory have entered the mainstream of legal scholarship, even though the magnitude and scope of their formative influence can be hard to detect. While often unannounced, the debt to law and literature held by many legal scholars and within multiple areas of legal scholarship is a profound one— a debt that the chapters included in this volume consider.

TAXONOMIES OF LAW AND LITERATURE

In the decades since its inception, law and literature has, with remarkable frequency, prompted two noteworthy and interrelated impulses. First, it has spawned an unusual number of taxonomies: efforts to devise conceptual frameworks for identifying, differentiating, and classifying the various kinds of scholarship that make up the interdiscipline. Critics have asked: Is law and literature scholarship united by shared questions, interests, or commitments? What are the key features that distinguish one basis for analyzing literature alongside law from the next? As an enterprise, is law and literature composed of different variants or genres, and how do those categories meaningfully diverge from and/or intersect with one another? What assumptions about law and literature alike do alternate types of scholarship implicitly marshal? Second, law and literature has met with an exceptional volume of internal objections and critique—critique that has often forecasted the field's obsolescence or even its demise.

These dual impulses tell us a lot about the preoccupations, concerns, and points of friction that have driven the field—as well as the hopes and uncertainties that have colored it. Classification, no doubt, can serve an authorizing or justificatory function; it can shore up bodies of knowledge with legitimacy, intelligibility, and verifiability. One story of the origins of law and literature cites to a sense of mutual lack: to anxieties about the perceived deficiencies and insularities of the two disciplines. The classificatory impulse might seem perfectly geared to quell those anxieties, although it has simultaneously instilled law and literature with a proclivity for often reflexive self-examination. Nonetheless, the sheer profusion of attempts to categorize law and literature over the past two decades invites its own scrutiny—the need to dissect and examine (or, we might say, to taxonomize) the taxonomic impulse. Of multiple delineations of law and literature, four have prevailed, and it is one item of this Introduction's agenda to evaluate them.

One frequent approach to mapping the variants of law and literature has been historical; critics have developed genealogies of law and literature over the years following James Boyd White's landmark 1973 *The Legal Imagination* in order to understand the interdiscipline. A second common angle has been to furnish a typology of the relationship between literary and legal objects, relating literary forms, genres, and structures to particular legal constructs, practices, or innovations. A third approach instead moves between the poles of "similarity" and "difference"; here, scholarship focuses on the extent to which law is viewed as symmetrical or complementary to literature and culture or instead should be contrasted with and opposed to those domains. And finally, a fourth approach emphasizes audience, asking about the relevant audience for and intended benefit from the interdisciplinary encounter. Each approach boasts some merits but also carries with it considerable drawbacks.

Jane Baron (addressing a largely legal audience from the pages of the *Yale Law Journal*) and Julie Stone Peters (speaking primarily to literary scholars in *PMLA*'s section on the profession) both described the early trajectory of the law and literature movement or enterprise as consisting of three principal strands.[15] The first was "humanist" and, in Julie Peters's words, expressed a "commitment to the human as an ethical corrective to the scientific and technocratic visions of law that had dominated most of the twentieth century."[16] Exemplified by the work of Richard Weisberg and James Boyd White, humanist law and literature scholarship often sought to shed light on the imaginative, cultural, and ethical dimensions of law and legal process. Martha Nussbaum's many interventions in the field, with their emphasis on empathy, compassion, and the significance of emotional life to the law, have similarly embodied the investments of humanistic variants of law and literature.[17] The recent turn to human rights within literary study might also be seen as a manifestation of this focus. Nonetheless, for many language and literature scholars working during the prime of postmodern and poststructuralist thought, "humanism" has carried more complicated associations, often signaling what theory foremost sets out to denaturalize and interrogate.

The second, "hermeneutic," strand drew on the interpretive turn within the humanities to study the techniques for meaning making within law.[18] While Ronald Dworkin analogized the common law to a chain novel in which each successive judgment and judge responds to and modifies the course of the plot, others considered the commonalities and distinctions between literary and constitutional interpretation.[19] Finally, what Peters and Baron describe as the third, or "narrative," strand of law and literature emerged in part out of feminist legal studies and critical race theory's efforts to expose the historical subject of Anglo-American law as white, male, straight, and economically entitled. Storytelling by individuals and groups structurally excluded from those privileged categories, it was believed, could remedy the biases and resultant injustices inscribed within the law, expanding the protections of rights and citizenship.[20]

Historicizing accounts of law and literature like Baron's and Peters's, however, tend to leave off around the turn of the millennium, neglecting subsequent developments within law and literature. In addition, these ways of subdividing the interdiscipline, while they capture much, tend to offer a rather partial portrait of the wide spectrum of eclectic methods that have characterized law and literature. Rarely does a given instance of law and literature scholarship fall neatly or tidily into only a single one of the foregoing categories, as they risk muting or discounting the variety, novelty, and excitement of the interdiscipline in its many incarnations.

Another common basis for categorizing the varieties of law and literature scholarship eschews this historical genealogy and instead considers the primary focus of the research—namely, whether its principal object of study involves legal or instead literary texts. For Guyora Binder and Robert Weisberg, there are two principal approaches, "law in" and "law as":

The Law and Literature movement embraces two distinct forms of scholarship. What is often called Law *in* Literature scholarship is a species of conventional literary history and criticism that treats works of imaginative literature that contain legal themes or depict legal practice. . . . Law *as* Literature . . . employs the techniques and principles of literary criticism, theory, and interpretation to better understand the writing, thought, and social practice that constitute legal systems and offer these techniques and principles as tools for reforming those legal systems.[21]

In addition to this dichotomy between "law in" and "law as,"[22] some include a third classification, "law of." "Law of" scholarship typically investigates the dynamics of laws that regulate the production and circulation of literature, whether obscenity laws or copyright restrictions.[23] Work in this vein demonstrates how legal rules both mold and constrain literary creation, just as those rules positively and negatively impact societal views about literature and culture.[24]

Such a classificatory framework helpfully highlights important features of law and literature scholarship that might otherwise go unremarked, asking about a scholar's priorities and the ramifications of that focus. However, these conceptual schemes can tend to circumscribe the complex, multifarious traffic between literature and law, imagining the route connecting the two disciplines to be something of a one- or two-way street. They can likewise presume that any given piece of scholarship will claim a primary audience, whereas much work in law and literature instead strives to intervene equally within both legal and literary studies.

To such ends, others have sought to categorize work in law and literature by asking how the ultimate relationship between the two disciplines is configured. In particular, scholars draw a distinction between assimilating law and literature, understanding those domains to be integrated or overlapping, and holding them apart, emphasizing their differences; indeed, assertions of and disputes about similarity and difference between law and literature as discrete modes of reasoning, thought, and discourse proliferate in law and literature scholarship.[25] This tendency may be connected to what Kenji Yoshino identifies as a divide between particularizing and generalizing conceptions of literature. Drawing on Timothy Reiss's historical account of the term "literature," Yoshino contrasts a "generalizing" view that literature "encompasses all texts of scholarly value or, in its fullest ambit, all texts" with the "particularizing" one that arose in the late seventeenth century and "held that literature was a belletristic discourse, containing 'works having formal beauty and emotional effect.'"[26] Whereas a generalizing perspective might incline a critic to emphasize the resemblances between law and literature, attention to the particularity or singularity of literature would amplify their divergences.

Other competing orientations within literary and especially critical theory over the decades since the emergence of the law and literature movement can help us further grasp such tensions. On the one hand, certain schools of theory have, in varying ways, contended with the larger political, social, and institutional structures—like law—that enable or constrict literary-cultural production and are themselves in turn shaped by cultural artifacts. For some critics, Michel Foucault's mode of genealogy has provided a model for demonstrating how legal and literary developments were forged under the same historical conditions, rendering their dual evolutions enmeshed.[27] Hence Foucault's classic 1975 *Discipline and Punish: The Birth of the Prison*, which charts the evolution of modern philosophies of criminal punishment and their role in the production of disciplinary knowledge, proved formative for innumerable law and literature scholars.[28] Along other lines, Marxist theorists have long insisted on the invariably economic or materialist and hence political or legal aspects of art, literature, and aesthetics. Whereas Walter Benjamin famously called for the Marxist politicization of art in response to both its commercialization and the rise of fascism in mid-century Europe in his 1936 essay "The Work of Art in the Age of Mechanical Reproduction," Fredric Jameson's analysis of the commodification of culture in his seminal *Postmodernism: The Cultural Logic of Late Capitalism* begins with the caution that "as throughout class history, the underside of culture is blood, torture, death, and terror."[29]

On the other hand, alternate schools of theory including poststructuralist thought have often asserted literature's difference or separation from the spheres of politics and law. For example, some deconstructive accounts of ethics have celebrated the singularity or Otherness of literature and "justice" in ways that segregate or oppose them to legal and other institutions. Such variants of thought have reinforced the common view that law and literature not only furnish radically different versions of truth but also represent competing discourses and registers of thought. In fact, literature and art are frequently understood to acquire ethical value through their capacity to disrupt legal regimes—rules, norms, and the status quo—and thereby disclose what those systems of thought exclude or repress.[30] Such accounts of the ethics of literature thus valorize (rather than lament) its opposition to law as precisely what endows aesthetic experience with bearing upon and relevance to social justice. Literature's alterity to law and politics is what allows it to generate insight into law's constitutive failures and negative limits. Theorists have employed various terminologies to elucidate this difference—at times drawing on (and occasionally misappropriating) Jacques Derrida's language of impossibility, incalculability, untranslatability, and aporia.[31] Such a conceptual grammar, for example, is central to both Judith Butler's and Gayatri Spivak's highly influential thought.[32] Within the legal storytelling movement, deconstructive variants of ethics similarly offered one important model for explaining how encounters with narrative literature can expose law's historical crimes and omissions, laying bare those offenses while creating an ethical awareness of law's excluded Others.

The similarity/difference dyad for categorizing law and literature thus concentrates attention on what can seem like important fault lines within law and literature scholarship. And indeed, those contrasting views about the relationship between literature and law are often mirrored not only in conflicting justifications for the interdisciplinary encounter—or arguments about what is gained by bringing literature and law into conversation, whether in research for scholars or pedagogy for students—but also in defenses of the humanities. During an era witnessing increasingly dire threats to most humanities fields, one response has understandably been to buttress conventional arguments for the merits of humanistic inquiry. However, many literary and critical theorists have simultaneously been reluctant to resort to instrumental justifications, framed in strategic, pragmatic, or utilitarian terms.[33] To be sure, this reluctance importantly safeguards the crucial experimental, imaginative, reflective, and creative elements of critical inquiry and humanistic thought, qualities that do meaningfully distinguish the humanities from the sciences and other applied disciplines like law. But there is growing pressure to reassess those common explanations for the value of the humanities, asking whether they have somehow sanctioned or accelerated the humanities' institutional marginalization and diminishing relevance. It is within appraisals of interdisciplinarity, then, that such tensions come into especially high relief. By defining literature as separate or different from law, do we inadvertently enfeeble its ability to serve as an agent of resistance, change, and reform? Or instead, must art and aesthetics remain outside and dissenting from law in order to preserve their oppositional and visionary capacities?

By no means last, law and literature scholarship has also, although less explicitly, been classified according to the audience or audiences it aims to address, as well as its goals for those audiences. These goals have often involved forms of consciousness raising. From the movement's beginnings, one ambition of law and literature has been to reform the souls of legal practitioners, whether by rendering judges and lawyers aware of the emotions that law occludes or by revealing its hidden and disavowed subjects.[34] Such an ambition frequently unites what might otherwise appear to be divergent approaches, aligning, for example, what Peters and Baron differentiate as humanist versus narrative strands of law and literature.

Analogously, some such scholarship sets out to raise questions of justice in a manner salient for not only academics but also students, and accordingly it has proven especially influential in law-and-literature pedagogy. As Ian Ward has noted, law and literature has maintained an educative function since its institutional inception, one that he suggests should become the focus of the field.[35] A central project of many law and literature courses involves cultivating student awareness of the dark undersides and contradictions that haunt certain legal rules and procedures, whether to dramatize the problematically gendered dimensions of witnessing and testimony or how the institution of slavery fashioned the legal constructs of both property and citizenship.

Whereas certain law and literature scholarship tries to affect the attitudes of students, practitioners, or scholars, other research instead presents itself as explicitly engaged in programs of institutional reform, whether those programs are understood to complement or to supersede the goal of individual improvement. For some critics, the very genesis and evolution of certain literary forms and genres—like the novel—demand to be historicized as involving both reformist and consciousness-raising objectives. Hence, intellectual historians have recently connected the eighteenth-century rise of the novel and the modes of sympathy novel reading fosters to advancing awareness of legal and political principles tied to liberty, freedom, and equality.[36] Contemporary literature scholars have similarly documented how twentieth- and twenty-first-century cultural texts can fulfill the function of promoting public sympathy for issues such as human rights or the plight of refugees. For instance, Kay Schaffer and Sidonie Smith's *Human Rights and Narrated Lives: The Ethics of Recognition* studies a series of concrete scenarios in which human rights activism succeeded due to the public circulation and reception of first-hand stories of victimhood and abuse.[37]

Frequently scholars working in this vein have derived concrete inspiration directly from literature to suggest how law and legal norms might be altered.[38] Henry Turner's *The Corporate Commonwealth: Pluralism and Political Fictions in England, 1516–1651* provides one recent example of such an approach; Turner investigates the roots of the fiction of the corporation in early modern England in order to devise socially progressive alternatives to dominant legal definitions of the corporate form today.[39] This kind of work inherits many emphases of critical legal history, including awareness of the mutually constitutive relation of law and its sociopolitical contexts as well as how legal and cultural spheres collaborate in their joint evolutions.[40] While demonstrating law's alliance with politics and society in generating an array of core legal principles, such as sovereignty, contract, and intention, projects in this vein often leverage historical analysis to simultaneously render normative prescriptions aimed at unseating established understandings of law and exposing them as myths. As Brook Thomas explains, works of literature "can help us identify stories about national membership and national values that are only implied by citizenship laws," thereby enabling us to recognize the "civic myths" that underlie our legal cultures.[41] The hope often is that, once the contingent underpinnings of legal doctrines are revealed, better alternatives will become apparent and thus available as resources for institutional reform.

THE CRITIQUES

Over the years, the law and literature enterprise has met with a number of objections, often articulated in the same breath as its various strands are taxonomized. Hence, Jane Baron laments that much scholarship in law and literature takes as a given what law is, endowing law with a stable ontology to which literature can be either connected or juxtaposed.[42] In other words, there has been a tendency to define law in terms of a finite, unchanging, clearly identifiable set of institutions and doctrines, imagining law as a foil or antithesis to the indeterminacy, multiplicity, and heterogeneity of literary expression and experience. Yet as critics like Baron argue, such frameworks not only lead to simplistic, falsified ideas about law but also encourage overly celebratory, idealized portraits of literature.

A related complaint is that law and literature scholarship has often glorified narrative and storytelling as inherently ethical or salvific, failing to attend sufficiently to the potentially distortive effects of narrative within law. Yoshino, for instance, points to the deployment of victim impact statements in criminal sentencing to illustrate such a concern.[43] As these objections suggest, law and literature scholarship has at times imagined that law disproportionately benefits from the interdisciplinary encounter, or that it needs the superior insights of literature as a corrective to its errors and failings—hence, more than literature needs law.

Another way to construe the foregoing concerns is to say that law and literature scholarship as practiced in its first several decades has too often vacillated between the dual poles of what Binder and Weisberg refer to as sentimentalism and skepticism. As discussed above, law and literature scholars have often insisted on the inherently ennobling effects of literature for legal subjects, treating literature as a natural antidote to the many liabilities of law. On the one hand, one might thus be tempted to censure work predicated on notions about the radical Otherness of literature for beholdenness to such sentimentalizing tendencies. On the other hand, purified ideas about literature have often been partner to problematically skeptical, suspicious understandings of law and legality. Either law comes to be construed as inherently biased and corrupt or its negative limits are seen to overshadow its virtues and accomplishments. This instinct to vilify law is manifest in a range of contemporary theory, wherein a frequent premise is that legality and the juridical are effectively synonymous with injustice.[44] But as Binder and Weisberg argue, such expectations can betray "a facile sophistication that mistakes *skepticism* for criticism and dishonors good causes with bad arguments."[45]

This claim that law and literature scholarship suffers from a surfeit of skepticism echoes recent debates within literary and critical theory about the limits of what Rita Felski labels "critique" and what Eve Sedgwick famously termed "paranoid" styles of reading.[46] Indeed, one might say that law and literature has been regulated by its own hermeneutics of suspicion, a phrase coined by Paul Ricoeur. For Ricoeur, suspicious hermeneutics are governed by the onus to demystify, or to reduce "illusions and lies of consciousness."[47] Whereas Ricoeur identified Marx, Freud, and Nietzsche as the three primary architects of this style of analysis, suspicion of law has become—perhaps ironically—a hallmark of much law and literature criticism, leading to the overwhelming presumption that virtually all laws and legalities are invariably constituted through a series of distortions or fabrications of reality that become the critic's responsibility to unmask and denaturalize. This pervasive skepticism about law is, with great frequency, also internally self-directed, or targeted back at the law-and-literature critic through autocritique, a phenomenon Caleb Smith considers in chapter 2 of this volume. But even more centrally, it has generated the presumption that law and its procedures should, first and foremost, be objects of negative misgiving and even condemnation. Conversely, it has created the corresponding (if tacit) suggestion that to avow faith, hope, or belief in the normative or world-making capacities of law is to be somehow naïve or misguided—to be either oneself deluded by law's mystifications or, even worse, an apologist for law's historical crimes. As both Janet Halley and Wai Chee Dimock suggest in their contributions (chapters 7 and 21, respectively), that dominance of suspicion in humanities-based legal scholarship has resulted in what Dimock characterizes as overly "muscular theories" and Halley diagnoses as a tendency to read power and other struggles in terms of Manichean dualisms that elide the nuances and complexities of many legal and social practices. As Sedgwick herself put it, overemphasis on suspicion can have "unintentionally stultifying side effect[s]" that turn paranoid styles of reading into "a mandatory injunction rather than a possibility among other possibilities."[48]

Another problem with much existing law and literature scholarship has been what critics have described as its resolutely Anglo-American compass. As Greta Olson, writing as an American expatriate in Germany, explains, many American law and literature scholars have tended to extrapolate from the particularities of their own legal experiences as though they were universal. At the same time, many European critics have relied too narrowly on the groundwork established within an Anglo-American context.[49] A number of the interdiscipline's core debates, critics thus complain, have been generated with reference to the peculiarities of the Anglo-American legal scene. As such, it is not just a matter of expanding law and literature scholarship to other geographies or to comparative work on the legal systems of the global South. Rather, there is a need to provincialize the field's basic assumptions within a globalized frame.[50] The turn to internationalize law and literature thus promises not only to enlarge the field's ambit but also to challenge some of its entrenched priorities and preconceptions about the scope and nature of law, literature, and their intersections, as Elizabeth Anker argues in chapter 12 of this volume.

Finally, one of the most frequent and trenchant objections to existing configurations of law and literature has questioned the exclusivity of that pairing. For instance, both Austin Sarat and Julie Peters have argued that the field's difficulties stem not from an excess of interdisciplinarity but rather from the fact that it has not been interdisciplinary enough.[51] Hence, Peters concludes her influential essay "The Vanishing Real" by gesturing toward the idea of "law, culture, and the humanities"—the name of a now-prominent conference and association—as having the potential to rescue law and literature alike from their respective errors, which for Peters derive from unproductive efforts to locate the "real" within the contrasting discipline's purview.[52] In a similar vein, Binder and Weisberg have advocated for the need to situate law and literature within a broader conception of culture.[53]

REIMAGINING LAW AND LITERATURE

These critiques, taken in conjunction with the wealth of recent and emerging scholarship in law and literature, suggest that extant taxonomies are insufficient to describe the state of the field today. There are, however, several criteria that any new account of the field must meet. First, it must be capable of registering the vast diversity of excellent scholarship being produced under the rubric of law and literature. Second, such a framework must capture the ever-shifting, mutating, dynamic operations of literature and law alike, both independently and as those fields interact with one another in evolving ways. Third, it must keep in sight the variegated range of methods and techniques that make up the interdiscipline's toolkit. And, by extension, there is a need to pluralize the rationales that have conventionally justified law and literature as an enterprise. Those are the overarching goals that have also informed the organization and content of this volume.

As considered above, established typologies of the interdiscipline tend to produce rather limiting portraits of it, implicitly sidelining, overlooking, or minimizing important scholarship that fails either to display specific attributes or, by extension, to conform to their corresponding classifications. One frequent worry that has been voiced about law and literature over the years is that of lagging or lukewarm interest, as the movement has seemed to proceed in merely episodic, temperamental fits and starts. We might blame the very impulse to taxonomize for, ironically, creating this syndrome that can deplete law and literature of energy—in other words, for causing the field to look far more uniform and prosaic than it actually is. The reigning diagrams for making sense out of the interdiscipline have often seemed to pigeonhole scholarship into exaggerated categories, as different variants of law and literature are imagined to exist in binary or opposing relationships to one another: a critic posits either similarity or difference but not both; approaches law either narratively or hermeneutically; and so on and so forth. But in practice, law and literature criticism is far more ecumenical and heterogeneous than these frameworks conceive. Most law and literature scholars sample from a catholic mix of theories and approaches, merging perspectives and analytics that the field's dominant taxonomies have insisted must be held apart. In consequence, those rigid categories not only will be of minimal use for deciphering the actual tenor and texture of the scholarship they purport to diagnose but also have worked to dampen enthusiasm for law and literature in the very ways their proponents decry. To be sure, simplification might be explained as an inevitable byproduct of the basic effort to taxonomize. *New Directions in Law and Literature*, however, aims to reconceive law and literature in terms that do better justice to its motley, miscellaneous, creative assortment.

The second challenge facing any attempt to craft a typology of current law and literature scholarship is to resist the urge to impose what Baron referred to as a "stable ontology" on either discipline. That is, both law and literature must separately be recognized as the mobile, fertile, fluid, restless phenomena that they are. Yet at times, scholars have defined law, in particular, in terms that deceptively flatten, arrest, or curtail its actual operations. In practice, law and literature alike are active sites of innovation, transformation, and generation, and their boundaries are neither static nor finite nor readily discernable. In fact, the scope and parameters of law as well as literature and culture are perpetually under negotiation. Nor can the dynamism of law and literature easily be separated out from other disciplines and spheres of influence. The lives of literature as well as those of law depend on the capacity to be responsive: to move, to bend, to accommodate, to perceive, to react. Their synergies cannot possibly be comprehensively summed up in a single dyadic or triadic scheme, yet they are the essence of what has rendered law, literature, and their cross-pollinations fruitful, vibrant, and energetic.

In *Forms: Whole, Rhythm, Hierarchy, Network*, Caroline Levine describes the "iterability" of both literary and political forms in terms that can further elucidate these dynamics of law and literature.[54] In the book, Levine questions the tendency of some critics to define literary structures in overly totalizing, monolithic, and unyielding ways. To the contrary, Levine argues, literary and other forms are inherently aleatory, unstable, and composed of internal tensions, even while they endure and are portable in meaningful ways. For Levine, it also makes little sense to think of forms—whether juridico-political or aesthetic—as singular or unitary. Rather, in any given time or context, a multiplicity of forms coexist and vie with one another for authority, entering into collision and contestation. Those collisions are what enable institutional and other forms and structures to mutate, evolve, and undergo transformation over time, a process that Levine explains in terms of their inherent "affordances." Importantly, Levine's description of these mobile interactions constitutive of forms contains within it a model of sociopolitical—and, for our purposes, legal—change, suggesting how the individual can intervene with agency in such processes. Jacques Rancière's insistence on the aesthetic dimensions of politics is here important to Levine, allowing her to examine how "aesthetic and political forms may be nested inside one another, and . . . each is capable of disturbing the other's organizing power."[55] Levine's description of the multiple and heterogeneous forms and formal migrations that together propel literary history and analysis as well as the operations of politics and law thus offers an analytic lens through which to refract the spectrum of working paradigms that have comprised law and literature. Beyond how law and literature alike resist stabilization or pinning down, *Forms* suggests why their multiform interactions will continually mutate and travel. Taking inspiration from Levine's analysis, it makes little sense to speak of a single or comprehensive basis for categorizing law and literature.

Third, it is crucial to recognize that the sporadic, fluctuating liaisons that comprise the interdiscipline are not constant or invariable across either geography or history, as a number of this volume's chapters likewise suggest. It is a truism that law is a situational, problem-solving, practice-based discipline that answers to the specific conflicts that enter its jurisdictional arena. While also forward-looking, its practitioners ultimately employ and perfect the law's rules, techniques, and precedents with reference to the particularity and happenstance of circumstance. It goes without saying that a legal scholar or judge will enlist different precedents and methods of analysis depending on the issue or question at hand, and no single decision, rule, procedure, or mode of reasoning and jurisprudence could possibly tackle or resolve even a small percentage of the full gamut of legal problems and cases. Something similar is true of literary study: it would make little sense to apply the conventions of lyric poetry, for instance, to explicate contemporary science fiction, at least without substantially rearranging one's hermeneutic expectations. So the techniques of literary analysis are also, to a great degree, contingent on the peculiarities of text, form, genre, history, and location.

Fourth, what this all means is that our rationales for combining literature with law must be equally reactive and receptive; they must equally adjust to the accidents they chance to encounter. Insofar as any taxonomy will marshal implicit justifications for law and literature, those reasons must also be attuned to the vagaries of time, place, and context. No single basis or explanation for the interdisciplinary encounter will capture every, or even most, examples of scholarship within the field. This is also to say that method can be a tactical choice, or a strategy for approaching the unique problems, issues, and concerns that present themselves.

THE NEW DIRECTIONS

With these guiding principles in view, it becomes possible to describe a number of new directions that have recently engaged law and literature scholars, as each chapter in this volume traverses one or more of those paths. These new directions are not discrete or capable of being partitioned off from one another but rather include several itineraries tracing intersecting routes. The numerous critiques of the law and literature enterprise have motivated some adjustments of course, requiring critics to shift their goals and expectations for literature as well as law. Perhaps most notably, the pathways forged within the interdiscipline have branched and extended beyond narrow conceptions of either law or literature. Nevertheless, the old roads long shaping law and literature scholarship remain visible and influential, even as they continue to be recharted and reworked.

New Directions falls into three sections. The first, "Genealogies and Futures," accounts for the past, present, and future of law and literature, asking about its histories, its current formations, and its ongoing possibilities. It highlights the continuities but also the breaks characterizing these different stages or episodes within the interdiscipline. The next, "Methods," focuses on the diversity of methodological approaches to law and literature over the years, and it explores both established and more recently developed frameworks. The final section, "Cases," investigates specific questions or sites of analysis to which the methods of law and literature have been applied. Overall, many of the ensuing chapters follow similar paths, just as their inquiries require them to pursue more than one of the new directions this Introduction maps. Among those many avenues traveled by law and literature, five emergent directions have become particularly visible and salient. Those directions include work that is shaped by history and political theory, that questions either the textual basis of law and literature or the hermeneutics of legal texts, that globalizes the field or considers it from a comparative perspective, that seeks to transcend a hermeneutics of suspicion, and that revisits and reinvents the role of the imagination in law and literature.

In recent years, law and literature scholars have often adopted historical approaches, drawing on developments in New Historicism and post–New Historicism within literary studies, as well as the ascendancy of legal history in research about law. Early modern and Victorian studies have been perhaps most heavily influenced by these historiographical developments, as Bernadette Meyler's "Law, Literature, and History: The Love Triangle" (chapter 9) discusses. Scholarship that adopts a historical frame often delves deeply into the mechanisms of the relation between legal and literary institutions, in a sense fulfilling Brook Thomas's call to cross-examine literature and law. For example, Lorna Hutson's *The Invention of Suspicion* both investigates the role of forensic rhetoric in the development of early English drama and situates developments in English neoclassical plotting within the fertile institutional context of the Inns of Court, whose members were simultaneously adapting Latin plays, studying law, and participating in parliamentary politics.[56] Here the relation between law and literature is concretized into particular episodes where techniques from one field are drawn into the other and the intersection of personnel between institutions produces complicated and fascinating results. In chapter 8 of this volume, "Proof and Probability: Law, Imagination, and the Form of Things Unknown," Hutson traces the movement of legal conceptions of human motive or *causa* to the imaginative world of sixteenth-century drama and, ultimately, Shakespeare's plays, which themselves in turn engendered new cultural understandings of human inwardness.

A longer overview of this historical orientation within law and literature is offered by Brook Thomas in chapter 1, "Minding Previous Steps Taken." Revisiting the 1980s, Thomas describes how growing interest in legal rhetoric and continental theory merged with a larger shift in literary studies from formalism toward history to help precipitate the law and literature movement. Turning to contemporary law and literature scholarship in "Who Wouldn't Want to Be a Person? Histories of the Present in Law and Literature" (chapter 2), Caleb Smith relatedly emphasizes the various modes of historicism that inform law and literature. In so doing, Smith in particular demonstrates how historicist work has called into question the category of legal personhood; as he submits, "[L]aw and literature make persons who are neither masterfully self-possessed (autonomous subjects) nor stripped of all agency (socially or civilly dead)."

The histories that gave rise to the interrelated legal constructs of the person, subject, and citizen also feature prominently in several of the other chapters that follow. In "Ornament and Law" (chapter 13), Anne Anlin Cheng investigates the strange role played by bodily adornments and sartorial choices in generating an understanding of legal personhood through examination of the nineteenth-century habeas corpus and immigration case of *Chy Lung v. Freeman* (1875). Focusing instead on the present, Imani Perry's "The Flowers are Vexed: Gender Justice, Black Literature, and the Passionate Utterance" (chapter 14) draws on Colin Dayan's *The Law Is a White Dog* to suggest that "[r]ecognition [as a person] disciplines as it excludes" and "demands a capitulation to the order of the society"; Perry asserts by contrast the need to develop "the alternative grammars and reordering that emerges from embodied truths."

As these explorations of personhood illustrate, political theory has exerted a powerful influence over recent work in law and literature. Among other developments in political theory, the concepts of biopower and sovereignty have commanded increased interest since the publication of Michel Foucault's late seminars and Giorgio Agamben's writings, from his 1995 *Homo Sacer* to the 2005 *State of Exception* and beyond.[57] Debates about biopolitics are central to the two chapters in this volume that address intellectual property law. Paul Saint-Amour's "Copyright and Intellectual Property" (chapter 19) illuminates how "copyright has enacted, over the course of its history . . . the biologization of property" and suggests that scholarship in copyright should enlarge its focus on the individual author to consider the study of populations proposed by Foucault's late work.

Adopting quantitative methods, for Saint-Amour, might further display the mechanisms through which intellectual property establishes the parameters of legal formulations of life. Looking instead to the issues surrounding the patentability of living organisms, Priscilla Wald's chapter 20, "Replicant Being: Law and Strange Life in the Age of Biotechnology," draws on science and technology studies to chart how the 1982 film *Blade Runner* critiques the law's response to scientific advances that altered legal definitions of and ideas about the human.

Wald's attention to the genre of science fiction highlights another characteristic of recent work in law and literature, which has inquired in more detail into the specificity of disparate literary genres while also broadening the range of work conventionally characterized as law and literature. This scholarship has responded to the critiques of law and literature that insist, on the one hand, that it takes the object of law for granted and, on the other, that it conflates a particularizing with a generalizing understanding of literature. One such approach has involved expanding the reference of "literature" beyond the novel or poem to include studies of law and performance or law and the image. These efforts to enlarge the purview of literature likewise challenge conceptions of what law is, showing that examining law through its appearance or performance can alter our understanding of its nature.

Along these lines, in "Law as Performance: Historical Interpretation, Objects, Lexicons, and Other Methodological Problems" (chapter 11), Julie Stone Peters asks what we might learn about law from investigating it not simply through legal texts or literary performances but instead the course of legal events as they have unfolded. While the attempt to reconstruct distant legal occurrences can pose difficulties from a historical vantage point, Peters demonstrates how studying law as performance can enable both historically situated and transhistorical insights into law.

Attending to the visual dimensions of law, Peter Goodrich argues in "Pictures as Precedents: The Visual Turn and the Status of Figures in Judgments" (chapter 10) that courts' increasing reliance on imagery has ushered in new habits of legal reasoning that have not been reckoned with fully. In particular, for Goodrich, the precedential value of pictures and other images should be recognized and understood in a manner that respects the uniqueness of the visual. As both Peters and Goodrich demonstrate, the object called "law" is constituted differently when examined in light of either its scopic or its performance-based aspects, as opposed to its strictly doctrinal and textual elements.

Legal hermeneutics, a methodological approach that typically concentrates on legal texts, has displayed interest in recent years both in the distinctiveness of legal as opposed to other styles of interpretation and in the variety of techniques for analyzing law. Martin Jay Stone's "There's No Such Thing as Interpreting a Text" (chapter 4) hence resists the prospect that a single thing called "interpretation" can elucidate the operations of both literature and law. He argues instead that "one always interprets for a reason," and that different reasons distinguish not only literary and legal analysis but also varying types of legal interpretation. Hence, authorial intention might be irrelevant in some legal contexts but matter for analyzing legislation, since the legitimacy of statutes' applications is predicated on the notion that the appropriate body intentionally passed the relevant laws.

Seizing more on parallels connecting literary with legal texts, Peter Brooks's "Retrospective Prophecies: Legal Narrative Constructions" (chapter 5) evaluates the various techniques that literary criticism brings to law and legal scholarship. Brooks wrestles in particular with the role of narrative in legal decision making, as well as its frequent disavowal by legal practitioners. For Brooks, the law therefore needs a narratology, and his chapter demonstrates how such a narratology can illuminate the narrative structure of the Fourth Amendment doctrine of "inevitable discovery," which "involve[s] a 'retrospective prophecy,' a construction of the story of the past by way of its outcome."[58]

Another related basis for conceiving the often unacknowledged literary or fictional components of law and legal texts can be found in recent work on legal fictions, which for Annelise Riles "bring to light . . . the technical source of law's agentive power."[59] In his "Legal and Literary Fictions" (chapter 18), Simon Stern analyzes the resemblances between legal fictions and literary fictions. Whereas some scholars locate the power of legal fictions like corporate personhood and civil death in their narrative structure, for Stern legal fictions instead should be explained by their peculiar ability to engross and maintain attention.

Taking another new direction, much recent law and literature scholarship has expanded to a global or international arena. Whereas some such work enlists a comparative perspective to analyze the laws of different domestic nations or regions alongside one another, other critics have contended with the role of law in the intertwined institutions of slavery, empire, and settler colonialism—both from a historical viewpoint and with reference to neo-imperial practices continuing into the present. Much scholarship within this vein employs literature as a mechanism for critiquing the racialized, gendered, and other violence that underwrites different legal institutions and practices, as in Caleb Smith's discussion of legal personhood in American law and literature and Imani Perry's examination of the passionate utterance. In "Genocide by Other Means" (chapter 15), Eric Cheyfitz and Shari M. Huhndorf likewise confront the ways that federal Indian law has historically served as an instrument of both oppression and colonial expansion. Their chapter understands Louise Erdrich's award-winning novel *The Round House* as both an attempt to reckon with the legal and political disempowerment of Native American tribes and a defense of tribal law as the sole path to justice in a settler colonial context.[60]

Just as Cheyfitz and Huhndorf demonstrate why federal Indian law is a product of settler colonialism in the Americas, other law and litera-ture scholars have shed light on the imperial or colonial designs of other legal institutions and constructs, whether in local or global settings. For instance, scholars of international human rights have shown how rights discourses and principles remain haunted by the long history of empire.[61] Importantly, scholarship on law, literature, and religion has ventured anal-ogous critiques of secularism as a legal regime. Just as recent work reani-mates questions that critical legal studies scholars earlier raised about the nature, scope, and desirability of rights, debates about the status of the veil contemplate the extent to which rights principles should protect individ-ual choices tied to self-presentation or attire.[62] As Cheng's chapter about immigration suggests, scholarly disputes over the veil erode many of the clear-cut distinctions on which law often relies, whether between surface and depth or public and private. In "Pluralism, Religion, and Democratic Culture" (chapter 16), Elliott Visconsi extends these debates through a reading of British-Pakistani novelist Nadeem Aslam's *Maps for Lost Lovers*, a novel that grapples with shifting legal protections for religious free expression in Europe under the jurisprudence of the European Court of Human Rights. As Visconsi maintains, Aslam's novel addresses the failures of democratic pluralism within an incompletely secularized polity, even while it imagines viable alternative routes to sociopolitical change.

Some law and literature critics have lately responded to Binder and Weisberg's charge of an excessive skepticism about law, while simultane-ously taking cues from efforts to move beyond or rethink the influence of negative critique and hermeneutic suspicion under way in literary circles. Elizabeth Anker's "Globalizing Law and Literature" (chapter 12) appraises the growing orientation toward the global South within law and literature from such an angle, asking why law and literature critics working within postcolonial studies have frequently envisioned law as the oppressing force and literature as the liberator. As Anker argues, through a reading of Nuruddin Farah's novel *Gifts*, the multiple and crosscutting sovereignties and legalities that comprise "law" within the postcolony "suggest an alter-nate framework for explaining the law-and-literature nexus in the midst of intensifying globalization" that, moreover, challenges assumptions implicit to much scholarship on neoliberalism by instead imagining law as potentially capacitating and generative.

Janet Halley's "Paranoia, Feminism, Law: Reflections on the Possibilities for Queer Legal Studies" (chapter 7) similarly questions the frequent emphasis on suspicion, although through an engagement with Eve Sedgwick's thought and life as well as Halley's own dialogue with queer theory over the course of her career. For Halley, Sedgwick's late work on the reparative suggests a "plural, sliding, additive, '. . . and others,' middle-term, midrange, horizontal aesthetic" that provides one model for transcending the chronic paranoia about law that has at times characterized work within the interdiscipline. Halley regrets, however, what she views as Sedgwick's own blind spot regarding law, which remained an object of suspicion despite her insistence on the reparative labor of criticism. Taking the example of current debates over sexual assault on campuses, Halley instead contends that "legal-realist understandings of law . . . can carry the plenitude of Eve's sliding lists into legal life."

It is with similar goals in mind that Wai Chee Dimock builds upon Sedgwick's appeal to the reparative to envision the workings of reparative justice, which Dimock contrasts with punitive justice (chapter 21). For Dimock, reparative justice "multiplies complexities and prolongs the input process, thanks to a multilayered and multivariable commutating network." Drawing on Bruno Latour's actor-network theory, Dimock considers how literature can facilitate such an endeavor through her analysis of novelist William Faulkner's reparative project, which aimed to redress both the humiliation of Japan after the Second World War and the displacement of American indigenous populations. For Dimock, efforts like Faulkner's succeed when they are "crowd-sourced over time" into weak networks, something her essay achieves by thereafter looking to Native poet Jim Barnes.

For some scholars, affect theory has provided a framework for departing from exclusively critique-based modes of analysis (although many affect theorists are invested in suspicion and other "negative" affects).[63] While there is a long tradition of law and literature criticism that examines the relevance of different emotions to law, affect studies often explicitly distinguishes affect from emotion, as Ravit Reichman explains, by "focus[ing] not on emotions strictly defined, but on the relations between mind and body, culture and individual subjectivity." In "Law's Affective Thickets" (chapter 6), Reichman explores the role of "reasonableness" as not only a powerful legal concept with potentially grave consequences, such as sanctioning police brutality, but also a specific affect accompanied by a distinct style and tone. To assess these dual senses of reasonableness, Reichman analyzes three seemingly distant legal and literary examples; she reads the ostensible absence of affect in Kazuo Ishiguro's *The Remains of the Day* in conjunction with both episodes from the HBO serial *The Wire* and the 2015 Supreme Court decision *Mullenix v. Luna*, which granted qualified immunity to an officer who shot a fleeing suspect six times after the majority of the Court judged his actions to be reasonable.

What many of these shifts and new directions augur further invites being described as a return to the imagination within law and literature. Given how James Boyd White's *The Legal Imagination* helped to catalyze the emergence of law and literature as a movement, recent appeals to the imagination might seem to signal forestalled progress or a mere revisiting of the interdiscipline's origins. As White announced almost forty years ago, the main focus in his book was "the life of the imagination working with inherited materials and against inherited constraints."[64] But whereas White was focused on "develop[ing] a way of thinking about the activities of mind and imagination that lie at the heart of the law—at what happens when a lawyer or judge is faced with a real problem in the world,"[65] the contributors to *New Directions* extend White's focus on legal actors to consider how legal imaginaries affect literary and cultural ones and how the legal and literary imagination intersect and work together. Indeed, recent attention to the imagination is a testament to the countless ways that legal imaginaries can and do continue to shape literary ones and vice versa—as well as to the elaborate interplay of both fields within other domains of culture. This is to say that current work on literary and legal imaginations alike points to the mobile, evolving, animated nature of these respective disciplines and their meaning-making capacities.

Responding to the seeming routinization of law and literature, Austin Sarat, in chapter 3 of *New Directions*, foresees three potential futures for the interdiscipline. The first, normalization, would treat law and literature as a kind of "normal science," thereby segregating it from other interdisciplinary approaches to law while scholars would continue to investigate further dimensions of established questions. Another possible future would conceive of law as performance, seeing law as a collection of collaborative performance processes and events. In addition, Sarat considers how future work in law and literature might understand the literary life of law as encompassing a broader definition of culture—or of "the imagination, invention, creativity, and improvisation that are culture itself." Several chapters included in this volume relatedly defend expanded ideas not only of culture but also of the imagination: they urge more elaborate, nuanced accounts *both* of the cultural terrain of law *and* of the vibrant, dynamic contours of the literary imagination. Many of the new directions explored in this collection chart untraveled routes for venturing into and navigating that widening landscape. The numerous methodological and other approaches developed in this volume—approaches that are both well trodden and more recently forged—all in their different ways propose techniques for negotiating the workings of the imagination, as a component of literature as well as of law. Hence, Lorna Hutson investigates how forensic rhetoric shapes the dramatic imagination, and, in turn, how Shakespeare's intervention into the dramatic tradition affected later cultural imaginings of interiority. Likewise, Elizabeth Emens's "Regulatory Fictions: On Marriage and Countermarriage" (chapter 17) seeks to supplement relatively impoverished views about the structure and nature of marriage with alternatives to marriage derived from literature. Emens enlists literature as a vehicle for enhancing the legal imagination with the hope that it will inspire the creation of new legal forms.

Taken together, the chapters in *New Directions in Law and Literature* offer a wide range of perspectives on the imagination and its countless pathways, as those routes continue to cross-section the varying jurisdictions of law, literature, and culture in unexpected ways. Those shifting domains at times overlap; at others are contiguous; and at yet others can appear rigidly separated or even segregated. Their many parallels, frictions, symmetries, tensions, fault lines, and gaps are the province of the imagination. They also alert us to the insurrectionary nature of the imagination: to why the imagination will always be poised to break down unhelpful barriers and borders, to refuse intellectual and other kinds of quarantine. And as such, these many intersections between law and literature further return us to the basic goals of interdisciplinarity, with its abiding promise to unsettle—to unsettle whatever boundaries and confines may unwittingly restrain us. It is in such a spirit of imagination that this volume invites you to participate.

NOTES

1. For a helpful bibliography of early work on law and literature, including that of Wigmore, see David R. Papke, "Law and Literature: A Comment and Bibliography of Secondary Works," *Law Library Journal* 73 (1980): 421–37. Richard Weisberg's "Wigmore and the Law and Literature Movement," *Law and Literature* 21 (2009): 129–45, discusses in more detail the nature of Wigmore's contribution to thinking about law and literature, as well as that of Benjamin Cardozo's influential 1931 essay "Law and Literature," in *Law and Literature and Other Essays and Addresses* (New York: Harcourt, Brace, 1931).

2. Peter Goodrich addresses claims of the death of law and literature; see "Screening Law," *Law and Literature* 21 (2009), 1–3.

3. Debates over the digital humanities, a field emerging at the intersection of computing and the humanities, have often provided a forum for negotiating such tensions. See, for example, the critique of the field in Daniel Allington, Sarah Brouillette, and David Golumbia, "Neoliberal Tools (and Archives): A Political History of Digital Humanities," *LA Review of Books* (May 1, 2016), https://lareviewofbooks.org/article/neoliberal-tools-archives-political-history-digital-humanities/; and the response by Matthew Kirschenbaum, "Am I A Digital Humanist? Confessions of a Neoliberal Tool," https://medium.com/@mkirschenbaum/am-i-a-digital-humanist-confessions-of-a-neoliberal-tool-1bc64caaa984#.m43nryfc8.

4. For a few influential examples that have helped to inaugurate such debates, see Sara Ahmed, *Strange Encounters: Embodied Others in Post-Coloniality* (New York: Routledge, 2000); Eve Kosofsky Sedgwick and Adam Frank, "Shame in the Cybernetic Fold: Reading Silvan Tomkins," *Critical Inquiry* 21 (1995): 496–522; Jacques Rancière, "The Misadventures of Critical Thought," in *The Emancipated Spectator* (New York: Verso, 2009), 25–50; Ann Cvetkovitch, *Depression: A Public Feeling* (Durham, NC: Duke University Press, 2012); José Esteban Muñoz, *Cruising Utopia: The Then and There of Queer Futurity* (New York: New York University Press, 2009); Bruno Latour, "Why has Critique Run out of Steam? From Matters of Fact to Matters of Concern," *Critical Inquiry* 30 (2004): 225–48; Stefano Harney and Fred Moten, *The Undercommons: Fugitive Planning and Black Study* (New York: Autonomedia, 2013); Heather Love, "Close Reading and Thin Description," *Public Culture*, 25 (2013): 401–34; Sharon Marcus, *Between Women: Friendship, Desire, and Marriage in Victorian England* (Princeton, NJ: Princeton University Press, 2007); and Stephen Best and Sharon Marcus, "Surface Reading: An Introduction," *Representations* 108 (2009): 1–21.

5. See Orin Kerr, "The Rise of the Ph.D. Law Professor," *Washington Post*, October 22, 2015; Lynn LoPucki, "Dawn of the Discipline-Based Law Faculty," *Journal of Legal Education* 65 (2016): 506–42.

6. For example, in 2014, the American Bar Association adopted a new requirement that law schools mandate "six credits of instruction in an experiential course or courses. To qualify, the experiential course or courses must be a simulation, law clinic, or field placement"; see American Bar Association, Section of Legal Education and Admissions to the Bar, "Explanation of Changes from 2014 Comprehensive Review of the Standards," available at http://www.americanbar.org/content/dam/aba/administrative/legal_education_and_admissions_to_the_bar/council_reports_and_resolutions/201408_explanation_changes.authcheckdam.pdf: 7. In 2013, the State Bar of California approved an even more rigorous set of requirements for those wishing to be admitted to the California Bar, including either taking "at least 15 units of practice-based, experiential course work" or "participat[ing] in a Bar-approved externship, clerkship or apprenticeship at any time during or following completion of law school"; see http://www.calbar.ca.gov/AboutUs/BoardofTrustees/TaskForceonAdmissionsRegulationReform.aspx.

7. For a representative chiding of the legal academy, see David Segal, "Law School Economics: Ka-Ching!," *New York Times*, July 16, 2011: BU 1.

8. Only seven of the 102 JD/PhDs Lynn LoPucki analyzed (including a 2010 faculty sample and 2011–15 entry-level hires) received PhDs in fields related to

literature (including American Culture, English, Classics, Germanic Studies, and Linguistics); LoPucki, "Dawn of the Discipline-Based Law Faculty," 40.

9. LoPucki, "Dawn of the Discipline-Based Law Faculty," 40

10. As Martha McCluskey writes in "Thinking with Wolves: Left Legal Theory after the Right's Rise," *Buffalo Law Review* 54 (2007): 1194–95: "CLS quickly lost its influence and visibility—which had rarely reached far beyond the margins of a few elite law schools. Later-formed branches of critical legal theory have survived and even thrived by focusing on particular problems of race, gender, and sexual identity. However, it seems that these often fragmented offshoots have not succeeded in building and disseminating a jurisprudence that comprehensively challenges the foundations of centrist or right law and policy." Janet Halley and Wendy Brown themselves assert, in the introduction to their volume surveying the post-CLS heritage, that "The work gathered here indicates that left internal critique is alive and well, if dispersed and perhaps undervalued," Brown and Halley eds., *Left Legalism/Left Critique* (Durham, NC: Duke University Press, 2002), 34.

11. See, for example, Sameer Ashar's call for increasing critical engagement within law schools: Sameer M. Ashar, "Deep Critique and Democratic Lawyering in Clinical Practice," *California Law Review* 104 (2016): 227–229.

12. Jeannie Suk, *At Home in the Law: How the Domestic Violence Revolution Is Transforming Privacy* (New Haven, CT: Yale University Press, 2009).

13. See, e.g., Elizabeth Emens, "Monogamy's Law: Compulsory Monogamy and Polyamorous Existence," *New York University Review of Law and Social Change* 29 (2004): 277–376.

14. Simon Stern, "From Author's Right to Property Right," *University of Toronto Law Journal* 62 (2012): 29–91.

15. See Julie Stone Peters, "Law, Literature, and the Vanishing Real: On the Future of an Interdisciplinary Illusion," *PMLA* 120 (2005), 442–53; Jane B. Baron, "Law, Literature, and the Problems of Interdisciplinarity," *Yale Law Journal* 108 (1999): 1059–85.

16. Peters, "Law, Literature, and the Vanishing Real," 444; see also Baron, "Law, Literature, and the Problems of Interdisciplinarity," 1064.

17. See, for example, Martha C. Nussbaum, *Poetic Justice: The Literary Imagination and Public Life* (Boston: Beacon Press, 1995).

18. Peters, "Law, Literature, and the Vanishing Real," 445–446; Baron, "Law, Literature, and the Problems of Interdisciplinarity," 1064–65.

19. Ronald Dworkin, *Law's Empire* (Cambridge, MA: Harvard University Press, 1986), 228–75. Sanford Levinson and Steven Mailloux, eds., *Interpreting Law and Literature: A Hermeneutic Reader* (Chicago: Northwestern University Press, 1988), conveys the range of related approaches to the enterprise.

20. Peters, "Law, Literature, and the Vanishing Real," 446–48; Baron, "Law, Literature, and the Problems of Interdisciplinarity," 1065–66. Robin West and Richard Delgado are among the most prominent exemplars of the narrative school of law and literature.

21. Guyora Binder and Robert Weisberg, *Literary Criticisms of Law* (Princeton, NJ: Princeton University Press, 2000).

22. Ian Ward discusses in depth both "law in" and "law as" in the first chapter of his book *Law and Literature: Possibilities and Perspectives* (Cambridge: Cambridge University Press, 1995), 3–27.

23. See Paul K. Saint-Amour, ed., *Modernism and Copyright* (New York: Oxford University Press, 2010); Paul K. Saint-Amour, *The Copywrights: Intellectual Property and the Literary Imagination* (Ithaca, NY: Cornell University Press, 2003); Robert Spoo, *Without Copyrights: Piracy, Publishing, and the Public Domain* (New York: Oxford University Press, 2013).

24. See Thomas Morawetz, "Empathy and Judgment," *Yale Journal of Law and the Humanities* 8 (1996): 518.

25. For a discussion of this quality in law and literature scholarship, see Bernadette Meyler, "Law, Literature, and History: The Love Triangle," chapter 9, below.

26. Kenji Yoshino, "The City and the Poet," *Yale Law Journal* 114 (2005): 1837 (citing Timothy J. Reiss, *The Meaning of Literature* [Ithaca, NY: Cornell University Press, 1992]). Brook Thomas makes a similar point in his introduction to *Cross-Examinations of Law and Literature: Cooper, Hawthorne, Stowe, and Melville* (Cambridge: Cambridge University Press, 1987), 15, about the initial union of "law-and-letters" and the subsequent "establishment of disciplines each with its own criteria for legitimate knowledge."

27. For example, see, Joseph Slaughter, *Human Rights, Inc.* (New York: Fordham University Press, 2007); Inderpal Grewal, *Transnational America: Feminisms, Diasporas, Neoliberalisms* (Durham, NC: Duke University Press, 2005).

28. Michel Foucault, *Discipline and Punish: The Birth of the Prison*, trans. Alan Sheridan (New York: Vintage, 1995).

29. Walter Benjamin, "The Work of Art in the Age of Mechanical Reproduction," in *Illuminations: Essays and Reflections*, ed. Hannah Arendt, trans. Harry Zohn (New York: Schocken, 1969), 219–53; Fredric Jameson, *Postmodernism: The Cultural Logic of Late Capitalism* (Durham, NC: Duke University Press, 1991), 5.

30. See Derek Attridge, *The Singularity of Literature* (New York: Routledge, 2004); Derek Attridge, *J. M. Coetzee and the Ethics of Reading: Literature in the Event* (Chicago: University of Chicago Press, 2004); Gayatri Chakravorty Spivak, *An Aesthetic Education in the Era of Globalization* (Cambridge, MA: Harvard University Press, 2012).

31. See Jacques Derrida, *Sovereignties in Question: The Poetics of Paul Celan* (New York: Fordham University Press, 2005), 87.

32. See Gayatri Chakravorty Spivak, "Righting Wrongs," *South Atlantic Quarterly* 103, nos. 2–3 (2004): 523–81; Judith Butler, *Undoing Gender* (New York: Routledge, 2004); Butler, *Giving an Account of Oneself* (New York: Fordham University Press, 2005); Butler, *Antigone's Claim: Kinship between Life and Death* (New York: Columbia University Press, 2002). See also Drucilla Cornell, "Post-Structuralism, the Ethical Relation, and the Law," *Cardozo Law Review* 9 (1988): 1587–628.

33. As Richard Howells writes, "There is . . . something of a backlash brewing over both the economic and instrumental justifications of the arts and humanities in both practice and research." "'Sorting the Sheep from the Sheep': Value, Worth, and the Creative Industries," in *The Public Value of the Humanities*, ed. Jonathan Bate (London: Bloomsbury, 2011), 239.

34. For such an argument see Peters, "Law, Literature, and the Vanishing Real," 447.

35. Ian Ward, *Law and Literature: Possibilities and Perspectives* (Cambridge: Cambridge University Press, 1995), 22–25.

36. Lynn Hunt, *Inventing Human Rights: A History* (New York: Norton, 2007).

37. Kay Schaffer and Sidonie Smith, *Human Rights and Narrated Lives: The Ethics of Recognition* (New York: Palgrave Macmillan, 2004). Schaffer and Smith describe

the Holocaust as the "premier instance of traumatic remembering." Ibid., 21. In *That the World May Know: Bearing Witness to Atrocity* (Cambridge, MA: Harvard University Press, 2007), James Dawes similarly considers the many impediments to humanitarian advocacy.

38. Thomas Morawetz describes a fourth category of law and literature scholarship as "law *as influenced by* literature (examination of the role of literature in affecting legislation, judicial practice, political attitudes, and so on)"; Morawetz, "Empathy and Judgment," 518.

39. Henry Turner, *The Corporate Commonwealth: Pluralism and Political Fictions in England, 1516–1651* (Chicago: University of Chicago Press, 2016).

40. For a discussion of the impact of critical legal history, see Christopher Tomlins, "After Critical Legal History: Scope, Scale, Structure," *Annual Review of Law and Social Science* 8 (2012): 31–38. Robert Gordon announced the approach in "Critical Legal Histories," *Stanford Law Review*, vol. 36 (1984): 57–124.

41. Brook Thomas, *Civic Myths: A Law-and-Literature Approach to Citizenship* (Chapel Hill: University of North Carolina Press, 2007), 13.

42. As she argues, in many versions of law and literature, " 'law' is treated as a largely empty domain composed mainly of rules, a barren realm of technocratic doctrinal manipulation. This depiction resonates strongly with a widely accepted story of law's development as an 'autonomous' discipline." Jane Baron, "The Rhetoric of Law and Literature: A Skeptical View," *Cardozo Law Review* 26 (2005): 2274.

43. See Yoshino, "City and the Poet," 1868–1885. Yoshino expresses sympathy for the Platonic critique of poetry as potentially destructive of the state and views the role and effect of victim impact statements as confirming the continued salience of this critique.

44. For a complicated discussion of this link, see Giorgio Agamben, *Remnants of Auschwitz: The Witness and the Archive*, trans. Daniel Heller-Roazen (New York: Zone, 1999); Alexander G. Weheliye, *Habeas Viscus: Racializing Assemblages, Biopolitics, and Black Feminist Theories of the Human* (Durham, NC: Duke University Press, 2014).

45. *Literary Criticisms of Law*, 16. As they put it, law and literature also risks "a *sentimentalism* in which passion is never cruel or self-indulgent or muddle-headed, invention is never destructive or dishonest, and civility is always inclusive and never elitist."

46. Rita Felski, *The Limits of Critique* (Chicago: University of Chicago Press, 2015); Eve Kosofsky Sedgwick, *Touching Feeling: Affect, Pedagogy, Performative* (Durham, NC: Duke University Press, 2003).

47. Paul Ricoeur, *Freud and Philosophy: An Essay on Interpretation*, trans. Denis Savage (New Haven, CT: Yale University Press, 1970), 32.

48. Sedgwick, *Touching Feeling*, 124.

49. Greta Olson, "De-Americanizing Law and Literature Narratives: Opening Up the Story," *Law and Literature* 22 (2010): 339.

50. For such a claim about the field of history, see Dipesh Chakrabarty, *Provincializing Europe: Postcolonial Thought and Historical Difference*, 2nd ed. (Princeton, NJ: Princeton University Press, 2007).

51. Austin Sarat, Matthew Anderson, and Cathrine O. Frank describe and praise the move from law and literature to law and the humanities in their introduction to *Law and the Humanities: An Introduction* (Cambridge: Cambridge University Press, 2010), 1–46.

52. Peters, "Law, Literature, and the Vanishing Real," 453.

53. Binder and Weisberg, *Literary Criticisms of Law*, 463–464.

54. Caroline Levine, *Forms: Whole, Rhythm, Hierarchy, Network* (Princeton, NJ: Princeton University Press, 2015).

55. Levine, *Forms*, 16.

56. Lorna Hutson, *The Invention of Suspicion: Law and Mimesis in Shakespeare and Renaissance Drama* (Oxford: Oxford University Press, 2007).

57. As Vernon Cisney and Nicolae Morar explain, "the disciplinary power mechanisms of the body and the regulatory mechanisms of the [population] constitute the modern incarnation of power relations, labeled as *biopower*"; "Why Biopower? Why Now?," in *Biopower: Foucault and Beyond*, ed. Vernon Cisney and Nicolae Morar (Chicago: University of Chicago Press, 2016), 5.

58. Brooks, chapter 5, 137–138; Peter Brooks, "Narrative Transactions—Does the Law Need a Narratology?," *Yale Journal of Law and the Humanities*, vol. 18, no. 1 (2006): 1–38.

59. Annelise Riles, "Is the Law Hopeful?," in *The Economy of Hope*, ed. Hiro Miyazaki and Richard Swedberg (Philadelphia: University of Pennsylvania Press, 2017), 125–46; for a volume that explores legal fictions, see Maksymilian Del Mar and William Twining, eds., *Legal Fictions in Theory and Practice* (Cham: Springer International, 2015).

60. See also Christopher L. Tomlins and Bruce H. Mann eds., *The Many Legalities of Early America* (Chapel Hill: University of North Carolina Press, 2001); Gregory Ablavsky, "The Savage Constitution," *Duke Law Journal* 63 (2014): 999–1089.

61. See Elizabeth Anker, *Fictions of Dignity: Embodying Human Rights in World Literature* (Ithaca, NY: Cornell University Press, 2012); Pheng Cheah, *Inhuman Conditions: On Cosmopolitanism and Human Rights* (Cambridge, MA: Harvard University Press, 2007); Joseph Slaughter, *Human Rights, Inc.: The World Novel, Narrative Form, and International Law* (New York: Fordham University Press, 2007).

62. For contrasting perspectives on this question, see Richard Thompson Ford, *Rights Gone Wrong: How Law Corrupts the Struggle for Equality* (New York: Farrar, Straus and Giroux, 2011), and *Racial Culture: A Critique* (Princeton, NJ: Princeton University Press, 2005); and Kenji Yoshino, *Covering: The Hidden Assault on Our Civil Rights* (New York: Random House, 2006).

63. As Emma Mason writes, "Affect theory has helped to shift the hermeneutics of suspicion that surrounded authenticity by working with phenomenology, psychology, [and] ethnography . . . to address how emotions circulate and adapt to material spaces and places, as well as how they are transmitted, expressed, constructed, and felt"; Mason, "Religion, the Bible, and Literature in the Victorian Age," in *The Oxford Handbook of Victorian Literary Culture*, ed. Juliet John (Oxford: Oxford University Press, 2016), 347.

64. James Boyd White, *The Legal Imagination: Studies in the Nature of Legal Thought and Expression* (Boston: Little, Brown, 1973), xii.

65. James Boyd White, "The Cultural Background of *The Legal Imagination*," in *Teaching Law and Literature*, ed. Austin Sarat, Cathrine O. Frank, and Matthew Anderson, 29–39 (New York: Modern Language Association, 2011).

PART 1
Genealogies and Futures

CHAPTER 1
Minding Previous Steps Taken

BROOK THOMAS

After the Second World War, East Germans rebuilt the main building of Berlin's Humboldt University. Opposite the entrance to the foyer, steps lead to a small landing, then divide, one set to the left and another to the right, giving access to the second floor. On the wall behind the landing is Karl Marx's famous Eleventh Thesis on Feuerbach: "Philosophers have only interpreted the world; the point however is to change it." Reunification prompted a debate over the inscription. Rejecting the precedent of Nazis and Communists, who often erased the past, authorities had a contest to create a new context for the quotation. The winning design places in front of each step leading to and from the landing the phrase *Vorsicht Stufe*: "Mind the step." We need to bring about change, but we should be careful about the steps taken in doing so.

Practitioners moving a field of study in legitimately new directions also need to mind previous steps taken. Thus, the coeditors asked me to provide a brief overview of work done between the 1973 publication of James Boyd White's *The Legal Imagination: Studies in the Nature of Legal Thought and Expression*, a textbook for legal writing often credited with initiating the law and literature movement, and Julie Stone Peters's 2005 *PMLA* essay "Law, Literature, and the Vanishing Real: On the Future of an Interdisciplinary Illusion," which polemically announced its end. My by necessity simplified review will hopefully help us take new steps with care.

Let me start by comparing the works bookending the years I was assigned to cover. Far from trying to inaugurate a new beginning, White, trained in the classics and the law, emphasized traditional legal study. "It is," he recounts, "only in the rather odd intellectual climate of the mid-twentieth century and beyond that it would have been possible to think that the law had no connection with the other arts of language and disciplines of thought we normally think of as constituting the humanities."[1] People had lost sight of that ancient connection, on the one hand, because of the formal method of teaching law—and legal writing—and, on the other, because most seeking an alternative to formalism turned to law and society, not to law and the humanities.

Whereas White initiated a movement by being old-fashioned, Peters was intent on proclaiming an end to a movement she claimed was motivated by a political desire to change the world. Peters starts her account with a self-consciously fictional anecdote about a meeting between a caricatured literature professor who, dissatisfied with literature's fictional status, turns to the law and its power to effect "real" political change and a caricatured law professor who, dissatisfied with the law's abstraction, turns to literature and its representational access to "real" life. But their movement was bound to self-destruct as each discipline came to realize that the "real" it sought in the other was illusionary. Thus, "the proliferation of essays over the past five years or so looking back at law and literature as a phenomenon might be taken as a sign that we are moving beyond it as a cognizable interdisciplinary formation." Nonetheless, "in its end may be its beginning," and Peters notes how Guyora Binder and Robert Weisberg had recently celebrated "cultural criticisms of law" and how law and literature was being melded into Austin Sarat's "law, culture, and the humanities."[2]

As this volume indicates, Peters's polemical pronouncement of an end proved premature. Since 2005, studies of law and literature have increased along with, and sometimes as part of, developments in law, culture, and the humanities. Institutionally, law and literature has become more entrenched with the MLA's recognition of an official discussion group, a proliferation of new courses, and a "literature and law" major at John Jay College. One reason law and literature thrives along with other developments in legal humanities is the slippery definition of literature. A standard early formula distinguished between analysis of "law in literature" and analysis of "law as literature." The first assumed a somewhat narrow, post-Romantic notion of literature as works of fiction. The second assumed a more capacious view of literature, because what people really advocated was a rhetorical analysis of legal documents. Peters generally opts for the more narrow view. White, in contrast, assumes the broader view of literature linked etymologically to "letters." For him, there is no need to distinguish "law and literature" from "law, culture, and the humanities." Looking back on "The Cultural

Background of *The Legal Imagination*," he uses interchangeably "law and literature," law and the "literary humanities," "law and the arts of language," and "law and humanities."[3] He especially emphasizes the importance of rhetorical training for lawyers.

A second reason law and literature persists is that, although some practitioners hoped for political outcomes, it cannot be reduced to a political movement. Its scholarship is not confined to a metaphysical quest for the "real," vanishing or otherwise. Instead, it is an interdisciplinary mode of inquiry designed to produce new knowledge of law, literature, and the cultures both inhabit. Methodologically, it is distinguished most obviously from law and society, which was an alternative approach to legal formalism in the 1960s. The Law and Society Association was founded in 1964 by law professors and social scientists intent on applying empirical methods of the social sciences to legal inquiry. Initially supported by grants from the Russell Sage and Walter E. Meyer Foundations with graduate centers at the University of California, Berkeley, the University of Denver, Northwestern University, and the University of Wisconsin, law and society has generated other PhD programs and over sixty undergraduate programs. Law and literature cannot match that institutional success, and White's insistence that law is an art, not a science, is in part a response to that imbalance.

The opposition between law as art and law as science is a relatively recent one, dating to the rise of the professional social sciences in the late nineteenth century. In his inaugural address at Harvard Law School in 1827, Justice Joseph Story insisted that every student should "addict himself to the study of philosophy, of rhetoric, of history, and of human nature" and should be in "full possession of the general literature of ancient and modern times."[4] For him, as for those who came before him, classical study was the best means to give the law a foundation based on eternal principles guiding human governance and behavior. But the view of law as embodying timeless principles was challenged in the late nineteenth century by Oliver Wendell Holmes Jr. The son of a famous writer, Holmes began his 1899 speech "Law in Science and Science in Law" with "[t]he law of fashion is the law of life," followed by the claim that "artists and poets, instead of troubling themselves about the eternal, had better be satisfied if they can stir the feelings of a generation." Dismissing efforts to base the law on eternal principles, Holmes urged a turn to the social sciences and their reliance on statistics, which could replace the "unreal explanations," "unreal formulas," and "inadequate generalizations" on which the law was too often based.[5] The first extensive use of statistics in a Supreme Court case was by Holmes's colleague Justice Louis Brandeis in *Muller v. Oregon*,[6] which helped give rise to legal realism and its reliance on the social sciences.

Peters cites the "memory of civil rights battles won in the courts" as political inspiration for the law and literature movement; in fact, with its use of psychological evidence in footnote 11, *Brown v. Board of Education*,[7] is the most famous social science case.[8] Soon, however, economics became the social science exerting the most influence in legal education and scholarship. Law and economics was a prime target of founding figures in law and literature. They were joined by Owen Fiss, who from the start embraced law and the humanities. In turn, Judge Richard Posner, the most vocal proponent of "law and economics," wrote *Law and Literature: A Misunderstood Relation*, insisting that literature is of little practical use for understanding the law. "Law is a system of social control as well as a body of texts, and its operation is illuminated by the social sciences and judged by ethical criteria. Literature is an art, and its best methods of interpreting and evaluating are aesthetic."[9]

The methodological divide between law and society and law and humanities is similar to ones that developed between social and cultural historians, analytical and continental philosophers, empirical and cultural anthropologists, and quantitative and theoretical political scientists. The institutional consequences of those divides persist today. They help explain two different institutional histories. Without institutional structures, movements do not last. As an alternative to the Law and Society Association, Richard Weisberg, a law professor with a PhD in comparative literature, helped found the Law and Humanities Institute, a reminder that the move from "law and literature" to "law, culture, and the humanities" had in some respects taken place from the start. Nonetheless, Sarat's Association for the Study of Law, Culture, and the Humanities has a different history. Sarat is not trained in literary studies. Nor is he based in a law school. On the contrary, he is a political scientist at an elite liberal arts school. As with many in both the "law and society" and "law and literature" movements, he believes that the law is too important for its study to be left to lawyers. Nonetheless, unlike White and Weisberg, he did not initially turn to the humanities. His first affiliation was with law and society, and only later did he became concerned with gaps the statistical measures of the social sciences left in our understanding of law's social and cultural role. The organization he founded is best understood as a splinter group from the Law and Society Association. Its first meeting was held at Georgetown Law School in 1998. Although its umbrella is large enough to include work in law and literature, its institutional history indicates significant differences.

Peters produces a narrative in which a unified movement moves from an emphasis on humanism to hermeneutics to narrative before collapsing. In contrast, I see all three taking place simultaneously in different institutional spaces. The first location was law schools, where other professors joined White and Weisberg in emphasizing a twentieth-century version of the Ciceronian tradition. *The Legal Imagination*'s founding premises are that legal language is a particular version of rhetoric and that lawyers will be better writers and more aware of the consequences of their words when they understand them as part of a "language in a universe of languages."[10] Weisberg made his first contribution by calling attention to and revising John H. Wigmore's list of legal novels that every lawyer should read, published in 1908 and updated in 1922. Weisberg justified his effort by lamenting the surrender of the humanistic lawyer to his "empirically armed rival," the social scientist, who "successfully courts and engages the legal profession."[11] The work of pioneers like White and Weisberg found a following; law review essays were published; and courses on law and literature began to be offered as electives at various law schools.[12]

Second, in both law schools and in literature departments, there was a heightened interest in theory, for the most part continental theory. Among those most interested were members of the critical legal studies movement, which certainly was politically motivated. Since literature departments were the clearinghouses for poststructuralist thought, these legal scholars, some of whom had turned to law when the job market in literary studies collapsed, read literary theorists. At the same time, as Peters notes, some literary scholars calling for a political turn in criticism saw the law as a discipline with much more direct influence on politics than literature. For them, the work of critical legal studies was a fruitful place to explore the political implications of various new theories. These theories, it was found, could be profitably applied to interpretations of legal documents as well as to works of literature.

Deconstruction attracted special interest. An influential essay for legal scholars was Jack Balkin's "Deconstructive Practice and Legal Theory" (1987). Also important were Derrida's comments on Walter Benjamin's 1921 "Critique of Violence" in "The Mystical Foundations of Authority" (1989), which has spawned a series of commentaries that continue today. But deconstruction was not the only topic of interest. Equally important was the application of narrative theory to the law. In "Nomos and Narrative" (1983), Robert Cover participated in and helped to launch analysis of the narrative component of the law. Peter Brooks followed suit in the collection of essays he coedited with law professor Paul Gewirtz, *Law's Stories: Narrative and Rhetoric in the Law* (1996), and his own *Troubling Confessions: Speaking Guilt in Law and Literature* (2000).

The third development was within literature departments. In 1982, Richard Weisberg and comparative literature professor Jean-Pierre

Barricelli produced "Literature and the Law" for an MLA volume on *Interrelations of Literature*.[13] About this time, others tried to move beyond formalism in literary study by turning to history. Engagement with legal history was one way to provide a new sense of literature's relation to culture in general. A groundbreaking work was Robert A. Ferguson's *Law and Letters in American Culture* (1984), which restored to our attention a "now-forgotten configuration of law and letters that dominated American literary aspirations from the Revolution until the fourth decade of the nineteenth century."[14]

The mid-1980s saw a flurry of activity in all three areas. Milner Ball drew on theology in *The Promise of American Law: A Theological, Humanistic View of Legal Process* (1982) and *Lying Down Together: Law, Metaphor, and Theology* (1985). The year 1984 produced Richard Weisberg's *The Failure of the Word* and White's *When Words Lose Their Meaning*. In 1985, Robin West used Kafka to challenge Posner's method of law and economics. Posner responded in 1986, reviewed Weisberg's book in 1987, and published his book the next year. In 1986, Ferguson's and Peters's colleague at Columbia Kathy Eden produced *Poetic and Legal Fiction in the Aristotelian Tradition*, which anticipated work on law and equity while tracing the influence of Greek tragedy on the law. My *Cross-Examinations of Law and Literature: Cooper, Hawthorne, Stowe, and Melville* came out in 1987. Having met at the School for Literary Theory and Criticism, literary critic Steven Mailloux and law professor Sanford Levinson edited *Interpreting Law and Literature: A Hermeneutic Reader* (1988), which included work by Stanley Fish and Walter Benn Michaels.

The synergy these three developments could produce was on display at a 1987 conference on *Billy Budd* at Washington and Lee University Law School. It brought together, among others, Richard Weisberg, Posner, West, Michaels, Mailloux, and me. Papers from that conference constituted the first issue of *Cardozo Studies in Law and Literature* (1989), which is now called simply *Law and Literature*. About the same time, Fiss successfully launched the *Yale Journal of Law and the Humanities*. With professional journals and professional organizations, a law and literature movement was well underway.

Nonetheless, differences between the three developments remained. Legal scholars focused primarily on classics with legal themes or conflicts, such as *Antigone*, *Measure for Measure*, *Bleak House*, *The Trial*, and *To Kill a Mockingbird*. One reason the conference on *Billy Budd* proved productive was that Melville's work was both part of the standard law and literature canon and a work that received a large amount of attention in English departments. Yet frequently in law schools, a work like *Billy Budd* was taught to raise philosophical and ethical issues about the role of the law, the nature of legal judgment, and standards of justice. In contrast, with the rise of the new historicism, the trend in literary studies was toward historical analysis. After Ferguson's book, the focus turned to more specific topics in their historical context. Laura Hanft Korobkin looked at storytelling and famous cases of adultery, including the Beecher affair, in *Criminal Conversations: Sentimentality and Nineteenth-Century Legal Stories of Adultery* (1998). Nan Goodman turned to torts in *Shifting the Blame: Literature, Law, and the Theory of Accidents in Nineteenth-Century America* (1998).

To be sure, there were exceptions. Whereas Wai Chee Dimock's *Residues of Justice: Literature, Law, Philosophy* (1996) seems historical because its literary examples come from nineteenth-century America, in fact, Dimock drew more on philosophers such as Kant. In this regard, she anticipated some of the most famous continental political philosophers of our generation. Melville's "Bartleby, the Scrivener" became the literary work of choice for Derrida, Deleuze, Agamben, Žižek, and Negri, all of whom provide provocative readings of Bartleby's "I would prefer not to," while ignoring the historical legal work done by Americanists. In a different fashion, the philosopher Martha Nussbaum had an impact in both law schools and literature departments with *Love's Knowledge* (1990) and *Poetic Justice: The Literary Imagination and Public Life* (1995). Like White and Richard Weisberg, whose second book was *Poethics: And Other Strategies of Law and Literature* (1992), Nussbaum turned to literature to find an ethical foundation for the law as opposed to the cost-benefit accounting of law and economics. But already in 1991, my *Critical Inquiry* essay "Reflections on the Law and Literature Revival" anticipated Binder and Robert Weisberg's 2000 criticism of the revivalist enthusiasm of ethical moralizing. It also anticipated their criticism of the endlessly skeptical questioning of literary and legal foundations. The task is not simply to deconstruct the law but to cross-examine law and literature to come up with alternative possibilities for justice within the legal system unimaginable if we limited ourselves to one discipline. In literature departments, that search involved evoking the holy trinity of "race, class, and gender" to expand the canon.

A great deal of attention was paid to race and racial relations. In *Whispered Consolations: Law and Narrative in African American Life* (2000), Jon-Christian Suggs argued that the African American literary tradition cannot be understood without knowledge of legal issues facing black Americans, whether the laws of slavery, the Civil Rights Amendments, Jim Crow laws, or rulings in the era since *Brown v. Board of Education*. In *Race, Citizenship, and Law in American Literature* (2002), Gregg Crane identified a

tradition of lawyers and writers, black and white, evoking higher-law principles to work for emancipation and civil rights. Stephen Best's *The Fugitive's
Property: Law and the Poetics of Possession* (2004) provocatively examined
how the conditions of African Americans affected and were affected by the
law of property. Earlier my *American Literary Realism and the Failed Promise
of Contract* (1997) expanded a 1989 essay comparing the fiction of Homer
Plessy's attorney, Albion W. Tourgée, with Mark Twain's *Puddn'head Wilson*,
and included a chapter on the legal argument of African American novelist Charles W. Chesnutt. William Moddelmog's *Reconstituting Authority:
American Fiction in the Province of the Law, 1880–1920* (2000) looked at
both Chesnutt and Pauline Hopkins. The use of literature to explore legal
issues facing African Americans and vice versa was not confined to literature departments. Alfred L. Brophy published the best accounts we have
of Stowe's use of the law in *Uncle Tom's Cabin* and *Dred, A Tale of the Great
Swamp* in law reviews.[15] In *Law and the Company We Keep* (1995), Aviam
Soifer used works by William Faulkner to explore law's relation to racial
violence.

Law is as formative in the development of the Native American, Asian
American, and Latino literary traditions as it is in the African American
tradition. Elizabeth Villiers Gemmette included works by Louise Erdrich,
Linda Hogan, and Leslie Marmon Silko in *Law in Literature: An Annotated
Bibliography of Law-Related Works* (1998). Lisa Lowe used works of litera-
ture to document the repressive effects of the state's regulation of Asian
American immigration in *Immigrant Acts* (1996). Although the lives of
Asian Americans were determined by repressive laws and administrative
structures of this sort, Asian Americans were also determined not to be
simply victims of the law. David Li's *Imagining the Nation: Asian American
Literature and Cultural Consent* (1998) explored how Asian American writers
appropriated the ideology of consensual citizenship to combat the reality
of exclusion. Carl Gutiérrez-Jones's *Critical Race Narratives: A Study of Race,
Rhetoric, and Injury* (2001) dealt with Chicano/Latino issues and more.

Gutiérrez-Jones's title alludes to critical race studies that developed
in law schools as critical legal studies began to wane. Arguing that the
American legal system does not allow the stories of people of color to be
heard, Derrick Bell, Kimberlé Crenshaw, Richard Delgado, and Patricia
Williams told personal stories about race and the law that exposed the system's exclusions. With Jean Stefancic, Delgado put together a collection
called *Critical Race Theory: The Cutting Edge* (1995). Crenshaw and others
followed with their own collection, *Critical Race Theory: The Key Writings
That Formed the Movement* (1996). Critical race studies did not invent the
idea that the law leaves stories untold. Feminist scholars have long argued

that the legal system does not adequately listen to concerns of women. As with those addressing issues of race, the work of these scholars coincided with expansion of the canon. An influential essay coauthored by distinguished legal and literary scholars Carolyn Heilbrun and Judith Resnik was "Convergences: Law, Literature, and Feminism" (1990). Susan Sage Heinzelman and Zipporah Batshaw Wiseman edited the important collection *Representing Women: Law, Literature, and Feminism* (1994).

Once a field of law and literature was established, work proceeded in all areas of literature written in English. Emily Steiner and Candace Barrington edited the wide-ranging *The Letter of the Law: Legal Practice and Literary Production in Medieval England* (2002). Major new work was produced in Renaissance studies. In *Kill All the Lawyers? Shakespeare's Legal Appeal* (1994), Daniel Kornstein, former president of the Law and Humanities Institute, extended a long tradition of lawyers turning to the bard's works initiated by Germans Rudolf von Jhering and Joseph Kohler. Law professor Paul Kahn followed *The Cultural Study of Law: Reconstructing Legal Scholarship* (1999) with *Law and Love: The Trials of King Lear* (2000). Within literature departments, Constance Jordan wrote *Shakespeare's Monarchies: Ruler and Subject in the Romances* (1997), and Julia Lupton's *Citizen-Saints: Shakespeare and Political Theology* (2005) helped spark interest in Carl Schmitt's theories of sovereignty. Victoria Kahn would also focus on political theology while working primarily in the seventeenth century. Her early contributions were a review essay in *Diacritics* in 1989 called "Rhetoric and the Law," the Pocock-inspired *Machiavellian Rhetoric: From the Counter-Reformation to Milton* (1994), and *Wayward Contracts: The Crisis of Political Obligation in England, 1640–1674* (2004). Along with Lorna Hutson, Kahn edited *Rhetoric and Law in Early Modern Europe* (2001). New historicist works include Luke Wilson's *Theaters of Intention: Drama and the Law in Early Modern England* (2000) and Richard Burt's *Licensed by Authority: Ben Jonson and the Discourses of Censorship* (1993), which looked at Jonson's works in relation to the licensing acts.

Burt's work reminds us that law and literature is concerned not only with how the law is represented in literature and rhetorical analysis of the law but also with how law affects the production of literature. William B. Warner carried that concern into the eighteenth century with *Licensing Entertainment: The Elevation of Novel Reading in Britain, 1684–1750* (1998). Paul Vanderham's *James Joyce and Censorship: The Trials of Ulysses* (1998) looks at obscenity charges against *Ulysses*. Those charges and ones against D. H. Lawrence's *Lady Chatterley's Lover*, Radclyffe Hall's *The Well of Loneliness*, and others are treated in Edward de Grazia's *Girls Lean Back Everywhere: The Law of Obscenity and the Assault on Genius* (1992). The case against *The Well of Loneliness* for its lesbian theme recalls the famous Oscar Wilde trial and serves as a reminder of work starting in this period on issues of law, literature, and sexuality. In the United States, the law interweaves questions of sexuality with the right to privacy. In *Pursuing Privacy in Cold War America* (2002), Deborah Nelson provides a provocative reading of Paul Monette's *Love Alone: Eighteen Elegies for Rog* (1990), along with more general comparisons between changes in the legal concept of privacy and the construction of the private in confessional poets after the Second World War.

If censorship is one way the law affects literary production, copyright is another. Copyright's effect on the idea of authorship was the topic of two studies of the eighteenth century: Mark Rose's *Authors and Owners: The Invention of Copyright* (1993) and Martha Woodmansee's *The Author, Art, and the Market: Rereading the History of Aesthetics* (1994). Susan Staves produced a pioneering study of the legal and literary implications of the institution of coverture in *Married Women's Separate Property in England, 1660–1833* (1990). Wolfram Schmidgen focused on property law in *Eighteenth-Century Fiction and the Law of Property* (2002). Alexander Welsh's *Strong Representations: Narrative and Circumstantial Evidence* (1991) examined the rise of techniques of literary realism in conjunction with the development of criteria for circumstantial evidence in the law from the eighteenth to the nineteenth century. In 1999 Hilary Schor contributed "Show-Trials: Character, Conviction, and the Law in Victorian Fiction." Criminal law was the topic of Lisa Rodensky's *The Crime in Mind: Criminal Responsibility and the Victorian Novel* (2003). Theodore Ziolkowski's *The Mirror of Justice: Literary Reflections of Legal Crises* (1997) traced the German tradition of *Dichterjuristen*, authors trained in the law, culminating with a brilliant discussion of *The Trial*.

There was also extensive work done outside the United States. The Department of Law, Birkbeck College, London, generated important theoretical pieces, especially by Costas Douzinas and Peter Goodrich, its founding dean. Goodrich's *Oedipus Lex: Psychoanalysis, History, Law* (1995) and *Law in the Courts of Love: Literature and Other Minor Jurisprudences* (1996) drew on psychoanalysis to argue that law denies heterogeneity by repressing its metaphorical and rhetorical components. In Wales, Martin Kayman contributed important essays on eighteenth-century British literature and commercial law, such as "The Reader and the Jury: Legal Fictions and the Making of Commercial Law in the Eighteenth Century." Australia formed its own association for the study of law and literature. In 1995 it joined forces with the Law and Humanities Institute for a conference and simultaneous publication. Kieran Dolin wrote *Fiction and the Law: Legal Discourse in Victorian and Modernist Literature* (1999). Shaun McVeigh stressed the importance of jurisdiction as opposed to Schmitt's emphasis on sovereignty.[16] McVeigh's work had implications for the *Mabo* case involving the rights of aborigines and anticipated law and literature work in postcolonial studies that built on pioneering essays by Ambreena Manji. There was also important work produced in continental Europe. The Dutch judge Jeanne Gaakeer wrote *Hope Springs Eternal: An Introduction to the Work of James Boyd White* (1998). In Italy Daniela Carpi published *The Concept of Equity in Law and Literature* in 2005 and later, in 2008, helped to found the Italian Association of Law and Literature.[17] Germany's Dieter Polloczek also explored questions of equity in *Literature and Legal Discourse: Equity and Ethics from Sterne to Conrad* (1999). Denmark's Helle Porsdam and Germany's Peter Schneck added to our understanding of American law and literature.[18] In Germany, Anselm Haverkamp edited an essential volume on Derrida's and Benjamin's views of violence and the law: *Gewalt und Gerechtigkeit: Derrida—Benjamin* (1994).[19]

I could go on. Law and literature deals with almost all aspects of life, and in these years a wide range of topics was covered: gender, race, and sexuality; politics, ethics, and aesthetics; narrative, drama, and interpretation; the construction and admissibility of evidence; famous trials and trial scenes; equity, sovereignty, and jurisdiction; capital punishment and pardoning; citizenship; torts and contracts; the law of property, commerce, marriage, inheritance, labor, and crime.

Having provided a partial sketch of work on which a newer generation of scholars can build, I want to close by returning to my beginning. As law and literature was gaining force, David Cole, now a celebrated civil liberties attorney, applied Harold Bloom's "anxiety of influence" to the law in "Agon at Agora: Creative Misreadings in the First Amendment Tradition" (1986). Bloom argued that the literary canon was formed when "strong" poets, competing with powerful predecessors, repressed their debt to the past in order to appear original. The desire to strike out in new directions can also cause scholars to misread—and even to ignore—what came before in order to make their work look new. That tendency is exacerbated by the different institutional places in which work is conducted. Despite the creation of interdisciplinary journals and organizations, too many literary and legal scholars remain unaware of much work in the other's disciplines. Likewise, disciplinary-based publications and work outside the United States are too often slighted in accounts of a collective "movement." My chapter is designed to urge those intent on forging new directions in the study of law and literature to mind—and not to skip—the steps that came before.

NOTES

1. James Boyd White, "The Cultural Background of *The Legal Imagination*," in *Teaching Law and Literature*, ed. Austin Sarat, Catherine O. Frank, and Matthew Anderson (New York: Modern Language Association, 2011), 30.
2. Julie Stone Peters, "Law, Literature, and the Vanishing Real: On the Future of an Interdisciplinary Illusion," *PMLA* 120 (2005): 451–52. Guyora Binder and Robert Weisberg, *Literary Criticisms of Law* (Princeton, NJ: Princeton University Press, 2000).
3. White, "Cultural Background," 29–31.
4. Joseph Story, "Value and Importance of Legal Studies," in *The Miscellaneous Writings of Joseph Story*, ed. William W. Story (Boston: Little, Brown, 1852), 527, 529.
5. Oliver Wendell Holmes Jr., "Law in Science and Science in Law," *Harvard Law Review 12* (1899): 443, 455–56.
6. 208 U.S. 412 (1908).
7. 347 U.S. 483 (1954)
8. Peters, "Law, Literature, and the Vanishing Real," 443.
9. Richard Posner, *Law and Literature: A Misunderstood Relation* (Cambridge, MA: Harvard University Press, 1988), 7.
10. James Boyd White, *The Legal Imagination: Studies in the Nature of Legal Thought and Expression* (Boston: Little, Brown, 1973), viii.
11. "Wigmore's 'Legal Novels' Revisited: New Resources for the Expansive Lawyer," *Northwestern Law Review* 71 (1976): 17.
12. For a survey of courses, see Elizabeth Villiers Gemmette, "Law and Literature: An Unnecessarily Suspect Class in the Liberal Arts Component of the Law School Curriculum," *Valparaiso University Law Review* 23 (1989): 267–340. See also C. R. B. Dunlop, "Literature Studies in Law School," *Cardozo Studies in Law and Literature* 3 (1991): 63–110.
13. Richard Weisberg and Jean-Pierre Barricelli, "Literature and Law," in *Interrelations of Literature*, ed. Jean-Pierre Barricelli and Joseph Gibaldi, 150–75 (New York: Modern Language Association of America, 1982).
14. Robert A. Ferguson, *Law and Letters in American Culture* (Cambridge, MA: Harvard University Press, 1984), 5.
15. Alfred L. Brophy, "'Over and above . . . There Broods a Portentous Shadow— The Shadow of Law': Harriet Beecher Stowe's Critique of Slave Law in *Uncle Tom's Cabin*," *Journal of Law and Religion* 12 (1996): 457–506, and "Humanity, Utility, and Logic in Southern Legal Thought: Harriet Beecher Stowe's Vision in *Dred: A Tale of the Great Dismal Swamp*," *Boston University Law Review* 78 (1998): 1113–61.
16. Shaun McVeigh and Shaunnagh Dorsett, "Just So: The Law Which Governs Australia Is Australian Law," *Law and Critique* 13 (2002): 289–309.
17. Daniela Carpi, *The Concept of Equity in Law and Literature* (Verona: University of Verona Press, 2005).
18. Helle Porsdam, *Legally Speaking: Contemporary American Culture and the Law* (Amherst: University of Massachusetts Press, 1999), and Peter Schneck, "*Wieland*'s Testimony: Charles Brockden Brown and the Rhetoric of Evidence," in *Law and Literature*, ed. Brook Thomas, *REAL* Yearbook 18 (Tübingen: Gunter Narr, 2002), 167–213.

19. Indulging in some broad generalizations, Greta Olson tries to distinguish between different approaches in the United States, Great Britain, and Germany in "De-Americanizing Law and Literature Narratives," *Law and Literature* 22 (2010): 338–64. See also Christine Corcos, *An International Guide to Law and Literature Studies* (Buffalo, NY: W. S. Hein, 2000).

CHAPTER 2

Who Wouldn't Want to Be a Person?

Histories of the Present in Law and Literature

CALEB SMITH

A little more than a decade has passed since Julie Stone Peters analyzed the condition of law and literature scholarship and offered her prognosis for the future of our "interdisciplinary illusion." According to the story Peters told in her landmark *PMLA* essay "Law, Literature, and the Vanishing Real" (2005), the law and literature encounter had begun with high expectations but ended by leaving both parties unsatisfied. Law professors had looked to literature, and especially to literary theory, for a style of critical sophistication and a real connection to humanity that seemed unavailable inside the legal academy. Literature professors had sought in the law's institutions a normative clarity and a real-world efficacy that criticism could not achieve on its own. Peters saw the law and literature movement as a thwarted romance, an affair of "projections" and "illusion," where each side wanted something that the other knew it couldn't really give. "The real" vanished and so, as it turned out, what the lawyers and the critics shared was not "content" but a condition of unfulfilled "longing."[1]

Peters's essay bears the clear markings of the interpretive mode that has come to be known as "symptomatic reading." "All interdisciplinarity, one might argue, is disciplinary symptom: somatization, in the disciplinary body, of some invisible pain, thwarted desire being acted out as neurosis."[2] Peters brings the diagnostic vocabulary of psychoanalysis to bear on academic departments and schools, making law and literature itself the target of her critique. She analyzes dim, half-conscious fantasies and attachments that we scholars have sometimes nursed without really examining them in the light of day. One of her most compelling arguments is that law professors and literary critics were attracted to each other because of frustrations they felt at home. "Thwarted desire" tended to fester in law schools increasingly dominated by styles of thought imported from economics and the social sciences; "neurosis" accompanied the decline, in colleges of arts and sciences, of the prestige that literary studies had once been able to take for granted.

Happily, though, Peters is not the kind of therapist who tries to chasten her clients into the routines and the tedium of domesticated life. In the end she prescribes more, not less, promiscuity among the disciplines: a "more comfortable habitation in disciplinary mobility" that would enable us to range beyond law and literature, into other fields like history, philosophy, and cultural studies.[3] Along the way, Peters invites us to see how our own fields had been interdisciplinary all along, drawing from various intellectual traditions and pursuing a wide range of questions. In moving from "law and literature per se" to a broader "disciplinary multiplicity," Peters argues, each side has a chance to lose its illusions not only about the other but also about itself.[4]

At the same time, though, Peters does recommend a lowering of expectations; she asks us to give up on our fantasy of earth-shattering, "revolutionary" contact with the real, to adjust ourselves to more modest scholarly discoveries and pleasures. This is the remedy she proposes for what she calls law and literature's "hysteria." Not every critic has been ready to follow Peters's recommendations. Some of the leading lights in law and literature have insisted that the enterprise will become unrecognizable if it gives up on the basic attachment that Peters sought to dissolve. "The movement has a single core," Martha Nussbaum and Alison LaCroix argued in 2013: "all its participants believe that attending to the stories told in literary works gives the law something that it needs."[5] Without this faith—without a view of literature as a corrective and a supplement—what would be the reason for teaching novels and plays in law schools? Peters, for her part, was willing to take the risk that law and literature in its twentieth-century form would cease to exist, and the new research and teaching programs she imagined for the twenty-first century would be better suited to humanities departments than to the legal academy. The program in Law, Jurisprudence, and Social Thought pioneered by Austin Sarat and his colleagues at Amherst is a promising model of what such a curriculum might look like.

For better or for worse, something like the future that Peters foresaw has in fact taken shape, and it characterizes the present situation in law and literature. Over the past decade or so, legal scholars interested in the critical humanities have not limited themselves to literature or literary theory, and literary critics interested in legal matters have found resources in fields (history, sociology, philosophy) beyond the law. It is probably fair to say, too, that a certain humility, even a kind of delicateness, has tended to replace the grasping for the impossible real—the "revolutionary," earth-shattering ambitions—that Peters saw in the previous generation's projects. Revisiting "Law, Literature, and the Vanishing Real" more than a decade after its publication, then, we see not only its dazzling display of symptomatic reading but also something more surprising: how Peters's call for a more patient, perhaps more humble criticism harmonizes with the styles of "postcritique" that have come to prominence in literary and cultural studies in recent years. Even as Peters's essay performs an almost parodic kind of suspicion, it feels its way toward an alignment with the varieties of reparative reading, surface reading, description, and new formalism.[6]

A more inclusive interdisciplinarity and a more open, humble approach to our objects of study: Peters, writing just after the turn of the century, hoped that these shifts in the orientation of law and literature would be healing, even liberating, for scholars, and the chapters in this volume do show how some kinds of postcritique, especially Eve Sedgwick's theorization of "reparative reading," have reanimated our work in the twenty-first century. Thus Wai Chee Dimock (this volume, chapter 21) invites us to imagine "weak reparation," a kind of justice that "multiplies complexities and prolongs the input process, thanks to a multilayered and multivariable commutating network," rather than rendering a decisive, punitive verdict. And Janet Halley (chapter 7), reflecting on her own long engagement with Sedgwick's writing and teaching, suggests that moving beyond the hermeneutics of suspicion can open readers up to the possibility of being "surprised by joy."

As Halley's own account of her initial resistance to reparative reading attests, though, it can be tempting to view new methods with some of the suspicion that Peters brought to bear on the "romance" between the law professors and literary critics of the previous generation. Could the willing surrender of our disciplinary identities and our revolutionary critical ambition itself be interpreted as symptomatic of new institutional conditions? If you're reading this, you probably don't need to be reminded that the present in law and literature is unfolding within a context of political, economic, and administrative crisis for the university system in the United States. As legislators and administrators shift resources away from the humanities and, in some cases, shutter longstanding departments and programs, the old-fashioned singularity of our disciplines looks, to some of us, less and less like a prison we would wish to escape, and more like a crumbling pillar of institutional security.

As for the humility that characterizes postcritique, Robyn Wiegman has argued that the rise of practices like reparative reading can be seen "not as an alternative to critique but as a means to compensate for its increasingly damaged authority."[7] Surveying the field, Jeffrey J. Williams has called the present a time of "new modesty," a kind of caution in response to "the shrunken expectations of academe, particularly the humanities, and a decline in the social prestige of literary criticism."[8] If we were telling the story in the mode of psychoanalytically informed satire that characterizes Peters's essay, we might cast the postcritical scholars as neglected suitors who console themselves for their lack of cultural capital with the notion that humility is an intellectual and ethical good. Mortified, they make a virtue out of an austere necessity imposed from without.

Whether we read for surfaces or for symptoms, in our time of precariousness and transition in the academy we are learning about the impermanence, perhaps even the frailty, of institutions. Over the past decade or so, scholars have recognized, with a growing consensus, that law and literature are not permanent, unchanging entities. They are contingent formations that take on different characters and enter into different relations with each other at different times, in different places. Reckoning with this contingency, law and literature scholarship tends toward one or another kind of historicism. As recently as 2000, Guyora Binder and Robert Weisberg were pointing out that law and literature had not always acknowledged the histories of fields and disciplines that enabled its own interdisciplinary endeavor: "A precondition of the application of literary theory to legal interpretation is their initial separation. Yet before the nineteenth century, literature was less the discrete enterprise it is today. Fiction, poetry, and drama were continuous with philosophy, history, and other learned discourses, including the more intellectually ambitious legal writing."[9] Lately, though, as Bernadette Meyler shows, the romance between law and literature that Peters analyzed has come to look more like a "love triangle" that includes history as its third party.[10] More and more, it is history that serves as the ground upon which scholars stage and play out the dramas of literature's dynamic engagement with legal thought and systems.

In the rest of this brief chapter, I consider the state of law and literature since the turn of the twenty-first century by exploring how historicist work in our interdiscipline has reconsidered one of our key problems, the character and limits of legal *personhood*. In particular, I examine how recent scholarship has attempted to move beyond personhood, seeking other conceptions of agency and responsibility. Traditional law and literature scholarship had aligned itself with movements for civil rights by critiquing systems and practices of exclusion from personhood—dehumanization, social death, civil disability—and by making moral arguments for legal reform; literature was thought to provide the ethical vision that could make such reforms imaginable. Recently, however, law and literature has become more interested in modes of action that do not depend on the integrity of the will and in versions of connection that do not presuppose the coherence of the self. Whether these mixed, unheroic kinds of being and belonging can become ideals for legal transformation, or whether they remain figures for our own diminished status, is still an open question.

Charting new directions for law and literature in this volume, Bernadette Meyler and Elizabeth Anker suggest the breadth of our interdiscipline's historical sweep, reaching from the early modern period of Shakespeare and the rise of the common law through the contemporary era of globalism and struggles over human rights. Debates about personhood in law and literature have often circled back to the middle phase, the eighteenth and nineteenth centuries, an epoch sometimes associated with the slow, uneven transition "from status to contract" or "from bondage to contract."[11] Scholars have long recognized that modernity's liberal, contractual subject took its distinctive shape in this era and in relation to many other figures of abjection and dispossession, and some of law and literature's most profound reckonings with matters of race, gender, and sexuality have depended on case studies from the eighteenth and nineteenth centuries.

As settler colonialism continued to expand and to divide the territories under the jurisdiction of Anglo-American legal systems, as the Atlantic revolutions and the Indian Wars threw sovereignty into jeopardy, as the violence of slavery provoked unceasing resistance, as the scaffold in the public square gave way to the prison interior behind stone walls, as social life seemed to divide itself into public and private spheres, as the condemnation of sin yielded to the classification and stigmatization of sexual identities (marked most spectacularly by Oscar Wilde's trials at the fin de siècle)—as the modern world took shape, lawyers and writers alike participated in the invention of new kinds of persons, endowed with new capacities and responsibilities, vulnerable to new injuries. By the early 1800s, on both sides of the North Atlantic, the individual citizen-subject, bearing the rights and obligations of legal personhood, had been defined in opposition to the many nonpersons and not-quite-persons who constituted, in fact, the majority of human lives that law would govern.

Meanwhile, the secular writing that would come to be known as literature had given a central role to the interior lives of ordinary people, organizing its plots around dramas of contract and harm. The epic fell into obsolescence (so the story goes), and in its place rose the novel, whose protagonists were known for their ordinariness and their vulnerability. Legal rationalism and literary sentimentalism took shape alongside one another. By the middle of the nineteenth century, it had become more or less routine for literature to define its moral vision against the cold logic of the law, often by way of human characters who stood outside the law's protections.

"Over and above the scene there broods a portentous shadow—the shadow of *law*. So long as the law considers all these human beings, with beating hearts and living affections, only as so many *things* belonging to a master, ... it is impossible to make anything beautiful or desirable in the best regulated administration of slavery."[12] Harriet Beecher Stowe's analysis of the slave system in the antebellum United States is a classic, highly conventional account of the vulnerabilities that come with exclusion from legal personhood. In *Uncle Tom's Cabin*, the paternalistic affection of the master lasts only as long as his good health and good fortune. The condescension of the mistress depends on her moods. Even economic self-interest is unreliable in restraining the violent passions of overseers and slavecatchers. The law divides the world into two classes, those who live in the light of its recognition and those who live under the shadow, appearing not as persons but as property, "so many *things*."

When literature claims the authority to expose this harsh contrast, it casts itself as a different kind of writing, critically estranged from law. Provisionally and strategically aligning itself with the private, domestic sphere—against a public sphere of legislators and businessmen—it offers a compensatory kind of recognition, attuned to the "beating hearts and living affections" of the enslaved. Yet the long-term project is to reclaim a kind of public and political authority: literature endeavors to bring the law into line with its own more capacious vision of the human community. In Stowe's liberal-sentimental project, the novel attempts to refashion the readers' sensibilities in order, ultimately, to expand the circle of legal personhood.[13]

A good deal of law and literature work has attempted to extend the same project into the twentieth century. Thus, Nussbaum in *Cultivating Humanity* argues, by way of Ralph Ellison's *Invisible Man*, that "narrative art has the power to make us see the lives of the different with more than a casual tourist's interest—with involvement and sympathetic understanding, with anger at our society's refusals of visibility."[14] In the same spirit, Teresa Godwin Phelps introduces a recent special issue of *Studies in Law, Politics* and *Society* (devoted to "Law and Literature Reconsidered") by announcing the high hope that literature might "offer a remedy to the malignities of the current legal culture," which has allowed itself to justify torture and other "ongoing, unspeakable, human rights violations."[15] Even after the absorption of poststructuralism and postcolonial theory into law and literature in the 1980s, many critics held fast to the same opposition between legal violence and literary dissent. As Elizabeth Anker's chapter in this volume (chapter 12) observes of the first wave of work on law, literature, and globalization, "literature, in contrast [to law], is celebrated as an antigen that counteracts law's toxicities and instead purveys justice and ethics."

Stowe practiced a Protestantism, stoked in the revivals of mid-nineteenth-century Connecticut and Ohio, that could see itself as timeless and universal, encompassing all of humanity. Nussbaum is a humanist and a classicist, but she is explicit about the far-reaching expansiveness of the ethical vision she draws from the study of literature. (In the chapter from which I quoted, above, she insists on the point by reading Ellison alongside Socrates.) Historicist scholars of law and literature, especially in humanities departments, have tended to be more circumspect, even relativist. Take, for instance, Bradin Cormack's cautious account of his own scholarly procedure in *A Power to Do Justice*: "I make no claim that either my readings or the texts that are their objects offer a universalizing account of literature's relation to law. The chapters develop, each along its own trajectory, more local claims about how different kinds of literary production grappled with kinds of legal discourse and legal problems."[16] *Grappled*: Cormack's use of the simple past, not the literary present, places the action at a distance from our own situation. In this kind of work there is no aspiration toward a transcendent ideal; there is an effort to analyze how particular institutions and assumptions took shape in certain historical situations.

The turn to historicism in law and literature has enabled scholars to raise some fundamental questions about the origins and character of legal personhood. Indeed, we can make a fair sketch of some of the most influential recent work in the interdiscipline by charting out the various positions that have defined themselves against the liberal ideal. First, and perhaps most familiarly, there is the argument that the individuated, rights-bearing legal person is a historical product of patriarchy, imperialism, and slavery.[17] Of legal thought in eighteenth- and nineteenth-century slaveholding societies, Colin Dayan observes, "the limits of personhood and the extension of thinglikeness became oddly coextensive in this landscape of coercion. New taxonomies had to be created. They formed the conditions for systematic abasement."[18] Building on Dayan's work, Imani Perry's chapter in this volume (chapter 14) shows how the law's invocation of a "reasonable person" summons various figures of unreason and nonpersonhood. According to this line of critique, banishment and dehumanization are not the signs that the work of making legal persons is incomplete; they are precisely the ways persons get made and unmade. It is by attending to "exclusion," to borrow an evocative formulation from Anne Anlin Cheng's chapter (chapter 13), that law and literature "reveals the artifice animating the heart of modern natural persons." If our work has become more and more interested in the possibilities that might be available without or beyond the fiction of personhood, it is at least in part because we have come to see how that fiction was forged in injury and dispossession.

Who wouldn't want to be a person? According to the conventional view, personhood provides the condition for the law's recognition and protection, the status of being one who can act with deliberation and consequence, one whose injuries will be taken seriously. From this perspective, personhood would appear to be a precious good, perhaps most of all to those who have never been entitled to take it for granted. Yet law and literature has come to the conclusion that legal violence operates not only by withholding the blessing of personhood but also by bestowing and manipulating it. Drawing from a theoretical tradition that extends from Butler back through Foucault to Fanon and Nietzsche and Freud, working through the paradoxes of subjectivity and subjection, law and literature finds that the passage from bondage to contract is something other than a full emancipation.

Thus Saidiya Hartman's field-changing study *Scenes of Subjection* tracks the continuities that link antebellum slavery to the legal and racial violence of the later nineteenth century. After the Civil War, an industrial capitalist society that had been built on slavery "found it impossible to envision freedom independent of constraint or personhood and autonomy separate from the sanctity of property and proprietorial notions of the self."[19] Even before legal emancipation, the slaveholding order itself had never effected a total abjection; it had always relied on the making and manipulation of subjects, for instance through "the inscription of agency as criminal or, at the very least, as deserving of punishment."[20] In a devastating account of antebellum rape cases, Hartman shows how the legal system endowed enslaved women with will and power so that it could hold them culpable and exonerate their rapists. Hartman goes on to read Harriet Jacobs's *Incidents in the Life of a Slave Girl* as a critique and subversion of the law's notion of seduction.

Revisiting the intertwined histories of criminalization and African American authorship, Jeannine DeLombard makes the unsettling argument that the attribution of criminal guilt, in formal trials but also in early America's vibrant and sensational gallows literature, was the very precondition for the rise of a publicly recognizable black personhood. As DeLombard sees it, the heroic figure conceived in the fugitive slave narratives of the antebellum decades was the direct descendent of the previous generation's condemned convicts.[21] On the surface of things, this argument looks almost like a reversal of Hartman's. Where Hartman emphasizes the kinds of dehumanization and vulnerability that follow from the attribution of responsibility to African American subjects, DeLombard understands criminal culpability as a mode of agency (however compromised) that could be expanded and refashioned for the purposes of public protest, even liberation.

How can we account for this apparent impasse? Both Hartman and DeLombard are historicists of law and literature, but they take different approaches to the archive. Hartman seems most keenly interested in the silences and gaps, the conditions for the impossibility of autonomous self-expression. As she writes in *Lose Your Mother* (2007), "The archive dictates what can be said about the past and the kinds of stories that can be told about persons cataloged, embalmed, and sealed away in box files and folios. To read the archive is to enter a mortuary; it permits one final viewing and allows for a last glimpse of persons about to disappear into the slave hold."[22] DeLombard, by contrast, reassembles the texts and ephemera that have survived, not to recover private histories but to account for the emergence of public ones. Rather than emphasizing the repressions that limit our access to the histories of the excluded, DeLombard asks how African American personhood, virtually unthinkable from within the slave law, was ever able to become imaginable in the sphere of letters. Finally, though, both Hartman and DeLombard find something generative in the most constrained forms of legal agency, forms that have little in common with the fiction of a self-possessing and autonomous personhood that is associated with liberalism and contract law. As Hartman argues in her treatment of Jacobs, even the notorious double bind of slave law—constituting the enslaved as property to strip away rights but as persons to hold them culpable for crimes—created openings that could be exploited for expression and resistance.

One of the insights of the historicism in law and literature scholarship, then, is that much of life plays out in the space between two stark opposites. Law and literature make persons who are neither masterfully self-possessed (autonomous subjects) nor stripped of all agency (socially or civilly dead). Edlie Wong's *Neither Fugitive nor Free* (2009), a study of the freedom suits that enslaved plaintiffs brought against their masters, is exemplary here. Focusing on men and women whose passage across jurisdictional borders gave them a claim to emancipation, Wong writes, "The paradoxical dimensions of the traveling slave's liminal position both inside and outside the category of the human confounded the geographical and ontological boundaries between freedom and slavery."[23] Even the jurisprudence of slavery in the antebellum United States, notorious for its fictions of absolute mastery and total subjection, was also a scene of "everyday animism," in Stephen Best's phrase.[24]

For obvious reasons, the colonial and postcolonial societies of the eighteenth- and nineteenth-century Atlantic world have been a key site for histories of personhood in law and literature. But they have not been the only sites. Scholars have also turned their eyes back to the European metropoles. In a critical revision of Foucault's account of subjection, Frances Ferguson's *Pornography, the Theory* (2009) reads eighteenth-century prison reform documents by Jeremy Bentham and others alongside novels from the same era to show how utilitarian social structures like the panopticon, far from isolating and fixing individuated subjects, can be understood as theaters for the performance and appraisal of action; the self that appears to cohere before the inspector's eye is not permanent but temporary and provisional, eventually moving on to try its luck in a different situation. Along the way, Ferguson makes an ally of the Marquis de Sade, hardly the kind of author who would provide the moral insights that would encourage liberal reformers to expand the circle of personhood.[25]

"Attending to the logic of strict liability," Sandra Macpherson writes in *Harm's Way* (2010), "requires us to rethink the question of the person in the history and theory of the novel. It also requires us to rethink the question of the nonperson."[26] The "person" Macpherson invites us to rethink is the protagonist of an older story about law and literature, one in which the law's contractual subject and the novel's private consciousness grew up together, kin to each other and to philosophical liberalism's figures of secular selfhood. The characters who interest Macpherson take shape elsewhere, not in the putatively equal partnerships of contracts but in the retroactively imposed bonds of strict liability. "Relationship on this account is profoundly nonvolitional, emerging independently of any prior connection between the parties other than that brought about by accident, harm, injury. Injury *produces* relationship, enforcing obligations between those who have not chosen or wanted to belong to one another."[27] These entangled, tragic creatures do not offer themselves up in the marriage plot. Their actions are not the effects of their conscious volition; nearly the opposite is true. They loom in ghost stories; they are made in disasters.

Macpherson's arguments have important consequences for how we think about eighteenth-century British legal and literary history. Rather than a movement from status to contract, we see how new kinds of status—of noncontractual affiliation—took hold and replaced older, feudal ones. In reconstructing the history of the relationships that injury produced, though, Macpherson is also using an unfamiliar version of the past to think her way out of some of the conceptual binds of the present. This is a historicism that discovers, in the archives, certain roads not taken, occluded possibilities that might be reanimated now as a usable past (usable at least for theory). Like several other recent works in law and literature, *Harm's Way* aligns itself with modes of acting and of belonging that do not depend on the fiction of a prior, coherent, self-determining subject.

As I see it, our era in law and literature has been characterized by a shift away from universalism and strong normative claims, toward a historicism that views the liberal-humanist promise of personhood with a critical, sometimes suspicious eye. Some scholars have recused themselves altogether from normative position taking, preferring a kind of antiquarian approach to the histories of legal and literary formations. Elsewhere, though, we see the return of an ethical imperative that would affirm nonpersonhood, perhaps even subpersonhood, as an ideal. I've suggested that a paranoid reading of this new work might view it as symptomatic of the marginalized, minoritized status that the interpretive humanities now occupy within the university and the public sphere: humbled professors finding historical and literary figurations of their own damaged authority. In the end, though, the promise of a law and literature that is moving beyond the ideal of personhood may be less in its ethical posturing than in its capacity to think about large-scale systems and collective fates: mass media, mass migration, mass incarceration.

NOTES

1. Julie Stone Peters, "Law, Literature, and the Vanishing Real: On the Future of an Interdisciplinary Illusion," *PMLA* 120 (2005): 442–53.
2. Ibid., 448. The term "symptomatic reading" is most strongly associated with criticism that has combined the insights of Marxism and psychoanalysis, especially Fredric Jameson, *The Political Unconscious: Narrative as a Socially Symbolic Act* (Ithaca, NY: Cornell University Press, 1981). The most influential recent revision is Stephen Best and Sharon Marcus, "Surface Reading: An Introduction," *Representations* 108 (2009): 1–21.
3. Peters, "Law, Literature, and the Vanishing Real," 451.
4. Ibid.

5. Martha C. Nussbaum and Alison L. LaCroix, "Introduction," in *Subversion and Sympathy: Gender, Law and the British Novel*, ed. Martha C. Nussbaum and Alison L. Lacroix (New York: Oxford University Press, 2013), 11.

6. On "reparative reading," see Eve Sedgwick, "Paranoid Reading and Reparative Reading, or, You're so Paranoid, You Probably Think This Essay Is about You," in *Touching Feeling: Affect, Pedagogy, Performativity* (Durham, NC: Duke University Press, 2003), 67–92. For an introduction to and defense of this and other "post-critical" reading methods, see Rita Felski, *The Limits of Critique* (Chicago: University of Chicago Press, 2015).

7. Robyn Wiegman, "The Times We're in: Queer Feminist Criticism and the Reparative 'Turn,'" *Feminist Theory* 15 (2014): 7.

8. Jeffrey J. Williams, "The New Modesty in Literary Criticism," *Chronicle of Higher Education Review*, January 5, 2015.

9. Guyora Binder and Robert Weisberg, *Literary Criticisms of Law* (Princeton, NJ: Princeton University Press, 2000), 7.

10. Bernadette Meyler, "Law, Literature, and History: The Love Triangle," *UC Irvine Law Review* 5 (2015): 365–91. See this volume, chapter 9.

11. The argument for a movement, in modernity, "from status to contract" traces its origins back to Henry Sumner Maine, *Ancient Law: Its Connection with the Early History of Society, and Its Relation to Modern Ideals* (London: John Murray, 1861). A major intervention, giving special attention to race and gender in the modern world, is Amy Dru Stanley, *From Bondage to Contract: Wage Labor, Marriage, and the Market in the Age of Slave Emancipation* (Cambridge: Cambridge University Press, 1998).

12. Harriet Beecher Stowe, *Uncle Tom's Cabin*, ed. Elizabeth Ammons (New York: Norton Critical, 1994), 8.

13. I give an account of secularization and the shifting relations between law and literature in Caleb Smith, *The Oracle and the Curse: A Poetics of Justice from the Revolution to the Civil War* (Cambridge, MA: Harvard University Press, 2013).

14. Martha Nussbaum, *Cultivating Humanity: A Classical Defense of Reform in Liberal Education* (Cambridge, MA: Harvard University Press, 1997), 88.

15. Teresa Godwin Phelps, "'Reading As If for Life': Law and Literature is More Important than Ever," in "Law and Literature Reconsidered," ed. Austin Sarat, special issue, *Studies in Law, Politics and Society* 43 (2008): 134.

16. Bradin Cormack, *A Power to Do Justice: Jurisdiction, English Literature, and the Rise of Common Law, 1509–1625* (Chicago: University of Chicago Press, 2007), 22.

17. Two of the most concise formulations of this argument are to be found in Carole Pateman, *The Sexual Contract* (Stanford, CA: Stanford University Press, 1988) and Charles Milles, *The Racial Contract* (Ithaca, NY: Cornell University Press, 1997).

18. Colin Dayan, *The Law Is a White Dog: How Legal Rituals Make and Unmake Persons* (Princeton, NJ: Princeton University Press, 2011), 140. Law and literature scholarship informed by Giorgio Agamben has extended this line of critique back to ancient Greek conceptions of democracy and citizenship.

19. Saidiya V. Hartman, *Scenes of Subjection: Terror, Slavery, and Self-Making in Nineteenth-Century America* (New York: Oxford University Press, 1997), 115.

20. Ibid., 62

21. Jeannine Marie DeLombard, *In the Shadow of the Gallows: Race, Crime, and American Civic Identity* (Philadelphia: University of Pennsylvania Press, 2012).

22. Saidiya V. Hartman, *Lose Your Mother: A Journey along the Atlantic Slave Route* (New York: Farrar, Strauss and Giroux, 2007), 17.
23. Edlie Wong, *Neither Fugitive nor Free: Atlantic Slavery, Freedom Suits, and the Legal Culture of Travel* (New York: New York University Press, 2009), 5.
24. Stephen Best, *The Fugitive's Properties: Law and the Poetics of Possession* (Chicago: University of Chicago Press, 2004), 2.
25. Frances Ferguson, *Pornography, the Theory: What Utilitarianism Did to Action* (Chicago: University of Chicago Press, 2004).
26. Sandra Macpherson, *Harm's Way: Tragic Responsibility and the Novel Form* (Baltimore, MD: Johns Hopkins University Press, 2010).
27. Ibid., 182.

CHAPTER 3

From Charisma to Routinization and Beyond

Speculations on the Future of the Study of Law and Literature

AUSTIN SARAT

Writing about law and society studies a decade and a half after the founding of the Law and Society Association, Richard Abel, by then a former editor of the association's journal, *Law and Society Review*, argued that "social studies of law have reached a critical point in their development. The original paradigm is exhausted. Until new ones are constructed, scholarship will be condemned to spin its wheels, adding minor refinements to accepted truths, repeating conventional arguments in unresolvable debates."[1] He went on to say that law and society studies were "running so smoothly along familiar tracks that the questions and answers have begun to sound a comfortable, but rather boring 'clackety-clack.'"[2]

What Abel wrote three decades ago might seem to be an apt description of the current situation of law and literature as a field of interdisciplinary endeavor. By now the field is well established and well delineated. The conventional markers of academic success (e.g., journals, book series, scholarly meetings) are amply attached to law and literature. Thus, *Law and Literature*, founded in 1988, is now in its twenty-seventh volume, and John Jay College of Criminal Justice holds an ongoing series of Literature and Law conferences.

There is, moreover, a pretty clear law and literature canon, a touchstone of works foundational in, and of continuing importance to, the field. All of this is to be celebrated. Law and literature has made substantial and important contributions to our understanding of law and opened up new avenues of inquiry in literary studies.

Yet as the field has moved from charisma to routinization, it runs up against the Richard Abel question. Is the field "running so smoothly along familiar tracks that the questions and answers have begun to sound a comfortable, but rather boring 'clackety-clack'"? And, if so, is this future one to which law and literature scholars should aspire?

More than forty years ago, James Boyd White published *The Legal Imagination* and launched the law and literature movement in the United States.[3] White's book treated legal and literary texts as mirror images of each other in the ways they constitute the identities of characters and invite their readers to assume certain kinds of characters. The publication of White's book coincided with developments in literary and legal theory that emphasized certain reading strategies to take advantage of the indeterminacy of texts in both domains and fueled interest in exploring the intersections of law and literature. Among these, the most important were associated with poststructuralism and deconstruction. These approaches decentered the author and shifted attention to communities of readers as sources of meaning.[4]

What happened next is a well-rehearsed story. Law and literature studies proliferated.[5] They quickly became an alluring type of interdisciplinary legal scholarship, compelling to those in and out of the legal academy for whom the turn to law and economics seemed arid at best and pernicious at worst. Legal scholars, like Owen Fiss, claimed that the turn to literature and humanistic approaches to law might help to free "contemporary law from its own barrenness."[6] Former Yale Law School Dean Calabresi said that literary and humanistic study in law might have a profound impact on the character of legal practitioners. He recounted how former Supreme Court Justice Hugo Black told him, on the second day of his clerkship, that if he had "never read Tacitus . . . then, you are not a lawyer."[7] The hopes of Fiss and Calabresi depended on a trope of rescue or recuperation, a trope that was crucial to the attractiveness of law and literature during its early, charismatic stages.

Turning to literature and to literary readings of law might help rescue law or, depending on one's historical perspective, help recuperate parts of law that would otherwise be lost. This trope was perhaps most visible in White's work. He contended that attention to literature would be an antidote to a conception of law as a machine operating on society. As White put it, "To imagine the law as a rhetorical and literary process may help us to see each moment in the law differently. . . . It leads to a different conception of the teaching of law and may help the practitioner conceive of its practice differently too. . . . [T]he poems by Frost, Dickinson, and Keats do much to suggest standards by which we might learn to do . . . law better."[8] Reading "great" literature expands the imagination and, as a result, enables lawyers and judges to make more impartial, yet empathetic, judgments.

The 1970s and 1980s were a heady time for literary and humanities scholars who seemingly had something of relevance to contribute to an institutional domain, namely law schools, which scored higher in the prestige and power hierarchy within universities than departments of English, classics, or comp lit. This period seemed to herald an end to the marginalization of law professors with a literary bent and, at the same time, to open a space for people in the humanities to make inroads into the legal academy. But all this came at a price.

Closely related to the trope of recuperation, the charismatic period of law and literature was dominated by a "high culture" conception of literature. Literature, specifically, and the humanities, generally, were said to provide uplift and inspiration; they raise the deepest questions about our lives and the values we pursue. It is, I suspect, not coincidental that Calabresi named Kant, Bentham, Captain Vere, and Athol Fugard, in addition to Tacitus, as examples of key literary and humanities texts that lawyers should read.[9]

This brief narrative of the early period is, of course, too linear and smooth to capture the dynamism and energy of the burgeoning law and literature movement. There were lively polemics and contestations about the forms and political implications of law and literature scholarship. Those polemics were an important part of the charismatic appeal of law and literature studies. Among the most influential was Richard Posner's criticism of the notion that literary analysis could add anything meaningful to the understanding of law.[10] Posner described what he called "the great false hope of law and literature—that it will change the way lawyers think about the interpretation of statutes and the Constitution."[11] He went on to say that he did not think that "law is a humanity. It is a technique of government."[12] Robert Cover's famous 1986 intervention "Violence and the Word"[13] also offered a biting critique of the law and literature approach, suggesting that it dangerously underplayed the fact that "legal interpretation plays on a field of pain and death."[14]

Today, the charismatic period of law and literature scholarship and the days when some turned to literature as a template for legal thinking are long gone. The crisis in, and of, the humanities has taken its toll, as have the threats to law schools posed by declining enrollments and difficulties in placing lawyers. Few, if any, still believe that reading novels is an unproblematic way to redeem lawyers and legal scholarship from narrow instrumentalism. Law schools generally have abandoned literary interdisciplinarity in favor of a back-to-basics approach.

I am of course not the first to notice or comment on this situation. As Kenji Yoshino has noted, the early division in the field between law *in* literature and law *as* literature has been exhaustively explored. "Three decades after James Boyd White's *The Legal Imagination* inaugurated it," Yoshino observed,

> the law-and-literature enterprise presents conflicting symptoms of health. On the one hand, the field appears to be flourishing as never before. Recent years have seen a spate of books taking law-and-literature approaches. The enterprise has penetrated the legal academy. Conferences on the subject occur with some frequency and attract renowned literary scholars, legal scholars, and jurists. On the other hand, the field continues to be plagued by skepticism. It has achieved more status than other interdisciplinary curiosities like law and music or law and mathematics. Yet it has never achieved the status of law and economics, legal history, and jurisprudence.[15]

Yoshino concludes that law needs, but has a deeply ambivalent relation to literature such that law and literature is "a distinctively fraught enterprise."[16]

So now what? There are, as I see it, three alternative futures for law and literature. There are choices to be made, the most important of which involves the issue of how bounded and distinctive law and literature scholarship should be.

The first possibility, which I label "normalization," would see the field emphasizing its distinctiveness and resisting incorporation into broader interdisciplinary explorations of law. It would mean continuing in the vein of a kind of normal science, adding "minor refinements to accepted truths, repeating conventional arguments in unresolvable debates." Following this path, new paradigms might emerge, but scholars would likely continue to turn out readings of the legal themes in this or that literary text and illuminate the literary qualities of this or that legal phenomenon. They would borrow from mainstream literary scholarship and fill gaps in existing knowledge.

The second possible future, what I call "selective assimilation," would see law and literature studies embedded in broader analysis of the relationship of law and cultural production. In this future, literary scholarship would borrow heavily from cultural analysis and cultural studies. Indeed, there are signs that this kind of selective assimilation already has an important place in the broader domain of law, culture, and humanities.

One can see incorporation of literary study of law into more of a historically specific and culturally attuned set of inquiries in which the literary text is not the primary object of inquiry but one resource for understanding a broader historical or cultural problem.[17]

A broadened cultural studies approach might give new energy and life to the study of law and literature by radically extending what counts in the analysis of literature beyond the realm of "high culture."[18] It would invite study of the quotidian world and connect literary study of law to analysis of film, advertising, and pop art. But, in addition to this liberating expansion in the objects of study, linking law and literature to cultural studies would also link it to the study of questions of social stratification, power, and social conflict and to "historical forms of consciousness or subjectivity, or the subjective forms we live by, or . . . the subjective side of social relations."[19]

Treating law's literary life as part of a more encompassing cultural reality would mean looking at the material structures of law and literature to see them in play and at play, as signs and symbols, fantasies and phantasms.[20] It requires examining the ways that the cultural lives of law contribute to what Johnson calls "asymmetries in the abilities of individuals and social groups to define and realize their needs."[21]

An expanded conception of law and literature would bring literary and legal scholars into a broader dialogue within the humanities and would resist the dichotomization of the symbolic and material. This would mean following Cover and examining how legal interpretation is shaped and reshaped by its relationship to violence. It would also marry literary and sociological perspectives. As Susan Silbey puts it, "[L]aw does more than reflect or encode what is otherwise normatively constructed; . . . law is part of the cultural processes that actively contribute in the composition of social relations."[22]

In this future, scholars of law and literature would attend to the ways law's power and meaning are continually renewed, recreated, defended, and modified but also to the ways they are resisted, limited, altered, and challenged in literary treatments of law and in the literary dimensions of legal life. It would remind us that law's cultural lives are not placid and calm. They are alive with the push and pull of contestation that always marks what Johnson has called "the subjective side of social relations."[23]

Embedding law and literature within a broader cultural study of law is then important as a way of unpacking what Rosemary Coombe calls "the signifying power of law and law's power over signification."[24] It invites us to acknowledge that legal meaning is found and invented in the variety of locations and practices that comprise culture and that those locations and practices are themselves encapsulated, though always incompletely, in legal forms, regulations, and legal symbols. But thinking about law and literature as part of a broader analysis of law's cultural role also highlights the limits of law's ability to constitute, regulate, or contain the imagination, invention, creativity, and improvisation that are culture itself.

The third route to the future also involves pushing the boundaries of law and literary study, only this time beyond the humanities and culture. This "law as performance" perspective brings literary and cultural analysis together with social studies of the way law performs in a variety of domains, from the appellate court to the cop on the beat, from stories about law in great literature to moments when law is silent. In this imagined future, law and literature gives up any claim to distinctiveness as a field of inquiry and contributes to analysis of enactment and performance. This analysis directs attention to text as well as context, role, and action, without privileging the word over the world or the world over the word. Here law and literature scholars might join in studying the human actions that go into giving a performance, thinking not only about texts and language, but staging, symbolization, and relation to audience.

In this imagined future, law might be treated as a domain for exploring the desires that performances seek to satisfy and the pleasures that legal performances provide. As Jack Balkin and Sanford Levinson have suggested, "The basic idea is that law, music, and drama . . . are similar . . . insofar as they involve the transformation of ink on a page—call it a statute, a score, a script—into complex social action."[25] Judges interpreting a statute must take into account their audience, anticipating its likely reactions, staging their decisions in such a way as to enable particular connections between the law's pronouncement and the pleasures that audience members may be expected to derive from the performance of law. Like conductors of symphony orchestras, they may begin with the score, but they must also concern themselves with the skills of the musicians with whom they work and the expectations of their audience, with staging, with sound, with the way the score can be enacted and through its enactment, brought to life.

Thinking about law as performance would bring the study of law and literature into dialogue with scholarship on theatre, dance, music, ritual, carnival, and spectacle, and draw on work in linguistics, anthropology, sociology, and theatre history in order to explore performance events and the collaborative work processes which produce them.[26] It would require law and literature scholars to join with people in the social sciences as well as the humanities to engage with performance practices of various legal actors, some of whom produce and interpret texts, some of whom seem less textually engaged. Law and literature scholars would help observe, document, analyze, and theorize about the various performance practices of law as well as the meaning-making processes of performance itself.

In linking the future of law and literature to the question of boundary maintenance, I am merely restating a point Fiss made long ago when he warned that scholars of law and literature "will have to struggle with the question of domain and definition, perhaps more so than is usually the case."[27] Here I have marked three possible futures, three paths with different relationships between law and literature and other interdisciplinary studies of law. The brightest future for the field seems to me to be one in which the distinctiveness of law and literature scholarship fades so that its contribution to broader understandings of law can be enhanced.

NOTES

1. Richard Abel, "Redirecting Social Studies of Law," *Law and Society Review* 14 (1980): 826.
2. Ibid., 805.
3. James Boyd White, *The Legal Imagination: Studies in the Nature of Legal Thought and Expression* (Boston: Little, Brown, 1973).
4. See, for example, Paul De Man, *Blindness and Insight: Essays in the Rhetoric of Contemporary Criticism*, 2nd ed. (Minneapolis: University of Minnesota Press, 1983).
5. See James Seaton, "Law and Literature: Works, Criticism, and Theory," *Yale Journal of Law and the Humanities* 11 (1999): 479–508.
6. Owen Fiss, "The Challenge Ahead," *Yale Journal of Law and the Humanities* 1 (1988): ix.
7. Guido Calabresi, "Introductory Letter," *Yale Journal of Law and the Humanities* 1 (1988): vii.
8. James Boyd White, "Imagining the Law," in *The Rhetoric of Law*, ed. Austin Sarat and Thomas R. Kearns (Ann Arbor: University of Michigan Press, 1994), 29, 55.
9. Calabresi, "Introductory Letter," vii.
10. See Richard A. Posner, "Law and Literature: A Relation Reargued," *Virginia Law Review* 72 (1986): 1351.
11. Ibid., 1360.
12. Ibid., 1392.
13. Robert M. Cover, "Violence and the Word," *Yale Law Journal* 95 (1986): 1601.
14. Ibid.
15. Kenji Yoshino, "The City and the Poet," *Yale Law Journal* 114 (2005): 1836.
16. Ibid., 1837.
17. See, for example, Eric Slauter, *The State as a Work of Art: The Cultural Origins of the Constitution* (Chicago: University of Chicago Press, 2011).

18. Herbert Gans, *Popular Culture and High Culture: An Analysis and Evaluation of Taste* (New York: Basic Books, 1974).

19. Richard Johnson, "What Is Cultural Studies Anyway?" *Social Text* 16 (1986): 39, 43.

20. For a general discussion of the materiality of cultural life see Raymond Williams, *Problems in Materialism and Culture: Selected Essays* (London: Verso, 1980).

21. Johnson, "What Is Cultural Studies Anyway?," 39.

22. Susan Silbey, "Making a Place for a Cultural Analysis of Law," *Law and Social Inquiry* 17 (1992): 39.

23. Johnson, "What Is Cultural Studies Anyway?," 43.

24. Rosemary J. Coombe, "Contingent Articulations: A Critical Cultural Studies of Law," in *Law in the Domains of Culture*, ed. Austin Sarat and Thomas R. Kearns (Ann Arbor: University of Michigan Press, 1998), 46.

25. Jack M. Balkin and Sanford Levinson, "Interpreting Law and Music: Performance Notes on 'The Banjo Serenader' and 'The Lying Crowd of Jews,'" *Cardozo Law Review* 20 (1999): 1513.

26. See Julie Stone Peters, "Legal Performance Good and Bad," *Law, Culture, and the Humanities* 4 (2008): 179–200.

27. Fiss, "Challenge Ahead," ix.

PART 2

Methods

CHAPTER 4

There's No Such Thing as Interpreting a Text

MARTIN JAY STONE

What we do is to bring words back from their metaphysical to their everyday use.

Wittgenstein[1]

Literary interpretation has been making regular appearances in the accounts of those who write about legal interpretation.[2] Sometimes what is proposed is an analogy, but sometimes it is more than that: some theorists begin by asking what interpretation-in-general is and then locate law and literature as two domains in which their account applies. Part of my aim is to somewhat break up such ideas of unity by making clear why differences are inevitable and, indeed, why "interpreting a text" is an abstraction and not the primary thing if you want to understand interpretation—what it is or how to do it—in any domain. I'm influenced by an idea of Joseph Raz: Our reasons for interpreting are different in different domains; and where our reasons are different, what it is to succeed at interpreting must differ as well.[3]

It makes sense that law and literature have been focal points for reflection on interpretation, for these kinds of work are created with the very aim of creating an object for interpretation. Interpretation self-consciously pervades these domains.[4] This contrasts with (say) conversational remarks, instructions, and historical events: these do come in for interpretation, but that isn't normally *why* people make them. Indeed, sometimes—for example, when I order a latte and all goes well—no interpretation is needed.

Or at least that is how things appear from a practically engaged point of view—the point of view we have when we are going about our activities rather than theorizing about interpretation. In contrast, there is today a *philosophical* use of the term "interpretation." Here the theorist speaks not of understanding this or that poem, rule, or instruction, but of interpretation as a condition of understanding *as such*: no "text" is present except by way of interpretation, we hear; and even "plain meanings" are interpretive products,[5] for it is "interpretation that gives us the rule, not the other way around."[6] Or (in a different idiom): all texts are instances of "generalized writing," "generalized literature," or "arche-literature," a mark of which is its polysemy.[7] In the broadest formulations, interpretation is present in any experience of the world—for example, Nietzsche: "There are no facts, only interpretations."[8] Such theses sound provocative because they seem to undermine our workaday distinctions (e.g., between cases where interpretations are needed and cases where they are superfluous) or at least to suggest that such distinctions lack the substance we are inclined to credit them with.

How did "interpretation" come to seem serviceable for expressing such philosophical insight into the world-as-a-whole or into any representation of it? Can the content of this insight be explained, or should we say, rather, that the meaning of some things must be available *without* interpretation if interpretation is to be possible at all? Wittgenstein asks this question,[9] and it is connected to one of his larger themes: that of philosophy as speech dislocated from—yet still depending on—its everyday contexts.

Depending on: For, after all, someone who employs "interpretation" in order to express "philosophical" insight isn't merely intending to introduce a new *technical* term but is relying on our familiarity with a term we already have. Even a philosopher like Derrida who favors new technical terms (like "arche-writing") will be found *explaining* his ideas in ways like this: "it does mean ... that one cannot refer to [anything] except in an interpretive experience."[10] This appeal to something as familiar as "interpretation" was bound to occur. For one difference between the terms "arche-writing" and "interpretation" is that the former but not the latter is clearly useless for purposes other than philosophy. Technical terms in philosophy can come in extended, mutually-referring chains, but if the chains didn't touch down in *some* terms with which we have an everyday, working familiarity, we couldn't even imagine that we were following along, much less gaining insight.

Hence, the everyday contexts of "interpretation"—the contexts in which we already know how to employ the term—are relevant to understanding why a philosopher is attracted to this particular expression. Moreover, there are *many* everyday contexts of interpretation and we lack a clear view of them: misunderstandings arise from associations the word carries in one context that don't actually characterize its work in another. Indeed, the fog which surrounds the term interpretation (for lack of a clear view of its different contexts) may be partly just what makes the term seem potent for expressing deep insight. That is, if someone *did* have clearly in view what "interpretation" is when it is at work in a particular domain—e.g., for lawyers, an interpretation is often a reformulation of a rule—she might no longer find it compelling or insightful to say "it is interpretation that gives us the rule" (or various similar theses), for of course she doesn't mean her expression like *that*: she doesn't mean you can apply a rule only by first reformulating it or by putting some additional gloss on it.

I won't pursue these points (about the relation between "interpretation" in its everyday and philosophical employments) further here.[11] They indicate my motivation for what I will do, which is to sketch an approach to legal and literary interpretation that doesn't begin with a philosophical thesis about how texts (in general) can mean something at all. My sketch will allow the differences between legal and literary interpretation to come into sharper view. And if someone says that interpretation is really ubiquitous and endless, my sketch suggests a partially sympathetic response: "That's an apt of description of *literary* interpretation, but there are other kinds of texts as well. You could make what you say correct by expressly restricting it to those texts."[12] To someone already committed to the thesis that all texts are instances of a generalized literature (i.e., that literary interpretation is exemplary of interpretation-in-general), my response might, of course, sound *naïve*.

1. INTERPRETIVE SETTINGS AND KINDS

Conversation, laws, poems, dreams, oracles, history, social practices, forms of relationship and cultural ideals all come in for interpretation. The term also describes uncertain inferences ("as I interpret the X-ray . . ."), translations of living speech, music and theater performances, and pure stipulations of meaning (e.g., what logicians do with variables). Such variation in the use of a word isn't surprising, but only loose analogies run through all this. The disanalogies are more impressive: The logician who 'interprets' a variable doesn't purport to *understand* anything; the physician who interprets an X-ray does purport to understand something, but unlike some of the other cases, the possibility of radiological "interpretations" would vanish if all the relevant facts were known. (Indeterminacy concerning the "meaning" of an x-ray is merely epistemic.) At the same time, the uniformity of a single word ("interpretation") is apt to disguise differences and thus to mislead us once a domain is branded an "interpretive" one.

I will leave aside X-rays, translations and some other contexts in which the term interpretation is commonly employed. Misconstructions of literary interpretation on the model of legal hermeneutics (and vice versa) are my main concern. These types of interpretation *do* share a concept, I think. But many people underestimate the structuring role that genre (or *kind of thing* being interpreted) must play here. Before the nineteenth century, almost nothing was said about interpretation-in-general: "hermeneutics"— always adjectively qualified as biblical, legal, etc.—referred to special techniques for understanding specific types of texts. Schleiermacher (1819): "Hermeneutics . . . does not yet exist *in a general manner*, there are instead only several forms *of specific hermeneutics*."[13] What changed has something to do with the success—and apparent unity—of natural science; this created a pressure to ask whether the *Geisteswissenschaften* (the "human sciences," where *meaning* becomes a question) have a like unity. But what Schleiermacher looked for—an "art of understanding" common to the *Geisteswissenschaften*—does not exist; and what *can* be said about interpretation-in-general should make clear why this is so.

2. "READING AS" AND THE QUESTION WHY

Start with the commonplace:

(1) The role of a judge is to interpret the law.

Here, to "interpret" means to *apply*—to say what the law requires in a particular case. Interpretation is a standing legal concern because the law, as a general norm, must also be heard in judgments about innumerable particulars. Hence, legal interpretation aims to spell things out, to *preserve* meaning rather than to make things up: the judge is not to decide, if the law already has decided, which features of the situation should guide her judgments. Of course, it could be asked why this is. Since the law might be unjust, it might be better if judges didn't have to *interpret* the law but could revise it, like a legislator. Why should judges say what the law requires when they could change it for the better? (Judges *do* sometimes interpret to avoid unjust results, but obviously this aim couldn't get (1)—judging as an *interpretive* attitude—up and running all by itself.)[14]

Contrast:

(2) Criticism: Stanley Cavell's interpretation of *King Lear* presents Shakespeare's figures of seeing and blindness in terms of the play's exploration of shame.
(3) Performance: Branagh's interpretation of *Hamlet* presents a less conflicted character than Olivier's. (Glenn Gould's late interpretation of the "Goldberg" Variations reveals the melancholy of Bach's Aria.)

In criticism, an interpretation is a verbal *take* on an earlier work. Interpretive performances, on the other hand, are *tokens* of a work. And there are other possibilities.

What is happening in all of these cases of "interpretation" is some way of bringing out the meaning of an antecedent object. But there is also this striking difference: literary interpretation isn't an endeavor to *follow* or *apply* a text—to say what it means or requires in some particular circumstance or *case*. Similarly, performances elucidate the meaning of an object, but not by presenting a *case* of it. Perhaps all interpretation has some applicative structure: for example, a director might endeavor to make *Antigone* come alive for an audience today. But terms like "contemporary audience" (or "contemporary significance") betoken the standing condition of interpretation—an interpreter always brings his own questions to the text[15]—whereas talk of *cases* indicates interpretive questions of a distinctive kind.

Someone might object that literary works have been followed (e.g., the Bible), just as laws (or notes about plums in the icebox) can be read "as literature." Does the possibility of "reading as" undermine my claim that interpretation is different in these domains? No, but it indicates how to understand it. It suggests that legal and literary texts are *functionally*—not ontologically or semantically—distinctive: we make different *uses* of them; they play different roles in our lives. To read something "as literature" is to take a certain kind of interest in it. And a partial specification of what this means is: one is not trying to follow it in particular cases. Of course, law demands just the kind of attention that literature puts out of play: there is no law without asking how to follow it. (Ancient legal codes—which may be of literary interest—are legal codes because they were *once* followed.)

The general point here is that "kind of text" is to be understood in terms of our reasons for paying attention. "Legal" describes both a kind of text and a space of interpretive reasons—each notion can explain the other. And the text at hand is always a text of *some* kind or other. That is, one always interprets for a reason. Interpretation isn't something that happens, like a chemical reaction, when readers and texts come together, nor a mere receptive capacity, like perception. It is an intentional activity. Hence it always makes sense to ask: "*Why* interpret?" To say that you interpret in order to "understand what something means" isn't wrong but a radical underspecification, like saying that you generally leave the house in order to go outside. Both statements invite reiteration of the question: why do that? And the further answers that can be given will be specifications of *what* you are doing (in interpreting or in leaving the house): for example, "I'm deciding the legal rights of the parties," "I'm walking to work."[16] *What you do in interpreting, reasons for interpreting,* and *kind of text* are mutually explanatory notions. Errors arise from failing to appreciate the unity of this trinity, as it were.

I will illustrate these claims by considering two controversial theses about interpretation-in-general: its necessary pluralism and creativity (section 3) and its circumscription or regulation by an author's intention (section 4). It will be seen that these theses don't describe interpretation-in-general, but only interpretation in one or another of its specific settings.

3. PLURALISM AND CREATIVITY

Interpretive pluralism says that there can be good but incompatible interpretations of the same object.[17] Incompatible interpretations aren't merely a matter of *different* interpretations. Difference is unremarkable, since there can always be different elucidations of almost anything. For example, why did so many people die in the earthquake? The size of the quake, the nature of the human body, the building materials used, the repeal of the zoning laws, and the lack of local doctors are all good answers (for different purposes). But these answers aren't incompatible; to the contrary, they might be combined in a single, more encompassing explanation. Similarly, sociology, neuroscience, and the lover's own discourse all tell us something about why John loves Mary, but perhaps their answers can live together. Much of the so-called conflict of interpretations is like this—merely compatible emphases on different aspects of a text.

When *are* two interpretations incompatible? A logical contradiction will always suffice to render interpretations incompatible, but incompatibility appears to be a broader notion than this. For example, that an object can't be both red and blue at the same time isn't a (truth-functional) tautology (no contradiction appears in saying that an object is both colors at once); instead, determinations of color appear to *exclude* each other in some other way.[18] The same is true with people's *moods*, their character traits, and other categories as well. Thus, some writers say that the basic idea of interpretive incompatibility is simply the uncombinability of two interpretations.[19] This seems unimpeachable, but how illuminating it is depends on whether there are any criteria (beyond logic) for interpretive combinability. Perhaps there aren't any. It seems very intuitive, at any rate, to think that combining different readings of a literary text might sometimes give you neither an outright contradiction nor a more complete view of things but just a *mess*.

Perhaps some interpretations don't exactly exclude each other (as colors do), but rather—think of good ways of life, kinds of relationship, architectural styles, or emotional attitudes—*occlude* each other: that is, to some (itself *indeterminate*) extent, the condition of having some actual one of these is that you don't have others. Thus, someone's expressing moral feeling in a particular statement seems incompatible with their simultaneously expressing murderous rage—until someone like Nietzsche or Freud shows how these can go together. What seemed incompatible becomes compatible by means of further interpretation. And, arguably, that further interpretation was creative: it doesn't leave "moral feeling" as it was before.

Interpretive creativity says that objects come to have certain meanings in virtue of their actually being interpreted—meanings they wouldn't otherwise have. Here again, this should be distinguished from a more anodyne idea: that interpreters reveal meanings that were already "in the object" but previously unnoticed. Novel aspects of something—in the sense of previously unnoticed ones—are nothing remarkable: the atomic structure of gold was once novel in this sense. But interpretive novelty doesn't all seem to be like this. If a director shows us that *Hamlet* is not a drama of indecision, as Olivier would have it, but of the loss of desire, as Lacan suggests, or of Christian redemption (Walter Benjamin), or of disgust at the *vita activa* (Nietzsche),[20] it would be odd to say: "Wow, I hadn't *noticed* all that." One problem is that while it needs only common sense to speak of natural facts that go unnoticed (or that are even permanently unknowable), meaning's *conceptual* tie to *understanding* renders the parallel thought—ungraspable meanings that forever lie waiting in the text (what if Freud and Lacan hadn't developed psychoanalysis?)—problematic. Undiscoverable meanings seem mysterious. Perhaps there's a way to make sense of undiscoverable meanings—they are meanings, at least, in God's eye—but it won't be very realistic. ("God's grasp of things" can of course make all kinds of strange philosophical theses work, as Berkeley illustrates.) And, anyway, there's a second problem: it seems that you *couldn't* have simply "*noticed* all that" since these readings occlude each other.

Pluralism and creativity thus seem closely related, if not mutually entailing. If you suppose that two good interpretations can be incompatible, it seems odd to think that incompatible meanings were merely *retrieved* from the text: for how can the selfsame text both say *x* and something incompatible with *x*? A text *can* be self-contradictory, ambiguous, or equivocal, but that is different: in such cases, it says nothing (very clear) about some matter. Thus, pluralism pushes you toward thinking that interpreters sometimes play a more creative (active) role. Conversely, if you suppose that interpreters can create meanings, then pluralism would seem to be a possibility: pluralism results when interpreters create in incompatible ways. Why shouldn't they?

But there are puzzles, as Joseph Raz has stressed, about how interpretive pluralism and creativity are so much as *possible*.[21] Perhaps the bright light of natural science makes it hard to see clearly here. For our notion of what natural science is to understand ("nature") is partly constituted by the idea of the compatibility of all good explanations of it; and, correspondingly, our idea of scientific "explanation" is of something inert: saying "this X-ray shows a fracture" doesn't affect or alter what it *does* show; that depends only on whether the bone is fractured. Yet interpretations are explanations too: they aren't pure makings—making a bowl (or a man) from clay isn't *interpreting* the *clay*—but elucidations of some prior object. How then, as Raz asks, can an *explanation* also be *creative*? To the extent that an interpretation creates meaning, it would seem that it couldn't be explanatory; to the extent it is explanatory, it would seem that it couldn't be creative. Putting the puzzle another way: If a successful interpretation elucidates the meaning of a text, but it is intolerable to think that the "text itself" means incompatible things, how can interpreters create in incompatible ways?

Answering this challenge might be partly a matter of dispelling the scientific image of things, and I'll make a suggestion about how to do this, with respect to interpretation, in section 7.[22] But for the moment my point concerns not the very *possibility* of interpretive pluralism and creativity but rather their variable *actuality*: leading the interpretive attitude in some settings, they understandably play only supporting roles in others.

Interpreting-by-performing is impossible without them.[23] "Branagh's *Hamlet*," for example, *always* implies that, at another time, the play may be interpreted in incompatible ways. (It also implies that Branagh is *present* in the interpretation in a way that contrasts with the discovery of as-yet-unnoticed facts, such as *Einstein's* "theory of relativity.") Performances make the fact of interpretive pluralism especially transparent because they are in *principle* (not just in fact) uncombinable: that is, anything you might call "combining" Branagh's and Olivier's *Hamlet* wouldn't be either actor's performance, but that of another actor who reworked something from each—just like "Greco-Roman" style. Does this *necessary* uncombinability trivialize pluralism by making it true as a matter of course?

No: performances determine a more abstract determinable. If *Hamlet* is to be seen at all, there must be innumerable decisions (not all conscious) about intonation, emphasis, mood, emotion, timing, speed, movement, staging, and so on. Such decisions all: (1) carry meaning, (2) *have* to be some way or other (i.e., no intonation *is* an intonation), and (3) exclude other decisions. A condition of the possibility of performance is that you can't have it every way.

This doesn't make interpretive pluralism trivially true because the pluralist thesis was not merely that there are *incompatible* interpretations, but that such interpretations can all be *good* ones. Yet once it is seen that to perform is (willy-nilly) to "determine," the truth of pluralism (viz., that different determinations don't call each other into doubt) flows naturally from commonplaces about the point or value of performance in the first place. As T. S. Eliot remarked, "novelty is better than repetition"[24]—that is, new orientations against the background of tradition are *valued*, not just tolerated here. Eliot's remark—part of an answer to the question 'why interpret a literary work'—explains why it seems absurd to say that different performances of *Hamlet* are merely epistemically "reasonable" (i.e., given the imperfect state of our knowledge of Shakespeare and his text). No performer so much as aims for *the* correct interpretation of a play – and understandably so, given what we value about performance. Could it be different with criticism? When literary interpretive monism is proposed and defended, the focus is naturally on criticism. But it would be odd if pluralism held for performative *tokenings* of a literary work but not for critical *takings*. After all, both of these are ways of exhibiting the meaning of the work. And performances are influenced by critical takes (which are sometimes even expressed as performance directions), just as performers draw out meanings that influence criticism: these ways of exhibiting a play's meaning are hardly alien to each other.

In this account, interpretive pluralism isn't grounded in distinctive semantic properties of literary texts (e.g., their ambiguity or absence of illocutionary force), much less in structural features of language use. Pluralism is a practical matter: why take a text in hand? The point therefore becomes clearer in contrast to law (section 5). But first I turn to a second claim about interpretation-in-general—one often favored by the interpretive *monist*.

4.   DOES A TEXT MEAN WHAT ITS AUTHOR INTENDED IT TO MEAN?

The right answer is: sometimes. "Sometimes" admittedly doesn't make for exciting philosophy—the truth here is boring.

Consider a thesis that has been put forward from many different orientations: Our interest in literary and other artworks is an interest in cultural items which are relatively autonomous of their author's intentions (the autonomy thesis, AT).[25] It could have been otherwise, but as it is, we have the idea of works that express aspects of the world, that are available for criticism from various orientations (social, psychological, philosophical, . . .), and that are capable of being appreciated without knowing much about their authors. You might disagree with this as a description of art, but I only need it to be a *conceivable* description. And it *is* conceivable, because many objects that are available for interpretive elaboration don't have authors or express anyone's intention. For example, the British Constitution is a set of long-standing social practices, not an authored text, but that's no bar to interpretive engagement with it.

An "intentionalist" might object that this example only *seems* to make AT conceivable by means of an equivocation: "Interpretation" as applied to social practices only shares a *word* with textual "interpretation" (his topic), he might say. It is true that theories of interpretation are not obliged to account for every use of the *word* "interpretation" (section 1). But—in view of the similarities of American and British "constitutional law"—on what grounds are interpreting a text and interpreting a social practice supposed to be categorically different activities? I find I don't know. And is "interpreting" history a further equivocation? To say that that just one of these cases of "interpretation" has an author and the others don't is true enough—but that's *my* point. Interpretation doesn't need an author to get going. Hence AT is at least conceivable.

If AT is right, we obviously can't expect "authorial intention" to play the same role in literary interpretation that it plays in the interpretation of (say) legal *wills* or *testimony*, where there are special reasons for being interested in what an author meant to say. Even if it is true, as some have stressed, that there would be no meaningful text to interpret apart from an author's intention to mean something,[26] the authorial intention relevant to a work of *literature* is, for AT, an intention to produce a work which—just like a social practice—is interpretable independently of what an author meant to express. This shouldn't seem mysterious or a mere play on words. A psychoanalytic patient is in the same boat as a literary author (according to AT): She *intentionally* presents what she says as something to be interpreted in ways that are not limited by her intentions, by what she means to say. And this is possible, not because her "unconscious" is a sort of backstage orator, but because what people say and do always expresses more than they mean, and (to approach the psychoanalytic situation) some of those unmeant things are structurally outside of awareness. In any case, given that people generally express more than they mean to express, it makes sense that it is really only in certain cases (or for special reasons) that interpretation becomes a matter of construing their intentions.

AT has been called "the death of the author." But here this is neither a conceptual truth (e.g., about graphemes or dissemination) nor something that somehow overtakes the author from behind: it describes the shape of a cultural practice—a practice which authors, intending a novel or a poem, *intend* to participate in. Literary authors aren't subordinated by this practice for the greater glory of criticism; it is this practice which makes it possible to be a *literary* author.

Again, the question isn't whether this is true, only whether it is possible. If AT is not a description of literature as it exists today, it *could* be (i.e., the formal dependence of the concept "text" on the notion of "someone's intention to say something"—the fact that you can apply the former concept only where you can apply the latter—doesn't settle the matter). In fact, I think AT affords a better description of all artworks than one which makes their interpretation a matter of retrieving authorial intentions. But even if I'm wrong about this, the fact that there *could* be such a practice (and such works) is sufficient to show that the relevance of authorial intention is a question about what *literary interest* is, not a question about what a text in general is. And that's the main point. We should be suspicious of any argument that purports to move from an account of how (or through what conditions) meaning-bearing marks are possible to conclusions about what interpretation is or the conditions of its success. (From some such account, the "deconstructive" theorist concludes that interpretation must *always* exceed the author's intention,[27] while the intentionalist concludes that it *never* can.[28] Both are mistaken.) For except by way of abstraction from what people do with legal, literary or other specific kinds of texts, there is no such thing as interpreting *a text*.

5. LAW AS A CONTRASTING CASE

In some areas of law authorial intentions *do* have the role which the intentionalist describes. But this is not because the law is sometimes a *text* (and, as such, has an author), but because we look to legal officials to make determinations that are binding regardless of what may seem right to you or me, and it wouldn't make sense to have such *authorities* if one weren't interested in what they mean to say.

Imagine that a general is appointed to lead our little army into battle. What would be the point of giving someone this position if, when he gave a command ("you three take the left flank") we were not interested in what he intended to say? Similarly, what would be point if the general's commands were always published through a mediating agency which altered them in random ways?[29] Obviously, authorities are pointless if they can't succeed in making the very commands they intend to make; and they can do *this* only if the agencies receiving and interpreting their commands are oriented to their intentions. Hence, the fact that law is a public authority provides a domain-*specific* reason for a collaborative activity of a certain shape: in the standard case, a statutory authority expresses intentions in anticipation of the methods and conventions through which those intentions might be construed. Literary interpretation, as described by AT, is also self-consciously collaborative. That is, the procedures and questions of criticism aren't something alien to a literary author—as if he were just trying to get his intentions across, against all the apparent odds. Literary interpretation would look very different—perhaps like a nonprotestant theology of some kind—if there were such a thing as literary authority. But, as we have it, the impossibility of authority is as fundamental to literature as it is to secular "morality." That is, there are no authors or readers (or even "communities" of readers)[30] whose pronouncements, just as such, are reasons for taking the text to mean *this* rather than *that*, quite apart from how the text seems to you. (This isn't to say that what others say can't influence you.)

Once we are free to approach "authorial intention" in this "let's *look and see*" kind of way, it should naturally appear that "legal text" is itself an inadequate basis for theorizing about *legal* interpretation. For example, while talk of the lawmaker's "intention" is always at home in applying *statutes*, doctrines of "the text's reasonable *public meaning*" (i.e., something different from what an author may have intended) intelligibly come into the interpretation of *contracts*, precisely because here *two* "authors" comprise the poles of a relation of *right*, and it would be unfair, in a dispute, to allow the idiosyncratic intentions of one to unilaterally determine the rights of the other.[31] Or again, interpreting *constitutions* may be something different yet from interpreting statutes or contracts, since it might be said that the constitutional framers' *general* intention (if there are "framers") was to create a morally valid political framework rather than to entrench any specific conflicting views they might have held.[32] These are just the kinds of differences we should expect once we no longer approach interpretation with some uniform, a priori idea of how it must work. For natural as it may be to speak of "law" when contrasting it with "literature," the legal subgenres aren't just convenient classifications of the state's exercise of a generic authority but different spaces of reasons.

What about creativity in legal interpretation? Creativity *may* be needed in saying what the law requires—e.g., where there are gaps in the law, or the law conflicts with itself or with morality—but creativity may also *not* be needed. The idea of a legally "hard case" presupposes that of an easy one:[33] interpretation succeeds in hard cases partly by making the law easier to apply thereafter. Relatedly, judicial creativity isn't always a virtue. One reason for the judge's *interpretive* attitude is continuity with precedent authority: *stare decisis et quieta non movere*[34]—the reverse of Eliot's "novelty is better than repetition." Further, the advantages of having authoritative rules would be defeated by a general practice of creatively "interpreting" them to reflect the (equitable) reasons revealed by each case. Hence—as literature itself has sometimes been drawn to consider—the *absence* of creativity becomes a value in legal interpretation. When judicial creativity does appear, its point is limited, viz., to make the law morally better or more coherent, not to exhibit novelty or individuality for their own sake: there is no legal parallel to the familiar criticism of literary and performing interpretations as uninformative, hackneyed, or slavish.[35]

6. INDETERMINACY AND HAVING TO DECIDE: SOME CONTRASTS

Judges must come to a nonarbitrary decision for one of the parties. Given the much-noted difficulty of codifying standards in advance of particular cases ("indeterminacy"), this means that judges must sometimes be creative.[36] It looks like there is room for judicial pluralism too, on the pattern previously noted: for even apart from disagreements about the law's overall aims, concrete determinations of more abstract ideas—choices among options that are equally "reasonable" (at least before an authoritative choice is made)—are often needed. Judges constantly gloss the law, and it is here that they seem most like literary critics.

Yet even here there are differences. Not all legal interpretation is garden-variety applicative judgment, but there would be no point to any legal interpretation unless some of it was. Just as hard cases have their background in easy ones, so legal glosses presuppose the possibility of cases in which the rules are clear and no further glosses are needed. *Clara non sunt interpretanda, Interpretatio cessat in claro*—such formulas appear and are valid wherever "following the text" is a reason for interpreting.

Correspondingly, the specificity of literary interpretation lies partly in the inaptness of such formulae. They are inapt not because criticism aims to make things *harder* (which might also be true), but because what it is for a text to be *unclear* or *indeterminate* doesn't appear, apart from the practical endeavor to follow it. In applicative discourses, terms like "indeterminate" or "unclear" characterize a rule's usefulness as a standard of correctness in a range of normal or foreseeable cases (not *all* cases). In contrast, when Olivier and Branagh interpret *Hamlet* in incompatible ways, are we really to say that Shakespeare's text is indeterminate? Unclear? Uncertain? That sounds as if Shakespeare left something out or gave inadequate directions; whereas, in truth, nothing Shakespeare *could* have put into the play would have sufficed to make it *determinate* for purposes of literary interpretation. Talk of "indeterminacy," though natural among lawyers, draws no contrast here. (In a different use, "indeterminacy" might describe the literary situation where we lack a definitive manuscript—but, clearly, interpretive pluralism does not entirely stem from indeterminacy in this sense.)

Given this, might it be said that some influential forms of literary theory come trailing inappropriate clouds of legality? Consider a climactic passage in Paul de Man's celebrated reading of Keats's "The Fall of Hyperion":

> Faced with the ineluctable necessity to come to a decision, no grammatical or logical analysis can help us out. Just as Keats had to break off his narrative, the reader has to break off his understanding at the very moment when he is most directly engaged and summoned by the text.[37]

The impotence of "grammar" and "logic" to decide how a text (any text) is to be understood is one of de Man's signature ideas—he explains this idea in terms of the unruly "rhetorical" ("figurative" or "tropological") aspects of language use. And literature, de Man suggests, is privileged to thematize and reveal the unstable nature of "reading," by making such unruliness especially transparent.[38]

What I've said already about *text* might be said as well about what de Man seems to mean by *reading*. The "infinity" of "potentially catastrophic confusions" a reader faces (on de Man's description) seems to be partly a product of de Man's imagining a confrontation with "texts," conceived as mere grammatical patterns: for example, the sentence type "What's the difference?" can be employed either to ask a genuine question or to deny there's a relevant difference.[39] But does the possibility of putting this sentence to use in these different ways make any *actual* use of it even *potentially* confusing? *No*, we might answer—not if this means that it always makes sense, whatever the circumstances are, to raise a doubt. When de Man says "potentially confusing," this is apparently spoken from some perspective other than the everyday (practically engaged) one of linguistic exchange. Just so, *reading* (a word on which de Man puts great emphasis) is theorized (1) under *abstraction* from the practical circumstances of an utterance (which often make interpretation of the utterance superfluous) *and*—more to the present point—(2) under abstraction from the *genre* of utterance (which means, according to my argument, under abstraction from what interpretation would specifically aim to do, should an interpretation be needed). Thus, all the concepts in this passage on Keats (the need to decide, the indeterminacy of the text) sound familiar: they *are* familiar (from *legal* hermeneutics), but are they apt in a description of interpreting a poem?

Whence, I want to ask, "the ineluctable necessity" to *decide*? Is that really what I was trying to do with Keats's poem? (Has the poet indeed become "the legislator of the world" and criticism a form of judicial review?) Or why does de Man take the grammatically allowed possibilities of meaning he uncovers to indicate that interpretive understanding has *failed* (it must be "broken off")? I need to know what de Man's idea of interpretive *success* with a poem might be. He seems to imply that a successful interpretation, if there could be one, would resolve ambiguity or would "authoritatively decide"[40]—in some nonarbitrary way—among the different grammatical possibilities. Again, that's a familiar enough idea of what interpretation does in some settings, but can it be an account of interpretation-in-general? If we hear in a business meeting, "You're going to do business with *Tokyo*?!"—in a way that is illocutionarily uncertain (a question, a statement, a warning?), the successful interpreter (translator) will use tone and pitch (or punctuation) to make the different possibilities apparent. Similarly, psychoanalytic interpretations often aim to preserve (and even create) ambiguities. Since it is *literature* we are interpreting here, isn't there, then, another option? Instead of saying that interpretive understanding must be "broken off," why not say that—in de Man's reading—interpretation has succeeded brilliantly? I hear someone welcoming this as a deconstructive paradox: "De Man has shown that readers can't *decide* between various meaning possibilities, that interpretation must fail. But if readers *could* decide, then the poem wouldn't bear the interpretation (i.e., an allegory of reading) that de Man has successfully put on it. So interpretive failure is really interpretive success. Or: we can't ever 'authoritatively decide' which it is." But the appearance of paradox here is only the criss-crossing of different forms of description—juridical and literary—where different notions of interpretive "success" apply. (Success in juridical contexts always involves a non-arbitrary decision; but de-Man's reading of Keat's poem may be counted successful even though it resolves none of the meaning-possibilities it exhibits.) Adjectivally unqualified terms like "text" and "reading" (texts and readings of no specific kind) are thus good for *purposes* of paradox, but such purposes seem optional.

Someone who wanted to give "indeterminacy" some work to do in the literary context might prefer to say simply this: "A literary text is 'indeterminate' insofar as there are incompatible but equally successful ways of exhibiting its meaning."[41] This rendering of "indeterminate" doesn't alter the previously noted asymmetries between law and literature, for now it will have to be said: *all* literary texts are "indeterminate." And this "all" expresses something special about literature. A literary text doesn't *happen* to be "indeterminate" (in the present sense): unlike a legal rule, its openness to interpretation isn't a contingent function of language, syntax, or context. Indeterminacy is rather its birthright, a reflection of the interest we take in it *as literature*. Relatedly, literary interpretation doesn't aim to *remedy* indeterminacy, as legal glosses do: it *multiplies* readings (it *celebrates* the work, in a literal sense) and thereby makes indeterminacy *appear*. And this is related to the *value* of indeterminacy in the two cases. It is usually of negative value in the law,[42] as in any text (a shopping list, instructions from the flight tower) made to be followed. Not so in criticism, where a history of incompatible readings is precisely the mark of the "classic."

There is a related contrast. The existence of interpretive incompatibility in literary criticism ("indeterminacy" in the present sense) is often difficult to discern. Are readings of a work from different orientations in conflict, or are they just emphasizing different aspects of the text in light of different questions? In criticism, the answer to this question often seems to be itself a matter of interpretation: that is, it is only by way of an *argument*—an argument clarifying entailments, presuppositions, implicatures, grounds, purposes, etc.—that claims about compatibility or incompatibility can be made. All this appears to be productive for literary criticism (and part of its engine of development), as critics interpret and reinterpret both primary texts and each other. But how singular all this is appears in contrast to law, where interpretive conflict is a comparatively *simple* matter. Inconsistent applicative judgments are the necessary and sufficient sign of it. For example, if under one interpretation of the First Amendment you have the right to march in a particular case, while under another you don't, there is a conflict. (Such conflicts may not always be immediately apparent, but the law aims to make them so.)

Thinking of the juridical significance of *interpretatio cessat in clara*, we might give criticism a corresponding maxim: *Every reading of a text is an interpretation.*[43] These old saws say "what kind of thing" an interpretation in a particular setting is; they express its grammar. Of course, a great deal of literary theory already affirms that interpretation is ubiquitous. So all that is needed to make good what this says is to remember that it applies not to all texts but to *literary* texts—it characterizes what they are.

7. INTERPRETATION-IN-GENERAL

On the argument I have made, "text" is as an abstract genus, like "color" or "animal": no one interacts with colors or animals in general, only with some determinate species of them. The verb phrase "interpreting a text" is just like "the self-moving of animals." The latter is a perfectly serviceable idea ("an animal's way of moving is related to how it thrives in its environment"), but analyzing it won't teach you anything about how any particular animal moves— that depends on what kind it is.

Should interpretation-in-general be set aside as an unhelpful abstraction then? Compare "explanation." Aristotle noted that there are as many kinds of explanation "as can be comprehended under" the question "why?"[44] And even if his *four*fold "why" (his *aitia*) does capture all uses of "explanation" in English (which seems doubtful), it seems unpromising to expect a rich account of the unity of this fourfold: one ends up stuttering or speaking, as Heidegger does, of "bringing forth," "revealing," or "making present."[45] Perhaps these terms do help exhibit explaining as a species of something even more general, but it also seems plausible to say that "explaining," like "reason," is among the most basic notions there are. Should one say that about "interpreting" too?

Not quite. For, over a core range of cases, interpretations are a *species* of explanation:[46] all interpretations are explanations (they aim to elucidate something), but not all explanations are interpretations. For example, Lévi-Strauss's "structuralist" account of the Oedipus myth in terms of combinations of "mythemes" (analogous to the linguist's phonemes)[47] is an explanation of the myth but not an interpretation of it. Since interpretations are a kind of explanation, it seems that there should be something, of a general nature, to say about what *kind* they are.

Admittedly, "interpretations are explanations" sounds awkward in English. Depending on the setting, terms like elucidation, explication, exposition, exhibition, application, determination, illustration, rendition, or elaboration might be more idiomatic. Nonetheless, all of *these* words have something in common: they characterize a response to meaning that isn't simply inventive but that also doesn't merely re-present what is already apparent. Kant can be found complaining that the German language is poor because, for the expressions "exposition," "explication," "declaration," and "definition," it has "nothing more than the word 'explanation'"

(*Erklarung*).[48] But one could reverse Kant's point: German is (philosophically) rich because, where Latinate languages submerge the connections between those four ideas, German has a term that exhibits their unity. In a broad sense of "making clear," interpretations are a kind of *Erklarung*. They bring meaning out of concealment.

Hence, even Branagh's performing interpretation is an "explanation" because it reveals something that might not otherwise be heard or understood (unlike the teacher's iteration of a script by calling roll). And judges are "interpreters" because their decisions disclose meanings which are not (all at once) apparent or surveyable (unlike a flight-attendant handing out a beverage at your request). A standard way to explain a rule is to say how it applies in a hypothetical case, as law professors know. But if hypothetical cases can serve to explain what the law means, then real ones can do so too.

This should lead us to say: interpretations are wanted just where explanations are wanted. And explanations, as Wittgenstein says, "come to an end somewhere."[49] (If an interpretive explanation was everywhere needed, nothing could ever be interpreted—meaning could never be revealed.) If literary criticism does traffic in endless interpretation, this indicates something about the nature of literary interest in terms of the practice of explanation that befits it. But such a practice is possible only if meanings are sometimes available without interpretation. One way to put this would be to say that not everything is "literature." Literature is not a higher genus, of which all other texts are species.

As was said, the very idea of interpretation as (1) a kind of explanation that is (2) sometimes pluralistic and creative can seem puzzling, and various theories of interpretation seem to register awareness of this difficulty by explicitly rejecting either (1) or (2). Thus, the deconstructivist who sees "active interpretation" at work everywhere is not alone in implying that interpretations are not essentially "explanations," while the intentionalist is apt to deploy his thesis (that all interpretation aims to recover an author's intention) against pluralism and creativity. Perhaps the term "interpretation" was only invented to answer a need: it lets us *imagine* there's a bit of both explanation and creativity, while hiding the fact that we don't really know what we're talking about. But I agree with Joseph Raz (who has foregrounded this puzzle) that what theorists say about interpretation should try to account for its commonplaces, not deny them. Reflection on the everyday practice of explaining action might help with this, I will briefly suggest.

"Why are you standing on that stool?"—"I'm getting the bowl down."— "I'm doing my balancing exercises."—"This is how we worship around here." Familiarly, action is often explained by locating it as a *part* of something else the agent is doing: an action is, in effect, the agent's answer to the question of how to do *that*.[50] Now your understanding of why you are, for example, standing on the stool doesn't exactly leave the object unaffected: it's not as if we can dispense with that understanding and still have in view the self-same matter to be explained. For your understanding of *why* you are doing something also determines just *what* you are doing—a bit of cooking, exercise, or worship. It would not be correct to say that you are (in any case) standing on the stool, whatever the further significance of this may be. For you are intentionally doing *that* only if standing on the stool *is* part of your answer to a *question* about how to do something else (like getting the bowl down to start cooking)—otherwise, you might be just involuntarily stuck there, who knows how.[51] Hence, Anscombe (following Aquinas) describes practical knowledge (i.e., an agent's grasp of what they are doing and why) as "the cause of what it understands," in contrast to speculative knowledge, "which is derived from the object known"[52]: that is, but for your grasp of what you're doing, you wouldn't be doing *that*. Understanding here plays a constitutive role; it might be called an *effective* understanding.

Action thus looks promising as a way of easing worries about the potential creativity of interpretation because it presents a familiar case in which (unlike knowledge of "nature"), understanding *is* effective. Could an interpreter's relation to a text be clarified through some extension of this paradigm of sense making?

I say "extension" because we don't generally think of action-explanation as interpretation. Perhaps this is because such explanations usually aim to express the agent's intention, and the agent is generally knowledgeable about that. Hence, I don't generally need to "interpret" your standing on a stool—I can just ask you what you're doing, if I can't (as is often the case) just see for myself. But we might well speak of action-*interpretation* where intentions or motives are opaque, or where the nature of our interest in action is such that first-person authority concerning what is going on is suspended—as, for example, when a psychoanalyst "interprets" the meaning of his patient's being late. Literature, I suggested, is like this: authority isn't suspended here; it never applies in the first place.

Why, then, shouldn't we expect literary interpretations/explanations to be both creative and pluralistic? Where our reasons for interpreting don't tie interpretive success to the recovery of what an author intended to say – that was the thesis of AT (section 4)— it makes sense that interpreters might sometimes render the author's "action" intelligible in incompatible ways, by exhibiting it as an answer or response to different questions. It won't do to say "yes, but what about the meaning of the text itself?"—any more than it makes sense to speak of "the action itself," apart from an effective understanding of it as the answer to some question (or as part of some larger purposive endeavor). In short, what we know about action and its everyday explanation helps here, because it helps break the hold of the idea that meaning is either in "the text itself" or in the understanding of the interpreter. It offers a different picture: meaning lies in text's capacity to appear as an answer (or a response) to a question the interpreter is asking, and to be exhibited as such.

"Texts" don't appear at all apart from reasons for taking them in hand—and then they appear as legal, literary, or other kinds of texts. Legal and literary interpretations aren't accidental specifications of a generic activity of interpreting or reading. To interpret is to be with some object (or person) in a domain of reasons where questions arise.

My survey points to the constitutive presence in law—and the absence in literature—of an interest in following or applying the text. This makes literature *not*-law, or better *otherwise*-than-law, for the point is not that you *don't* apply literature, but that the question of application doesn't arise. If law and literature seem to call for each other, this is no doubt because literature thinks about law (just as law does) but without having to resolve its applicative questions.

A further specification of literary interest might be in terms of the questions you *do* ask. And here the point is often made that these questions are innumerably many—the questions of all the disciplines. So much can already be heard when literary criticism readily accepts qualification in such terms as historical, sociological, Marxist, psychoanalytic, queer, and so on. (The list is as open-ended as the questions that might come to seem significant.) But if literature's porousness to all kinds of questions—its *motley*, as Shakespeare might say—registers a constitutive feature of literary interest, *law* is otherwise than literature, for it is impossible to qualify "legal interpretation" with the name of another discipline: at most you succeed in making an expression for a new topic. This manifests a truth about "Law and . . .," however the blank is filled in: the basic questions that orient law's elaboration of meanings do not depend on what any of the conjoined disciplines may reveal. Instead, the conjunction "Law and . . ." presupposes that the first term, law, is antecedently present and can take care of itself. Shouldn't we therefore say that the conjunction "law and literature" contains an asymmetry? Law is autonomous but literature is not. Literature thinks about law; law does not return the favor. Reading from the other direction—"*literature* and . . ."—you could fill in the blank with almost anything you like and you would be naming one of literature's own concerns.

NOTES

1. *Philosophical Investigations*, trans. G. E. M. Anscombe (Oxford: Blackwell, 1958), §116 (hereafter, *PI*).
2. Parts of this chapter previously appeared in James Conant and Andrea Kern, eds., *Varieties of Skepticism: Essays After Kant, Wittgenstein, and Cavell* (Berlin: De Gruyter, 2014), 216–247. My thanks to Stanley Fish and Moshe Halbertal for comments on an earlier draft of this chapter.
3. See Joseph Raz, "Why Interpret?" in *Between Authority and Interpretation: On The Theory of Law and Practical Reason* (Oxford: Oxford University Press, 2009), 223–40.
4. Laws aren't created *solely* for interpretation, but all legal systems look to officials to say what the law requires in particular cases.
5. Stanley Fish, "Force," in *Doing What Comes Naturally: Change, Rhetoric, and the Practice of Theory in Literary and Legal Studies* (Durham, NC: Duke University Press, 1989), 503–25.
6. Drucilla Cornell, *The Philosophy of the Limit* (New York: Routledge, 1992), 101–02.
7. See, e.g., Jonathan Culler, *On Deconstruction: Theory and Criticism after Structuralism* (Ithaca, NY: Cornell University Press, 1982), 181.
8. Friedrich Nietzsche, *Writings from the Late Notebooks*, ed. Rudiger Bittner (Cambridge: Cambridge University Press, 2003), Notebook 7, p. 139.
9. See *PI* §§85, 185–201.
10. Jacques Derrida, *Limited Inc.*, ed. Gerald Graff, trans. Jeffrey Mehlman and Samuel Weber (Evanston, IL: Northwestern Univ. Press, 1988), 148.
11. See Martin Stone, "Wittgenstein on Deconstruction," in *The New Wittgenstein*, ed. Alice Crary and Rupert Read, 83–117 (New York: Routledge, 2000).
12. Cf. *PI* §3.
13. Cf. Freidrich Schleiermacher, *Hermeneutics and Criticism and Other Writings*, ed. and trans. Andrew Bowie (Cambridge: Cambridge University Press, 1998), 5.
14. Cf. Raz, "Why Interpret?"
15. Cf. Hans-Georg Gadamer, *Truth and Method* (New York: Crossroad Publishing Company, 1982), 274–341.
16. This reflects a general feature of intentional action, as Anscombe taught.
17. My description of pluralism and creativity follows Raz, "Interpretation: Pluralism and Innovation," in *Between Authority and Interpretation*, 299–322.
18. See, e.g., Wittgenstein, "Some Remarks on Logical Form," Supplementary Volume, *Proceedings of the Aristotelian Society* 9 (1929): 162–71.
19. See, e.g., Raz, *Between Authority and Interpretation*, 226, 270–271, 302; P. D. Juhl, *Interpretation: An Essay in the Philosophy of Literary Criticism* (Princeton, NJ: Princeton University Press, 1980), 199.
20. See Simon Critchley, "It's Time to Make Shakespeare Dangerous," *The Guardian*, September 20, 2013.
21. See Raz, "Interpretation."

22. Raz's solution says that a successful interpretation makes sense of the text's features in a way that is sensitive to the interpreter's reasons for interpreting: different reasons for interpreting make for different (and sometimes incompatible) interpretations. See Raz, "Why Interpret," 231. The possibility of creativity, in turn, emerges by regarding meaning as neither just "in the text" nor "in the reader" but as a reason-mediated relation between the two; see "Interpretation."

23. I build here on Raz's suggestive comment in *Between Authority and Interpretation*, 271 and 307–09.

24. T. S. Eliot, "Tradition and the Individual Talent," *Perspecta* 19 (1982): 36–42.

25. See, e.g., Joseph Raz, "Interpretation without Retrieval," in *Between Authority and Interpretation*, 241–64; William K. Wimsatt and Monroe C. Beardsley. "The Intentional Fallacy," in William K. Wimsatt, *The Verbal Icon: Studies in the Meaning of Poetry* (Lexington: University Press of Kentucky, 1954), 3–18; Roland Barthes, "The Death of the Author" in *Image, Music, Text*, trans. Stephen Heath (New York: Hill and Wang, 1977), 142–48.

26. See, e.g., Stephen Knapp and Walter Benn Michaels, "Against Theory," *Critical Inquiry* 8 (1982): 723–42; Stanley Fish, "Intention is All There Is: A Critical Analysis of Aharon Barak's Purposive Interpretation in Law," *Cardozo Law Review* 29 (2008): 1109–46.

27. See, e.g., Derrida, "Signature, Event, Context," *Glyph* 1 (1977): 172–97.

28. See Knapp and Michaels, "Against Theory," and Fish, "Intention is All There Is."

29. I'm following Raz's thought-experiment in "Intention in Interpretation," in *Between Authority and Interpretation*, 265–99.

30. Cf. Stanley Fish, *Is there a Text in this Class: The Authority of Interpretive Communities* (Cambridge, MA: Harvard University Press, 1982).

31. See my "Introduction" in *Freedom and Force: Essays on Kant's Legal Philosophy*, ed. Sari Kisilevsky and Martin Jay Stone (Oxford: Hart Publishing, 2016), 3–15.

32. See, e.g., Ronald Dworkin, "Comment," in Antonin Scalia, *A Matter of Interpretation: Federal Courts and the Law* (Princeton, NJ: Princeton University Press, 1998), 115–28.

33. See Martin Stone, "Focusing the Law: What Legal Interpretation is Not," in *Law and Interpretation: Essays in Legal Philosophy*, ed. Andrei Marmor, 31–96 (Oxford: Clarendon Press, 1995).

34. Spicer v. Spicer, 79 Eng. Rep 451 (1620).

35. This is not to say that art *couldn't* be more law-like: my remarks concern our practices, not the concept of art.

36. Cf. H. L. A. Hart, *The Concept of Law* (Oxford: Clarendon Press, 1961), chap. 7.

37. Paul de Man, "The Resistance to Theory" in *The Resistance to Theory* (Minneapolis: University of Minnesota Press, 1986), 16.

38. See esp., de Man, "Semiology and Rhetoric," *Diacritics* 3, no. 3 (1973): 27–33.

39. Ibid.

40. Ibid., 29.

41. Cf. Raz, "Interpretation," 307–09.

42. "Usually": see my "Focusing the Law."

43. This shouldn't be heard as saying that there aren't facts about the literal content of a literary work that are available without interpretation.

44. Aristotle, *Physics* 2.3; *Metaphysics* 5.2.

45. See Martin Heidegger, "The Question Concerning Technology," in *Basic Writings*, ed. David Farrell Krell, 307–41 (London: Routledge, 1993).

46. Cf. Raz, "Intention," 301; Stuart Hampshire, "Types of Interpretation" in *Art and Philosophy: A Symposium*, ed. Sidney Hook, 101–08 (New York: New York University Press, 1966).

47. Claude Lévi-Strauss, *Myth and Meaning* (New York: Schocken, 1978).

48. Immanuel Kant, *The Critique of Pure Reason*, ed. and trans. Paul Guyer and Allen W. Wood (Cambridge: Cambridge University Press, 1998), A 730; thanks to James Conant for pointing out this passage.

49. *PI* §1.

50. This is the meaning of Aristotle's point in *Nicomachean Ethics* 3.3 that an agent's deliberation concerns the *means* of action.

51. In the limit case, you might be standing on the stool "for no reason." But that can't be the general case. The present point is even more obvious with actions that can *only* be done intentionally, like replying to someone's text: you're not *replying* at all if what takes place isn't such that "why are you doing it?" applies.

52. G. E. M. Anscombe, *Intention* (Cambridge, MA: Harvard University Press, 2000), §48; quoting Aquinas, *Summa Theologica*, Ia IIae, Q. a. S, obj. 1.

CHAPTER 5

Retrospective Prophecies

Legal Narrative Constructions

PETER BROOKS

I currently teach an undergraduate course called "Clues, Evidence, Detection: Law Stories." It does not aim to be a "pre-law" course, or to claim any true legal expertise—yet nor is it a "law in popular culture" kind of course (of which there are plenty of examples), since I do want to teach my students something about how "the law" goes about thinking about certain kinds of problems, in this case ones concerned largely with criminal procedure and the use of evidence. Discussion of these legal matters leads me into narrative analysis: the way in which the law understands discovery and recites the meanings derived from evidence raises problems in narrative telling of the sort studied by some narratologists: an understanding of how narrative presentation shapes events recounted, for instance, and of how anticipated ends shape story events. For, after all, the narratives presented in law as well as in literature are not themselves events in the world but rather the way we speak events, the way we give them significant order—a distinction too easily forgotten. Here there might be a productive meeting of legal and literary traditions.

I have long thought that the place and status of narrative in the law, and in legal studies, are strangely uncertain and ambiguous. On the one hand, trial advocates know—have known, presumably, since antiquity—that success in the law court depends upon telling an effective and persuasive story. The discipline of rhetoric originated essentially to teach courtroom practitioners how to do just that. Law schools courses on advocacy and legal writing necessarily pay attention to narrative skills, urging the importance of "controlling the narrative," though such courses are not generally thought to be central to the legal curriculum. Academic study sympathetic to "law and literature" has by now given considerable attention to narrative and its uses throughout the law, as institution and as praxis.[1] Still, one looks in vain within legal doctrine, and in judicial opinions, for any explicit recognition that "narrative" is a category for adjudication, that it is something that needs to be talked about and brought to bear analytically: that rules of evidence, for instance, implicate questions of how stories can and should be told. Not so long ago, Justice David Souter evoked a concept of "narrative integrity" in one of his Supreme Court opinions—so far as I can tell, the first overt recognition that the literary and cultural category of narrative needs to be imported into legal thinking, and one that thus far has had little in the way of sequel.[2]

The detective story is the most literary of genres (and the one most often written by academics) for a reason: its processes of investigation and detection touch on the very rationale of narrative; it very often gives narratives that speak to and exemplify the narrative process, or what is sometimes called "narrativity." To the extent that this narrative process is about discovery and the creation of a meaningful sequence, it touches closely upon a subject at the center of criminal justice. So before returning to generalities, let me try an example:

> "I knew we should find a ventilator before ever we came to Stoke Moran."
>
> "My dear Holmes!"
>
> "Oh, yes, I did. You remember in her statement she said that her sister could smell Dr. Roylott's cigar. Now, of course that suggested at once that there must be a communication between the two rooms. It could only be a small one, or it would have been remarked upon at the coroner's inquiry. I deduced a ventilator."[3]

Some readers may have recognized this exchange, from Arthur Conan Doyle's *The Adventure of the Speckled Band*. The ventilator is crucial since it suggests a communication between Dr. Grimsby Roylott's bedroom and that in which Julia Stoner died of mysterious causes. Add to the ventilator a dummy bell pull that hangs down from it to a bed that itself is clamped to the floor. And then find in Dr. Roylott's adjacent bedroom an iron safe, a bowl of milk, a horsewhip tied back to itself, and footmarks on the seat of a chair under the other end of the ventilator. Now you have a bridge along which the loathsome swamp adder can travel, from its home in the safe through the ventilator down the bell pull to the immovable bed.

Such moments are repeated throughout the Sherlock Holmes corpus. "I think we may safely deduce a cab," says Holmes after looking over the layout of the rooms, corridors, and staircases in the Foreign Office, in *The Naval Treaty*, all covered in a "creamy linoleum" that would have shown marks of wet boots on this rainy night had the thief come on foot. But what Holmes calls "deduction" really fits better into the discovery procedure that C. S. Peirce called "abduction," often glossed as "inference to the best explanation." If for most contemporary scientists abduction belongs to the "context of justification," for Peirce it was explicitly part of the context of discovery: "Abduction is the process of forming explanatory hypotheses," he wrote. "It is the only logical operation which introduces any new idea."[4] A perfect Holmes example comes in *Silver Blaze*, where he says of the wax vesta match he finds buried in the mud at the crime scene: "It was invisible, buried in the mud. I only saw it because I was looking for it." You would not have found it without first hypothesizing that it had to be there, since the criminal would have had to strike a light to perform his dastardly act of wounding the race horse. The inferential process of abduction interests me, not so much on philosophical grounds, but because it seems to characterize a form of legal narrative reasoning that finds its hyperbolic statement in the doctrine of "inevitable discovery."

I have written about "inevitable discovery" elsewhere.[5] In very brief definition, it is a doctrine that allows the prosecution to use results of an illegal search, one in violation of the Fourth Amendment rules on searches and seizures, if it can show that what was found would inevitably have been discovered if legal means had been used to discover it. This makes pretty good sense in the case in which the Supreme Court signs on to the doctrine, *Nix v. Williams*, in which there was a search party on the ground, marching westward through Iowa, some two and a half miles from the place where the murdered child lay—a search called off when the perpetrator told the police where the body was after an interrogation judged to be illegal.[6] In other cases, it has at times been a convenient way of saying that the finding of the goods (drugs, very often) by whatever means is justified because if the correct, warranted means had been used you would certainly have found it.[7] This sounds to me very much like the logic of a certain kind of narrative explanation that derives beginnings and middles from ends. It is the inferential logic of the: "it must have been like this." It may be the logic of *telling* rather than of *happening*, and the law can at times confuse the two, turning the way events are told into the way things happened. I want to pursue and refine this question by way of Carlo Ginzburg's ambitious essay on "Clues."

In a sinuous argument that touches on Sherlock Holmes, on Freud, and on the prototype of a kind of discovery procedure used by both that was elaborated by the art historian Giovanni Morelli—whose premise was that in order to authenticate a painting, one should look to minute details such as ear lobes and fingernails, where an artist's unique characteristics would be better revealed than in the ensemble—Carlo Ginzburg undertakes to isolate and define a special form of cognition by way of clues.[8] Knowing by way of clues—following the traces left by one's quarry—is of course the detective's method. It doesn't work by deduction from a general law (though it may call upon fragments of general wisdom, e.g., "the horse is a gregarious animal"), nor does it quite work inductively from part to whole. It is rather a science of the concrete and particular that achieves its discoveries through putting particulars together in a narrative chain.[9] Ginzburg identifies this science with the huntsman's lore:

> Man has been a hunter for thousands of years. In the course of countless pursuits he learned to reconstruct the shapes and movements of his invisible prey from tracks in the mud, broken branches, droppings of excrement, tufts of hair, entangled feathers, stagnating odors. He learned to sniff out, record, interpret, and classify such infinitesimal traces as trails of spittle. He learned how to execute complex mental operations with lightning speed, in the depth of a forest or in a prairie with its hidden dangers. (*Spie*, 166; *Clues*, 102)

Even in a post-hunting society, searches reach their discoveries by such tracking of details, making them into a chain of meaning, uncovering their connections. Ginzburg speculates that this kind of knowing may in fact lie at the inception of narrative itself:

> This knowledge is characterized by the ability to move from apparently insignificant experiential data to a complex reality that cannot be experienced directly. And the data is always arranged by the observer in such a way as to produce a narrative sequence, which could be expressed most simply as "someone passed this way." Perhaps the very idea of narrative (as distinct from the incantation, exorcism, or invocation) was born in a hunting society, from the experience of deciphering tracks. (*Spie*, 166; *Clues*, 103)

On Ginzburg's hypothesis, narrative would be a cognitive instrument of a specific type, one "invented" for the decipherment of details of the real that take on their meaning only when linked in a series, enchained in a manner that allows one to detect that "someone passed this way." This is what Sherlock Holmes's searches—for a wax vesta in the mud, for a ventilator high up in the wall—are all about. And the "huntsman's paradigm" may indicate in more general terms the use-value of narrative as a form of speech and cognition: it is the instrument we use when the putting together of particulars into a meaningful sequence seems to be the only way to track down our quarry, whatever it may be. Working from Ginzburg's suggestions, Terence Cave argues that the huntsman's or "cynegetic paradigm" points us toward that most basic and enduring and useful of plots: the story that leads to *anagnorisis* or recognition. "The sign of recognition in drama and narrative fiction belongs," says Cave, "to the same mode of knowledge as the signature, the clue, the fingerprint or footprint and all the other tracks and traces that enable an individual to be identified, a criminal to be caught, a hidden event or state of affairs to be reconstructed."[10] Signs of recognition in literature reach back to antiquity and forward to modernity: see the scar on Odysseus's thigh that enables his old nurse Eurykleia to recognize him by touch, see the hidden birthmark of Shakespeare's *Cymbeline*, see the notorious *la croix de ma mère* of nineteenth-century melodrama, the token which at the denouement allows the orphan to be recognized, true identities established. It is easy to recognize that the law, particularly when dealing with issues of evidence, must make use of the huntsman's paradigm, seeking to show how finding signs and deciphering tracks will lead to the apprehension of what passed that way.

Fingerprinting, from early in the twentieth century onward, assumed dominant importance in the tracking and identification of criminals. It was imported by the British raj from Bengal and immediately accepted in Europe and America: other systems of identification, including the complex measurements of "Bertillonage," were never wholly reliable. It is interesting, in the context of Ginzburg's paradigm, that a decision by federal judge Louis Pollak in 2002, in *United States v. Llera Plaza*, cast doubt on our dependence on fingerprinting.[11] Pollak ruled that fingerprint evidence does not meet the criteria for scientific evidence established in *Daubert v. Merrill Dow Pharmaceuticals*. He noted that other recent federal cases called fingerprint identification "the very archetype of reliable expert testimony" and "scientific knowledge," but that it failed on the grounds of testability and especially falsifiability: it is the test of falsifiability that allows one to know not only that a proposition is true a good deal of the time but that it is universally true. Fingerprint identification, while mustering a considerable body of expertise, does not in the final analysis meet this standard. The final step in fingerprint identification—the determination of a match between two sets of fingerprints—involves a subjective judgment rather than a scientific procedure: "it is a subjective determination without objective standards to it" (at 37–38, citing expert witness David Stoney). Therefore, Pollak ruled that experts may present analysis of fingerprints, and point out observed similarities between prints, but "will not be permitted to present testimony expressing an opinion of an expert witness that a particular latent print matches, or does not match, the rolled print of a particular person and hence is, or is not, the fingerprint of that person" (at 69). This I think had the effect of moving fingerprint evidence from the domain of science to the realm of Ginzburg's "conjectural knowledge." But Pollak's decision inevitably met with ferocious resistance in the police and prosecutorial communities, and he reversed himself three months later. The absolute accuracy of the clues registered by our digital imprints remains in doubt.[12]

Ginzburg notes an early relation of the huntsman's paradigm to law in his discussion of Mesopotamian divination, based on the minute investigation of seemingly trivial details: "animals' innards, drops of oil on the water, stars, involuntary movements of the body." According to Ginzburg, Mesopotamian jurisprudence was similarly oriented toward the interpretation of particulars: "Mesopotamian legal texts themselves did not consist of collections of laws or statutes but of discussions of concrete examples" (*Spie*, 168–69; *Clues*, 104). So that the same paradigm can be found in the divinatory and jurisprudential texts, with this difference that the former are directed to the future, the latter to the past. Ginzburg then stretches his hypothesis to suggest that narrative modes of knowing (such as archaeology, paleontology, geology) all make what he calls "retrospective prophecies" (183; 117), which he sees as the key to the popularity of detective fiction.[13]

What Ginzburg calls the "conjectural paradigm" means that when "causes cannot be reproduced, there is nothing to do but to deduce them from their effects." That working backward from effects to causes characterizes psychoanalysis in its entirety, as Freud was very much aware, and possibly much legal analysis as well. The "case method" of American legal study—introduced by C. C. Langdell at Harvard Law School shortly before Conan Doyle began his Sherlock Holmes tales—resembles the Mesopotamian approach in its insistence that argument be worked up from concrete particulars.[14] And here, too, the concept of "retrospective prophecy" is relevant: that which is plotted forward to the predictable outcome can be so ordered because one in fact stands at the point of the outcome. The causes become apparent in light of their effects.[15] Langdell of course thought the study of cases ought to lead to a legal science. Holmes suggests the same thing in a late story, *The Adventure of the Abbey Grange*, when he complains that Watson's "fatal habit of looking at everything from the point of view of a story instead of as a scientific exercise has ruined what might have been an instructive and even classical series of demonstrations."[16] He querulously proposes "to devote my declining years to the composition of a textbook, which shall focus the whole of detection into one volume." His reproach to Watson misunderstands—and allows his creator to emphasize—the genius of the case method. The point of the exercise, in a pedagogical and cognitive sense, is to retrace how the outcome can be drawn, with the logic of inevitability, from the "facts of the case" by the plotting of the story. And if we enjoy the mental processes activated by detective fiction and legal argument, it must be in part because of the satisfaction derived from the demonstration of inevitability: it had to be this way, and no other way.

Searches for evidence may always include a "retrospective prophecy" factor. Consider that application for a search warrant must contain a prediction of what is to be found. The warrant application sets forth the evidence that the police believe they (inevitably) will find if given permission to search.[17] Warrants must be based on "probable cause" that what is sought will be found. In this sense, searches for evidence always involve a prior story, a probable, hypothetical story which the search intends to confirm. The doctrine of "inevitable discovery" offers a particularly clear instance of "retrospective prophecy." It makes the claim that a trail to the quarry exists, and that the (hypothetical) following of the traces and tracks making up this trail would (certainly) lead to the quarry. In other words, it takes the logic of the huntsman's paradigm—the logic of narrative knowing— and, in its hypothetical application of the paradigm to a case in which the quarry *was not* but *would have been* found, exposes the logic of discovery as a narrative process. In the doctrine of inevitable discovery, we know that the quarry is there, at the end of the trail. The question is whether following the trail would inevitably have led to it. When you decide—as in *Nix v. Williams*—that it would have, you sign on to the logic of narrative discovery in a particularly telling way, accepting that the huntsman's lore is infallible, and infallibly cognitive. When as a legal decision maker you so decide, you may be simply affirming the nature of the law as discipline: affirming its belief in evidence as the meaningful entailment of tracks and traces.

NARRATIVE RETROSPECT

All the practices of identification by way of signs interpreted as clues in the narrative of what happened, who passed by, involve a "retrospective prophecy," a construction of the story of the past by way of its outcome, what it was leading to. It is in the peculiar nature of narrative as a sense-making system that clues are revealing, that prior events are prior, and causes are causal only retrospectively, in a reading back from the end. The narrative theorist Gérard Genette argues that narrative offers the determination of means by ends and of causes by effects. If the narrative went nowhere, never became a complete story, there would be no decisive enchainment of its incidents, no sense of inevitable discovery; the units of the narrative would cease to be functional. Such, Jean-Paul Sartre argued, is the difference between living and telling. To tell is to conceive life as adventure, in the etymological sense of the *ad-venire*, that which is to come, and by its coming to structure what leads up to it. It is worth quoting at some length the reflections of Sartre's fictional spokesman Antoine Roquentin on the problem. When you begin to tell a story, you appear to start at the beginning. But, says Roquentin:

> In reality you have started at the end. It is there, invisible and present, it is what gives these few words the pomp and value of a beginning: "I was out walking, I had left the town without realizing, I was thinking about my money troubles." This sentence, taken simply for what it is, means that the guy was absorbed, morose, a hundred miles from an adventure, exactly in a mood to let things happen without noticing them. But the end is there, transforming everything. For us, the guy is already the hero of the story. His moroseness, his money troubles are much more precious than ours, they are all gilded by the light of future passions. And the story goes on in reverse: instants have stopped piling themselves up in a haphazard way one on another, they are caught up by the end of the story which draws them and each one in its turn draws the instant preceding it: "It was night, the street was deserted." The sentence is thrown out negligently, it seems superfluous; but we don't let ourselves be duped, we put it aside: this is a piece of information whose value we will understand later on. And we feel that the hero has lived all the details of this night as annunciations, as promises, or even that he lived only those that were promises, blind and deaf to all that did not herald adventure. We forget that the future wasn't yet there; the guy was walking in a night without premonitions, which offered him in disorderly fashion its monotonous riches, and he did not choose.[18]

On this statement, any narrative telling presupposes an end that will transform its apparently random details "as annunciations, as promises" of what is to come, and that "what is to come" transforms because it gives meaning to, makes significant the details as leading to the end.

Roland Barthes once suggested that narrative may be built on a generalization of the philosophical error of "post hoc, ergo propter hoc": narrative plotting makes it seem that if *b* follows *a* it is because *b* is somehow logically entailed by *a*.[19] And certainly it is part of the "logic" of narrative to make it appear that temporal connection is also causal connection. This indeed may be one of the uses of narrative: we need to be able to discover connections in life, to have it make sense, to rescue passing time from meaningless successivity. One of the projects of complex narratives—such as novels—has often been to question such connections, to ask about the possible randomness of existence. Novels often appear to stage a struggle between chaos and meaning. But their very existence as novels, as writing about life rather than life itself, must generally assure that they conclude, however tenuously, in favor of meaning.

In the inevitable discovery doctrine, the law comes down firmly on the side of meaning, conjuring away the specter of meaninglessness, a chaotic universe in which searches would not necessarily lead to anything. It presupposes an infinitely knowable world, one laid out in tracks and traces— like the gridlines marked off on the county map by Agent Ruxlow in his search for the young girl's body in *Nix*—waiting to be deciphered. If this is a contestable picture of the world, it may be an accurate picture of the law, which assumes that its quarry exists, and that its discovery procedures, if patient and thorough enough, will find it. In the doctrine of inevitable discovery, then, the law is merely affirming (in fairly spectacular form) its own nature. By this, I mean that law is inextricably bound up with the making of "retrospective prophecies," using the shaping force of outcomes to construct narratives from tracks and traces into a coherent plot with a meaningful ending. Inevitable discovery is in this sense what the Russian Formalists might have called a "laying bare of the device": one of those moments that images the procedures and the very nature of the text in question.

When we speak of "the narrative construction of reality"—in Jerome Bruner's terms, how narrative "operates as an instrument of mind in the construction of reality"[20]—we must mean, among other things, the ways in which narrative sequence, plot, and intelligibility are used by humans to make sense of their lives and their world. It was precisely his reflection on the workings of narrative structure in the creation of intelligibility and meaning in human action (a reflection continued in his autobiography, *The Words*) that led Sartre eventually to renounce the novel as a genre, since it came to appear to him a violation of existential freedom, a misrepresentation of the open-endedness of becoming. Yet one might respond that the renunciation of narrative is not an option, since narrative construction of reality is a basic human operation, learned in infancy, and culturally omnipresent.[21] For better or worse, we are stuck with narrative and its ways of making sense. The conclusion would then seem to be that we should become better narratologists—better analysts of the stories we tell, the ways they work, the effects they have.

Bruner notes that the way the human mind processes knowledge as story "has been grossly neglected by students of mind raised either in the rationalist or in the empiricist traditions."[22] One wonders if it has been neglected as well by students of the law. One tends to find attention to the creation and critique of legal storytelling mainly consigned to the courses on courtroom advocacy and legal writing, which often have marginal status within law school. And, as I suggested earlier, one scans legal opinions in vain for any mention of narrative as a category that needs thinking about.[23] Justice Souter's riff on "narrative integrity" in a case called *Old Chief v. United States* remains exceptional. It is the only moment I've encountered where the Court considers what has been called the "epistemology of the particular": the way in which stories create certain meanings that cannot otherwise be conveyed.[24] At issue in the case is whether defendant Johnny Lynn Old Chief can "stipulate" to a prior crime and conviction, thereby preventing the prosecution from presenting the details of that old crime, which is very similar to the new charge. Souter registers the need for "evidentiary richness and narrative integrity in presenting a case."[25] He goes on to say that "making a case with testimony and tangible things ... tells a colorful story with descriptive richness."[26] And he continues:

> Evidence thus has force beyond any linear scheme of reasoning, and as its pieces come together a narrative gains momentum, with power not only to support conclusions but to sustain the willingness of jurors to draw the inferences, whatever they may be, necessary to reach an honest verdict. This persuasive power of the concrete and particular is often essential to the capacity of jurors to satisfy the obligations that the law places on them.[27]

Souter's opinion develops into a striking reflection on the nature and the force of narrative:

> A syllogism is not a story, and a naked proposition in a courtroom may be no match for the robust evidence that would be used to prove it. People who hear stories interrupted by gaps of abstraction may be puzzled at the missing chapters. ... A convincing tale can be told with economy, but when economy becomes a break in the natural sequence of narrative evidence, an assurance that the missing link is really there is never more than second best.[28]

For Souter, the full and convincing tale must be responsive to the jurors' expectations "about what proper proof should be."[29] These expectations preexist service on a jury: jurors bring them to the courthouse, "assuming, for example, that a charge of using a firearm to commit an offense will be proven by introducing a gun in evidence." Failure to meet what we might call jurors' "narrative competence" can undermine the prosecution's proof.

The need for a complete and convincing narrative indeed has an ethical dimension for Souter. Pointing out that jury duty is unsought and often difficult:

> When a juror's duty does seem hard, the evidentiary account of what a defendant has thought and done can accomplish what no set of abstract statements ever could, not just to prove a fact but to establish its human significance, and so to implicate the law's moral underpinnings and a juror's obligation to sit in judgment.[30]

As I read this, Souter seems to be saying that the force of narrative evidence, the kind of evidence of guilty mind and act that it alone can provide, may be tied in a deep way to the very act of passing judgment on one's fellows. It is only on the basis of seeing and feeling what someone did in committing a crime that we can understand the morality of passing judgment. If that is what Souter means, he implies that law without narrative would be not only disabled but lacking in moral force.

Curiously, though, this major statement on the importance of narrative in the law is used in the instant case to claim that while a jury needs to hear a full narrative of events, too much story, for instance that of Old Chief's past felony and conviction, could "overpersuade" the jury. That might lead the jury to convict on evidence of his bad character, rather than on proof specific to the crime. Old Chief's past felony, Souter decides, is not a chapter in this story: it is "entirely outside the natural sequence of what the defendant is charged with thinking and doing to commit the current offense."[31] Story is dangerous as well as persuasive. The law needs to keep it channeled or, you might say, under erasure: visible when you look for it but only barely legible. If it is in some way fundamental to the morality of criminal law, to recognize its constitutive force might be to concede that law rests on rhetoric.

Certainly where Fourth Amendment jurisprudence is concerned—when we are talking about searches and seizures and how we understand their workings in relation to constitutional "rules"—the narrative construction of the reality *is* the reality, and how it is constructed makes all the difference in the defendant's story. And when we start probing the interesting piece of Fourth Amendment doctrine known as "inevitable discovery," we find implicated within it a larger problem of legal narrative, which is in turn a problem of narrative as a human function, cognitive instrument, and moral compass.

Stories are not events in the world, but rather a way in which we speak the world, and in so doing give it shape and meaning. Yet in their telling and their reception as the given story of what happened, they become events in the world. This issue extends far beyond Fourth Amendment cases. Consider the obvious instance of rape. I have taught the famous case from Baltimore, *Rusk v. Maryland* and *Maryland v. Rusk* (recently the object of a fine essay by Jeannie Suk[32]), where the "same story" is retold four times, by majority and dissent at two different appellate levels, with crucially differing outcomes. Rusk was convicted at trial; the Maryland Court of Special Appeals reversed and vacated his conviction; then the Maryland Court of Appeals (the highest court in the state) reversed again, reinstating the conviction. In both appeals courts, there was a majority opinion and a dissent: the story is retold four times, twice as "consensual sex," twice as "rape." "What happened" was never in dispute. What it meant made all the difference—and that meaning was all in the way the happening was told, with different narrative connectives, with a differing understanding of how events fit together to make the chain of meaning. And it is easy to see that in all branches of the law, from trial court to Supreme Court, the telling of "the facts" underlies all adjudication. If the need to "control the narrative" has become something of a cultural cliché, that should suggest the need to unpack and analyze the prevailing narrative.[33]

One more example (if that's needed) could be found in the writing of postconviction petitions, which must claim that a story officially proclaimed at its end should be reopened. In *Mickens v. Taylor*, which reached the Supreme Court as a case of conflicted representation (counsel who had been representing the murder victim on a charge of assault against his mother was, immediately after the murder, appointed to represent his alleged killer), Anthony Amsterdam had to produce a petition for a writ of certiorari that would forcefully suggest from the outset that the record compiled at trial by Mickens's counsel could have and would have been different with unconflicted legal representation.[34] The lawyer's conflict of interest was the legal entering wedge; the more compelling issue was that the lawyer had allowed Walter Mickens to take the stand and deny any involvement with the killing although he had already confessed to it and the evidence against him was overwhelming. Mickens was convicted of aggravated homicide, murder made "wantonly vile" by forcible sodomy on the victim, and sentenced to death. Amsterdam's petition retold the story to suggest forcefully that the sexual encounter of Mickens and his victim was consensual, occurring in a well-known trysting place, and that the victim was indeed probably a male prostitute, thus disqualifying Mickens for a capital sentence in the Commonwealth of Virginia.[35] All the other courts below had accepted the story created at trial. Amsterdam effectively demonstrated that it could be told otherwise, and with greater plausibility. That argument took the case to the Supreme Court, where a five–four majority decided that Mickens had to demonstrate that his legal representation had an actual adverse effect on his trial—a "but for" unprovable by its very nature. As Justice Stevens puts it in his dissent, "we will never know" what the story made at trial might have been (at 186). The stories told at law, once accepted by juries and judges and then retold and ratified by appellate courts, become inert realities, rarely revised.

Courtroom advocates, appellate judges—including justices of the Supreme Court—"know" in some unacknowledged way that there are moments when the particulars of how "the facts" are told make all the difference. There are times when they would subscribe to Joseph Conrad's famous dictum for novelists: "My task . . . is by the power of the written word, to make you hear, to make you feel—it is, before all, to make you see. That—and no more, and it is everything."[36] But an explicit awareness of the crucial, sometimes decisive role of narrative in passing judgment rarely is visible, and almost never discussed. If the law regularly issues "retrospective prophecies"—reaching back to show how the present outcome was necessarily entailed by happenings and decisions in the past—it doesn't recognize the kind of narrative act involved in this reasoning. For instance, an acknowledgment that usually there are no facts of a search independent of the narrative form given to them might seem to be an important element in the intellectual toolkit judges bring to the resolution of appellate cases. The narrative construction of reality as an explanatory system surely is omnipresent, and it needs to be recognized *as* a construction rather than accepted as one of the givens of the real. Narrative analysis needs to take a place within legal analysis.

NOTES

1. See, e.g., Guyora Binder and Robert Weisberg, *Literary Criticisms of Law* (Princeton, NJ: Princeton University Press, 2000); Anthony G. Amsterdam and Jerome Bruner, *Minding the Law* (Cambridge, MA: Harvard University Press 2000); Peter Brooks and Paul Gewirtz, *Law's Stories: Narrative and Rhetoric in the Law* (New Haven, CT: Yale University Press 1996); Richard Posner, *Law*

and Literature: A Misunderstood Relation (Cambridge, MA: Harvard University Press 1998).

2. See Old Chief v. United States, 519 U.S. 172, 183 (1997). I have also discussed *Old Chief* and some of the rare cases that cite it in Peter Brooks, "Law and Humanities: Two Attempts," *Boston University Law Review* 93 (2013): 1437.

3. Arthur Conan Doyle, *The Complete Sherlock Holmes* (New York: Gramercy, 2002), 417. My thanks to Georgetown Law student Elizabeth Sebesky for her fine research assistance on this chapter.

4. Charles Sanders Peirce, "Three Types of Reasoning," in *Collected Papers of Charles Sanders Peirce*, ed. Charles Hartshorne and Paul Weiss (Cambridge, MA: Harvard University Press, 1965), vol. 5, §172. Peirce continues: "Deduction proves that something *must* be; [i]nduction shows that something *actually is* operative; [a] bduction merely suggests that something *may be*"; ibid., vol. 5, §171. See also the seminal discussions in Umberto Eco and Thomas A. Sebeok, eds., *The Sign of Three: Dupin, Holmes, Peirce* (Bloomington: Indiana University Press, 1984): Umberto Eco, "Horns, Hooves, Insteps: Some Hypotheses on Three Types of Abduction," 198–220, and Thomas A. Sebeok and Jane Umiker-Sebeok, "'You Know my Method': A Juxtaposition of Charles S. Peirce and Sherlock Holmes," 11–54.

5. See Peter Brooks, "'Inevitable Discovery': Law, Narrative, Retrospectivity," *Yale Journal of Law and the Humanities* 15 (2003): 101–29. Also Peter Brooks, "Clues, Evidence, Detection: Law Stories," *Narrative* 25:1 (January 2017).

6. See Nix v. Williams, 467 U.S. 431 (1984).

7. See for instance United States v. Feldhacker, 849 F.2d 293, 296 (8th Cir. 1988); United States v. Andrade, 784 F.2d 1431, 1433 (9th Cir. 1986); United States v. Levasseur, 620 F. Supp. 624, 632 (E.D.N.Y. 1985); State v. Butler, 676 S.W.2d 809, 813 (Mo. 1984). On these and a number of other cases, see Jessica Forbes, "The Inevitable Discovery Exception, Primary Evidence, and the Emasculation of the Fourth Amendment," *Fordham Law Review* 55 (1987): 1221–38. It is important to note that United States v. Levasseur was abrogated by United States v. Heath, 455 F.3d 52 (2d Cir. 2006), which created a heightened standard for the government to meet in order to rely on the inevitable discovery doctrine. The Second Circuit in that case expressly eschews the "reasonable probability" standard, and states: "we conclude that illegally-obtained evidence will be admissible under the inevitable discovery exception to the exclusionary rule only where a court can find, with a high level of confidence, that each of the contingencies necessary to the legal discovery of the contested evidence would be resolved in the government's favor." Heath, 455 F.3d at 61.

8. Carlo Ginzburg, "Spie: Radici di un paradigma indizario," in *Miti Emblemi Spie* (Torino: Einaudi, 1986), 158–209; "Clues: Roots of an Evidential Paradigm," in *Myths, Emblems, Clues*, trans. John Tedeschi and Anne C. Tedeschi (London: Hutchinson Radius, 1990), 96–125. I have modified the Tedeschi translation in places in order to give a more literal rendition.

9. The method identified by Ginzburg here resembles what C. S. Peirce called "abduction," "hypothesis," or "guessing."

10. Terence Cave, *Recognitions: A Study in Poetics* (Oxford: Clarendon Press, 1988), 250.

11. The first Pollak opinion comes in United States v. Llera Plaza, 179 F. Supp. 2d 494 (E.D. Pa. 2002), vacated by 188 F. Supp. 2d 549 (E.D. Pa. 2002); see also

Daubert v. Merrell Dow Phamaceuticals, Inc. 509 U.S. 579 (1993) (subsequent page references are to the first Pollak opinion).

12. For a thorough study of the current situation of fingerprinting and similar forensic evidence, see Jennifer L. Mnookin et al., "The Need for a Research Culture in the Forensic Sciences," *UCLA Law Review* 58 (2011): 725–80. The best book on the history of fingerprinting that I know is Simon A. Cole, *Suspect Identities* (Cambridge, MA: Harvard University Press, 1986).

13. The Tedeschi translation says: "the ability to forecast retrospectively," which I think downplays the striking paradox of Ginzburg's "retrospective prophecy," which seems to me a key part of his argument.

14. I am grateful to Simon Stern for bringing this parallel to my attention.

15. I have argued that this is true also of the way in which legal opinions recount the history of the law as applied to the case at hand; this may be especially true when the history of constitutional interpretation is at stake: the result must seem the inevitable conclusion drawn from prior cases. See Brooks, "Law and Humanities," 1456–63.

16. "The Adventure of the Abbey Grange," in Arthur Conan Doyle, *Sherlock Holmes: The Complete Novels and Tales* (New York: Bantam Dell, 1986), 1:1010.

17. See, e.g., the standard form for a warrant in federal court: http://www. uscourts.gov/forms/law-enforcement-grand-jury-and-prosecution-forms/ search-and-seizure-warrant.

18. Jean-Paul Sartre, *La Nausée* (Paris: Gallimard, 1947), 59–60. My translation. See also Gérard Genette, "Vraisemblance et motivation" ["Likelihood and Motivation"] in *Figures II* (Paris: Editions du Seuil, 1969), 71–100.

19. Roland Barthes, "Introduction to the Structural Analysis of Narrative" (1966), in *The Barthes Reader*, ed. Susan Sontag (New York: Hill and Wang, 1982), 266.

20. See Jerome Bruner, "The Narrative Construction of Reality," *Critical Inquiry* 18 (1991), 6.

21. Alan Dershowitz makes an argument against narrative construction as creating juror expectations of a tidy narrative whereas life is largely chaotic: see Dershowitz, "Life Is Not a Dramatic Narrative," in Brooks and Gewirtz, *Law's Stories*, 99–105. But such construction seems to me inevitably part of our understanding of events. See also the comment on the recent sensational television documentary *The Jinx* (containing the apparent confession to murders by Robert A. Durst) by documentarian Joe Berlinger: "Real life doesn't necessarily mirror the arc of scripted drama, and yet there has been this push in television to bring those two kinds of storytelling together"; Jonathan Mahler, "Irresistible TV, but Durst Film Tests Ethics Too," *New York Times*, March 16, 2015. Will TV crime drama in turn inflect legal procedure?

22. Bruner, "Narrative Construction of Reality," 8.

23. Although mentions of narrative integrity as such are rare in jurisprudence, the idea that parties should be able to tell and juries to hear a complete story is more commonly iterated. See, e.g., *Lakeside v. Oregon*, 435 U.S. 333, 339–41 (1978) (cited by Souter in *Old Chief* for the proposition that a nontestifying defendant may demand that a jury be instructed not to draw any adverse inference from his silence based on the propensity of jurors to fill in the gaps of the story if certain evidence is withheld); United States v. Pepin, 514 F.3d 193, 207–208 (2d Cir. 2008) (citing *Old Chief* for the premise that the lower court abused its discretion in excluding evidence that the defendant dismembered the body after committing homicide because these details "form[ed] part of the res gestae, the narrative

that the government rightly seeks to tell at the guilt phase of a trial"); *United States v. Hill,* 249 F.3d 707, 713 (8th Cir. 2001) (citing *Old Chief* to hold that past criminal evidence can constitute the "story of defendant's criminal behavior" as long as it goes to the intent to commit the present crime); United States v. Rezaq, 134 F.3d 1121, 1142 (D.C. Cir. 1998) (applying narrative integrity analysis of *Old Chief* to stand for the right of defendants generally to receive evidence in the form of actual classified governmental documents rather than a summary). See also United States v. Saunders, 209 Fed. App'x 778, 782 (10th Cir. 2006); United States v. Gartmon, 146 F.3d 1015, 1021 (D.C. Cir. 1998); United States v. Inserra, 34 F.3d 89–90 (2d Cir. 1994); United States v. Fortenberry, 971 F.2d 717, 721 (11th Cir. 1992); United States v. Storm, 915 F. Supp. 2d 1196 (D. Or. 2012) (citing *Old Chief*); Michael S. Pardo, "Juridical Proof, Evidence, and Pragmatic Meaning: Toward Evidentiary Holism," *Northwestern University Law Review* 95 (2000): 399–442; Nancy Pennington and Reid Hastie, "A Cognitive Model of Juror Decision Making: The Story Model," Cardozo Law Review 13 (1991): 519–58; Philip Meyer, *Storytelling for Lawyers* (Oxford: Oxford University Press, 2014).

24. One might find some similarities between Souter's dicta on narrative integrity and the common law doctrine of res gestae, which has been defined in various ways, most recently as the "inextricable intertwining" of evidence of one crime with the evidence of other crimes, and which was laid to rest in federal jurisprudence by the Seventh Circuit prior to Souter's opinion. Stephens v. Miller, 13 F.2d 998 (7th Cir. 1994). State courts remain split, and use unusually vivid and vehement language, on whether the common-law concept of res gestae can be reconciled with state rules of evidence. Compare State v. Kemp, 948 A.2d 636, 652 (N.J. 2008) ("Res gestae is the moldy cardboard box in the basement, whose contents no longer have any utility but which we nevertheless fear discarding. The time has come for us to rid our evidence rules of this ancient doctrine that no longer has any contemporary relevance.") with State v. Nelson, 791 N.W.2d 414, 423–24 (Iowa 2010) ("Therefore, under this narrow interpretation of Iowa's inextricably intertwined doctrine that completes the story of the crime, we must analyze the State's argument that the evidence the defendant was a drug dealer is not evidence of other crimes, wrongs, or acts but is, in fact, intrinsic evidence completing the story of the charged crime of murder in the first degree."). See also Edward J. Imwinkelried, "The Second Coming of Res Gestae: A Procedural Approach to Untangling the 'Inextricably Intertwined' Theory for Admitting Evidence of an Accused's Uncharged Misconduct," *Catholic University Law Review* 59 (2010): 719, 722–23, 727–28, which argues that res gestae, and a recognition of the concept of narrative integrity introduced by *Old Chief*, has been revived through a use of Federal Rule of Evidence 404(b) and is recognized by most circuit courts.

25. Old Chief v. United States, 183.

26. Ibid., 187.

27. Ibid., 187.

28. Ibid., 189.

29. Ibid., 188.

30. Ibid., 187–88.

31. Ibid., 191.

32. See Jeannie Suk, "The Look in His Eyes," Harvard Law School Public Law and Legal Theory Working Paper Series no. 10–13; reprinted in *Criminal Law Stories*, ed. Donna K. Coker and Robert Weisberg, 171–211 (New York: Foundation Press, 2012).

33. I note that attorneys are now posting filings in civil suits on the Internet in an attempt to "control the narrative." See "Lawsuits' Lurid Details Draw an Online Crowd," *New York Times*, February 23, 2015, http://nyti.ms/17L2Lgn.

34. See Mickens v. Taylor, 535 U.S. 162 (2002).

35. See Mickens v. Taylor, Petition for Writ of Certiorari to the United States Court of Appeals for the Fourth Circuit, No. 00-9285. I speak of this petition as the work of Anthony Amsterdam because I had the good fortune to work with him in his Persuasion Institute at the time he was writing it.

36. Joseph Conrad, "Preface" to *The Nigger of the Narcissus* (New York: Doubleday Page, 1897), 3.

CHAPTER 6

Law's Affective Thickets

RAVIT REICHMAN

"Legal interpretation takes place in a field of pain and death," Robert Cover wrote in his seminal 1986 essay "Violence and the Word."[1] His claim that law is composed of rules backed by force was nothing remarkable—John Austin, and no shortage of legal philosophers in his wake, had said as much. But this was not exactly Cover's main point. His aim, rather, was to illuminate the irony that shapes a legal world, the way a defendant whose life has imploded "sits, usually quietly, as if engaged in a civil discourse. If convicted, the defendant customarily walks—escorted—to prolonged confinement, usually without significant disturbance to the civil appearance of the event."[2] If there is anything "civil" about law, Cover suggests, it is its form rather than its content. His issue is not with punishment as such—many sentences, he adds, are entirely fitting and just. But he does not want us to confuse compliance with persuasion, "to pretend that we talk our prisoners into jail."[3] His problem is with tone and style, with the pains legal discourse takes to address its affective thickets in neutral terms, scrubbing and sanitizing, distancing and depersonalizing.[4]

To say that "legal interpretation takes place in a field of pain and death," then, is to do more than argue that jurisprudence is held in place by violence. It is to claim that law ensnares us in a net of affects, from fear to dread, anticipation to guilt, relief to devastation. Law's "field" is nothing short of affect itself; one would be hard pressed to find a legal proceeding that did not traverse an affective terrain in some fashion. The driver who runs a red light when no police car is in view; the conscript who burns his military draft card on the courthouse steps;[5] the county clerk who refuses, in tones of aggressive equanimity, to issue same-sex couples marriage licenses despite a court order to do so[6]—such moments of stakes large and small occur in a world of affect, some of which is readily articulable and some much harder to name and define.

It is no stretch of imagination or intellect to say that law is built around, through, and in response to a potentially inflammatory, unwieldy core of affect. Yet the nature of this connection has often gone unspoken, coming into view more prominently only in the past twenty years of scholarship, decades after the emergence of critical legal studies, law and economics, and feminist jurisprudence. Such belated treatment suggests that the relationship between law and affect is both so obvious that it goes without saying—one can certainly find work on emotions in critical legal studies and feminist legal theory—and so thorny that it cannot be articulated with clarity worthy of its complexity.

Affect lies in both the drama and the banality of law. Even the most bureaucratic procedures—filing one's taxes, writing a will, obtaining a marriage license—can signal untold depths of feeling. Yet we still invest mightily in the belief that law is more rational than emotional, a faith founded on the historical separation of emotion and cognition.

Susan Bandes observes that the study of law and emotions has now come into its own as a distinct field: interdisciplinary at its core, but with enough critical mass among legal scholars that it can be counted as its own area of inquiry.[7] Yet even as the field has gained in prominence, Kathryn Abrams and Hila Keren note a boomerang effect in its influence, "a renewed tendency to dichotomize and hierarchize reason and emotion, and a related preference for analyses grounded in objective premises"—evidence, they believe, of the legal academy's ambivalence about the relevance of emotions to jurisprudence.[8] The law, it seems, remains stubbornly resistant to feeling.

Two main approaches define the bulk of law and emotions scholarship.[9] The first focuses on specific emotions such as disgust, shame, love, or vengeance, evaluating their positive and negative valences in the context of morality, and asking how they drive legal claims and influence our beliefs about justice.[10] The second analyzes how legal procedures harness and produce emotion, examining such practices as victim impact statements or executions in light of the vengeance, mercy, or compassion they elicit.[11] Cutting across these varied perspectives is an undeniable normative impulse: much of this work takes aim at the practice of law, at its flaws and possible reforms. While the problems it addresses may be cultural, political, or historical, the instrumental thrust of a good deal of law and emotions work sets it outside the purview of a cultural study of law, at least in

Paul Kahn's insistence that cultural study should be segregated from legal reform rather than tied to legal practice.[12] If there are new directions to be found in the study of law and affect, these may well lie in resisting the urge to make recommendations about what law should be. The turn away from this instrumental approach opens up avenues of engagement with questions of culture and language, the kinds of questions that tend to preoccupy affect theorists.

While many scholars, myself included, use the terms emotion, feeling, and affect interchangeably, we are also keenly aware that affect represents a separate notion. Some of affect's early theorists, notably Silvan Tomkins, argue for discrete, nameable affects.[13] But most affect studies scholars describe a process that cannot be named so succinctly.[14] When Lauren Berlant defines cruel optimism as a condition in which "something you desire is actually an obstacle to your flourishing,"[15] she is describing an affective state that needs an involved explication; unlike happiness or anger, its associated feelings and conditions are not immediately obvious. This is because affect studies focuses not on emotions strictly defined, but on the relations between mind and body, culture and individual subjectivity. Brian Massumi contends that affect exists outside language; he calls it intensity, contrasting it with emotion, which he views as "qualified intensity, the conventional, consensual point of insertion of intensity into semantically and semiotically formed progressions"[16]—that is, intensity framed and fixed in language. If emotion is the musical note, articulable and recognizable, affect functions something like volume or timbre (though it is less measurable than either of these qualities), or like articulation—a constant rather than an instant.

Affect comes closer to perceiving than feeling; we might also think of it as the way that emotional experience consolidates itself out of depths that move us, but that we cannot fully acknowledge or apprehend. Colin Dayan, connecting dogs to ethical and juridical life, suggests as much in seeking out

> another kind of experience that can be felt but not always understood. By concentrating on that aspect of the reader's mind that can perceive but not comprehend, I hope to sharpen the appetite for seeing and knowing, even while suggesting something indiscernible behind what is seen and known. Mood replaces certainty. We are left with an all but unintelligible feeling. Or is it another kind of intelligibility?[17]

Dayan's recent work brings affect together with law in explicit ways, but legal scholarship has had surprisingly little to do with affect in its more inchoate, "unintelligible" sense, perhaps because the fluid methodologies and registers of affect theory make for a complex fit with the more precise legal imagination. Among the most forceful engagements of affect in the legal context is Patricia Williams's hybrid work *The Alchemy of Race and Rights*, which brings law into closer contact with affect not only by taking aim at the sterility of legal language, but by bringing Williams herself— as a scholar and teacher of law, a legal subject, a black woman—into the forefront, making things personal, dropping the detached voice that traditionally serves as the bearer of authority. "So you should know that this is one of those mornings when I refuse to compose myself properly," she declares; "you should know you are dealing with someone who is writing this in an old terry bathrobe with a little fringe of blue and white tassles dangling from the hem, trying to decide if she is stupid or crazy."[18] It's not just what she says, in other words, but how she performs what she says: in a bathrobe, in the first person, with an edge in her voice.[19] In person, rather than just in voice, does she address "the way in which legal language flattens and confines in absolutes the complexity of meaning inherent in any given problem."[20]

Williams offers her account as an alternative to the legal fiction around which so much common law turns: the figure of the reasonable person—or more pointedly, the reasonable man. This legal fiction, known in British law as "the man on the Clapham omnibus"[21]—that unremarkable, predictable, imaginary individual who sets the terms of reasonability—has long been the standard against which to measure the behavior of real people.[22] Williams's narrative suggests that nowhere is an account of affect more necessary, or more studiously avoided, than when reasonableness is the matter at hand. From reasonable doubt to reasonable fear, reasonable provocation to the reasonable person, legal doctrine and discourse invokes the word as though its very utterance guarded against the opening of emotional floodgates. I want to consider, however, the possibility that reasonability is not a mitigation of feeling, a way that affect is tempered and domesticated, but an affect in its own right. I make the case for reasonableness as an affect rather than a quality of mind—for reasonableness rather than reason— because it registers most powerfully as tone rather than fact. This does not mean that reasonability is divorced from fact or reason, but that its full effect can be grasped most readily as tenor, tendency, or intuition. Put simply, a reasonable person is not necessarily someone who reasons well, or reasons at all; it is someone who behaves—and expresses himself—in a certain way. That expression can be sensed most readily in tone, which I examine along the lines set forth by Sianne Ngai, who explains tone as "a global and hyperrelational concept of *feeling* that encompasses attitude."

While Ngai examines tone primarily in literary texts, her aim is wider: "To speak of tone is thus to generalize, totalize, and abstract the world of the literary object, in a way that seems particularly conducive to the analysis of ideology."[23]

Reasonableness, I submit, operates as both tone and ideology in literature and law, functioning as a kind of blankness, a site of contestation where affect needs to be worked out, but where just as often the law will not probe. In these moments of resistance to affect, reasonableness becomes a fig leaf, covering an unsettling, inarticulate affective knot. What would it mean to look for affect here, in the very places where law seeks to excise it? By way of an answer, I pair two very different instances of affect in literature and law. I look first at the devotion to reasonableness and aversion to feeling in Kazuo Ishiguro's novel *The Remains of the Day*, after which I turn to the notion of reasonable force (and its close kin, reasonable fear) in the context of police violence. The points of contact between these seemingly disparate examples make the case for the relevance and depths of affect to law.

It should not surprise us that some of the most powerful examples of skirting, overriding, or managing affect come from novels about work, invested as they are in the paradoxes and necessities of doing one's job in a difficult world, where hard choices weigh on professions from housekeeping and advertising to policing and lawyering. Novels like J. M. Coetzee's *Waiting for the Barbarians*, Kazuo Ishiguro's *The Remains of the Day*, and to some extent Joshua Ferris's *Then We Came to the End* have in common a persistent tone of reasonableness, staging the tension between desire and duty, individual and professional life. Of these, *The Remains of the Day* cleaves most doggedly and desperately to this tone; indeed, its protagonist, the butler Stevens, never seems to break stride when it comes to talking about the painful past. It is with Stevens, then—the reasonable man of fiction—that we might ask: What does it feel like to be reasonable? What, and how, does a reasonable person feel?

WHAT REMAINS: ISHIGURO'S AFFECT-FREE ZONE

On the surface, *The Remains of the Day* makes for an idiosyncratic reference point in a discussion of law and affect. The story of an aging butler who travels across England to visit Miss Kenton, the woman who served as housekeeper in his early years at Darlington Hall, would seem to have little connection to legal matters. Thematically, this is true enough, although the narrative does contain a subtext in the form of a failed libel suit (mentioned briefly near the end), filed by Stevens's former employer, the disgraced

Lord Darlington, against the newspaper that had accused him of colluding with the Nazis. These political dealings cast a pall over the novel, fueling Stevens's uncompromising defense of Darlington in a loyalty that extends well past the point of necessity.

But this legal action is far from the heart of the matter. At the story's navel is the struggle over how one lives in the shadow of the life one might have had, and in this sense *The Remains of the Day* marks a triumph of reasonableness over regret. Stevens's account, ultimately, is that of life unlived: of a man who might have followed instinct rather than duty in serving a morally dubious employer; might have allowed himself to love a woman who, years later, is married to someone else and expecting a grandchild. But in the novel's present tense, it is 1956 and Stevens is serving his new American boss, Mr. Farraday, who has bought Darlington Hall after Lord Darlington's death, keeping its butler on as a testament to the estate's authenticity. Left with a skeleton crew and an unnervingly informal employer, who seems to expect his butler to engage in banter—an awkward new "task" to which Stevens takes pains to adapt—the postwar world has for Stevens been a bruising fall from grace.

There is enough smoldering passion in the novel to warrant the likes of a *Downton Abbey*. Yet Ishiguro's prose, far from touting its drama in plain sight, buries it under sediments of circumspection and propriety, keeping faith with the virtue to which Stevens aspires, one belonging to nation and profession alike. Reflecting on the nature of Great Britain's "greatness," he speculates:

> If I were forced to hazard a guess, I would say that it is the very *lack* of obvious drama or spectacle that sets the beauty of our land apart. What is pertinent is the calmness of that beauty, its sense of restraint. It is as though the land knows of its own beauty, of its own greatness, and feels no need to shout it. In comparison, the sorts of sights offered in such places as Africa and America, though undoubtedly very exciting, would, I am sure, strike the objective viewer as inferior on account of their unseemly demonstrativeness.[24]

These comparisons, of course, are the stuff of fantasy: Stevens has no more been to Africa or America than he has to Mars. But his encomium to understatement makes clear that greatness (and its relatives, power and authority) inheres more in style than substance. Two nations may be equally beautiful, and two butlers equally skilled, but it is their bearing that confers upon them the imprimatur of greatness.

Stevens takes his definition of a great butler from the Hayes Society, an organization for elite butlers, which described the quality of an exemplary servant as "a dignity in keeping with his position."[25] To avoid abstraction, Stevens illustrates this quality with a parable, passed down to him from his father, who had himself been a butler. The "apparently true" fable concerns a butler who had gone to India with his English employer, and who one day discovered a tiger under the dining room table. It was shortly before dinner, and his employer was entertaining guests. With utmost discretion, the butler apprised his employer of the situation and proposed a solution: "Perhaps you will permit the twelve-bores to be used?" Three shots then rang out from the dining room, and the butler reappeared to announce, "Dinner will be served at the usual time and I am pleased to say there will be no discernible traces left of the recent occurrence by that time."[26]

The irony is lost on Stevens; the story of brutality masked by style and neutralized by tone may be Ishiguro's point (and the novel's internal parable), but it is not his narrator's. For Stevens, the fable exemplifies the admirable capacity to remain impassive in the face of chaos, to dispatch the most outrageous obstacles with unflappable efficiency. Stevens never talks about reasonability, and this is precisely the point: he doesn't need to talk *about* it because it forms an inextricable part of *how* he talks: reasonableness is his raw material rather than his subject. Not that the themes he takes up have nothing to do with reason: restraint, dignity, and duty certainly come close enough. But it is not what the narrative addresses that accounts for its tone of reasonableness; it is what it studiously and painfully avoids. "We must not allow sentiments to creep into our judgement,"[27] Stevens cautions Miss Kenton when she expresses her dismay at Lord Darlington's insistence that Stevens fire two Jewish maids. The sentiments are there, he acknowledges, but so is the prohibition; the duty of a good servant lies in separating work from one's feelings about it.

In the emotions it denies, *Remains of the Day* offers a protracted meditation on reasonableness, an affective resistance to probing the tectonics beneath keywords like dignity or greatness. What interests me is not the undertow of dissent in the novel, with its intimations of what might have been, but the contortions through which it manages to elide the feelings that drive the narrative in the first place. It does so not by avoiding the subject; Stevens gives enough devastating particulars to indicate that he does not shy away from facing facts. But each detail arrives in the high polish of reasonableness, in the managerial, even-tempered tone of someone getting the job done. So encompassing is this tone that Stevens doesn't even recognize a barometric change in emotion when in its very grip: it takes a stranger to observe, at the end of the novel, that Stevens is crying.

It goes without saying that *The Remains of the Day* offers up a story of culture and memory, of English restraint and nostalgia. But what gives ballast to these themes is the centrality of work: at bottom, Stevens's narrative is about doing one's job— about the lengths we go to, the price we pay—to be reasonable in the hardest of times and conditions. In its tones of professionalism, its overlaying of the butler with the archetype of the reasonable man, Ishiguro's novel tells us something about the rhetorical work it takes to domesticate affect, mitigating it to such an extent that feelings may be sensed, like a pulsing vein, but they cannot be named or considered with anything resembling precision. What we learn from these moments of reported feeling is that reasonableness needs to be deduced, interpreted, observed; it cannot be reported by the individual who supposedly feels it. One does not say, in law and elsewhere, "I feel reasonable." The tone of reasonableness, paradoxically, thus hollows out the very possibility of feeling reasonable. In this way, it hews closely to Sianne Ngai's interpretation of confidence as a fake feeling in literature and ideology alike: the strength of its tone stands in inverse relationship to its experience, making it "a feeling that no one actually feels."[28] The reasonable man, we might thus understand, is like the confident one, built around the desire for a feeling that can be neither confirmed nor denied.

To understand the notion of reasonable not as a modifier but as affect (or more precisely, the *idea* of an affect) is thus to understand it both as a rhetorical means and an affective end—as a strategy for working around the tangled terrain of feeling. This "working around," in turn, characterizes the reasonable man of fiction: duty-bound, articulate yet evasive, self-conscious but not introspective—and always, ultimately, interpreted by others. But reasonableness has its own fictional place in law, one that finds foothold and traction in the force of narrative. It is this juncture of law, fiction, and fact that I now examine.

REASONABLENESS AS A WAY OF LAW

In the second episode of HBO's *The Wire*, detectives Thomas "Herc" Hauk, Ellis Carver, and Roland "Prez" Pryzbylewski, flush with bravado after being assigned to a new detail targeting Baltimore's drug dealers, roll into a West Side housing project, one of the Barksdale gang's strongholds. Far from Baltimore's finest, they have already grown weary of the menial tasks delegated to them. Their courage leavened by resentment, beer, and a desire to do something important, they decide to make a show of it, abusing a fourteen-year-old boy for talking back. Prez pistol-whips the teen, and moments later, a stream of objects—bottles, cans, a television set—rains down on the detectives. Shots are fired from somewhere; glass shatters; Herc is injured; they radio for backup. What begins as a naked display of power ends by staging the core tension of the *The Wire*, the moral and political quicksand on which power is grabbed, and grabbed back, with stunning unpredictability.

Daniels, the detectives' lieutenant, arrives the next morning, tense with anger as he prepares to deal with the brutality charge his officers now face. With the charred remains of their squad car as backdrop, he asks why they pistol-whipped the boy. Defiant and unapologetic, Prez does not balk: "He pissed me off."[29] Slowly, steadily, Lieutenant Daniels corrects him:

> No, Officer Pryszbylewski, he did not piss you off. He made you fear for your safety and that of your fellow officers. I'm guessing now, but maybe he was seen to pick up a bottle and menace officers Hauk and Carver, both of whom had already sustained injury from flying projectiles. Rather than use deadly force in such a situation, maybe you elected to approach the youth, ordering him to drop the bottle. Maybe when he raised the bottle in a threatening manner you used a Kel-Light, not the handle of your service weapon, to incapacitate the suspect.[30]

In passing the night's impulsiveness, anger, and cruelty through the sieve of verifiability, Daniels offers a user's manual on the legal doctrine of reasonable fear, outlined so clearly that the phrase itself need not enter it. The details may not be true, but their objectivity cancels out any facts on the ground: the alcohol-soaked swagger, entitlement, panic—and, of course, fear, which may or may not have risen to anything one might call reasonable.

His instructions come straight from the Supreme Court playbook of 1989, when the Court ruled in *Graham v. Connor* that claims of excessive force by police should be determined by the objective measure of reasonability in the Fourth Amendment rather than the Eighth Amendment's subjective standards of cruel and unusual punishment, since "the terms 'cruel' and 'punishments' clearly suggest some inquiry into subjective state of mind, whereas the term 'unreasonable' does not."[31] The matter of reasonable force would now hinge on telling a story in real time, "from the perspective of a reasonable officer on the scene, rather than with the 20/20 vision of hindsight."[32] Reasonableness, in other words, has a tense: its story may be told retrospectively, but its tense is always the present. "The calculus of reasonableness must embody allowance for the fact that police officers are often forced to make split-second judgments—in circumstances that are tense, uncertain, and rapidly evolving—about the amount of force that is necessary in a particular situation."[33] And yet *The Wire* reminds us of the fictional possibilities of a reasonable officer's perspective—a story told in the present tense *with* hindsight. "Maybe he was seen to pick up a bottle." "Maybe when he raised the bottle in a threatening manner you used a Kel-Light." The cascade of possibilities coalesces into a wall of objective facts—and as the Federal Law Enforcement Training Center instructs its officers, "Facts make force reasonable."[34] The initial effort to categorize force as excessive or reasonable thus expands to the realm of affect, a lens that views reasonable force through reasonable fear. What follows is something of a legal tautology, in which reasonable force is force used by a reasonable officer, who acts based on reasonable fear. This echo chamber of reasonability makes it difficult to discern what else might have gone into an act of violence, the slow burn or sudden igniting that leaves a wound or ends a life.

This echo chamber appeared to be very much in play in November 2015, when the Supreme Court ruled in *Mullenix v. Luna* that an officer who shot a fleeing suspect six times was entitled to qualified immunity. On March 23, 2010, Israel Leija Jr. resisted arrest in Tulia, Texas, and led officers on a high-speed chase, during which he twice phoned the police dispatcher to say that he had a gun and would use it if necessary. Officers set up spike strips at three locations to stop the car. At the same time, trooper Chadrin Mullenix positioned himself on an overpass near the road spikes. He radioed his superior officer requesting permission to shoot at the vehicle, but was told to wait and see if the spikes worked first. Mullenix fired six shots anyway, hitting and killing Leija, whose family sued for violation of his Fourth Amendment right to be protected from unreasonable searches and seizures. In his defense, Mullenix claimed qualified immunity, a claim that would absolve him of personal liability unless his action violated a statutory or constitutional right.

When the case reached the Supreme Court five years later, the Court ruled for Mullenix, citing his reasonable fear that Leija posed an imminent risk to police and to civilians who might be in harm's way. Put simply, "Leija was speeding towards a confrontation with officers he had threatened to kill."[35] But this logic fell short of satisfying Justice Sotomayor, who alone dissented. As she saw it, Mullenix had fired shots at a moving vehicle with no prior training in the maneuver; Leija's car was moments away from hitting the spike strips; and Mullenix had been instructed by his superior officer to stand down. Taken in context, the officer's decision was neither justified nor reasonable.

Thus Sotomayor's legal rationale. But she adds a postscript to her dissent, separated from the body of her argument by three asterisks. It is here, after her consideration of the case's legal facets, that she lodges her most blistering objection:

> When Mullenix confronted his superior officer after the shooting, his first words were, "How's that for proactive?" (Mullenix was apparently referencing an earlier counseling session in which Byrd suggested that he was not enterprising enough.) The glib comment does not impact our legal analysis; an officer's actual intentions are irrelevant to the Fourth Amendment's "objectively reasonable" inquiry. But the comment seems to me revealing of the culture this Court's decision supports when it calls it reasonable—or even reasonably reasonable—to use deadly force for no discernible gain and over a supervisor's express order to "stand by." By sanctioning a "shoot first, think later" approach to policing, the Court renders the protections of the Fourth Amendment hollow.[36]

Sotomayor's account reads like an off-the-record remark, which she herself admits; her reference to Mullenix's quip is a side note, a story from the other side of the legal balustrade. His throwaway line may have no legal sway, but it provides a backstory that exposes something other than the reasonable fear that, for the majority, qualified the shooting as an instance of reasonable force. This purportedly extraneous moment demands nothing less than a reading of tone, Sotomayor suggests. "How's that for proactive?"—a rhetorical question that calls for taking seriously the smug, cavalier, go-getting confection of affect that cannot be captured in one word ("glib" seems too quick, "enterprising" too blunt an instrument), illuminating the blind spots created by the slavish insistence on reasonableness, on the hall of mirrors that self-replicates into the "reasonably reasonable." Sotomayor's legally irrelevant point, moreover, links *Mullenix* to the growing number of "stand your ground" cases, with their similar tactic of "shoot first, think later," and their pattern of structural racism.[37]

Sotomayor's retelling of the story engages the complexity of affect in a legal moment: the intricate set of feelings and bodies, embodied wants and needs, that came together violently on a stretch of highway in Tulia, but that the legal account renders inscrutable (even in the dissent, Israel Leija's ethnicity remains unspoken). In making these dimensions legible and audible, Sotomayor not only gives them a place in law, or intimates that they should have one, but she also lays bare the willful separation of law and culture, the self-imposed, self-declared blindness—justice, after all, is blind—to the harm done in law's name, and for which reasonableness serves as delivery system.

POSTSCRIPT: REASONABLENESS IN CRISIS

The contention that "facts make force reasonable" finds its ironic, wrenching counterpoint both in Sotomayor's dissent in *Mullenix*, and more recently in the July 2016 killing of Philando Castile, the African-American man shot by a police officer after being stopped for a broken taillight in suburban Minnesota. Castile's girlfriend, who was also in the car, live-streamed the aftermath of the shooting on Facebook. The graphic footage of a blood-soaked Castile hunched over in the front seat, the life draining out of him as the officer's gun still points through the car window, is hard to watch. But what amplifies and frames the violence is Diamond Reynolds's tone: not the high pitch of emotion that one would expect, but the chilling, steady recitation of facts. "Stay with me," she says to Castile. Then, as she faces the camera, her tone turns unsentimental, unwavering, consummately reasonable. "He was trying to get out his ID in his wallet out of his pocket, and he let the officer know that he was . . . that he had a [licensed] firearm and that he was reaching for his wallet. And the officer just shot him in his arm." [38]

It is the officer who seems undone, his voice high-pitched, panic-stricken—"I told him not to reach for it. I told him to get his hands up." [39] To which Reynolds answers: "You shot four bullets into him, sir. He was just getting his license and registration, sir."[40] Her even repetition of "sir" registers both as performed deference and the recognition of a threat; whatever else she may be feeling, Reynolds knows that she needs to act a certain way, a way that would keep her from harm ("Yes, I will sir, I'll keep my hands where they are") and that, ultimately, would be legally serviceable. Contradicting the officer's account in real time, Reynolds seizes the facts before they slip further into the legal machine, where reasonable fear and reasonable force draw on each other in mutual reinforcement. As officers order Reynolds out of the car, yelling at her to keep her hands up, ordering her to get on her knees; as her cell phone falls to reveal a bright blue sky and we hear the clicking of handcuffs; as her poised narration gives way to sobs ("Please don't tell me he's gone."), it is hard not to sense piercingly the unreasonability of force and reasonableness, the welter of affects beneath the display of a reasonable person before the law. And it is hard not to sense, too, that affect is lodged most firmly, and most mutely, in the folds and facts of all that strains, in judicious tones, to be reasonable.

NOTES

1. Robert M. Cover, "Violence and the Word," *Narrative, Violence, and the Law: The Essays of Robert Cover*, ed. Martha Minow, Austin Sarat, and Aviam Soifer (Ann Arbor: Univ. of Michigan Press, 1996), 203. Essay originally published in *Yale Law Journal* 95 (1986): 1601–29.
2. Ibid., 210–11.
3. Ibid., 211.
4. Justice Sotomayor, dissenting in the recent Supreme Court decision *Utah v. Strieff*, added her own postscript to Cover's argument. "Do not be soothed by the opinion's technical language," she warns. "This case allows police to stop you on the street, demand your identification, and check it for outstanding traffic warrants—even if you are doing nothing wrong"; Utah v. Strieff, 136 S. Ct. 2056 (2016), Sotomayor, J., dissenting, 2064.
5. See United States v. O'Brien, 391 U.S. 367 (1968).
6. The reference is to Kentucky county clerk Kim Davis, who in August 2015 cited her religious convictions as grounds for refusing to issue marriage licenses to same-sex couples in spite of the fact that the Supreme Court, in *Obergefell v. Hodges*, had ruled in favor of same-sex marriage.
7. Susan Bandes, ed., *The Passions of Law* (New York and London: New York University Press, 1999).
8. Kathryn Abrams and Hila Keren, "Who's Afraid of Law and the Emotions?" *Minnesota Law Review* 94 (2010): 2002.
9. The field can be mapped much more intricately, however. Terry A. Maroney identifies six approaches to its study in "Law and Emotion: A Proposed Taxonomy of an Emerging Field," *Law and Human Behavior* 30 (2006):119–42.
10. See, for example: William Ian Miller *The Anatomy of Disgust* (Cambridge, MA: Harvard University Press, 1997), and Martha Nussbaum, *Hiding From Humanity: Disgust, Shame, and the Law* (Princeton, NJ, and Oxford: Princeton University Press, 2004).
11. See, for example: Susan Bandes, "Empathy, Narrative, and Victim Impact Statements," *University of Chicago Law Review* 63 (1996): 361–412; Austin Sarat, *Gruesome Spectacles: Botched Executions and America's Death Penalty* (Stanford, CA: Stanford University Press, 2014). While approaches to law and emotion often concentrate on negative feelings, usually in the context of criminal law, some scholars have sought to excavate the place of positive emotions. Two notable examples are Robin West, *Caring for Justice* (New York: New York University Press, 1999), and Linda Ross Meyer, *The Justice of Mercy* (Ann Arbor: University of Michigan Press, 2010).
12. Paul W. Kahn, *The Cultural Study of Law: Reconstructing Legal Scholarship* (Chicago and London: University of Chicago Press, 1999).
13. See Eve Kosofsky Sedgwick and Adam Frank, eds., *Shame and Its Sisters: A Silvan Tomkins Reader* (Durham, NC: Duke University Press, 1995).
14. Others define affect as the "force or forces of encounter" (Melissa Gregg and Gregory J. Seigworth, eds., *The Affect Theory Reader* [Durham, NC, and London: Duke University Press, 2010], 2) or that "faint whisper of emotion" (Paul Slovic, "What's Fear Got to Do With It—It's Affect We Need to Worry About," *Missouri Law Review* 69 [2004]: 971).
15. Lauren Berlant, *Cruel Optimism* (Durham, NC, and London: Duke University Press, 2011), 1.

16. Brian Massumi, *Parables for the Virtual: Movement, Affect, Sensation* (Durham, NC, and London: Duke University Press, 2002), 28. See also Theresa Brennan, who defines feelings as "sensations that have found the right match in words"; *The Transmission of Affect* (Ithaca, NY, and London: Cornell University Press, 2004), 5

17. Colin Dayan, *With Dogs at the Edge of Life* (New York: Columbia University Press, 2016), xvi.

18. Patricia J. Williams, *The Alchemy of Race and Rights: Diary of a Law Professor* (Cambridge, MA: Harvard University Press, 1991), 4.

19. Other scholars have since followed Williams's lead, most notably Kenji Yoshino, whose recent work takes root in the tension between the scholarly and personal. See *Covering: The Hidden Assault on Our Civil Rights* (New York: Random House, 2006), and *Speak Now: Marriage Equality on Trial* (New York: Crown, 2015).

20. Williams, *Alchemy of Race and Rights*, 6.

21. McQuire v. Western Morning News, 2 K.B. 100 at 109 (1903).

22. Pierre Schlag traces American law's devotion to reason in *The Enchantment of Reason* (Durham, NC, and London: Duke University Press, 1998).

23. Sianne Ngai, *Ugly Feelings* (Cambridge, MA, and London: Harvard University Press, 2005), 43.

24. Kazuo Ishiguro, *The Remains of the Day* (New York: Random House, 1993), 28–29.

25. Ibid., 33.

26. Ibid., 36.

27. Ibid., 148.

28. Ngai, *Ugly Feelings*, 69.

29. David Simon, "The Detail," *The Wire*, directed by Clark Johnson (New York: HBO Video, 2002), DVD.

30. Ibid.

31. Graham v. Connor, 490 U.S. 386 (1989), 398.

32. Ibid., 396.

33. Ibid., 397.

34. Federal Law Enforcement Training Centers (podcast transcript), https://www.fletc.gov/sites/default/files/PartIGrahamvConnor.pdf, 3.

35. Mullenix v. Luna, 136 S. Ct. 305 (2015), 311.

36. Ibid., 316.

37. See, for instance, Mario L. Barnes, "Taking a Stand? An Initial Assessment of the Social and Racial Effects of Recent Innovations in Self-Defense Laws," *Fordham Law Review* 83 (2015): 3179–3210.

38. http://www.bbc.com/news/world-us-canada-36733681.

39. Ibid.

40. Ibid.

CHAPTER 7

Paranoia, Feminism, Law

Reflections on the Possibilities for Queer Legal Studies

JANET HALLEY

Why has queer theory been so productive in the humanities and so scarce in law schools? Surely one reason is that the constellation of hyperrational styles currently expanding in the legal professoriate—neoliberal and center-left instrumentalisms and neoformalism, primarily, but also ostensibly theory-free legal history, combined with the aspiration for law that it, itself, is and should be rational—form very unreceptive ground for an intellectual and political project so attentive to, and often so appreciative of, the irrational forces in human life. Perhaps it is a tautology to add that the departments and disciplines to which law schools turn for interdisciplinary institutionalization are not the ones where queer theory was born and continues to thrive. Law schools are now deeply connected to economics, quantitative social science, and history departments purged of the interpretive turn, far less so to literature, ethnographic social science, cultural studies, and the movement-inspired departments like Gender and Sexuality Studies and African American Studies.

Another reason could be much simpler: the extreme transition, in a short twenty-nine years, from *Bowers v. Hardwick* to *Obergefell v. Hodges*[1] has meant that queer theory in the humanities tends to venerate rights while representing the actual state as an evil empire. Neither conception of "what law is" has any currency in American law schools today. Everyone except the neoformalists is legal-realist now; and legal-realist legal study does (or in my view, should) quickly disabuse any American law student of the notion that—except in extreme instances—the state is sufficiently monolithic to have a single moral valence, for good or for ill. Anyone trying to transplant work with these features from the humanities into a law school today, or doing it there, is up against a lot of resistance.

I think the first set of reasons captures a very large number of pathologies in the law schools, and the second a large number of pathologies in the humanities today. The result is the very slow growth of queer theory within law. I don't know how to work past this impasse other than by mentoring individual students with a queer intellectual bent into law teaching, a project I have engaged in with considerable success and some heartbreaking failures for more than twenty-five years now. Occasionally I can lure critically oriented legal scholars and humanities folks onto a single project with interdisciplinary dimensions, but even there, I am committed to respecting the disciplinary commands coming along with each person like a backpack. So this chapter is not about how to fix the institutional problem I've described: rather, it is about how I've lived in it.

I am one of the thousands of people whose lives were transformed by the intellectual, aesthetic, hedonic, depressive, and affectionate profusion that flowed from Eve Kosofsky Sedgwick, one of the inaugurating figures of American queer theory. We taught English together at Hamilton College in 1980 and stayed in touch until her death in 2009. During this time I went to law school and became a law professor. This chapter traces the trajectory of our friendship as a story about queer theory transiting from humanities to law.[2]

Eve often exemplified the profoundly resentful, profoundly trusting attitude about law that I see so often in humanities-based work on law. It's all pretty much encapsulated in a T-shirt which she sent round to some friends in 2003, when the US Supreme Court decided *Lawrence v. Texas*.[3] Since 1986, *Bowers v. Hardwick* had been the law of the land. It announced that the Constitution had no objection whatsoever to jailing people for acts of consensual homosexual sodomy. In *Lawrence*, the Supreme Court changed its mind: consensual homosexual acts done in private were constitutionally protected, could not be treated as crimes. To Eve, *Bowers* had been a perpetual, almost personal affront; *Lawrence* righted that, and got things right at last. The passage that Eve loved so much that she emblazoned it on these T-shirts is unique in American law: "*Bowers* was not correct when it was decided, and it is not correct today. . . . *Bowers v. Hardwick* should be and is now overruled."[4] Even *Brown v. Board of Education* doesn't say that *Plessy v. Ferguson* was wrong when it was decided, only that it had become wrong in the course of historical evolution.[5] For Eve at this joyous moment, law could be, should be, and was right; she celebrated the Supreme Court's announcement that law that was wrong wasn't law at all.

Almost no lawyer thinks about law that way. Here as so many times in my long friendship with her, I felt that my new discipline was opaque to her, incomprehensible, extremely occasionally liberating but mostly menacing. This was always a sad moment for me, because Eve's work had been the source of many of my most treasured *legal* ideas. From my third year in law school, when she would send me drafts of *Epistemology of the Closet*, I have hoarded her formulations, her ideas, her analytic moves, and worked them into my papers and books on law. What was that process? What does it say about the possibilities for the interdisciplinary transfer of ideas? What elements of Eve's work—from her feminist work, to her innovations in queer theory, to her development of affect theory, from her Buddhism to her work in textiles—could and could not be assimilated by me into a series of interventions in law?

Before I begin, I should emphasize that what I'm about to present is just simply what *I* was able to carry across the literary/legal frontier (and what I wasn't). I'm going back to work by Eve that mattered to me, so my selections among her writings are ultimately unjustifiable except by the plea that this is how I remember it.

GOVERNANCE FEMINISM

To anchor this project firmly in law, I'm going to focus on a large collective project in which I am involved, organized by myself, Prabha Kotiswaran, Rachel Rebouché, Hila Shamir, and Chantal Thomas. Our project began several years ago when we published an essay claiming that, in recent years, feminism had a new situation vis-à-vis law: specifically, *inside* it.[6] We think it is simply beyond doubt that feminists now walk the halls of power. By no means all feminists: some forms of feminism disqualify their proponents from inclusion in the power elite. But you can get a job in the UN, in the World Bank, in the International Criminal Court, in the local prosecutor's office, and in the child welfare bureaucracy for espousing various strands of feminism. We are asking ourselves and our collaborators: exactly what forms of feminism "make sense" to previously entirely male power elites, find their way into legal institutions, and change legal thought and legal operations? Whose NGOs get funding from international aid and development agencies and from ideologically driven private donors? Once feminists gain a foothold in governance, what do they *do* there and which particular legal forms are they most heavily invested in? What are the distributive consequences of the partial inclusion of some feminist projects? Where does feminism succeed in mainstreaming its policies and does this success also bear some traceable systemic costs? Can feminism foster a critique of its own successes?

We have dubbed our topic Governance Feminism (GF).[7] We initially focused on two large GF projects in international law: making rape a crime against humanity and a war crime when committed upon civilians in armed conflict; and getting the right relationship between new antitrafficking law and prostitution or sex work. The former feminist effort piggybacked on the international policy steamroller leading up to the establishment, via the Rome Statute, of an International Criminal Court; and the latter piggybacked on a parallel international steamroller leading to the construction of a new level of coordination among the world's nations to combat transnational organized crime.

As I discovered in the course of my independent research into the rape effort,[8] the feminist ideology that worked its way into the Rome Statute was remarkably radical in its vision of the problem, and criminal in its vision of law. Rape in wartime was, to these feminists, continuous with rape in "so-called peacetime": there was no real peacetime because life everywhere involved a male "war on women." This was a structuralist, dominance feminism that is everything queer theory wants not to be: knowing, deliberately self-limited to the distinction between men and women, male and female, masculine and feminine (m/f for short), which draws the only horizon for its normative work, committed to a vision of the world as unilaterally hierarchical, m>f, and intent on wielding the sword of criminal punishment to put an end to gender violence against women everywhere. It exemplifies what Elizabeth Bernstein has dubbed "carceral feminism."[9]

Thomas showed in our original joint article that trafficking was, by contrast, the site of intense conflict among feminists: abolitionists very similar in ideology to the "war on women" feminists at the Rome Conference regarded prostitution as by definition male dominance and sought its abolition (hence the moniker for their position); while liberal-individualist and sex-worker-oriented human rights feminists pushed for a distinction between forced and elected prostitution, looking to protect women's autonomy to determine their own sexual lives and/or their social leverage as workers, and sought to limit the new trafficking regime to punishing pimps and customers involved in genuinely forced prostitution only. In part because of this conflict among the feminists, and in part because the overriding impulse behind antitrafficking was not feminist at all but neoliberal economic policy seeking to make the world safe for the orderly globalization of cheap labor, the dominance feminists so far have not enjoyed the almost complete sweep to victory on the trafficking side that their sisters did in humanitarian law reform of the 1990s.

Our initial idea was that GF was intrinsically structural in worldview and carceral in its legalism. We could barely constrain our dislike of these orientations long enough to write about their successes accurately (though I do believe we managed that). But what we missed was the immense role of liberal feminists in creating GF, the role of liberal cultural feminists whose worldview was not as structural as the dominance feminists, and the growing role of sexual minorities—LGBT—inside legal power. Our description of GF *as* dominance-feminist exaggerated the importance of this segment of feminism that we tend, still, quite actively, to resist; and as a result we implied that, for feminism or any other emancipatory -ism, acquiring legal authority was necessarily a bad thing.

I now see that we were being paranoid about feminism. And we sounded paranoid about law. Eve asked me to detach myself from these errors, and—though it is sometimes impossible to do so—I try.

THE HAMILTON COLLEGE PHASE

I first met Eve when I joined the Hamilton College English Department, where she was teaching creative writing. Hamilton—up until then an all-male institution—had just taken over Kirkland College, the women's college across the street.

I'll never forget the first Faculty for Women's Concerns meeting I attended, the one at which Carol Bellini-Sharp announced: "What you new women need to learn is that this is war!" It was a fully dualistic political encounter, in which we feminist modernist/postmodernists found ourselves in a Manichean struggle of good (which was us) against evil (which was them). It was women against men—modern, experimental teaching against traditional, severely hierarchical pedagogy; traditional departments against interdisciplinary divisions like Humanities and Sciences—Jews and their friends against smug WASP anti-Semitism. (The chair of Hamilton College's board of trustees was reputed to call Kirkland Kikeland. There was one Jew and one woman on the Hamilton College faculty at the time of the merger, and she was the same person.) It was progressives against conservatives; postmodernists rebelling against modernists and classicists; the city versus the suburbs; antiformalism against formalism; the arts against (as we saw it) philistinism; young turk scholars against Mr. Chips.

Eve was a ferocious participant in this conflict. Once, a group of women faculty was standing in the quad talking about it, and up came a male colleague with the clever comment "Bubble bubble toil and trouble—what's up now ladies?" Eve shot back, "Oh it's just girl talk—lawsuits and such." And indeed we saw law as our friend, vowing to punish sexual harassers, prosecute fraternity rapists, and force equality down the institution's throat. We were feminists with a will to power and faith in the prohibitory effectiveness of law.

It was thrilling but also more than a little scary—Eve herself in this mode could be pretty scary. She later remembered that most of us were non-tenure-line faculty "so there was nothing to deter us from taking professional risks in our adversarial relation to this college."[10] But some of us (myself included) were untenured but tenurable; others were Kirkland tenured faculty who had to be *retenured* at Hamilton (some of whom did not make it); and still others were tenured Hamilton College faculty who were going to spend their entire careers picking up the rubble. Eve's intense, rageful, scornful, red-hot antagonism was not thoroughly affordable for all of us. The space between opposition and cooptation was so slim, so contingent, as sometimes to disappear altogether. Much of the anxiety I experienced then was generated not by our enemies but by my allies.

THE TURN TO QUEER

By 1990, Eve had produced an alternative to the Manichean governing aesthetic that I had shared with her in the fraught context of an institution at war and that survives today in and around so many dominance-feminist projects in law. I think of this alternative as the ". . . and others" sensibility[11] that animates so much of the most remarkable, most noticing, and most alive queer theory—the openness to seeing long sliding series where prevailing discursive habit sees pitched dualisms.

Whereas most laborers in the pro-gay vineyard post-*Hardwick* addressed the grand opposition supposed to exist between homosexual and heterosexual, Eve noted that—even if we posited the existence of people with identical gender, race, nationality, class, and "sexual orientation" identities—they would inevitably be *oriented* in sexuality in an infinitely long series of different ways. She ranged some of these ways in a list: "identical genital acts mean very different things to different people"; the intensity and importance of sexual acts, sexual identities, and sexual fantasies (not just the acts, identities, and fantasies) make people different from one another; so does their sense of the meaningfulness of sex, their sense of innateness and chosenness on any of these dimensions of sexual life ... and her list goes on ... and on ... registering ways in which sexuality both really really matters to people and utterly escapes the homo/hetero distinction.[12]

Later, in *Tendencies*, she pulled off this tour de force a second time but in reverse, mockingly presenting a list of ways in which the m/f distinction is supposed to (but she implies with almost palpable amusement, cannot) organize your "sexual identity": your biology, gender assignment, personality, and appearance traits are supposed to match; the same traits of your preferred partner are supposed to line up within that person and to be the opposite of yours; your self-perception as gay or straight is supposed to correspond perfectly with all of the above, as are your role models, your community and political affiliation, and your capacity to exercise power ... and, again, the list ... goes on .... [13] The sheer infinitude of ways in which gender and sexuality can deviate from dualistic prescriptions—in which the first list's others burgeon out of the silly suppositions of the second— creates in readers who like this kind of thing (and I am one of them) a profound sense of conceptual and sensual liberation, of lush possibility, of the aliveness of life.

These famous lists were only the most typographic way in which Eve conducted explorations in the ". . . and others" sensibility. In *Tendencies*, she gave a description of queer to include not only "same-sex sexual object choice, lesbian or gay" but also—*in addition*—"the open mesh of possibilities, gaps, overlaps, dissonance and resonances, lapses and excesses of meaning when the constituent elements of *anyone's* gender, of anyone's sexuality, aren't made (or *can't* be made) to signify monolithically."[14] She derived the word queer from old words for "across"—"from the Indo-European root -*twerkw*, which also yields the German *quer* (transverse), Latin *torquere* (twist), English *athwart*." She went on: "Titles and subtitles that at various times I've attached to the essays in *Tendencies* tend toward 'across' formulations: *across genders, across sexualities, across genres, across* 'perversions.' ... The *queer* of these essays is transitive, multiply transitive."[15] At the beginning of *Touching Feeling: Affect, Pedagogy, Performativity*, she set out to avoid reading "beneath" or "beyond"—undertakings presupposing that reading aimed to discover origin or telos—in favor of reading "beside": "*Beside* is an interesting preposition also because there's nothing very dualistic about it; a number of elements may lie alongside one another, though not an infinity of them."[16] She was ever alert for the "excluded middle," noting "middle ranges of agency," for instance, that could rearrange dualistic representations of power as an all-or-nothing scenario of domination and subordination.[17]

HOW AN ". . . AND OTHERS" SENSIBILITY PLAYS OUT IN CRITICAL WORK ON LAW

Many people, myself included, found these moves highly suggestive for work in law—in legal theory, in critical legal studies (CLS), in legal feminism, in queer work on law. They constituted for me a ground on which I could move away from the—to me—increasingly implausible formulations of dominance feminism; on which I could articulate alliances with men and masculinity; and in which I could find in the register of literary and social theory some important correspondences with moves I treasured in legal-realist inspired CLS. It was partly on the basis of these lists—plus the Second Axiom of *Epistemology of the Closet*'s introductory chapter[18]—that I formulated the idea that it might be good for some of the people laboring in the vineyard of sexual law, politics, and justice to take a break from feminism. F and its others? Feminism and its others? Both of these questions seemed to me to be deeply implicated in the queer governing aesthetic—an aesthetic of addition.

The "and others" sensibility of Eve's—and others'—work in queer theory fit in with a certain left, critical, legal realist way of assessing the GF projects I've mentioned. To abbreviate the process quite a bit: First, you identify the plural goods and bads at stake among a plurality of players (not just two, m/f) in a particular social context that has a legal element. Then you identify the many forms of power—not the single form—at play in the setting you are concerned with. Then you identify any legal rules that help distribute those goods, those bads, and that power, and then you try to see what the plural players do in the mesh of it all. Because you are a lawyer interested in justice, you try to see if a shift in the legal rule will enable the players to distribute power, goods, and bads differently. You are predicting without the warrant that you are right, because you know that your players are complicated, interdependent, and unpredictable.

This method actually does take on board the idea that power can be everywhere, fragmented, fluid, carrying its own resistances, and morally good, bad, or indifferent. It is quite at home with the idea that a coerced person can be exercising "agency"; that there are middle ranges of coercion and agency that meet each other complexly in a process like prostitution, labor migration, going on a first date. It pays respect to the staggering complexity of human interaction while seeking some justifiably bounded way of putting a frame down and seeing whether patterns emerge within it.

The plurality and horizontality of this approach continues as it asks how law might come into play to tilt the game among social players. Criminal law appears in the form of punishment of wrongdoers, of course, but also of innocents; and where criminal law runs out this method looks for the irrevocable but elastic level of tolerated violation—what Duncan Kennedy called the tolerated residuum of abuse.[19] But law is not exclusively criminal: there are also private law, administrative agencies, legal practices of inducing knowledge formation and respecting it as "expertise" with governance functions of its own.[20] The law is just as likely to be the social worker who smells the milk in your refrigerator to see if you are successfully managing to be a family in reunification—and the bureaucracy that monitors that social worker's reports to see if your state government is engaged in federally required "reasonable efforts" to achieve family reunification—as it is to be the officer who arrests and jails you for child neglect or abuse. And it is just as likely to be *you*, dear reader, writing an op-ed or a blog post or even a tweet exerting your will to power, as it is that resented government bureaucrat over there.

This approach in law draws from the toolkit of American legal realism the methodological preference for doing "is" before we get to "ought"[21]—to be morally engaged late in the analysis, not a priori. This part of the CLS thinking repertoire is often misconstrued as moral nihilism but it's not. It's certainly not amenable to moral crusades and stances of moral righteousness, but I think that's a plus. It frames the moment of "ought" as no more warranted than the moment of description—we think of ourselves as making decisions, not deductions, when we act.

EVE'S CRITIQUE OF PARANOID STYLES

Certainly by 1997, the year after her diagnosis of metastatic breast cancer, Eve experienced the governing aesthetic of Manichean dualism to be malign, entrenching, preclusive, and very possibly deadly. She diagnosed it, in turn, as paranoid and, following Melanie Klein, as "paranoid/schizoid."[22] I don't think the timing of this shift was accidental. She later wrote that she "knew for sure that the paranoid/schizoid was no place I could afford to dwell as I dealt with the exigencies of my disease."[23] But it was also a continuous outgrowth of the plural, sliding, additive, ". . . and others," middle-term, mid-range, horizontal aesthetic of her lists and I think she would have pursued it, though perhaps not with the same—may I say—ruthlessness, no matter what her health had been.

Eve's introduction to her 1997 anthology *Novel Gazing*—entitled "Paranoid Reading and Reparative Reading; or, You're So Paranoid You Probably Think This Introduction is About You"—is a full-scale attack on the reading protocol famously designated by Paul Ricoeur the "hermeneutics of suspicion."

In this essay, paranoid reading is reading *against* (or *beyond* or *behind*) any text, social or literary, to discover its denied, repressed, hidden, occluded, and almost always dread-inducing truth. Eve's three prime examples are her own prior work, presumably *Between Men* and *Epistemology*; a text that had inspired the latter, D. A. Miller's *The Novel and the Police*; and Judith Butler's *Gender Trouble*. Here we have Eve undertaking a profound self-remaking.

Her bill of particulars against paranoid reading does not include a claim that the things it detects—"systematic oppressions,"[24] deep contradictions, and immemorial antagonisms—don't exist; they do and in fact they are often pretty obvious. Her concern instead is that they should not be allowed reappear as our only *methodology* for reading them. We can also read otherwise.

Here is a brutally truncated recap of Eve's reasons for taking a stand against paranoid reading (a gesture which, of course, produced the very dynamics she objected to—but paranoia is like that, as we will see). Paranoid reading always already knows what it so vigilantly discovers. By anticipating this disclosure it intensifies its own necessity: "you can never be paranoid enough." By committing itself to mimetically and reflexively disclosing the supposed unknown and repressed, it entrenches the very things it purports to uproot. If this hidden substance produces bad affect—humiliation, shame, gender dysphoria—then paranoid reading can be depended on to intensify the very problem from which it purports to liberate us. And paranoid reading, banking all redemption on a strategy of exposure, invites its practitioners to imagine themselves fully redeemed: it is always *someone else* who needs to be disabused and shamed into the paranoid interpretive cycle. For all its vigilance and moral indignation—for all its fearfulness and underdog sensibility—it's ultimately smug, complacent, dogmatic, and thus politically disabling.

Worse, paranoid reading leaves important things out. For one thing, it can't notice when the text it is construing is intent not on hiding but on *displaying* its claims to truth. It is no good at propaganda or baroque profusion.

But most important for Eve, I think: paranoid reading, so committed in advance to avoiding all surprise, can never be surprised by joy. Reparative reading—reading in search of pleasure, positive affect, and ameliorative possibilities—is made more necessary, more urgent *and more impossible* by the affective tautology of paranoid styles.

To get a little more concrete, here's an example.

> The queer-identified practice of camp, for example, may be seriously misrecognized when it is viewed, as Butler and others view it, through paranoid lenses.

... [C]amp is currently understood as uniquely appropriate to the projects of parody, denaturalization, demystification, and mocking exposure of the elements and assumptions of a dominant culture; and the degree to which it is motivated by love seems often to be understood mainly as the degree of its self-hating complicity with an oppressive status quo. ...

The desire of the reparative impulse, on the other hand, is additive and accretive. ... [I]t wants to assemble and confer plentitude on an object that will then have resources to offer to an inchoate self. To view camp as, among other things, the communal, historically dense exploration of a variety of reparative practices is to be able to do better justice to many of the defining elements of classic camp performance: the startling, juicy displays of excess erudition, for example; the prodigal production of alternate historiographies; ... the rich, highly interruptive affective variety ....[25]

Once again I'm stopping mid-list. I will call this a "rereading strategy": switch out your theoretical presuppositions and the very same text—camp, a Supreme Court case—can look so completely different.

HOW READING "PARANOID READING" CHANGED MY LIFE IN LAW

I remember being a little indignant when I first read "Paranoid Reading." Eve, after all, had been one of my teachers in the fine arts of paranoid reading. I was a quick study, too. Here is an episode from my Hamilton College days. Eve was no longer teaching there, but I was definitely pitching for the approval of her spirit, which still hovered so palpably there after her departure. The aforementioned Faculty for Women's Concerns was persuading college administrators to adopt a sexual harassment policy. In its favor, I said—thinking myself extremely clever and effective at the time—"And if we don't get a lot of complainants coming forward, that will prove that the problem is much worse than we think." Now I blush to recount it. Eve described it perfectly: I was immersed in the paranoid "anticipatory mimetic strategy whereby a certain presumed, stylized violence ... must always be *presumed* or *self-assumed*—even, where necessary, imposed—simply on the ground that it can never be finally *ruled out*."[26]

Eventually I gave up my annoyance with Eve's disloyalty to her own past self and tried her playful translation of dark into bright possibilities and the power of the rereading strategy. I'll never forget the excitement I felt, following her example to reconstrue the Supreme Court's decision in *Oncale v. Sundowner Services*, the 1998 case in which the Court held that same-sex sexual harassment was actionable under Title VII. *Oncale* came down just months before I read "Paranoid Reading" and there was already in place a standard feminist construal of that case fitting it firmly into the dominance feminist account. I tried to give that reading some competition by transposing Eve's effort to find the openings for positive affect and to reread otherwise a text already made devastatingly intelligible on paranoid presumptions. You can read the results near the end of my book *Split Decisions*.[27] I felt while writing those pages that I was cracking myself out of a carapace of thought that had produced miseries like my infinitely regressing logic that "absent complaints prove uncounted violations." Getting out of that spiral, I could barely contain the joy I felt and the plural, horizontal possibilities that came into view about disputes like the *Oncale* case. And I know, for sure, that I made some people very indignant with me in the process.

Still, a vast chasm separates Eve's loving accretion of the ways in which camp houses endless possibilities for love and my much more stylized unraveling of the facts in *Oncale* to loosen the dominance feminist narrative and supplant it with pro-gay and pro-sex ones. No matter which way I turned the case, the inherent violence of the lawsuit was ineradicable: no matter whose side you were on, *someone* was badly wronged; the lawsuit either sought to redress—or was itself—an act of aggression. And in subsequent work, Eve apprehended this element in law and worked to push it out of her reparative vocabulary.

IN THE BARDO OF DYING

"Come as You Are" is a 1999 talk published after Eve's death in *The Weather in Proust*, a collection of work that remained unpublished at the time of her death.[28] In "Come as You Are," Eve reflected at length on life in the bardo of dying. A bardo in Buddhism, Eve tells us elsewhere in *The Weather in Proust*, is a space/time in which a person is open in particular ways to enlightenment. Bardos are "gaps or periods in which the possibility of realization is particularly available." All the ones she mentions are transitional, "across" states: meditation, sleep, dreams, and the instant immediately in or after death. "*Bar* in Tibetan means in between, and *do* means suspended or thrown."[29]

Buddhist thought focused intently on the bardo of after death—the privileged access to realization that opens up in the transit from life into death; but in "Come as You Are," Eve reflected on the bardo of dying, the time between one's diagnosis with a fatal illness and one's passage into the bardo of after death.[30] Eve wrote a lot about her illness, her awareness of her mortality, and her experience of dying—hard reading for her friends, of course. But in "Come as You Are," she hoped that, in an era of early diagnosis and semisuccessful treatment, the bardo of dying could become a capacious political space, a place of companionship and insight. "To say that there seem to be distinctive psychological and spiritual tasks to accomplish in the bardo of dying, for anyone lucky enough to be able to focus and be present to them, is only another way of saying that there are special freedoms to be claimed here: freedoms both of meaning, relation, and memory, yet also from them."[31]

One of the freedoms of meaning and relation she found was an ability to sidestep the fight against cancer. Though she had metastatic breast cancer, by my count, for almost thirteen years,[32] she never heeded or issued the cry: "What you new cancer patients need to know is that this is war!" Cancer was disorderly and "antinomian" to be sure, but its chaos was not the one attributed to it by Sherwin Nuland. As Eve observed, Nuland had represented cancer cells as possessed of a promiscuous, frenzied, rapacious, and racially malign fecundity—shades of the welfare queen with her "wilding" brood—that threaten the body's orderly society from below and that require firm repressive discipline from the doctors. Instead, cancer seen by Eve in the bardo of dying had the disorder of random horizontal progress, the sliding, accidental, ". . . and others" disorder of her queer lists: "[T]here is no organ, vital or vestigial, including the little toe and the heart, where it won't take hold if the tide of contingency and sheer unorganization drops it there. The disease's course depends much on the thinnest fabric of whimsy, and not at all on any law—except for the one law, of being fatal."[33]

The thinnest fabric of whimsy. Given the redemptive role that weaving and working fabric played for Eve in her years in the bardo of dying,[34] this phrase almost suggests that finding new tumors could be as amusing to the patient's Buddha-self as it is to the disease. Against that, note the malignancy, not of the disease itself, but of its law: the rule of cancer's fatality is self-executing, tautologically complete. Law and death come into perfect alignment. Together they block the redemptive sequence of Eve's paragraph, bringing it to an abrupt end.

For those of us who see ourselves as working critically in law, this imagery for law is not helpful and doesn't even seem slightly right. It makes me sad that law remained a thing that Eve could be paranoid about.

EVE AGAINST LAW

I'm going to jump to what may be the last piece Eve published in her lifetime—"Melanie Klein and the Difference Affect Makes"—to inquire further into her equation in "Come as You Are" of law with death, her continual routing of them both into the paranoid cycle, and her efforts to protect her reparative practices from the threats they posed.[35]

Here Eve turns her critique of paranoid reading on the Oedipal drama in Freud (she repeatedly admits, a Freud sometimes of her own making), on Michel Foucault's heroic but in her view ultimately unsuccessful attempt to undermine its authority in *The History of Sexuality*, volume 1, and on the persistence of the paranoid style in then-contemporary queer theory. She also sets up a much more elaborated reparative project based on Klein and Silvan Tomkins than anything she had had on offer at the time she wrote "Paranoid Reading."

What paranoid reading is to "Paranoid Reading," the paranoid/schizoid position is to "The Difference Affect Makes." Paranoia is no longer a self-limiting intellectual choice—it is now the original psychic position of all infants and a persistent, never-eradicable way of being for humans generally. And it is truly immiserating. It is made up of "five violent things." To brutally summarize again, these are: (1) all-or-nothing perceptions of gain and loss; there are only life and death; (2) a schizoid practice of splitting good and bad aspects of the subject and its objects into magical bits that carry life and death; (3) all-or-nothing attribution of omnipotence or powerlessness to the self, its others, and the fragmented bits broken off from them; (4) a greedy hunger to ingest magically powerful good things and objects so that they can do internal battle against the bad things and objects that also magically reside inside; and (5) projective identification, the propulsive ejection of good and bad parts of the self not so much onto as *into* frightening but desperately needed others. "Endogenous primary dread" is the ruling affect of the paranoid/schizoid position.[36]

What's redemptive for Eve's thinking about this is that Klein's infant can sidestep these ferocious dualisms by moving into the depressive position. Here the exhausted infant can see that its Manichean divisions are optional; that both self and its objects are good and bad at the same time, less perfect but also less fatal; indeed that good and bad continuously come together and exhibit middle ranges that make both of them less powerful; and that giving in, giving way to this depressive sensibility interrupts the cycle from omnipotence to powerlessness and back. From there, the infant can notice reality and can invest its "repaired" objects with love.[37] According to Eve, Klein thought that the depressive position provided the place for developing mature realism and generous and altruistic feelings; and through Thompkins, Eve added to these riches exploratory creativity and especially aesthetic invention. As Eve said in "The Difference Affect Makes," this account of depression corresponded profoundly with her own lifelong experience of it; and she looked to its reparative capacities as an "other room," if you will, for a psyche made brittle by paranoid/schizoid experience.

The depressive position thus provided Eve with a new way of doing work in her preferred governing aesthetic. In turning away from Freud and to Klein and Tomkins, Eve was attempting what she understood Michel Foucault to have attempted in volume 1:[38] to find an alternative to the confrontation of desire by prohibition which, for both Eve and Foucault, was the irreducible kernel of Freud's theory of psychoanalysis and his foundational error. Again, it wasn't that desire or prohibition didn't matter—they just didn't matter in the way she read Freud to say they did. She wanted to avoid

> some of the damaging assumptions that have shaped psychoanalysis in (what I think of as) its Oedipal mode: the defining centrality of dualistic gender difference; the primacy of genital morphology and desire; the determinative nature of childhood experience and the linear teleology toward a sharply distinct state of maturity; and especially the logic of zero-sum games and the excluded middle term, where passive is the opposite of active and desire is the opposite of identification; and where one person's getting more love means a priori that another is getting less.[39]

Klein's theory worked "not so much against the concept of repression as around it.... The whole Freudian dialectic between desire and prohibition is only a secondary development for Klein, and one among several such."[40] Faced with the vicious cycles of ressentiment and paranoia, Eve notes, "[c]haracteristically, Klein's resource ... is neither to minimize the importance of this circular mechanism nor to attack it frontally. Instead she contextualizes it newly—just as she had reshaped the view of repression by framing it as a defense mechanism among others rather than the master key to mental functioning."[41] Note these moves—not so much against as around; one among several such—which Eve treasured for their additive, horizontal, ". . . and others," sliding form as much as (or maybe more than) for their propositional contents. We have seen this complex maneuver before, in "Paranoid Reading" and going all the way back to Eve's queer lists.

This turn in Eve's work led her to push away Freud and Foucault and to disaffiliate from queer theory and from political engagement. Because many of us treasure precisely these resources, this was a painful lesson for us in her late work. I want to look directly at these disavowals and to argue that they made sense because of Eve's residual paranoia, and that her image of law as prohibition served to secure it. Law figures in Eve's late work as the baneful pole of a baneful dualism that cannot be unlocked, can only be evaded.

The Oedipal economy which Eve regarded as so impoverished was subservient to the central dualism pitting prohibition against desire. "To internalize societal prohibition in an effective but not paralyzing way is, for Freudian psychoanalysis, *the* maturational task of the individual."[42] Whether particular therapeutic practices promote "the repressive needs of civilization" or the "countervailing claims of individual desire," the whole schema "reinforce[es] a single structuring assumption: that psychic activity is ultimately, definitionally constituted by the struggle between intrinsic desire and imposed or internalized prohibition."[43] For all that Foucault strove in volume 1 to disable the "repressive hypothesis," Eve concluded that his opponent ultimately got the better of him. And once again, she understood that, for Foucault, it is the specifically *legal* authority of the repressive command that secures the repression/liberation dualism that he sought so relentlessly to escape but which, in Eve's diagnosis, he ultimately "propagate[ed]" further.[44] Quoting Foucault, Eve wrote:

> "Whether one attributes it to the form of the prince who formulates rights, of the father who forbids, of the censor who enforces silence, or of the master who states the law,"—or, we might add, that of the internalized superego—"in any case one schematizes power in a juridical form, and one defines its effects as obedience." In other words, Foucault describes the whole range of Western liberatory discourses—those of class politics, identity politics, Enlightenment values, and the project of sexual liberation including psychoanalysis—as being congruent and continuous with one another precisely in their dependence on the centrality of external and/or internal repression.[45]

Repression/liberation constituted in volume 1 a "performative continuity" which ensured that Foucault's every effort to wrest himself free of the repressive hypothesis effectively "function[ed] as near-irresistible propaganda for the repressive hypothesis itself."[46] To face it directly was always to be pulled back into the dualism prohibition/liberation with all of its paranoid/schizoid intensities. Foucault thus constitutes for Eve another example of law securing the need for paranoid styles which attach themselves permanently to their objects of resistance, entrenching and intensifying them, making liberation from them an almost definitional impossibility.

I think this is less a critique of Foucault than a restatement of his own problem with his achievement in volume 1. Biopower, bodies and pleasures, the care of the self, and governmentality were all additive moves of his own aimed to have the same sideways movement that Eve appreciates so much more when it brings into view Klein's depressive position.[47] The works in which Foucault developed these strategies need to be read very closely for the constant reemergence of prohibition/liberation within them. And I speculate—I could never prove this—that the grand difference between Foucault and Klein for Eve was precisely that Foucault kept trying to find the middle path in legal terms, while Klein did not.

Queer theory itself seemed to Eve to produce inevitable and unstoppable opportunities for the "terrifying contagion of paranoid modes of thought[.]"[48] The epidemic of homophobia that attended the early years of AIDS in the late 1980s and early 1990s "imprint[ed] a paranoid structuration onto the theory and activism of that period, and no wonder": political and medical life then fully justified paranoia. Then, officialdom appearing as law, bureaucracy, and public health all conspired to generate "fake-judicious, fake-practical, prurient schemes for testing, classifying, rounding up, tattooing, quarantining, and otherwise demeaning and killing men and women with AIDS[,]" ensuring that queer theory would be born bearing the mark of the paranoid/schizoid position. But Eve observed that, under then-current conditions in which an HIV diagnosis for most Americans meant nothing worse than life in the bardo of dying, queer work that retained an unrelenting grip on paranoia was increasingly unreal: "a lot of more recent queer theory has retained the paranoid structure of the earlier AIDS years, but done so increasingly outside of a context where it had reflected a certain, palpable purchase on daily reality."[49] Eve included her own work among the sources of this stuckness. "[T]he formative queer theory work of the 1980s, some of my own very much included, has generated a disciplinary space called queer, where those circular Foucaultian energies inhere with a striking distinctive intimacy." She was ready to move on.

For Eve, the paranoid/schizoid position was a constitutive element of life in political struggle, and she looked back on her own activist past[50] in sorrowful disavowal:

> As I understand my own political history, it has often happened that the propulsive energy of activist justification, of being or feeling united with others in an urgent cause, tends to be structured very much in a paranoid/schizoid fashion: driven by attributed motives, fearful contempt of opponents, collective fantasies of powerlessness and/or omnipotence, scapegoating, purism, and schism. Paranoid/schizoid, in short, even as the motives that underlie political commitment may have much more to do with the complex, mature ethical dimension of the depressive position.[51]

She could have been thinking of our political life together at Hamilton College when she wrote those words.

ASSESSING GF IN THE KEY OF QUEER CRITICAL LEGAL STUDIES

Years ago, when both Eve and I found it possible to savor the manic antagonism of the paranoid/schizoid position, I believed—and argued—that sexual-harassment enforcement on campus could never be strict enough. I was being a governance feminist, with the paranoid/schizoid commitments of dominance feminism as the beating heart of my will to power. In recent years, a lot of what I asked for has come about: campus sexual-harassment policies have become more inclusive, more powerful, and more punitive at the urging of new generations of feminists animated, as I was then, by dominance-feminist thinking. But having taken the queer turn in sexuality, and the realist/critical turn in law, I now sometimes feel that my work way back then helped to create a monster. The new systems fill me with primary endogenous dread. The paranoid/schizoid reemerges, with a new object—yet another evidence of the infinitely regressive, self-proliferating power of paranoia.

How to assess this dauntingly complex range of outcomes? It is partly *because* dominance feminism is saturated by the hermeneutics of suspicion, riven with paranoia, and nastily violent in the style of the paranoid/schizoid position that answering this question in anything like the plenitude it seeks seems so hard. Even asking it feels dangerous. "What you new feminists need to know is that this is war!" Eve's yearning to evade paranoia helps me see that the paranoid attitude of dominance feminism induces paranoia *in me*—along with an appetite for attributed motives, fearful contempt of opponents, collective fantasies of powerlessness and/or omnipotence, scapegoating, purism, and schism. My fear of dominance feminism induces me to entrench it, make it central, attribute to it magical prowess that it may not actually have—and also to imagine that the best way to fight it is to mimic it. "What is the most defining act, the conclusively diagnostic act of *ressentiment*? It is *accurately* accusing *someone else* of being motivated by it. Where then to find a position from which to interrupt this baleful circuit?"[52]

What Eve's long labor to find ways out of the paranoid/schizoid position suggests to me now is that the queer ". . . and others" sensibility can help here. Re-seeing these systems with loving awareness of the lush profusion of human sexualities and genders, and with realist/critical awareness of the consequential plenitude that even intentionally repressive legal orders can produce when diverse social actors actively engage them, stills the dread and produces a complex attitude to the systems. For they also express a deep and unsatisfied yearning for love and justice. And they have done a lot of good.

They have *both* emancipated women and created new forms of oppression for them; have *both* liberated and expunged sexual pleasure. They have vindicated some victims and prevented others—while creating new ones—male, female, and other. On the metric of Eve's queer ". . . and others" sensibility, they seem wonderful when they enable people to explore—and bad when they constrain and predetermine—sexual, erotic, and gendered life. In my long engagement with this issue as an English teacher, a law teacher, and an activist, I have, again and again, seen them do all of the above. Any interdisciplinary project in queer legal studies would—I hope—search for that proliferation of possibilities within the constraints of moral outrage and legal command.

NOTES

Thanks to Libby Adler, Aziza Ahmed, Duncan Kennedy, and Hal Sedgwick for help with this essay, and to the Boston University Faculty Group for Gender and Sexuality Studies for inviting me to deliver it as their third annual Eve Kosofsky Sedgwick Memorial Lecture in January 2013.

1. Bowers v. Hardwick, 478 U.S. 186 (1986); Obergefell v. Hodges, 135 S. Ct. 2584 (2015).
2. Janet Halley, Katherine M. Franke, Clare Huntington, Susan R. Schmeiser, Philomena Tsoukala, and Darren Rosenblum, "A Tribute from Legal Studies to Eve Kosofsky Sedgwick." Special issue, *Harvard Journal of Law and Gender* 33, no. 1 (2010): 309–356.
3. Lawrence v. Texas, 539 U.S. 558 (2003).
4. Lawrence v. Texas, 539 U.S. at 578.
5. Brown v. Board Of Education, 347 U.S. 483 (1954); Plessy v. Ferguson, 163 U.S. 537 (1896).
6. Janet Halley, Prabha Kotiswaran, Hila Shamir, and Chantal Thomas, "From the International to the Local in Feminist Legal Responses to Rape, Prostitution/ Sex Work, and Sex Trafficking: Four Studies in Contemporary Governance Feminism," *Harvard Journal of Law and Gender* 29 (2006): 335–423.
7. We are currently finishing two books on GF: Janet Halley, Prabha Kotiswaran, Rachel Rebouché, and Hila Shamir, *Governance Feminism: An Introduction* and *Governance Feminism: Notes from the Field* (Minneapolis, MN: University of Minnesota Press, forthcoming).
8. Janet Halley, "Rape at Rome: Feminist Interventions in the Criminialization of Sex-Related Violence in Positive International Criminal Law," *Michigan Journal of International Law* 30 (2008): 1–123.
9. Elizabeth Bernstein, "The Sexual Politics of the 'New Abolitionism,'" *differences* 18, no. 3 (2007): 128–151, 143.

10. Eve Kosofsky Sedgwick, "Thinking through Queer Theory," in *The Weather in Proust*, ed. Jonathan Goldberg (Durham, NC: Duke University Press, 2011), 191.

11. For examples, see Jonathan Goldberg, *Willa Cather and Others* (Durham, NC: Duke University Press, 2001); Michael Moon, *A Small Boy and Others: Imitation and Initiation in American Culture from Henry James to Andy Warhol* (Durham, NC: Duke University Press, 1998); Eve Kosofsky Sedgwick, "Willa Cather and Others," in *Tendencies* (Durham, NC: Duke University Press, 1993), 167–76.

12. Eve Kosofsky Sedgwick, "Introduction: Axiomatic," in *Epistemology of the Closet* (Berkeley, CA: University of California Press, 2008), 25–26.

13. Sedgwick, "Queer and Now," in *Tendencies*, 7–8.

14. Ibid. 8 (first italics added).

15. Sedgwick, foreword to *Tendencies*, xii.

16. Eve Kosofsky Sedgwick, "Introduction" to *Touching Feeling: Affect, Pedagogy, Performativity* (Durham, NC: Duke University Press, 2003), 8.

17. Eve Kosofsky Sedgwick, "Melanie Klein and the Difference Affect Makes," in *Weather in Proust*, 130.

18. Sedgwick, "Introduction: Axiomatic," 27–35.

19. Duncan Kennedy, "Sexual Abuse, Sexy Dressing, and the Eroticization of Domination" in *Sexy Dressing Etc.* (Cambridge, MA: Harvard University Press, 1993), 137.

20. David Kennedy, *A World of Struggle: How Power, Law, and Expertise Shape Global Political Economy* (Princeton, NJ: Princeton University Press, 2016).

21. Karl N. Llewellyn, "Some Realism about Realism," *Harvard Law Review* 44, No. 8 (1931): 1222–64, see especially 1236–37.

22. Sedgwick, "Paranoid Reading and Reparative Reading; or, You're So Paranoid You Probably Think this Introduction is About You," in *Novel Gazing: Queer Readings in Fiction*, ed. Eve Kosofsky Sedgwick (Durham, NC: Duke University Press, 1997), 15.

23. Sedgwick, "Melanie Klein and the Difference Affect Makes," in *Weather in Proust*, 139.

24. Sedgwick, "Paranoid Reading," 4.

25. Ibid., 27–28.

26. Ibid., 12.

27. Janet Halley, *Split Decisions: How and Why to Take a Break from Feminism* (Princeton, NJ: Princeton University Press, 2008), 290–303.

28. The chapter does not appear in the table of contents because Eve had so thoroughly mined it for passages in works that do appear there that reprinting it would have introduced a lot of duplication. Instead, Goldberg identifies for us where its contents appear in other chapters and provides footnotes holding all the material that didn't make its way to those berths. This explains why my citations to "Come as You Are" refer to other works.

29. Sedgwick, "Reality and Realization," in *Weather in Proust*, 210.

30. Ibid., 213n, 214n (restoring a fragment of "Come as You Are"). Here, Eve reflects on the bardo of dying originally noted by Rick Fields.

31. Ibid., 214n (restoring a fragment of "Come as You Are").

32. Sedgwick, "Melanie Klein and the Difference Affect Makes," in *Weather in Proust*, 138. Sedgwick was diagnosed with metastatic cancer in the summer of 1996 and died April 9, 2009.

33. Sedgwick, "Reality and Realization," 215n (restoring a fragment of "Come as You Are").

34. Sedgwick, "Making Things, Practicing Emptiness," in *Weather in Proust*, 69–122.

35. Before Sedgwick's death, Andrew Parker and I included this essay in "After Sex? On Writing since Queer Theory," ed. Janet Halley and Andrew Parker, a special issue of *South Atlantic Quarterly* 106, no. 3 (2007): 625–42, and soon after her death in a book, *After Sex? On Writing since Queer Theory* (Durham: Duke University Press, 2011), 283–301. But I rely here on the slightly expanded version that appears in *Weather in Proust*, 123–43.

36. Sedgwick, "Melanie Klein and the Difference Affect Makes," in *Weather in Proust*, 131–33.

37. Ibid., 136.

38. Michel Foucault, *The History of Sexuality*, vol. 1, *An Introduction*, trans. Robert Hurley (New York: Pantheon, 1978).

39. Sedgwick, "Melanie Klein and the Difference Affect Makes," in *Weather in Proust*, 129–30. Note the parenthesis—an acknowledgement that this is a strong reading of Freud and not a necessary one.

40. Ibid., 131.

41. Ibid., 134.

42. Ibid., 131.

43. Ibid.

44. Ibid., 134.

45. Ibid., 133 (quoting Foucault, *History of Sexuality*, 1: 82–85).

46. Ibid., 133.

47. On biopower, see Foucault, *History of Sexuality*, 1:140–45; on "bodies and pleasures," see 1:157–59; on the care of the self, see Foucault, *The History of Sexuality*, vol. 3, *The Care of the Self*, trans. Robert Hurley (New York: Pantheon, 1986); on governmentality, see Foucault, *Security, Territory, Population: Lectures at the Collège de France, 1977–1978*, ed. Michel Senellart, trans. Graham Burchell (New York: Palgrave Macmillan, 2004).

48. Sedgwick, "Melanie Klein and the Difference Affect Makes," in *Weather in Proust*, 135.

49. Ibid., 138–39.

50. Of course, Eve never moved entirely past activism. For a project still on her blotter when she died, see the aptly titled "Anality: News from the Front," in *Weather in Proust*, 166–82.

51. Sedgwick, "Melanie Klein and the Difference Affect Makes," in *Weather in Proust*, 137.

52. Ibid., 134.

CHAPTER 8

Proof and Probability

Law, Imagination, and the Forms of Things Unknown

LORNA HUTSON

LITERATURE'S REALISM V. LAW'S REALITY

In a vivid, satirical critique, Julie Stone Peters characterized the law and literature movement as the comic romance of each discipline's doomed longing for an illusory "reality" felt to be located in the other. Peters explained how, in spite of the law and society movement's challenge to an older legal formalism, the lure of the "humanist realism of law and literature" seemed to offer "an antidote to the sterile technicality of the social sciences."[1] An example of this kind of antidote can be found in James Boyd White's *The Legal Imagination*, which superbly demonstrates the rhetorical range and ethical complexity attainable in a legal practice attuned to literary analysis and imitation. The lawyer, White argues, needs these resources, for, from the moment he [*sic*] encounters a client, he has to draw on "a social and narrative imagination, a capacity to envision different versions of the future." Imagining the client is itself a part of this: "Who is this person and how shall I address him [*sic*]?," asks White. Or, as White goes on,

> suppose you are arguing a case: you must imagine ahead of time what the judge might say to this or that, or what the other lawyer might say in objection to the evidence or refutation of your position, and prepare to meet it.[2]

On the one hand, then, the lawyer needs to have the literary resources to give imaginative shape to other people's experiences, arguments, and thoughts. On the other hand, however, the literary critic, who is an expert in identifying these very resources, is confined to the classroom, to talking about how literature seems "real" in ways that nevertheless appear to lack practical consequentiality. Thus the literary critic, Peters observes, seeks the compensatory "real" of the law. So, for example, the brilliant narrative theorist and psychoanalytic critic Peter Brooks has turned his attention to how the devices that make novelistic narratives seem real or plausible work in the legal retellings of the "facts" of a case in the US law courts. Drawing on Wolfgang Iser's notion of the reader filling in *Leerstellen*, blanks or gaps in the text, as well as on Roland Barthes's notion of the reader bringing readerly and cultural expectations (the *déjà lu*) to the text, Brooks accounts for the different verdicts and sentences arising from the "same" facts by offering a literary analysis. In each telling, he suggests, "the narrative 'glue' is different: the way incidents and events are made to combine in a meaningful story, one that can be called 'consensual sex' on the one hand, or 'rape' on the other. In each case, the blanks ... of the story are filled in according to each of the judges' general understanding of human behavior and intent."[3]

So, in Peters's chiastic formulation, law supplements a social-scientific externality with the literary capacity to *imagine*, to body forth the inwardness of another person, to enter another person's mental world. Meanwhile literary criticism, adept at analyzing the disciplinary effects of such imaginings, turns its attention to the more dubious workings of *vraisemblance* and of stereotyping in police interrogations, the law courts and the media.

The chiasmus itself poses an interesting further question that I want to explore here. To what extent is it assumed that literature's special imaginative "reality" depends on its practical inconsequentiality, the self-sufficiency of the mimetic other world, the "imaginary world" that it is able to create? Not all literature is self-contained in this way, of course—there are many genres one might bracket off, such as occasional verse, *à clef* satires, civic pageants, and shows. But on the whole the great historical achievement of Western literature has been taken to be, in Erich Auerbach's words, "the representation of reality" ("mimesis"), and in Auerbach's compelling account this achievement involved the gradual breaking down of a classical separation of styles into a new universality of the human, dependent on "the Christian idea of the indestructability of the entire human individual."[4] Western European literature, from Dante onward, was thus, as Auerbach argued, able to endow the whole of life, in its concrete particularity and ordinariness, with the dignity of ethical significance.

Without necessarily invoking Auerbach, the law and literature movement has engaged profoundly with the ethical implications of the Auerbachian conception of Western literature as supremely mimetic, as *representative* of human reality rather than participating in direct social and political action. Robert Cover's "Violence and the Word" thus critiques facile analogies between law and literature by reminding us that the legal act of interpretation, unlike its literary equivalent, is morally unintelligible unless it can command real effects.[5] Kenji Yoshino's "The City and the Poet" extends Cover's inquiry further into the dubious ethics of permitting a genre of literary composition—the victim impact statement—to affect the outcome of a trial and have real consequences in sentencing.[6] Both Cover's and Yoshino's interventions rely, in different ways, on defining literature's imaginative self-sufficiency and ethical place in the polity *against* the idea of its direct participation in social and juridical action. Effects of realism, not real-world effects, are proper to literature; the opposite is true of law.

Historically, though, many literary historians have traced a process of development, in the Christian West, from forms of literary activity that involve participation in religious or legal ritual, toward forms of literary activity that are more imaginatively self-contained. So, for example, if we isolate drama as one of the Western literary genres Auerbach treats, we can see that critics have linked the increasing mimetic realism of drama's imaginative illusion with its increasing detachment from participation in the jurisdictional reality of actors and audience. Thus Anne Barton distinguishes the fifteenth-century English mystery play, in which "[i]t had always been possible for people . . . to recognize Christ on the cross as the local cobbler and still believe they are witnessing the actual Crucifixion of the son of God," from the classically influenced drama of the sixteenth century, in which the fictional story that the audience follows is "rigorously self-contained."[7] The imaginative experience of the fifteenth-century mystery play depended on its enactment of the community's experience of Christ's jurisdiction in the form of confession and absolution. Sarah Beckwith has described how Corpus Christi plays enacted the processes of forgiveness enjoined by the sacrament of penance and the mandatory annual confession that preceded the Easter Eucharist. Sacraments, Beckwith reminds us, are "actions not things" and are therefore best understood in terms of theatre's "phenomenality, in its central resource of the body of an actor."[8] Moreover, the sacrament of penance, which involved mandatory annual confession to a priest, was not merely a private ritual of forgiveness but a form of social (and juridical) action. "The person out of charity needs to restore charity by coming either by himself or with his priest to the person he has harmed," Beckwith writes.[9] Like the sacrament of penance, she argues, the York Corpus Christi plays, "radically conceive of the church as the body of Christ enacted among them [the people], incomprehensible except as the very product and horizon of their agreements or disagreements."[10] So where Barton describes the fifteenth-century audience as recognizing a neighbor as the actor playing Christ and yet "believing" they are witnessing the Crucifixion, Beckwith helps us to understand this "belief" in witnessing the Crucifixion as less like an abstract form of knowing than as a form of participatory juridical action, participation in a drama that conceives of the body of Christ as a jurisdiction of forgiveness and restitution.

But if drama increasingly becomes, in sixteenth-century England, self-sufficiently fictional, it seems that its increasing imaginative reality is achieved precisely at the expense of the audience's participation in its symbolic jurisdiction, its sacramental action. Belief is no longer a matter of participation in the theatrical event; the drama begins to acquire a separateness from the audience that requires that the drama itself should ask, as the Chorus does in Shakespeare's *Henry V*, that the audience bring "imaginary forces" to supplement what can't be staged. Each audience member will supply, from "talk of horses," a mental vision (itself evoked by synecdoche and hypallage) of "proud hoofs" printing themselves in the earth.[11] Imagination will also shape transitions of time and space into a unity, carrying the story "here and there" and "jumping o'er times." In this and many other instances, Shakespeare registers the new demands his plays make on the audience's readiness to conceive, to imagine, to turn the discontinuity of *sjuzhet* (the order or artifice of representation) into the *fabula* (the sense we have of a whole unseen, offstage "world" of motive, causality, of temporal and spatial hinterland).[12] Nor need the *fabula* itself be believable; it may be ostentatiously imaginary. Shakespeare's *A Midsummer Night's Dream* makes a joke of its own not-to-be-believed-in-ness when Theseus, both Duke and Judge over Athens, says that he "never may believe / These antique fables, nor these fairy toys" that the lovers' relate in explanation of the resolution of their differences.[13] Critics point out, of course, that Theseus thereby calls his own antique fable, Plutarch's life, and Seneca's plays, into question, relegating himself to the status of the "fantasies" ("phantasies" in Q) bodied forth and penned by the poet.

For Holger Schott Syme, cautioning against recent overstatements of the closeness of the relationship between law and literature in early modern England, the self-contained, acknowledged fictionality of the stage world is one obvious reason why it makes no sense to talk of the audience's judgment with respect to a play as being in any way comparable to legal judgment, to the work of the jury.

> Unlike juries, spectators do not "try" the facts of a play, even if some plots deliberately blur the line between truth and lies. . . . "We" might be convinced that Hamlet's mother was an accessory to his father's murder or "we" may believe her to be innocent, but either judgment is extrinsic to the play itself . . . members of the audience who storm on to the stage to declare, say, that Hermione is innocent, mistakenly cross over from the world of the theater into the world of the play. They do not pass judgment, they interrupt the scene.[14]

Crossing over from the world of the audience (rather than "the theatre") into the world of the play was, of course, essential to the fifteenth-century dramaturgy of the *platea*, which survives into the sixteenth century in morality plays and in the clowning elements of humanist drama.[15] In Sarah Beckwith's account of fifteenth-century mystery plays, this crossing over is essential to the plays' theological work. In the York Corpus Christi plays, she explains, the scene of the Crucifixion draws out the physical action of the job of nailing Christ to the cross in ways that insist on the actor's body's phenomenality and physicality, as well as its semiotic meaning as "the body of Christ." As Anne Barton said, people recognize Christ as their neighbor—a man physically hoisted high on a cross—and experience the meaning of that recognition as "belief" in crucifixion precisely because they cross over into the "world of the play," participating in its phenomenal reality as they recall the significance of their own participation.

With respect to late sixteenth-century drama, Holger Syme, like Robert Cover, insists on distinguishing literary interpretation and judgment from its legal equivalent. Legal interpretation has real effects: it judges, convicts, and sentences. Literary interpretation involves judging fictional characters while observing the boundary between fiction and reality. But if the spectator of a Shakespeare play is not to interrupt the scene, not to cross into the "world of the play" as the fifteenth-century spectator might, this does not mean that the mode of that spectator's judgment, his or her being "convinced" of an imaginary character's motivation, thoughts, reasons for behaving and speaking in a certain way, needs no analysis or has no cultural effect. The sixteenth-century playgoer's conviction of the mimetic self-sufficiency of the playworld needs to be distinguished from "belief" in the participatory sense outlined by Beckwith in her account of the phenomenal reenactment of the Crucifixion in the York Corpus Christi plays. The sixteenth-century audience member contributes, imaginatively, to the play's capacity to body forth "the form of things unknown," but does so by a process of judging and conjecturing motives for the staged action as the complex story unfolds. It is hard, in these contexts, to avoid mentioning Coleridge's formulation of "the suspension of disbelief" as a characterization of willingness to entertain wildly improbable representations by granting them a psychological truth. Coleridge speaks, in *Biographia Literaria*, of his need, in inventing a supernatural poetic world, to "transfer" from his own "inward nature a human interest and a semblance of truth sufficient to procure for these shadows of imagination that willing suspension of disbelief for the moment that constitutes poetic faith."[16] Thus, in Coleridge's terms, it is the poet's transference of human interest and *vraisemblance* from his own "inward nature" that permits readers and audiences to suspend disbelief, to disregard the absurdity of antique fables and fairy toys enough to pay them serious attention.

THE VIVID IMAGINATIVE PARTICULARITY OF THE FORENSIC

Spectators and audiences do not try the facts of a play. Actor-audience lines of communication, familiar from Corpus Christi drama or from moralities like David Lindsay's *Satyre of the Thrie Estaitis* (where the "real world" continually encroaches, as Dissait [Deceit] and Falset [Falsehood] refer by name to Cupar burgesses and craftsmen, or the pauper interrupts from the audience to make a legal complaint), are, in the drama Syme refers to, almost nonexistent.[17] It is this separation that both enables the Renaissance play to constitute "another world," a self-contained imaginative reality, and, at the same time, denies it direct reference to and efficacy in the world the audience inhabits. But if the self-contained play asks no less than that the audience grant it poetic faith—that is, bring it into imaginative being in their own minds, rather than participating in its action—what kind of judgment does this imagining involve? Certainly, as Syme says, it is not a trial of the facts, it is not a verdict and it is not legal. Nevertheless, it has, as I will show, a forensic basis. The sixteenth-century achievement of a drama that could create its own self-sufficient imaginative world, locating characters in imagined space and time, drew crucially on the techniques of forensic rhetoric, especially with respect to the forensic invention of motive, or *causa*.

Anne Barton noted that the first experiments in producing self-contained drama in English were deeply indebted to the classical Latin tradition, to Plautus and Terence and Seneca. This tradition tends to be talked about in terms of the "rules" it imposed—rules of temporal and spatial unity, for example. However, what dramatists writing from the mid-sixteenth century onwards learned from Plautus and Terence and from Seneca, as well as from the forensic rhetoric of Cicero and Quintilian, was not a series of rules or categories, but a way of composing which involved the *invention of arguments as forms of proof*.[18] The composition of arguments became, with the humanist reformation of dialectic, central to literary practice. In the 1970s, Lisa Jardine showed how, at Cambridge, Rudolph Agricola's pioneering reformed dialectic *De inventione dialectica* (1515) challenged the long didactic tradition of Peter of Spain's logic (1246) and introduced a new *ars disserendi* (art of discourse) anchored in the study of literature and promoting the topics as places from which to invent arguments and discover how to speak *probabiliter* (convincingly).[19] Agricola's reformed dialectic entered literary studies with Erasmus's *De Copia* and with Agricola's own Latin translation of Aphthonius, the elementary composition book used in grammar schools. And this reformed dialectic was concerned with using arguments to secure belief, or faith—*fides*. Agricola defined dialectic as that which is "concerned with speaking convincingly (*probabiliter*) and *probabile* will mean whatever can be said as suitably as possible for creating belief" (*quam aptissime ad fidem dicetur*).[20]

What might the inventing of arguments to secure faith or belief have to do with a theatre that can make us believe in a whole fictional world—including its wonders and impossibilities—and imagine the thoughts and feelings of its inhabitants? The answer lies in the connection between the invention of rhetorical and dialectical arguments that make a particular *causa* or motive seem likely as an explanation, and the realization of a coherently imagined scenario or coherently imagined spatiotemporal coordinates of human action. In classical forensic rhetoric, a particular set of argumentative topics or "places of argument" (*argumentorum loci*) were identified to help narrate and inquire into human actions and motives. They were called *peristaseis* or *circumstantiae* or (in dialectic) "accidents," and they were identified in forensic rhetoric as the major source of so-called technical or artificial proof, that is, proof created by the art of the orator. Quintilian lists the circumstances as including "causa tempus locus occasio instrumentum modus et cetera" ("motive, time, place, opportunity, means, method and the like").[21] While these topics informed the questions of confessors in the sacrament of penance from 1215 until the Reformation, their development in humanist literary culture produced something quite new. They were linked not only with dialectic and topics logic but also with the most intense poetic effects of arousing emotion and of bringing scenes before the mind's eye. Quintilian makes inventing from topics of circumstance—time, place, means, instrument—fundamental to the arousing of emotion through *phantasia*, or imagination in pleading a case:

> Suppose I am complaining that someone has been murdered. Am I not to see before my eyes all the circumstances (*omnia quae in re praesenti accidisse*) which one can believe to have happened during the event? Will not the assassin burst in on a sudden, and the victim tremble, cry for help, and either plead for mercy or try to escape? Shall I not see one man striking the blow and the other man falling? Will not the blood, the pallor, the groans, the last gasp of the dying be imprinted on my mind? The result will be *enargeia*, what Cicero calls *illustratio* and *evidentia*, a quality which makes us seem not so much to be talking about something as exhibiting it. Emotions will ensue, just as if we were present at the event itself. (6.2.31–32)

The key sixteenth-century school textbook on literary composition, the *De copia* of Erasmus, was very much indebted to both Quintilian and Rudolph Agricola. Erasmus draws attention to the twin powers of circumstances as both generators of arguments and as contributors to *enargeia/evidentia* or vivid imagining. Erasmus's chapter on *enargeia* footnotes it as "born of dialectical definition, especially that they call 'of accidents.'"[22] And Erasmus himself defines *enargeia* in drama as consisting, "chiefly in an explication of circumstances (*circumstantiarum*), and those in particular that bring the thing (*res*) most vividly before our eyes and give character to the narrative (*ac moratem reddunt narrationem*)."[23]

The contribution of "circumstances" to *phantasia*—to the vivid bringing of a whole scene before the mind's eye—is only part of the story, however. We see from the footnotes to Erasmus's own chapter on circumstances in the *De copia* that another key to their power is the fact that one of the topics—the topic of *causa*, or motive—is *only imaginable through the others*.[24] Arguments from the time, place, opportunity, or manner of a deed's doing are what make conjectures about motive possible. An open manner might argue an honest *causa*, but secrecy or stealth suggests its opposite, a furtive purpose. Against a person found in a solitary place at an obscure time (in a wood, at night) might be argued, in relation to signs of rape or murder, the guiltiness of their *causa*. In this way, as we can begin to see, the coordinates of a dramatic story—time, place, manner—might take the form of arguments about a cause. The space and time of the play, that is, might come into imaginative being in their relation, as arguments of proof, to those hidden, unknowable inferences of the motive, desires, and fears that we attribute to characters.

To see how the invention of circumstantial arguments began to figure in the composition of the self-contained fictional world of the play, it is helpful to look at Philip Sidney's comments on an early experiment in Senecan drama, Thomas Norton's and Thomas Sackville's *Gorboduc*, performed in 1561. Sidney says that *Gorboduc* climbs to the height of Seneca's style, but is "defectious in the circumstances" because it has "many days and places inartificially imagined."[25] Sidney's criticisms are technical; they use a vocabulary derived from dialectic and from forensic rhetoric, a vocabulary indicative of theories of how to invent deliberative arguments and proofs to secure *fides* and to create *enargeia* or *evidentia*—to bring a story or description vividly before the eyes. We can contrast what Sidney says about the other stage plays of the 1570s:

> But if it be so in *Gorboduc*, how much more in all the rest? where you shall have Asia of the one side, and Afric of the other, and so many other under-kingdoms, that the player, when he cometh in, must ever begin with telling where he is, or else the tale will not be conceived. Now ye shall have three ladies walk to gather flowers and then we must believe the stage to be a garden. By and by we hear news of a shipwreck in the same place, and then we are to blame if we accept it not for a rock. Upon the back of that comes out a hideous monster with fire and smoke, and then the miserable beholders are bound to take it for a cave. While in the meantime, two armies fly in, represented with four swords and bucklers, and then what hard heart will not receive it for a pitched field?[26]

Striking, here, is Sidney's reason for laughing at the vernacular romances that held the stage in the 1570s. We can see that Coleridge's "suspension of disbelief" gives, after all, too passive an impression of how the audience's imagination is to be engaged. It is not that people are unable to suspend their disbelief—no-one is so hard-hearted that they can't suspend their disbelief and accept the stage for a rock, a seashore, a garden, and battlefield in quick succession. But belief, to extend to the world of the fiction, needs to do some work, some active construing and inventing of the inner logic of motive and feeling, some projecting of the *fabula*, the world constructed by the characters' desires, fears, and memories of one another.

In this passage, Sidney is referring to plays such as the delightful *Sir Clyomon and Sir Clamydes* (ca.1577), a perambulatory romance in which the players are obliged, as they enter, to "ever begin with telling where" they—and the scene—presently are. The action opens with Sir Clamydes "Bringing my bark to *Denmarke* here," as he tells us. Once he's vowed to the Princess of Denmark that he'll slay a dragon for her, "To *Suauia* soile," he says, "I swiftly will prepare my foot-steps right." The next scene opens with Sir Clyomon

(Juliana's brother), who immediately lets us know that "being here in *Suauia* / And neare vnto the Court," he plans to deprive Sir Clamydes of his knighthood. This fraud naturally occasions a quarrel between the knights, and they vow to fight in fifteen days' time in the presence of King Alexander in Macedonia. But Sir Clamydes, imagining that fifteen days gives him ample leisure to make it to the forest, slay the dragon, and be back with time to spare for the combat, is sent into an enchanted sleep for ten of his precious days. Meanwhile, in the next scene, the seasick Sir Clyomon comes on stage and asks a sailor how far this ship is from Macedonia, only to be told that it has, in fact, just anchored at an island "More then twentie dayes sayling, and if the weather were faire" from Macedonia.[27]

It is evident that the dramatist wants to use the concept of time and place bound by exchanges of faith (the promise to fight in fifteen days in Macedonia) to structure the temporal and spatial experience of the plot, but he has no resources to offer the audience to help them "conceive" this spatio-temporal complexity as part of what the knights conjecture, imagine, or remember. There is no dialogue that, by debating likely outcomes of action or conjecturing interpretation, would enable an audience to imagine future directions of action and the emotional responses these might elicit. This is why the player must "ever begin with telling where he is or else the tale will not be conceived."

Gorboduc, by contrast, is a play in which movements across time and space are made conceivable or imaginable by way of deliberative arguments on the question of what is a most probable or most likely conjecture of another person's *causa* or motive. King Gorboduc has two sons, Ferrex and Porrex. He plans to divide his kingdom while he lives and give elder and younger sons equal shares. In the play's second scene the king takes advice on this plan from his counselors. One of these counselors opposes the plan by imagining the sons' emotional reactions to the division of the kingdom. Ferrex will think he suffers a greater wrong, because the custom of primogeniture would make him expect to inherit, whereas Porrex will be puffed up in importance and become arrogant. These emotional responses, he points out, will almost certainly precipitate violence, for flattering courtiers will soon see their way to encouraging King Ferrex's sense of injury and King Porrex's new self-importance. Finally, the counselor warns Gorboduc to keep his sons by him and not to "plant them out in further parts," where "traitorous corrupters of their pliant youth / Shall have, unspied, a much more free access."[28]

Act 1's scene of deliberation enables the audience to grasp immediately, as the second act begins to unfold, that the player who is busy aggravating Ferrex's sense of grievance and persuading him to prepare against Porrex's likely invasion is a courtier, and precisely the type of "traitorous corrupter of pliant youth" of which the counselor had spoken. We therefore easily "conceive" the change of scene and easily imagine that a certain amount of time has passed. We imagine that this dialogue—in which Ferrex is being persuaded to make secret preparations for war against his brother—must be taking place in the southern part of Britain, in Ferrex's kingdom, and that the time must be some months after Gorboduc's division of the kingdom into northern and southern halves. When the second scene of act 2 opens with Porrex's exclamation, "And is it thus? And doth he so prepare / Against his brother as his mortal foe?" (2.2.1–2), we are already fully on board, as it were, immediately ready to fill in and infer the events that must have passed. Porrex must be addressing a courtier (Tyndar) who has just come from Ferrex's court, with news of the "great preparèd store / Of horse, of armour, and of weapon there" (2.2.6–7).

It's important to stress, though, that our *phantasia* or imagining of the "jumping o'er times" and "carrying . . . here and there" of the action is the result of conjectures about *causa* or motivation, and not the other way around. In other words, inventing arguments of circumstance produces a *psychologizing* of dramatic action and its time and space. Tyndar's vivid account of the warmongering atmosphere of Ferrex's court would easily lead to Porrex's idea that it would be dangerous to go directly to Ferrex and find out exactly what he has in mind. Tyndar uses *enargeia* to persuade Porrex to imagine a pervasive national hostility in Ferrex's kingdom, based on a legitimate sense of grievance:

> Lo, secret quarrels run about his court
> To bring the name of you, my lord, in hate.
> Each man almost can now debate the *cause*
> And ask the reason of so great a wrong,
> Why he, so noble and so wise a prince,
> Is, as unworthy, reft his heritage . . .
> The wiser sort hold down their griefful heads;
> Each man withdraws from talk and company
> Of those that have been known to favour you. (2.2.10–20)

This vividly imagined scenario—which is, incidentally, an image of men *imagining* or debating Gorboduc's *causa* or motive for disinheriting Ferrex—then makes Porrex refuse the counsel that he should "Send to your brother to demand the *cause*" (2.2.30; my italics). Porrex argues that to do this would be unsafe and that to send to his father Gorboduc would be to give Ferrex leisure to invade (2.2.52–54).

What is almost schematically evident, then, is that, in a recursive fashion, the imagined distance of time and space between the brothers is deployed to motivate their receptiveness to highly colored conjectures about one another's predisposition to violence, which, in turn, produce further imagined reasons to act upon these hostile fantasies rather than dispel them by an attempt to reach one another's minds and "causes" directly. It would not be too much to say that *Gorboduc* is the first tragedy in English to produce *imagined and imaginative time and space*; indeed, in *Gorboduc* it is imagined time and space—in Porrex's conviction that to send for his father would turn time into the "leisure" Ferrex requires to execute his intended invasion—that brings about the tragedy of Porrex's fratricide.

LITERATURE'S REAL EFFECTS

In sixteenth- and seventeenth-century English drama, then, the imagined dramatic world acquires its own verisimilitude or inward truth (despite jumping oe'r times, or despite being full of fairy toys) to the extent that its times and spaces and the manner of its actions are conceived, poetically, as proofs of the characters' *causae*—their motivating fears and desires. *Gorboduc* represents an early and very interesting experiment in this circumstantial dramaturgy, but Shakespeare's development of it is far more complex and successful, as I have shown at length elsewhere.[29] Indeed, Shakespeare's success brings us back to the question of literature's special imaginative "reality" being dependent on the self-sufficiency of its mimetic other world. Holger Syme distinguished between the jury that tries facts and the audience that is conscious that its imagination helps body forth the form of things unknown. We assume, I think, that such a consciousness is what makes great literature avoid the charge of merely circulating the *doxa* or conventional beliefs of its own culture.[30] This is why, in Peters's terms, great literature is inwardly "real" to the very extent that it, unlike law, has no "real" effects.

Yet it is also possible to argue that Shakespeare's innovative development of the topics of circumstance—time, place, manner, and motive—so as to encourage us to imagine the play's time and space very largely in the subjective terms of the fears, desires, and motives we attribute to the characters, has also made his plays unusually capable of lending their "reality" to future forms of cultural *doxa*, producing beliefs that Shakespeare could not have anticipated. In *A Midsummer Night's Dream*, for example, the idea of a woman's fear is at the comic center of the play (for the mechanicals, worry about "fright[ening] the ladies" motivates all their dramaturgical ingenuity; 1.2.67–68). This comedy alludes to and veils the play's serious investment in the cultural, prophylactic value of women's fear with respect to the maintaining of chastity. No one, of course, is raped in *A Midsummer Night's Dream*, but the play is premised on *fears* of nocturnal abandonments, infidelities, rapes, and murders that do not actually take place. The invocation of fairy agency (being "taken with the fairies") was, as Mary Ellen Lamb has shown, a recognized way of masking the human shame, the inadmissible human narratives behind traumatized signs of sexual violence, abandoned infants, and illegitimate births.[31] In Shakespeare's play the supernatural agents traditionally called into being as cover stories for various kinds of shame and sexual transgression—that is, fairies and elves—are partly characters and partly complicit with the circumstances of time, place and opportunity (Night, Wood, and Moonlight), as quasi-animate *proofs* of human power and willingness to transgress, and corresponding proofs of human fears of humiliation. "Night" and "the Wood" are, of course, topics of Time and Place, but "by Moonlight" is linked to "Manner," the topic of how something is done. (Moonlight is frequently paired with *stealing* and *stealth*, that is, a furtive, clandestine manner. Thus Egeus accuses Lysander of having "stol'n" Hermia's fantasy "by moonlight"; 1.1.30–32; Lysander suggests he and Hermia "steal" through Athens' gates "when Phoebe doth behold / Her silver visage in the wat'ry glass"; 1.1.209–13.)

Night, Wood, and Moonlight all contribute to proofs of the possibility of violence and infidelity while exonerating the probable agents of that violence and infidelity. Demetrius accuses Helena of impeaching her modesty by committing "the rich worth of her virginity" to someone with a *causa* or motive to violate her ("one that loves you not") and by trusting "the opportunity of night / and the ill-counsel of a desert place" (2.1.214–19). Hermia awakes to find herself deserted by an unfaithful lover, in the midst of a chilling nightmare of that lover's smiling while a snake feeds on her heart (3.1.155). These fears are all "fairy toys" of course, quite unreal. Yet readers and audience have found various kinds of "inward truth" in them. The Victorians produced a childlike, fairytale truth by softening up the pent-up violence and hostility of the lovers in the forest, removing sexual references and "any shade of the suggestive and any shadow of the unpleasant."[32] However, twentieth-century, post-Freudian critics and directors were prompted to locate the play's inward truth in sexual repression and female sexual neurosis. They were responding to Shakespeare's brilliant relegation of the proofs of Demetrius's and Lysander's respective *causae* of sexual violence and sexual infidelity to the space of fearful feminine conjecture (Hermia's dream of the snake, Helena's fears of the men's sexual mockery). These female dreams, imaginings, conjectures were read as signs of repression or nymphomania. Hermia, refusing to allow Lysander "bed-room" (2.2.57) by her side, was "frigid"; Lysander's loathing and abandonment were therapeutic and Hermia's dream of the snake obviously phallic.[33]

A narrative about female sexual repression seems unlikely to be the human interest transferred from Shakespeare's inward nature to produce a willing suspension of disbelief for these fairy antics, especially as, in Shakespeare's day, women were thought to be sexually voracious, not sexually repressed. It is more likely that behind the story of the lovers in the woods lies a conjectural version of the story of Theseus's infamous rapes and abandonments, alluded to in the opening scene, and in Oberon's quarrel with Titania. One of Theseus's rape victims, Perigouna, had misguidedly put her trust (as Helena does) in the forest itself, thereby inviting her own violation, while the famous victim of his infidelity and abandonment, Ariadne, found herself, like Hermia, waking in the wilderness alone, her lover having deserted her.[34] Ariadne, according to Plutarch's *Life of Theseus*, dies in childbirth or hangs herself for shame and sorrow after Theseus's breaking of his faith. Hermia, though likewise deceived by Lysander's "two bosoms interchainèd with an oath" (in Plutarch, Lysander is an oath-breaker), has, by denying him bed-room, kept herself, unlike Ariadne, unpregnant.[35] So the snake in Hermia's dream, watched by a smiling Lysander, signifies not "an adolescent girl's oedipal fears ... about the opposite sex" but rather a vivid image, a *phantasia*, of Lysander's infidelity, the oath he would probably have broken had he slept with her. The form of the dream draws on an Aesopian fable of a farmer who warmed a dying snake into life in his bosom.[36] Shakespeare folds Lysander's probable infidelity into the private space of Hermia's fearful conjectures, her anxious dreams, thus keeping her character chaste and the play a comedy, and making a space for the future emergence of psychoanalytic criticism.

By this means, by animating the topics of proof (threatening Night, solitary Wood, deceiving Moonlight) and skeptically exposing the fairy world's prophylactic origins in the creative human mind, Shakespeare appears to render obsolete or invisible his own culture's profound difficulties with its investment in female sexual honor, its structural distrust of the deceptiveness of women's bodies and the testimony of women's language. But the fact that the play has invited successive generations to imagine, through it, the inward truth of their own culture and humanity gives it real-world effects arguably just as powerful, enduring, and far-reaching as any reality the law can claim.

NOTES

1. Julie Stone Peters, "Law, Literature and the Vanishing Real: On the Future of an Interdisciplinary Illusion," *PMLA* 120 (2005): 444.
2. James Boyd White, *The Legal Imagination: Studies in the Nature of Legal Thought and Expression* (Chicago: University of Chicago Press, 1985), 208–09.
3. Peter Brooks, "Narrativity of the Law," *Law and Literature* 14 (2002): 3–4.
4. Eric Auerbach, *Mimesis: The Representation of Reality in Western Literature*, trans. Willard Trusk (Princeton, NJ: Princeton University Press, 1953), 199.
5. Robert M. Cover, "Violence and the Word," *Yale Law Journal* 95 (1986): 1601–29.
6. Kenji Yoshino, "The City and the Poet," *Yale Law Journal* 114 (2005): 1835–96.
7. Anne Barton [Anne Righter], *Shakespeare and the Idea of the Play* (Westport, CT: Greenwood, 1977), 18, 53.
8. Sarah Beckwith, *Signifying God: Social Relation and Symbolic Act in the York Corpus Christi Plays* (Chicago: Chicago University Press, 2001), 59.
9. Ibid., 92.
10. Ibid., 116.
11. William Shakespeare, *Henry V*, ed. T. W. Craik (London: Bloomsbury Arden, 1995), Prologue, 18, 26–7, 29.
12. On *sjuzhet* and *fabula* in drama, see Keir Elam, *The Semiotics of Theatre and Drama* (London: Routledge, 1994), 120; Lorna Hutson, *Circumstantial Shakespeare* (Oxford: Oxford University Press, 2015), 5–17.
13. William Shakespeare, *A Midsummer Night's Dream*, ed. Peter Holland (Oxford: Oxford University Press, 1994), 5.1.2–3. (Further references in the text.)
14. Holger Schott Syme, "(Mis)representing Justice on the Early Modern Stage," *Studies in Philology* 109, no. 1 (2012): 79–80.
15. For the "platea," the space shared by audience and actor, see Robert Weimann, *Shakespeare and the Popular Tradition in the Theater: Studies in the Social Dimension of Dramatic Form and Function*, trans. Robert Schwartz (Baltimore, MD: Johns Hopkins University Press, 1987).
16. Samuel Taylor Coleridge, *Biographia Literaria*, ed. George Watson (London: Dent, 1965), 168–69.
17. Sir David Lindsay, *Ane Satyre of the Thrie Estaitis*, ed. Roderick Lyall (Edinburgh: Canongate Classics, 1989), 69–73, lines 1933–2043; 143–48, lines 4049–219.
18. On the connections between English Renaissance drama and forensic rhetoric, see Kathy Eden, *Poetic and Legal Fiction in the Aristotelian Tradition* (Princeton, NJ: Princeton University Press, 1986); Lorna Hutson, *The Invention of Suspicion: Law and Mimesis in Shakespeare and Renaissance Drama* (Oxford: Oxford University Press, 2007); Quentin Skinner, *Forensic Shakespeare* (Oxford: Oxford University Press, 2014); Hutson, *Circumstantial Shakespeare*.
19. See Lisa Jardine, "The Place of Dialectic Teaching in Sixteenth-Century Cambridge," *Studies in the Renaissance* 21 (1974): 31–64; Peter Mack, *Renaissance Argument: Valla and Agricola in the Traditions of Rhetoric and Dialectic* (Leiden: Brill, 1993), 168–73.
20. Mack, *Renaissance Argument*, 170.
21. Quintilian, *Institutia oratoria*, trans. Donald A. Russell, 5 vols. (Cambridge, MA: Harvard University Press, 2001), 2:5.10.23. (Further references in text.)

22. Erasmus, *D. Erasmi Roterdami de Duplici Copia Verborum ac Rerum* (London, 1573) fol. 127r.: *nascitur ex definitione Dial. praesertim illa quam accidentariam [sic] descriptionem vocant.*

23. Erasmus, *On Copia of Words and Ideas*, trans. Donald B. King and H. David Rix (Milwaukee, WI: Marquette University Press, 1999), 48–9; Erasmus, *De Duplici Copia*, fol. 122r.

24. See Hutson, *Circumstantial Shakespeare*, 83–84.

25. Philip Sidney, *An Apology for Poetry (or The Defence of Poesy)*, ed. Geoffrey Shepherd, rev. R. W. Maslen (Manchester: Manchester University Press, 2002), 110.

26. Ibid., 110–11.

27. *Sir Clyomon and Sir Clamydes* (1599), ed. W. W. Greg (London: Malone Society Reprints, 1913), lines, 9, 94, 156–57, 731.

28. Thomas Sackville and Thomas Norton, *Gorboduc, or Ferrex and Porrex* in *Drama of the English Renaissance*, vol. 1, ed. Russell A. Fraser and Norman Rabkin (Upper Saddle River, NJ: Prentice Hall, 1976), 1.2.313, 316–17.

29. Hutson, *Circumstantial Shakespeare*.

30. For a discussion of the charge that mimetic (realistic) fiction merely circulates the stereotypes of the culture, see Christopher Prendergast, *The Order of Mimesis: Balzac, Stendhal, Nerval, Flaubert* (Cambridge: Cambridge University Press, 1986), 45–48.

31. Mary Ellen Lamb, "Taken by the Fairies: Fairy Practices and the Production of Popular Culture in *A Midsummer Night's Dream*," *Shakespeare Quarterly* 51, no. 3 (2000): 277–312.

32. Gary Jay Williams, "Madame Vestris' *A Midsummer Night's Dream* and the web of Victorian Tradition," *Theatre Survey* 18, no. 2 (1977): 6.

33. See, for example, Peter Brooks on Hermia, in David Selbourne, *The Making of "A Midsummer Night's Dream"* (London: Faber and Faber, 2010), 87; Norman Holland, "Hermia's Dream," in *New Casebooks: A Midsummer Night's Dream* ed. Richard Dutton (London: Macmillan, 1996), 65.

34. See *Plutarch's Lives of the Noble Grecians and Romans, Englished by Sir Thomas North* [1579] (London: David Nutt, 1895), 1:116.

35. Lysander, according to Plutarch, was "indifferent to the obligations of an oath." See Plutarch's "Life of Lysander," in *Plutarch's Lives*, ed. Arthur Hugh Clough, trans. John Dryden (New York: Random House, 2001), 1:588–89.

36. T. W. Baldwin, *William Shakspere's Small Latine & Lesse Greeke* (Urbana: University of Illinois Press, 1944), 1:615; see Holland, "Hermia's Dream," 65.

CHAPTER 9

Law, Literature, and History

The Love Triangle

BERNADETTE MEYLER

At the end of her characteristically astute provocation of law and literature scholars in "Law, Literature, and the Vanishing Real," Julie Peters suggested moving beyond the law/literature dichotomy into both "law, culture, and the humanities" and global "disciplinary tourism."[1] By silently glossing over "literature" in favor of the broader terms "culture" or the "humanities," new formulations of the area of study might, she indicated, help to dispel the "interdisciplinary illusion" fueling the opposition between and relation of law and literature, dispensing with the notion shared by scholars of both law and literature that the "real" is located just over the methodological divide between the fields.[2] Peters's essay valuably rejected the binary that appears in far too many versions of law and literature scholarship. Its aspiration to put aside disciplinary boundaries among sectors of the humanities in studying "law, culture, and the humanities" or "law and the humanities" *tout court* has not, however, proved entirely feasible, nor is it necessarily desirable.

As those familiar with "law and society" know, the turn toward a broader category—like culture, or the humanities, or society—may not remain unvexed, as questions arise respecting the unity of the umbrella term and its framing in opposition to law. Moreover, from within the parameters of law, and particularly those of legal pedagogy, "law and the humanities" designates not precisely a decomposition of the boundaries between law and its outside, but a gesture toward one form of law's outside, the humanistic, as opposed generally to the social sciences. Despite the proliferation of the "law and" fields, many—including law and the humanities—still appear from the vantage point of legal pedagogy as a superficial carapace that can be shed when financial exigencies press law schools to cut costs and reduce tuition.

This chapter aims to demonstrate the centrality of the humanities to the core of law school pedagogy today. At the same time, by focusing on two areas within the humanities—literature and history—it tries to show how disciplines still matter, both as engines and impediments. Examining the shifting passions that bind law, literature, and history to each other, it foregrounds the dynamic quality of disciplinary relations as the attraction of fields for each other waxes and wanes. This dynamism itself advances the possibilities for new births of knowledge. Although unstable and of unknown fate, the love triangle of law, literature, and history continues to spawn fertile offspring.

The notion of the love triangle has captured the imagination of many writers, including Simone de Beauvoir, whose own experiences furnished material for her first novel, *She Came to Stay* (*L'Invitee*).[3] The heroine of the 1943 work, Françoise, resembles Beauvoir in a number of respects, including in her relationship with Pierre Labrousse, a thinly veiled version of Jean-Paul Sartre. Intimately involved with each other since their early twenties, Sartre and Beauvoir had agreed to renounce jealousy and act freely on their desires for others. One of the objects of these desires was Olga Kosakiewicz, a young woman of Russian parentage whom they supported so that she could live alongside them in Rouen and then Paris. Unsuccessful in seducing Olga, Sartre moved on to her younger sister, Wanda, with whom he proceeded to have an affair of several years. The character of Xavière in *She Came to Stay* (a work dedicated to Olga) collects attributes of both sisters. Despite the mutual involvement of the various protagonists, Sartre and Beauvoir—as well as their characters—found that "the most satisfying form of communication was tête-à-tête. If Sartre was eating with Wanda at the Coupole, or if Beauvoir was seeing Olga at the Dôme, there was no question of the other's spontaneously joining them."[4]

Beauvoir's reduction of Olga and Wanda to one character in the novel suggests the extent to which the idea of the love triangle—as opposed to a larger and messier mélange—proves imaginatively productive. Although isolating law, literature, and history may similarly elide characters affiliated with them, the stylization brings to the fore more clearly both the generative and the competitive aspects of the relations among the three. On a broader level, the figure of the love triangle insists that interdisciplinarity need not be conceived as either an exclusive connection between two or as an entirely open multiplicity; instead, intermediate arrangements may spur new developments.

BREAKING DOWN THE AFFAIRS

For a while Françoise gazed with a lover's eyes at this woman whom Pierre loved.

"On the contrary, everything could be so easy," she said. "A closely united couple is something beautiful enough, but how much more wonderful are three persons who love each other with all their being." She waited a while. Now the moment had come for her, too, to commit herself and to take her risks. "Because, after all, it is certainly a kind of love that exists between you and me."[5]

For any love triangle, a story can be told about how each pair within it came to know each other, whether through hushed whispers overheard from afar, a dramatic confrontation, or a chance encounter and exchange of glances. Often one of the three is a latecomer to the relationship between two, intervening to destabilize an established dynamic; how enduring the effects of the intervention will be can remain uncertain for quite some time. Law, literature, and history are no exception. As J. G. A. Pocock famously demonstrated in *The Ancient Constitution and the Feudal Law*, the origins of modern historiography are themselves almost coextensive with the beginnings of modern Anglo-American law in seventeenth-century England.[6] Despite this venerable heritage, legal history was not taught regularly in separate law school courses until after the First World War, when it became part of the curricula of some elite schools; in the 1960s, law schools finally embraced legal history more broadly.[7]

Law and literature as an area of study boasts an even more recent history, often dated back to the 1970s with James Boyd White's *The Legal Imagination*, which countered the emerging field of law and economics with a focus on the humanistic backdrop of law.[8] There were, of course, isolated earlier works, but none of these interventions attempted to engage literary studies as a disciplinary matter, unlike the scholarship that has proliferated since the 1970s. During this more recent period, the field of literary studies has attempted to seduce law away from history, or, perhaps more accurately, to seduce law and history together. In the process, it has frequently suffered rebuffs at the hands of one or the other. It remains to be seen whether the love triangle will become a true ménage à trois.

The early story of what has come to be known as the law and literature enterprise has been told, and told well. Many accounts of law and literature stop around its twenty-fifth birthday, either positing the death of the enterprise, insisting upon its survival, or presenting new possible paths. Within the past several decades, two developments have occurred, both of which opened new avenues for law and literature. Following the 1998 translation of Giorgio Agamben's *Homo Sacer* into English and the rise of interest in sovereignty and biopolitics within literature departments, political theory attracted adherents and generated concern with the connection between law and politics.[9] Even Agamben's own *State of Exception*, the sequel to *Homo Sacer*, addresses the provisions—or lack thereof—for states of emergency within various constitutional regimes.[10] Interest in sovereignty has prompted examination of legal and political theory by those working on contemporary globalization as well as on early modern monarchies.

Even before this turn to political theory, the arrival of New Historicism in literary studies brought with it a host of materials that might previously have been considered less relevant to scholarly endeavors. Early versions of New Historicism often focused on a particular period and tied analyses of literary with nonliterary works from the same era; the texts considered alongside classics of the literary canon included accounts of early modern colonial encounters and reports by Victorian reformers.

Despite emerging in opposition to formalism, the New Historicists' approach was text-based—too text-based for some, who argued that the method "amounts to a large claim about society or social relations based on some very close readings of tropes and figures in a number of parallel texts, say a novel, a medical treatise, a classic of political economy, and maybe some popular journalism" or that it simply exported techniques of reading from literary to other objects, which "can mean that the social text turns out to be read as [scholars] have been trained to read a literary text, that is, in traditional formalist terms."[11] Many of the most prominent works of the movement therefore put aside the question of whether a text had emerged out of some systematic framework—such as the legal—that shaped its mode of expression and even its meaning.

In the effort to distinguish itself from an older historicism and to avoid teleology, New Historicism also embraced the anecdotal. Instead of focusing on the question of how a phrase moved from one sphere to another, New Historicists concentrated on the narrative that a present observer might construct based on its occurrence in various domains. As Peter Hohendahl glossed it, "the agenda of the New Historians [is] a hermeneutic project, in which the critic is seen as locally situated, without absolute access to the truth, but at the same time motivated by his or her social and political concerns."[12]

Recent work in law and literature influenced by New Historicism has diverged from its forebears in several ways. It is characterized by a return to considerations of form—not only form as traditionally conceived within literary study, but legal form as well. These legal forms comprehend both the kind of legal work most accessible to literary scholars—the judicial opinion—and modes of procedure that call upon the more arcane knowledge of the legal scholar. The very title of Bradin Cormack's *A Power to Do Justice: Jurisdiction, English Literature, and the Rise of Common Law* indicates its interest in connecting the particularity of the legal mode of asserting authority—jurisdiction—with the literary.[13] While Max Brzezinski and others have critiqued the new literary formalism for focusing on form *instead of* content,[14] scholars operating within the encounter among law, literature, and history have tended to demonstrate the constitutive nature of the formal aspects of both law and literature, showing how literary and legal authority find themselves established through metaphor, precedent, and jurisdiction. This turn has, in effect, reconciled the dichotomy Robert Weisberg identified in speaking of the division of law and literature into "law as literature" and "law in literature."[15] If one takes seriously the formal aspects of the materials involved, the same project can both read law as literature and see law in literary form.

Scholarship in this mode also tends to focus on a particular theme that crosses over the legal-literary divide and to explore the development of the topic in question through the mutual operations of literature and law. In doing so, it raises questions about the mechanisms by which concepts circulate among sectors of society within a particular period. Luke Wilson's *Theaters of Intention: Drama and the Law in Early Modern England* and Oliver Arnold's *The Third Citizen: Shakespeare's Theater and the Early Modern House of Commons* both resonate with this approach. Finally, the tone of these works often bears a greater resemblance to that of historians' writings, generally framed without immediate reference to the situation of the critic herself.

While this type of law and literature scholarship—increasingly connected with close historical analysis or delving into law's relation with political theory—has made a significant mark in the academy, most of its practitioners have resided institutionally outside law schools. Hence, many law and literature courses taught to law students fall within older paradigms, like that embraced by Richard Posner's popular textbook *Law and Literature*, now in its third edition.[16]

Turning to the pairing of literature and history, what may be most striking is the paucity of actual dialogue between scholars of literature and history, despite literary studies' fascination with history and history scholars' interest in literary texts. Pedagogical endeavors to combine the study of history with literature, such as Harvard's History and Literature Concentration, have had great success, at least if measured by the number of students they have attracted. And yet history as conceived in literature departments, including the New Historicism and its descendants, and history as practiced by historians remain imperfectly linked. Based on a careful analysis of recent scholarship in Atlantic studies and a survey of cross-disciplinary book reviews between literary scholars and historians, Eric Slauter has concluded: "[L]iterary scholars now import more from historians than they export to them."[17] Treating potential explanations and remedies, Slauter contends that literary scholars still often rely on already familiar historical materials rather than "supply[ing] a real contribution to historical knowledge" or "advanc[ing] a powerful theoretical claim to be further developed and historicized."[18] For their part, historians could do more to recognize the theoretical insights furnished by the work of literary scholars. A less superable problem is perhaps presented by the move of history as a discipline away from text-based scholarship toward demographic and economic models.

At the same time, however, a newfound interest in text within legal history has the potential for reinvigorating the relation between literature and history, particularly as the history of the book has captured the imagination of literary scholars. Steven Wilf has explicitly thematized legal historians' relation to text, lamenting that "text is of essential importance to legal historians and at the same time underexamined," while suggesting a way forward in envisioning the "legal historian as an *interested reader* of text."[19]

Finally, law and history is the old, established pair, whose passions have ebbed and flowed with new interests and renewed affairs. The Anglo-American story of their relation could be narrated as a political history, connected with the establishment of the autonomy of law from politics or sovereignty within seventeenth-century England. The conventional tale, however, begins in the late nineteenth century, with F. W. Maitland.[20] As Michael Lobban has elaborated on the genealogies of legal history following Maitland, "legal historians working in law faculties tended to focus more on doctrinal histories. This was true on both sides of the Atlantic."[21] The work of the "law and society" movement and the writings of J. Willard Hurst shifted the scene within the US academy in the mid-twentieth century. As Lobban summarizes:

> Law, in the Hurstian view, was about the practice of government, at every level where law structured or regulated the exercise of power between people. In his view, the proper way to study legal history was not to look at the development

of single doctrines over the long term, but to look in great detail at the working of law in one particular context and era.[22]

With Bob Gordon's 1984 essay *Critical Legal Histories*, critical legal history broke onto the scene and disrupted the Hurstian vision, insisting upon the contingency of legal developments and the mutually constitutive relation of law and society.[23] In the wake of Gordon's foundational statement of antifoundationalism, legal historical narratives of the kind he advocated have proliferated, perhaps most prominently in the work of John Witt, including his book *The Accidental Republic*.[24]

A love triangle may also entail tensions and oppositions between the pairs that comprise it or contests over the affections of a central figure. Between law and literature and legal history at least two such struggles have occurred, one over authority and the other over normativity. Despite historians' ambivalent relation to law's normativity, both the legal academy and legal practitioners deem the expertise of historians central to the proper formulation and understanding of law. The status of the knowledge derived from literary disciplines remains much less exalted within legal institutions. At the same time, law and literature scholarship insists upon its normative positions and, in some respects, chastises legal history for maintaining a descriptive rigor that can be separated from normative claims.

Imagine, for example, the following scenario. A case reaches the US Supreme Court urging the reconsideration of the *D.C. v. Heller* decision holding that the Second Amendment protects an individual right to bear arms.[25] As in *Heller* itself, amicus curiae briefs arguing about the relevant history would proliferate. A literary critic's perspective on the meaning of the amendment would be given short shrift by the justices, however.[26] Even when Chief Justice Rehnquist invoked the dissemination of the Miranda warning into popular consciousness through its ubiquity in culture, he relied on personal experience rather than on disciplinary expertise.[27]

On first blush, one might imagine that the difference lies in the fact that the members of the Court already possess both interpretive acumen and cultural knowledge, whereas they require the specialized training of historians to uncover the relevant history behind constitutional provisions. As any reader of judicial opinions already knows though, the kind of history recited by judges often appears more like what has been disparaged as "forensic history" than the type of inquiry respected by historians.[28] Indeed, invocations of history within judicial decision making may appear to historians no less illegitimate than judicial interpretive practice seems to literary critics or the Court's account of popular consciousness looks to experts in cultural studies. The authority historians currently hold—at least nominally—in the judicial process hence stems not from the actuality of a specialized knowledge that lawyers do not already possess but from law's recognition of historians' knowledge as lending authority. Law has determined within the past decade or two that historians' mechanisms for ascertaining truth should be included as a part of the process of understanding the US Constitution. To realize that this conjunction is not inevitable one has only to look to the example of seventeenth-century English jurist Sir Edward Coke, who explicitly defined his own historical account of the common law against the work of chroniclers and annalists, historians he found lacking in the rigor of an internal perspective on the law.[29] The relation of legal institutions with the discipline of history hence possesses a particular salience today, one that literary studies lacks and envies. The next question, which is too involved to answer here, might be why history currently has such purchase for law and represents the kind of expertise to which the Supreme Court must at least pay lip service.

At the same time, the teaching of and scholarship on law and literature often adopt unapologetically normative positions, unlike most rigorous legal history. Robert Cover's classic writings on law and literature insisted upon the normative purchase of the endeavor. Nor has that tendency been entirely eclipsed within the law and literature enterprise. For example, Robin West concludes her recent essay on "Literature, Culture, and Law" by observing that "[p]opular narrative fiction, television shows, and films, no less than canonical literature, may, on occasion, have something true to teach us about law, life and sex."[30] What they have to teach consists partly in critique; as West had earlier explained, Tom Wolfe's novel *Charlotte Simmons* "should be read as a critique of potent and harmful—but nevertheless *legal*—sex, and the culture that legitimates, honors and encourages it."[31]

By contrast, for at least the past half-century, legal history has been characterized by an avoidance of normativity.[32] This should be no discovery for those who have been involved in legal history workshops, where disputes often rage over whether a project is excessively "presentist" in focus, spawned by a normative desire to use the past, or whether it can be considered more rigorously historical, its dominant question instead emanating from the archive. Wilf and others contend that alternative possibilities can be found within the history of legal history itself, particularly in the legal realists' aspiration for the normative potential of scholarship in legal history.[33] New approaches to legal history may be in the process of rethinking legal history's neglect of normativity; an opportunity for literature may, concomitantly, be on the way.

In Rouen, Sartre started to spend time with Olga Kosakiewicz. They enjoyed being together, and everyone benefited. Sartre felt reinvigorated in Olga's presence, Beauvoir was relieved to see Sartre more cheerful, and Olga liked to feel needed.

Before she even set eyes on Sartre, Olga had encountered the legend. Beauvoir had talked about him and the couple they formed. Sartre knew that. As he wrote later, his relationship with Beauvoir appeared "fascinating" and "crushingly powerful" to the people around them. "Nobody could love one of us without being gripped by a fierce jealousy—which would end by changing into an irresistible attraction—for the other one, even before meeting them, on the basis of mere accounts."[34]

Passions arise easily in the pedagogical context; hence it is there that the possibilities for the romance among disciplines may be most completely realized. Julie Peters is doubtless right to lament that the "real" always appears elsewhere within exchanges between law and literature. Nevertheless, in the classroom, it may be the desire for something outside of the discipline—whether "real" or imaginary—that most effectively propels interdisciplinary inquiry. The task of teaching law and the humanities consists, I contend, in inciting each audience—whether undergraduates in the humanities, law students, or graduate students—to experience a lack within their discipline, a lack that propels the passionate investigation of another field. Rather than, however, presenting each mode of inquiry as itself deficient, I would embrace a pedagogy that temporarily situates students entirely within the technical aspects of the local discipline. Only through fully entering into the consciousness of a particular field can one experience a desire for another discipline that follows not a path of assimilation or escape but rather one of embrace.

This point could be put in conceptual, rather than romantic, language. Niklas Luhmann persuasively did so in describing the relation between legal and social systems. In *Law as a Social System*, Luhmann posits law's "operative closure" with respect to its environment.[35] As Luhmann contends, "the legal system operates in a normatively closed and, at the same time, cognitively open way."[36] What this means is that stimuli from the environment can affect the legal system only indirectly, through the recursive operations of that system itself, which proceeds to include or reject components of the outside world. This approach reformulates the distinction between law and morality. Although morality is excluded under Luhmann's account from appearing without mediation in law, it can be integrated through the legal systems' own operations.[37] Even after becoming law, this and other material from law's environment retain traces of their location within another system and direct the legal actor toward an investigation of the relationship among these systems.

One consequence of invoking passion—or systems theory—might be a movement away from assertions of similarity or difference. Even the most sophisticated scholarship in law and literature tends to divide according to whether it places emphasis on the resemblance between legal and literary materials or insists upon their disparities. While legal and literary forms may, in fact, diverge, the significance of this phenomenon lies not in the divergence but rather in the institutional forces producing it. What counts as authority is determined within the particular system at issue, whether legal or social (or cultural), and stylistic discrepancies index those processes. At the same time, identical protagonists pass through these varied systems and may import techniques and tools from elsewhere.

All of this remains quite abstract though; how might a teacher actually serve as procuress of these passionate engagements? In order to suggest one possible answer, I will briefly describe a pedagogical experiment I began to undertake several years ago. Having taught introductory Constitutional Law for a number of years, often to students in the first semester of their first year of law school, I grew frustrated with some aspects of the various casebooks that I sampled in the effort to enhance students' experience. Many of the texts abbreviate cases so radically that it is impossible to recover alternate readings or to see disparate paths that the law might have taken. Other casebooks valuably furnish historical materials in conjunction with Supreme Court opinions, giving context for the development of law. Yet engaging in lengthy historical inquiry into the evolution of doctrine under the Commerce Clause frequently exasperates first-year students, who wonder about the relevance of this material to legal practice. It is simultaneously difficult to avoid the sense that the histories told in this setting are mere forensic history (as John Reid would call it), tending to naturalize the jurisprudential place where we have landed. Finally, despite the meteoric rise in theories emphasizing extrajudicial interpretation and implementation of the Constitution, these find little purchase within constitutional law casebooks, which still remain largely indebted to Supreme Court opinions.

Having previously attempted to supplement these texts with my own materials, from history articles, to statutory text, to essays on constitutional interpretation, I decided upon a counterintuitive solution. Instead of adding more and more context, I resolved to see what would happen if I presented the lawyers' lawyer version of the materials, fulfilling the presentist desires of the students more than they could ever have wished. To this end, I developed new materials around several Supreme Court cases that had either been decided in the past term or remained pending. We began with *National Federation of Independent Business (NFIB) v. Sebelius*, otherwise known as the healthcare decision.[38] Doctrinally, this allowed us to cover a number of the major congressional powers, including the Commerce, Necessary and Proper, and Taxation and Spending Clauses. Rhetorically, it presented a fascinating study in contingency, framing, compromise, precedent, concurrence, and dissent.

Prior to commencing the case, I asked the students to peruse the Constitution and to read the relevant sections of the Patient Protection and Affordable Care Act of 2010 ("Affordable Care Act"),[39] in order to situate them in the same textual position (absent Supreme Court precedent) as the justices would have been. We then sliced through the case, treating the opinions section by section, and covering them in their entirety.

Not only was the *NFIB v. Sebelius* decision preceded by substantial public controversy, but it also entailed a split between members of what was frequently considered the conservative wing of the Supreme Court. The heart of the disagreement involved the question of whether Congress possessed the authority to pass the so-called individual mandate provision of the Affordable Care Act, the section requiring everyone to purchase insurance or face a penalty.[40] Between the first challenges to the individual mandate as exceeding Congress's power and the time the Court issued its opinion in *NFIB*, avid Court watchers first derided the notion that the individual mandate would be struck down, deeming such an outcome impossible under current precedent, then became increasingly convinced that the Court would actually invalidate the provision. While the majority did not do so, the margin and grounds for reaching a different result were quite tenuous. Chief Justice Roberts disagreed with both Justice Ginsburg— who would have upheld the mandate under all justifications the government offered—and the four Joint Dissenters (Scalia, Roberts, Alito, and Kennedy)—who would have struck down the mandate under all available justifications.[41] Instead, he split the difference, agreeing with the dissenters that the Commerce Clause could not allow Congress to force individuals into activity and into participation in the healthcare market, but deeming the individual mandate justified under the Taxation Clause, despite Congress's efforts to represent the mandate as anything but a tax.[42]

The circumstances surrounding the healthcare decision, although contemporary rather than historical, dramatize the contingency of constitutional decision making and the role of social movements (such as the Tea Party) in the generation of constitutional shifts, aspects that legal historians have been emphasizing since Bob Gordon's "Critical Legal

Histories" and Reva Siegel's work on social movements, respectively.[43] When teaching the "switch in time that saved the nine"—the Court's supposed capitulation to FDR's New Deal and its concomitant decision to interpret Congress's economic powers expansively—it is difficult to convey to students anything but the feeling of the ineluctable march of historical change, economic expansion dictating the eventual demise of policies rooted in eighteenth-century realities. By contrast, the healthcare decision remains recent enough in public consciousness that several of the students in my class expressed great puzzlement about it on the first day, before realizing that we would be covering the case. The confusion these students voiced pertained not only to the media's framing of the case and predictions of what the outcome would be but also to the significance of the decision, once rendered. Rationalizations have proliferated since *NFIB* appeared, rendering the outcome more obvious in retrospect. Considering the healthcare decision so soon after its resolution allowed us to inhabit its contingency more completely.

Justifying the decision in light of this contingency required resort to a mechanism for constructing authority internal to the legal system, that of furnishing precedent. From each opinion, we generated a list of the five precedents that seemed most crucial to the historical narrative recounted for every constitutional clause. Unsurprisingly, these differed significantly between the Ginsburg opinion and the Joint Dissent, but there were also subtle disparities between the Joint Dissenters and Roberts as well. Taking our cue from the various opinions, we examined the several possible genealogies of the present. In the process, the question continually arose as to the relationship between the aims of a history of doctrine produced within the legal system and other versions of history.

By puzzling through the Roberts and Joint Dissenters' citations in the Spending Clause area, we also watched the seamless conversion of precedent from one area to another and the generation of constitutional meaning through judicial interpretation. In the process of finding that the Medicaid provisions of the Affordable Care Act engaged in unconstitutional "coercion" of the states in violation of the Spending Clause, the first time that such coercion had been discovered, Chief Justice Roberts cited extensively and without much fanfare to cases derived from the Commerce Clause area, particularly the "commandeering" decisions, *Printz* and *New York v. United States*.[44] In the confusion over differentiating "coercion" from "commandeering" and the attempt to discern what the extension of the metaphor from commerce to spending might signify, we watched the process of constitutional meaning making at work and observed the effects of constitutional rhetoric in action.

Finally, examining the language of the Affordable Care Act itself before turning to the case assisted in seeing the mechanisms behind the law's co-optation of facts. Whereas Roberts and the Joint Dissenters framed the individual mandate in terms of a distinction between activity and inactivity, insisting that requiring individuals to purchase health insurance or face a penalty resembled compelling broccoli consumption,[45] Ginsburg saw the individual mandate as a necessary part of a comprehensive legislative scheme, just as the Court had found the medicinal use of marijuana to be legitimately prohibited as part of the federal government's broader regulation of drugs.[46] Neither of these accounts was dictated by the prejuridical situation, but both served to narrate the facts to legal effect.

By foregrounding contemporary cases, I asked these first-year law students to move from the social system they had been inhabiting to the legal system and to observe the process by which that movement was taking place. Through carefully inspecting the mechanisms by which they could make themselves legal actors, they became aware of law as a discipline while simultaneously witnessing the distinctions law draws to render itself independent of its environment. It may be this very cognizance of disciplinarity that enables the passion for other disciplines to arise. Rather than being sated by the anodyne version of history that appears in casebooks, students were prompted to think about the competing forces of historical momentum and change that coalesced in the healthcare decision as well as about the extralegal implications of granting economic rights as the Affordable Care Act arguably did. By reading the passages of the opinion that cited to counterintuitive precedents and inquiring about the generation and co-optation of language like that of commandeering and coercion, they were incited to imagine a literary approach to legal opinions.

ACTING TOGETHER

Alone. She had acted alone. As alone as in death. One day Pierre would know. But even he would only know her act from the outside. No one could condemn or absolve her. Her act was her very own. *I have done it of my own free will.* It was her own will which was being fulfilled, now nothing separated her from herself. She had chosen at last. She had chosen herself.[47]

In the last chapter of *She Came to Stay*, Françoise does act—with disastrous consequences for Xavière and for the love triangle. Pierre and Xavière's liaison has been broken off, but Xavière has learned that Françoise betrayed her by carrying on a secret affair with Xavière's other lover, Gerbert.

Deeming her own guilt inexpiable as long as Xavière continues to exist and her consciousness persists in judging, Françoise opens the gas in Xavière's room as the latter is about to fall asleep and leaves Xavière to perish.

This chapter has suggested how the disciplines comprising one version of law and the humanities—law, literature, and history—might coalesce into a true ménage à trois rather than sacrificing one in service of another's autonomy while leaving the third out of the battle. In particular, immersion within a particular discipline may not exclude other areas but instead prompt more desire for those fields. Law, literature, and history find themselves at an opportune moment for joining together to act rather than remaining content with analyzing. I hope that they can act, in whatever form, together, not alone.

NOTES

1. Julie Peters, "Law, Literature, and the Vanishing Real: On the Future of an Interdisciplinary Illusion," *PMLA* 120 (2005): 442–53. Sections of this chapter are reprinted with permission from the *UC Irvine Law Review*, where a longer version appeared; Bernadette Meyler, "Law, Literature, and History: The Love Triangle," *UC Irvine Law Review* 5 (2015): 365–91.
2. Ibid., 452–53.
3. Simone de Beauvoir, *She Came to Stay*, trans. Yvonne Moyse and Roger Senhouse (Cleveland, OH: World, 1954), 210–11.
4. Hazel Rowley, *Tête-à-Tête: Simone de Beauvoir and Jean-Paul Sartre* (New York: HarperCollins, 2005), 73.
5. Beauvoir, *She Came to Stay*, 210–11.
6. J. G. A. Pocock, *The Ancient Constitution and the Feudal Law: A Study of English Historical Thought in the Seventeenth Century* (Cambridge: Cambridge University Press, 1987), 31.
7. See Joan Sidney Howland, "A History of Legal History Courses Offered in American Law Schools," *American Journal of Legal History* 53 (2013): 363, 375.
8. James B. White, *The Legal Imagination: Studies in the Nature of Legal Thought and Expression* (Boston: Little, Brown, 1973), xix.
9. Giorgio Agamben, *Homo Sacer: Sovereign Power and Bare Life*, trans. Daniel Heller-Roazen (Stanford, CA: Stanford University Press, 1998).
10. Giorgio Agamben, *State of Exception*, trans. Kevin Attell (Chicago: University of Chicago Press, 2005).
11. Regenia Gagnier, "Methodology and New Historicism," *Journal of Victorian Culture* 4 (1999): 116, 119; Carolyn Porter, "History and Literature: 'After the New Historicism,'" *New Literary History* 21 (1990): 253, 257.
12. Peter Uwe Hohendahl, "A Return to History? The New Historicism and Its Agenda," *New German Critique* 55 (1992): 87, 89–90.
13. Bradin Cormack, *A Power to Do Justice: Jurisdiction, English Literature, and the Rise of the Common Law, 1509–1625* (Chicago: University of Chicago Press, 2007).

14. Max Brzezinski, "The New Modernist Studies: What's Left of Political Formalism?," *Minnesota Review* 76 (2011): 109, 117.

15. See Robert Weisberg, "Law, Literature, and Cultural Unity: Between Celebration and Lament," in *Teaching Law and Literature*, ed. Austin Sarat, Cathrine O. Frank, and Matthew Anderson (New York: Modern Language Association, 2011), 86, 88.

16. See Richard A. Posner, *Law and Literature*, 3d ed. (Cambridge: Harvard University Press, 2009).

17. See Eric Slauter, "History, Literature, and the Atlantic World," *William and Mary Quarterly* 65 (2008): 135.

18. Ibid., 159.

19. Steven Wilf, "Law/Text/Past," *UC Irvine Law Review* 1 (2011): 543, 545–46.

20. Frederick Pollock and Frederic William Maitland, *The History of English Law before the Time of Edward I*, 2nd ed., vol. 2 (London: Cambridge University Press, 1911).

21. Michael Lobban, "The Varieties of Legal History," *Clio@Thémis* 5 (2012): 1, 9.

22. Ibid., 15.

23. See Robert W. Gordon, "Critical Legal Histories," *Stanford Law Review* 36 (1984): 57.

24. John Fabian Witt, *The Accidental Republic: Crippled Workingmen, Destitute Widows, and the Remaking of American Law* (Cambridge, MA: Harvard University Press, 2004).

25. District of Columbia v. Heller, 554 U.S. 570 (2008).

26. Peter Brooks has shown that this occurred in Heller itself with respect to the amicus curiae brief filed by Professors of Linguistics and English; "Literature as Law's Other," *Yale Journal of Law and the Humanities* 22 (2010): 349, 363–64.

27. See Dickerson v. United States, 530 U.S. 428, 430 (2000). For a discussion of the treatment of the cultural authority of Miranda in the *Dickerson* opinion, see Kenji Yoshino, "Miranda's Fall?," *Michigan Law Review* 98 (2000): 1399, 1412–14.

28. See John Phillip Reid, *The Ancient Constitution and the Origins of Anglo-American Liberty* (DeKalb: Northern Illinois University Press, 2005), 5–7; Reid, "Law and History," *Loyola of Los Angeles Law Review* 27 (1993): 193, 203–04.

29. For a discussion of Coke's treatment of historians unaffiliated with law, see Bernadette Meyler, "Towards a Common Law Originalism," *Stanford Law Review* 59 (2006): 551, 585–86.

30. Robin West, "Literature, Culture, and Law at Duke University," Georgetown Law Faculty, Working Paper, no. 75, 2008, http://scholarship.law.georgetown.edu/fwps_papers/75.

31. Ibid., 112.

32. Wilf, "Law/Text/Past," 562.

33. Ibid., 556–64.

34. Rowley, *Tête-à-Tête*, 57, quoting Jean-Paul Sartre, *War Diaries* (Quintin Hoare trans., Verso ed. 1984).

35. Niklas Luhmann, *Law as a Social System*, ed. Fatima Kastner et al., trans. Klaus A. Ziegert (New York: Oxford University Press, 2004), 105.

36. Ibid., 106.

37. 38 Ibid., 107–08.

38. National Federation of Independent Business v. Sebelius, 132 S. Ct. 2566 (2012).

39. 26 U.S.C. § 5000a (2012).

40. 26 U.S.C. § 5000a.

41. National Federation of Independent Business v. Sebelius, 132 S. Ct. at 2609, 2642.
42. Ibid., 2593, 2601.
43. See Gordon, "Critical Legal Histories"; Jack M. Balkin and Reva B. Siegel, "Principles, Practices, and Social Movements," *University of Pennsylvania Law Review* 154 (2006): 927.
44. National Federation of Independent Business v. Sebelius, 132 S. Ct. 2602–03; see also Printz v. United States, 521 U.S. 898 (1997); New York v. United States, 505 U.S. 144 (1992).
45. National Federation of Independent Business v. Sebelius, 132 S. Ct., 1 2591, 2650.
46. Ibid., 2609 (Justice Ginsburg, concurring in part and dissenting in part).
47. Beauvoir, *She Came to Stay*, 404.

CHAPTER 10

Pictures as Precedents

The Visual Turn and the Status of Figures in Judgments

PETER GOODRICH

In the fields with which we are concerned, knowledge comes only flashlike [*blitzhaft*]. The text is the long roll of thunder that follows.[1]

The advent of images in judicial opinions raises interesting questions of method. Those schooled in common law are very familiar with the binding character of prior decisions, and it is indeed the distinguishing feature of the system of precedent that defines the tradition, the *mos britannicus*, and now also the *mos americanus*, as a distinct form and practice of law. In the words of Mr. Justice James Parke, in the case that is the acknowledged source of the doctrine, the principle of subsuming novel facts under "rules of law which we derive from legal principles and judicial precedents" is of great importance "not merely for the determination of the particular case, but for the interests of law as a science."[2] It is on the strength of this principle that common lawyers distinguish the authority of prior cases and treat the *ratio decidendi*, the reason for the decision, as binding on subsequent coordinate and lower courts in the same jurisdiction. The remainder of the decision, the *obiter dicta*, the things said by way of justificatory argument, are treated as being of persuasive but not of binding authority. What then is a subsequent court to make of a decision that inserts pictures into the judgment?

Figure 10.1 Ostrich with its head buried in the sand. Courtesy of *Gonzalez-Servin v. Ford Motor Co.*, 662 F.3d 931 (7th Cir. 2011).

Start with an extreme instance of the judicial posting of images. *Gonzales-Servin v. Ford Motor Company* involved two consolidated appeals from District Court decisions dismissing class action lawsuits brought by foreign nationals, on the grounds of *forum non conveniens*. The Seventh Circuit Court of Appeals, in a decision authored by Judge Posner, dismisses the complaint fairly summarily. The decision relies upon precedents of the same court, and specifically *Abad v. Bayer Corp.*, decided two years earlier, that had dismissed appeals in circumstances "nearly identical" to those of the present case.[3] In justifying the dismissal of the appeals, the judge goes out of his way to censure the appellants' attorneys for failing to address the appropriate, binding authority. "Where there is apparently dispositive precedent, an appellant may urge its overruling or distinguishing or reserve a challenge to it for certiorari but may not simply ignore it."[4] Such a lesson is unremarkable in itself, but the judge then proceeds to reproach the appellants' advocacy as "unacceptable" and depicts it as "an ostrich-like tactic." He then inserts two pictures into the judgment (Figures 10.1 and 10.2).[5]

Figure 10.2 Man with his head buried in the sand. Courtesy of *Gonzalez-Servin v. Ford Motor Co.*, 662 F.3d 931 (7th Cir. 2011).

As the decision purports to offer a lesson on the importance of precedent and specifically asserts the dispositive quality of prior judgments in similar circumstances, it is unquestionably necessary to address the precedential status and import of the images that form the most striking aspect of the decision handed down. It is necessary to ask whether the pictures are part of the reasoning of the decision, whether they bind future courts, and what precisely is their priority and status in relation to apparently similar cases to come. In reading, or better, viewing the decision, it would be a grave error and indeed would exacerbate the poor advocacy denounced by the judge simply to ignore this visual depiction of willful ignorance. Such, however, has generally been the fate of images in judgments for the principal reason that lawyers have neither training nor skill in visual advocacy. More than that, legal method has no concept of how to incorporate images into the prosaic logic of precedent. In what follows I will suggest that the history of the use of images in legal texts can be used to construct a new version of the humanistic *mens emblematica*, a legally devised methodology that apprehends pictures not *ad similia*, as text, by way of analogy, which is generally the lawyer's rule, but *ad apparentiam*, by dint of how they appear. In conclusion, I will develop a distinct logic of visual authority which treats imagery according to the novel criteria of *imago decidendi* and *obiter depicta*, respectively the image determining decision, and things shown and seen along the way to judgment.

VISUAL AND VIRTUAL

The precedent decision requires that the judgment handed down be taken seriously and addressed as law. It may have its ludic dimensions, but wittingly or otherwise, the incorporation of images into legal texts belongs explicitly within the tradition of *serio-ludere*, the playfully serious, and so, even without the contemporary ruling, requiring attention and observance, the apprehension of the legal image has to be treated with a certain degree of sobriety and gravity, if not necessarily any full-blown solemnity.[6] The judge, in using images, is playing the law but then, of course, such is invariably the judicial function. It is just that it is not so often the case that the confluence of the serious and the ludic in the portrayal of the legal is made visible in judgment. Figures, the art and imagery of justice, have remained relatively familiar, and have recently been studied exhaustively in the encyclopedic treatise *Representing Justice*, but the visual depiction of doctrine, rule, norm and law, is less well known and so merits a brief reinscription.[7]

To know is first to imagine and then to reason or, as Aristotle puts it, to think is "to speculate in images."[8] The root of speculation lies in the specular, and has its source in the Latin *specere*, to look, and in *specula*, or watchtower. Rhetoric has long recognized such imperative of exterior projection and interior visualization, the imagination that precedes and accompanies thought, the dream and then the reverie or intuition that takes the form of invention, the sense and sensibility of an image that will impel and guide the process of argument. Even in law there is no escaping imagery, and there never has been, a fact that is ingrained in legal language, not simply in the concept of evidence, from the Latin *ex-videre*, from sight, a root that does much to explain the requirement of the visibility of legal process and the norm that trial take place *in vivo*, as a theatrical rite or, as Agamben has traced it, a liturgical performance.[9] The words of the law are literally visible signs, *verba visibilia* in the Christian tradition, meaning heralds of unseen causes, of angelological images, specular ideas that are made present and effective through their invocation in the legal process and according to the grave and learned, legitimate and authorized theatricality of their delivery.

The law is in its most general and accessible form the order of visible places and roles. This normative deployment of the visual is the object of the *ius imaginum*, the law of visual depiction of office and role that dates back to classical Rome but was inherited in the Renaissance in the form of the codification of the licit depictions and authorized signs of all the administrative places within the carefully ordered and lengthily transcribed hierarchies of the spiritual and civil polities. Sovereignty, which lies at the root of legality, is a spectacular affair, a profusion of visible signs and oneiric presences, because, to borrow a phrase, "a picture is worth a thousand words."[10] Lawyers have long been aware of that priority and power of the imaginal but have tended to hide such knowledge in the full view of practice as performance. The regal costumes and settings, the magisterial architecture and imposing portraiture all scream the visibility of power, and the depiction of the presence of law, but the legal curriculum traverses those settings in silence, with blindfolds, so as to proffer the proper attention to "written reason" and the protestant motif of the text alone. A little reconstruction and recuperation of law's visual rule, of the visiocratic regimen, is necessary to the understanding of the juristic manipulation of imagery.

The visiocratic refers to the history and rule of licit images, the dogmatic sources of legal rules and maxims. The licit or, in theological terms, iconic image represents the founding moment and the vanishing point of authority, and thus acts as both the representation and the veiling of the invention of the rule. The image is the first and last instance of the source of law and of its validity. If we return to the pair of images used in the case of *Gonzalez-Servin*, the ostrich and the kneeling figure with their heads in the sand, it bears immediate note that the legal tradition is far from deprived of images of ostriches in the early visiocratic regimes of vexillology—the encoding of the imagery of flags—as also of heraldry and emblematics, the legal disciplines that study the representation of offices and the depiction of norms. The very concept of visiocracy, of an order of images, in legal Latin, *iconomus*, a hierarchy and template of licit representations, already suggests that there is juristic significance to the figurative depiction of a norm. A judge who invokes the gravamen and power of precedent should thus himself pay attention to the visual precedents, the *imagines decidendi*, the prior depictions that define the image that is used as belonging within a prior order, *iconomus* or lexicon, of pictures.

First, a general and perhaps obvious though neglected point. The judge is not using the images evidentially but is rather inserting the pictures in the course of argument and decision. They are part of the judgment, not part of the proof, and in this regard they belong, as I hinted at the outset, to the reasoning of the case, but in a very novel and unprecedented way.

Here we have, in logical terms, an imagistic expansion of the *argumentum ad hominem*, in the mode of an *argumentum ad imaginem,* an argument to the image or, to be specific, an *argumentum ad struthiocamelum*—an argument to the ostrich. This might suggest that the argument to the image is reducible to the discursive rules of logic and as such arguments are well-recognized fallacies, it would suggest there is no single meaning or more properly signification to the picture, save that it is outwith the field of strictly rational, textual deliberation. The picture will require interpretive work, analysis, and critical response rather than simple assertion of an obvious and singular meaning. It is worth noting here that Judge Posner in fact treats the image as nontransparent, in that he notes parenthetically that ostriches do not "*really* bury their heads in the sand when threatened," and then adds, "don't be fooled by the picture below."[11] Posner does not, however, offer any account of how not to be duped, of how to view the image as someone other than a fool. He is seemingly unaware, despite his advocacy of the use of images in legal argument and in judicial opinion writing, of the precedential status of his pictures and the need to trace and detail their provenance and their effect.[12] The irony of placing an image of an ostrich, in his apprehension as a joke or playfully serious corrective, in a precedent that is concerned to dictate that attorneys take precedents much more seriously, seems to pass unnoticed and unremarked.

The importance that I have attributed to the pictures of ostrich and besuited figure with their heads buried is in large part a consequence of the novelty of the images as aspects of the reasoning of the decision. At the very least the *argumentum ad imaginem* reintroduces the humanistic and expanded scope of legal reasoning which historically included not inconsiderable attention to images both in the architecture, ceremonies, and dress of the law and in the use of pictures in legal texts in the form of emblem books and law treatises, which would include woodcut depictions as insertions (*emblemata* or *pegmata*) in the text. That imagistic relay and transmission belongs to the genre of *serio-ludere*, of the jointly playful and serious, and operates to introduce affect and desire, humor and gravity, enthusiasm and melancholy, in sum another scene, into legal reason.[13]

Pausing on the ostrich, we find the image in early modern heraldic works on vexillogy, the discourse of flags, as well as in a variety of emblem books. Its significations are well enough known and can be classed in four aspects. First, it is a hieroglyphic symbol, familiar and indeed popular among early modern lawyers who studied legal enigmas or, in the Roman tradition, *aenigmata iuris*.[14] Horapollo in his *Hieroglyphica* lists ostrich feathers as a symbol of justice as equal distribution: "for the ostrich has its wings more equally balanced than any other bird."[15] The imagery of flags and devices takes up this sense, and ostrich feathers with a sword between them, with the motto *nobiscum deus*, "God is with us," indicate the justice of a cause.[16] A comparable flag depicts an ostrich with a sword in its beak, with the motto *hoc nutrior*, "By this I am nourished." The bird as a sign of virtue transmits to the tradition of emblems a group of images which depict the ostrich with a horseshoe in its mouth or on the ground, signaling good luck or a faith that others will attend to its needs, and specifically its young. The law, *in nuce*, will render justice, and will shape our ends, rough hew them how we may.[17]

There is a second hieroglyphic signification to the image of the ostrich, which originates in Valeriano's *Hieroglyphica* of 1556.[18] In this version, the ostrich signifies the heretic (*haereticus*), "because it appears to have feathers of wisdom, but it cannot fly at all."[19] The ostrich in this conception appears wise but is not. It fools its viewers into believing that it has virtues and insight. It requires knowledge, perceptiveness, skill to see through this dissimulation, this appearance of having what it in fact lacks. From this root, the emblematist Peacham shows the ostrich challenging an eagle as to which bird deserved precedence by virtue of greater honor and rank.[20] It believes that it is beautiful (*pulchram*), and its fine figure (*formam*), its size, and strength make it an ornament of peace and war alike (Figure 10.3). The eagle, however, points out that it can fly, and further that Jupiter rides astride its wings. The eagle has the highest honor in that it carries on high the thunderbolt-wielding divinity and source of law. *Jus* is in this etymology an abbreviation of *Jupiter*. Finally, Abraham Fraunce, philosopher and lawyer, notes in his *Insignium armorum* that an ostrich with its head in the bushes is a symbol of foolishness. It thinks that it is hiding but it is not.[21]

I will not belabor the emblematical point too long, but it should be noted that these images, these visual relays *ad apparentiam*, are but a scratching of the surface of the visiocratic tradition.[22] Beyond the necessary observation of the plural significations of the first image, that of the ostrich hiding and yet also displaying its body, its *corpus* and plumage, we can briefly push further in the mode of critical analysis and note that this hiding of the head and display of the "other face" or, in the second image, the trousered moon, can introduce the relation of the figure to desire, and the proximity of the image to the erotic. Freud argues in *The Interpretation of Dreams*, that feathers, birds, and flying are erotic symbols.[23] The bird, in dreams, in the work of images, signals intercourse, and flight is indicative of erection of the phallus. The judge's symbolism thus becomes more complex still if we place the images in the figural domain of desire, as expressions of *eros* and of wish-fulfillment. There is an implicit sexuality which can again be figured visually, *ad apparentiam*, by looking, for example, at Giulio Romano's 1520

Figure 10.3 Henry Peacham, *Emblemata varia* [1621].

image of *Iustitia* in the Vatican Sala di Costantino (Figure 10.4). The right hand of Justice clasps the erect, naked, and elongated neck of the ostrich as significant of force and in the mode of analysis of dreams, of phallus and sexuality as well. While the surface meaning, the connotation by which one should not be fooled, is of justice, even-handedness, appropriate distribution, the oneiric significance is more probably of prowess, of virility, and by extension, of sexual charge. The judge, in inserting the picture of the ostrich, is by fairly close association in display mode, marking territory, signaling strength and a leonine pride.

It can be noted further and more briefly that the picture of a man with his head buried is cognate with a headless subject and is a hieroglyphic symbol of impossibility. So too the doctored image, the photoshopped representation of the ostrich with its head hidden marks the secretion of the end of the neck, the point of the phallus, out of view, impotent and lacking arousal. In this aspect, the comparison of the pictures suggests a transmission from bird to lawyer and so it is eros thwarted, desire buried or hidden, the symptom and its repression that is now conveyed. It is a small step to viewing the suited lawyer as castrated. If such is the view,

Figure 10.4 Giulio Romano, *Iustitia* ("Justice"; fresco, 1520), Sala di Costantino, Vatican. Courtesy of the Library of Congress.

then the judge, in using the image, is symbolically wounding the lawyer and excising his desire, his covert intention to make law rather than follow precedent. Law, after all, is in Aristotle's definition "wisdom without desire," and this might be the signification of the images, were it not for the complicating factor that they are part of a judgment, a facet of the precedent, the reasoning of a decision that chooses images precisely to convey a significance, a sensuous apprehension and so to mark an affect and express desire. To add the original or less than original intent of the author projects the analysis into the tenebrous dominion of the subject and can for my purposes here be restricted to the question of the relationship of the image to wish-fulfillment. At this point there is a pleasing enough paradox, in that the judgment and, being objective about it, the Court determined to use these images, to render justice visually, and in doing so introduced a different element, the pictorial, into the prose of judgment. In the words of the English editor of Ripa's *Iconologia*, "Images are the Representations of our Notions; they properly belong to Painters, who by Colours and Shadowing, have invented the admirable Secret to give Body to our Thoughts, thereby to render them visible."[24] To the extent that the images here are figures of erotic desire we are witness to the judge's desire and to the signification of its repression, at the same time as the image exposes the judicial imagination and its embodiment of the work of thought. It can be added that it is also pictures that signify the danger of pictures both to law and to lawyers, while ironically offering nothing by way of method, scheme, or other apotropaic device to avert, channel, ward off, or alternatively, faute de mieux, to enjoy the desires that the embodiment, the picturing of ideas, of thoughts grounded or failing to take flight may propel.

FIGURATIVE REASONING

My argument is that analyzing the use of the image is essential to a proper understanding of the judgment, to the reconstruction of its motivation, and to the apprehension of its scope. It is in Benjamin's terms the "flash," a momentary window onto the judge's motives, a glimpse of intent and desire, which will be formulated here as the *imago decidendi*, the image that portends and propels the judgment. It should first be acknowledged that the image has significance. Law denies the importance of the visual, and tends to denigrate the pictorial as an element of rhetoric, as ornament and lure, seduction rather than reason or argument. Even where images in advocacy and judgment are argued for, their actual use is neither analyzed by their proponents nor included in the explicit reasoning of the judgment. They subsist in an unspoken manner, as apparently self-evident affects, ornament and adornment, as lure and attractor of unspoken desire. This, of course, is a way of endeavoring to hide or repress the significance of the image, but this failure or blind spot, this acknowledgment of the figure only in its negation, in fact draws attention to the motive force and symptomatic importance of its use. Denial is a clue. A clue is a mode of expression, usually an unintended and unwitting one, of the motive for the decision. The *imago*, the butterfly, the nascent judgment is visible in the figure reproduced and so allows for the introduction of the category of *imago decidendi*, the image of decision.

Returning to Posner's depiction of ostrich and lawyer, a further feature merits note. The upending of the figures, the head in the soil, the rear raised calls upon a common emblematic theme of a world gone mad, unreason loosed, and judgment lost. It is pertinent to recognize the excitation and the disorientation, the disruption and the specifically visual intervention that the image introduces. As an image, seen *ad apparentiam*, in relation to, and association with other images, it borrows, again unwittingly, from

Figure 10.5 John Taylor, *Mad Fashions* (1642). Frontispiece emblem: *The World Turn'd Upside down*.

the visiocratic template, the history of the political theology of the image and we can take as an example an emblem from 1642 of the world stood on its head and thereby potentially destroyed (Figure 10.5).[25] In John Taylor's explanatory verses, it is as metamorphosis and as strangeness, monstrosity and transformation that the image of the upside down be comprehended. The picture is of time out of joint, and in the emblem this is visible in the legs coming out of the shoulders, the cart before the horse, the flying eels and fishes, the mouse chasing the cat, and plural further depictions of nature perverted. One might, parenthetically, here note a further implication of Posner's image of the lawyer upended, head in the sand, namely that humans are not birds, and that nature, *leges naturae*, or perhaps the laws of sand, *leges saburrae*, are infracted by the behavior of the attorney.

> Meane time, till wee amend, and leave our crimes,
> The Picture is the Emblem of the Times.
> FINIS.[26]

Denial, or in the Freudian argot negation, is a mode of negative acknowledgment, and signals both desire for and repression of the object denied. The denial is symptomatic in the sense that it energizes the repressed object and signals a degree of condensation, a compression of affect into the truncated form of the figure, the image that is the operative element in the primary process.[27] The figure, to paraphrase Ovid, is more than it seems and carries in condensed form a signal series of affective associations and connections that the viewer, the analyst, has to follow if she is to apprehend the sense of the pictorial and of the visual. Condensation displaces the content, the dream work or imagistic thought of the subject, it transposes the content into chains of association that rework and extend the condensations. The energy escapes the constraint but does so in transposed form. Which means that manifest content and sense are constantly at war with each other, and so too image and text in our judgments are at odds, and to borrow from Lyotard: "Writing belongs to a space of reading (letters without depth), the process of displacement has a kind of gesticulatory, visual scope, and the result of displacement, which encompasses both the readable and the visible, is illegible. It is this that constitutes a kind of murder: desire, with its dimension of depth, disfigures the table of the Law."[28] To put it aphoristically, the desire that escapes repression in the form of the image is the *imago decidendi*. It evidences, which is to say literally makes visible, the ground, the invention that occasions the decision.

At a broader level, the history of figuring, of giving body to thoughts, of enacting ideas and coloring intentions operates according to a well-expounded though now rather forgotten register of templates, or shadow archive of scenes and depictions that the theologico-legal tradition has handed down. I have made an effort here to set out the contours of such a history of images and its relay of figures and would now point out that this transmission is very far from a free play. The Reformation era in which early common law was formed, both as method and as doctrine, saw an extraordinarily intense war of images. That history has been rehearsed too frequently to bear repetition here, save to say that the war of images has seldom been extrapolated in its relation to and effect upon legal regimes of control.[29] It greatly restricted the use of imagery and the play of figures in texts and is in significant degree responsible for the unconscious Protestantism of much of the theory of simulation—the image is evil, it is false in a moralizing sense, it threatens concupiscence and incontinence, delusion and delirium, and other similar premises of analysis. It is also responsible for the blindness of legal doctrine in the sense of its complete unpreparedness to address and critically analyze the use of imagery, let alone its status as precedent in the formulation and dissemination of law.

The recovery and analysis of the image archive requires an appreciation of the *arkheîa*, which is etymologically a reference to the residences, the buildings where the magistrature resided, and where offices were located. It is a reference thus to the monumental, to buildings, to the spatial configuration of law and the spatial thinking that images require in their association and concatenation, their movement, which also moves us. It is to this history of the significance of the built environment of law that Resnik and Curtis have drawn attention in their encyclopedic study of courts as representations of justice, as spaces of the distribution of iconic images as well as being, to pun somewhat, the location where *imago hominis*, the image of the human, fashioned after *haec imago*, the image of the divine, is both empowered and incarcerated, ambulant and confined.[30] It is the built environment that constitutes the first source of imagery in the West, tropes being architectural ornaments, trophies on buildings, and figures and images being statues and other plastic representations, *stellae*, and portraits of the sovereign and the administration.[31]

CONCLUSION

I have argued that images think differently and that they therefore require a methodology appropriate to the visual. The legal tradition already provides significant elements for the development of a critical approach to viewing, as opposed to reading images. The classical use of images warned against the reduction of picture to text and the starting point of emblematics is precisely the distinction between the figurative and the lectoral. Art fights against discourse and the image too requires a viewing that inserts it into discourse but sees that insertion as a rupture in the linear flow of the text and the scopic restraint of reading. The lesson of history is that images cannot be read in the legalistic frame of scanned lines but rather must be apprehended *ad apparentiam*, in relation to other images, laterally, in associative and spatially conceived frames and networks. The eye walks and wanders, digresses, and circles in the image. Borrowing from the *Psalms*, we walk among images, as images among images and it is in that vein that we must understand the rhythm and tone, the intensity and energy that images bring and relay.

Acknowledgment of the *legal* import of images, of the juristic and also precedential value of pictures and depictions, of visual figures is the first move, yet to be taken in quite that form because no one has yet admitted that an image could be a part of the precedent. The recognition of difference, of the distinctive methodology, of viewing the decision *ad apparentiam*, is the second and equally crucial feature of progress. The ambulation of the eye over the picture is not the same as that of a traditional account of rational scanning of legal texts from left to right in their black and white array of lines. The text will have figures and intensities but legal method has generally attempted to constrain and exclude such affect and literary efflorescence. The image in the precedent text is ironically the revenge of rhetoric, the return of the art of delivery, of the *lex gestus* or law of gesture, and with it comes the necessary recognition of the performance that is law in the theatre of justice and truth, to borrow momentarily the title of an old collection of canon law (*theatrum veritatis et iustitiae*).[32]

The image in the judgment is a part of the precedent and so deserves equal treatment, its own analysis according to protocols and methods appropriate to apprehending the image through the history and associations, the intensities and affects that the visual transports and unleashes. The concept of *imago decidendi* is a start in the direction of elaborating and operationalizing such a methodology in the media-saturated, multiplying-platform, internet-driven, mobile-optimized, web-ready, contemporary public sphere. The mobile device may limit the cathartic impact of the image but it also distributes it exponentially and potentially sets it on fire. For a judge simply to insert an image in a decision, to cut and paste a picture because it amuses, because it reproves or incites, pleases, or wounds is not only aesthetically tragic but legally highly misleading. Similarly, to announce that the images presented to the court speak for themselves, as if images could speak, as if these were further words or texts, is again to fall into the trap, the seduction of taking the image as if it were an unproblematic surface to be read, as if it existed autonomously and alone, without extant chains of associations, without composition or technical distinctiveness. Such an uncritical judicial practice and such an uninformed approach to pictures and precedents is to be deplored in the context of the interpretation of the text and pictures that make up the decision, the precedent, that which binds. Such an attitude and hope, that the image in the age of social media is simply what it seems, can be likened, to borrow from the case where I began, to the attitude of an ostrich that sticks its head in the sand, an image, inter alia, of a world turned upside down and of a law hiding from the very act of law creation. It allows for the apprehension of a final significance to the ostrich and the lawyer.

The last connotation or visual association of the dual depictions of an ostrich and a man with their heads both buried in the sand is in all probability the most obvious. The missing head, the hidden *caput* or *chef*, signals not only death, in that one cannot breathe, but also deafness and blindness. It is the latter feature that should attract the jurist's attention even if it seems to have passed by the author of the judgment. To present pictures of an ostrich and a lawyer blinded, is to offer a fairly direct association to the blindness and blindfolding of justice. As stated, the ostrich is traditionally a variable symbol that accompanies the depiction of *Justitia*. While justice may sometimes be blindfolded, this is not the case in the pictures where she is accompanied by an ostrich. Here she is clear-sighted, as in Romano's depiction discussed earlier, and the figure of justice is by this token positive and effective. What then of a buried and blinded head, a flaccid and deflated neck? These, as in the final figure, from Giordano, last inclination to a picture, are signs of injustice and defeat. (Figure 10.6)

The foregrounded picture of the ostrich, either dead or deposed, below a troubled and fraught *Justitia*, signals the demise of justice, her dethronement and disarmament. The satyr on her right is taking her sword, the cherub to her left is unbalancing the scales, desire is everywhere encroaching. The figure of cupid flying on the right of the picture is intriguingly depicted covering his eyes with a blindfold but only appearing to do so, acting falsely in that the blindfold is not covering his left eye. The blindfold is a sham, a joke, a mistake. Consider, then, what this signifies when translated into the decision handed down in *Gonzalez-Servin*. It indicates that images are dangerous, and here full of injustice and desire, lust and wantonness. If we then address the fact that the image is not of justice or judgment, but

Figure 10.6 Luca Giordano, *Allegoria della Giustizia oppressa*. Courtesy of the Szépművészeti Múzeum, Museum of Fine Arts, Budapest.

rather is *in*, and an integral part of a judgment, its association is that of injustice, of desire amok, of the judge disarmed by his affect, law laid bare by dreams.

NOTES

1. Walter Benjamin, *The Arcades Project* (Cambridge, MA: Belknap Press of Harvard University Press, 2009), 456.
2. Mirehouse v Rennell [1833] 1 CL. & Fin. 527, at 546; 6 Eng. Rep. 1023.
3. Gonzalez-Servin v. Ford Motor Company 662 F.3d 931, at 933 (2011).
4. Gonzalez-Servin, at 934.
5. Gonzalez-Servin, at 935. The images are in black and white in the official report but are in color in 2011 U.S. App. LEXIS 23670.
6. On the tradition of legal images, originating in juristic emblems, see Peter Goodrich, *Legal Emblems and the Art of Law:* Obiter depicta *as the Vision of Governance* (New York: Cambridge University Press, 2014). An excellent introduction and overview of the emblem tradition is to be found in John Manning, *The Emblem* (London: Reaktion, 2002).
7. The reference is to Judith Resnik and Dennis Curtis, *Representing Justice: Invention, Controversy, and Rights in City-States and Democratic Courtrooms* (New Haven, CT: Yale University Press, 2011). For further discussion, specifically of imagery of justice, see Sionaidh Douglas-Scott, *Law after Modernity* (Oxford: Hart, 2013); and Desmond Manderson, "The Metastases of Myth: Legal Images as Transitional Phenomena" 26 *Law and Critique* 207 (2015); and in greater detail, Manderson, *Just in Time: Law in the Visual Arts* (Cambridge: Cambridge University Press, forthcoming).
8. Aristotle, *De Anima* 431 a 17.
9. Giorgio Agamben, *Opus Dei: An Archaeology of Duty*, trans. Adam Kotsko (Stanford, CA: Stanford University Press, 2013), 33–37.
10. The point is made at length in Costas Douzinas and Lynda Nead, eds., *Law and the Image: The Authority of Art and the Aesthetics of Law* (Chicago: Chicago University Press, 1999); and in a more contemporary vein in Richard K. Sherwin, *Visualizing Law in the Age of the Digital Baroque: Arabesques and Entanglements* (London: Routledge, 2011). For the law review literature, see, for example, Rebecca Tushnet, "Worth a Thousand Words: The Images of Copyright Law," *Harvard Law Review* 125 (2012): 683–759; Elizabeth Porter, "Taking Images Seriously," *Columbia Law Review* 114 (2014): 1687–1782.
11. Gonzalez-Servin, at 934.
12. Richard A. Posner, "Judicial Opinions and Appellate Advocacy in Federal Courts: One Judge's Views," *Duquesne Law Review* 5 (2013): 12–13.
13. For a highly detailed account of the ludic in *serio-ludere*, see Valérie Hayaert, "Serio-ludere et humanisme juridique: Les Gloses de Benoît le Court aux *Arrêts d'Amour* de Martial d'Auvergne," in *Des "Arrests Parlans": Les Arrêts notables à la Renaissance entre droit et literature*, edited by Géraldine Cazals and Stéphan Geonget (Geneva: Droz, 2014). On the genre, variously termed *serio-ludere* or *ex nugis seria*, useful introductions can be found in Michael Bath, *Speaking Pictures: English Emblem Books and Renaissance Culture* (New York: Longman, 1994);

Manning, *Emblem*. On the polemical motives of the *emblemata*, see Valérie Hayaert, "*Calumnia: De famosis libellis* et ripostes aux attaques injurieuses: La verve satirique de l'emblème," *textimage* 7, no. 2 (2010): 1–19.

14. Antionio Nebrija, *Aenigmata iuris* [1506], republished as *Vocabularium utrisuque iuris* (Venice: Zalterium, 1612); and for a general and important discussion, see François Menestrier, *La Philosophie des images* (Paris: Robert de la Caille, 1683); discussed in Peter Goodrich, "Legal Enigmas: Antonio de Nebrija, *The Da Vinci Code*, and the Emendation of Law," *Oxford Journal of Legal Studies* 30 (2010): 71–99.

15. George Boas, ed., *Horapollo's Hieroglyphica* (Princeton, NJ: Princeton University Press, 1968), 98.

16. Alan R. Young, ed., *The English Emblem Tradition*, vol. 3, *Emblematic Flags of the English Civil War, 1642–1660* (Toronto: University of Toronto Press, 1995), 137 (01251.0).

17. Jacques De Ville, "Mythology and the Images of Justice," *Law and Literature* 23 (2011): 324–64.

18. Piero Valeriano, *Hieroglyphica sive de sacris Aegyptiorum literis commentarii* (Basel: n.p., 1556), and see the commentary of Peter Manning in Abraham Fraunce, *Philosophiae symbolicae liber quartus* [1590] (New York: AMS Press, 1991).

19. Valeriano, *Hieroglyphica*, fol. 179r, *qui habere quasi videtur sapientiae pennas, volare tamen non potest.*

20. Henry Peacham, *Emblemata varia* [ca. 1621] (Ilkley: Scolar, 1976), 11v.

21. Abraham Fraunce, *Insignium armorum, emblematum, hieroglyphicorum, symbolorum* (London: Orwin, 1588), 67.

22. Peter Goodrich, "Visiocracy: On the Futures of the Fingerpost," *Critical Inquiry* 39 (2013): 498–531; and Goodrich, "The Visial Line: On the Prehistory of Law and Film," *Parallax* 55, no. 4 (2008): 55–76.

23. Sigmund Freud, *The Interpretation of Dreams*, trans. James Strachey (New York: Avon Books, 1965), at 429–30.

24. Cesar Ripa, "To the Reader," in *Iconologia: or, Moral Emblems*, ed. P. Tempest (London: Motte, 1709).

25. John Taylor, *Mad Fashions, Od Fashions, All out of Fashions, Or, The Emblems of these Distracted times* (London: John Hammond, 1642), frontispiece.

26. Taylor, *Mad Fashions*, n.p.

27. Freud, *Interpretation of Dreams*, 312–39.

28. Jean-François Lyotard, *Discourse, Figure*, trans. Antony Hudek and Mary Lydon (Minneapolis: University of Minnesota Press, 2011), 237.

29. Peter Goodrich, *Oedipus Lex: Psychoanalysis, History, Law* (Berkeley: University of California Press, 1995), covers much of that history and literature.

30. Resnik and Curtis, *Representing Justice*, 338ff., discussing the aspirational iconography of a democratic justice.

31. Guido Panciroli, *Notitia utraque dignitatum iuris* (Gabiano, 1618), *de imaginibus Principum*—on the images of the emperor.

32. J. Baptista (Cardinal de Luca), *Theatrum veritatis et iustitiae* (Cologne: Lit. Soc., 1685); and for discussion, Peter Goodrich, "The Theatre of Emblems," *Law, Culture and the Humanities* 11(2012): 47–67.

CHAPTER 11

Law as Performance

Historical Interpretation, Objects, Lexicons,
and Other Methodological Problems

JULIE STONE PETERS

In 1590–91, a series of witchcraft accusations swept the northern coast of
Scotland. Under torture, the accused confessed to: disinterring corpses
and making powders of the bodies, attempting to bewitch the king by
roasting a wax image of him, baptizing a cat in order to raise a storm to
prevent the king's new bride from reaching Scotland, and other "conjuring, witchcraft, enchantment, sorcery, and such like" (in the words of *News
from Scotland*, a pamphlet published at the height of the trials).[1] Agnes
Sampson, a healer, diviner, and midwife, confessed to collecting the venom
from a black toad in an oyster shell in order to do *maleficium* on the king
by means of a piece of his foul linen. John Fian, a schoolmaster and town
lothario, confessed to putting a hex on a love rival that caused him to "f[a]ll
into a lunacy" (318) (after, rumor had it, a failed attempt to bribe a pupil
to steal "three hairs of his sister's privities" [319] so that Fian could possess her by witchcraft). Most of the accused confessed to attending a mas-
sive witches' sabbat on All Hallows Eve at North Berwick Kirk, the church
to which they traveled over the North Sea in a sieve and where, accompanied by a young maidservant named Geillis Duncan on a "trump" (or
Jew's harp), led by Fian (in disguise), they "took hands" and "danced [a]
reel," back-to-back and "widdershins" (counterclockwise) with hundreds of

Figure 11.1 Witches in the examination chamber in *Newes from Scotland* (1591).

other witches, at the end enacting a mock sacrament that concluded with a dramatic performance of the *osculum infame* ("shameful kiss"): as Agnes Sampson's confession put it, the devil got up on the pulpit, "lifted up his gown[,] and every one kissed his arse" (138).

The twenty-four-year-old king (James VI, soon to be James I of England)—personally implicated, perhaps alarmed, but still more titillated by the wondrous stories—took the unusual step of calling the accused to Holyroodhouse (the royal residence in Edinburgh) in order to conduct pre-trial examinations in his own chamber (a woodcut in *News from Scotland* [Figure 11.1][2] appears to show James presiding from his dais, the accused on their knees before him). Not satisfied with merely interrogating the witches, however, James commanded them to reenact the witchcraft of which they were accused in order to prove the "verity" of their confessions (318), as *News from Scotland* puts it. Geillis Duncan (the first to be brought to the king's chamber) attempted to recreate the North Berwick sabbat, dancing the witches' dance and playing on a Jew's harp for the king (315). Agnes Sampson, the next, offered a clairvoyance demonstration, announcing to the assembly that she knew what the king and queen had said in their bedchamber on their wedding night, drawing close to him and whispering in his ear, causing him to cry out: "[A]ll the devils in hell could not have discovered the same[!]" (316). Following Sampson, John Fian brought his love rival (the man he had bewitched) before the king in order to display the "lunacy" that Fian's witchcraft had wrought:

> [B]eing in his Majesty's chamber, suddenly he gave a great screech and fell into a madness, sometime bending himself, and sometime capering so directly up that his head did touch the ceiling of the chamber, to the great admiration of his Majesty and others then present; so that all the gentlemen in the chamber were not able to hold him, until they called in more help, who together bound him hand and foot, and suffering the said gentleman to lie still until his fury were past, he within an hour came again to himself. (318–19)

These scenes give rise to many questions. For instance, the accused had confessed to roasting the king's image and trying to drown him at sea: Why risk exposing him to envoys of the devil who had confessed to seeking his destruction? *News from Scotland* in fact worries about just this: some (it speculates) might "conjecture that the king's Majesty would not hazard himself in the presence of such notorious witches lest thereby might have ensued great danger to his person and the general state of the land" (324). Leaving aside the hazard, why demand the repetition of the crime of witchcraft, a crime no less criminal when performed for the king? And why, when the king saw these fiendish scenes, did he not experience horror or terror, but instead (we are told) "wondered greatly" (316) and, "in respect of the strangeness of these matters[,] took great delight to be present at their examinations" (315)? How might we understand the Jew's harp, the song the witches allegedly sang ("Cammer go ye before, commer go ye . . ."), widdershins, and back-to-back dancing, Sampson's whispered aside to the king, the binding of Fian's love rival, and all the visceral details of these scenes? What were the legal effects of these demonstrations, and what did they mean for the law of witchcraft, treason, evidence, jurisdiction?

Before we can even begin to address substantive questions of this kind, however, we must face a series of methodological questions. What is the implied object of understanding here? (The events themselves? The representations of the events? How they reflect or shape social or legal classifications?) What can we know of that object from available historical sources? (How credible are the sources? If they serve as evidence, of what?) What kind of "meaning" do they bear? (Legal? Ideological? Rhetorical? Phenomenological? Aesthetic? Symbolic? Cognitive? . . .)

My description of the scenes in James's chamber is a fragment of a larger study investigating the role of performance in the historical production and reception of law. In the larger study, I offer close readings of a series of historical legal events and practices—trials, public punishments, police actions, and more—whose meaning was articulated not primarily through texts, doctrine, or rules but through what we have come to call "performance." At the same time, understanding these performances is inseparable from understanding the doctrines and institutional structures from which they emerged, and the historical attitudes that both shaped them and registered their meaning. Central to these attitudes was the figure of theatre. On the one hand, in the classic trope, law was supposed to act as a kind of theatre (a "Theatre of Justice and Truth," in the often-quoted phrase of the seventeenth-century lawyer Giovanni Battista de Luca).[3] On the other hand, law was *not* supposed to act like theatre (we must, at all costs, prevent the courtroom from becoming a "theater and spectaculum," "circus," or "carnival.").[4] If, unlike theatre, law was nasty, brutish, and long (and, oh yes, really boring), that's what it was supposed to be.

My claim (here and elsewhere) is not that all legal events and practices are theatrical, or even that they are performances or performative (critical truisms that I will address further below). But I hope to show how performance and theatricality (both as effect and idea) matter to law—to legal institutions, practices, and doctrines, to specific outcomes, to the broader meaning of law, to our understanding of how law achieves its effects, how it persuades people of the legitimacy of its use of force, and how it exerts (or fails to exert) power over us. My readings of events, practices, and historical views about legal performance are meant to suggest an alternative way of studying law: more attentive to the material, affective, and aesthetic textures of legal process, both complement and corrective to the doctrinal, institutional or intellectual history of law. While my initial description of the Scottish witch trials hints at the kind of reading I do in the larger project, this chapter does not offer an extended demonstration of that kind of reading. Instead, it attempts to explain the methodological choices, interpretive dilemmas, and implicit theoretical claims that undergird my work and that distinguish it from the study of law and literature, legal history, and previous studies of law and performance.

1. LAW IN LITERATURE AND LAW AS LITERATURE VERSUS LAW AS EXPRESSIVE EVENT AND PRACTICE

Some years ago, I wrote a semisatirical essay about law and literature as a subdiscipline, an affectionate critique of the field's primal longings, which were, of course, my own.[5] Chastened but not fully reformed by my own critique, the project I outline here continues to embrace the aspirations of law and literature (though perhaps its more modest ones). It shares one of law and literature's central motivations: the desire to offer a corrective to traditional legal scholarship's historical focus on doctrines or institutions alone, as if these were hermetically sealed off from the broader culture. Like other work in law and literature, it strives to offer "thicker descriptions" of law (to use Clifford Geertz's overused term)[6]—to escape the realm of concepts or rules and get further inside the experience and visceral effects of law. Like other work in law and literature (and unlike most legal history), it is attentive to law's aesthetic, symbolic, rhetorical, narrative, semiotic, phenomenological, and cognitive dimensions: the power of narrative and genre to shape legal events; the force and meaning of rhetoric, form, style, and structure; the work that symbolic substitution or figural slippage does; and more. Like other work in law and literature, it resists traditional views of law as a thing produced only within institutionally defined boundaries and forms (legislation, judicial decisions, institutional practices), recognizing the force of culture and representation to shape not only the legal subject but law itself.

However, my objects are neither of law and literature's traditional objects, as identified in the classic distinction: literary texts (the object of "law in literature") and judicial opinions (the object of "law as literature").[7] Instead, my objects are historical events and practices. That is, unlike law *in* literature (and such offshoots as law in film or law in art), I avoid extended analysis of what I will call "aesthetic" representations—literary texts, theatrical productions, films, or images—however relevant such representations may be, however expressive of the ethos from which they emerge.[8] For instance, in discussing the Scottish witch trials, it is tempting to discuss *Macbeth* (a play that explicitly draws on James's encounter with the North Berwick witches) or James's *Daemonologie* (1597), a highly literary expository text in which the witch trials play a major role. I resist this temptation not because I am skeptical about the capacity of literary texts (or other aesthetic representations) to tell us important things about legal history, but because I am wary of two scholarly tendencies: first, the tendency to use literary texts as straightforward evidence for a set of otherwise ungrounded legal or historical or political claims; second, the tendency to allow literary analysis to sideline the legal history that may have been the project's initial justification. As the literary (so rich in detail, so temptingly *interpretable*) grows larger, legal history (harder to access, more resistant to interpretation) grows proportionally smaller. The literary text initially holds itself out as the entry point to the legal ideas or events that are the chapter's main subject. But a kind of bait-and-switch occurs: legal ideas or events, briefly sketched, quickly give way to extended literary analysis, which becomes the sole foundation for historical claims. Analysis of historical events or practices disappears from view.

My object of study, then, is not law *in* literature, nor is it law *as* literature, which traditionally studies not legal events and practices but legal texts. What classically distinguished scholars of law as literature from legal historians was not merely their use of the tools of literary analysis, but their close attention to legal texts as critical objects in themselves, not as mere evidence of events, practices, or doctrines. Various subfields within both historical and literary studies (new historicism, *histoire des mentalités*, cultural studies) have, of course, long challenged the distinction between text as evidence and text as critical object, with some justification. As theorists in these fields have argued, it is predominantly through representations (largely verbal texts, but also images and recordings) that we know history.[9] Even the most purportedly documentary of sources is refracted through memory, judgment, and imagination. The Scottish witch trials' ostensibly verbatim depositions, for instance, probably represent not what the accused actually said but what those who took down the depositions *thought* they should have said. Moreover, even the most self-consciously aesthetic, or rhetorically readerly, of texts can provide evidence of historical events, practices, and meanings. If *Macbeth*, *Daemonologie*, or a judicial opinion offers us a representational world with its own logic, that logic is evidence of the meaning of the historical events it represents, however transformed through the process of narrative representation.

These views are in fact fundamental to my own work. And yet, the logic I seek in texts is the logic of historical events themselves, not the logic of authorial or textual consciousness (although these may overlap). For instance, *News from Scotland* is a paradigmatic new historicist law-and-literature text: flamboyantly expressive (rhetorically and visually), about as unreliable a witness to history as one can find, and thus revealingly symptomatic. Leaving aside its assertions about the witches' ability to conjure a raging storm in the North Sea, bounce a love rival off the ceiling, or kiss the devil's "arse," it is a piece of patent propaganda, inflated with lurid rumors about the accused (based largely on European witch lore, with a *soupçon* of Apuleius's *Golden Ass*), rumors that, of course, tell us more about belief than about actual events.[10] If we look instead to the images as historical evidence, we learn that the woodcut purportedly showing James presiding from his dais—the only one that seems to represent the legal scene itself— is actually a stock woodcut, repurposed for the pamphlet: it tells us nothing about James's actual chamber or what the accused did there.

Like other law-and-literature scholars, I might argue that, while the image does not represent James or the accused themselves, the printer's decision to include it does represent a set of attitudes, attitudes that may also have been at work in the trials and about which we can speculate. Perhaps, for instance, its inclusion offers a celebration of the subjection of the witches to royal legal power, or (on the other hand) a critique of royal legal violence. Perhaps it reminds readers that the trials were not merely enactments of legal judgment but demonstrative (a reminder emblematized in the royal minister's very indexical index finger). Like other scholars of law and literature, I might point to the pamphlet's stress on the king's "admiration," "wonder," and "delight," emotions replicated in the images, arguing that they reflect an affective logic that may also have been at work in the examinations themselves. Like other scholars of law and literature, I might dwell on the text and its images as a rich repository of the history of consciousness, history accessible only through interpretation.

That said, there is a difference between law and literature's reading of historical texts and images and my reading of historical events and practices *through* texts and images: a difference, perhaps, more of degree than of kind, or of foreground versus background, but a difference nonetheless. Looking at *News from Scotland* alongside the examinations, confessions, depositions, "dittays" (indictments), and other available historical evidence, unlike most law-and-literature scholars I try to bracket *News from Scotland*'s textual effects and the singularity of its imaginative world in order to focus on what it (in conjunction with other evidence) tells us of the trials themselves and *their* imaginative world. Trained in literary analysis, I often find myself tempted by texts. But I try to resist the text's seductions—to resist allowing it to sideline the harder-to-access historical events and practices it represents. I try to foreground not the representation of events and practices, but events and practices as, themselves, representations.

Legal historians, of course, similarly focus not on texts themselves but on historical events and practices. Earlier, I pointed out that my attention to the aesthetic, symbolic, or rhetorical features of legal events and practices differentiates my work from that of most legal historians. But there is a second important difference: I focus on events and practices that are expressive or demonstrative, events and practices that do not merely do law, but *show* the doing of law. The events and practices I examine are articulated and communicated in embodied ways in space and time: three-dimensional, extratextual, produced collectively in the moment. Investigating such events and practices necessarily includes an inquiry into backgrounds: how people and things got where they are; why they are as they are. But my primary focus is on the present of event and practice: moments that we might understand as "scenes" (and that are often understood as such by contemporaries). I am interested in the relationships and movements of people in space, their gestures and vocal effects (what the Greeks called *hypokrisis* and the Romans called *actio*), their projection of ethos and emotion through tone, duration, and tempo, the objects, architecture, sounds, and images that are in play in a given moment, the scene's production of embodied phenomenal, sensory, kinaesthetic, semiotic, psychic, affective, ritualistic, or other kinds of meaning. In short, I am interested in what has come to be called "performance."

"PERFORMANCE"

The word "performance" has been naturalized in a number of fields and subfields in the humanities and social sciences over the past few decades: cultural studies, literary studies, anthropology, microhistory, visual studies, theatre studies, and, not least, performance studies, with which (of course) my project can most readily be identified. However, the word presents certain problems. First, there is the notorious difficulty of defining it. Early theorists of performance studies, while acknowledging that any action might be a performance of sorts, strove to distinguish performance from other social phenomena, in the hope that the distinctiveness of the field's objects would establish the distinctiveness of the field itself.[11] For Richard Schechner, performance was (famously) "restored" or "twice behaved" behavior. At the same time, for Peggy Phelan, performance was what could not "be saved, recorded, documented, or otherwise participate in the circulation of representations *of* representations: once it does so it becomes something other than performance."[12] Meanwhile, poststructuralist discussions of "performativity" taught that performance could *not* be set apart as distinctive. As Jacques Derrida and Judith Butler (via Erving Goffman) taught, everyday life, utterances, identities, even subjectivities were produced through performance, or "performativity."[13]

These definitional difficulties have been compounded by the word's mutable history. The most common meaning of the word "performance" in English was—and in fact remains—"the accomplishment [or] doing of an action," or "[t]he quality of execution of such an action . . . when measured against a standard," as in the performance of a duty, promise, or cure.[14] Through the early modern period, title pages and advertisements for theatre, opera, or dance usually referred to these kinds of performances as "representations." If they used the word "performance" (as they did occasionally), the word did not identify the representation as belonging to a special class of arts, but merely signified that it was an "accomplishment" (an *ouvrage*, or work, as Abel Boyer's 1767 English-French dictionary translated the word).[15] Its meaning was the same as that in such phrases as a "philosophical performance" or a "performance of penmanship," or, for that matter, "the regular Performance . . . of the animal *Secretions*, and *Excretions*" so necessary to health.[16]

Only in the later eighteenth century did usage of the word "performance" begin to split, retaining its primary meaning but also taking on a specific association with public exhibition before spectators. Samuel Johnson's *Dictionary of the English Language* (1755) was the first to note this special secondary presentational and aesthetic connotation: the word "performer," Johnson explains, is "generally applied to one that makes a publick exhibition of his skill."[17] However, it was not until the 1828 edition of Noah Webster's American dictionary that we find a definition of "perform*ance*" registering this special secondary connotation, a connotation that does not appear in British dictionaries until the mid-nineteenth century.[18] In nineteenth-century aesthetics, theatre, opera, and dance were not treated as "performing arts" but still generally clustered under the word "representation."[19] In fact, the classification "performing arts" did not appear until well into the twentieth century.[20] In short, the aesthetic and presentational usage—in which "performance" connotes public exhibition and spectatorship—was a gradual formation, fully established only in the twentieth century.

One of the central innovations of performance studies has been to fuse the early (and still dominant) usage with the more recent aesthetic usage. On the one hand, performance studies is not theatre studies because it engages with a wide array of events, practices, and forms of expression, including nonaesthetic ones (such as political protests, football matches, zookeeping, or "the presentation of self in everyday life"). In fact, the "performances" performance studies analyzes (for instance, secret rituals, surgery, psychotherapy, masturbation, . . .) do not necessarily have spectators per se. On the other hand, in performance studies (as Schechner explains in his classic textbook), performance is not merely the *doing* of an action, as in early modern and much modern usage, but the *showing* of doing.[21] That is, if performance studies often focuses on nonaesthetic, nonpresentational being and doing, what it *highlights* in these is the aesthetic and presentational (associated with the modern secondary meaning of the word "performance"), frequently leaning heavily on the modern theatrical associations of the word.

In the early years of performance studies, "theatricality" was often vilified as the bourgeois twin of "performance": where performance was presentation, theatricality was representation; where performance was real, theatricality was false; where performance was raw, theatricality was overcooked.[22] But Judith Butler's discussion of the theatricality of drag performance helped redeem "theatricality," which, it turned out, had been the subversive twin of "performance" all along. For Butler, theatricality could be "a resignifying practice [that] contest[ed] the terms of [a norm's] legitimacy," allowing for "subversion," a "*working [of] the weakness in the norm*." The drag performer (for instance) could use theatricality to "*mim[e] . . . discursive convention[s]*" and "*rende[r] [them] hyperbolic*," thereby "*revers[ing]*" them. Theatricality thus became a practice not of compulsory repetition (as in the performance of normative gender) but of *citation*, a kind of citation of norms that rendered them visible and could thus "resignif[y]" them.[23]

Nevertheless, the word "performance" (or "performativity"), used as a form of ontological critique challenging the naturalness or inevitability of norms or analytic categories, has continued to play a key interpretive role, not only in performance studies but in the humanities and social sciences more generally. Over the past few decades, it has become axiomatic that all categories, and especially those things once thought natural, are really "performative"—that unveiling hidden "performativity" (especially of identities: racial, ethnic, gendered, sexual, . . .) can help us subvert coercive normativity and make visible a history of performative resistance. This usage is broad (in fact, universal) in its application: everything is performance, or performative. But it is narrow in its singular, politically charged critique: if we reveal the hidden performativity of the allegedly natural, we might free ourselves from its stranglehold.

The definitional quandaries surrounding the word "performance" have not disappeared. Is performance a distinctive kind of thing? Or is everything performance? Is it, by definition, twice-behaved? Or is it unrepeatable? And yet performance studies seems to have embraced its own ambiguities. The brochure for Performance Studies at NYU (where the field originated) describes it (and, implicitly, its objects) as a "provisional coalescence on the move," made up of "more than the sum of its inclusions."[24] In this, of course, performance is no different from the objects of any other field (literature, religion, art, philosophy, math, . . .), all of which remain manifestly undefined, in richly generative ways.

Thus disavowing the necessity of definition (in solidarity with my fellow scholars across the arts and sciences, who, mostly, do not feel required to define their objects), I do nevertheless tend to use the word "performance" in particular ways. Stressing the aesthetic and presentational over the ontological, I tend to use the word not as a tool for unveiling the pretense of naturalness but as a qualifier for identifying particular expressive or demonstrative effects. Rather than setting "performance" and "theatricality" in opposition (political or otherwise), I treat them as part of a continuum, using "theatricality" to describe more overt or conspicuous forms of "performance." I do look at legal ritual and *habitus* (to use Pierre Bourdieu's term)[25]—practices that often seem normal and are thus invisible to contemporaries—attempting to make their strangeness comprehensible or their familiarity strange. But I mostly focus on legal events and practices that are distinctively, often intentionally, sometimes embarrassingly theatrical. Poststructuralist theory is needed to expose invisible performativity, but once exposed, its lesson is simple: you thought it was real, but it's performative. Nothing is needed to expose overt theatricality: it is always already exposing itself. But, however raw its visibility, its meaning is a labyrinth of ambiguities: enigmatic, contradictory, equivocal, without determinate politics, often not reducible to a political proposition at all. In its peculiarities, its eccentricities, its sometimes outlandish caprices, conspicuous theatricality usually surprises us: we often don't know what to do with it, and thus it does things with us.

I cannot do without the words "performance" and "theatricality" as transhistorical shorthand for identifying the expressive legal events and practices that are the objects of my study. But neither word is perfectly satisfying: the modern presentational and aesthetic sense in which I use the word "performance" suffers from anachronism; the word "theatricality," with its historically negative associations, suffers from too much attitude. Thus, while I do use them as shorthand, they do little analytic work for me. The words that serve as my primary analytic tools arise instead from the historical lexicon. When a sixteenth-century Scottish polemicist describes the accused as "dancing," "playing," or "capering," or a seventeenth-century French judge calls a trial a *comédie*, or an eighteenth-century English prisoner describes the road to Tyburn as a "sad pageant," when observers describe legal events as "representations," "shows," "entertainments," or "dramas," "staged" or "acted" in "scenes" for "spectators," these words—often associated transhistorically with theatre and entertainment, but historically and geographically inflected in particular ways—are my primary keys to the events and practices they describe. Each of these words has a distinctive history and a distinctive valence, with its own temporal, spatial, ethical, and aesthetic associations. But together they form a lexical constellation, more useful than "performance" or "theatricality" for understanding legal events and practices, and the concepts, attitudes, and judgments inseparable from them.

LAW IN PERFORMANCE AND LAW OF PERFORMANCE VERSUS LAW AS PERFORMANCE

The only general book on law and performance is Alan Read's short guide, *Theatre and Law*,[26] but there is a small but growing body of scholarship that might be called law and performance studies. Largely under the influence of critical race and queer theory, many such studies address questions of identity formation; for instance, Joseph Roach's influential exploration of the creation of circumatlantic racial identities through both law and performance, or Joshua Takano Chambers-Letson's study of law, performance, and Asian American identity.[27] Some focus on legal processes (for instance, Catherine Cole's analysis of South Africa's Truth Commission), symbolic legal action (for instance, Robin Chapman Stacey's study of legal performance in early Ireland), or protest as legal counterperformance (for instance, Lucy Finchett-Maddock's study of illegal occupation as performance).[28] Traditional literary topics, such as the representation of law in drama, and traditional legal topics, such as the regulation of theatre and performance, have come to include work on the dynamic between legal and theatrical performance.

If we can no longer neatly divide law and literature into "law in literature" and "law as literature," neither can we neatly divide law and performance into object-defined categories: studies of law and performance tend to move freely among legal texts, their instantiation in legal performance, and representations of these in theatre, media, and popular culture. Nevertheless, attending to differences among kinds of objects in these studies can highlight crucial methodological differences. These objects might be separated into three broad categories: law *in* performance (theatrical, quasi-theatrical, or quotidian performances that represent or enact law and its effects); law *of* performance (legal texts and rules that construct or regulate performance and its effects); and law *as* performance (expressive legal events and practices themselves).

Like law *in* literature, law *in* performance might be defined by its concern with the representation or enactment of law in extralegal spheres (in, for instance, theatre, the streets, or everyday life). Such representations or enactments may be agents of law, creating legal subjects of their actors and spectators. But, like literature, they represent law outside its official institutional structures. Like law *as* literature (and the studies of the legal regulation of literature that have sometimes been called law *of* literature),[29] law *of* performance might be defined by its concern with legal texts. Looking at (for instance) judicial decisions and statutes dealing with theatre, obscenity, public speech, or religious attire, it focuses on their *textual* effects, their rhetorical postures, and the ideologies reflected in their language.[30] That is, the study of law *in* performance focuses on performative representations of law. The study of law *of* performance focuses on legal representations of performance. But neither examines legal events and practices as, themselves, representations, taking place in courtrooms, examination chambers, places of judicial torture, execution sites, police precincts, prisons. This kind of analysis, law *as* performance, is what I am attempting in my larger project.

Such distinctions, of course, rely on a set of artificial boundaries that depend on spatial and medium metaphors (inside/outside, text/performance),—metaphors that are, like the aesthetic/nonaesthetic distinction, subject to many qualifications. It is the virtue of most studies of law and performance to ignore such artificial boundaries, showing law to be created precisely through its refraction among various kinds of objects. Nevertheless, however artificial such distinctions may be, they do allow us to see how rare it is, in fact, to find sustained analysis of the visceral, kinaesthetic experience of legal events and practices: analysis of courtroom performances quickly disappear into readings of judicial opinions; analysis of police actions quickly disappear into readings of the performance pieces that represent them. Those who have worked on such material understand why: legal records do not tend to tell us about the viscera of event or practice; evidence is often maddeningly sparse and impenetrable; even when it can be found, its veracity is always suspect. But attention to such effects is uniquely valuable. If analysis of legal performance per se is routinely diverted into analysis of extralegal performance or the legal text, we cannot come to understand the specific narrative, structural, and kinaesthetic dynamics of law *as* performance. We cannot fully come to understand how legal events and practices work.

SOME LAW-AS-PERFORMANCE PARADIGMS

While each event or practice has its own historical particularities, a few transhistorical paradigms have come to shape my understanding of legal performance (paradigms that are not exclusive to law but particularly marked there). First, legal performances often attempt to reenact past events, whether literally (for instance, in trials) or symbolically (for instance, in torture or punishments). They are acts of conjuration: concretizing these events, relocating them in immediate time and space, transforming them into visually, spatially, kinaesthetically legible happenings, subject to the intervention of spectators. Attempting to root out outlawry, legal actors must also conjure it, and in so doing, they reproduce it, representing it in myriad forms. Scholars of law and literature often evoke narrative theory's classic dyads to describe the relationship between the background events leading up to a trial and the trial itself: the background events are the "story" (or *fabula* or *histoire*); the trial is the "plot" (or *sujet* or *récit*) that, effectively, narrates those events. But a dyadic analysis does not register the work that performance does. To understand this, we would arguably need to add a third term to narrative theory's classic dyad: "enactment," or "mimesis" in Aristotle's sense (that is, showing as opposed to telling). Legal examinations, or trials, or torture not only tell people what happened but *show* what happened. If legal narration elaborates, reorders, and resymbolizes the events it represents, so legal performance elaborates, reorders, and resymbolizes both background events and legal narratives.

Second (a point related to the first), in legal events, people regularly stand in for or represent others: lawyers stand in for plaintiffs or defendants; executioners stand in for the people or the princely power. What Joseph Roach has said of theatre and celebrity culture, one might also say of legal performance: it "generates a parade of substitutes, surrogates, stand-ins, body doubles, and knock-offs."[31] That is, legal performances are not only acts of conjuration but also acts of surrogation and symbolic substitution. Law seeks truth, but the mimetic substitutions that occur in legal events give that truth a multilayered fictionality. Law is supposed to be the institution in which language becomes reality through linguistic performatives, and decisions have the most real of bodily consequences. But, like theatre, it often works through representation or the staging of things that may be an illusion: figuring something absent (like metaphor or conjuration) or pointing to an elsewhere (like metonymy or the indexical). In this, law shares theatre's condition of simultaneous corporeality and illusoriness: it is real and happening here (in the bodies brought before those who watch), but it is also somehow always (to borrow from Schechner) in the subjunctive mood, the "as if."[32]

Third (and perhaps most important for my work), theatricality is not just a thing law does, but a thing toward which, in doing it, law expresses an attitude. That is, legal performances sometimes embrace their own theatricality, sometimes disavow it, or sometimes do both, acting out their ambivalence. Exploiting its performance medium, law may sometimes aspire to the power of theatre: its pomp and ceremony, its masquerades, its spectacular effects, its manipulation of the passions, its electric connection to the crowd of spectators. At other times, it may revile, rebuke, or disavow its own latent theatricality: enact its opposition to legal histrionics, or perform its own invisibility (visibly concealing its occult secrets in behind-the-scenes chambers). Law sometimes enhances its power by exploiting theatrical means. But it also sometimes enhances its power—its legitimacy (its law-ness)—by repudiating those means: to refuse to allow law to become a "circus," "carnival," "theater and spectaculum" is to proclaim one's superlegality. Overt theatricality appears in law as an embarrassing bit of supplementarity (law is, after all, supposed to be purely instrumental). And yet, that theatrical supplement sometimes turns out to be precisely the thing that is most instrumental to an outcome. Law oscillates between theatricality and antitheatricality, visibility and invisibility, make-believe and reality—an oscillation that is not an exception in law's history, but a chronic refrain, deep in the structure of its institutions, practices, doctrines, and, above all, the events and practices through which it unfolds.

Answers to the questions I raised at the beginning of this chapter about the Scottish witch trials will have to await an essay dedicated not to methodology but to the specific meaning of those events. Letting that essay-to-come serve as the conclusion to this one, I will merely say here that, in those trials—as in so many legal events—expressive, communicative, three-dimensional, sensory, kinaesthetic, embodied articulation mattered, not only to specific outcomes, but to issues in the broader history of law. Looking at legal performance there, as elsewhere, suggests one new direction for law and literature—a way of taking what law and literature has taught us about the importance of representation, the aesthetic, and culture and using it to look into the heart of legal events—in the process transforming our understanding of law.

NOTES

1. *News from Scotland* (originally 1591), in Lawrence Normand and Gareth Roberts, eds. *Witchcraft in Early Modern Scotland: James VI's Demonology and the North Berwick Witches* (Exeter: University of Exeter Press, 2000), 321 (quotations from *News* and trial documents hereafter cited to this collection in the text). The pamphlet was probably written by James Carmichael.
2. *Newes from Scotland* (London: William Wright, 1591?), sig. B1v.
3. Giovanni Battista De Luca, *Theatrum veritatis, et iustitiae*, 21 vols. (Rome: Corbelletti, 1669–81).
4. Estes v. Texas, 381 U.S. 532, 571, 605 (1965); and Sheppard v. Maxwell, 384 U.S. 333, 358 (1966).

5. Julie Stone Peters, "Law, Literature, and the Vanishing Real: On the Future of an Interdisciplinary Illusion," *PMLA* 120 (2005): 442–53.

6. Clifford Geertz, "Thick Description: Toward an Interpretive Theory of Culture," in *The Interpretation of Cultures: Selected Essays* (New York: Basic Books, 1973), 3–30.

7. The classic distinction has arguably been superseded, since most law and literature studies treat both literary and legal texts, but it is nonetheless useful for distinguishing the field's objects.

8. Bypassing a more extended philosophical discussion, my use of the word "aesthetic" in this chapter is shorthand for the kind of representations generally treated as either art or entertainment: literature, theatre, visual art, theme parks, and so on. This shorthand is intended to distinguish between these and legal texts or historical events and practices, which also, of course, have aesthetic and representational properties but are not institutionally framed as art or entertainment.

9. Material objects and remains are, of course, traditional sources for archaeologists and historians, and many performance historians (most notably Diana Taylor, Rebecca Schneider, and Joseph Roach) argue that the performed repertoire serves as a kind of alternative archive. See, for instance, Taylor, *The Archive and the Repertoire: Performing Cultural Memory in the Americas* (Durham, NC: Duke University Press, 2007), 20 (and throughout). That said, even performance historians tend to rely primarily on verbal texts, images, and recordings.

10. The tale recounted in *News* (319–20)—in which John Fian bewitches the hair of a "young virgin heifer" (thinking it is his beloved's pubic hair), and she proceeds to pursue him into his church, amorously mooing—appears nowhere in the legal documents. See the similar tale in *The Golden Ass* (Bks. 2.32 and 3.15–18), and the editors' discussion in Normand and Roberts, *Witchcraft in Early Modern Scotland*, 299, 308.

11. Richard Schechner, "Restoration of Behavior," in *Between Theater and Anthropology* (Philadelphia: University of Pennsylvania Press, 1985), 35, 52.

12. Peggy Phelan, *Unmarked: The Politics of Performance* (New York: Routledge, 1993), 146. Despite Phelan's repudiation of it, the claim has remained influential.

13. See especially Erving Goffman, *The Presentation of Self in Everyday Life* (Garden City, NY: Doubleday, 1959); Jacques Derrida, "Signature Event Context," *Glyph* 1 (1977): 172–97; and Judith Butler, *Gender Trouble: Feminism and the Subversion of Identity* (New York: Routledge, 1990).

14. "performance, n.," *OED Online*, September 2016. Oxford University Press, http://www.oed.com/view/Entry/140783?redirectedFrom=performance#eid.

15. Abel Boyer, *The Royal Dictionary Abridged* (London: Bathurst, et al., 1767) (no pagination).

16. Theophilus Lobb, *Rational Methods of Curing Fevers . . . Together with a Particular Account of the Effects of Artificial Evacuations by Bleeding, Vomiting, etc.* (London: John Oswald, 1734), 66. The *OED* cites earlier passages that associate "perform[ance]" with drama, ballet (etc.), but, in context, it becomes clear that only the general meaning (accomplishment) is at work.

17. Samuel Johnson, *A Dictionary of the English Language*, vol. 2 (London: J. and P. Knapton, et al, 1755) (no pagination).

18. Noah Webster, *An American Dictionary of the English Language*, vol. 2 (New York: S. Converse, 1828) (no pagination). After Webster's, I have found no dictionary giving "performance" this special meaning before Charles Fleming's

Royal Dictionary English and French and French and English, 2 vols. (Paris: Firmin Didot frères, 1846–60), 1:845.

19. In German, for instance, *die darstellenden Künste*.

20. The *OED* identifies an earlier instance in Shaftesbury's *Characteristics* (1711): "There must be an Art of Hearing found, e'er the performing Arts can have their due Effect" (1.3.240). However, given that Shaftesbury is referring primarily to criticism (with printed texts a central focus), and that "Hearing" is only a metaphor for critical reception, it becomes clear that he is not using the phrase in the modern sense, but means something more like "productive arts." The first instance I have found of the phrase "performing art" or "artist" to distinguish these from other arts is in "Hungarian Radio Co. v. Gramophone Co., Ltd., London," *American Journal of International Law* 29 (1935), 699. The *OED* offers no instance of the phrase "performing arts" between the Shaftesbury quote and 1946, when New York's High School of Performing Arts was founded.

21. "'Showing doing' is performing: pointing to, underlining, and displaying doing." "The underlying notion is that any action that is framed, enacted, presented, highlighted, or displayed is a performance." Schechner, *Performance Studies*, 28, 2.

22. The opposition between "theatricality" and "performance" was axiomatic in the early years of performance studies. See, for instance, the section on "*Performance*, or the Subversion of Theatricality," *Modern Drama* 25 (1982), 154–81.

23. Judith Butler, *Bodies that Matter: On the Discursive Limits of Sex* (New York: Routledge, 2011), 177, 181.

24. NYU Tisch School of the Arts, *Institute of Performing Arts Performance Studies B.A. M.A. Ph.D. Programs*, 3, http://www.flipsnack.com/NYUPerformanceStudies/department-of-performance-studies-brochure.html.

25. See, for instance, Pierre Bourdieu, *The Logic of Practice*, trans. Richard Nice (Stanford, CA: Stanford University Press, 1990), 52–65.

26. Alan Read, *Theatre and Law* (London: Palgrave, 2015) (a ninety-six-page contribution to Palgrave's "Theatre &" series).

27. Joseph Roach, *Cities of the Dead: Circum-Atlantic Performance* (New York: Columbia University Press, 1996); Joshua Takano Chambers-Letson, *A Race So Different: Performance and Law in Asian America* (New York: New York University Press, 2013).

28. Catherine M. Cole, *Performing South Africa's Truth Commission: Stages of Transition* (Bloomington: Indiana University Press, 2010); Robin Chapman Stacey, *Dark Speech: The Performance of Law in Early Ireland* (Philadelphia: University of Pennsylvania Press, 2007); Lucy Finchett-Maddock, *Protest, Property and the Commons: Performances of Law and Resistance* (New York: Routledge, 2016).

29. See, for instance, Kenji Yoshino, "The City and the Poet," *Yale Law Journal* 114 (June 2005): 1838.

30. Such studies do sometimes look at the performances that the relevant legal texts discuss, but these are generally extralegal (splitting off into law *in* performance analysis within law *of* performance analysis).

31. Joseph Roach, "Celebrity Erotics: Pepys, Performance, and Painted Ladies," *Yale Journal of Criticism* 16 (2003), 216.

32. Schechner, "Restoration of Behavior," 37.

CHAPTER 12

Globalizing Law and Literature

ELIZABETH S. ANKER

As a primarily American, and secondarily European, phenomenon, the law and literature movement has typically taken the national and local as its main points of reference, focusing on either United States jurisprudence or the domestic laws of various European nation-states. However, recent years have witnessed the globalization of the interdiscipline: its expansion to concerns of a worldwide or international scale, often from a comparative perspective. This deterritorialization of law and literature has opened the field to a wealth of new inquiries, including debates about method. Indeed, the globalization of law and literature represents one of the field's most comprehensive recent transformations—a transformation that productively challenges many orthodox ideas about law, literature, and their cross-pollinations.

The factors motivating this turn to the global—both within law and literature scholarship and the academy at large—are multiple. It responds most immediately to the changing nature of sovereignty in a post-Westphalian world order. The past decades have been characterized by the growing juridification as well as influence of supranational law and policy-making bodies, whether the courts of the European Union or human rights monitoring agencies or quasi-legal institutions created by treaties and nongovernmental agreements. These developments have understandably shifted the jurisprudential gaze from nation-state law and diplomacy to other vectors of regional, global, and nonstandard sovereignty. Meanwhile, the birth of postcolonial studies in the 1980s electrified many fields within the Anglo-American academy, especially literary studies. Scholars of postcolonial or world Anglophone and Francophone literature began to investigate the instrumental role played by law under empire and in the tumultuous wake of decolonization, as is dramatized in many widely read and taught literary texts. More recently, scholarly emphasis on "neoliberalism" has further trained attention on geopolitics. With its own colonizing logic, neoliberalism is typically understood to subsume all legal-economic-political-social activities within its orbit.[1] Yet while totalizing, neoliberalism has equally spawned unofficial, contraband, and illicit channels and flows of people, goods, and information that progressively subordinate the nation-state to their rival jurisdictions. These conduits are themselves facilitated by quasi-juridical, binding regulations and rules, even if are not formally codified in law.

Clearly, many of the above are recent and hence historically specific developments. Nonetheless, they find roots in, and accordingly demand analysis with reference to, law's long history of entanglement with imperial dispossession. Studies of sovereignty under colonization, in one sense, suggest that it was never unitary or monolithic; rather, pre-colonial and colonial territories alike were cross-sectioned by multiple overlapping and contested sovereignties, just as today fiefdoms and overlords often wage warfare over and control substantial areas of the global South.[2] In another sense, many authoritative legal devices and constructs—whether the "corporate" form, or principles of humanitarianism, or risk-based insurance law (as I'll consider below)—were devised and perfected in the imperial theater. These imbrications reveal the current guises of globalization to be far from unprecedented or original, while also pointing to the tainted genesis of international law in practices of disenfranchisement and injustice.

An acute awareness of these dark pasts has guided the methodology of much law and literature scholarship that adopts a global frame, frequently rendering the law and literature critic's primary task one of excavating and interrogating the law's troubling histories. A number of common rationales for placing literature into dialogue with law are shaped by not only such goals but also the assumptions they marshal about the two separate disciplines. Typically, literature is enlisted as a vehicle for exposing and decrying law's many wrongs and failures, causing law to be regarded in an overridingly ominous, suspicious light. Globalization, likewise, is typically scripted as the inevitable march of power, domination, and neoliberalization—of corporatization, rationalization, instrumentalism, and capitalist exploitation—to which law is a mere handmaiden. Especially studies of law in the global South have tended to therefore submit law to a thoroughgoing process of debunking and negative critique, as the critic uncovers the many exclusions, crimes, and complicities written into law's basic architecture. Law is accordingly pronounced to be constitutively fraudulent and corrupt—often beyond salvaging. Whereas literature, in contrast, is celebrated for counteracting law's liabilities and instead purveying justice and ethics. This common way of explaining the interdisciplinarity nexus, however, opposes literature to law in unilateral and imbalanced terms, privileging the former while supplying a caricatured, reductive, inaccurate portrait of the latter.

Yet a different story—a less bleak, less singularly threatening one—can simultaneously be told about law in an ever-more enmeshed, interdependent world. This is not to deny either how the law historically structured the colonial encounter (as the next section considers) or its ongoing neoimperial violence. Rather, recent scholarship on globalization conceptualizes law as a complex, multifaceted, fluid, and fluctuating conglomeration of practices that are simultaneously synergistic and diffuse, centralized and centrifugal, networked and compartmentalized. Whereas "law" is often theorized as clearly localizable, definable, and delimitable, it more accurately represents a multinodal, far-flung, layered phenomenon that includes within its provenance an array of irregular, informal, bootlegged, and extrajuridical spheres of rule making, dominion, and exchange. On one hand, the proliferation of these illegal profit centers and renegade authorities can and should be worrisome, given how black markets and local despots are not only prone to abuse but often sustained by duplicity, vice, and exploitation. But on the other hand, those unsanctioned axes of governance, fiscal productivity, and norm construction can be deeply capacitating. Enabling alternate economies of collaboration and trade, nonstate sovereignties are ripe for harnessing and manipulation in ways that escape the reach and parameters of neoliberalism—indexing the limits of neoliberalism as an analytic.

In the global South, law is increasingly regulated by informal, contraband economies, and some theorists have therefore looked to the postcolony as a harbinger of the larger world's legal, political, and fiscal futures.[3] Within such analyses, "law" per se becomes something of a misnomer, given how the many sovereignties that cross-section any given geographic space are not totalizable, monolithic, or static. The meaning of "legality," too, must therefore be reconceived as intersectional, interstitial, uneven, mutating, and dynamic—carrying significant implications for our existing conceptual models. Such an expanded understanding of law and legality suggests why an exclusive focus on law's sinister duplicities can perpetuate inaccurate, simplistic, and exaggerated accounts of law that miss or gainsay the nuances of its real-world operations. In addition, a strictly skeptical view of law is prone to overlook the ethical, communal dimensions of its growing deterritorialization, insofar as within such a process all laws and legalities (whether corporate or state) become provisional, contextual, and contested. No doubt, here again there are important exceptions. Development regimes, for instance, frequently inflict forms of fiscal servitude on community-based, local patterns of coexistence, causing neoliberal power structures to encroach on them even as they defy external influence. These and other tools of extortion and control do require vigilant critique. That said, theoretical analysis must also document and affirm the matrices of mutual benefit, generosity, and sharing that productively elude the profit-driven, market-based appetites of global capital. These countervailing energies of globalization are valuable for numerous reasons. They can effectuate non- or countercapitalist practices of equitable partnership and trade that are exportable to other regions and contexts. Those modes of reciprocal indebtedness can furthermore cultivate habits of resistance that thwart full assimilation into neoliberal economic systems. Perhaps counterintuitively, the untapped ethical promise latent in these alternate vectors of sovereignty has, by many accounts, multiplied under globalization. Globalization, in other words, does not entail a single, unbroken narrative of homogenization, conformity, incorporation, and power imposed by Northern profit centers on the South; to the contrary, it simultaneously proliferates exceptional, insurgent zones and liaisons that are pregnant with opportunity.

The remainder of this chapter evaluates how law and literature scholars have tended to assess both the globalization of law and the status of law in the postcolony. Within many widely read and taught texts of postcolonial and world literature, the law functions as a something of a main character. With frequency, law and judicial process are depicted as, even as they lend sanction to colonial rule, actively guaranteeing its hierarchical and oppressive logic. These portrayals of law have understandably helped to create the expectation that, for the law and literature critic, law should foremost occasion skepticism and mistrust, given its historical support for imperial domination. The next section of this chapter therefore examines a series of literary texts that characterize law in such overwhelmingly negative terms. But in addition, literature can reflect the variegated, ambivalent aspects of globalization in ways that complicate a narrowly condemnatory view of law and legal process. This chapter therefore concludes by discussing a novel that requires a significantly more ambivalent as well as balanced view of law and legality in the global South. Although Nuruddin Farah's 1993 *Gifts* protests the coercive lending practices that usually accompany foreign aid and relief packages, it simultaneously contemplates the local, networked economies of mutual benefit, gift giving, and exchange that are motored by globalization yet evade neoliberalism's logic. Within the novel, these countervailing dimensions of globalization inspire unexpected, clandestine loyalties and extralegal yet meaningfully binding bonds and accords. *Gifts* thereby offers a complex, dense portrait of globalization that contends with not only its risks but also its many opportunities.

The disciplinary force of law looms large in a number of classic literary texts about empire. Indeed, a preoccupation with law has shaped received ideas about the colonial encounter since the emergence of anti- and postcolonial Anglophone and Francophone literature. We can think of E. M. Forster's 1924 *A Passage to India*, the entire plot of which hinges on the outcome of a visible and controversial trial.[4] Following a spelunking adventure to the local Marabar Caves, the Indian Dr. Aziz is wrongly accused by the young Englishwomen Adela Quested of assault. When the legal system gets ahold of these accusations, they spiral out of control, incensing the British community. Even though Adela eventually retracts her erroneous charge on the witness stand, law is shown in Forster's novel to be a central technology of imperial domination with its own independent force and momentum. And precisely its spurious neutrality is what enables law to manage deeper anxieties of empire while seamlessly and efficiently carrying out the project of colonial governance.

In many respects it is this impersonal, abstract, rationalist character of law that permits it to effectuate the work of imperial domination. The law's anonymous, detached authority renders it unassailable and absolves individual actors of blame. Many acclaimed texts dealing with the colonial encounter wrestle with that very ruse—and in turn with the isolated individual's moral responsibility relative to law's objective, measured violence. For instance, J. M. Coetzee's 1980 *Waiting for the Barbarians* investigates the ethical quagmire faced by an unnamed Magistrate—a designation clearly marking him as law's representative—when imperial forces descend upon the remote, ordinarily peaceful outpost he administers.[5] The wrath inflicted by the imperial army on effectively harmless "barbarians" reveals the ruthless cruelty at the heart of empire, cruelty ordinarily suppressed in its mundane operations overseen by the Magistrate. These events confront the Magistrate with his own moral implicatedness and, by extension, the disconnect between law and justice. While the Magistrate publicly denounces the empire's atrocities, those efforts are fruitless, exposing imperial law as polluted to its core. Although the Magistrate attempts to extricate himself and flee, Coetzee's novel instead dramatizes the futility of both principled resistance and his disavowal of moral accountability. *Waiting for the Barbarians* thus lays bare what is often described as the ontology of empire; however, it does so only to demonstrate law's fatal complicity with empire's crimes. In Coetzee's novel, the law is neither ancillary nor a mere helpmate to but fully constitutes the central machinery of imperial dispossession.

A long and wide-ranging story could be told about how colonization and slavery incubated and fashioned multiple legal institutions and constructs. Whether the corporation, the legal person or subject, or human rights, many contemporary legal forms and fictions were directly borne out of those dual institutions. Law and humanities scholars have sought to excavate those fraught geneses, showing how empire and slavery were more than licensed by but fully wrought a number of foundational legal principles and categories. For instance, Saidiya Hartman's 1997 *Scenes of Subjection: Terror, Slavery, and Self-Making in Nineteenth-Century America* was seminal in displaying such connections. Hartman studies law under American slavery and into the reconstruction era to show how legal notions tied to liberty and citizenship were, throughout that period, "consolidated by the mechanisms of racial subjection that [they] formally abjured."[6] Slavery, in other words, was "the object or the ground that makes possible" various tenets of American legal culture that exist yet today (62). Hartman thus arraigns the ostensible neutrality and universality of law and its classificatory systems for, first, shoring up slavery as an institution and, second, actively necessitating practices of enslavement for their basic intelligibility and coherence.

As I've suggested, conclusions akin to Hartman's have represented the dominant view within much law and literature scholarship, especially work concerning the twinned histories of slavery and empire. And just as suspicion of law emerges in many now canonical critical-theoretical texts, contemporary authors of imaginative literature continue to confront the law's stained, even criminal design. To such ends does M. NourbeSe Philip's acclaimed 2008 long poem *Zong!* explore the origins of risk-based contract and insurance law in the eighteenth-century transatlantic slave trade.[7] Philip contemplates how the perils of the Middle Passage gave rise to new forms of speculative finance that reduced human lives to chattel or property capable of being indemnified against loss. *Zong!* is a book-length volume, and the majority of it is composed of a multisegmented poem that recreates the imagined scene aboard the slave ship the *Zong*, whose captain notoriously decreed the murder of 150 slaves when he interpreted the provisions of an insurance agreement to deem their death by drowning more profitable than by natural causes (i.e. thirst or starvation) after unexpected delays on the journey. That act of violence was memorialized in the historical record when the ship's owner sued to collect on the insurance contract, a claim initially upheld by a jury but remanded for retrial by the English Court of King's Bench in the published legal decision *Gregson v. Gilbert*. Scholars have approached the decision as both formative in the history of opposition to slavery and emblematic of the tainted roots of risk-based lending and finance.[8]

One noteworthy feature of *Zong!* is its unusual structure. While a 182-page poem opens the volume, a series of postscripts or addenda follow it. First comes a Glossary translating the non-English words populating the text—words that derive from a total of fourteen languages. Those languages include not only six African tongues but also Arabic, Latin, and Hebrew, complicating whatever boundary might separate Old World from New, or modern from premodern civilizations. Next comes a strange "Manifest": by dictionary definition, a catalog of cargo produced for customs. However, this itemized list includes categories for "Body Parts," "Nature," and "Women Who Wait." Highly ambiguous, those designations illustrate the indeterminate status of ideas about property and self-ownership at the very historical moment when the institution of slavery consolidated their contemporary meanings. The Manifest thus stages a separate indictment of the legal classification of the Zong's human-slave cargo. As vehicles for retroactively deciphering the poem, the Glossary and Manifest are succeeded by a longer prose section "Notanda," in which Philip performs a type of autocriticism of her own poetry. Although she recounts her decision to compose and publish the volume, Philip also explicates her aesthetic strategies and symbolic gestures. Autobiographical, this segment of *Zong!* recalls the agony of "not tell[ing] the story that must be told" (189), although by enlisting almost academic prose, including multiple footnotes.

Philip's self-commentary explicitly reflects on the poem's antagonistic relationship to the decision *Gregson v. Gilbert*, a reproduction of which ends the volume. While thereby withholding the voice of law, the lyric and creative portions of *Zong!* conduct self-conscious dialogue with the decision's specialized idiom. As Philip explains, in the poem she sought to both "lock" or imprison herself within the "particular and peculiar discursive landscape" of the legal opinion (191) and to "mutilate the text" in ways analogous to the slave trade's destruction of African life (193). Philip relates those efforts in visceral, graphic language, as requiring the legal text's "castrati[on]" and "mayhem" that leaves her "hands bloodied" (193). Yet although the law's grammar pervades the poem, *Zong!* relegates the archival and official record to the position of an afterthought or footnote. This strategy subordinates the law to alternate modes of telling while yet preserving it as the tragically controlling version of events. Such an organizational scheme also places the law's structural violence into high relief, rendering that violence all the more horrific. It likewise imposes circularity on the volume. Insofar as *Gregson v. Gilbert* in hindsight elucidates Philip's allusions and preoccupations (with the language of "necessity," "weight," "circumstance," and so forth), it directs the reader back into the poem: it demands that we reencounter the poem anew as a prolonged assault on the dehumanizing, objectifying language of law. Hence, *Zong!* invites its own rereading, a rereading that itself enacts the cyclical, interminable nature of historical trauma. Although the legal decision might appear to establish closure, the volume's organization actively subverts any such pretense of finality or resolution.

Inextricable from this assault on the grammar and reasoning of law is *Zong!*'s conjuring of the affective and visceral immediacy of experience on the ship. Much as *Zong!* purports to summon the submerged past, Philip disavows her own individualized authorship, as the title page reads: "As told to the author by Setaey Adamu Boateng." Yet the poem's opening one- or two-page segments (numbered through 26, at which point that ordering impulse falls apart) simultaneously mimic the balancing act of an accounting ledger, visibly dividing up words into columns on the page. Philip here reproduces the structure of both economic and judicial calculus, offsetting and counterpoising "the weight in want" with "in sustenance" over against "the loss" and then "the order in destroy" (5). However, Philip quotes the operational logic of law only to turn it on its head, quantifying loss in order to display how that logic masks and condones moral wrongdoing. *Zong!* critiques law precisely by parroting the law's abstract, measured, disengaged rationality, excavating its underlying violence.

Thereafter, ensuing sections of Philip's poem build into escalating chaos and vertiginous unreality. The body of the poem incorporates a cacophony of voices, languages, and perspectives, merging the many viewpoints aboard the ship into a single multivocal chorus. The text recurrently lapses mid-line or mid-stanza from one language into another, with the further effect of collapsing one subject position (slave versus captor) into the next. This mounting confusion conveys various phenomena at once: the desperation of a crew (and cargo) on the brink of dehydration and starvation due to diminishing supplies; the moral agony of crew members tasked with sacrificing the slaves; the general trauma of the Middle Passage; and the death throes of the drowning victims. The poem's emotion intensifies, and Philip materializes that pain not only in the aural and lyrical qualities of *Zong!*'s poetry but also in the visual layout of words on the page. While *Zong!* opens with sparsely populated pages that resemble the columns of a bookkeeping ledger, that semblance of reason and equanimity is eroded. Progressively, volumes of words come to be distributed over entire pages with what looks like growing pandemonium and incoherence. By its conclusion, a diminished typeface causes individual words to fade away, with some portions of text superimposed on top of others. As such, *Zong!* visually enacts the destruction of language that Philip describes as retribution for what that very language wrought in the hands of the law.

Zong! thereby unfolds an affectively charged denunciation of the legal system for not only sanctioning but directly authoring some of the most egregious crimes associated with the joint legacies of slavery and empire. Within Philip's text, the law elicits recrimination and attack as an active instrument of racialized terror. A text like Philip's accordingly reinforces what has been a common view for law and literature scholars: that law primarily demands censure and critique. It is relatedly with reference to those corruptions that *Zong!*, as for other literary texts, acquires its ethical-political-critical value and merits. One of *Zong!*'s overt goals is to exhume the historical traumas perpetuated and ratified by the legal system, and the corresponding conceit is that this labor of historical recovery will concentrate attention on analogous wounds inflicted by law in the present. *Zong!* channels not only the imagined spirits invoked in Philip's dedication but also the ongoing, lived realities of racial and other oppression presumably shared by many of Philip's readers.

While literary texts like *Zong!* thus offer productive avenues for grappling with law's routine violences, *Zong!* does so to unfold a near-uniformly damning account of law and legality. That focus on the distortions, biases, and injustices constitutive of law has, I've suggested, been widespread within law and literature scholarship. To be sure: the dual aftermaths of slavery and colonization make such wariness necessary and even commendable. Yet when such a mindset becomes the exclusive or predominant one, it can nonetheless encourage reductive or misleading ideas about law's actual, real-world operations. When a critic's main impetus involves disclosing the harms and exclusions inscribed within law, those negative limits come to be privileged—at the expense of the positive, salutary features of any given legal order. While not to gainsay the important labor of critique, a singular emphasis on negative exposure can encourage reductive, unidimensional, and clichéd understandings of law that downplay or neglect its virtues and accomplishments. Pathologizing law can furthermore lead to limiting (and overly gratifying) explanations of the law-and-literature nexus. When the fraudulent, broken aspects of law are granted hermeneutic priority, literary study finds justification in relation to—and can seem to need or depend upon—those failures. Law thus provides a foil or antithesis to the contrastingly redemptive properties of literature, installing something of a binary code of "law bad / literature good." Such black-and-white configurations of the interdisciplinary juncture—wherein law is fatally flawed and literature latent with ethical promise—not only purvey idealized fantasies about the salvific attributes of aesthetic experience but also misrepresent the complex workings of law in an increasingly intertwined, globalized world. The machinations of law—especially in the context of waning national sovereignty—are rarely so one-sided, straightforward, or strictly pernicious. Nor is the complex traffic between literature and law so polarized, imbalanced, or predictable.

In recent years, some humanities-based studies of law in international and postcolonial contexts have therefore sought to develop theoretical frameworks better calibrated to conceptualizing emergent types of contra- and extralegal dominion. For instance, the 2006 essay collection *Law and Disorder in the Postcolony* investigates the unprecedented forms of lawlessness that have, ironically, accompanied post–Cold War democratization in formerly colonized states. As Jean Comaroff and John L. Comaroff contend in the Introduction, the rise of market fundamentalism has paradoxically blurred the lines separating law from illegality to propagate "outlaw cultures . . . infused with the spirit of law."[9] Under neoliberalism, ambiguous zones of jurisdictional indistinction—or what they term "twilight markets"—have become highly lucrative, often motivating North-South collaboration that exploits those ambiguities.[10] These jurisdictional aporias, the Comaroffs argue, splinter or dissipate the sovereignty of the state by transferring modes of quasi-legal authority to counterfeit, piratical, or forged economies that acquire influence precisely by mimicking or impersonating statehood. While eroding the legitimacy of law and its protections, these growing areas of deregulation can simultaneously be "spaces of opportunity, of vibrant, desperate inventiveness and unrestrained profiteering."[11] Although artifacts of neoliberalism, the modes of lawlessness overtaking the postcolony are ripe for maneuvering in ways creatively defiant of neoliberalism's scope and logic. Importantly, the Comaroffs herald these proliferating spheres of liminal, contested jurisdiction as the eventual path of all law under globalization. Rather than treating the postcolony as an aberrant site of legal anarchy, they understand it as a forerunner of juridical realities destined to become globally ubiquitous.

In *Extrastatecraft: The Power of Infrastructure Space* (2014), Keller Easterling similarly explores the burgeoning of a different but related phenomenon that she terms "extrastatecraft." Extralegal yet claiming state and official sanction, the primary examples Easterling studies are export processing and free trade zones, global broadband networks, and various transnational standard-making organizations.[12] Like the piratical economies of the postcolony, these technologies of "infrastructure space" usurp and evade the prescribed channels of law, at the same time as they impose binding regulatory procedures that act as blueprints for state planning and decision making. Such new engines of clandestine governance can, on one level, carry dangerous consequences, either because they lack the checks and balances intrinsic to formal legal systems or because they camouflage yet consolidate the power of both states and capital. Supported by powerful legal-economic enticements and exemptions alike, extrastatecraft can override or circumvent local law and its safeguards, akin to how free-trade zones provide safe harbor for human rights abuses. Even mere informational conduits like broadband marshal powerful, material effects—redistributing resources and reterritorializing space.

Yet on another level, Easterling examines how extrastatecraft is manipulable, dynamic, and open to active molding and intervention. Easterling thereby challenges the tendency to decipher such practices as straightforward, unilateral vectors of militarism, liberalism, or rationalization. Rather, infrastructure space carries untapped, undisclosed political bearings with resistant and even activist potential.[13] Extremely malleable, the very properties of extrastatecraft that render it a vehicle of political and economic power can be leveraged to divergent ends, for Easterling, through unexpected tactics like counternarratives, gossip, the gift, comedy, distraction, and exaggerated compliance. Indeed, Easterling demonstrates how extrastatecraft can supply latent ethical resources and opportunities. As she argues, extrastatecraft can cultivate interdependencies that broker "a more reciprocal disposition" and "interplay" entailing a "politics of balance rather than control."[14] Insofar as these webs of governance are becoming progressively dominant and authoritative, they do not, for Easterling, spell doom. To the contrary, they assemble capacities that can be harnessed to refute or escape the machinery of neoliberalism. Easterling's account of extrastatecraft thus further illustrates why law's globalized activities are not unambiguously lethal or colonizing but instead layered, multifaceted, networked, and dense with possibility. New conceptual schemes are needed to map those insurgent energies—as they both incapacitate and empower.

Just as new models for grasping the status of law in a globalized world are needed, the role of literature relative to law's increasingly polyvalent, dispersed, and contraband energies must be rethought. The Somali author Nuruddin Farah's *Gifts* suggests one basis for thus reenvisioning law and literature. Farah's depiction of life in the postcolony echoes both Easterling's and the Comaroffs' analyses. *Gifts* follows the plight of recently bereaved, single mother Duniya as she attempts to make ends meet in Mogadishu during the early 1990s—and hence against the backdrop of the Somali famine. Notably, Duniya does not herself experience starvation or extreme poverty. However, *Gifts* interweaves her plight with that of the nation through self-consciously political dialogue and by periodically interspersing excerpts from alleged news media within the narrative. These plot interludes analogize Duniya's predicament as an unmarried women to the comparatively vulnerable African state. Duniya's marital status renders her understandably self-protective and wary of dependency or indebtedness, and that reluctance allows *Gifts* to reflect on the different economies of generosity, reciprocity, exchange, and debt that oversee existence within Somali culture. While *Gifts* evolves into a love story culminating with Duniya's marriage, its opening sequence finds her defensively negotiating with a male friend, Bosaaso (eventually turned suitor), over whether or not she can accept a ride to work from him and under what terms of repayment. Although they ultimately deem the arrangement a reciprocal gift, *Gifts* foregrounds Duniya's onus to guard herself against apparent kindness that in fact disguises domineering or extortionist behavior.

Countless other plot incidents surround types of gift giving and donation, some welcome and some not. An early chapter finds Duniya's daughter Nasiiba pale after donating blood (13), and even gonorrhea is construed as something one is unwittingly "given" by another (16). Duniya's supervisor at work has just returned from twenty years abroad having "donate[d] his services to the government and people of his country, accepting no payment" (17). Duniya, moreover, is by profession a midwife and nurse in an obstetrics ward—thus herself implicated in the webs of charity and obligation that *Gifts* contemplates. With Duniya's employment, Farah enlists a common trope in literatures from the global South, namely to liken the developmental woes of the postcolonial state to the birth of a human infant. Perhaps most memorable of such analogues is found in Salman Rushdie's 1980 *Midnight's Children*, whose protagonist and first-person narrator enters the world at the precise instant of Indian independence. This parallel is further developed in *Gifts* when Duniya is mysteriously bequeathed an unidentified, orphaned infant, whom she has no choice but to care for. This and other related incidents complicate the meaning of the novel's title: is the infant a gift or a burden? When and why do so many gifts, in *Gift*'s own language, come with "strings attached" (48)? And are those strings useful or disabling?

These quasi or debatable gifts that fuel Farah's plot on one level occasion a meditation on the double bind of Somalia under a system of Western aid that instates new kinds of indentured servitude. Published on the heels of the famine, an episode that rendered Somalia's reliance on foreign assistance a matter of sheer survival, the characters in *Gifts* repeatedly parallel their own day-to-day choices and interactions with the quandaries faced by the nation. As Duniya justifies herself, "Because unasked-for generosity has a way of making one feel obliged, trapped in a labyrinth of dependence. ... [H]aven't we in the Third World lost our self-reliance and pride because of so-called aid we unquestioningly receive from the so-called First World?" (22). In this way, *Gifts* unfolds a scathing critique of the fiscal and legal enslavement that development and foreign aid packages frequently impose on the global South. "Generosity" in such contexts becomes a ruse masking usurious lending practices that merely perpetuate the hierarchies of privilege and dispossession historically installed under empire. Sections of Farah's dialogue explicitly associate the contemporary dilemmas faced by the struggling African state with earlier imperial tactics that equally masqueraded as dubious gifts. Characters reflect on the legacies of cultural imperialism, wherein economic domination was inseparable from the "giving of worldviews" and religious beliefs that subsequently became integrated into Somali culture (96). In such ways does *Gifts* liken Duniya's position to that of the nation-state to highlight the paternalistic, condescending stereotypes and predatory, self-interested motives that frequently underlie Western beneficence. *Gifts* accordingly exhibits the profound suspicion about international politics and law that has been *de rigueur* for many postcolonial writers and critics. In particular, Farah's novel exposes humanitarianism to be merely the latest ideology enforcing both the fiscal subjugation of Africa and other global wealth disparities.[15]

But at the same time, *Gifts* affirms the tangled webs of mutual indebtedness and interdependence that internally regulate coexistence within the postcolony. Those intricate networks of precarity and obligation extend from formally and informally juridical practices and also impose near-contractual bonds; yet they are recurrently cast as bountiful, generative, and enabling. From one vantage point, *Gifts* contrasts Northern or European lifestyles with Somali custom, and the characters actively debate those alleged differences. Reciprocal gift-giving, Farah's characters attest, is engrained within Somali culture, and they celebrate the bonds and loyalties it fosters. To be sure, the narrative also reckons with certain liabilities of those norms, for instance by recalling Duniya's first arranged marriage to a blind, elderly man who had been a friend of her deceased father's. Against the cautions of her siblings and peers, Duniya opted to comply with her father's dying wish, which promised her "hand in exchange for a handsome horse" (38). Subsuming the bartering and exchange of women into the habits of reciprocal trade that its title simultaneously applauds, *Gifts* refuses to blithely romanticize those practices, underscoring their costs and contradictions.

Because whereas some such bargains enforce gender and other subordination, others carry substantial promise. Indeed, precisely the blurred boundaries separating welcome gifts from those that impose burdens or liabilities seem to be what endows them with their community-engendering power. The orphaned baby bestowed on Duniya represents one such example of a mixed blessing, and the characters extensively deliberate over their motives for keeping him, asking whether they emanate from "pure kind-heartedness," "goodwill," "mercy," or other factors (83). The baby, moreover, complicates the premise that debts are invariably unidirectional or imbalanced, as Bosaaso comments: "he is keeping us, in the sense of cementing [our] friendship." Bosaaso's statement in addition emphasizes the collectivizing impact of the gift, since caring for the baby becomes a prelude to their marriage. Although the child eventually dies (in another allegorical commentary on the troubled Somali nation-state), his community-building impact is momentous. Here, the baby's indeterminate status becomes a lesson in the disconnect separating the technical mechanisms of law from ordinary social practice. When Duniya and Bosaaso initially contact the police to check for reports of a missing infant, the inspector requires them to submit to the state bureaucracy and register as coguardians (72). On one hand, the law's supervision of their parentage foists artificial strictures on their investment in the child (and new relationship). But on the other, this oversight is capacitating, given how it formalizes and hence nurtures their budding partnership. The institutions of law are neither solely malevolent nor strictly disciplinary within *Gifts*; rather, juridical and contractual accountabilities embolden Farah's characters, whether to induce generosity or successful collaboration.

Gifts thereby contemplates a wide array of illicit yet socially binding gifts and debts that cohere the community constituted over the course of its plot. Its narrative traces a dense matrix of interlocking bonds and allegiances that exceed the jurisdiction of law yet carry near-juridical authority and force. These irregular, contraband norms and economies are what facilitate coexistence within the postcolony: economies predicated on informal, nonmonetary, organic fabrics of beholdenness and exchange that resist quantification or rationalization via the dual logics of capitalism and neoliberalism, yet are enforceable through their own enabling logics and customs. While those many local, clandestine, interwoven, and yet diffuse ties are suggested to emerge naturally from Somali culture, *Gifts* simultaneously construes them as part and parcel of globalization and its vast constellations. In such ways does *Gifts* dramatize the ethical as well as resistant opportunities that reside within globalization's many tributaries, some of which confound international law and order (with its overridingly capitalist orientation) and others of which leverage sovereignty in unexpected ways—to adopt Easterling's terms, to broker interplay and reciprocities. Within the novel's imaginative universe, gifts and the near-contractual burdens accompanying them propagate as much as they restrict, contributing to a vision of law as productive and fertile even under the long shadow of imperialism.

Along the way, *Gifts* suggests an alternate framework for explaining the law-and-literature nexus in the midst of intensifying globalization. Its plot does critique the neocolonial, paternalistic, imbalanced legal architecture that supports development and humanitarian regimes as well as international fiscal policy. However, its narrative simultaneously charts the quasi-legal force of the debts and solidarities that congregate community, affirming those synergies and connections. As a literary text, *Gifts* demonstrates how and why law and other expressions of sovereignty—not in spite of but precisely because those orders are riddled with innumerable pressures and tensions—can be sociopolitically capacitating. Indeed, Farah's characters exploit the latent frictions within the diverse sovereignties that enmesh them to ends that nourish their own precarious relationships. While not uncomplicated, legal and economic gifts, along with the complex textiles of indebtedness they produce, are not hostile or threatening in *Gifts* but instead make up the backbone of Farah's imagined community.

NOTES

1. See Wendy Brown, *Undoing the Demos: Neoliberalism's Stealth Revolution* (New York: Zone, 2015).
2. See Lauren Benton, *A Search for Sovereignty: Law and Geography in European Empires, 1400–1900* (New York: Cambridge University Press, 2010).
3. See Jean Comaroff and John Comaroff, eds., *Law and Disorder in the Postcolony* (Chicago: Chicago University Press, 2006).
4. New York: Mariner, 1965.
5. Reprint ed. (New York: Penguin, 2010).
6. New York: Oxford University Press, 1997, 118. For other important scholarship on law, literature, and slavery and its aftermath, see Orlando Patterson, *Slavery and Social Death: A Comparative Study* (Cambridge, MA: Harvard University Press, 1982); Stephen Best, *The Fugitive's Properties: Law and the Poetics of Possession* (Chicago: Chicago University Press, 2004); Jeannine DeLombard, *Slavery on Trial: Law, Abolitionism, and Print Culture* (Chapel Hill, NC: University of North Carolina Press, 2007); Colin Dayan, *The Law Is A White Dog: How Legal Rules Make and Unmake Persons* (Princeton, NJ: Princeton University Press, 2011); Lisa Marie Cacho, *Social Death: Racialized Rightlessness and the Criminalization of the Unprotected* (New York: New York University Press, 2012).
7. Middletown, CT: Wesleyan, 2008.
8. For example, see Ian Baucom, *Specters of the Atlantic: Finance Capital, Slavery, and the Philosophy of History* (Durham, NC: Duke University Press, 2005).
9. "Law and Disorder in the Postcolony: An Introduction," in *Law and Disorder in the Postcolony*, 19.

10. Ibid., 8.
11. Ibid., 9.
12. Keller Easterling, *Extrastatecraft: The Power of Infrastructure Space* (New York: Verso, 2014).
13. Ibid., 92.
14. Ibid., 136.
15. For other analyses of the politics of humanitarianism in *Gifts*, see Elizabeth S. Anker, "Teaching the Legal Imperialism Debate," in *Teaching Literature and Human Rights*, ed. Elizabeth Swanson Goldberg and Alexandra Schultheis (MLA Options for Teaching Series 2015); Pheng Cheah, *What is A World? On Postcolonial Literature as World Literature* (Durham, NC: Duke University Press, 2016).

PART 3
Cases

CHAPTER 13
Ornament and Law

ANNE ANLIN CHENG

Yes, sir; that is what distinguishes them from the virtuous female—that style.

Dr. Otis Gibson, clergyman, 1874

Figure 13.1 Arnold Genthe, *Dressed for the Feast, Chinatown, San Francisco* (1896–1906). Courtesy of Library of Congress Prints and Photographs Division, Washington DC.

The eminent English legal historian Frederic William Maitland once asserted, "The only natural persons are men. The only artificial persons are corporations."[1] While the concept of legal personhood, especially of abstract corporate personhood, has long been a subject of study for legal historians (Kennedy, Maitland, Noonan, Pocock, Wolin) and more recently for scholars in the humanities interested in notions of persona or artificial persons (Johnson, Slaughter, Turner), less attention has been paid to the constitutive and conjoined presences of race and sexuality in the making of this artifice.[2] Almost every term of Maitland's assertion comes into question when we introduce these two supposedly most biological of categories. Who constitutes "natural persons," and how do we move from a biological to a legal standing? What legal alchemy enables the transformation from singularity to collectivity, from embodiment to abstraction? And what does the "feminine"—simultaneously erased by Maitland's calculus and implicitly relegated to the realm of unnatural artifice—do to this equation? The exclusion of women and in particular women of color from discourse about legal personhood may not surprise us, but the critical agency that their presences lent to the adjudication of what counts as a person in US legal history may.

This chapter takes us back to a little-known nineteenth-century immigration case and the eccentric role that Asiatic female artifice played in order to bring into view some unexpected interconnections among ideas of natural and unnatural persons, legal and illegal subjects, citizenship and criminality. In particular, we will be tracking the insistent yet mercurial association between Chinese femininity and ornaments during the course of the trial. It is my gambit that the unlikely eruption of the ornamental in this heated immigration case can be highly instructive in showing us how a body comes to be legible to law. Indeed, I argue that ornamentation crystallizes the logic through which the *decoration* (rather than biology) of race is legally constructed. Ornament, which in this chapter encompasses both small and seemingly peripheral objects of decoration and the broader notion of clothing, plays a vital function in the legal production of race which in turn sanctions categories and hierarchies of oppression and affirmation. Throughout the chapter, I allow the term "ornament" to draw from and weave together several registers: a category of physical object; a logic of embellishment; a performance of self-marking; and a larger metaphysical debate about essence versus superficiality that has always attended to Western philosophic discussions about personhood. If masculinized natural personhood, itself the product of a long line of Enlightenment thinking about the human, provides the foundation on which legal personhood is built, because it is a body imagined to be imbued with essential and natural rights, then I offer in what follows a different genealogy of modern personhood: one that is deemed particularly artificial, feminine, partial, illegal, and non-European. This synthetic or criminalized figure, relegated to the margins of modernity and discounted precisely as a nonperson, nonetheless holds a key to the formative terms of modern citizenship and attending personhood. In other words, I want to trace not just an exclusion but also how that exclusion reveals the artifice animating the heart of modern natural persons. By turning our attention to a case that is little known but arguably one of the most significant habeas corpus cases in the second half of the nineteenth century, I want to retrieve a lost "body" in the history of the making of American legal personhood through the engine of citizenship, a moment furthermore that reveals the collusion of law, visuality, race, and gender. In the end, I suggest that it is at the seemingly superfluous periphery of ornamental details that the solemn stakes of legal personhood can be played out.

AT THE HARBOR

In August 1874, an American steamer named the SS *Japan*, carrying almost 600 Chinese passengers traveling from Hong Kong to America, docked in the San Francisco harbor after thirty days at sea (Figure 13.2). According to the National Climatic Data Center, it was a sunny balmy day, and for those with cabin fever, the sight of the sprawling city beyond the harbor must have offered a welcoming even if, for most, an unfamiliar sight.

That afternoon, Rudolph Piotrowski, the California commissioner of immigration and himself an immigrant from Poland, went aboard the ship and after a brief inspection allowed everyone to disembark, except a group of twenty-two young women ranging in ages from seventeen to twenty-three. Why not? "They were lewd," he said (Figure 13.3).[3]

Piotrowski thought the women were prostitutes. He based his judgment on two criteria: first, he found the women traveling alone (we might say, *undecorated* by husband or children); second, upon cursory visual inspection and a brief interrogation through translators, he found their appearances to be "perfectly unsatisfactory."[4] Moral delicacy, however, did

Figure 13.2 W. Endicott & Co. (lithographer), Pacific Mail Steam Ship Company's Steamer, Japan (New York, ca. 1868). Courtesy of Huntington Library, John Haskell Kemble Collections, Prints.

not prevent the commissioner from asking the ship's master, a Captain John Freeman, to pay a bond of $500 in gold coins (roughly equivalent to $10,000 today) for each woman to disembark.[5] When the Pacific Mail Ship Company for whom Freeman worked refused to pay, Piotrowski ordered the women detained on board and forcibly returned to Hong Kong on the ship's next voyage.

No one came forward to claim the women, but someone did obtain legal counsel for them.[6] In the four-day trial that followed in the Fourth District Court of San Francisco, Judge Robert F. Morrison agreed with Piotrowski's assessment and reaffirmed the state's right to protect itself from "immoral, pestilential visitation."[7] This decision was then echoed by the California Supreme Court. Both Piotrowski and the California Supreme Court turned to the 1874 State Political Codes that granted the commissioner of immigration the right to "satisfy himself whether or not any passenger who shall arrive in this State by vessel from any foreign port . . . is lunatic, idiotic, deaf, dumb, blind, crippled, or infirm . . . or is a convicted criminal, or a lewd or debauched woman."[8] Apparently, for California officials and in the eyes of the law, there was little difference between disability, immorality, and Chinese femininity.

The case then went before the Circuit Court for the District of California, where Justice Stephen Field, to the surprise and distress of some, ruled in

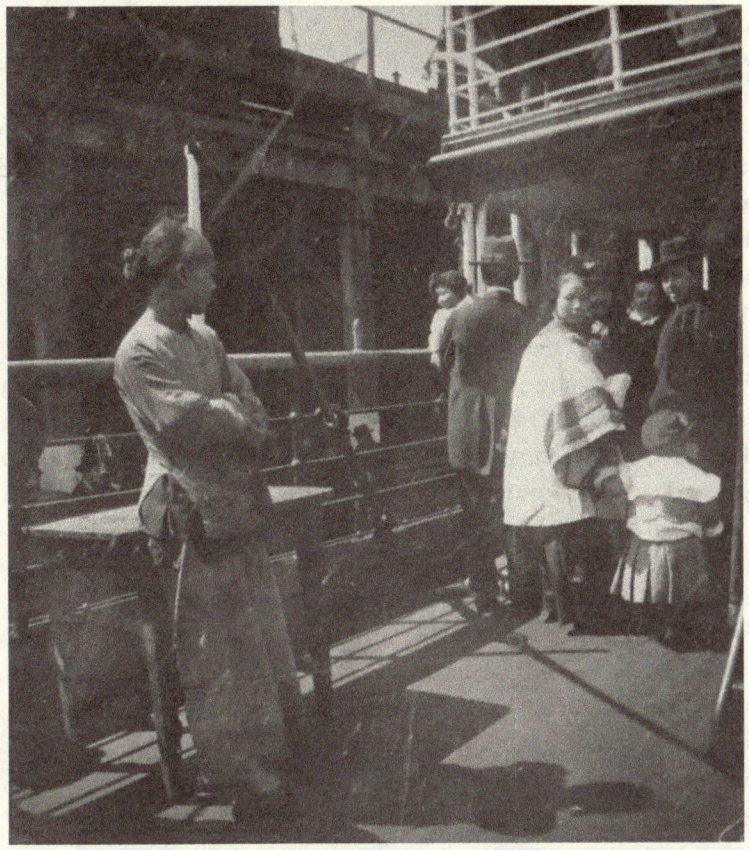

Figure 13.3 Unknown photographer, Chinese passengers on ferry in San Francisco Bay (ca. 1900). Courtesy of UC Berkeley, Bancroft Library, Burckhalter Family Collection.

favor of the women. Field, however, did not see this as a case about the women's personal or immigrant rights; instead, he saw the case as a dangerous instance of the state overstepping its power, and because of this, he recommended that the government take the case to the Supreme Court. The case, now known as *Chy Lung v. Freeman* (1875), subsequently went before the US Supreme Court, marking the first time that a Chinese litigant had brought suit before America's highest court. There, Fields's ruling was upheld and the women finally released ... only, it seemed, to disappear into the streets of San Francisco.[9]

It is worth noting that the women in question actually possessed the proper paperwork. As Judge Leander Quint, who was at the time acting as counsel on behalf of the women, pointed out during the trial, the women had a right to enter the country under the sixth article of the 1868

Burlingame Treaty between China and the United States. They all possessed signed travel documents and had been interviewed several times by both Chinese and US officials at Hong Kong. And the captain of the ship had testified that the women behaved with decorum throughout the journey and exhibited no signs of lewd behavior. Yet they were treated like criminals nonetheless.

At first glance, this case of discrimination against a little group of Chinese women is hardly surprising. Contrary to the welcoming banner of the Burlingame Treaty, anti-Chinese sentiments in California had long been brewing. California had already spent the previous decades passing laws with the goal of getting rid of the Chinese after having solicited their labor: the Foreign Miners Tax had siphoned off roughly one-half of Chinese miners' already low wages; the Chinese Police Tax had been charged to persons of the "Mongolian race"; Chinese adults were prohibited from testifying against whites in criminal or civil cases; Chinese children were denied access to the public school system. Legal, cultural, and pragmatic situations were such that it was extremely difficult for Chinese women to immigrate to America, whether to be with their husbands or to find work. During the course of the women's litigation, the Page Act (1875) would come into effect and, within a decade, the infamous 1882 Chinese Exclusion Act as well.[10] Indeed, we might see the Page Act as responding precisely to a ruling like *Chy Lung v. Freeman*. This is why the final victory for the Chinese women in this case may have been pyrrhic, because it spurred the backlash of racial-sexual panic to follow, a panic that would form the moral and legal basis for legislations during the Progressive Era.[11] Thus *Chy Lung*, also known as the "Case of the Twenty-Two Lewd Chinese Women," took place at that pivotal moment of transition when the Chinese were transitioning in the American national imaginary from "Celestial Beings" to the "Yellow Peril."

What is unexpected and puzzling about this case, however, is the intense and what turns out to be surprisingly complex visual component in the deliberations in the California courts and the complication that this focus produces at the intersection of raced bodies and the definition of a legally recognizable person. Unlike African Americans, whose legal racialization was based on something beyond visibility alone—that is, the 1/16th "blood" rule intended to bypass the deceptive potentials of the visible, as in the cases of passing—the racialization of the Chinese was historically tied to their physical appearances and their inescapably "foreign-looking" bodies. From political rhetoric to popular press, the discourse of Chinese difference has always been tied to a visual and corporeal vocabulary about highly visible differences in physiognomy and costumes of dress. And these differences are often cited as rationales for the inassimilability of the Chinese in American polity and culture.[12] But, as we shall see in a moment, the issue of ostentatious visibility would take on a series of twists and turns during this trial.

In the face of the burgeoning tension between state anxiety about Chinese immigration and American diplomacy in China, the Fourth District Court of San Francisco pursued what would at first appear to be a highly eccentric line of inquiry: the issue of the twenty-two young women's relationship to ornaments, including decorative objects and other sartorial styles. During the course of the trial, much if not most of the attention was paid to the question of decoration: detailed discussions about forms of costume; the colors, patterns, and feel of fabrics; the cuts of sleeves; and even categories of hair dressing. Thus, although this case invokes serious concerns about immigration policy and even thornier arguments about state versus federal power, these issues appear to have been sidetracked by the trial court's exceptional interest not in actual biological components or in the interpretation of the law but instead in the question of superficial, feminine style.

In order to determine the difference between "Chinese wives" and "Chinese prostitutes," the young women were displayed in court and several expert witnesses were called to provide accounts of Chinese courtesan sartorial style. Most of these witnesses were white men who did not know any of the women, did not speak Chinese, and were not on board the steamer, but whose sole qualification appeared to be that they resided in China at one point or another, or, as was the case with our first witness below, the fact that he, as he claimed, happened to have come to port to see, in his words, the curious sight of "a hundred or eighty Chinese women arriving in a ship"[13] According to these testimonies, certain sartorial practices offered tell-tell signs. One particularly animated witness, a Dr. Otis Gibson, who was a missionary in China, after reassuring the court that he has "no familiarity with prostitutes in any country," nonetheless offered the following detailed analysis:

> courtesans are in the habit of wearing a kind of flowered garments generally—not always, but generally. You will find silk; you will find silk yellow & figured, & things of that kind, which are not worn so much by the wives; the wives wear plain colors, except on gala days, when there is a great deal of dressing up for company.[14]

He also made observations about hair styles and decorative accessories:

> There is a certain class of prostitutes, boat-women, that wear handkerchiefs on
> their heads; the same women here do not always do it; the same class in every
> other respect do not always wear the handkerchiefs on their head.
>
> . . .
>
> the manner of dressing the hair is somewhat different, though I could not well
> explain it. They have many modes of doing the hair in different places.[15]

A Mr. Ira M. Condit followed and concurred that a penchant for festive and
bright colors (not surprisingly, especially the color yellow) indicates disso-
lute character. Prostitutes, he testified, wear:

> gayer style of dress, a dress with yellow in it, & brighter colors. There is no defi-
> nite dress which distinguishes them as such from the others more than that
> general feature of dress . . . [and again, later] they wear a great deal of bright
> yellow. . . . On occasion they ["the wives"] dress up very gayly; that is, when they
> go to the theatre, or to the burying-ground to feed the dead, and Josh days.[16]

The first thing that strikes us about these testimonies is their incoherence: signs of respectability (the silks worn by respectable wives of mer-
chants) resemble signs of debauchery (the silks worn by prostitutes); some
women definitely always sometimes wear certain hair dressing; "wives"
dress up on special occasions, but then so do "courtesans," and so forth.[17]
As the trial went on, even a respectable category like "Chinese wives"
became unreliable. A local police officer who oversaw the Chinatown
beat testified that he rarely saw anything untoward in Chinese familial
relations, though he also thought that the uncommon (that is, crowded
tenement) living arrangements in Chinatown made it very difficult to
ascertain "proper" familial relations, suggesting that the non-Christian
(that is, "heathen") Chinese may not in fact have understood the notion of
a proper marriage at all.

The weaknesses of the testimonies did not loosen the association
between Asian femininity and debauchery, nor at any point did anyone ascertain whether or not these women were in fact prostitutes
before they were treated as such. And while the women eventually won
their case, they were never explicitly exonerated from the presumptions made about them. The real circumstances of these women remain
shrouded in mystery, unavailable to history. It was wholly possible that
these women came, as they all testified, to find their spouses and to find

work. At the same time, the situation of Chinese women in America at the time was precarious, haunted on one side by the specter of human trafficking and on the other by the fracturing impact of Chinese male transpacific labor migration on Chinese familial structure in response to.[18] Many of the Chinese men living in the United States at that time had for all practical purposes abandoned their wives back in China and started new lives here, at times taking up new or second common-law wives. This may explain why the women in this case were not claimed by doting spouses or seemed not to know the exact whereabouts of the said partners. In short, little was known about these women, yet much was presumed.

Regardless of whether the women were or were not "licentious," the presumptions about their character, which here is directly linked to presumptions about their eligibility for legally recognizable personhood, rest on the seemingly frivolous category of ornaments.[19] At a time when the increasing influx of Chinese laborers into the United States was causing labor competition and when Euro-American views of China had started to shift from one of acquisitive fascination in the previous century to one of suspicion and contempt, this association between ornamentation and debauched femininity came to coalesce around—indeed, became synonymous with—the Chinese woman herself. So what is the relationship between (gendered and racialized) ornament and law? What does it mean to say that the law is indebted to a sartorial logic?

While it has often been observed that legal rhetoric has a penchant for sartorial metaphors (we speak of "the cloak of justice," "vested interests," "to pin a crime on someone," and so forth), the case of *Chy Lung* shows that that relationship may be, not simply rhetorical, but *structural*. The trial of *Chy Lung* shows us that the questions of habeas corpus (what it means to have a body) and "personhood" (what it means to be legally recognized) are far from given at the site/sight of the biological raced body. The most telling of all evidences in that courtroom—the materiality of the women's bodies—turns out to be the most spectral. For halfway through the trial, we discover that the counsel and witnesses for the state had a bit of a challenge: the much-cited ornaments were in fact rather elusive. Our good clergyman, Dr. Gibson, for example, had to reach for what is not readily available to the eye:

> They are accustomed to wear flowered gaudy kind of clothing—clothing that is not worn by respectable wives. There is no indelicacy in seeing or examining them; those women will show it if the'[sic] exposed there [sic] arms; & you will

find that under their outside clothing in 9 out of 10 cases some of this variegated silk or imitation of silk, some fancy clothes that has a bright color.

. . .

They have a black one on the outside, but just under that you will see the kind of cloth I was describing.[20]

This then led Mr. Ryan, the counsel for the state, to call forth several of the women in a row, in order to raise and peek into their sleeves. More eye-balling investigations ensued, with the men attending to the hems of the women's gowns, examining their hair, and there was even a heated debate about just how wide a sleeve can be before it tips into licentiousness.

According to court recording and press coverage, the women in question mostly wore uninteresting, black, loose-fitting clothes. All the categories that the California courts took to be *visually* and hence *materially* evident in this case—the citation of corporeality as evidence for racialized subjectiv-ity, the sociology of feminine decoration, the relations between skin and what rests on it—turn out to be not evident. The invocation of ostentatious female ornamentation—that most visible and material of categories—turns out to pivot on an elaborate articulation between imagined presence and projected absence. The women were simultaneously dressed up and stripped down. The evidence of an overmaterialized and scopically available body emerges, not out of bare flesh or real ornaments, but from their fan-tasmatic conflation, an overlapping of surfaces located in teasing peripher-ies: the borders of a collard, the peep of a hem, the gleaming edge of a sleeve.

To dismiss this scene as simply yet another regrettable example of racist prurience or Puritanical conservatism is to miss the extraordinary negotia-tion of the visible and the invisible at play here. What constitutes visual evidence? What does it mean to produce bodies as evidence, and what hap-pens to visuality itself in relation to the raced and gendered bodies? The California court took the Chinese female body to be self-evident. But how that body evidences the invisible in its visibility or vice versa has yet to be fully examined. What happens when we consider the ideas of "body," "skin", "cloth," and "ornament" as interrelated metaphors for thinking about "per-sonhood" in social and legal realms in the nineteenth century, and what are the legacies of these entwined ideas for the twentieth century?

AT THE EDGES OF OUR CIVIL BODIES

This little-known immigration case takes us far into our past and well into our future. In March of 1876, Justice Samuel Miller of the US Supreme

Court articulated three reasons for overturning the California Supreme Court ruling: first, the California state law allows petty state officials such as Piotrowski to extort money; second, the law produces shallow profiling; and third, the state does not have the power to determine immigration policy. As historian Paul Kramer puts it, "A legislative recipe for extortion; a capricious exercise of perception and power; a dangerous usurpation of federal law: What was *not* wrong with California's immigration law?"[21] Yet the lucidity of Miller's 1876 decision would seem to bear repeating, given, for examples, California's Proposition 187 in 1994 and Arizona's infamous immigration law in 2000. Both sought to allow state laws to intervene in federal immigration policy, and both profiled "illegal aliens" in ways that were finally found to be unconstitutional. Indeed, we might see the 1876 Supreme Court case as an ongoing rebuke to the practice of racial profiling from California to New York to this day.

Moreover, this 1876 case raises larger, theoretical concerns about our present conceptualizations of constitutional rights. What does it mean that our civil rights resort to a language and an ideal about "natural person-hood" when legal personhood is anything but natural? The Anglophone, Enlightenment conception of philosophic and hence legal personhood, from Thomas Hobbes to John Locke to William Blackstone, is indebted to a dominant fiction about natural personhood: the person as a living, organic, and organized human body "such as the God of nature formed us."[22] Obviously, the practice of slavery poses a challenge to this ideal. The recent works of scholars such as Stephen Best and Monique Allewaert, for example, focus on how the enslaved black body challenges this philosophic or legal construction of personhood.[23] Best contends that the conceptions of slave property are indebted to abstract rather than biological aspects of personhood, while Allewaert argues that plantation labor practices and ecological peculiarities compel us to reconsider the idea of a person as a discrete, purely biological agent. Here I suggest that the Asiatic body—especially the feminine, Asiatic ornamental body—sheds light as well on the particularly synthetic and sartorial roots of legal personhood with pro-found implications for contemporary conceptualization of the "natural" person and "natural" rights.

In the orientalism of the nineteenth-century California court, it is the *virtual ornamentality* of the women's bodies that allows the judges and lawyers to plunge into the "real" possibility of bearing witnesses to Asiatic femininity, to make the necessary slippage between the biological and dis-cursive body. But these "exceptional" bodies must compel us to reconsider to what extent is this slippage always already the condition of legal person-hood. The questions of *what is a natural body* and *what are its natural rights* have a long and troubled history in US legislation, especially when it comes to adjudicating which body counts and which does not. The writ of habeas corpus, for example, means literally in Latin "may you have the body." Yet what are the terms of this "body"?[24] Indeed, what "natural" bodies have what rights has been a constant problem for the courts when it comes to a racialized or gendered body. In *Roberts v. City of Boston* (1849), the desegregation case which served as a precedent for the "separate but equal" doctrine of *Plessy v. Ferguson* (1896), Justice Lemuel Shaw states:

> The great principle, advanced by the . . . advocate of the plaintiff, is, that . . . all persons without distinction of age or sex, birth or color, origin or condition, are equal before the law. This, as a broad general principle . . . is perfectly sound . . . *But*, when this great principle comes to be applied to the actual and various conditions of persons in society, it will not warrant the assertion, that men and women are *legally clothed* in the same civil and political powers. (emphasis added)[25]

All bodies may be considered equal, but their civil covering is not. Thus the issue here extends beyond legal personhood to what *lies on top* of that "person."

Is "skin" a natural attribute or a cloak of negating distinction? The court appears to be confirming equality before the law based on the commonality of naked bodies, but it immediately delimits that universality by subsuming the biological body to social cladding—or, more accurately, social ornamentation. Moreover, that social ornament is gendered and racialized: male versus female and white versus racial otherness. Thus, what starts out as potentially an affirmation of natural bodies as all equal before the law turns out to deny equality and to reconstitute the very powers and privileges of social construction to which race and gender are both subject.

In proclaiming that rights and personhood are decorative rather than biological or essential, *Roberts* reminds us that **constitutional personhood is a function of legal ornaments.**[26] Racialized skin, that most biologized of surfaces, is here implicated by the ornamental logic and subject to refabrication in the history of citizen making. Historian Mae Ngai has pointed out that, prior to the Johnson Reed Act of 1929, racial categories in the United States were far from rigid and that it took a great deal of juridical wrangling to make them so.[27] Legal categories of personhood are thus constructed along a series of delicate, necessary slippages between bodies and their surfaces, between essence and attribute. The marking of an unmarked body into a visible state of idealization or denigration relies on these conflations that the law both instantiates and represses.

This sartorial cladding of a person—a fundamentally decorative gesture that simultaneously effects embodiment and disembodiment—in order to render that subject visible in the eyes of the law reminds us that legal rights have very little to do with "natural" bodies even as this legal fiction has very real effects on very real bodies. Let us remember that those (unadorned and yet too-adorned) female bodies had already been subjected to other forms of erasure: imprisoned and stripped of rights (consider the duration of these women's ordeal in uncertain detention—even imprisonment—after already having been on board very cramped quarters for thirty days);[28] bodies that had been profoundly dislocated as products of transpacific labor migration. The ghosting of these women's bodies—through both physical custody and the cloaking logic of orientalist female visuality—veils the profound crisis of mobility that in fact conditions these women's lives on quotidian and global levels. In addition to the question of what was presumably shown on the surfaces or edges of these women's bodies as indexes for imagined character and interiority, there was also a long line of inquiry during the trial speculating on the question of "permission" given or not given to Chinese women (both in China and in Chinatown) to be walking on the streets at all. The quotidian constraint of female movement speaks to more than gender inequality; it also reminds us that these women, who had exiled themselves to embark on this daunting journey, had had to place themselves in the new global economy as both agents *and* commodities. The melancholy of this doubleness runs through *Chy Lung*. Some of these women came in search of husbands they barely knew and whose whereabouts they could only ascertain through hearsay; others came alone in a wild gambit for work and a better life, just like the men who had put themselves in the maelstrom of what Zygmunt Bauman calls "liquid modernity";[29] yet others most likely have been sold, with or without their knowledge and at times by their own families, into human traffic. Caught between a dream of self-fashioning and a legal system that cloaked them in racialized transparency, these women had to navigate a difficult, if not impossible, set of constraints conditioning the personal, cultural, social, and legal fabrications of their personhood.

This case registers a delicate moment—prior to the full denial of legal personhood that we see in the Exclusion Act of 1881 and on the cusp of the solidification of racial categories through the process of increasing race-based immigration restriction—when the issue is not quite yet so much legal personhood per se as what *kind* of person is or is not acceptable, that is, the *preconditions* for legal personhood. This case thus signals the beginning of a legal process of person categorization that will become the foundation for solidifying the modern racial categories as we know them today, which will in turn justify more stringent constitutional denials to come. Thus, while the Chinese women in this case were not denied legal personhood per se, their story shows that they were already being excluded from the narrative and idea of *modern personhood*, in so far as the latter implies property, family, civil society, and state. Those twenty-two young women did in the end win their writ for habeas corpus, but it is *how* that corpus gets spectrally produced as material evidence in the courtroom that sheds light on the sartorial (and, we might say, orientalist) logic informing the conceptualization of personhood and rights to this day.

Today, the language of the sartorial resurfaces in both critical legal studies and colloquial conversations, but this language is mostly invoked symptomatically to refer to the mourned divide between individual authenticity and social coercion, whereas I see a case such as *Chy Lung* as doing the important work of compelling us to see that: first, the sartorial as a function of the ornamental is more than rhetorical and speaks to something crucially structural about the law's imagination; second, more importantly, the relation between personhood and its external covers or decorations must be understood as vitally, even if disturbingly, imbricated.

Oriental sartorialism—or, what we might call *"ornamentalism"*— survives in our contemporary legal imagination in strange and convoluted ways. In his enormously popular study *Covering: The Hidden Assault on Our Civil Rights*, critical race theorist and constitutional scholar Kenji Yoshino astutely reminds us that contemporary antidiscrimination laws are specifically based on the protection of what are understood to be so-called natural and immutable traits (such as blood, chromosome, skin color, etc.); they do not protect what are thought to be "superficial" characteristics: behaviors, style, cultural practice, and other, we might say more "ornamental," practices.[30] Thus, an individual might not be able to get fired for being black or gay, but that same person can be fired for wearing corn-rows or for "flaunting" his or her gay marriage—in short, for style. And, for Yoshino, one of the tasks of formulating the new civil rights must be the freedom to exercise one's vision of one's sense of authenticity, the right to self-fashioning.

This call for authenticity, social visibility, and self-making is, of course, enormously appealing for anyone who has enjoyed neither. But the history of the delineation of racialized bodies that we have been studying here suggests that something more fraught is at stake here than notions of authenticity, or of suppressed or ineluctable visibility for that matter. Covers and ornaments can indeed enact a "hidden assault on our civil rights," but as we have seen (via the "clothing" of race), they also form the basis for anchoring our rights . . . and perhaps even our embodied sense of ourselves. It is beyond the scope of this chapter, but this discussion bears relevance for other "ornamental" practices such as the veil. More than simply a marker of racial and epistemic otherness, the veil also invokes complications about surface and essence, about the relationship among ornament, performance, embodiment, and agency, or lack thereof. Some feminists have long identified the patriarchal and religious discipline embedded within the practice, but others have also pointed out that the relationship between institutional demand and self-performance may be much more complex than simply an issue of external disciplinary covering versus an oppressed self, or a true self versus the false consciousness of internalized patriarchal norms.[31] The ideal of a naked or unornamented self, seductive as it may be, cannot be the solution to the problem of racism, oppression, or discrimination, for that ideal denies how the (racialized) "self" is always already an effect of the ornament worn. This is not simply a theoretical insight or an insight derived from theoretical privilege; this is a critically important understanding that goes straight to the heart of the complex reality of our everyday senses of our own embodiment. The ornamental and clothing can offer the performance, the *habitus*, through which we acquire our sense of selfhood. The separation of essence from performance, assumed by our very formulation of our civil rights, elides this insight: that our experiences of our own racial, sexual, and ontic identities arise most acutely precisely at the intersection of *being* and the *doing* that supposedly decorates it. Our sense of our racial and sexual ontologies emerges most intensely *as* and *through* performances in a social context. Given this, we are effectively legally protected exactly where our racial and sexual identities do *not* live.

It is sobering to think that the concept of covering has surpassed the trope of passing in our contemporary society because the intervention of nineteenth-century orientalism into our legal imaginary about natural personhood has remained and morphed into the peculiar (double-layered?) discourse of our "authentic" civil rights. When we return to Yoshino's intriguing text, we will see that under the cover of its call for authenticity there lies an intricate narrative that suggests a much more fraught picture of our relations to our sartorial selves. The most haunting and stirring aspects of that book arise out of those moments when the narrator helps us to see, not the opposition between authenticity and false covers, but the active negotiation between the experience of subjectivity and acts of social performance. Almost every single personal account in this poignant book suggests that authenticity is not an integral or a priori entity but a palimpsest of identifications, layered and ridden with internal contradictions. If anything, Yoshino demonstrates the psychoanalytic insight that we are every one of us the sum of the history of the ghosts of others whom we have taken in. When, for example, the narrator realizes that, after years of Japanese school training, his sister "is no longer passing as Japanese, but that she was Japanese," he has located a highly imbricated dynamic between essence and performance, between body and discipline.[32] What it means to be at home in your own skin turns out to signal the necessary distance between ontology and its ornaments.

Even more tellingly, when Yoshino describes the critical moment of his coming out, he gives us a rather Lacanian mirror scene with sartorial roots:

> One Saturday, [Maureen] and I wandered into a haberdashery . . . I found a vest—gold lions ramping through a cobalt brocade . . . as I ran the brittle fabric between my thumb and finger, I experienced a jackdaw craving for it. I slipped it on . . . . "It becomes you," the shop keeper said gruffly through his waxed mustache. I realized it did become me, and that I could become it. It did the work of . . . [driving] my invisible difference to the surface and held it there. . . . The shop did not take checks, so Maureen put the vest on her credit card, and I signed away an alarming portion of my living stipend to her. By next mail, she sent back my pale green check cut in half and folded into two origami cranes.[33]

Is it an accident that this challenge to the limits of personal liberty is being articulated here by an Asian American legal subject confronting his gender difference, mediated through a mirror image (at once personal and social) and through a series of recognizable orientalist tropes (gold brocade, jackdaw, origami)? Synthetic and natural personhood converges vertiginously in this scene; both bring productive as well as limiting capabilities. We cannot fail to note that that this scene of coming out is taking place in a literal closet (that is, the dressing room) and that this scene of discovery is facilitated by covers and ornaments. What enabled the narrator to come out to himself is not nakedness, literally or otherwise, but the agential work of a piece of clothing and a highly decorated and racialized one at that.[34] Moreover, we might remember that the word "vesture" is linked to the notion of legal power as something that can be "invested": we speak, for example, of "vested interests."[35] Here, the vested interests of personal liberty and selfhood acknowledge the very logic of ornamentation that the discourse of covering had set out to redress. Finally, this moment of self-possession and self-investment is, significantly, also a moment of debt, of becoming indebted to another. This is why the "gift of selfhood" is such a paradoxical and revealing phrase, for self-possession is often made possible through the layers and mediations of "otherness."

In this extraordinarily layered scene of revelation, mediation, recognition, projection, self-owning and self-giving-away, we are presented with covers that uncover. Psychoanalytic insights would tell us that fantasy occupies a constitutive place in the imaginary act of self-recognition; what the legal imaginary teaches us is that what allows the subject to emerge from the closet is not liberating nakedness, but social ornamentation. At the same time, that ornament is never "just" a costume. As Yoshino tells us, "it did become me, and . . . *I could become it*" (italics added).

All of this is not to deny the importance of authenticity as an ideal or as a necessary fiction of our lives. But, like all ruling or originary fantasies we have about ourselves, these fictions are at once tenacious and fragile, insistent and susceptible. This is why "subjective agency" is at once so valuable and yet so deceptive a notion for an individual who is already suffering under the violence of a compromised individuality. My point here and throughout this chapter is, I hope, not a pious one about the shallowness of mistaking surface for person; on the contrary, I want to underscore the disquieting insight that personhood—on ontological, social, and legal levels—has always been implicated by its external vestment. To spell it out: ornament is never mere ornament. **It is an add-on that allows us, retroactively, to fantasize about natural personhood.** And the challenge that we must confront for the future is: can our law and can our civil rights accommodate the profundity and the dilemmas of our sartorial personhood?

Yes, the orientalism that fueled *Chy Lung* allowed the men in power to make categorical mistakes and remain blind, but it also reveals something critical about the making of personhood in the eyes of the law. We have to ask ourselves what are the visual conditions under which a (raced and gendered) body comes into visibility? This question touches on the very fiber of how we today imagine the psychological, social, and even legal basis for forging identity and its concomitant rights. To think about law and the ornament is therefore to confront a whole set of political dilemmas that structure personhood and, by implication, racial materiality. The case of the "twenty-two lewd Chinese women" reminds us that **being seen is not a condition of the visible but of the law** and that **how a body matters is a less a function of flesh than of ornament**. In the end, the case of *Chy Lung* enacted a vertiginous drama about the "layeredness" of legal visibility. Let me conclude with yet another little-noticed but dramatic turn in the story of the visible in this case. Not only did the men during the trial contort themselves and their female subjects to see what was not there to be seen, they also had to labor to not see what was there. Here I am referring not to the legality of the Burlingame Treaty that granted these women the right to come to America, nor to the certified, legal papers that the women possessed and displayed in their defense, but to what turned out to be under (or up) their sleeves. In a last twist, we learn that the women's bodies did have something to say. During the trial, Captain Freeman described the layered procedures the women underwent prior to boarding the transpacific steamer:

> [In Hong Kong] the women were all obliged to go to the counsel's, and are there interviewed by him and his interpreters. He satisfies himself that they are respectable women, & he gives them a permit to buy a ticket. At that time, *he stamps them upon their arm*; from there they are obliged to go to the harbor-master, and [there] he satisfies himself on the same grounds & *he stamps them [again]*, then they go to the office and buy their tickets. The day the ship leaves Hong Kong the harbor master . . . & the counsel himself come on board and see that the women . . . are the same; they are again interviewed . . . & *the stamps are still upon their arm*. (emphasis added)[36]

In other words, these women's bodies *were* in fact literally decorated: indelibly imprinted by legal ornaments that the law both imparts and erases. Retrieving this last and lost ornamental detail compels us to confront the invisibility of the visible on the one hand and the visibility of the invisible on the other. Or, to put it differently, what we have here is a parable for the modern visuality of race: one that is based, not on the visible or the corporeal, but on the invisible markings that stand in for the flesh.

NOTES

My gratitude to Judge Denny Chin of the US Court of Appeals for the Second Circuit for first bringing my attention to, and for his generous conversations about, this fascinating and haunting case.

1. Frederic William Maitland, "The Corporate Sole," *The Collected Papers of Frederic William Maitland*, vol. 3, ed. H. A. L. Fisher (Cambridge: Cambridge University Press, 1911), 200.
2. For an exception, see Carole Pateman's important study *The Sexual Contract* (Stanford, CA: Stanford University Press, 1988), which examines the constitutive role of gender within contract theory. For studies of corporate personhood, especially in relation to English common laws, see John T. Noonan Jr., *Persons and Masks of the Law: Cardozo, Holmes, Jefferson, and Wythe as Makers of the Masks* (Berkeley: University of California Press, 2002); Duncan Kennedy, "The Structure of Blackstone's Commentaries," *Buffalo Law Review* 28 (1979): 209–382; J. G. A. Pocock, *The Machiavellian Moment: Florentine Political Thought and the Atlantic Republican Tradition* (Princeton, NJ: Princeton University Press, 2003); and Sheldon S. Wolin, *Democracy Incorporated: Managed Democracy and the Specter of Inverted Totalitarianism* (Princeton, NJ: Princeton University Press, 2008).

For recent scholarship on legal personhood in the humanities, see Barbara Johnson, *Persons and Things* (Cambridge, MA: Harvard University Press, 2008), which explores the relationship between corporate personhood and lyrical personhood; Joseph R. Slaughter, *Human Rights, Inc.: The World Novel, Narrative Form, and International Law* (New York: Fordham University Press, 2007), which examines the convergence between international human rights law and an ideology of the enlightened individual, as revealed through the rise of the *Bildungsroman*; and Henry Turner, *The Corporate Commonwealth: Pluralism and Political Fictions in England, 1516–1651* (Chicago: University of Chicago Press, 2016), which traces the evolution of corporations during the English Renaissance.

3. Chy Lung v. Freeman, 92 U.S. 275 (1875). Transcript of Record/U.S. Supreme Court/1875/478/92 U.S. 275/23 L. Ed. 550/1-8-1987; also reprinted in *The Making of Modern Law: U.S. Supreme Court Records and Briefs, 1823–1978*, edition 5. Hereafter cited as *Transcript*.

This case was also described by Charles J. McClain in his study *In Search of Equality: The Chinese Struggle against Discrimination in Nineteenth-Century America* (Berkeley: University of California Press, 1994). It came back into attention in recent years in relation to contemporary immigration reform controversies such as the 2000 Arizona immigration law. See Paul A. Kramer, "The Case of the 22 Lewd Chinese Women: A Crazy 19th-Century Case Shows How the Supreme Court Should Deal with Arizona's Immigration Law," *Slate. com*, April 23, 2012, http://www.slate.com/articles/news_and_politics/jurisprudence/2012/04/arizona_s_immigration_law_at_the_supreme_court_lessons_for_s_b_1070_via_the_case_of_the_22_lewd_chinese_women.html. Finally, the case received recent attention through a dramatic reenactment of this trial, written and organized by the Asian American Bar Association of New York, in collaboration with Judge Denny Chin and Kathy Hirata. See Elizabeth Yuan, "'22 Lewd Chinese Women' and Other Courtroom Drama," *The Atlantic*, September 4, 2013.

4. *Transcript*, 12.

5. As prostitutes, the women would be treated as commodities subject to taxes. There were many of these kinds of "taxes" placed on arriving immigrants under varying rationales. Section 70 of the 1874 Amendments to the Political Code reads: "[N]o person who shall belong to either class, or who possesses any of the infirmities or vices specified herein, shall be permitted to land in this State, unless the master, owner, or consignee of said vessel shall give a joint and several bond to the people of the State of California, in the penal sum of five hundred dollars in gold coin of the United States." Clearly the purpose was to extort money from a large class of passengers or to prevent their immigration to California altogether.

6. We do not know for certain who this person was, though some of the local papers speculated that it might have been a man named Ah Lung, described by some as a local merchant and by others as a trafficker in Chinese prostitutes, reminding us that the presumably respectable category of the Chinese "merchant" (and soon to be one of the few categorical exceptions during the Chinese Exclusion) is itself often imputed with its own dark notes.

7. Transcript of Ex parte Ah Fook case file, No. 10114, California Supreme Court, California State Archives, Sacramento. Also quoted in the article "The Chinese Maidens," *Daily Alta California*, 26:8915, August 29, 1874.

8. *Amendments to California Political Code* § 69–71 (1874). For more on the long history of anti-Chinese sentiments, especially around the figure of the Asian woman, see Sucheng Chan, "The Exclusion of Chinese Women, 1870–1943," *Entry Denied: Exclusion and the Chinese Community in America, 1882–1943*, ed. Sucheng Chan, 94–164 (Philadelphia, PA: Temple University Press, 1991); McClain, *In Search of Equality*.

9. Although almost entirely forgotten today, the "Case of the 22 Lewd Chinese Women" generated a media storm at the time, soliciting almost daily reporting for months in the local press, such as *Daily Alta, S. F. Chronicle, Sacramental Daily Union*, and others. This intense prurience, however, ceased almost overnight after the case was ruled in favor of the women. There seems to be, to my knowledge, no records of the women after they left the courtroom.

10. The Page Act preceded the 1881 Chinese Exclusion Act and was the first restrictive federal immigration law. It prohibited the entry of immigrants considered "undesirable" and imposed a steep fine and maximum jail sentence of one year on anyone who tried to bring a person from China, Japan, or any Asian country to the United States "without their free and voluntary consent, for the purpose of holding them to a term of service." Although the rhetoric is about protecting laborers, the goal was to end the danger of cheap Chinese labor and reputed immoral Chinese women. The Page Act made it very clear that gender as well as race has been a significant factor in immigration policy. The 1882 Chinese Exclusion Act is infamously the first and only race-based immigration restriction in the United States and one that lasted until 1943. For a historical overview, see Ronald Takaki's definitive study *Strangers from a Different Shore: A History of Asian Americans*, rev. and updated ed. (New York: Little, Brown, 1989). For a new and comprehensive volume on anti-Chinese sentiment and specifically its visual legacy, see John Kuo Wei Tchen and Dylan Yeats, eds., *Yellow Peril! An Archive of Anti-Asian Fear* (New York: Verso, 2014).

11. There is a rich body of scholarship on the larger picture of how sexual reform during the Progressive Era drove racial legislations and vice versa: Kevin Mumford, *Interzones: Black/White Sex Distrcts in Chicago and New York in the Early Twentieth Century* (New York: Columbia University Press, 1997); Mary Ting Yi Lui, *The Chinatown Trunk Mystery: Murder, Miscegenation, and Other Dangerous Encounters in Turn-of-the-Century New York City* (Princeton, NJ: Princeton University Press, 2007); Pamela Haag, *Consent: Sexual Rights and the Transformation of American liberalism* (Ithaca, NY: Cornell University Press, 1999); Kathy Peiss and Christina Simmons, eds., *Passion and Power: Sexuality in History* (Philadelphia, PA: Temple University Press, 1989); Margot Canaday, *The Straight State: Sexuality and Citizenship in Twentieth-Century America* (Princeton, NJ: Princeton University Press, 2009); George Chauncey, *Gay New York: Gender, Urban Culture, and the Making of the Gay Male World, 1890–1940* (New York: Basic Books, 1995).

12. Ideas about slanted eyes, pug noses, bow-legs and notions of outlandish clothes populate images of the Chinese in nineteenth-century American press and popular culture. See Philip P. Choy, Lorraine Dong, and Marlon K. Hom, eds., *Coming Man: 19th Century American Perceptions of the Chinese* (Seattle: University of Washington Press, 1994); Takaki, *Strangers from a Different Shore*, on the persistent trope of the Chinese as "perpetual strangers" in American polity and culture; James S. Moy, *Marginal Sights: Staging the Chinese in America* (Iowa City: University of Iowa Press, 1993).

13. *Transcript*, 16. It turns out that Gibson was hardly an accidental witness. He ran a missionary in Chinatown and, in spite of his damaging testimony here, saw himself as advocate for the Chinese. Like many Christian progressive reformers of the time, Gibson was an ambivalent and complex figure. Although he was known to have been active in helping Chinese male immigrants who had troubles with the immigration authorities (see a case with his involvement in McClain, *In Search of Equality*, 49–52), Gibson also operated on Victorian stereotypes about the "Oriental," especially when it comes to women, as we see here in Chy Lung v. Freeman.

14. *Transcript*, 17–18.

15. *Transcript*, 17–18.

16. *Transcript*, 23–26.

17. The history of Chinese immigration regulation also tells a story about "exemptions" to the rule: the so-called merchant class that was exempted from this exclusion. Paul A. Kramer argues that this focus on "merchant class" partakes of a discourse about the American civilizing project that is not only imperial but also specifically corporate. See Kramer, "Imperial Opening: Civilization, Exemption, and the Geopolitics of Mobility in the History of Chinese Exclusion,1868–1910," *Journal of the Gilded Age and Progressive Era* 14 (2015): 317–47.

18. Since the majority of early Chinese immigrants and gold-rush participants were male, the shortage of women created new global markets for the trafficking and exploitation of women, with prostitutes arriving from many different countries. In the burgeoning "yellow slave trade" in Asia, thousands of Chinese women and girls were kidnapped or deceived by procurers in China and some were sold by their families. By the 1850s, the prostitution industry in cities like San Francisco had become sufficiently embarrassing that local officials, while still unwilling to call prostitution illegal, passed statutes designed to penalize prostitutes, brothel owners, and landlords—but not their patrons. Although initially worded to attack prostitution generally, the laws were directed principally against the Chinese. At the same time, Chinatown's so-called Bachelor Society and US immigration restrictions severed traditional family relations and kinship system. These twenty-two unclaimed women were a symptom of this complex history.

19. It is beyond the scope of this chapter, but the ornament has long been employed to signal moral decay. In speaking of the tricks and ornaments of sophistic oratory, Plato called the ornament false, oriental, and misleading. In *The Merchant of Venice*, Shakespeare famously warns us that "the world is deceived with ornament." In colonial America, sumptuary laws often centered on sartorial adornment and practices (the prohibition against the making and wearing of lace, for example) were meant to regulate not only social hierarchies but also moral conduct. For the enduring philosophic connection between ornament and gender, see Alina Payne, *From Object to Ornament: Genealogies of Architectural Modernism* (New Haven, CT: Yale University Press, 2012); Naomi Schor, *Reading in Detail: Aesthetic and the Feminine* (New York: Routledge, 2007); and Mark Wigley, *White Walls, Designer Dresses: The Fashioning of Modern Architecture* (Cambridge, MA: MIT Press, 2001). For the racialized aspect of that connection, especially its legacy in the twentieth century, see Anne Anlin Cheng, *Second Skin: Josephine Baker and the Modern Surface* (New York: Oxford University Press, 2011).

20. *Transcript*, 27.

21. Kramer, "Case of the 22 Lewd Chinese Women."

22. William Blackstone, *Commentaries on the Laws of England, 1765–79*, 15th ed. (London: T. Caddell and W. Davides, in the Strand, 1765), 123. See also Kennedy, "Structure of Blackstone's Commentaries."

23. Stephen Best, *The Fugitive's Properties: Law and Poetics of Possession* (Chicago: University of Chicago Press, 2004); Monique Allewaert, *Ariel's Ecology: Plantations, Personhood, and Colonialism in the American Tropics* (Minneapolis: University of Minnesota Press, 2013.)

24. The fact that the women could bring a habeas corpus and brave a court hearing implies a personhood status, but the lower court ruled that these women's personhood was not one entitled to the legal benefits that they sought. So the issue is really more nuanced than just "personhood," it is also the classification of "persons."

25. Sarah C. Roberts v. The City of Boston, 59 Mass. (5 Cush.) 198 (1850) was a court case seeking to end racial discrimination in Boston public schools. The Massachusetts Supreme Judicial Court ruled in favor of Boston, finding no constitutional basis for the suit. The case was later cited by the US Supreme Court in *Plessy v. Ferguson*. The case centered on Sarah Roberts, a five-year-old African American girl enrolled in Abiel Smith School, an underfunded all-black common school, far from her home in Boston, Massachusetts. Her father, Benjamin F. Roberts, also African American, attempted to enroll her at closer, whites-only schools. After Ms. Roberts was denied on the basis of her race, and was physically removed from one school, Roberts wrote to the state legislature to seek a solution. The Supreme Court of Massachusetts heard the case, in which Benjamin Roberts listed his daughter Sarah as the plaintiff and the City of Boston as the defendant. Judge Lemuel Shaw ruled for the defendant.

26. For more on the relations between legal personhood and dress, see Gary Watt, *Dress, Law and Naked Truth: A Cultural Study of Fashion and Form* (London: Bloomsbury Academy, 2013). Where Watt posits law and dress as two cultural equivalences (in that both the judicial and the sartorial aim to regulate and order the body, which is why his study focused on the regulation of literal dress, such as uniforms, judicial robes, etc.), I would suggest that the relationship is not simply analogous but structural. I pinpoint the *act* of "dressing" and "putting something on" as fundamental to the ornamentation or fabrication of judicial personhood.

27. Mae M. Ngai, *Impossible Subjects: Illegal Aliens and the Making of Modern America* (Princeton, NJ: Princeton University Press, 2014). Landmark cases such as Takao Ozawa v. U.S. (No. 1. Supreme Court of the United States, 260 U.S. 178; 43 S. Ct. 65; 67 L. Ed. 199; 1922) and U.S v. Bhagat Singh Thind (No. 202. Supreme Court of the United States. 261 U.S. 204; 43 S. Ct. 338; 67 L. Ed. 616; 1923) reveal the vicissitudes of "Asian" as an American racial category.

28. The profound dislocation of these women finds its most literal expression in what happened to them after the commissioner of immigration detained them. Between the times the women were detained by Piotrowski and before they went to court, they were basically unwanted. According to the *Los Angeles Herald* (August 26, 1874), "a proposition was made to remand [the women] to the custody of the captain, but he declined saying that he produced the women in Court, and the Court could take care of them. Judge Morrison then ordered that the whole gang be taken to the County Jail."

29. Zygmunt Bauman, *Liquid Modernity* (Cambridge: Polity, 2000).

30. Kenji Yoshino, *Covering: The Hidden Assault on Our Civil Rights* (New York: Random House, 2006)

31. For the latter, see Saba Mahmood's work on the rituals of Islamic revival in works such as "Feminist Theory, Embodiment, and the Docile Agent: Some Reflections on the Egyptian Islamic Revival," *Cultural Anthropology* 16 2 (2001): 202–36; and Joan Wallach Scott, *The Politics of the Veil* (Princeton, NJ: Princeton University Press, 2010).

32. Yoshino, *Covering*, 35.

33. Ibid., 11–12.

34. For a wonderful history of the vest as itself an article of clothing that originated in Asia, see Adam Geczy, *Fashion and Orientalism: Dress, Textiles and Culture from the 17th to the 20th Century* (London: Bloomsbury Academic, 2013).

35. For a rich account of the etymology of the word "vesture," see Watt, *Dress, Law and Naked Truth*, 2–3.

36. *Transcript*, 8.

CHAPTER 14

The Flowers Are Vexed

Gender Justice, Black Literature,

and the Passionate Utterance

IMANI PERRY

Like most students at the beginning of law school, I learned about the "reasonable man" standard. This standard of analysis emerged in nineteenth-century Anglo-American jurisprudence. The reasonable man, a subject guiding interpretation, is imagined as dispassionate and measured. He appears as an everyman of sorts, although not quite in the circumstance of every man because he appeared not to be burdened with the urgencies caused by poverty and desperation. His gaze became the traditional standard for legal decision making. What would the reasonable man do or think in a given situation had bearing upon the appropriate interpretations of the rule of law.

We learned further, that over time this standard was no longer construed in ways that were gender (and race) specific. And that the law itself has expanded to include women and people of color, and a panoply of different sorts of others. For some people this seems to be enough, a pathway toward emptying out the reasonable one of his identifying traits, making him truly neutral. This immediately triggered my skepticism as a student because I agree with Simone de Beauvoir's assertion that "The point is not for women simply to take power out of men's hands since that wouldn't change anything about the world. It's a question precisely of destroying that notion of power." The chapter that follows is, however, not so much about destroying a notion of power. It entails two distinct yet related movements. First, it makes a critical intervention into feminist jurisprudence, by calling into question the ideal of the reasonable man or ideal citizen as a patriarchal figure not solely or even primarily due to gender, but rather due to the relations with others. The second movement looks to the philosophical work of Black women's fiction, work that challenges the failures in the concept of the "reasonable man," work that imagines and describes reforms and reconfigurations of human relation in the pursuit of justice, to extend this intervention.

Reading Colin Dayan's book *The Law is a White Dog*[1] helped me understand how the structural relations of domination that lie as raw naked power are scaffolded by what appear to be abstractly good legal principles and ideas of citizenship, once shorthanded as that which would serve the status of the reasonable man. The model citizen for whom the law of the sovereign nation, which theoretically protects its borders and people, is made in relation to others who are constantly being unmade. Dayan describes legal nonpersons: humans in detention, incarcerated, in torture, geopolitically quarantined, and at the other side of the technologies of necropolitics, or in other words, subject to the death machines of a sovereign authority to which the murdered don't belong.[2] This current reality is unsurprising because as the reasonable man was being created by law and social practice, the slave was as well, by the same means. The legal person (today emptied somewhat of his nominal whiteness and maleness) and the nonperson human sit at opposite ends of the spectrum of power even in the twenty-first century. The legal person is protected and rights-bearing, the nonperson human is shielded from the view of public life by bars and oceans and veils of ignorance, although also ever present in our consciousness as a threat, justifying the police and military power of the state.

Another approach to thinking about the reasonable man is to locate him not simply legally but economically. And to that extent the historical figure who best represents him for me is the patriarch of the plantation household in American slavery. Of course, patriarchy took different configurations in the West, dependent upon local economies. But the plantation household is so effective as a means of thinking about patriarchy because there was a spatial contraction of the range of beings in the structure of power. But of course, colonial power and industrial power have repeating analogous structures in which the patriarch exists as representative citizen. Recognized intimates, like wives and children, were dispossessed but with some degree of comfort. And then there were those outside of the home, some with a degree of autonomy due to being the subjects of exploitation but not complete economic domination. And then there were the enslaved, nonpersons. This was patriarchy.

The reasonable man is also the patriarch, and I would argue that figure remains our primary unit of citizenship and rights, notwithstanding expansions of what kind of person can be that figure, as well as various expansions and contractions of the subidentities and rules sitting within, outside, and—to use Hortense Spillers's phrase from her classic essay "Mama's Baby, Papa's Maybe: An American Grammar Book,"[3]—in the vestibule of the house. Spillers described slavery. Things are different now in many ways. The physical form of the reasonable man is no longer limited to the cis male white body (there are people of various hues and bodies and histories who can occupy that space). This is what we take to be the great gain of the women's movement and independence movements and civil rights. But those transformations don't resolve the original sin the reasonable man represents. The reality of partial persons and nonperson humans finds new forms today. And there is no sign of this status waning. In fact, it seems to be increasingly codified and obscured.

As individuals we stand in communities, and before the state, and the world. We each occupy a position in relationship to these institutions that may or may not entail membership, and the capacity to live a full and rewarding life in which one is heard, loved, and granted the opportunity to pursue one's goals. As we stand, our lives are at once shaped by the forces of capital, gender, race, disability, and sexuality, and as well are profoundly individual. Intimacy, interiority, and power are intertwined in our existences as gendered subjects.

Gender is the most core form of inequality, an *ur*-inequality, as it were, but also it animates other forms of social stratification. Inequalities are systematized and essentialized in the West by means of the logic and language of gender. What do I mean by this? Colonialism and slavery depended upon an ideology naming othered men as insufficient as men, unreasonable, guided by passions and bruteness (masculine, but of an undeveloped sort), as "failed men."[4] Women who were not the wives of patriarchs were failures as well, as women, ambiguously gendered, cast into chattel-like conceptions of gender and flexibly gendered. Women in public, poor women, also were failures for not fitting the code of women of the household. At the same time, the ladies of the household had a fixed role, idealized and yet marginalized, possessed of a power that was only ancillary, that which accrued from the patriarch.

In mainstream feminism today we hear endless discussions that, to put it bluntly, are really all about the grappling between the patriarch and the lady, particularly with respect to those who own the biggest plantations, symbolically and economically speaking. That is what we are supposed to lean in to witness how they can have it all. Efforts to move us out of the wrangling within the plantation household through the pathways of feminist of color thought, Marxist feminism, postcolonial theory, critical race theory, queer theory, and now transtheory, have generally been ghettoized, despite the fact that they engage the difficulties of gender and sexuality for a large majority of the world, while patriarchs and ladies are a small (albeit powerful) group.

In addition to the popular discourse, there is a lot of policy research that describes how poorly women fare around the world. But so often that line of inquiry flattens global relations of power that are gendered. (Take, for example, the saying that the United States is the world's daddy.) To focus on the women of poor countries and communities often enables us to evade questions of global capitalist power that would reasonably lead us to question our role in their sufferings. Moreover, feminism has recently been enlisted as part of the justification for neoimperialist incursions into less powerless nations by global powers. So while gender inequality and oppression merit local and domestic forms of examination, we must also rethink international relations of power as a gendered project. And therefore we see that the fact of one's citizenship or statelessness, how these statuses can be exercised, what power they force you to submit to, how much closer to untimely death you are because of statelessness, are concerns appropriately pursued by feminist jurisprudence.

What I am sharing is a brief gesture toward a feminist analytic that understands both the structure of international domination of the poorer and internal domination of women and sexual-identity minorities. Such a move is necessary because behind our ideals of status or personhood are people excluded from status or recognition. Our proclamations of virtue often destroy them.

If we read the many layers of relations of power, behind the big house (to the field and the outhouse), and behind the political representative, or representative reasonable citizen (to the interior, to the many), we find ourselves compelled to move beyond looking at gender as a set of binary analogies always reducible to an essential codependent conflict between men and women. We are challenged to resist monolithic understandings of the interests of "communities" that are marginalized or oppressed. Rather we are moved toward ethics that are at once intimately and structurally understood.

For my purposes, it is quite useful to extend Hortense Spillers's germinal concept of vestibularity (standing at the threshold) in order to think about the legal, economic, and political structures through which we decide to count who counts as human beings and who falls outside of those logics. I want to begin by centering a vestibular existence. Rather than the body politic here, we might think of ourselves as being situated in "the gaps" and minding them. The gaps are a geographic metaphor for Spillers's vestibularity and Dayan's non-personhood in human encounters. The gaps are everywhere yet out of view because outside of the traditional forms or processes of legal recognition. They are after-hours spots, prisons, the back rooms of strip clubs, detention centers, rooms of solitary confinement, and truck stops. They are social spaces that are unprotected by the logic of rights and recognition, either because by being there you are automatically on the wrong side of the regulatory state or because they are spaces in which the regulatory state does not extend protection.

Gap spaces are ominous. And similarly ambiguous, they are places of danger but also of possibility. Outside of the articulation of order, but repressed, they are a no-man's-land (pun intended) of our human experiences. To understand the potential of gap spaces, we might turn to Angela Davis's 1970 essay "Women and Capitalism," in which she identifies the alienation from the means of production experienced by oppressed people of color in the United States as providing opportunity for more humane and less patriarchal interaction than that led to by the clear structural relationship to capital and the means of production for the proletariat. She writes this idea, however, with some skepticism about the prospect for this liberatory potential to be widely realized without major social transformation or revolution. But the sense of creative possibility is a compelling one. I would argue, for instance, that the development of fictive kinship among African American and LGBT communities is something produced by meaningful ethical creation in the absence of formal constrictions, born in the gaps. And yet the greatest abuses of these very same communities so often occur in the gaps as well. We have to sit there and think.

Locating that place to "sit and think" in literature is archaeological. For example: the most-remembered part of Virginia Woolf's *A Room of One's Own* is the formulation that gives the essay its title. That for a woman to write she must have real property and money to spend. But digging, I found another part of the essay even more important for this chapter:

> genius of a sort must have existed among women as it must have existed among
> the working classes. Now and again an Emily Brontë or a Robert Burns blazes

out and proves its presence. But certainly it never got itself on to paper. When, however, one reads of a witch being ducked, of a woman possessed by devils, of a wise woman selling herbs, or even of a very remarkable man who had a mother, then I think we are on the track of a lost novelist, a suppressed poet, of some mute and inglorious Jane Austen, some Emily Brontë who dashed her brains out on the moor or mopped and mowed about the highways crazed with the torture that her gift had put her to.[5]

any woman born with a great gift in the sixteenth century would certainly have gone crazed, shot herself, or ended her days in some lonely cottage outside the village, half witch, half wizard, feared and mocked at.[6]

In reading this part, I am doing what Thadious Davis calls a compensatory reading[7] of those paragraphs. Filling in the gaps of this important essay, I am arguing that to invoke the witches is not simply taking note of misguided or stagnant creative energy. Witches, metaphorically speaking (but also as a category of people treated in Anglo-American history as a threat to order, and frequently associated with non-European influence), bend the naturalized landscape. They have transformative power. They can show us another way. The conditions of what we accept as normal, the logic that dominates our understanding, is disrupted by their existence. What I am encouraging here is a reading of Black women's literature that facilitates a challenge to the exclusionary logics of the reasonable man. The tradition recommends seeking, to borrow the words of my friend Ashon Crawley, the "otherwise."[8] Woolf, it seems, wanted us all to become reasonable men. But in contrast, we read this distinct intervention, seeking the otherwise, from Toni Morrison, Walker, Ayana Mathis, Jamaica Kincaid, and many more.

A bewitching creative energy appears in Jamaica Kincaid's story "In the Night," where a Caribbean girl dreams of growing up to marry a "red skin woman with black bramblebrush hair and brown eyes, who wears skirts that are so big that I can easily bury my head in them."[9] Her interior queer yearning occurs in a small place at the crossroads of race, gender, sexuality, and empire. As such, she breathes in a matrix. And like the flowers in her midst, she is shaped by the beings, earth, air, and sea, growing and living, alternately pruned and reckless. Caught in an underbrush, she is vexed. Writing of her environs, and their mirroring effect, Kincaid says, "In the night the flowers close up and thicken. The hibiscus flowers, the flamboyant flowers, the batchelors buttons . . . the flowers on the dumps tree, the flowers on the papaw tree, the flowers everywhere close up and thicken. The flowers are vexed."[10] The heroine's yearnings chafe against all maternal efforts to discipline her according to gender rules that failed her sense of self.

The analogy between self and nature is extended in this story: At night in the Caribbean, the flowers are vexed, unlike the tamed English garden. And on her small island, duppies, legal nonpersons, literal nonhumans, but as alive as anyone else, walk among the wild flowers here, and also in Toni Morrison's novel *Tar Baby*, in which they haunt the lead character, Jadine. They are concerned with settling past scores, reminding us of their presence. The reader is drawn into their vexations. Such seductions are not simply an intoxication, they are also an argument.

An element of that argument is related to a point made by philosopher Richard Rorty that language is contingent,[11] and that we can use vocabularies to create meanings. The statements and personalities and relations provided in Black literature of a gender-liberationist sort are in some significant measure ways of providing alternative grammars through which to develop values. This thematic alone provokes a challenge to the oft-presumed ideal of our given (and abstracted) political and legal order in the United States. The creation of alternative grammars, or we might say "constitutions"—a set of human relations—for the moral universes of the novels and their characters is an invitation to readers to think in different ways. And to me, most importantly, in these works the alternative grammars refuse any possible reduction of the moral claims of the novel to mere requests for inclusions in the political and intellectual grammars of Western legitimacy.

THE PASSIONATE UTTERANCE

I find philosopher Stanley Cavell's concept of the passionate utterance quite useful as a term for what I am describing in this literature. He explains that the idea of passionate utterance is an extension of J. L. Austin's concept of the performative utterance (which is essentially a statement intended to lead to some conventional outcome according to appropriate procedure, such as "with this ring, I thee wed"). Literary theorists and cultural studies scholars have done a great deal of exploration of the performative utterance and its constraints already, The passionate utterance, in contrast, is a form of invitation for which there is no existing conventional procedure to produce a particular effect. The speaker is using emotion to assert standing before the one who is being spoken to, and doing so vulnerably and yet also with assertive demand. Cavell describes the passionate utterance as an invitation into the disorders of desire, to something possible but not probable.

J. L. Austin's conception of performative utterance is found in the utterance "I am free," which may or may not be effectively true. The passionate utterance, in contrast, is acting upon one's humanity freely, in ways that disrupt convention. The performative utterance obscures the fact that all legal decision making is emotional, making it look like a set of dispassionate procedures. The passionate utterance uses emotion and humanity to force a reconsideration of the sedimented abstract proceduralism of law masquerading as pure reason. In times and places when "freedom" may be formally institutionalized but effectively denied (because of categories of difference, or differences in categorical meanings), then the passionate utterance is an argument for a particular kind of witnessing and acknowledgment as expressed in the improvisational reordering of dominant grammars of human interaction.

In Toni Morrison's *Song of Solomon*, the heroine, Pilate Dead, is born without an umbilical cord (no navel gazing for her). She climbs out of her mother's womb like Athena from Zeus's head. Pilate is an outcast. A migrant worker who gets expelled several times once her unusual body is revealed. Cast out of outcasts. She is the moral center of the novel. She is magic. Magic, however, in this and similar works doesn't provide a simple remedy to bad things. Pilate can't save all the children she loves, or her own life. Magic is a gesture, but never promises utopia or peace. Pilate survives by the grace of her grace. Pilate revels in the beauty of nature; witch-like and bewitching. And Pilate's operative logic is to love the marginal, a logic that fails in its capacity to create justice or fairness or a felicitous conclusion writ large, but which we as readers are confronted with and, as Cavell articulates, a demand is made upon us to do something about it.

At her crossroads or conversion moment, after enduring so much cruelty, Pilate's new approach to the world is described like this:

> Although she was hampered by huge ignorances, but not in any way unintelligent, when she realized what her situation in the world was and would probably always be, she threw away every assumption she had learned and began at zero. First off, she cut her hair. That was one thing she didn't want to have to think about any more.
>
> Then she tackled the problem of trying to decide how she wanted to live and what was valuable to her. When am I happy and when am I sad and what is the difference? What do I need to know to stay alive? What is true in the world? Her mind traveled crooked streets and aimless goat paths, arriving sometimes at profundity, other times at the revelations of a three-year-old. Throughout this fresh, if common, pursuit of knowledge, one conviction crowned her

efforts: since death held no terrors for her (she spoke often to the dead) she knew there was nothing to fear.[12]

In this moment, Pilate identifies knowledge in the wake of her psychic emancipation as something wholly different from preexisting rules. We can read her as a figure in conversation with Frederick Douglass who, in his classic narrative, frees himself with the classic chiasmus of man enslaved transforming from slave to man. Pilate is transformed in a way that doesn't expand the category "Man" or "citizen," as Douglass the abolitionist, intellectual, and activist did when confronting the law of slavery. Instead Pilate starts fresh.

She is asymmetrical. With a snuffbox earring on one side and a smooth belly, her body does not adhere to the cycle of life. Even her name is disruption, spelled P.I.L.A.T.E. but really a P.I.L.O.T., whose maps are written in song and improvisation. As an old woman, her strength is supernatural; she can fly without leaving the ground.

Pilate's spirit rejects the rules of science and society. Her embodiment contradicts the way we learned high school biology and the drawings of the natural human body that hung on the wall in our classrooms: those images of slim, well-muscled, and perfectly symmetrical bodies—usually a man with an outline of Ken doll hair, and sometimes a woman with a flip. Pilate's disruption guides a revelation. How much more would we learn in biology from witnessing the range of figures and experiences we have in the flesh? From a practice of refiguring. Imagine a series of drawings, dozens, hundreds, in a single anatomy book, each an example of the striking distinctiveness of each body, filled with the things that make us: short legs, long neck, one arm, wide waist, flat feet, appendectomy, a goiter, a hump, a growth, a long trailing scar, a chokecherry tree on the back. The reality of natural bodies is that they are alarmingly specific. Breasts, penises, waistlines, feet, hands noses, their shape, color, size, and proportion are wildly divergent. According to Anne Fausto Sterling, close to 2 percent of the population doesn't even fall into the two sex classification.[13] Additionally, once we understand bodies as not static, but ever-changing, the binary conception of gender is increasingly unsatisfying. Over the course of one's life one may not have breasts, have breasts, and then no longer have breasts. Bunions grow. People, desperate people, sell organs and rent their wombs. Our reproductive functions change in the longer terms of a lifespan, but also in the shorter cycles of menstruation. Bodies change as a result of temperature, sexual excitement, illness, dietary habits, surgery, hormones, and aging. A person may begin their life classified as able-bodied, and may later be blind, or an amputee. Disease and disability are universal and herald discoveries in the lives of those who confront them. And that is everyone on God's green earth. The ability spectrum is not fixed in any person's life. Those considered fully able are only fully able for a portion of their lives. The truth is, our capacity shifts over the course of days, weeks, months, and years, with the changes in, and demands of, our flesh and innards, and the wounds and gifts of our experiences working upon our minds and bodies. Everyone has lived without the ability to walk, whether in infancy, or old age, or injury, or permanent loss. Everyone has been debilitated by confusion, whether from exhaustion or medication or Alzheimer's or schizophrenia. Depression strikes many of us, some due to grief and heartbreak, others due to an unexpected upheaval in the body chemistry.

In Pilate we see this human vulnerability. Lovers leave her (who loves bigger and wider than anyone) because her body frightens them. We find ourselves constantly seeking and validating simplistic oppositions and figurations and therefore misapprehending all sorts of complexity and inner workings.

I am reading this novel as a philosophical intervention. The analogies one might draw between Pilate and others who are making their way in the gaps unrecorded and unrecognized so often by legal doctrine are powerfully instructive. Pilate deserves more than our recognition, she demands that we receive her insight.

In the Ayana Mathis novel *The Twelve Tribes of Hattie*[14] we encounter another example of a passionate utterance. One chapter features a man named Floyd, a musician, who has sexual encounters with men under the cover of night, but is a rather average heterosexual philanderer in public. But then he meets Lafayette: "The man couldn't have been more than eighteen. But he was not a boy, that is to say his lips were red and voluptuous and he held them slightly apart. It was a mouth as ripe as a strawberry; the young man was not unaware of this"[15] Floyd is drawn in by Lafayette's beauty and the possibility of life with him. They make love. He later invites Lafayette to hear him play, but when Lafayette arrives he gets kicked out of the club and beaten for entering a space in which as a gay man he is not allowed. Floyd doesn't intervene. He tries to find Lafayette after the set, but he fails. So he simply leaves town. Before his departure he encounters two people: one a woman who is his former lover and another, a friendly man. Both of them confront him with his moral failure, his refusal to protect Lafayette. In this moment, even for two people whose words are couched in homophobic language, passion, not gender doctrine, drives the sense of morality. This vignette is rife with strangeness, and I use the term "strangeness" not as a pejorative, but I want to use it in the sense of outside of convention, which is part of what makes each expression of desire, one for the other, a passionate utterance.

I think such passionate utterances matter so much as a site of inquiry because the writers aren't simply saying prejudice is bad and here are its effects, but they are proposing, I think, that we consider some broader ambivalence about the political appeals to recognition. And what I mean is this: Recognition disciplines as it excludes, it demands a capitulation to the order of the society. In these books all the idealized values of the West, of the United States, are directly challenged in the form of conventional characters who are ultimately not the moral centers of the works. Rather, those who are othered, on the margins, in the gaps, suggest a distinct project of human relation. It is the women who are disordered, disabled, and cast off, and beautifully so, who are sage. On the maps of these remappers, plant life is sentient, disability is sapience, justice is improvisational, the dead and unborn are welcome companions, queer love is everywhere, family holds no biological or juridical presumptions, it becomes repeatedly. Their alternative grammars defy the fetishes of reasonability, respectability, and rules of stratification.

They challenge doctrine and toggle the handle on our ethical imagination. So we are called to ask, what happens if we start here instead, and build out upon the alternative grammars and reordering that emerges from embodied truths? Such an approach allows us to think through the fact of forms of embodiment that are feminine, irrational, inferior, according to the nineteenth-century standards for reasonable, to, as Cavell describes, "acknowledge[e] my desire in confronting you, [to] declare my standing with you and single you out, demanding a response in kind from you, and a response now, so making myself vulnerable to your rebuke, thus staking our future."[16] This is done doubly, both in the characters' encounters in the text, in which they often meet with actual rebuke, and as well in the intimate confrontation with the reader. The utterances described here are not presented in the classic form of appeal, their seduction is not pursued by a contortion into being cognizable, but rather in the form of an invited and naked speculation about other possibilities of being human, and in that way they do what philosopher Sylvia Wynter proclaimed as our duty, to displace the idea/ideal of MAN as if it were the only mode of full humanness.[17] There is human possibility beyond efforts to approximate the ideal of "MAN." In addition to necessarily displacing logics of gender and race, passionate utterances can remind us that our expressions of what are naturalized human performances of right and wrong are in fact not natural at all but created and matters of faith.

We are all ultimately bricoleurs. We quilt, we "rig," we are making do in this project of living with what we have at our disposal. This at once affirms Judith Butler's argument about the predetermined grammar of gender, and explodes it with an understanding of the potential of bricolage, improvisation, and subversion within the intellectual and political radicalism necessary to even imagine gender liberation in this age.

We can build our ideas and values, collaging, from the stuff of imagination, experience, and knowledge. They grow in our encounters with the world as we know it, the very world we seek to change. Therefore we ought to be sensitive to the gaps and passions in our own bricolage houses and those of others as well, and resist doctrines that render them invisible.

NOTES

1. Colin Dayan, *The Law is a White Dog: How Legal Rituals Make and Unmake Persons* (Princeton, NJ: Princeton University Press, 2011).
2. See Achille Mbembe, "Necropolitics," *Public Culture* 15, no. 1 (2003): 11–40.
3. Hortense J. Spillers, "Mama's Baby, Papa's Maybe: An American Grammar Book," in "Culture and Countermemory: The 'American' Connection," *Diacritics* 17, no. 2 (1987): 64–81.
4. See Jeffrey Q. McCune Jr., *Sexual Discretion: Black Masculinity and the Politics of Passing* (Chicago: University of Chicago Press, 2014).
5. Virginia Woolf, *A Room of One's Own and Three Guineas* (Oxford: Oxford University Press, 1992), 63.
6. Ibid., 64.
7. See Thadious M. Davis, *Games of Property: Law, Race, Gender and Faulkner's "Go Down, Moses"* (Durham, NC: Duke University Press, 2003).
8. See Ashon T. Crawley, *Blackpentecostal Breath: The Aesthetics of Possibility* (New York: Fordham University Press, 2016).
9. Jamaica Kincaid, "In the Night," in *At The Bottom of the River* (New York: Farrar, Strauss and Giroux, 1978), 11.
10. Ibid.
11. See Richard Rorty, *Contingency, Irony, and Solidarity* (Cambridge: Cambridge University Press, 1989).
12. Toni Morrison, *Song of Solomon* (New York: Vintage, 2004), 149.
13. Anne Fausto-Sterling, *Sexing the Body: Gender Politics and the Construction of Sexuality* (New York: Basic Books, 2000), 51.
14. Ayana Mathis, *The Twelve Tribes of Hattie* (New York: Alfred A. Knopf, 2013).
15. Ibid., 15.
16. Stanley Cavell, *Philosophy the Day after Tomorrow* (Cambridge, MA: Belknap Press of Harvard University Press, 2005), 148.
17. See Sylvia Wynter, "Unsettling the Coloniality of Being/Power/Truth/Freedom: Toward the Human, after Man, Its Overrepresentation—An Argument," *New Centennial Review* 3 (2003): 257–337.

CHAPTER 15

Genocide by Other Means

US Federal Indian Law and Violence against Native

Women in Louise Erdrich's The Round House

ERIC CHEYFITZ AND SHARI M. HUHNDORF

To begin, two questions. What is literature? What is the law? While in the West both literature and law have long oral traditions, typically in the modern era they have come to refer to what is written. In Indigenous communities, traditionally—that is, prior to colonization and in ongoing resistance to it—there was/is neither literature nor law in the Western sense. There were/are stories, conveyed orally or in forms of nonalphabetic writing such as wampum.[1] Thus, what the West terms the law is one kind of story in Indigenous terms. In his 2008 collection *Survivance*, the Anishinaabe scholar, novelist, and poet Gerald Vizenor gives us a telling example in the testimony of Anishinaabe Charles Aubid:

> This inspired storier was a sworn witness in federal court that autumn more than thirty years ago in Minneapolis, Minnesota. He raised his hand, listened to the oath for the first time in the language of the Anishinaabe, Chippewa, or Ojibwe, and then waved, an ironic gesture of the oath, at United States District Judge Miles Lord. . . .
>
> Aubid was a witness in a dispute with the federal government over the right to regulate the *manoomin*, wild rice, harvest on Rice Lake National Wildlife Refuge in Minnesota. Federal agents had assumed the authority to determine

the wild rice season and to regulate the harvest, a bureaucratic action that decried a native sense of survivance and sovereignty.

Aubid, who was eighty-six years old at the time, testified through translators that he was present as a young man when the federal agents told old John Squirrel that the Anishinaabe would always have control of the *manoomin* harvest. Aubid told the judge that the Anishinaabe always understood their rights by stories. John Squirrel was there in memories, a storied presence of native survivance. The court could have heard the testimony in a visual trace of a parol agreement, a function of discourse, both relevant and necessary.

Justice Lord agreed with the objection of the federal attorney that the testimony was hearsay and therefore not admissible and explained that the court could not hear as evidence what a dead man said, only the actual experiences of the witness. "John Squirrel is dead," said the judge. "And you can't say what a dead man said."

Aubid turned brusquely in the witness chair, bothered by what the judge had said about John Squirrel. Aubid pointed at the legal books on the bench, and then in English, his second language, he shouted that those books contained stories of dead white men. "Why should I believe what a white man says, when you don't believe John Squirrel?" Judge Lord was deferential, amused by the analogy of native stories to court testimony, judicial decisions, precedent, and hearsay. "You've got me there," he said, and then considered the testimony of other Anishinaabe witnesses.[2]

As an aside, we should note that Judge Lord is an anomaly in the annals of US federal Indian law, where oral testimony has typically not been admitted in the courts or not accorded the same validity as written documents.

Aubid points to the irony governing the disciplinary separation of law and literature, which is that Western law is itself nothing but a set of stories, distinguishing itself from literature by function more than form. That is, when the West speaks of literature today it tends to mean nonfunctional, in the sense of aesthetic, fictions of one kind or another: novels, poems, plays, short stories, and belle-lettristic essays, which have no practical force in the world. On the other hand, legal fictions have a function; they are instrumental in the criminal and civil justice system.[3] The law is not understood as literature in the West, as stories, unless of course one studies it as such, concentrating on its narrative structure, its rhetorical agendas: its evasions and contradictions, that is, its fictions in a literary not legal sense. Put another way, today in the West, the law and its fictions have a particular political or juridical force that literature does not possess because of the way the West has increasingly compartmentalized knowledge over time, whereas in traditional Indigenous life, both philosophically and practically, stories have what the West might understand as juridical force, which is to say they prescribe behavior. Unfortunately, colonialism has skewed the traditional though not thwarted it, precisely because the traditional is dynamic: it adopts without necessarily adapting.

US federal Indian law and US American Indian literatures have a very precise relationship with each other. For the one cannot be understood without the other.[4] The reason for the inseparability of the two is the colonial condition that has persisted from 1789, when the first US Congress was seated under the auspices of the Constitution and defined the boundaries of Indian Country, to the present. Today Indian Country includes the 336 federally recognized tribes in the lower forty-eight states (and one reservation in Alaska) that are defined oxymoronically as "domestic dependent nations," the phrase articulated by Chief Justice John Marshall in his 1831 opinion in *Cherokee Nation v. Georgia*.[5] This phrase is *dicta* that in effect has become *doctrine*, as has Marshall's statement noting that this "relation to the United States resembles that of a ward to his guardian."[6] Thus the tribes are minors before the law that governs them, even though the treaty relationship, from which this law springs, suggests a relationship between sovereign nations. It follows, then, that the language of "consent between equals" that informs the treaties is no more than an alibi for the genocidal violence that compelled the treaties and the ceding of Native lands that was their purpose.

However, the language of federal Indian law erases the genocide that grounds it, beginning with the Supreme Court decision in *Johnson and Graham's Lessee v. M'Intosh*,[7] which translated nonfungible Native communal lands into *property*, the very essence of which is fungibility, so that the federal government could claim title, actually and virtually, to these lands. The Lumbee legal scholar Robert A. Williams Jr. calls *Johnson* the "legal basis" of "genocide."[8] To say, then, that US federal Indian law and Native literatures are inseparably bound, means that on the one hand a person cannot understand Native literatures without understanding the colonial context in and to which they are responding, a context structured by federal Indian law; and on the other hand, a person cannot understand federal Indian law without reading Native literatures, which make legible, as in a palimpsest, the genocidal violence that federal Indian law, taken by itself, erases. From the writings of the antebellum Pequot human rights activist William Apess to Louise Erdrich's 2012 National Book Award-winning novel *The Round House*—a story of the jurisdictional traps that spring in trying to prosecute the rape of a Native woman by a non-Native man on a North Dakota Anishinaabe reservation—US American Indian literatures articulate a rigorous critique, explicitly and implicitly, of US federal Indian law. Thus, not to understand federal Indian law and Native literatures as a single story of conflict is to leave gaps in the narrative of this law and these literatures taken separately that render them, literally, incomprehensible.

In *Worcester v. Georgia*,[9] the third of the "Marshall trilogy" (*Johnson* and *Cherokee Nation* being chronologically the first two cases), Chief Justice Marshall, writing for the Court, recognized in his opinion a separate, inherent, if subordinate, sovereignty in the tribes (subordinate to the federal government but not to the states). But, in the way that federal Indian law takes away with the left hand what it gives with the right, the history of this law is the history of the Supreme Court narrowing the reach of Native sovereignty without Congress—which, as affirmed by the Court, has "plenary power" in Indian affairs—intervening, except in one notable instance.[10] The Lumbee scholar of federal Indian law David Wilkins points out that the "judiciary has never voided a single congressional act that diminished or abrogated any inherent or aboriginal tribal rights."[11] In effect, then, there is no judicial review in federal Indian law. If the lower federal courts find for tribal interests, which they do on occasion, the Supreme Court will grant certiorari and reverse in keeping with what it understands as congressional intent expressed in treaties and statutes. In this system, the Court acts as Congress's proxy, its alibi in the colonial policing of the tribes. As Wilkins points out, "'federal Indian law' as a discipline having coherent and interconnected premises is wholly a myth."[12] The law's incoherence is a mark of its violence, of the genocide by other means it visits on the tribes.

A series of Trade and Intercourse acts, promulgated by Congress between 1790 and 1834, and one Supreme Court decision, *Oliphant v. The Suquamish Indian Tribe*,[13] handed down in 1978, mark the federal subversion of tribal sovereignty in the area of criminal jurisdiction, which is the focus of Erdrich's novel. In section 25 of the Trade and Intercourse Act of 1834, Congress states:

> That so much of the laws of the United States as provides for the punishment of crimes committed within any place within the sole and exclusive jurisdiction of the United States, shall be in force in the Indian country: *Provided*, The same shall not extend to crimes committed by one Indian against the person or property of another Indian.[14]

The Major Crimes Act of 1885 vitiated if it did not technically erase this Indian-on-Indian-crime exception and thereby extended federal jurisdiction over all major crimes in Indian Country, with some subsequent exceptions.[15] Interpreting both treaties and congressional statutes of the kind just cited, the Supreme Court, with Chief Justice Rehnquist writing the opinion of the Court in *Oliphant* and Justices Marshall and Burger dissenting, reversed two lower federal courts in finding "that Indian tribes do not have inherent jurisdiction to try and to punish non-Indians."[16] In *dicta*, the opinion argued that only Congress had the power to grant such jurisdiction, thus, once again, affirming the "plenary power" doctrine. However, in reaching the majority opinion, the Court

> recognize[d] that some Indian tribal court systems have become increasingly sophisticated and resemble in many respects their state counterparts. We also acknowledge that with the passage of the Indian Civil Rights Act of 1968, which extends certain basic procedural rights to anyone tried in Indian tribal court, many of the dangers that might have accompanied the exercise by tribal courts of criminal jurisdiction over non-Indians only a few decades ago have disappeared. Finally, we are not unaware of the prevalence of non-Indian crime on today's reservations which the tribes forcefully argue requires the ability to try non-Indians.[17]

By "sophisticated" here the Court, exhibiting its colonial mentality unselfconsciously, meant "Westernized." But what is noteworthy is the Court's recognition "of the prevalence of non-Indian crime on today's reservation," which its decision only encouraged, a brutal irony that seemed to escape the majority. Commenting on the Major Crimes Act, for which the Bureau of Indian Affairs (BIA) had lobbied forcefully, Sidney Harring notes:

> Though pleased that the final act followed closely their original proposal, BIA officials were concerned that without a substantial appropriation of funds, the legislation would have no impact. Local federal, state, and territorial authorities were often not interested in crimes on Indian reservations and might be deterred from pursuing felons under the act by the high cost of such prosecutions.[18]

The situation described in 1885 by Harring was implicitly noted in 1978 by the Rehnquist court when it remarked on "the prevalence of non-Indian crime on today's reservations." That is, having assumed jurisdiction of major crimes in Indian country, the federal government failed to commit the necessary resources, both human and financial, to effectively police this jurisdiction. This failure continues to the present moment. On November 12, 2012, the *New York Times* ran a story by Timothy Williams titled "Washington Steps Back from Policing Indian Lands, Even as Crime Rises." The first paragraph of the story tells the story: "The federal government has cut the size of its police force in Indian country, reduced financing for law enforcement and begun fewer investigations of violent felony crime, even as rates of murder and rape there have increased to more than 20 times the national average, according to data."[19] What is the message in this trajectory from 1885 to 2013? That one can commit genocide by means other than preemptive war and ethnic cleansing. Active neglect of literally murderous conditions, which one has created by promulgating a series of unenforced laws, is certainly another way.

While the *Times* story does not break down the crimes demographically, we have such a breakdown with the crime of rape, where, as Louse Erdrich points out in her "Afterword" to *The Round House* and in an op-ed piece, "Rape on the Reservation," published in the *New York Times* on February 26, 2013, two days before the House passed the Senate version of the Violence Against Women Reauthorization Act of 2013 (VAWA), "[m]ore than 80 percent of sex crimes on reservations are committed by non-Indian men, who are immune from prosecution by tribal courts."[20] Contextualizing this statistic within the legal framework elaborated here, Erdrich notes in her op-ed that "federal prosecutors decline to prosecute 67 percent of sexual abuse cases, according to the Government Accountability Office." In its Title IX, "Safety for Indian Women," VAWA now provides a partial fix for *Oliphant*, but the range in which it provides for the prosecution of non-Indian offenders is very narrow. In an analysis of VAWA, which he published prior to the passage of the bill, Thomas F. Gede gives an accurate summary of S.47:

> [T]he bill provided a "partial" *Oliphant*-fix, giving tribes "special domestic-violence criminal jurisdiction" to hold non-Indian offenders accountable, but only for crimes of domestic violence, dating violence, and violations of protection orders that are committed in Indian country. It would cover only those non-Indians with significant ties to the prosecuting tribe, those who reside in the Indian country of the prosecuting tribe, are employed in the Indian country of the prosecuting tribe, or are either the spouse or intimate partner of a member of the prosecuting tribe.[21]

With all of these limitations, Title IX of VAWA will do little to diminish the tsunami of violent crime against Native women in Indian country. The tribes can still not try the major crime of rape as rape but must try it as a lesser crime and then hope that under the dual sovereignty doctrine affirmed in *U.S. v. Wheeler*[22] the feds will try it as a major crime. But, as we know, because of the lack of resources and political will, that hope is illusory. One can also expect challenges to the constitutionality of the "*Oliphant*-fix," as well as a hopeless overload in the underresourced tribal courts. So the question remains: Where in the haystack of federal Indian law do we find the needle of justice? Erdrich's answer in *The Round House* is "nowhere." That is, the novel tells us, we find justice elsewhere, in traditional tribal law. But even there, because of colonialism's violence, justice cannot be separated from vengeance, a point among others that the next section of this chapter discusses.

FEDERAL INDIAN LAW, SEXUAL VIOLENCE, AND LOUISE ERDRICH'S *THE ROUND HOUSE*

Erdrich's *The Round House* illuminates the connections between genocide and federal Indian law in a story about sexual violence on an Anishinaabe reservation in North Dakota. The novel opens with the brutal rape and attempted murder of Geraldine Coutts, the tribal enrollment officer and wife of tribal judge Bazil Coutts.[23] The story about what happened—what brought Geraldine to the site of the rape, who attacked her and why—unfolds as a mystery, disclosed piece by piece, that ultimately brings into focus the multiple colonial dimensions of the attack and its legal aftermath. As *The Round House* thus brings public attention to the alarmingly high rates of violence against Native women and legal barriers to prosecuting these crimes, it exposes the political investments of federal Indian law by narrating its social effects and its roots in histories of overt colonial violence. Fiction also enables Erdrich to limn the differences between Indigenous and Western legal traditions, and *The Round House* ultimately positions Indigenous law as offering a path to justice denied by colonial law.

Although many forms of colonial violence could have grounded the critique of federal Indian law, the rape narrative carries special significance in part because it draws together multiple, intersecting dimensions of ongoing colonization. Because Native women experience sexual assault at far higher rates than any other group of women,[24] rape shows particularly clearly how the disempowerment of tribal legal systems has rendered Native people vulnerable to violence. The extent of Indian victimization and limits on tribal jurisdiction bear on a range of crimes, but "the problem is greatest in the realm of sexual violence," contends legal scholar N. Bruce Duthu, "because rapes and other sexual assaults on American Indian women are overwhelmingly interracial," so that these crimes fall outside of tribes' prosecutorial authority. Racism, according to Amnesty International, counts among the primary reasons for attacks on Native women, the brutality of these attacks, and the failure of federal and state agencies to investigate or prosecute these crimes.[25] Finally, colonial policies designed to undermine the political autonomy and economic self-sufficiency of Native communities have disproportionately affected Native women, leading to poverty, dislocation, and violence. Indeed, Amnesty International has labeled the vulnerability of Native women a "legacy of history" brought about by these policies.[26] In *The Round House*, the crime of rape thus facilitates the novel's critique of a wide spectrum of colonial attitudes, practices, and policies in which the law is implicated.

In the story, such connections between law and colonization emerge from the reasons for the rape, the place where it occurs, and the insurmountable barriers to prosecuting the rapist. "I suppose I am one of those people who just hates Indians generally," admits rapist Linden Lark as he holds Geraldine captive, because "they were at odds with my folks way back."[27] While racism with deep roots in the past provides one reason for the attack, Linden's family histories underscore continuities between the rape and broader colonial processes, especially as they come to bear on law. These include two legal cases, both heard by Geraldine's husband Bazil, brought against the Larks for attempting to use legal loopholes to swindle the tribe. The Larks lose both cases, and Linden's anger provides yet another reason for the rape. The cases repeat colonial histories about dispossession and economic exploitation, and such connections between past and present underlie another, more distant family tale, one that underscores the racial dimensions of the rape because it involves the participation of Lark's great-uncle in the lynching of innocent tribal members. Lark, in Bazil's words, "[k]nows we can't hold him. Thinks he can get away. Like his uncle."[28]

These same colonial processes of racialized violence, disempowerment, and dispossession—all sanctioned by federal Indian law—bear on the assault itself. "I've been boning up on law," Linden taunts Geraldine, "I know as much law as a judge. . . . [You] have no standing under the law for a good reason and yet have continued to diminish the white man."[29] Here, the novel points to the ways that federal Indian law has weakened tribal sovereignty so that women in particular become vulnerable, while the site of the rape recalls colonial histories that have enabled the attack and show its full political significance. The rape occurs at the round house, a site with multiple political and cultural meanings. Although it is located on the reservation, the round house is a place where tribal, federal, and state landholdings converge, divisions that stem from appropriations of Native territory that continued even after the establishment of the reservation. The place, then, represents colonial dispossession as well as the diminishment of sovereignty because here tribal legal powers, such as they are, come into conflict with those of state and federal governments. Law thus figures as the nexus of violence, dispossession, and political disempowerment, and this is also true of the litany of legal cases the novel cites, from the Marshall decisions to *Lone Wolf v. Hitchcock* (1903), previously cited, which asserted the "plenary power" of Congress in Indian affairs, to *Tee-Hit-Ton Indians v. United States* (1955), which denied Native title to historic land because such title had not been recognized by Congress.[30] Such histories lead directly to the attack. Understanding the legal loopholes created by conflicting legal jurisdiction, Linden blindfolds Geraldine so that she is unaware of the location where the rape takes place, thereby making it impossible to prosecute. The round house is significant for another reason as well. As the place for performing traditional ceremonies, it is a sacred site ordained as "the body of [our] mother,"[31] its beginnings entwined with the origins of the tribe. The resonance with Geraldine, the primary mother figure in the novel, is unmistakable, so that the rape constitutes a violation of cultural traditions and an assault on the community itself. The rape, in other words, is not merely a *consequence* of historical assaults on land, culture and political power but rather *the very paradigm* of ongoing colonial power enacted through violence.

As *The Round House* thus utilizes the rape narrative to expose and condemn colonial power, the novel calls up another gendered narrative at the heart of federal Indian law: that of paternalism. Familial metaphors that position the US government as a father to his Indian children run throughout federal Indian law and policy, finding their most famous expression in the 1831 *Cherokee Nation v. Georgia* decision in which, as noted in the first part of this chapter, Chief Justice John Marshall described Indians as being in a "state of pupilage" and their relation to the United States as "that of a ward to his guardian."[32] Federal Indian law, in other words, obscures US power over tribes by invoking a Western kinship system that aligns Native interests with those of the federal government. In fact, however, *Cherokee Nation* redefined the status of tribes as "domestic dependent nations" to dramatically weaken their sovereignty and claims to land. Familial metaphors obfuscated the colonial nature of *Cherokee Nation* by naturalizing Indian subordination (because Indians are like children) and recasting colonial power as benevolence (because the federal government is like a caring parent). Erdrich's novel exposes the violence of paternalism and denaturalizes the kinship system on which it is based, thus unraveling the logic that positions federal Indian law as politically neutral and benevolent. The patriarchal nuclear family is a colonial imposition tied to other forms of power. The history of the round house itself, narrated by the elder Mooshum, describes a traditional Indigenous form of kinship, the clan system, that underlies tribal law and provides possibilities for justice denied by federal Indian law.

The Round House exposes and refutes the consequences of federal paternalism through its narrative structure and its plot. The story is told from the perspective of Geraldine and Bazil's thirteen-year-old son Joe, whose coming of age entails political understanding and disillusionment. When Bazil, the tribal judge, solicits Joe's help in reviewing past cases to seek clues about the rapist's identity, Joe realizes the limits of his father's power and, by implication, that of the tribe: "I had imagined that my father decided great questions of the law," ruminates Joe, "that he worked on treaty rights, land restoration, that he looked murderers in the eye . . . but as I read on I was flooded by a slow leak of dismay. . . . My father was punishing hot dog thieves and examining washers—not even washing machines—just washers worth 15 cents apiece."[33] Because the adolescent Joe is the story's narrator and its center of consciousness, focusing his growing political awareness on revelations about "our toothless sovereignty" recalls the positioning of Indians as children under colonial law and challenges the structures of authority that it permits.[34]

Further challenging the notion of benevolent paternalism, The Round House represents, and Joe understands, paternalism as brutality enacted on the body of a woman. Not only does federal Indian law create Native women's vulnerability, but also the gendered dynamics of paternalism themselves constitute a form of colonial violence. The novel's critique of paternalism bears on the story of Geraldine as well as that of Mayla Wolfskin, whose murder is entangled with Geraldine's rape. The path that leads to Mayla's murder begins when she finds employment as an intern for South Dakota governor Curtis Yeltow. In the novel, Yeltow appears as a quintessential colonial figure, a government official who is "well known for [but tries to conceal] his bigoted treatment of Indians."[35] Mayla, for her part, represents the "Indian as child" at the center of the discourse of paternalism. As her age and gender make clear, Yeltow's sexual relationship constitutes power and exploitation, though he uses the hiring of an Indian intern for positive publicity. His subsequent attempt to adopt Mayla's child constitutes a strike against tribal sovereignty because it violates the Indian Child Welfare Act,[36] while Linden Lark's jealous response to their relationship reiterates colonial desires for power and possession and ultimately results in Mayla's death. Linden murders Mayla, and the place where her body is unearthed, a federal construction site on tribal land, further underscores connections between the law, dispossession, and violence against Native women.

The narrator Joe rejects the role of child assigned to colonial subjects under federal Indian law when he refuses its authority and the injustice it creates. Realizing that Linden will go free, he sets out to kill his mother's rapist. The killing exposes the impossibility of justice under colonial law: it is "a wrong thing which serves an ideal justice," in Bazil's words, "it settles a legal enigma. It threads that unfair maze of land title law by which Lark could not be prosecuted."[37] The police suspect but can never prove Joe's involvement in the killing, so he is never prosecuted, and in this way the story shows the limits of the law's authority and the possibility of its subversion. The narrative structure of *The Round House* also refutes the positioning of the Indian as a child. Although the story is told from his point of view of Joe as an adolescent, it is narrated retrospectively after he has become an adult. He has followed in his father's footsteps by becoming a lawyer and a tribal judge, influenced perhaps by Bazil's wishful optimism about the possibility of using law to subvert colonial authority: "We are trying to build a solid base here for our sovereignty. We try to press against the boundaries of what we are allowed, walk a step past the edge. Our records will be scrutinized by Congress one day and decisions on whether to enlarge our jurisdiction will be made. Some day."[38] As a child who has become an adult and as a character who transgresses, in multiple ways, the authority of colonial law, Joe redefines in theory the political position of tribes in relation to the federal government in a way that supports self-determination.

The killing defies colonial authority in yet another way because, in the novel's rendering, it falls within the system of traditional Indigenous law that federal Indian law seeks to displace. In the story, federal Indian law creates a legal impasse that denies a justice that only traditional law can redeem. The killing, as Bazil describes it, is an act with a "traditional precedent": "It could be argued that Lark met the definition of a wiindigoo [a being akin to a cannibal]," he explains to Joe, "and that with no other recourse, his killing fulfilled the requirements of a very old law."[39] Here, the novel harkens back to a tribal origin story told by Mooshum, Geraldine's father and a traditional elder, that Joe later understands as "a reading of traditional case law."[40] The story begins in the early reservation period, when the upheavals brought by land loss and starvation disrupt the social life of the community. The husband and brothers of Akiikwe turn against her, accusing her of turning wiindigoo. "Some people in these hungry times became possessed," Mooshum explains, "A wiindigoo could cast its spirit inside of a person. That person would become an animal, and see fellow humans as prey meat."[41] When the men try to kill Akiikwe, only her son Nanapush remains loyal. By saving her, he brings about events that return harmony to the community, affirm the clan system ("the first system of Ojibwe law" that governs human relationships with one another and with animals),[42] and establish the round house. Joe's story follows this one in several respects. Both unfold in the context of social disruptions brought by colonization, and like Nanapush, Joe saves his mother, who remains paralyzed by fear of Linden. This killing not only brings justice but also draws together Joe's family and community, who conspire to protect him from unfair legal consequences. The novel underscores the connection between Joe's story and the one told by Mooshum when, as an adult, Joe marries a member of the Nanapush family so that his story facilitates community connections and cultural continuities over time that colonialism aims to sever.

By describing the clan system as "the first system of Ojibwe law," *The Round House* shows the differences between tribal law and federal Indian law as arising in part from divergent systems of kinship. As the novel thus calls further attention to the social entanglements of the law, it condemns paternalism, along with the patriarchal nuclear family on which it is based, as fundamentally hierarchical and exploitative, whereas the clan system is premised on reciprocal obligation and respect. Additionally, the story of Akiikwe draws out the implications of paternalism for violence against women. In the story, the act that disrupts the social fabric is the attempt by Nanapush's father to kill his mother, and order returns when she is restored to her position and the clan system is established. The attempted killing of Akiikwe resonates with colonial displacements of and violence against Indigenous women, and because the Ojibwe clan system is matrilineal, such contemporary violence constitutes an attack on Ojibwe traditions. Linden's assault on Geraldine repeats the story of Akiikwe, the "unkillable mother",[43] not only because Geraldine is the primary mother figure in the novel but also because, as the tribal enrollment officer, she is the person who holds community memory and establishes community belonging (roles that are tied up with the purposes of the clan system).

Although the killing of Lark constitutes an enactment of traditional law, the colonial predicament leaves little room for self-determination and so renders impossible the proper enactment of traditional law. Joe must act secretly, telling only his best friend Cappy (who becomes complicit in the murder and fires the shot that ultimately kills Linden). Joe never admits the killing even to his parents, although they nevertheless realize his involvement. Because the killing cannot be processed by the community as traditional law requires, Joe's dreams become haunted by Linden, prompting him to worry that he too now possesses the soul of a "wiindigoo." In this way, the novel extends its critique of paternalism by drawing out the injurious effects of colonial law on the Indian child (or the Indian-as-child).

In *The Round House*, this critique of federal Indian law is inextricably bound to stories, metaphors, and literary form. The rape narrative brings to light the violence enabled by federal Indian law and its ruinous political, social, and psychological consequences, thus exposing the role of law in the ongoing colonization of Native communities. Additionally, by calling up the literary dimensions of federal Indian law itself—the metaphors and narratives that ground paternalism and give it material force—the novel further disputes its neutrality and its standing outside the social relations of colonialism. In this way, too, the novel draws federal Indian law into comparison with traditional law. In Indigenous contexts, law, as it is expressed through oral traditions, writes John Borrows, "does not stand alone" but rather "is given meaning through the context of the larger cultural experiences that surround it."[44] As the rape narrative places federal Indian law in its relevant social and cultural contexts, both the Nanapush tale and the story of the novel itself privilege Indigenous traditions as providing a path to justice and social restoration. As *The Round House* thus overturns colonial hierarchies that undermine Indigenous authority, it unsettles distinctions between law and literature at the heart of the Western tradition.

NOTES

1. There is a growing body of scholarly literature concerning Indigenous "writing." See, for example, Birgit Brander Ramussen, *Queequeg's Coffin: Indigenous Literacies and Early American Literature* (Durham, NC: Duke University Press, 2012).
2. Gerald Vizenor, *Survivance: Narratives of Native Presence* (Lincoln: University of Nebraska Press, 2008), 5–6, 389.
3. Robert Cover makes a similar point in his essay "Violence and the Word," where he notes that word and act are one in legal interpretation, producing violence, whereas in literary production, "It will not do to insist on the violence of strong poetry, and strong poets. Even the violence of weak judges is utterly real." *Narrative, Violence, and the Law: The Essays of Robert Cover*, ed. Martha Minow, Michael Ryan, and Austin Sarat (Ann Arbor: University of Michigan Press, 1995), 213. Essay originally published in *Yale Law Journal* 95 (1986): 1601–29.
4. Eric Cheyfitz, "The (Post)Colonial Construction of Indian Country: U.S. American Indian Literatures and Federal Indian Law," in *The Columbia Guide to American Indian Literatures of the United States Since 1945*, ed. Eric Cheyfitz, 1–124 (New York: Columbia University Press, 2006).
5. Cherokee Nation v. Georgia, 30 U.S. 1, 17 (1831).
6. Ibid.
7. Johnson and Graham's Lessee v. M'Intosh, 21 U.S. 543 (1823).
8. Cited in David Getches, Charles Wilkinson, and Robert A. Williams Jr., *Cases and Materials on Federal Indian Law* (St. Paul, MN: West Group, 1998), 71. For more on *Johnson*, see Eric Cheyfitz, "The Post(Colonial) Construction of Indian Country," 48–50; Eric Cheyfitz, "Savage Law: The Plot against American Indians in *Johnson and Graham's Lessee v. M'Intosh* and *The Pioneers*," in *The*

Cultures of United States Imperialism, ed. Amy Kaplan and Donald E. Pease, 109–128 (Durham: Duke University Press, 1993); Cheyfitz, *The Poetics of Imperialism: Translation and Colonization from "The Tempest" to "Tarzan"*, expanded ed. (Philadelphia: University of Pennsylvania Press, 1997), 10–11; Lindsay G. Robertson, *Conquest by Law: How the Discovery of America Dispossessed Indigenous Peoples of Their Lands* (New York: Oxford University Press, 2005).

9. Worcester v. Georgia, 31 U.S. 515 (1832).

10. The Supreme Court affirmed the "plenary power" doctrine in two cases: United States v. Kagama, 118 U.S. 375 (1886), and Lone Wolf v. Hitchcock, 187 U.S. 553 (1903). The one notable instance of Congressional intervention is the so-called Duro fix (1991), which reversed the Court's decision in Duro v. Reina, 495 U.S. 676 (1990). The *Duro* decision interdicted tribal courts from asserting criminal jurisdiction over non-member Indians. The congressional "fix" reversed that decision in order to fill the jurisdictional gap created by it. For a discussion of the controversial "plenary power" doctrine, see Gregory Ablavsky, "Beyond the Indian Commerce Clause," *Yale Law Journal* 124 (2015), 1012–1089.

11. David E. Wilkins, *American Indian Sovereignty and the U.S. Supreme Court: The Masking of Justice* (Austin: University of Texas Press, 1997), 10.

12. Ibid., 2.

13. Oliphant v. The Suquamish Indian Tribe, 435 U.S. 191 (1978).

14. Francis Paul Prucha, ed., *Documents of United States Indian Policy*, 3rd ed. (Lincoln: University of Nebraska Press, 2000), 67. This is now codified as General Crimes Act, 18 U.S.C.§ 1152, also known as the Federal Enclaves Act or the Indian Country Crimes Act.

15. See United States v. McBratney, 104 U.S. 621 (1882), holding that, absent treaty provisions to the contrary, the state has exclusive jurisdiction over a crime committed in the Indian country by a non-Indian against another non-Indian. Public Law 280 enacted by Congress in 1953 gave five states criminal jurisdiction in Indian country and an option to the other forty-four to assume criminal jurisdiction in whole or in part if they wished. Few have taken up that option and in 1968 Congress amended Pub. L. 280 so that the tribes had to consent to such an assumption from that point on (see Stephen L. Pevar, *The Rights of Indians and Tribes*, 3rd ed. [Carbondale: Southern Illinois University Press, 2002], 122–27).

16. 435 U.S. at 212.

17. Ibid.

18. Sidney L. Harring, *Crow Dog's Case: American Indian Sovereignty, Tribal Law, and United States Law in the Nineteenth Century* (New York: Cambridge University Press, 1994), 140.

19. Timothy Williams, "Washington Steps Back from Policing Indian Lands, Even as Crime Rises," *New York Times*, November 12, 2012; http://www.amren.com/news/2012/11/washington-steps-back-from-policing-indian-lands-even-as-crime-rises/.

20. Louise Erdrich, "Rape on the Reservation," *New York Times*, February 26, 2013; http://www.nytimes.com/2013/02/27/opinion/native-americans-and-the-violence-against-women-act.html?hp.

21. Thomas F. Gede, "Criminal Jurisdiction of Indian Tribes: Should Non-Indians Be Subject to Tribal Criminal Authority Under VAWA?," *Engage* 13, no. 2 (2012): 40–44; http://www.fed-soc.org/publications/detail/criminal-jurisdiction-of-indian-tribes-should-non-indians-be-subject-to-tribal-criminal-authority-under-vawa.

22. United States v. Wheeler, 435 U.S. 313 (1978).

23. Louise Erdrich, *The Round House: A Novel* (New York: Harper Perennial, 2012).

24. Native women in the United States are at least 2.5 times more likely to be raped than any other group of women, and one in three will report being raped during her lifetime. See Amnesty International (AI), *Maze of Injustice: The Failure to Protect Indigenous Women from Sexual Violence in the USA* (New York: Amnesty International, 2007), http://www.amnestyusa.org/pdfs/MazeOfInjustice.pdf; and AI, *Stolen Sisters: A Human Rights Response to Discrimination and Violence against Indigenous Women in Canada* (New York: Amnesty International, 2004), https://www.amnesty.ca/sites/amnesty/files/amr200032004enstolensisters.pdf; N. Bruce Duthu, "Broken Justice in Indian Country," *New York Times*, August 11, 2008, A17.

25. See AI, *Maze of Injustice*.

26. AI, *Stolen Sisters*, 6–7. Although this report refers specifically to Canada, most of the policies it describes were also enacted, in similar form and to similar effect, in the United States.

27. Erdrich, *The Round House*, 161.

28. Ibid., 211.

29. Ibid., 161.

30. Tee-Hit-Ton Indians v. United States 348 U.S. 272, 228–29 (1955).

31. Erdrich, *The Round House*, 214.

32. Cherokee Nation, 30 U.S. at 17.

33. Erdrich, *The Round House*, 48.

34. Ibid., 142

35. Ibid., 157.

36. The Indian Child Welfare Act was passed in 1978 to end the widespread removal of Native children from tribal homes. Because the Act grants tribal governments jurisdiction in child custody proceedings, it constitutes a key dimension of tribal sovereignty as well as efforts to sustain traditional communities and cultures.

37. Erdrich, *The Round House*, 306.

38. Ibid., 229.

39. Ibid., 306.

40. Ibid., 307.

41. Ibid., 180.

42. Ibid., 154

43. Ibid., 187.

44. John Borrows, "Indigenous Legal Traditions in Canada," *Washington University Journal of Law and Policy* 19, no. 13 (2005): 191.

CHAPTER 16

Pluralism, Religion, and Democratic Culture

Nadeem Aslam's Maps for Lost Lovers

ELLIOTT VISCONSI

A novel is a democracy.

Nadeem Aslam

Burkini bans, headscarves, and ostentatious religious garb. Immigrant and refugee camps. Terrorism and violence. Xenophobia and ethnonationalism. Brexit. At this writing in late 2016, the United Kingdom—like other European countries and the United States—is witnessing the reassertion of forceful challenges to the underlying value of racial, ethnic, and religious pluralism within the democratic state. Fueled by anxieties about demographic change, geopolitical unrest, and economic uncertainty, an intemperate and illiberal vocabulary of anti-immigrant nativism has reappeared in mainstream political discourse across the European Union, in the UK, and in the United States. The brutal violence (terrorism, drones, mass shootings) that punctuates geopolitical life has amplified this highly wrought language in contemporary public discourse, where it usually drowns out appeals to shared but evidently bloodless political norms of justice and pluralism.

Corollary crises of free expression are an epiphenomenon of a broader crisis of liberal democracy. Toleration of extreme and often seditious speech is cast as weak-kneed and naïve loyalty to a rights regime dismissed with contempt by the speakers themselves. And as the state discards civil liberties in notorious and persistent security campaigns, the broader state institutions and legal-juridical procedures so essential to a functioning civil society are eroded by an unsurprising and pervasive feeling of public distrust. Diminished in status within public discourse, the liberal state and its procedures are often described as overreaching and impotent, as a tool of manipulative elites rather than an instrument of the popular, safely homogenizing will. Finally, in the public discourse of the moment, blame for this apparent crisis of political liberalism is set at the feet of the very minority groups who are repulsed from entry into public life or not recognized as legitimate participants therein. Pluralism has come to seem like a political problem to be solved through the instrumentality of the state or through the implementation of naked political will, rather than an underlying norm constitutive of vibrant democratic liberalism itself.

The felt absence of robust pluralism in the UK in 2009 prompted Rowan Williams (then Archbishop of Canterbury) to argue notoriously that the United Kingdom was composed of "non-communicating little groups of people locked up in their corners, dominated by their own prejudices and their own superstitions, among which the state has somehow to keep the peace."[1] As part of his contemplation of the possibility of introducing specifically confessional courts to adjudicate specifically confessional matters (sharia, *beth din*), Williams lamented the fact that religious Britons felt increasingly alienated from the law and the democratic process: "if the law of the land takes no account of what might be for certain agents a proper rationale for behavior—for protest against certain unforeseen professional requirements, for instance, which would compromise religious discipline or belief—it fails in a significant way to communicate with someone involved in the legal process (or indeed to receive their communication)."[2] The condition Williams laments is not only a needless dismissal of religious expression, but also a lost opportunity for meaningful democratic self-government. A polity divided into antagonistic and noncommunicating little groups, without the presence of productive struggle and a shared underlying commitment to democratic principles, is the precondition for the collapse of public culture and of democratic institutions.[3]

Britain has a long history of violent struggle around questions of domestic religious pluralism; the seventeenth century is ample, vivid testimony of such a durable historical pattern, but postwar and postcolonial immigration flows have transformed that pattern into its contemporary shape, in which race and religion are the most prominent and indelible markers of difference.[4] The questions: to what degree, if at all, should Britain accommodate the preferences of religious minorities, especially when those preferences seem to strike at the very core of liberal and democratic values? Can race and religion be conflated, or untethered from each other? To what extent is the persistence of isolated minority groups a threat to the social fabric or to a transcendent conception of the state? Upon whom should any burden of accommodation or assimilation be placed? How asymmetrical can such a burden be, before it becomes openly violative of the rights conventions and aspirational values to which the United Kingdom subscribes? The contemporary United Kingdom, post-Brexit, is teetering on the brink of backsliding into ethno-nationalism; the answer to these and similar questions, for many Britons, is unflinching and inhospitable.

The latest recrudescence of hostility toward Muslim Britons in the era of al-Qaeda and ISIS is, in part, legible as a phase in a long-term oscillation of crisis and accommodation in regard to religious difference, a wave that rises and falls in rhetorical amplitude in line with geopolitical, cultural, and economic contingencies. The wave of hostility and skepticism toward pluralism is now amplifying, fueled by the double-headed beast of "immigration and terrorism." But popular hostility toward the norm of democratic pluralism (e.g., the notion that difference has unimpeachable value to the process of democratic self-government) also has features specific to post-1989 politics, the newly multilateral and neoliberalizing era, in which civil rights and fundamental liberties are protected and promoted in a trans-European context by the European Court of Human Rights (ECHR) and others.[5]

The holdings of the ECHR on questions of religious expression are rendered in reference to Article 9 of the European Convention on Human Rights:

> Section 1. Everyone has the right to freedom of thought, conscience and religion; this right includes freedom to change his religion or belief, and freedom, either alone or in community with others and in public or private, to manifest his religion or belief, in worship, teaching, practice and observance.
>
> Section 2. Freedom to manifest one's religion or beliefs shall be subject only to such limitations as are prescribed by law and are necessary in a democratic society in the interests of public safety, for the protection of public order, health or morals, or the protection of the rights and freedoms of others.[6]

The right to freedom of thought, conscience and religion (the *forum internum*) is inviolable and largely beyond the reach of law, being an internal condition; indeed extremely few cases are brought under this area. However, the right to "manifest ... belief ... in worship, teaching, practice, and observance" is another matter, for in some circumstances, the manifestation of belief can provoke a collision with public order or an infringement upon the rights of others. Section 2 of Article 9 provides the participating states with latitude to enforce public order by restraining or interfering with specific manifestations of religion. Such latitude is called the "margin of appreciation."[7] Balancing generally applicable Article 9 rights with the specific local particulars, the margin of appreciation is itself arguably a technology of pluralism.

As a doctrine, the margin of appreciation permits political difference among states but appeals to a shared underlying conception of justice (universal rights and liberties) as well as a fundamental legal regime (the European Convention on Human Rights). So in ECHR jurisprudence shaped by the margin of appreciation, it is possible to discover potentially incommensurable, or at least inconsistently aligned, holdings around religious expression and the manifestations of religion. Thus the ECHR upheld the prior restraint of *Das Liebeskonzil*, a film that was demonstrably upsetting to a Tyrolean Catholic majority and which was described as blasphemous and threatening to social tranquility.[8] And the ECHR likewise upheld a Turkish university's ban on Islamic headscarves, seeing that policy as a justified interference with Leyla Şahin's Article 9 rights. In *Leyla Şahin v. Turkey* (2005), the court afforded Turkey an especially large margin of appreciation because of the central place of secularism in the fundamental law of the Turkish republic: secularism "is undoubtedly one of the fundamental principles of the Turkish State which are in harmony with the rule of law and the respect for human rights" [and as such] the state's interference with Sahin's article 9 rights must be permitted.[9] Academics such as Susanna Mancini and Joan Scott have been critical of the ECHR's willingness to provide a wide "margin of appreciation" in cases of interference with religious expression, especially insofar as such interferences fall disproportionately in their view upon European Muslims and Muslim women in particular.[10]

Despite the elasticity of the margin of appreciation principle, the ECHR has in a string of decisions, beginning with *Kokkinakis v. Greece* and including *Supreme Holy Council of the Muslim Community v. Bulgaria*, consistently has articulated the deep and valued tie between democracy, pluralism, and religion:

> The Court reiterates that the autonomous existence of religious communities is indispensable for pluralism in a democratic society. . . . What is at stake here

is the preservation of pluralism and the proper functioning of democracy, one of the principal characteristics of which is the possibility it offers of resolving a country's problems through dialogue, even when they are irksome.[11]

Such a promise does not always feel realized in the daily experience of religious minorities. Indeed, some religious actors might agree with the 2007 UNHCR report which contends that, in European law and political culture, "aggressive secularist rhetoric" and "increasing hostility toward religious symbols" are flourishing.[12] As religion is diminished within public discourse, so fares pluralism.

The strict exclusion of individual and group manifestations of religion in French public life, advanced under the banner of *laïcité* and animated by the spirit of horizontal republican confraternity, is for many scholars the signature feature of liberal political secularism.[13] For critics such as Talal Asad and Bill Connolly, strong secularism diminishes religious expression as a valued feature of a pluralist state.[14] Secularism, for Saba Mahmood, is built upon a robust separation of church and state and yet also structures and reorganizes "substantive features of religious life, stipulating what religion is or ought to be, assigning its proper content, and disseminating concomitant subjectivities, ethical frameworks, and quotidian practices."[15] In her account, moreover, secularity is self-regenerating—"any incursion of the state into religious life often engenders the demand to keep church and state separate, thereby replenishing secularism's normative premise and promise." Symbolic displays of religious belief (clothing, in particular) thus take on added gravity in public discourse, for they invite regulatory intervention or illustrate the fact of minority religious difference as a provocation to the public at large. Mahmood's analysis, on its face, resonates with the portrait of truncated pluralism and alienation of which Rowan Williams writes. By privatizing religious belief while subjecting religious manifestations to the regulatory and definitional attention of the state, secularism clusters observant believers together into isolated communities huddled in defensive resistance and alienated from public discourse.[16] Secularism, on this account, hinders the flourishing of democratic pluralism by hardening identitarian and confessional boundaries rather than inviting all into a capacious and inclusive vision of public discourse.

The situation is a bit more nebulous in the United Kingdom, in which there is neither a presumption of secular neutrality, as in France, nor a US-style generalized liberty of religious expression. Insofar as the head of the established church is also the sovereign, the UK is far from state secularism, even if the practice and prestige of religious belief is on the wane. Despite the political headwinds of the post-Brexit environment, the UK is equipped with a constitutional posture relatively congenial to religion (an established church, meaningful and persistent religious diversity). It is even plausible to imagine the nonrevolutionary development of a "civil religion" along American lines where the functional separation of church and state is complemented by rituals, ceremonies, and gestures that recognize the role of religion in the history and lived experience of the nation. If French or Turkish *laïcité* negates religious difference in the desire to promote horizontal republican confraternity, UK law might be more readily deployed to nurture democratic pluralism and the affirmative celebration of religious difference often promoted by the ECHR in decisions such as *Supreme Council v. Bulgaria* and many others.

It is into these waters that the British-Pakistani novelist Nadeem Aslam has waded. Aslam is an avowedly political writer; he eschews "Muslims are people too" Booker-bait fiction built around geopolitical grand narratives and charismatic struggles for personal liberty set against a cardboard cut-out of Islamic culture. "A novelist doesn't tell you what to think; a novelist tells you what to think about," he has remarked, seeing his fiction as a stimulus for collective engagement with the world. In his own account, Aslam implements a traditional fictional method built around style and finely grained characterization, designed to cultivate a deeper acquaintance with and empathy for individual human action within the eye of history:

> I won't say this or that American character is bad, or a Pakistani character is bad. I will show you their history, beliefs, and conduct, and then let you make up your mind about him. A novel is a democracy—if it is about two characters then you cannot have character A be fully developed and character B poorly developed. The reader would feel the lack. . . . I don't look at my characters as representatives of a religion, nation, or ideology. I don't really care about countries—I am more interested in people.[17]

Such an approach, building from the ground up around the fine particulars and contextual details of everyday life, is a consistent feature of Aslam's novels. His two most recent novels, *The Wasted Vigil* (2008) and *The Blind Man's Garden* (2013), pursue this method through the setting of post-9/11 Afghanistan, particularizing that ostensible clash of civilizations into affective moving local contingencies. It is not controversial to suggest that fiction can be an instrument of sympathy and of cultural memory, a site where communities develop, negotiate, and transmit identity. Simon

During has put it well: "Modern serious fiction, in its virtuality, has the capability to report what it is like to live now—to feel, think, share, love, hate, dream, hope, despair, drift, remember— and it does so across a range of situations, identities and types, while essaying unrealized experiential possibilities."[18]

Left unsaid so far is a question fundamental to law and literature as an academic enterprise. Is the literary merely a charismatic and involving fact pattern, potentially of a piece with other particular records of experience that prompt or solicit legal remedies? Or does the literary (narrative, fiction, epic) enjoy special status as a constitutive element in the formation of the nomos we inhabit? These questions were pioneered by Robert Cover in his generative article "*Nomos* and Narrative." For Cover, "law and narrative are inseparably related." On this account, law obtains and sustains its normative meaning from cultural narratives, which are in turn shaped by law:

> No set of legal institutions or prescriptions exists apart from the narratives that give it meaning. For every constitution there is an epic, for every decalogue a scripture. . . . Every prescription is insistent in its demand to be located in discourse—to be supplied with history and destiny, beginning and end, explanation and purpose. And every narrative is insistent in its demand for its prescriptive point, its moral. History and literature cannot escape their location in a normative universe, nor can prescription, even when embodied in a legal text, escape its origin and its end in experience.[19]

Nadeem Aslam's 2004 novel *Maps for Lost Lovers* is an intervention into the public argument about pluralism and assimilation in the United Kingdom, a narrative that illuminates the prescriptive regimes and structuring epiphenomena of law in post-9/11 Britain. *Maps* is also a thick description of the lived experience of being a stranger in the land, inhabiting a "noncommunicating little group" within the vast and anonymous British state. In the pages that follow, I take Aslam's stated approach at face value. The novel is an agenda-setting narrativization of a legal regime, and specifically a richly textured and individuated account of the failures of democratic pluralism and social relations within an incompletely secularized polity.[20] Like Aslam's other fiction, *Maps for Lost Lovers* seeks to cultivate those habits of thought that can lead to collective engagement and political change. As such, it is legible as part of a broader cultural initiative, no less valuable or effective than the Article 9 decisions of the ECHR, to enrich democracy by provoking a more capacious vision of public culture and beyond it of the pluralist state.

Maps for Lost Lovers delivers a powerful vision of life in "the desert of solitude" that is contemporary England; the novel describes a world in which alienation and despair trump political belonging and the promise of democratic pluralism. But Aslam's novel is more than a mere representation of lived experience; it is a carefully crafted diagnosis of the structure of social and political relations in contemporary Britain, in which Muslim immigrant communities are alienated from full participation in the procedures of the state and the affective experience of public life. Focused on a single immigrant family and its penumbra, *Maps* organizes its account around the master trope of solitude.

In the contemporary United Kingdom, Muslim immigrants and in some cases second-generation Muslim Britons are routinely cast as disaffected aliens severed by custom and choice from full participation in the democratic machinery of the state. Such claims routinely overlook the invidious machinery of quotidian discrimination (hate speech, refusals to hire or admit minorities, and the like). But to be sure, there are also plenty of normative pressures on Muslim Britons, and especially on first-generation immigrants whose ties to their original country are more durable, that can compel individuals to seek less than full membership in the political community. In some cases, participatory disincentives for Muslim Britons are explicitly religious.

English law, which is trending secular since the 2008 abolition of the blasphemy laws, describes a normative universe often quite distant from the familiar terrain of sharia law, even if from one perspective the English state is more congenial to religion than, say, France. In such circumstances, many Muslim Britons seek the guidance of sharia and the counsel of scholars and imams even if it means incurring additional risk and further alienation from democratic processes. There are also functional disincentives to political assimilation: traditional customs, organizations, and kinship structures both licit and illicit are often valued for their utility in negotiating a hostile polity.

Maps for Lost Lovers is an account of two generations of an extended Pakistani-British family as they experience the aftermath of an honor killing; their brother and uncle Jugnu and his girlfriend Chanda are murdered by her unrepentant brothers. The novel is written in a Jamesian mode focusing with intense, almost lapidary, detail on the closed universe of Dasht-e-Tanhaii, the anonymous postindustrial city that the family inhabits as "strangers in the land." Indeed, with the exception of a few references to the distant London, the novel rarely refers outside of its narrowly delimited world; only the machinery of English law (in the form of criminal process) and the experience of racial discrimination intrude upon this closed world.[21] Although the city evolves, there is one constant: "as more and more people came, the various nationalities of the Subcontinent have changed the names [of streets and neighborhoods] according to the specific country they themselves are from . . . [but] only one name has been accepted by every group, remaining unchanged. It's the name of the town itself. Dasht-e-Tanhaii. The Wilderness of Solitude. The Desert of Loneliness" (29).

The master trope of crushing solitude governs the intergenerational struggle between the immigrant parents—Kaukab the strictly religious mother and Jugnu's brother, Shamas, the patriarch and central figure of the novel—and their assimilated and apostate children. Shamas is a highly respected community leader, a former communist, and a religious skeptic who works doggedly as an advocate for and organizer of immigrants; despite his distinguished position, Shamas is a figure of tragic stasis. He remains tethered to the poor neighborhood in which he and his wife Kaukab have lived since their arrival, and resists, out of indifference, honors and preferments that might offer a path to material comfort and assimilation. Shamas demonstrates little interest in the consolations of Islam, and despite his status, he is targeted and beaten by a gang of kidnappers who specialize in "family reunification"— these thugs return wayward children by force into the coercive bosom of their families, whose honor is at stake. The gang offers to revisit the beating with greater force: "next time we'll deal with you in a Pakistani way," they warn. Shamas fails to inform the police; he is victimized by the customs and usages of the old country but still beneath the notice of the legal machinery of the English and as such his emblematic status as a lonely "stranger in the land" is amplified.

Kaukab, Shamas's wife, is much more at home with "the Pakistani way"—indeed, she visits the kidnappers with the vain hope of bringing her assimilated son Ujala back home—and she seeks the consolations and guidance of a narrow reading of Islamic law at every turn. She rebukes her daughter Mah-Jabin for deserting her abusive fundamentalist husband: "you may have divorced him under British law, but haven't done so in a Muslim court. My religion is not the British legal system, it's Islam" (118). Kaukab is tethered to Pakistan by language, religion, custom, and nostalgia; she seeks no accommodation with English law or culture and views the West as a site of godless pollution: "for the people in the west, an offence that did no harm to another human or to the wider society was no offence at all, but to her—to all Muslims—there was always another party involved— Allah" (44). But despite—or, the novel implies, perhaps because of— her apparent comfort in the strict authority of Islamic law, Kaukab suffers from a familiar crushing loneliness:

here Kaukab is, away from her children, away from her customs and country, alone and lonely, and yet He [Allah] tells her to have faith in His compassion. And that is what she should do uncomplainingly, reminding herself that she is not lost, that He is with her in this strange place. And yet she doesn't know what to do about the fact that she feels utterly empty almost all of the time, as though she has outlived herself, as if she stayed on the train one stop past her destination. (276)

Within the desert of solitude, Dasht-e-Tanhaii, the honor killings of Chanda and Jugnu make a muted but slowly resonant impact; the crime itself is unfolded gradually and without procedural intrigue, the effect of which is to focus attention away from any investigation and to keep it on the emotional density of the crime. Aslam resists the impulse to unfold an illuminating collision of normative orders, and the brothers are instead blundering thugs incapable of any charismatic language of justification. They find encouragement in Pakistan: Chanda's brothers "knew the law of [England] would not view their crime indulgently. They boasted of having killed her and Jugnu—but only in Pakistan, where the laws and the religion and the customs reinforced their sense of having acted properly, legitimately, correctly" (357). The novel demonstrates the awful hypocrisy of the brothers (one keeps a mistress, the other aborts a girl fetus only to discover to his chagrin that it was a boy) but the trial itself is almost an afterthought, intruding into the narrative incrementally. The verdict earns a short paragraph

the judge [said] that the killers had found a cure to their problem through an immoral, indefensible act; a cure, a remedy—and their religion and background took care of the bitter aftertaste. Their religion and background assured them that, yes, there were murderers but that they had murdered only sinners. The judge said that Jugnu and Chanda had done nothing illegal in deciding to live together . . . but the two brothers feel that the fact that an act is legal does not mean it's right. (286)

This is as close to *Antigone* as we are to get, and when the next account of the verdict comes in a hundred pages, it too is affectively inert:

Here in England, the judge, batting down all talk of "code of honour and shame" would call them "cowards" and "wicked" on the day of the trial. . . . A distinguished Pakistani commentator on the Asian radio too would be forthright: "some immigrants think that just because they belong to a minority they are nice people, that they should be forgiven everything just because they were oppressed." As for the murderers themselves, after the verdict had been announced they would begin to shout in the court the litanies, including words like "racism" and "prejudice." The judge's remarks would be deemed to have "insulted our culture and our religion." They'd said England was a country of "prostitutes and homosexuals." Being led away, the younger, Chotta, would shout "it's a kangaroo court!" (357)

Here Aslam illustrates the manner in which both the court and the criminals are speaking in "litanies," each actor using a kind of knee-jerk boilerplate (which Aslam sets off in scare quotes). The judge's admonition provides no consolation, no feeling of compensatory justice to the victimized family, and Chotta's outburst is not entirely wrong—insofar as the court has failed in one duty. Although it delivers a proper verdict, the court acts finally in its own interest, without communicating either inclusion or satisfaction to the victims; this scene passes without comment and only heightens the feelings of individual alienation from the machinery of law and beyond it the democratic process.

Aslam's wilderness of solitude is pitiless; no one who inhabits the closed universe of Dasht-e-Tanhaii has access to any form of meaningful belonging. Neither sharia nor British law delivers a feeling of compensatory justice for loss; punishment is never consolation. The durable customs and traditions of Pakistan are either tainted by naïve nostalgia or polluted by barbarism. Second-generation children reject these traditional forms of belonging but sit uneasily within a British society that can't clear the hurdle of race and religion. The immigrant community—potentially a source of horizontal comradeship—is merely proximal and contingent. In Aslam's vision, there are no communities of affirmative belonging available to Pakistani Britons, just deep, crushing loneliness. Neither first- nor second-generation Pakistani Britons have meaningful access to the machinery of democratic decision-making, and the feeling of alienation from such processes is absolute.

Maps for Lost Lovers describes in precise detail the attenuated pluralism and partially implemented pseudosecularity that structures the experience of immigrant groups and religious minorities in the United Kingdom. Public discourse is distant from view, legal procedures are opaque, and the community huddles together in desperate but weak solidarity bereft of any of the consolations of community. Unlike France, where the principle of *laïcité* is announced in the fundamental law, in Aslam's Britain, the presence of immigrant communities and the fact of their religious difference is a regrettable postimperial hangover. These communities are not traumatized by aggressive state intervention nor described as combatants in a charismatic struggle over conceptions of the state. They are instead ignored or resented as parasites on the social body, unassimilable strangers in the land rather than contributors to the democratic process and a richly textured and inclusive conception of the state.

Republican neutrality (as in French or Turkish *laïcité*) asks some minorities to travel too far in the quest for horizontal national community. Expressive freedom, as, for instance, in the wearing of garb signaling religious observance, invites all citizens into the same sphere of public discourse on equal terms, free to manifest their commitments and have those commitments valued as contributions to robust democratic pluralism. Within such a vision of the state, a shared underlying conception of justice, perhaps a Rawlsian conception of fundamental intuitive ideas of rights and liberties shared in common, becomes the essential precondition. "Embedded pluralism" of this kind, for Bill Connolly, is a developmental process that should be nurtured in culture and underwritten through regulatory state action. The result, he writes, "of such a process is to transfigure the myth of a uniform majority that tolerates or represses a set of discrete minorities ranged around it into a visible culture of interdependent minorities of multiple types negotiating a generous ethos of governance between them."[22] *Maps for Lost Lovers* is poised at an early stage in Connolly's developmental process, in which the begrudging tolerance and intermittent hostility of the "uniform majority" dominate and structure the everyday life of the Pakistani immigrant community in Dasht-e-Tanhaii. The novel's charge to its readers—perhaps its political imperative—is to continue the work of building a meaningful pluralism, replacing isolation with interdependence by imagining and creating a more capacious British state.

Connolly's embedded pluralism is a theoretical aspiration rather than a description, although he hopes it will be "a viable corrective to cultural relativism, shallow secular diversity, and national models of exclusionary politics."[23] Most crucially, such a posture amplifies the *feeling* of democratic legitimacy—it communicates the state's endorsement of pluralism to minorities and it helps the state to recognize, or hear, the communications of those same groups. But free expression, on this reading, is free— with that liberty also comes blasphemy, and exposure to the speech that demeans or provokes. In a public realm broadly permissive of symbolic expression, exposure to blasphemy and offensive speech are the entry cost that some must pay. Democratic legitimacy within a pluralist state not only depends upon regulatory permission for religious free exercise. Also it hangs on cultivating the feeling of access to public discourse and to the machinery of decision making.[24] Solitude is its antithesis, the alienation from such processes. Conversely, a legal regime that provides wide latitude for religious speech of all kind reduces solitude and alienation by offering each citizen equal access to democratic discourse while manifesting their full capacities and habits of belonging. Put another way, the cure for solitude is blasphemy.

A goal of this chapter has been to position Aslam's affectively involving *Maps for Lost Lovers* within its wider British and European theoretical and legal conversation about religion, immigration, and the failed promise of pluralism. My claim that the novel sits within this context is, I hope, faithful to Aslam's own intentions as a political writer seeking to provoke collective engagement through a cultivated imagination. On this account, the novel is an exercise in humanist pedagogy, designed to provoke in its readers identification, sympathy, and the therapeutic enhancement of the political imagination. Fiction has long been an available technology through which may be cultivated those intellectual habits of mind, creative faculties, and political dispositions so central to flourishing liberalism.[25] Specific legal doctrines, conceptions of the state, and discursive structures of power are revealed in their operational effects within *Maps*, and the novel itself is legible as an affective description sharing a common vocabulary and set of allusions with legal decisions and theoretical studies concerned with the limitations of British pluralism. But fiction is not evidence, nor does fiction have regulatory power. It certainly does possess cultural authority; the market often provides works such as *Maps* with prestige and visibility, amplifying the political engagements so central to Aslam's stated method.

In composing this chapter, one of my aims has been modest—to summon the politico-legal context and analytical vocabulary that structures the contemporary public conversation about democratic pluralism, religious diversity, and the conceptions of the state—and demonstrate how *Maps for Lost Lovers* participates in and contributes to that shared public discourse. In so doing, I have tried to avoid replicating the purely instrumental use of the literary as charismatic evidence within a jurisprudential or sociological argument, a maneuver that asks fiction to account for itself as a utility in the service of the law.[26]

By revealing the operations of power in richly textured ways, and describing the discursive structures that shape individual experience, fictional works such as *Maps for Lost Lovers* may be able to redirect public discourse, change the tone or content of the political vocabulary, or potentially inspire steps toward a shared underlying conception of justice.

NOTES

1. Rowan Williams, "Faith in the Public Sphere," lecture at Leicester Cathedral, March 22, 2009; http://rowanwilliams.archbishopofcanterbury.org/articles.php/817/faith-in-the-public-square-lecture-at-leicester-cathedral.
2. Rowan Williams, "Civil and Religious Law in England: A Religious Perspective," *Ecclesiastical Law Journal* 10 (2008): 262–82.
3. Chantal Mouffe, "Religion, Liberal Democracy, and Citizenship," in *Political Theologies: Public Religions in a Post-Secular World*, ed. Hent de Vries and Lawrence E. Sullivan, 318–26 (New York: Fordham University Press, 2006); William E. Connolly, "Pluralism and Faith," in de Vries and Sullivan, *Political Theologies*, 278–97.
4. Randall Hansen, *Citizenship and Immigration in Postwar Britain* (Oxford: Oxford University Press, 2000); Paul Gilroy, *There Ain't No Black in the Union Jack* (Chicago: University of Chicago Press, 1987); Enda Delaney, *The Irish in Postwar Britain* (Oxford: Oxford University Press, 2007); Kathleen Paul, *Whitewashing Britain: Race and Citizenship in the Postwar Era* (Ithaca, NY: Cornell University Press, 2014).
5. Bernadette Meyler, "Law, Literature, and History: The Love Triangle," *UC Irvine Law Review* 5 (2010): 365–91.
6. Article 9 of the European Convention on Human Rights.
7. Andrew Legg, *The Margin of Appreciation in International Human Rights Law: Deference and Proportionality* (Oxford: Oxford University Press, 2012); and Eyal Benvenisti, "Margin of Appreciation, Consensus, and Universal Standards," *NYU Journal of International Law and Politics* 31 (1998): 843–54.
8. Otto-Preminger-Institut v. Austria, no. 13470, ECHR (1994).
9. Leyla Şahin v. Turkey, no 44774/98, ECHR XI (2005).
10. Susanna Mancini, "The Power of Symbols and the Symbols of Power: Secularism and Religion as Guarantors of Cultural Convergence," *Cardozo Law Review* 30 (2009): 2665; Joan Wallach Scott, *The Politics of the Veil* (Princeton, NJ: Princeton University Press, 2009).
11. Supreme Holy Council of the Muslim Community v. Bulgaria, no 39023/97 ECHR IX (2005). Cf. Bernadette Meyler, "The Limits of Group Rights: Religious Institutions and Religious Minorities in International Law," *St. John's Journal of Legal Commentary* 22 (2007): 535–58.
12. Doudou Diène (Special Rapporteur on Contemporary Forms of Racism, Racial Discrimination, Xenophobia and Related Intolerance), *Racism, Racial Discrimination, Xenophobia and Related Forms of Intolerance: Follow-Up to and Implementation of the Durban Declaration and Programme of Action*, A/HRC/6/6, United Nations Human Rights Council (August 21, 2007), https://documents-dds-ny.un.org/doc/UNDOC/GEN/G07/137/32/PDF/G0713732.pdf?OpenElement.
13. Patrick Weil, "Why the French Laïcité Is Liberal," *Cardozo Law Review* 30 (2009): 2699–714.
14. Mouffe, "Religion, Liberal Democracy and Citizenship"; Connolly, "Pluralism and Faith"; and Talal Asad, *Formations of the Secular: Christianity, Islam, Modernity* (Stanford, CA: Stanford University Press, 2003).
15. Saba Mahmood, *Religious Difference in a Secular Age* (Princeton, NJ: Princeton University Press, 2015), 4.

16. Ibid., 3–4.
17. Terry Hong, "An Interview with Nadeem Aslam," *Bookslut*, July 2013, http://www.bookslut.com/features/2013_07_020162.php; "Mystery Is All There Is: Michael E. Halmshaw Interviews Nadeem Aslam," *Guernica*, August 15, 2015, https://www.guernicamag.com/interviews/mystery-is-all-there-is/.
18. Simon During, "Completing Secularism: The Mundane in the Neoliberal Era," in *Varieties of Secularism in a Secular Age*, ed. Michael Warner, Jonathan Vanantwerpen, and Craig Calhoun, 105–25 (Cambridge, MA: Harvard University Press, 2010). See also Justin Neuman, *Fiction beyond Secularism* (Evanston, IL: Northwestern University Press, 2014), 14.
19. Robert M. Cover, "The Supreme Court, 1982 Term. Foreword: *Nomos* and Narrative," *Harvard Law Review* 97 (1983): 4–5.
20. On the utility of counterstories for members of religious and racial minorities, see Richard Delgado, "Storytelling for Oppositionalists and Others: A Plea for Narrative," *Michigan Law Review* 87 (1989): 2411–41.
21. Nadeem Aslam, *Maps for Lost Lovers* (New York: Knopf, 2004), 182.
22. Connolly, "Pluralism and Faith."
23. Ibid., 14.
24. Robert Post and Reva Siegel, "Democratic Constitutionalism," in *The Constitution in 2020*, ed. Jack M. Balkin and Reva B. Siegel, 25–35 (New York: Oxford University Press, 2009).
25. This claim has been advanced by many, including Martha Nussbaum, *Poetic Justice: The Literary Imagination and Public Life* (Boston: Beacon, 1995); Kathy Eden, *Poetic and Legal Fiction in the Aristotelian Tradition* (Princeton, NJ: Princeton University Press, 1986); Victoria Kahn, *Wayward Contracts: The Crisis of Political Obligation in England, 1640–1674* (Princeton, NJ: Princeton University Press, 2004); and Elliott Visconsi, *Lines of Equity: Literature and the Origins of Law in Later Stuart England* (Ithaca, NY: Cornell University Press, 2008). It is not without adversaries. Cf. Richard A. Posner, "Against Ethical Criticism," *Philosophy and Literature* 21 (1997): 1–27.
26. Julie Stone Peters, "Law, Literature and the Vanishing Real: On the Future of an Interdisciplinary Illusion," *PMLA* 120 (2005): 442–53.

CHAPTER 17

Regulatory Fictions

On Marriage and Countermarriage

ELIZABETH F. EMENS

The debates in the public sphere over the future of marriage have spurred theoretical debates in the academy over the value of marriage.[1] Even as some scholars have debated whether gay people's relationships are worthy of marriage—sometimes before large crowds hosted by student organizations—arguably the most robust theoretical debates have occurred among academics who all fall on the pro-gay side of the political spectrum. Specifically, pro-gay scholars have engaged in heated exchanges over whether marriage should be the political goal of LGBT and leftist thinkers. Some of these scholars want to imagine intimate possibilities apart from marriage,[2] while others think marriage is the most practical way to organize our intimate lives.[3] And several scholars have identified the current period as a rare window for imagining a space beyond marriage—a space where intimate relationships previously deemed illegal are not yet fully embraced by the long regulatory arm of marriage.[4]

Those who question marriage ask: If marriage urges us to organize our lives in certain conventional ways, then what might society look like in its absence? For some of these scholars, a world beyond marriage sounds hopeful, expansive, or at least interesting for its possibilities. This hypothetical world without marriage stands in sharp contrast to the dim, painful, dignity-deprived world that was typically represented by the plaintiffs' briefs in the same-sex marriage cases. In a sense, then, for the pro-gay scholars who seek to look beyond marriage, the argument is not over whether gay people are worthy of marriage but, rather, whether marriage is worthy of gay people—and thus of everyone.

This chapter imagines a world beyond our current marriage regime by looking to some unusual sources: works of fiction. Literature seems the obvious place to look when we are trying to imagine new possibilities, but we rarely look to literature as a source for new laws. This use of fiction to imagine new legal regimes adds to the tools of law and literature as a discipline. Law and literature generally comprises categories such as "law in literature" (think trials in Dickens), "law as literature" (think deconstructive critique of legal opinions), and "law of literature" (think copyright law).[5] In contrast, by looking to fiction for ideas for new laws, this chapter engages in an enterprise we might call "literature as law."

Literature as law bears some relation to the category of law in literature, but the aim here is not to study how law operates in literature but rather to draw from literature inspiration for novel laws. Literature is thus mined for its original contributions to legal innovation. These contributions may arise more or less directly from their fictional sources. Some of the legal regimes offered in this chapter appear explicitly in the relevant literary text; others are extrapolations of an arrangement embedded in the text.

In this chapter, the inquiry into literature as law yields a variety of intriguing *countermarriage* possibilities. By countermarriage, I mean the vast range of alternative ways we might regulate intimate relationships, from tweaks of existing marriage law to wholesale replacement of marriage with some other regime. *Exploding marriage*, for instance, offered by Goethe, alters the expected time horizon of a marriage, whereas *a world without marriage*, invited by Hamlet, upends it all.

I invite the reader into this exploration of countermarriage possibilities for reasons both general and specific. Generally, this chapter is an exercise in innovative thinking. Recent work in behavioral science has shown how much our decisions are determined by the frames surrounding them.[6] Thinking along unusual pathways may help free us from our assumptions so that we may view the status quo with fresh eyes. Inventing and considering alternatives to current practice may benefit both our descriptive and our normative analyses across areas of law. In addition, exploring different types of sources for legal thinking, such as literature, may give us new tools for innovation—a topic I revisit in the conclusion. More specifically, this chapter urges the reader to think innovatively about marriage. In light of the academic and popular interest in considering marriage's aims, functions, and value to society, this seems a critical moment for sharpening and expanding our thinking in this area.

Of course, we may continue to accept marriage in its current form even after we question our assumptions about it. Considering alternatives to an institution may lead us to embrace a different approach, or such a process may lead us to conclude that the institution has value, perhaps with greater confidence than if we had remained tied to our assumptions.[7] This chapter offers an array of inventive variations on our current marriage regime to help free our minds for that evaluative process.

Lastly, but not trivially, I hope this experience of engaging the imagination, of entertaining visions of a world slightly or wildly different from our own, will be pleasurable. For many of us, the simple act of opening our minds to previously unimagined possibilities can be a delight. Pleasures vary, however, and this endeavor will not be everyone's idea of fun. Though the hedonic aim of the chapter is not insignificant to the author, for those readers whose tastes differ, I hope the other aims will be sustaining.

Before beginning, I offer a caveat for the normatively inclined reader: this chapter explores but does not prescribe. Though discussions of marriage are typically normative, this chapter resists drawing conclusions about whether we should have marriage and in what form. The aim here is instead to step away from that prescriptive project and generate a broad range of countermarriage regimes inspired by unlikely sources. What follows is a selection of fictional possibilities that I hope will be provocative and perhaps even delightful for their distance from the regimes we generally consider in our debates over marriage.

EXPLODING MARRIAGE AND THREE-STRIKES MARRIAGE: PLAYING WITH PERMANENCE

Goethe's novel *Elective Affinities* entertains two different countermarriage regimes that play with the permanence of marriage.[8] A core aspiration of marriage is that it last forever: *till death do us part*. The reality is of course rather different, with divorce rates for first marriages at 45–50 percent in the United States.[9] And yet couples continue to enter marriage optimistic about their prospects for staying together, as reflected in their reluctance to sign prenuptial agreements.[10] Goethe's countermarriage regimes play with this assumption of permanence.

Goethe's first countermarriage idea is what we might call *exploding marriage*. In this regime, marriage expires after a fixed term of years. The character of the Count in *Elective Affinities* explains to an assembled dinner group that "[o]ne of [his] friends, whose high spirits mostly express themselves in suggestions for new laws, claimed that every marriage should only be contracted for a period of five years."[11] Five years, the friend thought, "was a nice odd number, a sacred number, and a period just sufficient to get to know one another, produce a number of children, separate, and, the nicest part of it, become reconciled again."[12] In explaining his proposal, the friend would "exclaim":

> "How happily the first years would pass! Two or three years would go by very pleasantly. Then one party, eager to see the relationship continue, would become increasingly attentive the closer the end of the contract approached. The indifferent or even dissatisfied partner would be charmed and won over. They would forget, as we do the hours in good company, that time was passing, and would be most pleasantly surprised to notice, after the deadline was already passed, that the contract had been extended without a word having ever been spoken."[13]

The Count's friend implicitly critiqued the ways married people sometimes come to take each other for granted, and cease to invest in the marriage or to appreciate their spouse. Hence the expiration date. The looming deadline forces the partners to consider each other closely again, much as one might energetically consume—or discard—an overlooked item in the refrigerator upon noticing it expires tomorrow. Interestingly, although the friend's proposal seems to imply that the default rule is for the marriage to explode at the five-year mark, he also seems to suggest that the couple can opt out of that presumption and silently ratify their relationship through the behavior of renewing their enthusiasm for each other and continuing together past the deadline.

The Count offers another marriage alternative, *three-strikes marriage*. Here, only marriages involving someone who has been married twice before are legally permanent:

> "That same friend," [the Count] went on, "made yet another suggestion for a new law: a marriage should only be regarded as indissoluble when it was the third marriage of one or both. For this was incontrovertible evidence that marriage was something this person could not do without. Now it would also be known how they had behaved in their previous relationships, and whether they had bad habits, which more frequently lead to separations than do bad characters. We should find out about one another; and we should keep an eye on married people as well as unmarried ones, since we could not know what might come to pass."
>
> "That would greatly increase society's interest," said [another character]; "for indeed, when we are married, nobody bothers about our virtues or faults anymore."[14]

The suggestion that marriage should be permanent only if at least one party has been married twice before seems, in a way, perverse. It seems to assume the impermanence of marriage, at least of first (and second) marriages. And it emphasizes desire for marriage itself—as "something this person could not do without"—rather than for the individual partner. And where the Count does attend to the individual, he focuses on habits rather than character. Such an account is surprising because a lover is typically expected to adore the essence of the person. Habit seems superficial, relative to character, though a long tradition of writers has argued otherwise.

Both of these countermarriage possibilities resist the usual sentimentality that presumes some people are meant for each other or even that the heart of marriage is necessarily love. On the other hand, the two alternatives may be read to push in opposite directions, with three-strikes marriage focused on a party's reaffirming their commitment to the *institution* time and time again, and exploding marriage focused on the parties' reaffirming their commitment to *each other* time and time again. By contrast to three-strikes marriage, exploding marriage might seem highly romantic in its emphasis on the partners' affirmative desires, rather than on other values. Thus, both of these countermarriage possibilities vary our current regime, with one favoring the institutional over the romantic dimensions of marriage and the other favoring the reverse.

The novel implies that it is dangerous to question the commonplace pieties about love, marriage, and permanence. The source of these marriage variants is a controversial character, someone who has been burned by marriage in its current form. The Count has been unhappily married for years but unable to get out of his unhappy marriage and marry the woman he loves; he thus spends as much time as he can traveling the country with his beloved and is a scandalous, as well as dissatisfied, figure.[15] The text thereby creates some distance from the proposer of countermarriage possibilities by presenting him as bitter and cynical. And yet Goethe also portrays the questioner of marriage as hopelessly in love, suggesting that his cynicism might be a cover for his deeply romantic nature. Rather than being the most *cynical* about love and relationships, then, the marriage critic might in fact be the most *romantic*. This tension gives the reader ample space to consider the countermarriage proposals, unencumbered by any clear judgment from the text. The reader can make what she will of the proposals and of their various suggestions, taken together, that the institution of marriage may be the true object of love, or that love may be more important than commitment in marriage, and that, in either case, a marriage's structural features may determine its success or failure.

LINE MARRIAGE: RECONCEIVING THE BASIC STRUCTURE

Robert Heinlein's novel *The Moon Is a Harsh Mistress* offers us the idea of *line marriage*.[16] Real-world marriage typically imposes expectations along the dimensions of numerosity (permitting only two persons per marriage) and exclusivity (permitting erotic intimacy only within marriage). Line marriage necessarily violates the numerosity requirement, and it may also depart from the exclusivity requirement: in this fanciful marital form, spouses of both sexes are added to the marriage, one by one, over time. Line marriage bears a similarity to what we generally think of as polygamy, except that it is symmetrical and (at least structurally) egalitarian, with multiple spouses of both sexes. It is a "line" in its continuity over time: adding new spouses one after the other makes it possible that the marriage could continue interminably, like a corporation.

The form is introduced in the novel by a participant who emphatically characterizes it as "nice"—a high compliment in his distinctively clipped speech. He says,

> "Our marriage nearly a hundred years old ... —twenty-one links, nine alive today, never a divorce. Oh, it's a madhouse when our descendants and in-laws and kinfolk get together for birthday or wedding—more kids than seventeen, of course; we don't count 'em after they marry or I'd have 'children' old enough to be my grandfather. Happy way to live, never much pressure. Take me. Nobody woofs if I stay away a week and don't phone. Welcome when I show up. Line marriages rarely have divorces. How could I do better?"[17]

His interlocutor concurs, "I don't think you could."[18] Their dialogue further elucidates the variation available within that line structure. The marriage accommodates new spouses at any time because "[s]pacing has no rule, just what suits us."[19] And individual families may create their own patterns, and deviations from those patterns. For example, one family institutes a requirement to alternate the sex of each new spouse, but treats it flexibly: "Been alternation up to latest link, last year. We married a girl when alternation called for boy. But was special."[20] Throughout the book, line marriage repeatedly engenders praise, for its "financial security, fine home life it gives children, fact that death of a spouse, while tragic, could never be tragedy it was in a temporary family, especially for children—children simply could *not* be orphaned."[21] Such analytic praise is underscored by the emotional context in which it is offered— as in the statement following this list of benefits: "Suppose I waxed too enthusiastic—but my family *is* most important thing in my life."[22]

Even greater sexual openness characterizes relationships of more than two elsewhere in Heinlein's work. In his best-known novel, *Stranger in a Strange Land*, the characters organize their intimate relationships on a variety of models, including apparently monogamous pairings.[23] The most significant and best-loved characters, however, revel in a combination of love and sex with a range of devoted partners and friends in a communal setting.

Traditional polygamy, more precisely termed polygyny, in which one man is married to more than one woman, appears elsewhere in fiction and in fact, and has been explored in detail by other sources. But the line-marriage structure in particular highlights the possibilities for varying marital structure along a range of dimensions. Within Heinlein's imagined universes, countermarriage possibilities vary the number of partners (numerosity) and the openness of their relationships (exclusivity) in both structured and unstructured ways.

WHO CAN ENTER: FLIPPING THE PRESUMPTIONS

In an essay in the *Boston Evening Transcript* on August 18, 1900, African American[24] fiction writer Charles Chesnutt imagined a kind of racial utopia.[25] He predicted that "the future American" would be a mixture of the current races, and he hypothesized a legal regime that would speed us to this conclusion:

> We will assume ... that the laws of the whole country were as favorable to ... amalgamation as the laws of most Southern States are at present against it; i.e. that it were made a misdemeanor for two white or two colored persons to marry, so long as it was possible to obtain a mate of the other race—this would be even more favorable than the Southern rule, which makes no such exception.[26]

Even if we erroneously assume two pure races at the start, Chesnutt concluded, "in three generations the pure whites would be entirely eliminated, and there would be no perceptible trace of the blacks left."[27]

This imagined regulatory regime, akin to one elaborated in slightly different form by legal scholar Geoffrey Stone a century later, flips the presumption as to who qualifies to enter a marriage.[28] Instead of our historical legal prescription—and ongoing majority social practice—of racially homogamous marriage, Chesnutt's law (partially) prescribes racially heterogamous marriage.

Various works of science fiction alter other conventional expectations of entrants into marriage, such as the widely held presumption of adult age (by making the threshold younger out of necessity in a society decimated by plague[29]), or the traditional assumption of the sex of the participants (by, for instance, encouraging or even mandating same-sex relations to stem population growth in a society facing resource depletion[30]). Unlike the science fiction variations on this theme, which tend to present new presumptions about who should enter marriage in functional terms, Chesnutt and Stone offer political justifications. In both cases, the fictional nature of the work provides an opportunity for variations that challenge assumptions about the entrants to marriage.

Moreover, Chesnutt's version of this altered reality invokes the criminal law, making certain kinds of marriages misdemeanors. Compared with the softer version of a rule presented in Goethe's exploding marriage, Chesnutt's criminal prohibition highlights the ways the rule can vary—from criminal prohibition of one sort or another, to civil fines, to regulatory approval, to default rules (creating a presumption, which parties can overcome by speaking to the contrary), to forced choosing (requiring parties to choose an option, either of their own design or off a menu), to framing rules (framing parties' decisions with particular words or context). The Chesnutt essay, though far from inventing these sorts of variations, calls our attention to degrees of regulatory strength through its invocation of the harshest state regime, criminal prohibition.

Renewable Marriage: Buying an Option

Shakespeare's *The Winter's Tale* provides the inspiration for a form of countermarriage that, generalized, we might call *renewable marriage* (or perhaps, more playfully, *take-a-break-from-marriage marriage*).[31] This countermarriage form plays with the permanence, not of the marriage commitment, but of its termination. Extrapolating from *The Winter's Tale*, we can imagine marriage as a renewable resource: mistreatment by one spouse of the other leads to a term of years apart which, if it leads to remorse, can end with vibrant reunion.

King Leontes, thinking his wife Hermione unfaithful with his friend, and desperately jealous, jails her, holds a trial in which he disregards the oracle that declares her innocent, and then orders the murder of their newborn daughter, Perdita (though she is secretly hidden rather than killed). His actions lead to the death of their fragile son and the eventual proclamation of Hermione's death from grief as well. After sixteen years pass, Perdita is recovered, and Hermione's friend Paulina elicits from the remorseful King both an admission that he effectively killed his wife through his cruelty and a promise that he would never marry again. The King and Perdita come, with other assembled guests, to ask Paulina to show them a statue of the Queen in her possession. Paulina presents the statue to the visitors, and as they admire the likeness, Paulina promises to bring the Queen back to life: "It is requir'd / You do awake your faith. Then all stand still: / Or— those that think it is unlawful business / I am about, let them depart."[32] The King orders Paulina to proceed:

> Paul[ina]:
>> Music, awake her; strike!　　　[*Music.*]
>
> 'Tis time; descend; be stone no more . . .
> Bequeath to death your numbness; for from him
> Dear life redeems you. You perceive she stirs:
>> [*Hermione comes down*]
>
> Start not; her actions shall be holy as
> You hear my spell is lawful. [*To Leontes*] Do not shun her
> Until you see her die again; for then
> You kill her double. Nay, present your hand:
> When she was young you woo'd her; now, in age,
> Is she become the suitor?
>
> Leontes:
>> Oh, she's warm!
>
> If this be magic, let it be an art
> Lawful as eating.[33]

The play offers language at various points to suggest that Hermione has been in hiding all these years, cared for by Paulina, but it also leaves open the possibility that her statue has truly been brought to life.

Unlike some of our other fictions, which explicitly offer countermarriage regimes, *The Winter's Tale* offers merely an anecdote of renewable marriage played out between these lovers. The closest we might come to an affirmative regulatory vision comes in the possible element of magic: the suggestion that magic might assist the Queen's return hints at the possibility of an approving universe—a kind of supernatural regulatory body—that looks on and enables the reunion.

Extrapolated from Shakespeare's approving frame, the idea of renewable marriage plays with the presumed continuity of marriage, suggesting that marriage could be intermittent, or terminated and then resumed.[34] It suggests a structure for the unfolding of relations between lovers over time, after growth and new appreciation of one for another. One might imagine variations: from the mistreated spouse who eventually forgives and returns but only after remorse and recuperation by the abusive spouse, to the perhaps more fantastical permanent presumption in favor of a former spouse. Such a permanent presumption might confer privileges, such as ongoing access to a sexual relationship—that is, the former spouse might be an exception to new commitments of exclusivity or monogamy by the ex.

A formal legal version of this is even more implausible, though not impossible. For instance, we might imagine a regime in which relations with a former spouse would not legally constitute adultery. The path of the older relationship worn into the new one would create a kind of sexual easement that persists despite new ownership.

This romantic elaboration of renewable marriage reads the play only through horizontal relations—that is, intimate, as opposed to parental, relations. But The Winter's Tale does not focus merely, or even principally, on Hermione's relation to Leontes. Hermione gives us only one reason why she has returned to life: "to see the issue."[35] Her dead son is gone for good, but her daughter Perdita has come back (bringing a spouse, who may be read as a kind of replacement son), and Perdita's return coincides with Hermione's. Perdita's reunion with Hermione is figured almost romantically. After her father notes that Perdita "stand[s] like stone with" her mother,[36] in essence taking on her aspect, Perdita speaks to the statue: "Lady, / Dear queen, that ended when I but began, / Give me that hand of yours to kiss."[37] Perdita's words literally describe the gap between them, in that mother and daughter just missed each other in time, with mother dying just after daughter was born. But her wording suggests romantic union: one person ends where the other begins. Perdita's final and only other line in the scene comes twenty lines before her mother's awakening. She sighs: "So long could I / Stand by, a looker-on."

The play's emphasis on the vertical (parental) relation over the horizontal (intimate) relation may bring us to the more practical reason that spouses commonly reunite after breaks: to try again for the sake of the children. Even more, in contrast to the sexual easement I proposed above, the most common kind of easement a former spouse might have on the other takes the form of the dialogue, negotiation, and detailed knowledge of each other's lives necessary to coordinate their relationships with the children that came from their marriage. As noted elsewhere, family constructions in the contemporary United States look more transgressive when viewed through a child's eyes: the children of serial monogamists accumulate multiple parents, creating a kind of structural polyamory (or polyantipathy) from the child's perspective. Thus, the renewable marriage possibilities discussed here—while inviting us to reconsider our expectations about the conditions and terms of exiting marriage—may also be less radical than they at first appear.

SOLITARY MARRIAGE: ISOLATING AND SELF-MARRIAGE

Marriage is generally conceived of as a joining together. It thus seems contrary to, or at least apart from, solitude. But fictional and philosophical sources—low and high—invite us to consider solitude through marriage.

The poet Rilke, writing in an epistolary mode, urges a view of the good marriage as a path to solitude:

> It is a question in marriage, to my feeling, not of creating a quick community of spirit by tearing down and destroying all boundaries, but rather a good marriage is that in which each appoints the other guardian of his solitude, and shows him this confidence, the greatest in his power to bestow.[38]

Rilke eschews the idea of a "togetherness" between people, viewing it as hindering "freedom and development."[39] But, Rilke concludes,

> [O]nce the realization is accepted that even between the *closest* human beings infinite distances continue to exist, a wonderful living side by side can grow up, if they succeed in loving the distance between them which makes it possible for each to see the other whole and against a wide sky![40]

Rilke's metaphor of the lovers always appearing to each other against a vast sky is not a form of structural countermarriage. He embraces our standard marital form—of two people facing each other and (presumably) only each other—but his rendition of marriage also imagines each spouse's role in the other's life not as coentrant into a union but as a protector of the other's isolation.

The relation between marriage and solitude can take a bolder structural form: marriage to oneself. References to self-marriage appear occasionally in parodic criticism of same-sex marriage—as another place on the slippery slope that allegedly runs from same-sex marriage to polygamy. In popular fiction, the idea of marrying oneself is elaborated slightly more seriously in an episode of the HBO series *Sex and the City*.[41] There, the lead character, Carrie, decides to announce to a friend that she is marrying herself and registering for a particular pair of shoes. Carrie's intention is to make her friend realize how much Carrie has spent on the friend's life events, from wedding presents to baby showers. The friend had insulted Carrie for spending too much on a pair of Manolo Blahnik shoes that went missing at the friend's baby shower, where guests were required to remove their shoes for the health of the resident toddler. On learning the shoes were gone, and after some prompting, the friend had offered to pay for Carrie's missing shoes. But when the friend heard they cost nearly $500, she reneged, intimating that her own grown-up married life with children leaves no room for such trivial expenditures. Carrie fumes as she adds up how much she has spent on her friend's life choices—engagement, wedding, and babies—expenditures that may never come back to Carrie. So Carrie decides to leave a voicemail for her friend, announcing her marriage to herself and her registry at one place: the shoe store Manolo Blahnik. The friend finally seems to understand Carrie's point of view and buys the shoes, sending a note saying she hopes that "you and you will be very happy."[42]

The episode's flirtation with self-marriage has a serious side: the wealth transfer from single people to married people that custom often dictates. That wealth transfer has legal and institutional dimensions, in terms of the state and workplace benefits that marriage provides to married couples. Social status also accompanies marriage, as is often noted in contemporary marriage debates; for many it signifies, among other things, entry into stable adult life. In this light, that someone might want to marry herself sounds, though still fanciful, like less of a joke.

EXCULPATORY MARRIAGE: THE ULTIMATE BENEFIT

In *Never Let Me Go*, Kazuo Ishiguro applies his subtle appreciation of human relations to a subject more typical of science fiction.[43] Ishiguro portrays a dystopic society where the powers that be have created a race of clones. These clones are kept in institutions so that eventually their organs may be harvested for the benefit of the regular citizens. Society exploits some of the clones not only for their bodies but for their labor: these latter clones act as caregivers for others who, as a result of the organ harvesting process, are growing gradually weaker on their road to an early death (or "completion," as the novel puts it).

The novel's poignancy turns on two of its features. One is the gradual unfolding for the narrator, Kathy, of the truth of her own identity as a clone and of this grotesque societal arrangement. The other is the love between two of the clones—Kathy and Tommy, a boy with whom she went to "school" before either knew they were clones—and the rumor that emerges about love as a way out of the early death to which clones are consigned. As Kathy cares for a childhood friend before the latter's completion, the friend reveals the underhanded way in which she had long ago come between Kathy and Tommy, who had always loved each other. She urges Kathy to reconnect with Tommy, to pursue their love, and to seek from the authorities a special dispensation rumored among the clones.

The rumor is that clones can have their organ donations, and thus their premature death, "deferred"—"if they're really in love."[44] Tommy and Kathy journey to the authorities who had run their school so many years ago. The lovers plead their case, only to learn that the rumor is false. There is no way to defer their donations; their love cannot save them. The novel thus beautifully renders, and then shatters, a classic and deeply human fantasy: that love can save us from our own mortality.

In so doing, the novel also portrays a fantastical vision of the benefits the state could bestow on deserving lovers. State-recognized relationships— that is, what we currently tend to call marriage—can involve any number of state-sponsored benefits (and burdens). In Ishiguro's rendering, the state is rumored to have a regulatory regime that bestows the ultimate benefit on deserving couples: life. Those scheduled for execution, for an untimely death by order of the state, could be pardoned, spared—if their love takes the right form. We might call this *exculpatory marriage*. The novel rejects this rumor, but nonetheless leaves us with a striking vision of a state that could select a chosen few for a kind of marriage whose benefit is the right to live.

The possibility of exculpatory marriage drawn from Ishiguro's world, though extreme, looks less absurd if we recognize the ways that our current legal system allows people effectively to "contract around" the criminal law. For instance, in some states, the relationship of marriage is a defense to statutory rape. Consent to sex might similarly be understood, though it sounds crass to many ears, as a form of contract that converts rape into legal sex. Contracting to make pornographic films can allow one to pay others to have sex without running afoul of prostitution laws. The Ishiguro example draws our attention to this feature of existing law and urges us to imagine the broadest possible range of benefits that marriage law could confer.

THE END OF MARRIAGE

Following this brief tour of fictional rewritings of our marriage regime, let us return to Shakespeare for the ultimate countermarriage proposal— Hamlet's call for the end of marriage:

> *Ham*[*let*]: I have heard of your paintings well enough. God hath given you one
> face, and you make yourselves another. You jig and amble, and you lisp, you

nick-name God's creatures and make your wantonness your ignorance. Go to, I'll no more on't, it hath made me mad. I say we will have no mo[re] marriage. Those that are married already—all but one—shall live; the rest shall keep as they are. To a nunn'ry, go.[45]

"We will have no more marriage," says Hamlet. Simple enough, though he does address the regulatory detail that existing marriages are grandfathered in (as it were), even as new entrants are not permitted.

We need not linger over the basic idea of ending marriage, as it has been addressed at length in the same-sex marriage debates. Much attention has been paid to the question whether we should get the state out of marriage altogether and just permit adults to organize their intimate affairs through private contract. Scholars have proposed various rationales for this contractual regime, including refocusing the state's attention and resources on relations of dependency;[46] getting the state out of an institution historically associated with legal impairments for women;[47] paving the way for religions to define marriage more purely according to their faith;[48] and prompting partners to make more active choices about the kinds of relationship they want to have under law as well as the role they want law to play in their relationship.[49]

It is hard to read Hamlet's imagined world without marriage positively, given its inclusion in his rant against Ophelia. Hamlet's spiteful railing against marriage may remind us of Goethe's Count, whose own embitterment may fuel his personal interest in alternatives to marriage. Remember, however, that the Count's story of exploding marriage invites us to view as close cousins the cynical and the romantic. Hamlet and the Count remind us that while imagining alternative social structures may seem the terrain of the brave adventurer, such searching and imagining may stem as much from romantic idealism as from irreverence.

CONCLUSION: OF LAW, LITERATURE, AND INNOVATION

Marriage is the triumph of imagination over intelligence. Second marriage is the triumph of hope over experience.[50]

These lines, often mistakenly attributed to Oscar Wilde, present ordinary marriage as an imaginative endeavor. It may be so, at least for some. And it is certainly possible that little should change in our current marriage regime. As I noted at the start, my aim has not been to argue for one or another countermarriage regime, but to excavate possibilities from some unlikely sources. I thus conclude with a few reflections on these sources, and on the relationships among law, literature, and innovation.

Various justifications may be offered for the status quo. For some traditions and thinkers, the way things *are* is the way they *should be*—"Whatever is, is right."[51] Burke famously extolled the virtues of tradition as the accumulated wisdom of the centuries.[52] More recently, there's the joke about the (old school) Chicago economist:

> A Chicago economist and a friend were walking along the street when they spotted a $20 bill. The economist kept walking. The friend turned to him and asked, "Aren't you going to pick that up?" "Of course not," said the economist. "It's fake. If there were a real $20 bill on the sidewalk, someone would have picked it up already."[53]

The joke plays off classical economic principles, which suggest that the current state of affairs cannot be improved upon, because the market has already perfected it. The efficient-markets hypothesis, for instance, posits that prices accurately reflect all available information and indeed instantly incorporate any information that becomes newly available. Similarly, in the joke, money could never be available for free.

The joke may be read as a fable about how certain assumptions about economics can impoverish our sense of what is possible. The efficient-markets hypothesis and its ilk have of course been criticized from within economics and not just by behavioral economics.[54] And various forms of economic thinking have been the source of highly innovative and provocative ideas.[55] But the pervasive use of certain concepts from economics, stripped of context or crucial critique, may constrain our exploration of alternatives. For example, the so-called Coase theorem, which is widely taught in law schools, has been frequently mischaracterized as a theory of how legal rules might not matter to outcomes, even though Coase actually meant to highlight the importance of transaction costs, not to posit their nonexistence.[56] Why the slippage exists is an interesting question; there are apparently disciplinary and context-specific reasons for it,[57] but perhaps there is also something alluring about the idea that things are as they should be, that private parties will work them out unaided by law.[58] Regardless, the slippage surrounding Coase is one example of how watered-down principles of classical economics—at least in legal education—may hinder legal thinkers' appreciation of law's imaginative possibilities, of the potential benefits, as well as the costs, of innovation.

Research in fields ranging from social psychology (on system justification and status quo bias) to organizational theory (for example, on the so-called dark side of organizations) has documented the ways we become stuck in the present configuration of things.[59] What allows us to think beyond the ruts we create for ourselves, to imagine and examine other possibilities?

In their different ways, both literature and law are realms of the imagination, both mechanisms for innovation. Both urge us to expand our thinking beyond the status quo. Literature is obviously a realm of the imagination. Scholars have already written about the political possibilities of the literary imagination, for instance, in helping to facilitate empathy with diverse others.[60] But literature has been underutilized as a source of legal innovation.

Literature allows us to imagine entirely new regulatory worlds because fictional worlds are also rule-bound. Literary texts create fictional worlds with internal rules that dictate what is possible within that world. It is for this reason that we can say something is "unrealistic" or "would never happen" even within a work of science fiction; what we mean is that the particular event violates the rules of that fictional world. The need for a nuanced rendering of a rule-bound universe—but where the usual nonfiction rules need not apply—makes fiction a space for testing out regulatory possibilities.

Law seems a less likely candidate for an imaginative realm, yet law can also force us out of the status quo. It can force us to change practices, sometimes on the level of the minute details of our lives. Think of sexual harassment law, which changed everyday workplace interactions in previously inconceivable ways. Law can work against status quo bias; for better or worse, it can force change where social pressures cannot reach. In this way, law and literature have more in common than they appear, as both invite innovation by spurring us to move into uncharted territory. Literature does this by permission and imaginative license; law may do so by mandate.

None of these considerations indicates that things should change. Sometimes the way things are is, indeed, the way things should be. But as Justice Holmes famously wrote, "[i]t is revolting to have no better reason for a rule of law than that so it was laid down in the time of Henry IV."[61] As scholars and students, we should consider the range of alternatives to the present state of things before reaching a conclusion about the normative merits or demerits of keepings things as they are. We cannot know how long our collective ruminations on marriage will last. We should therefore look to whatever sources we can find to open our minds to every imaginative possibility. We should look to literature as law.

NOTES

1. This chapter is a version of an earlier article, Elizabeth F. Emens, "Regulatory Fictions: On Marriage and Countermarriage," *California Law Review* 99 (2011): 235–72, which contains extensive citation material largely omitted here at the request of the editors. Interested readers might consult the earlier article. For excellent research and editorial assistance on this version, my thanks go to Logan Gowdey and Kelsey Ruescher.

2. Martha Albertson Fineman, *The Neutered Mother, the Sexual Family, and Other Twentieth Century Tragedies* (New York: Routledge, 1995); Mary Lyndon Shanley, "Afterword," in *Just Marriage*, ed. Joshua Cohen and Deborah Chasman, 109–16 (New York: Oxford University Press, 2004).

3. Carol Sanger, "A Case for Civil Marriage," *Cardozo Law Review* 27 (2006): 1311–23; Elizabeth S. Scott, "A World without Marriage," *Family Law Quarterly* 41 (2007): 539, 565–66.

4. Although same-sex couples in the United States now have the constitutional right to marry (see Obergefell v. Hodges, 135 S. Ct. 2584 [2015]), this continues to be a critical period for imaginative discourse because same-sex couples around the world continue to be prohibited from marrying. See "Gay Marriage around the World," *Pew Research Center*, June 26, 2015, http://www.pewforum.org/2015/06/26/gay-marriage-around-the-world-2013/. For an example of a source noting the importance of the window between decriminalization and regulation, see Katherine M. Franke, "Longing for Loving," *Fordham Law Review* 76 (2008): 2685–707.

5. Robert Weisberg, "The Law-Literature Enterprise," *Yale Journal of Law and the Humanities* 1 (1988): 1–67; Kenji Yoshino, "The City and the Poet," *Yale Law Journal* 114 (2005): 1835–96.

6. Amos Tversky and Daniel Kahneman, "The Framing of Decisions and the Psychology of Choice," *Science* 211 (1981): 453–58; Ian Ayres, "Menus Matter," *University of Chicago Law Review* 73 (2006): 3–15; Cass R. Sunstein and Richard H. Thaler, "Libertarian Paternalism Is Not an Oxymoron," *University of Chicago Law Review* 70 (2003): 1159–202.

7. Elizabeth F. Emens, "Monogamy's Law: Compulsory Monogamy and Polyamorous Existence," *New York University Review of Law and Social Change* 29 (2004): 286.

8. Johann Wolfgang von Goethe, "Elective Affinities," in *Goethe: The Collected Works*, ed. David E. Wellbery, trans. Judith Ryan (Princeton, NJ: Princeton University Press, 1995), 11:11.

9. Linda A. Jacobsen and Mark Mather, "U.S. Economic and Social Trends since 2000," *Population Bulletin* 65 (2010): 1–16.

10. Heather Mahar, "Why Are There So Few Prenuptial Agreements?" *Harvard Law School John M. Olin Center for Law, Economics and Business Discussion Paper Series*, Paper 436, 2003, http://lsr.nellco.org/cgi/viewcontent.cgi?article=1224&context=harvard_olin; D'Vera Cohn, "The States of Marriage and Divorce," last modified October 15, 2009, http://pewsocialtrends.org/pubs/746/states-of-marriage-and-divorce.

11. Goethe, "Elective Affinities," 139.

12. Ibid.

13. Ibid.

14. Ibid., 140.

15. Ibid., 136.
16. Robert Heinlein, *The Moon Is a Harsh Mistress* (New York: Orb, 1997).
17. Ibid., 42.
18. Ibid.
19. Ibid.
20. Ibid.
21. Ibid., 260.
22. Ibid.
23. Robert Heinlein, *Stranger in a Strange Land* (New York: Ace, 1987).
24. Chesnutt considered himself African American, as did the one-drop laws of various jurisdictions, though his paternal grandfather was a white slave owner and he could apparently pass for white (though he chose not to do so). See Pauline Carrington Bouvé, "An Aboriginal Author," *Boston Evening Transcript*, August 23, 1899, 16; and David Perlmutt, "Stamp Honors Black Author with N.C. Roots," *News and Observer* (Raleigh, NC), October 7, 2007, B3.
25. Charles W. Chesnutt, "The Future American," *Boston Evening Transcript*, August 18, 1900, http://www.online-literature.com/charles-chesnutt/wife-of-his-youth/11.
26. Ibid.
27. Ibid.
28. Geoffrey R. Stone, "If America Only Had One Mixed Race," *Chicago Tribune*, March 30, 1999.
29. George Stewart, *Earth Abides* (New York: Random House, 1949).
30. Joe Haldeman, *The Forever War* (New York: St. Martin's, 1974).
31. William Shakespeare, *The Winter's Tale*, ed. J. H. P. Pafford (London: Arden, 2006).
32. Ibid., 5.3.94–97.
33. Ibid., 5.3.98–111.
34. Of course, at present, marriages can be terminated and then resumed, but this is done through divorce and remarriage, which follows the usual procedures for any new marriage, rather than invoking any special practice of renewing the first marriage. In principle, the closest legal analog to renewable marriage might be the phenomenon that Jeannie Suk has termed "state-imposed de facto divorce," in which courts issue restraining orders in domestic violence situations, thereby prohibiting contact between the parties for a specified period ranging from two to eight years; Jeannie Suk, *At Home in the Law: How the Domestic Violence Revolution Is Transforming Privacy* (New Haven, CT: Yale University Press, 2009): 40n55, 40–50).
35. Shakespeare, *Winter's Tale*, 5.3.121–28.
36. Ibid., 5.3.41.
37. Ibid., 5.3.44–46.
38. Rainer Maria Rilke, *On Love and Other Difficulties*, trans. John J. L. Mood (New York: Norton, 1975), 28.
39. Ibid.
40. Ibid.
41. HBO, "A Woman's Right to Shoes," *Sex and the City*, August 17, 2003.
42. Ibid.
43. Kazuo Ishiguro, *Never Let Me Go* (New York: Knopf, 2005).
44. Ibid., 174.
45. William Shakespeare, *Hamlet*, ed. Harold Jenkins (London: Arden, 1982), 3.1.144–51.

46. Martha Albertson Fineman, *The Autonomy Myth: A Theory of Dependency* (New York: New Press, 2004); Fineman, *Neutered Mother*; Nancy D. Polikoff, "Why Lesbians and Gay Men Should Read Martha Fineman," *American University Journal of Gender, Social Policy, and the Law* 8 (2000): 167–76.

47. Patricia A. Cain, "Imagine There's No Marriage," *Quinnipiac Law Review* 16 (1996): 27–60; Cass R. Sunstein, "The Right to Marry," *Cardozo Law Review* 26 (2005): 2081–120.

48. Douglas W. Kmiec and Shelley Ross Saxer, "Equality in Substance and in Name," *San Francisco Chronicle*, March 2, 2009; Martha C. Nussbaum, *From Disgust to Humanity: Sexual Orientation and Constitutional Law* (New York: Oxford University Press, 2010): 163.

49. Joshua Cohen and Deborah Chasman, eds., *Just Marriage* (New York: Oxford University Press, 2004).

50. This popular phrase has variously been attributed to diverse sources, including Oscar Wilde. The attribution appears to be apocryphal, and the phrase a paraphrase and amalgamation of separate witticisms by Samuel Johnson and H. L. Mencken.

51. Alexander Pope, *Essay on Man* (1734), 6th edition, ed. Mark Pattison (Oxford: Clarendon Press, 1881): line 294.

52. Edmund Burke, "Reflections on the Revolution in France," in *The Portable Edmund Burke*, ed. Isaac Kramnick (New York: Penguin, 1999), 456.

53. Robert Roy Britt, "Laughter Soothes the Wounded Heart," *Flatrock*, http://flatrock.org.nz/topics/humour/no_joke.htm.

54. Ronald Coase, "The Problem of Social Cost," *Journal of Law and Economics* 3 (1960): 1–69.

55. Gary S. Becker, *A Treatise on the Family* (Cambridge, MA: Harvard University Press, 1991), 81–104; Elisabeth M. Landes and Richard A. Posner, "The Economics of the Baby Shortage," *Journal of Legal Studies* 7 (1978): 323–48.

56. Coase, "Problem of Social Cost"; Robert C. Ellickson, "The Case for Coase and Against 'Coaseanism,'" *Yale Law Journal* 99 (1989): 614.

57. Michael R. Butler and Robert F. Garnett, "Teaching the Coase Theorem: Are We Getting It Right?" *Atlantic Economics Journal* 31 (2003): 133–45.

58. John J. Donohue III, "Opting for the British Rule, or if Posner and Shavell Can't Remember the Coase Theorem, Who Will?" *Harvard Law Review* 104 (1991): 1115.

59. Gary Blasi and John T. Jost, "System Justification Theory and Research: Implications for Law, Legal Advocacy, and Social Justice," *California Law Review* 94 (2006): 1119; Russell Korobkin, "The Endowment Effect and Legal Analysis," *Northwestern University Law Review* 97 (2003): 1228–91; Diane Vaughn, "The Dark Side of Organizations: Mistake, Misconduct, and Disaster," *Annual Review of Sociology* 25 (1999): 271–305.

60. Martha C. Nussbaum, "Narratives of Hierarchy: *Loving v. Virginia* and the Literary Imagination," *Quinnipiac Law Review* 17 (1997): 337–55.

61. Oliver Wendell Holmes, "The Path of Law," *Harvard Law Review* 10 (1897): 469.

CHAPTER 18

Legal and Literary Fictions

SIMON STERN

If law and literature share certain kinds of imaginative capacities, as much recent scholarship contends, legal fictions seem to offer a promising means of exploring this kinship, and particularly its narrative dimensions. Commentators on legal fictions often apply the term to doctrines that make the law's image of the world seem fanciful or distorted, with fascinating and often worrisome consequences that form the contours of a story, as the fictional premise yields one bizarre result after another. Jeremy Bentham famously criticized legal fictions of all stripes, insisting that they were invariably "employed ... with a bad effect," and that their polluting effects went far beyond the fiction's immediate purpose: "[E]verything is sham that finds its way into that receptacle, as everything is foul that finds its way out of Fleet-ditch into the Thames."[1] More recent commentators do not necessarily share Bentham's antipathy to legal fictions as a class, but many nevertheless share the view that legal fictions proceed from a false premise to produce results that percolate throughout the legal domain, generating an array of consequences that may have no clear stopping point. One scholar, for example, associates legal fictions with "seriously flawed" assumptions whose "premises ... inform and shape doctrine in diverse areas of the law."[2] Another writes that "legal fictions allow the courts to tell a story that is imagined," thereby serving to "set norms for human behavior and social conduct" and "work[ing] as support structures to the law" that may "transform into binding legal principles" and influence "arguments about fundamental legal, historical, and sociological truths about human ontology."[3] A third warns that fictions in law are dangerous because "any deviation from the principle of meaning what one says must be carefully circumscribed. Without limitations set on the use of false statements, we run the risk of linguistic anarchy."[4] In these accounts, the falsehood at the fiction's base carries a risk because of its unpredictable career: once it has been launched, it may entrench itself in various legal domains that carry its implications even further. This uncertainty about what the hypothesis will yield explains why legal fictions are sometimes analogized to literary narratives, whose allure similarly consists in showing how an event may set off a whole chain of results, some predictable and others unforeseen. In what follows, I challenge this view of legal fictions, arguing on the one hand that these concerns about the premise's consequences apply to legal facts and doctrines generally, instead of being restricted to the ones that are usually characterized as fictions, and on the other hand that the conventional definitions of legal fictions, if taken seriously, demarcate a small group of legal rules and doctrines with an unusually constrained narrative structure that differentiates them from literary fictions rather than suggesting a kinship between the two.

My aim is to refocus the discussion of legal fictions and their significance for literary scholars. To that end, I develop three arguments in the course of this chapter. First, I suggest that narrative logic is an essential and commonplace feature in law, rather than being confined to a particular set of doctrines. It is a mistake to think of doctrines that appear fanciful or manifestly imaginative as somehow exceptional, because the law's usual processes of reasoning by analogy have similarly narrative qualities. Second, I suggest that if certain legal fictions have a distinctive narrative form, it is because they proceed by arbitrarily curtailing the chain of causal effects that flow from the premise, displaying a highly artificial kind of truncated causation that we rarely, if ever, find in imaginative literature. Finally, if law only occasionally manipulates narrative logic in the fashion that distinguishes this group of doctrines, we may ask what value there is in applying the label of legal fiction to anything else. Returning to the examples that most frequently attract the interest of modern commentators, I propose that these doctrines are seen as displaying their artifice in a way that other doctrines do not, and that this feature explains why they provoke so much concern. Their ostentatiousness makes these doctrines seem brazen about their fabricated status—and thus emphatically capricious and fallacious—even if they otherwise resemble the seemingly prosaic and inconsequential doctrines that surround them. Because all doctrines are similarly consequential (or have the potential to be), the difference is one of neither degree nor kind, but instead of visibility. In bringing their artificiality to the surface, the more ostentatious doctrines call attention to the creative operations that pervade the legal realm but that usually pass unnoticed in the guise of merely technical routines.

THE PLOT OF THE LAW

In scholarship that weaves together strands from legal and literary texts, the term "legal fiction" is usually connected to narrative inquiry. In this usage, a legal fiction begins as a metaphor, asserting an equivalence, and yields a series of far-reaching implications that radiate out from the premise. Corporate personhood is called a legal fiction (according to this view) because the label is taken to present corporations as embodied entities. This proposition may lead to conjectures about exactly which human traits might be attributed to a corporation, or what other entities are also endowed with these traits. The ultimate product might be a world populated by animate objects, like an eighteenth-century "it-narrative" gone wild.[5] Examined through a critical lens, the imaginative world inhabited by these legal persons would open up the kinds of questions about "character-space" and competition that Alex Woloch considers, as aspects of sparsely and densely populated novels, in *The One vs. The Many*.[6] The world that legal doctrine creates—and the world of legal doctrine itself—might thus be considered not only in terms of narrative structure but also in relation to character, perhaps the most important means of creating that structure, and one that has not commanded much attention in narrative studies of legal texts.

Again, civil death is called a legal fiction because it treats convicted criminals as if they were dead for certain legal purposes, rendering them incapable of bringing a civil action, for example.[7] Once recognized as figurations of the undead, they might be thought to take on other zombie-like features as well, and that suggestion might raise any number of comparisons with recent novels and television series, and might also prompt reflection on how law, as well as literary fiction, can manipulate the flow of time and even its direction. Temporality, like character, has long been an object of literary research on order and causation in narrative, but rarely figures in discussions of legal narrative.[8] The examples of corporate personhood and civil death show how ways of linking doctrines to literary genres, and to familiar questions in the study of narrative more generally, have a crucial role to play in research on legal doctrines and devices, whose distinctive narrative attributes seldom receive more than passing notice, even in work that investigates the law's imaginative dimensions. At the same time, these inquiries do not need to rely on the legal fiction as a framing device, because they find their root in the analogical basis of legal reasoning as a routine practice.

Lon Fuller, in one of the best-known discussions of the subject, explains that a legal fiction is "adopted by its author with knowledge of its falsity. A fiction is an 'expedient, but *consciously* false, assumption.'" Fuller adds that a fiction "is not intended to deceive"; rather, he writes, its falsity is tolerated because the fiction is "recognized as having utility."[9] What, then, is the falsity in the doctrines just mentioned? Both could be described as correct statements of law that do not purport to describe nonlegal phenomena. Corporations are classified as "legal persons"—that is, they have standing to be parties in legal disputes.[10] Convicted criminals are deprived of certain legal rights. Whether there is a falsity depends on whether the doctrine is seen as making a claim about natural (nonlegal) persons or whether the doctrine simply *is* the legal conclusion ("corporations have standing"; "convicted criminals may not bring civil actions"). Just as some philosophers of aesthetics argue that whatever is asserted in a story is "true in the fiction,"[11] we might say that the doctrine simply sets out what is "true in law" and that it does not purport to go outside the law. I will argue for this view, but will also consider the implications of the account that would characterize corporate personhood and civil death as legal fictions.

It will help to contrast those examples briefly against a few of the kind that Fuller and others have offered when considering legal fictions as consciously false assumptions. A concise illustration is found in the doctrine of *filius nullius* ("child of no one"), which was used to deny illegitimate children any share in a father's estate, if the father died intestate. The proposition might be articulated in precisely this fashion—as a doctrinal statement about the legal result. In some instances, however, courts felt it necessary to reach that result by way of the assertion that, for the purpose of this legal question (and for this purpose only), the child has no father.[12] Similarly, according to the "attractive nuisance" doctrine, when a hazardous object on a landowner's property injures a child, the owner is made liable on the ground that the child was "invited" onto the property.[13] Rather than simply explaining that strict liability applies in such cases, courts achieved the same result by way of a factual claim that, like the claim about illegitimate children, has only this one legal effect. In both examples, this claim advances a (consciously false) assertion about the world outside the courtroom as a means of reaching the legal conclusion, rather than moving directly to the conclusion.[14] This form of explanation has a narrative structure that differs significantly from that of the examples presented at the outset. After looking more closely at the view that would treat those earlier examples as legal fictions, I will return to the kind of legal fiction that Fuller and others have explored.

In the cases of corporate personhood, civil death, and the like, the significance of the legal fiction lies not only in its starting point but also in what flows from it. When considered in this way, the fiction holds the seed of a plot. The latent narrative potential of the doctrinal premise explains why legal fictions are sometimes likened to literary fictions. That analogy would reveal something important, if corporate personhood were unusual in its ability to spawn a series of other legal consequences, such as that corporations have the same rights of speech and expression as other legal persons (and thus various other rights, in turn, entailed by that proposition). The plot of corporate personhood might thus recall the plot of *Frankenstein* or *The Matrix*, which describe the conflicts that arise when human attributes are conferred on artificial creations. However, corporate personhood is not unusual in that respect. Given that common-law judgments present themselves as rooted in precedent and are written in anticipation of their own use as precedents, this narrative potential is an ordinary feature of the common-law mode of conflict resolution, not a distinctively imaginative quality of a certain subset of judgments or doctrines. To single out, as fictions, a few that are wrapped in openly metaphorical language would implicitly reaffirm the view that other doctrines, sparer of their means and more banal in their mode of expression, are meager fare for the legal narratologist. As a tool for legal analysis, the work of critics such as Woloch would thus be reserved for doctrines whose names happen to call attention to their status as products of invention, fabrication, and imagination. The law's imaginative domain is vast and so far has been largely exempt from narratological inquiry, which should operate on a much wider range of materials than those that are seen as highlighting their fictional qualities.[15] To question the characterization of corporate personhood as a legal fiction, therefore, is not to limit the scope of narrative inquiry in legal analysis, but to broaden that scope to include areas not usually considered to exhibit such self-consciously literary features as metaphor.[16] As to legal fictions in particular, I will argue that if they display a generative potential that invites analogy to literary fictions, that kinship owes more to the ways in which both fictional modes solicit a particular kind of attention than to a shared ability to spin out narrative arrays.

According to one view, then, a legal fiction proceeds from a stipulation that generates absurd or at least implausible results—such as that corporations are legal persons, or that under the law of *feme covert*, "the very being or legal existence of the woman is suspended during the marriage, or at least is incorporated and consolidated into that of the husband," or that control of an object, even without physical custody, is deemed to be possession under the doctrine of constructive possession.[17] The fiction articulates a hypothetical which, once it has been postulated, may deliver all kinds of unanticipated consequences. The potential dangers of this process are a frequently rehearsed theme in the commentary on legal fictions. One version of this warning was quoted at the outset; another version may be found in Lord Mansfield's insistence, in 1761, that "fictions of law hold only in respect of the ends and purposes for which they were invented" and should not be extended to achieve "purpose[s] not within the reason and policy of the fiction."[18] This warning reflects the intuition that fictional premises are easily accepted and, if they are not properly monitored, may be readily integrated with existing assumptions. That intuition has been borne out in research by cognitive psychologists on fiction and imaginative engagement, showing that "[r]eaders will initially accept the assertions in a fictional work as true and will ... reject those assertions only if [the reader is] motivated and able to evaluate their veracity."[19] Whereas Coleridge described a "willing suspension of disbelief," implying that readers must exercise a certain kind of effort to become capable of assenting to the fiction's premise, this research suggests that belief comes readily, and that active effort is required to reject the premise—just as the commentators on legal fictions suggest, when emphasizing the need to be vigilant in circumscribing the fiction's ambit.

As noted earlier, the common-law method of problem-solving depends fundamentally on the suggestive powers of a premise to yield new and unanticipated analogies. Consider the case of a court that takes the equitable doctrine of patent abuse and applies the doctrine to copyrights. Patent abuse (or patent misuse) is an affirmative defense that can be used to mitigate damages when a party is charged with infringement. The defense applies when the patent owner has engaged in an antitrust violation or has improperly sought to expand the scope of the patent or its term. While there is disagreement about the use of this defense in copyright cases, some federal circuits have permitted it.[20] This extension from patent to copyright does not appear to present an inviting opportunity to study the workings of the legal fiction (e.g., a fiction premised on the assumption that copyrights are patents). Instead, the example offers a mundane illustration of what courts do all the time: they take existing doctrines, seek to discern their grounds and limits, and then decide, in light of those considerations, how the doctrine applies in a new context. For one who understands legal fictions as having distinctive imaginative qualities, perhaps the answer would be that copyrights, patents, and their owners' abusive efforts all lack any such quality, because they are creations of law to begin with. Accordingly, a court has not done anything very imaginative by changing the scope or application of a doctrine that never had any basis outside the law, whereas corporate personhood appears more self-consciously creative precisely because it seems to refer to nonlegal entities. Legal fictions, it might be argued, are fictional because they identify legal actors, or objects of legal analysis, in ways that are inconsistent with our experience when we consider them from a nonlegal perspective. That would explain why doctrinal modification, as in the case of patent abuse, has no fictional quality, but the label could apply to the corporate person.

This explanation quickly crumbles, however. First, as noted above, nonlegal persons do not figure in the doctrine of corporate personhood. Moreover, in most of the analyses that actually refer to nonlegal entities, when articulating the kind of equivalence we have just observed, no legal fiction is created. Consider the case of a court that must decide whether steamboat operators are liable for property theft onboard. The New York court that addressed this question in 1896 had already held that innkeepers were liable for the losses of their guests because of policy concerns about the dangerous temptations that might otherwise motivate the staff to rob their guests with impunity.[21] The court concluded that the same concerns applied to steamboat operators and their passengers. The owners of inns and steamboats, according to the court, had the same opportunities to steal from their customers, and in both cases the better policy was to make the owners liable for all thefts, regardless of who actually committed the crime, because the alternative would inevitably prompt the management to prey on their guests (or passengers). The case has become a classic in discussions of legal reasoning,[22] but nowhere in the commentary on this case has anyone suggested that the court created a legal fiction in which steamboats are inns.

Indeed, commentators have refrained from characterizing the opinion in this fashion even though the court, in formulating the analogy, observed that "[a] steamer carrying passengers upon the water, and furnishing them with rooms and entertainment, is, for all practical purposes, a floating inn."[23] While the opinion traffics in nonlegal entities such as steamboats and inns, this formulation is simply a way of asserting an identity between them in light of a particular legal problem. The court does not assume that steamers are inns, but instead reasons that they present the same policy concerns. Courts routinely speak in this fashion when they consider extending or modifying doctrines, but commentators have not treated the process as an exercise of the capacity for fiction-making, even though any comparison inevitably requires an element of creativity or imagination, and often encompasses nonlegal entities. In short, analogies and equivalences—both mundane and far-fetched—are essential ingredients of legal reasoning, and the lines of argument they will ultimately support are rarely discernible in advance. Judgments, like Tribbles, are born pregnant, always capable of spawning. The doctrines most often classified as legal fictions are not unusual, either in their ability to drive a plot or in their means of slotting nonlegal phenomena into legal analyses.

2. THE ARTIFICIAL LIMITS OF LEGAL FICTIONS

If plot-like structures abound in legal analysis, the falsity at the fiction's base, and particularly the role that the falsity plays in advancing the fiction's utility, may offer a more promising means of understanding what differentiates the "consciously false assumptions" cited earlier—the examples of *filius nullius* and attractive nuisance. Those examples require the court to disregard a fact that it already knows (that is, the person seeking a share of the intestate estate is actually the decedent's child, and that the land owner never invited the plaintiff onto the property).[24] In these examples, the legal fiction proves singularly immune to the logic of plot. The falsehood yields exactly one conclusion, and is barred from yielding any others that might seem to follow. The claimant who is called *filius nullius*, for example, cannot parlay that ascription into the result that he is free to marry one of his half-siblings (since they are unrelated), nor, at common law, was the father even entitled to disclaim responsibility for supporting the child.[25] Similarly, the fact of the property owner's invitation cannot be used for other evidentiary purposes, such as to show that she was already acquainted with the plaintiff before the accident occurred. This truncated form of causation, in which the stipulated fact motivates a single conclusion and excludes any others, distinguishes legal fictions (on Fuller's definition) from literary fictions.[26]

To be sure, literary texts often achieve similar effects by using narrators and characters who strategically withhold information. However, this method nevertheless assumes that the concealed details, once released, will ramify out to the full extent of their explanatory reach. They do not operate selectively to yield one result while being cordoned off from others, unless the plot itself justifies this constraint (for example, by keeping some characters unaware of the revelation and therefore unable to act on it). While there are numerous works of fiction in which the ordinary logic of entailment goes haywire, one would have to search far and wide for a literary plot in which an event produces results along a particular vector, while all other consequences that would normally follow are arbitrarily disallowed. Even in recent research on "unnatural narrative," which studies narratives featuring "scenarios and events . . . [that are] impossible by the known laws governing the physical world, as well as logically impossible ones," scholars have discussed examples in which the principles of causation are revised (for example, by making time go backwards) but none in which they are curtailed in the manner of a legal fiction.[27] A narrative exhibiting this feature would provoke the reaction that philosophers have called "imaginative resistance": readers would refuse to accept this truncated view of causality, even though "for the most part we have no trouble fictionally entertaining all sorts of far-fetched and implausible scenarios."[28] Nothing in the argument here requires that an "unnatural narrative" could *not* readjust causal logic in this fashion, but it is telling that few if any stories have tried the experiment.[29] Without a significant amount of explanatory preparation, bafflement would be the likeliest result. Far from cutting the chain of causal inference, the trend in recent fiction has been in the other direction—that is, to minimize the information offered directly to the reader, while leaving increasingly more to be inferred from the details that are presented explicitly.[30] This method depends precisely on letting the reader see how far implications will carry.

By contrast, the facts that come into being through the doctrines of *filius nullius* and attractive nuisance generate only one result—the legal consequence for which they were created in the first place. This feature also distinguishes legal fictions from various other legal devices that they resemble in certain respects. Presumptions of law, for example, are used to create facts, but once they have been accepted, they may be integrated with all the other facts that form part of the evidentiary record and were established by legal proof.[31] The same treatment applies to deeming provisions, which stipulate that a certain entity or action is to be treated as if it were something else; the result is that not only the legal consequence, but also the stipulated fact, may be used to achieve any other relevant purpose. Thus, for instance, once control is deemed to be sufficient for possession, the fact that a party "possessed" an item might help to show not only that the party used it to commit a crime, but also that she owes taxes on it, or that it is an asset of her bankruptcy estate. These legal devices obey the same narrative logic that typically governs imaginative literature, offering premises to be integrated with other details to see what conclusions they will yield. The consciously false assumption in Fuller's definition of the legal fiction obeys a markedly different logic.

3. THE LANGUAGE OF THE LEGAL FICTION

If legal fictions prove to be most unusual when considered as narrative formations, perhaps the consciousness that accompanies the consciously false assumption offers a more promising means of explaining why corporate personhood, *feme covert*, and numerous other doctrines are so frequently characterized as fictions, and why this tendency is significant. Perhaps, when commentators quote Fuller's definition, the important aspect is not so much the falsity of the doctrine's premise as the consciousness that attends its use, which for some is an index of the self-consciousness they discern in certain doctrinal formulations. That is, the court that adopts a "consciously false assumption" conveys something about its own attitude toward the law and the judge's ability to manipulate the law at will, and this understanding of the court's demeanor means that the terms can be flipped: when a court uses language that openly displays a doctrine's artificiality, the court is resorting to a fiction.

Fabrication is the very stuff of law, and it may seem paradoxical to single out, as particularly notable, the instances that call attention to their artifice (through the use of personification, or deeming provisions, or terms like "constructive"), when the more successful contrivance is the one that conceals its imaginative origins. This tendency is not paradoxical, however, if the self-consciously inventive style that these doctrines affect is taken to reflect a kind of fascination with the law's constructive abilities. Literary scholars, no matter how attuned to the ways in which texts muse self-consciously about their fictionality, would not regard this as a definitive trait of literary fictions, such that a story counts as a fiction only if it is presented self-consciously. Rather, in the case of literary self-consciousness, a text that lays bare the means of its own fashioning offers a means of exploring its attitude toward its imaginative status. Similarly, then, perhaps various doctrines that have often been called legal fictions might be arranged according to the ways in which they signal or conceal their imaginative origins. A spectrum that encompasses modes of legal fictionality might reveal otherwise obscured connections between the more openly creative doctrines and the ones tacitly relegated to the category of legal truths or facts (or merely lackluster technicalities). This approach would continue to highlight the concern with contrivance and creativity that accounts for so much of the scholarly research in this area, while dispensing with the suggestion that a doctrine's name, or expressly constructive effect, determines its status as a fiction.

When we consider a doctrine such as corporate personhood in this fashion—as a display of fictionality—its distinctive features are illuminated at least as well by analogy to works like Marcel Duchamp's *Fountain* (1917), as by the label of fiction. Duchamp transfigured the urinal, endowing it with a new significance and soliciting a kind of attention that it would not receive when seen as merely a commonplace object. Presented as art, the urinal invites us to consider it as a part of a system and to interpret it in relation to other objects in the system. Moreover, in failing to decorate or alter the urinal (except for the addition of the date and the signature "R. Mutt"), Duchamp highlighted the gesture itself, the movement of the urinal from its familiar location to the gallery, as the act that invests the object with this meaning. Similarly, doctrines like corporate personhood show us how law takes seemingly ordinary terms and attaches them to a system where they take on a different meaning, yielding new and often unforeseen results as they interact with the rest of the system. The artifice is readily visible when the terms are widely used outside of the courts, while there may seem to be no artifice at all in terms cultivated within the legal sphere, such as "patent" and "copyright." Precisely because legal language varies in the means and degrees by which it exhibits its own artifice, these doctrines might be considered along a spectrum of fictionality rather than simply labeling some as fictions *tout court*.

Finally, even for those who remain unpersuaded that the legal fiction (as opposed to legal fictionality) should be identified with a distinctive narrative structure, this analysis may nevertheless help to show that narrative merits more attention in the study of legal fictions. Commentators generally treat the falsity of the doctrinal name (or of its premise) as the only feature worth examining, before turning to the dangerous consequences that the falsehood might engender. This approach assumes that the study of narrative is largely irrelevant, because only one narrative structure is possible—namely, a tragicomic one in which the absurd premise is fully exploited, harming whatever it encounters. In short, "fiction" is simply equated with "narrative," as if the latter could offer no particular methods of analysis. The tools developed by students of "unnatural narrative," and by other narrative scholars, can help us look more closely at the forms of legal artifice, such as the different tools by which the law seeks to effect its exclusions and the different temporal rules by which they operate. This kind of research might yield new discoveries both about relations between legal and more conventionally aesthetic modes of fictionality, and also about unrecognized affinities among familiar legal devices.

NOTES

For comments on earlier drafts, thanks to Gregg Crane, Jeannine DeLombard, Markus Dubber, Maks Del Mar, Peter Goodrich, Robert Spoo, Bill Warner, and especially to Elizabeth Anker and Bernadette Meyler.

1. Jeremy Bentham, *Works*, ed. John Bowring (Edinburgh: Tait, 1838–43), 9:77, 8:284; quoted in C. K. Ogden, *Bentham's Theory of Fictions* (Paterson, NJ: Littlefield, Adams, 1959), cxvii, 142.

2. Peter J. Smith, "New Legal Fictions," *Georgetown Law Journal* 95 (2007): 1435–95, at 1438.

3. Alina Ng Boyte, "The Conceits of Our Legal Imagination: Legal Fictions and the Concept of Deemed Authorship," *New York University Journal of Legislation and Public Policy* 17 (2014): 707–62, at 720, 713.

4. Louise Harmon, "Falling Off the Vine: Legal Fictions and the Doctrine of Substituted Judgment," *Yale Law Journal* 100 (1990): 1–71, at 59.

5. On this genre, which featured coins, coats, coaches, and the like as narrators, see the essays in Mark Blackwell, ed., *The Secret Life of Things: Animals, Objects, and It-Narratives in Eighteenth-Century England* (Cranbury, NJ: Associated University Presses, 2007). Jeannine DeLombard hints at the possibilities of such a world when she describes "the doctrinal and practical dilemmas that first slavery and then the corporations posed to the common-law tradition," and considers the genre of the it-narrative in relation to the problem of "artificial or natural bodies that incorporat[e] a bundle of legally defined rights and responsibilities." *In the Shadow of the Gallows: Race, Crime, and American Civic Identity* (Philadelphia: University of Pennsylvania Press, 2012), 7; see also Lisa Siraganian, "Theorizing Corporate Intentionality in Contemporary American Fiction," *Law and Literature* 27 (2015): 99–123.

6. Alex Woloch, *The One vs. the Many: Minor Characters and the Space of the Protagonist in the Novel* (Princeton, NJ: Princeton University Press, 2003).

7. Some discussion of these issues may be found in Colin Dayan, *The Law Is a White Dog: How Legal Rituals Make and Unmake Persons* (Princeton, NJ: Princeton University Press, 2011), 21–22; and Caleb Smith, "Detention without Subjects: Prisons and the Poetics of Living Death," *Texas Studies in Literature and Language* 50 (2008): 243–67, at 253. Today, the legal restrictions once associated with civil death are statutorily specified, and there is no premise about the felon's death that figures in the list of individually enumerated legal consequences. For a survey, see Kathleen M. Olivares, Velmer S. Burton Jr., and Francis T. Cullen, "The Collateral Consequences of a Felony Conviction: A National Study of State Legal Codes 10 Years Later," *Federal Probation* 60, no. 3 (1996): 10–17.

8. Alison L. LaCroix, "Temporal Imperialism," *University of Pennsylvania Law Review* 158 (2010): 1329–73, offers a provocative discussion of temporality that does not expressly consider its narrative relations but might be usefully juxtaposed with literary scholarship. Peter Brooks discusses some aspects of narrative temporality in law, in his writing on "retrospective prophecies"; see, e.g., *Enigmas of Identity* (Princeton, NJ: Princeton University Press, 2011), 134.

9. Lon L. Fuller, *Legal Fictions* (Stanford, CA: Stanford University Press, 1967), 7, 9 (quoting Hans Vaihinger, *Die Philosophie des Als Ob*, 4th ed. [Leipzig, F. Meiner, 1920], 130).

10. For a useful survey of accounts of corporate personhood, see Susanna K. Ripken, "Corporations Are People Too: A Multi-Dimensional Approach to the Corporate Personhood Puzzle," *Fordham Journal of Corporate and Financial Law* 15 (2009): 97–177.

11. See, e.g., Gregory Currie, *The Nature of Fiction* (Cambridge: Cambridge University Press, 1990).

12. Pierre J. J. Olivier, *Legal Fictions in Practice and Legal Science* (Rotterdam: Rotterdam University Press, 1975), 133. That this kind of fiction also has literary implications—albeit of a different narrative status than is usually

supposed—may be seen from discussions such as Homer Obed Brown, "*Tom Jones*: The 'Bastard' of History," *boundary 2* 7 (1979): 201–34, at 203; and Michael Neill, "'In Everything Illegitimate': Imagining the Bastard in Renaissance Drama," *Yearbook of English Studies* 23 (1993): 270–92.

13. Fuller, "Legal Fictions," 372, 378; Maksymilian Del Mar, "Legal Fictions and Legal Change in the Common Law Tradition," in *Legal Fictions in Theory and Practice*, ed. Maksymilian Del Mar and William Twining (Cham: Springer International, 2015), 235. Peter Karsten gives an excellent account of the doctrine's history in "Explaining the Fight over the Attractive Nuisance Doctrine: A Kinder, Gentler Instrumentalism in the 'Age of Formalism,'" *Law and History Review* 10 (1992): 45–92.

14. Of course, one might also say that it is "true in law" that the child has no father, and hence this statement has the same status as the assertion that corporations are legal persons. As will become clear, however, the need to advance this provisional claim about the child, as a means of reaching a generalizable doctrinal truth about inheritance and intestacy, bespeaks such a different understanding of the claim's truth-status that it seems misleading to call it "true in law." The point of a doctrinal proposition is its generalizability, and that is what makes it "true in law."

15. For recent scholarship that examines law's narrative dimensions, see, e.g., Greta Olson, "Narration and Narrative in Legal Discourse," in *The Living Handbook of Narratology*, ed. Peter Hühn, et al., 371–83 (Hamburg: Hamburg University Press, 2014); Monika Fludernik, "A Narratology of the Law? Narratives in Legal Discourse," *Critical Analysis of Law* 1 (2014): 87–109 (http://cal.library. utoronto.ca/index.php/cal/article/view/21024/17173); Peter Brooks, "Narrative Transactions: Does the Law Need a Narratology?," *Yale Journal of Law and the Humanities* 18 (2006): 1–28; Simon Stern, "The Third-Party Doctrine and the Third Person," *New Criminal Law Review* 16 (2013): 364–412; Joseph Slaughter, *Human Rights, Inc: The World Novel, Narrative Form, and International Law* (New York: Fordham University Press, 2009).

16. Geoffrey Samuel offers a penetrating analysis of the fictional nature of legal concepts and doctrines as a general matter, in "Is Law a Fiction?" in Del Mar and Twining, *Legal Fictions in Theory and Practice*, 31–54.

17. William Blackstone, *Commentaries on the Laws of England*, ed. David Lemmings (Oxford: Oxford University Press, 2016), 1:284; Markus Dirk Dubber, "Policing Possession: The War on Crime and the End of Criminal Law," *Journal of Criminal Law and Criminology* 91 (2001): 829–996, at 938.

18. Morris v. Pugh (1761) 3 Burr. 1241, 1243; 97 Eng. Rep. 811 (K.B.).

19. Deborah A. Prentice, Richard J. Gerrig, and Daniel S. Bailis. "What Readers Bring to the Processing of Fictional Texts," *Psychonomic Bulletin and Review* 4 (1997): 416–20, at 417. Similarly, in *Experiencing Narrative Worlds* (New Haven, CT: Yale University Press, 1993), Richard J. Gerrig argues for an account that "replaces a 'willing suspension of disbelief' with a 'willing construction of disbelief.' The net difference is that we cannot possibly be surprised that information from fictional narratives has a real-world effect" (230).

20. For patent abuse, see, e.g., Morton Salt Co. v. G. S. Suppiger Co., 314 U.S. 488, 493 (1942); for copyright abuse, see, e.g., Practice Mgmt. Info. Corp. v. Am. Med. Ass'n, 121 F.3d 516, 521 (9th Cir. 1997), amended by 133 F.3d 1140 (9th Cir. 1998). Robert Spoo has shown how copyright misuse could apply to the conduct of the James Joyce estate; see Spoo, "Three Myths for Aging

Copyrights: Tithonus, Dorian Gray, Ulysses," *Cardozo Arts and Entertainment Law Journal* 31 (2012): 77–112, at 101–04.

21. "[G]reat temptation to fraud and danger of plunder exists by reason of the peculiar relations of the parties." Adams v. New Jersey Steamboat Co., 45 N.E. 369, 369 (N.Y. 1896).

22. Possibly because of its inclusion in Jingxiong Wu, *Cases and Materials on Jurisprudence* (St. Paul, MN: West, 1958), 596.

23. Adams, 369.

24. Michael Neill, "In Everything Illegitimate," succinctly makes this point when he observes that "[t]he *filius nullius* . . . was not so much the son of nobody, as the *heir* of nobody" (273).

25. On the latter point, see Richard H. Helmholz, "Support Orders, Church Courts, and the Rule of *Filius Nullius*: A Reassessment of the Common Law," *Virginia Law Review* 63 (1977): 431–48.

26. For fuller discussion of this point, see Simon Stern, "Legal Fictions and Exclusionary Rules," in Del Mar and Twining, *Legal Fictions in Theory and Practice*, 157–73.

27. Jan Alber, "Impossible Storyworlds—and What to Do with Them," *StoryWorlds: A Journal of Narrative Studies* 1 (2009): 79–96, at 80. Alber discusses several examples of "antichronological narrative" in "Unnatural Narratives, Unnatural Narratology: Beyond Mimetic Models," *Narrative* 18 (2010): 113–36, esp. 116–17. As he explains, "one way of dealing with unnatural narratives is to try to approach the unnatural on the basis of pre-existing cognitive parameters" (118)—an approach that includes assuming that the ripple effect of causal events operates as widely as it does in conventional fiction.

28. Tamar Szabó Gendler, "The Puzzle of Imaginative Resistance," *Journal of Philosophy* 97 (2000): 55–81, at 55. Research in this area usually asks why readers reject certain moral judgments for which a fiction might invite assent, but the question also applies to causal claims, as Kathleen Stock implies when arguing that "in central cases of imaginative failure, the basis for the failure is the contingent *incomprehensibility* of the relevant propositions"; Stock, "Resisting Imaginative Resistance," *Philosophical Quarterly* 55 (2005): 607–24, at 608 (emphasis added).

29. Stories with "plot holes" are perhaps the most obvious counterexamples, but the tendency to diagnose them as flaws shows that readers reject such efforts rather than taking them to exemplify an unfamiliar but intriguing kind of causal logic. Some examples are discussed in Marie-Laure Ryan, "Cheap Plot Tricks, Plot Holes, and Narrative Design," *Narrative* 17 (2009): 56–75.

30. Much of the research on this topic has been done by scholars interested in how fictional characters are presented as inferring each other's mental states, and how they are to be inferred by the reader. See, e.g., Alan Palmer, *Fictional Minds* (Lincoln: University of Nebraska Press, 2004). Mark McGurl has discussed the process by which minimalism came be treated as a sign of literary craftsmanship in MFA programs toward the end of twentieth century; McGurl, *The Program Era: Postwar Fiction and the Rise of Creative Writing* (Cambridge, MA: Harvard University Press, 2009), esp. 292–320.

31. Yan Thomas, "*Fictio Legis*: L'empire de la fiction romaine et ses limites médiévales," *Droits* 21 (1995): 17–63, at 18.

CHAPTER 19

Copyright and Intellectual Property

PAUL K. SAINT-AMOUR

Copyright is literature's most inherent law. Other areas of law, such as censorship, defamation, and contract, affect some literary works. But no work of literature is exempt from copyright's jurisdiction. Unpublished works are provided for by copyright law. Works in the public domain have that status thanks to copyright's provisions, which can also protect new works that transform public domain material. Even literature written centuries or millennia before 1710, when the first copyright statute was adopted, has a status, now, in respect to copyright. What's more, to the extent that law is thrashed out, encoded, contested, and studied in written language, law too unfolds within copyright's jurisdiction. Copyright is among the sites where law and literature are most intimately and obviously entangled.

So in a way it's surprising that interdisciplinary scholarship on law and literature didn't get its *start* in copyright. In fact, copyright didn't begin attracting interdisciplinary scholars until the mid-1980s. There are several reasons for this belatedness. Since literary writers started to become involved in copyright debates in the 1700s, they have been much likelier to lecture or testify about the law than to write about it, and likelier to write about it in contexts not conventionally deemed literary—in broadsides, columns, and articles. Compared with, say, criminal or inheritance law, there just aren't many novels, short stories, plays, or poems that allude to copyright, much less thematize it. Scholars interested in "law in literature" naturally went elsewhere. Literariness, meanwhile, has been a more prominent legal criterion in obscenity law than in copyright, whose jurisdiction includes but is not limited to literary works. For much of the twentieth century, literary scholars treated copyright as a technicality of interest primarily to biographers, bibliographers, and editors, while legal academics writing about copyright tended to regard literature as an amusing but analytically inert subset of the law's objects.

Benjamin Kaplan's *An Unhurried View of Copyright* (1967) was among the first works by a legal academic to view literature as more than an object of copyright. Kaplan saw a symbiosis between copyright and what he called the Romantic "cult of originality," and he went on to call for a retirement of that cult and its legal prop, copyright maximalism.[1] In the world he imagined superseding them, collaborative, aleatory, and networked forms of expression would prevail. Citing the likes of electrical engineer Carl Overhage and media critic Marshall McLuhan, he predicted:

> [I]n full-scale "on-line" operations with computers ... not only is the relationship between author and audience radically changed but the author's pretensions to individual ownership and achievement are at a discount: his [sic] dependence on the past is better appreciated; he is seen somewhat as a tradition-bearing "singer of tales," as a kind of teacher peculiarly indebted to his teachers before him. (118)

Such a discounting of the originality cult, Kaplan concluded, would probably "abate feelings of proprietorship and modify conceptions of copyright, especially those bearing on plagiarism"—a possibility he welcomed, given his stated "low-protectionist bias" (125). The Romantic individualist versus the bardic conduit of tradition: this opposition, central to *An Unhurried View*'s predictions about copyright law, amounted to a difference in literary ethos. By thus envisioning literary and legal change as coeval, Kaplan helped open the door to further questions about the reciprocal shaping energies of literature and the law.

Even more generative for later scholars of copyright and its cultural correlates was another late-sixties' text, Michel Foucault's "Qu'est-ce qu'un auteur?" (1969), which first appeared in English translation in 1979.[2] It's difficult to imagine the last thirty years' worth of interdisciplinary law and humanities scholarship on copyright having developed as it did without the following sentence—fascinatingly, one in which Foucault's essay projects a course it then declines to follow:

> Certainly it would be worth examining how the author became individualized in a culture like ours, what status he has been given, at what moment studies of authenticity and attribution began, in what kind of system of valorization

the author was involved, at what point we began to recount the lives of authors rather than of heroes, and how this fundamental category of "the-man-and-his-work criticism" began. (141)

Foucault's brief suggestion has enjoyed a long critical afterlife, prompting work on the history of the writerly profession, literary property law, the publishing industry, and mythologies of authorship. The earliest of these studies understandably gravitated toward the birth-century of modern copyright. Martha Woodmansee's classic 1984 article "The Genius and the Copyright" traced the exchanges among early copyright statutes, German Romanticism, the economics of the book trade, and the model of original genius that precipitated out of these crossings.[3] Mark Rose's 1993 study *Authors and Owners: The Invention of Copyright* took a sustained look at decisive eighteenth-century British copyright cases to illustrate the contingencies of the law's founding decisions, and finally to argue that copyright is "an archaic and cumbersome system of cultural regulation" and "an institution built on intellectual quicksand: the essentially religious concept of originality, the notion that certain extraordinary beings called authors conjure works out of thin air."[4] By demonstrating how copyright law and literary culture interdependently construct the author as original genius and as possessive individual, Woodmansee's and Rose's studies helped draw attention within legal scholarship to the biases the Romantic author-figure builds into intellectual property law.[5] Subsequent work by Peter Jaszi, James Boyle, Rosemary Coombe, and other legal scholars looked to more recent eras, often criticizing copyright's enduring reliance on individualist models of authorship and their resulting inability to reward collective innovation.[6]

All of the scholars I've mentioned so far, even those trained in the humanities, tended to foreground legal over literary discourse to learn how the laws pertaining to the literary marketplace underwrote aesthetic categories and criteria that had conventionally been seen as remote from the market. Their work inaugurated a still-growing body of scholarship that looks at copyright's history and central concepts as they affected both the economics and the evaluative paradigms of the literary marketplace. In attending to copyright as a base or footing of cultural production, however, such work can treat literary texts as epiphenomenal to copyright—as passive counters circulating on a field constituted and delimited by intellectual property law and other market forces. Responding to this tendency, a second generation of interdisciplinary scholarship argued that copyright's presence *within* literary texts is both pervasive and consequential. Rather than view copyright as an external ground of literariness and literary culture, this work recognized the law as mutually constitutive with the literary. It recognized, too, that copyright need not be accorded a naturalized, nonnegotiable facticity or sovereignty over literary contingency, but that it might be a crucial subject of literary meditation and contestation. Literary texts, for their part, could be understood anew as spaces where lettered discourse wrestles, or is made to wrestle, with its own vexed status as property.

In asking how literature engages internally, as it were, with its intellectual property status, this second generation has found it reasonable to reach for a small but growing number of texts that overtly thematize copyright, especially those that do so in a polemical spirit. Scholars have attended closely to Wordsworth's pro-copyright-extension sonnets, "A Plea for Authors, May 1838" and "A Poet to His Grandchild"; to an 1889 piece called "An Animated Conversation," a six-character colloquy on the pros and cons of international copyright by Henry James; and to Mark Twain's unpublished procopyright dialogue "The Great Republic's Peanut Stand," written in 1898.[7] We know that when in *Finnegans Wake* James Joyce calls a book "Cowpoyride by Twelve Acre Terriss in the Unique Estates of Amessican," he's referring to *Ulysses*, which forfeited its copyright status in the United States when a court declared it obscene in 1921.[8] The list of novelists who treat copyright as a major plot element is lengthening, although less quickly than the list of writers who treat it more glancingly. And we know of an increasing number of speculative fictions, from Spider Robinson's "Melancholy Elephants" (1982) to the two *Future of Copyright* anthologies (2012 and 2013) that project ever-strengthening copyright laws into the future in order to warn us about the cultural, psychological, and political consequences of overpropertizing expressive works.[9] Although in one respect such works comport with a "law in literature" approach, in another they trouble the very distinction on which that approach is premised—the distinction between law as content and literature as container, or between law as a represented object and literature as the medium of its representation. Literature about copyright is always self-referential, always metafictive: it calls attention to the fact that it is shaped and governed by the intellectual property laws it represents. In a physics only M. C. Escher could draw, the content contains the container.

Even as we've expanded our census of literary works that muse explicitly on copyright as diegetic premise or polemical topic, literary scholars have found other ways to "read for" intellectual property law. Robert Spoo, for example, has read Oscar Wilde's *The Picture of Dorian Gray* as allegorizing the heavy toll copyright takes on the communal lives of cultural works without ever mentioning the law explicitly, instead shifting some of its core dynamics into more dramatic registers and genres.[10] Caren Irr sees works by Ursula LeGuin, Andrea Barrett, Kathy Acker, and Leslie Marmon Silko as modeling alternatives to private intellectual property—and to private property full stop—through their utopian premises, their emplotments around the property rights of women and indigenous people, and (in Acker's case especially) their textual practices of appropriation.[11] Joseph Slaughter reads the plagiarist poetics of Yambo Ouologuem's 1968 novel *Le Devoir de violence* as parodying copyright's idea/expression dichotomy and the culturally appropriative practices it licensed in European modernist work. *Le Devoir*, for Slaughter, holds the mirror up to copyright regimes originating in the global North, exposing their role in abetting the abstraction and extraction of cultural wealth from the global South.[12] As Irr and Slaughter exemplify, we're learning to see how certain radically intertextual literary practices can engage critically with copyright law. These engagements take a variety of forms, from pointed mimicry of copyright's central categories and distinctions to assertions of a strong theory of fair use; from transgressive recombinations of protected works to alternative models of the law, the commons, and the work of culture.

Despite the growing number of ways humanists have of scrutinizing literature's engagement with copyright law, our interpretive lenses still tend to be individualist ones, focusing our attention on one writer or work at a time. This owes partly to a strong disciplinary bias toward the singular over the aggregate, the particular over the universal, the anomaly over the norm. I'd add that it's also a byproduct of Foucault's highly influential "What Is an Author?" As I said above, that essay's call to investigate "how the author became individualized" engendered crucial work on the rise and persistence of a possessive-individualist model of authorship, and on that model's coemergence with the Romantic figure of original genius. This body of scholarship necessarily focused on copyright's individualist dimensions in the course of historicizing and critiquing them. As the beneficiaries of that work, we are now in a position to attend to the stones it left unturned. Chief among them is the fact that copyright, for all the individualist formations it came to support, has also been intimately, and increasingly, linked to the masses, and particularly to questions of population, generation, and mortality. To pursue this insight is to turn the conversation toward a different Foucault, the Foucault of biopolitics. Having begun to call for such a turn a couple of years ago, I'd like to renew and extend that summons here.[13] Not as a flight from literature or culture, however: my claim is, rather, that one of the roads to the next generation of work on literature and copyright lies through the biopolitical.

In his lectures at the Collège de France during the mid-1970s, Foucault defined biopolitics in contrast to the disciplinary modality of state power. Whereas the disciplinary mode isolated individual bodies the better to train, inspect, and punish them, the biopolitical mode has sought since the late eighteenth century to manage the lives of whole populations, a project aided by the concurrent rise of sciences such as demography, epidemiology, and statistics. Instead of isolating individuals in order to cultivate their habits of self-surveillance, biopower regulates masses of citizens by compelling the parameters and conditions of their living. It adjusts a citizenry's aggregate natality, fertility, and mortality. In this shift to state-controlled biology, death itself gets resignified: "Power no longer recognizes death," writes Foucault. "Power literally ignores death."[14] At one time, sovereign power had ignored living subjects until they needed to be compelled or punished through death or the threat of execution. Under biopower, that sovereign "right to take life or let live" has been superseded by the state's "power to 'make' live and 'let' die."[15] Yet the biopolitical state remains prepared to take the lives of certain others—and in the era of genocidal weapons, of certain other *populations*—in order to ensure the security of its own. This, for Foucault, is the function of state racism, which turns the adversary, whether external or internal, into a biological other whose life can be taken, effaced, or nakedly compelled in the name of making a better, purer life for a citizenry.

So far, Foucault's discussion of biopolitics seems to have informed intellectual property scholarship exclusively in the area of patents, which in the case of "bioproperty" confer upon the patent holder exclusive rights in a life form, as it were—in a reproducible genetic code that, when activated, produces a particular strain or species of life. If patent law's creation of bioproperty has initiated a new phase in the propertization of life, we might say that copyright has enacted, over the course of its history, the reverse: the biologization of property. At British copyright's inception in 1710, the fourteen-year term granted by the law derived from the existing patent term of that length, which in turn had been computed as twice the seven-year term of trade apprenticeships. Measured by analogy with apprenticeship, and from publication rather than from the author's death, copyright at that point resembled organic forms only in its temporariness. Although the first US Copyright Act also adopted a term of fourteen years, Thomas Jefferson had initially calculated a term of nineteen years by consulting French mortality tables to determine the length of a generation.[16] Jefferson's actuarial reasoning didn't persuade the congressmen who gave the US Copyright Act the British term plus minor modifications. But as US, UK, and European terms grew over the course of the nineteenth century and eventually came to be measured from the author's death, the demographic approach to determining copyright's duration gained wide acceptance. One thing, however, sets Jefferson crucially apart from those who recently argued for European Union (EU) and US copyright term extensions based on growing life-expectancies.[17] Whereas the latter group deploys its life tables to argue for longer postmortem terms, Jefferson's figuring proceeded from a premise he supposed "to be self-evident: that the *earth belongs in usufruct to the living*; that the dead have neither powers nor rights over it." No generation, he maintained, had "the right to bind another"; each generation must receive the earth "clear of the debts and encumbrances" of its forerunners.[18]

If we want to see the present-day ascendancy of the demographic logic Jefferson used, we do well to look at the 1990s debates over term extension. The EU's Commission on copyright made two main arguments in favor of "harmonizing upward" from the standard postmortem term of fifty years to the German and Austrian postmortem term of *seventy* years. Both arguments had to do with generations and mortality. First, the commission surmised that postmortem copyright was "intended to provide for the author and the first two generations of his [*sic*] descendants"—and that because the average lifespan in the EU had grown, the old term of the author's life plus fifty years was no longer sufficient to fulfill that intention. Second, the commission favored a term extension in order to "offset the effects of the world wars on the exploitation of authors' works."[19] The unusually long German and Austrian terms that other countries would adopt resulted not from longstanding legal traditions but from 1960s *années de guerre* measures designed to compensate authors and rightsholders in those countries for the premature deaths and lost productivity caused by the world wars.[20] The EU tends as a rule to generalize the most comprehensive national rights to all member states. For that reason, a copyright term that stemmed from two nations' temporary provisions for wartime generations became the permanent Euro-American standard, and is rapidly becoming the global one. In other words, much of the world has now been conscripted to a perennialized mourning for two generations of German and Austrian war dead.[21] At the same time, corporate "work for hire" copyright terms also gained twenty years, even though the demographic rationales invoked on behalf of individual creators were irrelevant to corporate "authors," who have neither the incentive of heirs nor the need to be compensated for lost productivity in wars.

Copyright is clearly entangled in what Foucault called biopolitical techniques, as witnessed by the fact that even opponents of the recent term extensions did not reject the relevance of demographic arguments as such.

But to what extent can we really call copyright biopolitical in its function? Is literary property law a technology of state bioregulation? Here let me contrast copyright to the state censorship regime from which it both emerged and differentiated itself. Like the disciplinary regime of which it is a part, censorship individuates, subjecting to a visible discipline the bodies of both the transgressive work and the transgressive author. Censorship, in Foucaultian terms, either lets live or makes die. Early copyright may have served a censorship function by making attribution a precondition of the monopoly right. But as it becomes more actuarial, copyright participates in what Foucault called "a second seizure of power that is not individualizing but, if you like, massifying, that is directed not at man-as-body but at man-as-species"; it becomes a device not for singling out anomalies but for managing the balance, at the level of population, between innovation and legacy, access and incentive, public good and private monopoly, even natality and mortality.[22] The subject imagined by copyright is a biopolitical subject, one that can be compelled to live and create in particular ways through the regulation of the fields and systems it shares with its population. And if the *subject* that copyright comes to imagine is a biopolitical one, the *work* that copyright protects is, oddly, its doppelgänger—a property form endowed with the lineaments of a life form. By regulating the conditions of an intellectual property's creation and vitality, copyright makes property live; by making regulation coterminous with that vitality, copyright lets property die. And the death into which the work passes is, like the death into which its author retreats, an escape into a "privacy" where power ceases to recognize it, a privacy-from-power called, only a little paradoxically, the public domain. What clearer illustration of Foucault's thesis do we need than the fact that copyright law, in the age of biopolitics, can imagine propertizing a work only by first constructing it as a life?

The conflation of intellectual property estates with an artist's legacy, privacy, and integrity may seem to issue from copyright's encounter with Romantic individualism, but it belongs equally to the law's more recent shift to the biopolitical. We speak readily of "revived" or "zombie" copyrights and "orphan" works because intellectual properties whose duration is measured from the author's death are envisioned in the eerily organic ways I have been discussing. At the same time, the more postmortem copyright acts as a surrogate for the authorial organism, the more intellectual property becomes a receptacle for fantasies of transcending that organism's mortal condition. Because copyright likes to linger in the graveyard, it entertains a dream fostered by that place: the dream of eternal life, or at least of an eternally visited tomb. The crucial point here is that one of copyright's most powerful affective externalities—its quasi-religious role of protecting, commemorating, and even conferring a kind of immortality upon creative individuals—is not incidental to the law's regulatory and demographic logic but deeply enmeshed in that logic.

It goes without saying that copyright's biopolitical logic should become an object of critique. But it might also become a critical tool, one that equips us to question legal maximalism in terms that its advocates have already embraced. We might build on the work of the "Copyleft" in graphically representing how successive copyright term extensions have diminished both the existing and the prospective public domain. Here, Figure 19.1 is one such image, by Tom W. Bell, that was widely circulated in the United States in the wake of the 1998 Bono Act.

More forcefully than descriptive language can do, this image portrays the time-lapse progress of copyright maximalism and its power to hinder the growth of the public domain. The law's deepening reliance on demographic and actuarial logics is legible in the fact that Bell must make assumptions about average life expectancy and age of most productive work in estimating the length of postmortem copyright protection. (He assumes that authors create their works at age thirty-five and live for seventy years). Imagine how much more vivid such an image would be if it also conveyed the degree to which the growth of copyright has outpaced the growth in life expectancy to which it is rhetorically pinned. Or if, along the lines of a 2009 study, it could show us how the annually increasing quantity of new copyrighted works is a function not of longer copyright terms but

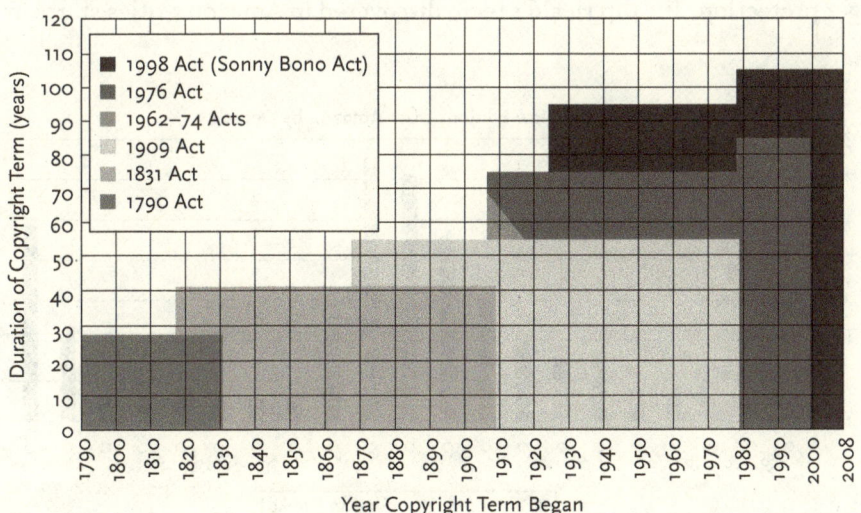

Figure 19.1 Trend of maximum general copyright term. Graphic by Tom W. Bell. Creative Commons Attribution-ShareAlike 3.0 Unported License (CC BY-SA 3.0).

of population growth, and how the incentive-based argument in favor of term extension is thus an empty one.[23] Imagine the force of such an image if it could illustrate the effects of term extension on successive generations of cultural producers whose would-be transformations of public-domain works are "let die" by a biopolitical copyright regime. By allowing us to approximate the sheer number of creative and scholarly projects foreclosed by term extension, such a study would give us a haunting counterfactual to the maximalist present, a sense of what the growth of copyright has cost us collectively.

A 2014 quantitative analysis by Paul J. Heald has explored new ways to illustrate strong copyright's chilling effect, in this case on the availability of print works.[24] Heald's research assistant generated random ISBN numbers and fed them into Amazon.com's application programming interface, which provides access to the company's product catalog data. The total of 2,266 discrete ISBNs corresponded to actual new (as opposed to used) books, and these were then sorted by decade of the work's initial publication. The raw results, based on data current as of fall 2012, showed a high number of recent titles precipitously declining through the preceding decades into the mid-century period, then even more dramatically increasing through the 1920s into the 1910s (see Figure 19.2).

In the United States, works published before January 1, 1923, are in the public domain. Works published between 1923 and the end of 1977 are protected for ninety-five years, so will not begin entering the public domain until 2019. Works published from 1978 on enjoy, in many cases, even longer protection. The dip Heald's team discovered in Amazon's titles starts in

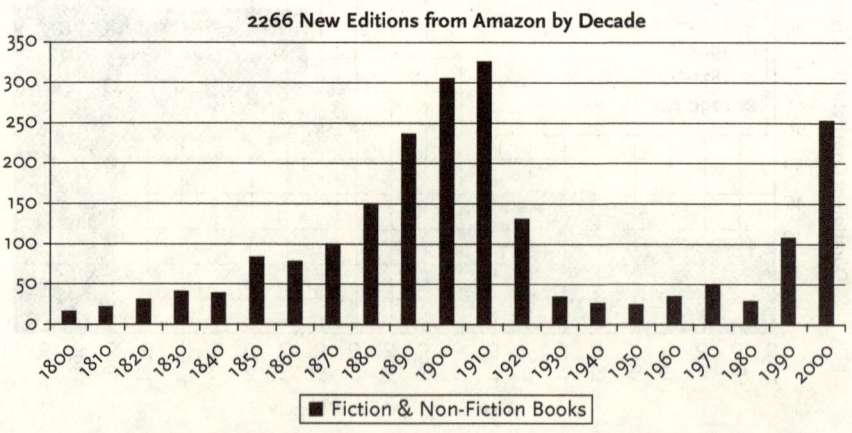

Figure 19.2 2266 New Editions from Amazon by Decade. From Paul J. Heald, "How Copyright Keeps Works Disappeared," *Journal of Empirical Legal Studies* 11 (2014).

the 1920s because the moving wall of copyright protection currently begins there, in the year 1923. Contradicting rightsholders' claims that copyright provides incentives to keep works in print, Heald's work suggests that lengthy terms result in the underexploitation and unavailability of protected works until they enter the public domain. Even adjusting for multiple editions of the same work and for longitudinal changes in the total number of works published, the dip in in-print works first published during the mid-century decades is dramatic. Again, far from spurring rightsholders to keep their intellectual properties available, lengthy copyright terms appear to have prevented all but the most durably popular works from remaining in print longer than a decade after their initial release. If this is the case, then long copyright terms on the vast numbers of out-of-print works benefit no one—neither rightsholders, who receive no sales, nor the public, who cannot obtain new copies of the work. In contrast, works that have entered the public domain are being widely republished, often in multiple editions and formats, including print-on-demand and eBooks. As Rebecca J. Rosen sums up Heald's findings, "A book published during the presidency of Chester A. Arthur has a greater chance of being in print today than one published during the time of Reagan."[25]

Heald's research raises more questions than it answers.[26] When it comes to accessibility, with how much accuracy can we extrapolate from 2,266 new titles on Amazon.com to cultural works writ large? Even if we found Heald's dip in a much larger sample, with how much certainty could we impute causality to excessive copyright over other factors, such as low demand for older works and variations in their cultural shelf lives? And in the era of large-scale digitization projects such as Google Books, how much of a given work's availability to readers will depend on its being currently in print? My point in discussing the study isn't to herald its findings as unassailable but to suggest that other scholars of law and literature should ask similarly large-scale, longitudinal questions, and be open to using quantitative methods in pursuit of them. To do so wouldn't require abandoning analyses of copyright's relationship with individual texts. But in supplementing those close readings, it would enable us to match the gauge of our analysis to some of the large scales at which copyright is most influential—the scales of genre, generation, nation, population, century, and cultural sphere.

I've so far keyed this discussion to the US context I know best, but the prospective use of quantitative methods to oppose copyright maximalism on its own terms only increases in critical amplitude as we scale up to international and global frames. At such scales, we might ask which populations are most benefited by long postmortem copyright laws and thereby most effectively "made live," to use Foucault's expression. To the extent that longevity is correlated with socioeconomic status, copyright gives the greatest "incentive" to those who will tend to need it least—that is, to highly educated, economically secure people living in politically and environmentally stable communities. If growing life expectancy has driven copyright term extension in developed nations, should countries where life expectancy is shorter (say, in Mozambique, where the average life expectancy is now 52.94 years, versus 77.4 years in Poland or 79.68 in the United States or 84.68 in Singapore)—have commensurately shorter copyright terms?[27] If not, what does it mean that copyright terms in the developing world are driven by life expectancies in developed countries? Should one lament or celebrate the fact that intellectual property's long duration in Mozambique results from the greater life-expectancies in nations whose development was fueled, in many cases, by racist, often genocidal imperialist projects followed by a postindustrial phase of net intellectual property export? To what extent has the hemispheric (and concomitantly racial) imbalance in intellectual property fields—one of imperialism's most durable legacies—been underwritten by a demographic logic that, starting from different, more Jeffersonian premises, might have secured the resources of the global South for the usufruct of the global South?

Now that we're acquainted with the biopolitical rationales and functions of copyright, how might we fold this new understanding back into our engagement with the contents of literary and other cultural works? One obvious place to begin is with "distant reading," the aggregative, usually computer-assisted methodology that also goes by the name of quantitative formalism. It's "distant" in contrast to close reading, a more institutionally embedded method that calls for slow, detailed, elaborative engagements with a given passage. Close reading tends to extrapolate large-scale claims about a period or genre from a handful of (mostly canonical) works. Distant reading has computers trawl through much larger samples to test hypotheses or identify lexical, syntactic, and other formal patterns in a more quantitatively rigorous manner. For many devotees of close reading, distant reading isn't reading at all. But if copyright's dominant logics and primary effects have indeed become more and more demographic with time, then the tools of close reading will sometimes be too fine to show us how copyright structures literary practices at the scale of a whole period or a generic or demographic field. Distant reading, in contrast, is ideally suited to such projects, and we might expect its practitioners to have begun tracking copyright's effects on literary practices. But so far, on the rare occasions when distant readers speak of intellectual property law at all, they tend to be complaining about how extensive copyright regimes impede the creation of literary data sets, those collections of digitized texts on which the quantitative humanities rely.[28] It seems a good bet that Franco Moretti has intellectual property in mind when he asks, in the concluding sentences of his book *Distant Reading*, "Will we, as a discipline, be capable of sharing raw material, evidence—*facts*—with each other? It remains to be seen. For science, Stephen Jay Gould once wrote, fruitful doing matters more than clever thinking. For us, not yet."[29] For the distant reader, "fruitful doing" can depend on access to proprietary data sets, which can depend in turn on access to protected material. Both legal and informal constraints on digitized texts may be the difference between distant reading's clever thinking and its actualization.

If we let ourselves imagine a moment in which copyright no longer impedes the quantitative study of its own effects on literary practice, what kinds of questions would we ask? We could begin, plainly enough, by tracking the appearance of "copyright," "patent," "trademark," "infringement," "piracy," and other related intellectual property (IP) terms within a given set of texts. This would give us a way to assess the law's prominence as a narrative premise and diegetic object, as a search for "copyright" reveals it to be in William Gaddis's *A Frolic of One's Own* (1994) and Michael Chabon's *The Adventures of Kavalier and Clay* (2000), both of which feature infringement plots. We would also want to learn to identify the lexical indicators of property plots that might more obliquely engage questions of intellectual property, through allegory or analogy. We might harness the computational methods currently used in plagiarism detection software—substring matching, fingerprinting, bag-of-words analysis, stylometry—to assess the prevalence of quotation, allusion, parody, pastiche, and, yes, plagiarism within a field of literary texts. Having conducted such analyses, we could mesh them with the kinds of analyses distant reading is already starting to produce—quantitative stylistics, for instance, or network mapping—and learn which literary practices "close to" copyright are positively correlated with those at a greater distance from it. Whether, for instance, intellectual property plots tend to occur more in certain genres, or to be accompanied by particular kinds of textual practice, or to produce intergenerational character maps. And we could apply these methods to years' or decades' worth of texts so as to track longitudinal mutations in literary practices and to ask which of these happen in discernible relation to legislative changes, developing case law, and shifts in the law's cultural uptake, as well as to standard demographic metrics such as population growth and average life-expectancy.

As we distant-read large sets of cultural works in relation to such data, we would also want to renew our close attention to how individual works dwell on the biopoliticization of copyright and other intellectual property regimes. By what narrative and other formal means, we would want to ask, does a given work address property's regulation of life? Which works from earlier periods anticipate the biologization of property? Which imagine an intellectual property regime decoupled from biopolitical logic? And how do contemporary cultural works constellate biology, property, and power? As one brief response to this last question, consider this message, found encrypted in a human clone's genetic sequence in the season one finale to the TV series *Orphan Black*:

> THIS ORGANISM AND DERIVATIVE GENETIC MATERIAL IS RESTRICTED INTELLECTUAL PROPERTY.

The human clones in the series have been patented under a fictional top-secret military IP regime. Although in reality both reproductive human cloning and the patenting of naturally occurring human genes are illegal in many jurisdictions, some of the same jurisdictions have issued biological patents on all sorts of genetically modified non-human organisms. For our purposes, however, the key words in *Orphan Black*'s big reveal are "derivative genetic material." Although in the story-world of the series this means that the children of clones are also the intellectual property of the patent holder, we know that "derivative works" is a term of art in copyright law, not patents. What the writers of *Orphan Black* imply here is a melding of copyright and patent such that the offspring of a patented organism can be considered a derivative work. If, as I suggested earlier, patent propertizes life and copyright biologizes property, we find here the imagined fusion of those two IP regimes. And we don't find it only in *Orphan Black* but in growing numbers of dystopian, speculative, and counterfactual fictions.

That includes the two *Future of Copyright* anthologies I mentioned earlier, both of them resulting from crowd-funded contests supported by the Trust for Civil Society in Central and Eastern Europe, and published by the Modern Poland Foundation.[30] Hailing from many countries, the contributors to these anthologies imagine a wide array of scenarios in which life is propertized and property biologized, offering us a glimpse of copyright's biopolitical imaginary in the present. In Jesse Betteridge's "The Brick in Room 207," a man is killed by his virtual reality implant when the gizmo's parent company discovers it running unlicensed software. In Eddie's "In Session," a court awards 75 percent of an unborn child's lifetime wages to the corporate rightsholder of the child's DNA. And in Alf Melin's "Remote Kill," a patient finds out that his dental implants were unlicensed and have been remotely deactivated by the rightsholder, prompting him to seek out "OpenTeeth" implants licensed, like the anthologies themselves, by Creative Commons. Read individually, these fictions offer us the immersive and particular rewards that distant reading cannot deliver, and that we shouldn't relinquish even as we explore the potential of the quantitative humanities. Taken together, however, these speculative fictions and their predecessors have been telling scholars something about copyright for a while now that we have been slow to realize. It's this: copyright can no longer adequately be thought about outside the nexus of biology and power— outside the lives it makes live, the lives it mimics, the lives it mourns, and the lives it may one day propertize. From here on out, literary property *is* bioproperty.

NOTES

1. Benjamin Kaplan, *An Unhurried View of Copyright* (New York: Columbia University Press, 1967), 117. Further references cited in the text.
2. Michel Foucault, "What Is an Author?" in *Textual Strategies: Perspectives in Post-Structuralist Criticism*, ed. Josué V. Harari, trans. Josué V. Harari, 141–60 (Ithaca, NY: Cornell University Press, 1979). Further references cited in the text.
3. Martha Woodmansee, "The Genius and the Copyright: Economic and Legal Conditions of the Emergence of the Author," *Eighteenth-Century Studies* 17 (1984): 425–48. See also Woodmansee, *The Author, Art, and the Market: Rereading the History of Aesthetics* (New York: Columbia University Press, 1994).
4. Mark Rose, *Authors and Owners: The Invention of Copyright* (Cambridge, MA: Harvard University Press, 1993), 142.
5. Even as later scholars would call into question this use of "Romantic." See, for example, Tilar J. Mazzeo, *Plagiarism and Literary Property in the Romantic Period* (Philadelphia: University of Pennsylvania Press, 2006).
6. See Peter Jaszi, "Toward a Theory of Copyright: The Metamorphoses of 'Authorship,'" *Duke Law Journal* (1991): 455–502; Jaszi, "On the Author Effect: Contemporary Copyright and Collective Creativity," in *The Construction of Authorship: Textual Appropriation in Law and Literature*, ed. Martha Woodmansee and Peter Jaszi, 29–56 (Durham, NC: Duke University Press, 1994); James D. A. Boyle, *Shamans, Software, and Spleens: Law and the Construction of the Information Society* (Cambridge, MA: Harvard University Press, 1996); and Rosemary J. Coombe, *The Cultural Life of Intellectual Properties: Authorship, Appropriation, and the Law* (Durham, NC: Duke University Press, 1998). For a thorough, full-length overview of interdisciplinary law and humanities scholarship on copyright, particularly as it informs the field of book history, see Meredith L. McGill, "Copyright and Intellectual Property: The State of the Discipline," *Book History* 16 (2013): 387–427.
7. On Wordsworth, see Susan Eilenberg, "Mortal Pages: Wordsworth and the Reform of Copyright," *English Literary History* 56 (1989): 351–74; on James, see Robert Spoo, "Ezra Pound's Copyright Statute: Perpetual Rights and the Problem of Heirs," *UCLA Law Review* 56 (2009): 1808–09; on Twain, see Siva

Vaidhyanathan, *Copyrights and Copywrongs: The Rise of Intellectual Property and How It Threatens Creativity* (New York: New York University Press, 2001), 62, 78–80.

8. James Joyce, *Finnegans Wake* (London: Faber and Faber, 1939), 105, lines 35–36.

9. Spider Robinson, "Melancholy Elephants" (1982), rpt. in *Melancholy Elephants* (New York: Tor, 1985). I discuss Robinson's story in the conclusion to Paul K. Saint-Amour, *The Copywrights: Intellectual Property and the Literary Imagination* (Ithaca, NY: Cornell University Press, 2003).

10. Robert Spoo, "Three Myths for Aging Copyrights: Tithonus, Dorian Gray, Ulysses," *Cardozo Arts and Entertainment Law Journal* 31 (2012): 77–111.

11. Caren Irr, *Pink Pirates: Contemporary American Women Writers and Copyright* (Iowa City: University of Iowa Press, 2010).

12. Joseph R. Slaughter, "'It's Good to Be Primitive': African Allusion and the Modernist Fetish of Authenticity," in *Modernism and Copyright*, ed. Paul K. Saint-Amour, 275–301 (New York: Oxford University Press, 2011). See also Slaughter, "World Literature as Property," *Alif: Journal of Comparative Poetics* 34 (2014): 39–73.

13. See my "Introduction: Modernism and the Lives of Copyright," in *Modernism and Copyright*, ed. Paul K. Saint-Amour, 21–30 (New York: Oxford University Press, 2011), from which this section of the present chapter is drawn.

14. Michel Foucault, *"Society Must Be Defended": Lectures at the Collège de France, 1975–1976*, ed. Mauro Bertani and Alessandro Fontana, trans. David Macey (New York: Picador, 2003), 248.

15. Ibid., 241.

16. See Thomas Jefferson to Richard Gem, undated [September, 1789], *The Writings of Thomas Jefferson: Memorial Edition*, vol. 7 (Washington, DC: 1903), 462–63.

17. These arguments were on the winning sides in both jurisdictions—in EU Copyright Directive 93/98/EEC, passed in 1993 and implemented in 1995, and in the Sonny Bono Copyright Term Extension Act, passed and implemented in the United States in 1998. Both laws prolonged the term of copyright protection by twenty years, to the length of the author's life plus seventy years.

18. Thomas Jefferson to James Madison, September 6, 1789, *Writings of Thomas Jefferson*, vol. 7, 454–56.

19. European Union Directive 93/98/EEC on Copyright Term of Protection, Recitals 5 and 6; quoted in Brad Sherman and Lionel Bently, "Balance and Harmony in the Duration of Copyright: The European Directive and its Consequences," in *Textual Monopolies: Literary Copyright and the Public Domain*, ed. Patrick Parrinder and Warren Chernaik (London: Office for Humanities Publication, 1997), 24–25.

20. Belgium and France had made similar, albeit slightly shorter, compensations for the war years. See Julian Barnes, "Letter from Paris," *Times Literary Supplement* (December 21, 2001), 13.

21. Peter Baldwin, *Copyright's Wars: Three Centuries of Trans-Atlantic Battle* (Princeton, NJ: Princeton University Press, 2014), takes up the *années de guerre* measures briefly (246–47), but we still lack a full-length study of their impact on the global standard.

22. Foucault, *"Society Must Be Defended,"* 243.

23. Raymond Shih Ray Ku, Jiayang Sun, and Yiying Fan, "Does Copyright Law Promote Creativity? An Empirical Analysis of Copyright's Bounty," *Vanderbilt Law Review* 62 (2009): 1669–746.

24. Paul J. Heald, "How Copyright Keeps Works Disappeared," *Journal of Empirical Legal Studies* 11 (2014): 829–66.

25. Rebecca J. Rosen, "The Hole in Our Collective Memory: How Copyright Made Mid-Century Books Vanish," *Atlantic Monthly*, July 30, 2013.

26. For a skeptical response to Heald's article, see David Newhoff, "Don't Blame Disposability on Copyright: Part II," *The Illusion of More: Dissecting the Digital Utopia*, November 13, 2015, http://illusionofmore.com/dont-blame-disposability-on-copyright-part-ii/.

27. Life expectancies at birth, estimated for 2015 for both men and women together, are taken from US Central Intelligence Agency, *The World Factbook 2013–14* (Washington, DC: US Central Intelligence Agency, 2014). See online version: https://www.cia.gov/library/publications/the-world-factbook/fields/2102.html.

28. Presumably a crucial reason Heald's team used Amazon.com's API for their 2014 study is *because they could*.

29. Franco Moretti, *Distant Reading* (London: Verso, 2013), 240.

30. Modern Poland Foundation, *The Future of Copyright* (Warsaw: Modern Poland Foundation, 2012), and *The Future of Copyright 2.0* (Warsaw: Modern Poland Foundation, 2013). The prompt asked: "What should a good copyright system look like? Is it possible to live without sharing? Will artists disappear if we make copyright less strict? Can we make culture without artists?" http://infojustice.org/archives/29769. I'm grateful to Maciej Jakubowiak for introducing me to these anthologies.

CHAPTER 20

Replicant Being

Law and Strange Life in the Age of Biotechnology

PRISCILLA WALD

In the June 1987 *Christian Science Monitor*, Alvin Toffler issued a stark warning. Asking "What is Human Now?," the author of the international best-seller *Future Shock* urged readers to consider how "the full glare of global publicity" focused on the world leaders who "presumably make the 'really' big decisions affecting today's world" was obscuring "a tiny group of men and women, virtually unknown" who were "busy making even bigger decisions."[1] The group was not a conspiracy. Most had no knowledge of each other and were "undoubtedly well intentioned," but these "businessmen, bureaucrats, judges, doctors, and scientists" were creating policies "for the biological revolution about to engulf us" that "could affect human destiny for all time" (20).

Despite the label "biological revolution," the concern registered in the titular question quickly moves Toffler out of the laboratory and into the legal and political arenas, where the basic definitions and moral principles on which social relations rested were suddenly in question (20). A woman pregnant with her grandchild, a dog returned from a state of frozen suspended animation, a human cell line at the center of a patent battle all embody, for Toffler, the dilemmas emerging from entities lacking legal and social as well as biological precedents. "It is now possible, in principle," he worries, "to transfer human traits into animals and animal traits into humans. If we do this, or create new life forms with genes drawn from humans, we can, also in principle, reach a point at which the common (mainly implicit) definition of 'humanness' becomes blurred. What traits ultimately define a human? Where is the borderline of 'humanness'"? (20).

Toffler was not alone in his depiction of a world careening into a science fictional future. Anticipating his screed by a decade, for example, the science writer June Goodfield broods similarly about the trend in patents on living organisms: "We can no longer possess, in the legal sense, a slave or a wife, or any category of living things," she chastens. "But if we now can *possess* a group of living molecules and be protected by patent, is it not possible that commercial companies could slowly 'climb' the evolutionary ladder with living organisms, whose rights and development they wish to have solely?"[2] Cautioning against *Playing God*, she worries "we are losing our respect for each other, and for what it means to be human" (71).

A keen cultural observer, Toffler was sensing a change in what the legal scholar James Boyd White calls "constitutive rhetoric," the language and narratives through which communities shape common values and beliefs. For Toffler, that change was at least as important to the emergence of the biotech industry as the laws and policies under discussion. Drawing on the specters of Nazi Germany and the South Africa of his own day, he worries that "murder can be redefined if the victim is regarded as 'not human.'" And for a more imminent example, he summons the language of a legal case, *Moore vs. Regents of the University of California*, that was moving through the California courts at the time: "Slave labor is not slavery if the slaves are 'not human,'" he admonishes. And "if we can sell parts of our cells . . . why not the entire body? And if body parts can be sold separately, why not the whole—for 21st-century bioslavery?" (21). If the biological revolution was poised to "shape the future of evolution," it was the lexical implications that threatened to "knock the props out from under traditional morality and institutions from the United States to Central Africa, from Europe and Japan to Latin America" (20). The consequences were too important to leave to legal and political systems where special interests could too easily shape policy to their advantage. Accordingly, he advocated worldwide debate and a global effort to agree on "a common definition of human" (22).

Toffler was right about public attention. While cases such as *Roe v. Wade* inspired debate about the irresolvable question of when life began, the biotech revolution emerged less publicly through cases involving more technical legal issues, such as *Diamond v. Chakrabarty*, which facilitated the emergence of biotechnology as big business in a five–four Supreme Court decision in 1980 by affirming the patentability of living organisms, and

Moore, which determined who should profit from such patents (here, of a human cell line). Yet, as Toffler forecast, the impact of these cases was much greater than the public notice they attracted. Their considerable economic effects were complemented by their contribution to the changing "constitutive rhetoric" of communal self-definition that accompanied the biotech revolution.

Jurists seeking to define such unprecedented entities as engineered bacteria and immortal cell lines and to address the ethical dilemmas they raised exposed what White calls "the condition of radical uncertainty in which we live: uncertainty as to the meaning of words, uncertainty as to their effect on others, uncertainty even as to our own motivations."[3] Uncertainty of "we" itself, which depends on the "comprehensible relations and shared meanings," constituting "the kind of community that enables people to say 'we' about what they do and to claim consistent meanings for it" (37). The historians William McNeill and Joseph Mali call such "we" narratives mythistories to mark how collective beliefs and values endowed with qualities of the sacred shape accounts of a group's past.[4] Although inevitable and constantly in flux, these stories change more rapidly and visibly when new discoveries challenge conventional definitions. The legal cases concerning biotechnology registered the instability of definitions of the human and of life itself.

The turn to historical examples such as racial slavery and Hitler's Final Solution suggest memories flashing up, in Walter Benjamin's formulation, at a moment of danger. In his posthumously published meditation "Theses on the Philosophy of History," Benjamin muses on two ways of engaging the past. The historicist fashions a progressive narrative that links the present causally to the past. The historical materialist, by contrast, illuminates "the constellation which his own era has formed with a definite earlier one."[5] For the historical materialist, the flashing memory manifests a pattern of resemblance rather than progress or causality: the social hierarchies and inequities in the present are not caused by past events, they reproduce them. The "danger" of the flashing memory lies in its precarity: it can expose or foreclose the repetition of the past that perpetuates oppressive structures.

Legal narratives derive power for White in warding off the "evils" of uncertainty and senselessness, while maintaining the "integrity" of the self "in the face of threats of total destruction"—efforts, in effect, to sacralize the law.[6] While it would seem those efforts would work through concealment of the uncertainty, court cases in fact expose it, dramatizing both the moment of danger and its foreclosure. While jurists work to fashion narratives that resolve the issues before the court, the case as a whole, from a Benjaminian perspective, shows how law bleeds into theology, potentially exposing the workings of mythistory. While White does not share Benjamin's messianic materialism, he recognizes the potential for insight and transformation in such moments. Viewing the "law as rhetoric," he contends, "might enable us to attend to the spiritual or meaningful side of our collective life."[7]

Insight does not necessarily lead to change. The irrepressible image of its precarity—Benjamin's "danger"—can compel belief in as much as challenge mythistories. *Chakrabarty* and *Moore* show how legal cases can become entangled in mythistories and with what consequences. The new creatures emerging from the labs embodied challenges emanating from the geopolitical and socioeconomic transformations of a globalizing world that were more difficult to name. They gave the uncertain directions of humanity a science fictional inflection. In turn, science fiction fleshed out the mythistorical contours of the narratives emerging from the courts and media. Trafficking heavily in corporate science and the mythic, Ridley Scott's 1982 cult classic *Blade Runner* offers an especially prescient engagement with the issues raised by the patent debates surrounding *Chakrabarty* and *Moore*. The film anticipates *Moore* in the figure of the bioslave through which it explores the concepts of life and humanity in a degraded world. As it follows the transformation of one such figure from avenging angel into agent of redemption, *Blade Runner* illuminates how two landmark patent cases register the pull of the sacred through which mythistory expresses its theology. Contra the science fictionalization of the cases that deflect the socioeconomic questions of an "intensifying global competition," however, the film shows how a dangerous embracing of uncertainties is the most ethical position in a fallen world.

CASE BY CASE

Ananda Mohan Chakrabarty, a biochemist, was not trying to fuel an emerging industry. He had spent his postdoctoral years working to engineer a new species of *Pseudomonas* bacteria that would more efficiently degrade hydrocarbons and "digest" large oil spills. He continued the research on his own time after beginning a job at the General Electric Research Center in Schenectady, New York, in 1971. The next year, he successfully engineered the *Pseudomonas putida*, but when his boss learned of his intention to present his research publicly, he sent Chakrabarty to the GE patent lawyers, which was how attorney Leo I. MaLossi first learned that living creatures were excluded from patent law. The restriction seeming outmoded to him, he decided to challenge the law by having Chakrabarty file for a patent not only on the process by which he had created the bug (as a biotech firm likely would have done), but also on the bacterium itself. The patent examiner's refusal of Chakrabarty's patent on the organism began the seven-year legal process that eventually led to the US Supreme Court.[8]

MaLossi continued to challenge the ruling throughout the 1970s, against the backdrop not only of media accounts of recombinant DNA but also of other biotech innovations and the rapid proliferation of biotech companies. The public encountered tales of "immortal life in the test tube" and "a monster in the pyrex," for example, when the story of Henrietta Lacks and the HeLa cell line surfaced in the mid-1970s.[9] The successful birth of a "test-tube baby" in July 1978 invigorated debates about the creation of a genetic master race and whether such babies would have souls. Technologies extending the survival of premature babies amplified the already intense debates surrounding *Roe v. Wade*. Most dramatically, journalistic accounts of the creatures produced in laboratories through recombinant DNA in the mid-1970s anxiously heralded the "modern Frankenstein creations" that "scientists will literally be loosing . . . on the world," and the "strange life" that bore comparison most nearly to "interstellar 'monsters'" that may be "brought to earth from other planets."[10] As one scientist lamented, humanity was engaged in "a destructive colonial warfare against nature."[11]

MaLossi strove to keep the narrative focused on the narrow points of law by distinguishing Chakrabarty's cross-bred bugs from the creatures produced through recombinant DNA. The US Supreme Court justices who supported the five–four decision that "a live, human-made organism is patentable subject matter" insisted "the question" was "a narrow one of statutory interpretation."[12] They intended, they claimed, only to interpret the meaning of constitutional language about patents, not to make policy. Their demurral, however, evades what they knew to be the broader implications of the case, as they facilitated the growth of the industry, assuring, in the words of a spokesperson from Genentech, Inc., "this country's technology future."[13]

Where they saw a policy vacuum, the other justices saw clear rulings limiting the patenting of living organisms. Writing for the dissenters, Justice William J. Brennan took issue with the use of the 1930 and 1970 Congressional Plant Patent Acts as precedents. In those acts, he averred, Congress had "chosen carefully limited language granting protection to some kinds of discoveries, but specifically excluding others . . . strongly evidenc[ing] a congressional limitation that excludes bacteria from patentability." Brennan also underscored that the patent extended only to plants that are "asexually reproduced" and was not intended to interfere with the functioning of living organisms.[14]

Scientists and ethicists expressed similar reservations about the erosion of the definitions of life and of the human and especially the exclusion of these concepts from the realm of the sacred. What for some was a narrow point of patent law was to others the prelude to an ontological crisis. "The Brave New World that Aldous Huxley warned of is now here," lamented the nonprofit People's Business Commission, which filed the sole amicus brief on behalf of the government.[15] "The ethical and spiritual hazards are less obvious [than the physical hazards], but perhaps even more significant," warned one journalist, summarizing the concern, articulated broadly following the case, "that once science becomes accustomed to manipulating and even creating life (including human life) in the laboratory, it increasingly will tend to view that life as a mere substance for experimentation, simply a means toward its own ends."[16] The decision was an "ominous harbinger of a technological nightmare waiting just down the road," according to Johns Hopkins biophysicist Richard Cone. Yale professor of molecular biophysics and biochemistry Harold Morowitz similarly worried that the narrowness of the point of law involved in the decision would mask its "deep philosophical implications. . . . Millennia of awe and respect for the special character of life, dating back to biblical times, or before, are being discarded if that life has any element of biological or genetic engineering in its synthesis," he laments. "The ruling by the highest court . . . goes far beyond the confines of patent law and, ultimately, may find its way back to our view of humanity."[17]

If patents tested the definition of life in *Chakrabarty*, *Moore* showed how the memory of slavery flashed up when the legal question concerned not the patentability of living things—human-derived, in this case—but their definition as property. Unusual immunological properties in his cells put John Moore, a man undergoing treatment for hairy-cell leukemia, at the center of this case, which turned on Moore's claim that medical researchers at UCLA had improperly "converted" his lawful possession into their property when they applied for a patent on an immortal cell line derived from the cells of his cancerous spleen. Moore had never granted permission for the cell line, which he discovered only when doctors asked him to sign a consent form after the fact.[18]

The consent issue loomed large for Moore, who had been misled about the need for semiannual doctor visits involving travel to UCLA from Seattle and invasive procedures. His lawyers, however, believed the unresolved property issues—who should profit from the patent; who "owned" the cells—were the key questions of a precedent-setting case. Once again the question of patents—and, in this case, evident confusion in the judicial opinions about the nature of intellectual property—generated a narrative that inflected the legal issues of the case. Lawyers on both sides invoked a slippery slope to bioslavery. Moore's attorneys summoned the specter of patented cells leading to an "owned" donor; the defense attorneys, distinguishing between intellectual and material property, argued that any slippery slope began with the identification of cells as "owned" even by the donor himself. The majority of the Los Angeles County Superior Court concurred with the defense and dismissed the case. An appeals court sent the case back to court with the judgment that "the essence of a property interest—the ultimate right of control . . . exists with regard to one's own human body."[19] But Justice David M. Rothman offered the crux of the emerging narrative when he conceded, in the majority opinion, that the issue should be approached "with caution," since "the evolution of civilization from slavery to freedom, from regarding people as chattels to recognition of the individual dignity of each person, necessitates prudence in attributing the qualities of property to human tissue."[20]

Although acknowledging the "dramatic difference between property rights in one's own body and being the property of another," the statement nonetheless manifested the emerging narrative as the case made its way through both the courts and the popular press. Following a year and a half of deliberation, the California Supreme Court in 1990 found that while the researchers had not discharged their disclosure obligations and therefore deserved censure, Moore nonetheless had no conversion claim. While the justices' opinions, as in *Chakrabarty*, register a debate concerning the emergence of the biotech industry, as it made its way into the mainstream media the slippery-slope argument entangled the technical legal terms in an ontological discussion of human dignity and worth. Although concurring with the majority, Justice Armand Arabian chose to file a separate opinion in order "to give voice to a concern that . . . informs much of that opinion but finds little or no expression therein." Moore has brought the court to the very limit of the law, he admonishes. "Plaintiff has asked us to recognize and enforce a right to sell one's own body tissue *for profit*. He entreats us to regard the human vessel—the single most venerated and protected subject in any civilized society—as equal with the basest commercial commodity." The stakes for him extend beyond oppressive power relations, beyond even the challenge to the most fundamental definitions of the human. Moore has stepped into another realm entirely: "he urges us to commingle the sacred with the profane. He asks much."[21] The question haunting *Moore* concerned the definition rather than creation of the cell line.

From the beginning of the nineteenth century, when Victor Frankenstein realized his ambition to create life in the laboratory, through Giacomo Rappaccini's cross-pollination of his daughter with poisonous flora, to Dr. Moreau's horrific metamorphoses of animals into people at the century's end, literary works registered a concern with scientists' hubristically interfering too radically with Nature's handiwork. Emerging as a recognizable mass genre against the backdrop of the acceleration of science and technology between the two world wars, early science fiction summoned those prototypes, which in turn inflected popular perceptions of biotechnology, as creatures seemed to step out of those literary works and into the laboratory.

The rise of the biotech industry, however, replaced the laboratory with the boardroom as the profit motive displaced—or, at least, supplemented—scientific hubris. Thus Goodfield expresses concern less about the creation of new entities than about the effects of patenting them, and Toffler worries about the unstable definitions surfacing in legal and political debates. Works of science fiction similarly registered the shift in their preoccupation with these new life forms. But the fears articulated by Goodfield, and later, Moore's attorneys, Toffler, and others are nowhere more vividly dramatized and intricately explored than in the 1982 biotech fable *Blade Runner*. Adapted from Philip K. Dick's 1968 novel, *Do Androids Dream of Electric Sheep?*, the film explores the loss of humanity and devaluation of life in a dystopic future, but with a more pronounced emphasis on the biotech industry than Dick's novel. While nuclear war has caused the novel's all but uninhabitable Earth, the film opens with the image of an industrial wasteland that seems to be the cumulative effect of indifference and neglect rather than the result of a particular event, "wreckage upon wreckage," as Benjamin might say, "in a pile of debris growing skyward."[22]

In both cases, environmental degradation has prompted the formation of Off-world colonies, which, coming with their own hardships, have given rise to the need for cheap expendable labor and the consequent production of Dick's androids and Scott's deliberately renamed Replicants. But Dick's innuendo—an advertisement for androids that summons "the halcyon days of the pre-Civil War Southern states"—becomes the film's full-blown scenario.[23] The genetically engineered Replicants are human entities mass produced explicitly as slaves. The circumstances of their creation allow their creators to overlook their human attributes, hence to justify their inhumane treatment. In staging these debates through the experience of sentient characters, however, *Blade Runner* allows for their exploration in the context of the human need for meaningful existence that makes mythistories so powerful.

An Off-world slave rebellion commences the action of the film, which pits Blade Runner Rick Deckard against the four Replicants who have subsequently returned to earth to find the head of the Corporation that produced them, hoping to extend their four-year life span. The drama of the film inheres in the bioslaves' efforts to claim their humanity in a world in which degradation extends to the term "humanity" itself. The film intensifies the characterization of the novel. The Replicants manifest more emotional complexity than the androids, and Eldon Tyrell is a more sinister corporate head than Eldon Rosen. The Replicants Deckard has been assigned to "retire" are all Nexus 6s, Tyrell's new line, and the Blade Runner learns how difficult his task will be when he is nearly fooled by Tyrell's Nexus 6 assistant, Rachael, who is unaware of her heritage. As Tyrell chillingly explains, "Commerce is our goal here at Tyrell. 'More human than human' is our motto—Rachael is an experiment, nothing more."[24]

An exceptionally cruel feature of the Tyrell Corporation's design makes the subterfuge possible. "We began to recognize in them a strange obsession," Tyrell explains, "after all they are emotionally inexperienced with only a few years in which to store up the experiences which you and I take for granted. If we gift them with the past we create a cushion or pillow for their emotions and consequently we can control them better." Deckard's outburst—"memories, you're talking about memories"—signals the master Blade Runner's increasing sense of a violation. The Tyrell Corporation engineers the "failsafe device" of the four-year life span to protect humanity from the "emotional responses" these engineered enslaved beings "might develop." Rachael poignantly tries to convince Deckard of, and reassure herself about, her humanity by producing a photograph of herself as a child with her mother. Deckard taunts her with irrefutable evidence in his identification of her childhood memories—things she has told no one—as those of Tyrell's six-year-old niece. Her devastation moves him, however, initiating a process through which he will come to regard the corporation's exclusion of the Replicants from the basic terms of humanity as an act of violence.

Violence begets violence. Deckard is called back from retirement because of the near-fatal shooting of the top Blade Runner while administering a test to determine which employees of the Tyrell Corporation are the Nexus 6 infiltrators. Seeking to measure empathy (ostensibly the distinction between human beings and Replicants), the examiner asks the subject, Leon, a series of questions, culminating in one about his mother, which prompts him to shoot the Blade Runner. The unfolding film makes retrospective sense of this act as it educates us, along with Deckard, about the nature of human-on-Replicant violence. Leon's anguish implies that the charged icon of "mother" prompts an unbearable reminder of his exclusion from history and humanity. The memories flashing up for Replicants are only empty signifiers: lies that mark the Replicants' preclusion from the terms of mythistory.

Photographs depict distinctive moments of danger in the film, both literal—Leon is willing to risk capture to save the photographs through which he seeks to fashion a past—and in Benjamin's sense of a flash of insight. The Replicant leader, Roy Batty, scoffs at Leon's attachment to the photographs. After all, they represent the Replicants' internalization of the fictions of the Tyrell Corporation: their longing for a past—for inclusion in a mythistory—which is to say, the emotional terms of their enslavement. But Roy, like Benjamin's historical materialist, comes to understand how the corporation's violence inheres in converting the defining features of the Replicants' humanity into the terms of their enslavement. Their desire for inclusion in the mythistory explains why the idea of the sacred, and all it implies, might surface in a legal case concerning the fundamental definitions of life and the human.

The script of *Blade Runner* draws on the prophetic books of the poet William Blake to show how Roy's bid for survival becomes a quest for humanity, experienced as a transcendent sense of belonging. "Fiery the angels fell," Roy intones, invoking, and altering, a line from Blake's 1793 *America: A Prophecy*, as he enters the factory that produces Replicant eyes in his search for Tyrell.[25] "Deep thunder rolled around their shores burning with the fire of Orc." Blake's Orc, a revolutionary figure who eschews the deadening attributes of both religious commandments and secular law, appears sinister to the oppressive forces of civilization. *America: A Prophecy* begins with his breaking his chains and inspiring the American Revolution. Throughout the poem he embodies the creative human spirit struggling for liberation. The association identifies Roy and his fellow Replicants as angels of revolution. Capable of raw brutality and fierce love, Roy is nonetheless the moral center of *Blade Runner* and its prophetic voice.

The ruse through which Roy finally gains access to Tyrell also strikingly echoes the parable of a ventriloquized chess game that opens "Theses on the Philosophy of History." Benjamin describes the illusion of a chess-playing puppet manipulated by a hidden expert ("a little hunchback") as an obscure analog of how historical materialism must enlist the services of a hidden theology. Roy uncannily penetrates the fortress of Tyrell Corporation by orchestrating a chess game that he plays with an unwitting Tyrell through the decoy of the reclusive magnate's usual chess partner, the meek toymaker Sebastian.[26] On seeing Roy, Tyrell expresses surprise only that he had not come sooner, to which Roy replies, "It's not an easy thing to meet your maker." The intensity of Roy's emotions in his subsequent confrontation with Tyrell gives the lie to Replicants' alleged affectlessness. Roy is at once suppliant and rejected child; his request for extended life is at the same time, like Frankenstein's creature, a plea to turn his maker into a father. The hopelessness of Roy's quest is evident even in Tyrell's name, which, again drawing on one of Blake's prophetic poems, evokes Tiriel, the tyrant king who enslaves his many children and eventually causes most of their deaths.[27]

Tyrell of course misses Roy's point. The request for more life, he chides, is "a little out of [his] jurisdiction," and he enumerates dangers that could have been lifted from the transcripts of the 1975 Asilomar conference at which scientists debated a research moratorium in light of the potential dangers of recombinant DNA experiments. Efforts to alter an organic life form have produced "a lethal mutagen, . . . a virus so lethal the subject was dead before he left the table." Looking proudly, even lovingly at Roy, he assures him, "You were made as well as we could make you" to which Roy replies, "But not to last."

In his effort to console his creature, Tyrell reveals the nature of his violence. "The light that burns twice as bright burns half as long," he tells Roy, "and you have burned so very, very brightly, Roy. Look at you, you're the prodigal son. You're quite a prize." To Roy's pained confession, "I've done questionable things," he counters, "Also extraordinary things," and he advises Roy to "revel in [his] time." Roy's icy response—"Nothing the god of biomechanics wouldn't let you in heaven for"—suggests he apprehends his maker's lack of humanity as well as the violence of the institutions that perpetuate it. The depth of Roy's emotion is evident in the metamorphosis of a passionate kiss into a graphically intimate blinding culminating in Tyrell's death. Gruesome as the scene is, the punishment fits the crime. Tyrell has failed him as father, maker, and human being. He has not only failed to understand Roy's anguished regret for the crimes Tyrell's work has forced him to commit, but he is also blind to the agon of Roy's existence as a sentient being without a past, which is to say an enslaved person longing for, but excluded from, the most fundamental terms of history and the most intimate relationships of humanity.

Yet, if Roy's act of violence grows out of his recognition that Tyrell is motivated not, as many of his science fiction predecessors, by the passion of a mad scientist, but by the dispassion of a corporate head ("Rachael is an experiment, nothing more"), it is also an act of vengeance. Any moral edge is undercut by his ostensible murder of the one witness to his act: the sympathetic Sebastian. The lingering close up of the eye of an unseeing (because mechanical) owl, with which the scene ends, signals the missed possibility of the act in the surrender to the vengeance motive and the destruction of the only possible witness. There is no one to benefit from a lesson learned. Roy's puzzling decision to save Deckard at the end of what appears to be a bloody fight to the death in the penultimate scene makes sense if the regret he expresses to Tyrell at what he has had to do to survive is ultimately a turning point.

Roy had come to Earth to protest Replicant treatment and demand more life. When his encounter with his father and maker becomes a meeting with a corporate head, however, he comes to understand the structural violence that has created the depleted world in which others—the toymaker, the Blade Runner, the engineer in the Eye Works factory, the pickpockets and street urchins—not just Replicants, are trying to survive. Earlier, he had taunted Chew, the eye engineer, with his near-sightedness, quipping, "If only you could see what I have seen with your eyes." But his final words suggest the cosmic perspective he has achieved: "I've seen things you people wouldn't believe. Attack ships on fire off the shoulder of Orion. I watched C-Beams glitter in the dark near the Tannhäuser Gate. All those moments will be lost in time like tears in rain. Time to die." Capable of discerning astral figures, a transformed Roy expresses resignation but not despair. His earlier taunt gives way to his expressed desire to transmit his vision and his acceptance of the limitations in doing so. Acknowledging that he is out of time, he bequeaths what he can of his cosmic perspective to Deckard, whose subsequent revelation that he may himself be a Replicant proves his fitness for the inheritance. Association with the eponymous (and mythistorical) figure of Wagner's opera, Tannhäuser, imparts to Roy the redemptive power of sacred (and sacrificial) love.

The decision to save Deckard makes sense, that is, if we understand Roy not only as Blake's angel, but also as Benjamin's. Benjamin embodies his messianic view of history in the by now iconic form of the Angel of History, whose "face is turned toward the past. Where we [with our limited human perspective] perceive a chain of events, he sees one single catastrophe which keeps piling wreckage upon wreckage and hurls it in front of his feet." The angel offers the possibility of revelation and redemption ("only a redeemed mankind receives the fullness of its past"), but is forestalled by "a storm . . . blowing from Paradise [that] has got caught in his wings with such violence that the angel can no longer close them." He "would like to stay, awaken the dead, make whole what has been smashed," but the "storm [called progress] irresistibly propels him into the future to which his back is turned, while the pile of debris before him grows skyward."[28] Humankind's belief in "progress," in the idea of civilization as inevitable enlightenment, obscures the Angel's effort to tell the stories of those, living and dead, who have been forgotten by history, as it endlessly defers the Angel's revelation. Benjamin's flashes of memory mark fleeting moments of insight into the angelic perspective.

Roy's transformation from the Angel of Revolution into the Angel of History parallels the arc of Benjamin's piece. Having come to rebel against this world, Roy learns he must also seek to redeem to it. He must, that is, restore life to a deadened humanity. With its emphasis on Replicants as enslaved beings excluded from a collective sense of belonging to humanity, *Blade Runner* is a memory flashing up in the dangerous moment of the emergence of the biotech industry, and Roy's encounter with Eldon Tyrell mediates the nature of the constellation. The corporate magnate is more monstrous than his eighteenth- and nineteenth-century predecessors because of the venality, and ordinariness, of his motivations. Lacking the Romantic ambitions of Dr. Faustus and Dr. Frankenstein, he embodies the diminished priorities that underpin corporate science. No slope slips from patenting life to owning a human being. That conceit is the historicist's Romantic vision of a science fictional future. Rather, the Replicant Angel sees in Tyrell the institutionalized indifference to human or any other life that has yielded the blasted world of *Blade Runner*: the wreckage upon wreckage of slavery, colonialism, genocide, but also, more mundanely although no less violently, of the inequities of lived experience that continue to trace the historical contours of exploitation. That is what is obscured. Where, for example, both sides in *Moore* decried the (science fictional) scenario of the slippery slope of bioslavery, no one followed the logic of the flashing memory to where I am suggesting *Blade Runner* leads us: the constellation formed between the differential value of human life that enabled the colonization and enslavement of populations and the socioeconomic inequities among the descendants of the oppressors and the oppressed that are perpetuated by the institutions of global capital, or, in Toffler's words, the "intensifying global competition" in which "giant corporations and nations alike [were] jockeying for position to cash in on the enormous profits" (20).

It is, of course, important to remember that the Angel Roy is also and always a Replicant, whose memories, flashing or otherwise, are implanted. Yet, he is throughout the visionary—who sees with the engineer's eyes, who witnesses the cosmic spectacles we "people" can only imagine—and through whose eyes Deckard, and we, come to see ourselves. The vision bequeathed to us, as to Deckard, is the uncertainty of our humanity. Replicants all, we dwell in history, which is to say our memories—at least collectively—are indeed implanted. As Replicant, slave, and angel, Roy reveals the ontological investment in memory—collective and individual—that would make someone risk everything for a photograph, even while knowing it as a fiction: a futile effort to construct a past. He shows us, that is, our own investments in mythistory.

The extended scenario of *Blade Runner* draws out the complexities of those investments as they surface in the flashing memories of the landmark patent cases of *Chakrabarty* and *Moore*. The extralegal responses to both cases evince a longing for an understanding of life and the human that would put both terms ineffably beyond definition—in the realm of the sacred. That is the longing for an ontological investment in something beyond law and policy, something beyond question and debate to which law and policy have to answer. That (impossible) longing explains the power of the mythistorical and the danger, as Benjamin would have it, when its terms become visible—at moments of social, political, and legal transformation. Roy's bequeathing of his cosmic memories in the penultimate scene of the film marks a dangerous moment of precisely such clear-sightedness. Irresistibly propelled into the future, the Angel of History—in the legal cases as in the film—heralds the longing for the sacred that endlessly dangles redemption in the elusive definition of the human.

NOTES

1. Alvin Toffler, "What Is Human Now?" *Christian Science Monitor*, June 4, 1987, 20–22, at 20. Further references cited in the text.
2. June Goodfield, *Playing God* (New York: Harper Colophon, 1977), xiii.
3. James Boyd White, "Rhetoric and Law: The Arts of Cultural and Communal Life," *Heracles' Bow: Essays on the Rhetoric and Poetics of the Law* (Madison: University of Wisconsin Press, 1985), 28–48, at 40.
4. See William H. McNeill, "Mythistory, or Truth, Myth, History, and Historians," *The American Historical Review*, Vol. 91, No. 1 (Feb., 1986), pp. 1–10 and Mythistory and Other Essays (Chicago: University of Chicago Press, 1986); Joseph Mali, Mythistory: The Making of a Modern Historiography (Chicago: The University of Chicago Press, 2003).
5. Walter Benjamin, "Theses on the Philosophy of History," *Illuminations: Essays and Reflections*, ed. Hannah Arendt, trans. Harry Zohn (New York: Schocken, 1969), 253–64, at 255, 263.
6. James Boyd White, "The Judicial Opinion and the Poem: Ways of Reading, Ways of Life," in *Heracles' Bow*, 107–38, at 137; "Telling Stories in the Law and in Ordinary Life: The *Oresteia* and 'Noon Wine,'" in *Heracles' Bow*: 168–91, at 172.
7. White, "Rhetoric and Law," 42–43.
8. On the history and significance of *Chakrabarty*, see Daniel J. Kevles, "Ananda Chakrabarty Wins a Patent: Biotechnnlogy, Law, and Society, 1972–1980," *Historical Studies in the Physical and Biological Sciences* 25, no. 1 (1994): 111–35.
9. Laurence E. Karp, "Immortal Life in the Test Tube," *Washington Post*, April 18, 1976, B1; Michael Rogers, "The Double-Edged Helix," *Rolling Stone*,

March 21, 1976, 51. While George and Margaret Gey produced the HeLa cell line in 1951, the flurry of articles about HeLa in the 1970s followed the discovery that the unusually robust HeLa cells had contaminated multiple subsequent cell lines.

10. Peter Gwynne, "Genetic Watchdogs," *Newsweek*, July 4, 1976, 106; and John A. Conway, "Safe Houses for Strange Life," *Newsweek*, June 28, 1976, 15.

11. Erwin Chargaff, "On the Dangers of Genetic Meddling," Letter, *Science* 192, no. 4243 (1976): 938–39 at 939.

12. Diamond, Commissioner of Patents and Trademarks v. Chakrabarty 447 U.S. 303; 318 (1980).

13. Linda Greenhouse, "Science May Patent New Forms of Life, Justices Rule, 5 to 4: Dispute on Bacteria: Decision Assists Industry in Bioengineering in a Variety of Projects," *New York Times*, June 17, 1980 (late edition), A1.

14. Diamond v. Chakrabarty at 447 U.S. 319.

15. Cited in Greenhouse, "Science May Patent New Forms of Life." On the role of the PBC in the Chakrabarty case, see Kevles, "Ananda Chakrabarty Wins a Patent."

16. Tom Nugent, "Engineering Life: Boon or Nightmare?" *Baltimore Sun* July 13, 1980, K1.

17. Cone quoted in Nugent, "Engineering Life," and Harold Morowitz, "Reducing Life to Physics" *New York Times*, June 23, 1980, A23; and "Is High Court Blind to Life?" *Chicago Tribune*, June 27, 1980, d3.

18. For my discussion of *Moore*, I am drawing on work I did for two previous essays, "What's in a Cell? John Moore's Spleen and the Language of Bioslavery," in "Essays Probing the Boundaries of the Human in Science and Science Fiction," special issue, *New Literary History* 36, no. 2 (2005): 205–25; and "Cells, Genes, and Stories: HeLa's Journey from Labs to Literature," in *Genetics and the Unsettled Past: The Collision of Race, DNA and History*, ed. Keith Wailoo, Alondra Nelson, and Catherine Lee, 247–65 (New Brunswick, NJ: Rutgers University Press 2012).

19. Moore v. Regents of the University of California, 249 Cal. Rptr. at 506.

20. Moore v. Regents of the University of California, 249 Cal. Rptr. at 504.

21. Justice Armand Arabian, Concurring, Moore v. Regents of the University of California, Supreme Court of California, 51 Cal. 3d 120, 148 (1990).

22. Benjamin, "Theses on the Philosophy of History," 257–58.

23. Philip K. Dick, *Do Androids Dream of Electric Sheep?* (New York: Doubleday, 1968).

24. *Blade Runner*, directed by Ridley Scott (1982); *Blade Runner: The Final Cut* (Warner Home Video, 2007), DVD.

25. The misquotation of William Blake's *America: A Prophecy*—"Fiery the angels rose, & as they rose deep thunder roll'd / Around their shores: indignant burning with the fires of Orc"—has been much remarked. *The Complete Poetry and Prose of William Blake*, ed. David V. Erdman (newly revised edition) (New York: Anchor Books [Random House]), 1988: 51–59, 55.

For excellent extended discussions of the film's use of Blake, see Alexis Harley, "'America, a Prophecy': When Blake Meets *Blade Runner*," *Sydney Studies in English* 31 (2005): 62–76; and Mark Lussier and Caitlin Gowan, "The Romantic Roots of *Blade Runner*," *Wordsworth Circle* 43 (2012): 165–72.

26. The parallel is striking and tempting to read as homage, but I have been unable to establish any firm connection.

27. *Tiriel*, ca. 1789, was the first of Blake's prophetic books.

28. Benjamin, "Theses on the Philosophy of History," 257–58.

CHAPTER 21

Weak Reparation

Law and Literature Networked

WAI CHEE DIMOCK

Two kinds of reading: one strong and one weak, one damaging the world, and the other trying to make amends, Eve Kosofsky Sedgwick argues in her now-classic essay. The strong theory she has in mind is the version that Paul Ricoeur calls a "hermeneutics of suspicion," and that she herself calls "paranoid reading." Such readings require a postulate of global symptomaticity, in turn requiring a postulate of global mystification. They are "strong" (or not) depending on the absoluteness of these two claims. Lapse on either front would weaken the case, so evidence to the contrary is not exactly welcome here; in fact, it is routinely dismissed, discounted, urged not to be taken at face value. Since it is the case, and since this practice has dominated literary studies for some time, the field of affect is now winnowed down to this single, powerful, and powerfully negative one. What results is the equivalent of the loss of biodiversity, Sedgwick says, the overwhelming ability of one dominant gene to eliminate all others, leaving us with a "shallow gene pool" that seriously undermines our "ability to respond to environmental (i.e., political) change."[1]

Given such losses, reparative reading has no choice but to be "additive and accretive." It has to do a different kind of evidentiary bookkeeping, making the discounted once again count. Taking the world not as a seamless mask but as a torn web with gaping holes—the result of failed efforts and missed connections—it proceeds with the repairs, and often with not much supervision, prompted more by rumblings from the ground up than edicts from the top down. It sees weak mastery as a small price to pay for the job at hand. Rather than stripping away what mystifies, reparative reading wants to add layers of mediation to the world. It "wants to assemble and confer plenitude on an object that will then have resources to offer to an inchoate self."[2] And, toward that end, it is willing to err on the side of tangentialness and inconclusiveness, bringing more to the table than strictly necessary, canvassing more than would clinch the case, giving up the time-honored satisfaction of the compact punch line for the uncertain benefit of scattershot input, too-widely distributed agency, and less-than-guaranteed verdicts.

Focusing on the reparative/paranoid duo, Sedgwick does not consider another pair of terms equally pertinent to her analysis and perhaps having more direct impact on the world: the reparative versus the punitive. In this chapter I'd like to open up that conversation as a methodological debate within law and literature, a debate between two different conceptions of justice and two different attendant outcomes—mediating circumstances versus punishable deed, extensive commutation versus discrete verdict—at work in both literary history and criminal law. One cuts through the evidence and delivers a clean, finalized, individualized judgment, while the other multiplies complexities and prolongs the input process, thanks to a multilayered and multivariable commutating network. Taking the former as a strongly institutionalized norm, and the latter as a weakly experimental alternative, I'd like to make a case for reparative justice as weakly experimental in just that second sense: an unorthodox but not implausible form of networked mediation, its scope and efficacy as yet to be tested, but with consequences already palpable for law and literature both.

On the law side, an especially interesting example of reparative justice is a program called Alternatives to Incarceration (ATI). ATI is any informal program of activity required of offenders, a substitute for penal action and leading to reduced jail time. Given the well-documented abuses of US prisons, ATI was a high priority for the Obama White House.[3] Many cities have such a program; New York City leads the way, boasting an ATI rehabilitation rate of 60 percent. According to a study commissioned by the city, New York

> has expanded the network of actors in the courtroom to encourage the use of alternative sentences. City officials have created an ATI system that includes not only programs for offenders, but also court representatives whose job is to persuade even reluctant judges, assistant DAs, and public defenders to use these programs routinely in appropriate cases. As a result, the ATI system plays a dual

role in the criminal justice process, trying to shape plea bargains and sentencing decisions in court as well as administering the sentences themselves.[4]

Active both inside and outside the courtroom, before, during, and after sentencing, the ATI as implemented in New York is a crowd-sourced network dedicated to turning jailed offenders into ordinary citizens. Community groups, working together on an ad hoc, case-by-case basis, spearhead the action here, guided by the understanding that punishment is only a small and mechanical part of criminal justice, that the most necessary, and necessarily collaborative, work is in fact that of repairing lives, giving a second chance to those who perhaps have never had much of one to begin with. Networked mediation in this form has already borne fruit in law. What might a parallel effort in literary studies look like?

LOW-BAR NETWORKS

Bruno Latour's actor-network theory is especially helpful here. Latour distinguishes between two ways of networking, done by *intermediaries* and by *mediators*—the former, passive vehicles, rubber stamps that transmit existing decisions without altering them; and the latter, actively intervening forces that dynamically alter the relation between input and output in any social aggregate.[5] A literary history networked in this second sense, by way of input-bearing mediators, gives the last word neither to institutions, nor to individual texts as free and sovereign products of single authors, but remains in progress, with actively contributing sites still being added. What this suggests about individual authors is that any existing corpus is bound to be incomplete—in the sense that it cannot be its own endpoint—precisely because it is singular, the work of one pair of hands, and arrested at one particular moment in time. This is not a lapse requiring punitive action, since the shortfall here is in fact generative, a built-in limit that makes room for a reparative sequel, making the perennially not-done perennially input-accepting. Buried nuances subsequently brought to light, roads not taken subsequently visited—these time-delayed amendments make literature a nontrivial player in reparative justice, joining it as part of an extended mediation, crowd-sourced over time.

In particular, I am interested in extended mediation achieved by networks that most would call "weak": ad hoc, minimalist, backed neither by restrictive membership nor by institutional grounding. Networks of this sort are accretive by nature. Not overly efficient in gatekeeping, their low-level multiplication might be our best bet for an unsponsored, unregulated, but nonetheless reliably incremental form of reparative action. I'd like to test their capabilities and limits through the example of Faulkner: a Southern writer trying to make amends for his region's past through imaginary ties and long-distance atonement, and, in not quite succeeding, in not even being clear about what it was that he was trying to do, also making way for input from others, an accretive vitality born of its reparative weakness.

Here, I'd especially like to draw on the work of sociologist Mark Granovetter, whose memorable oxymoron—"the strength of weak ties"— captures just this odd resilience of low-bar networks, the resilience of nonselective crowdsourcing. Granovetter coined this phrase back in 1973, inspired by the role of "informal interaction in systems that are formally rationalized."[6] Focusing on the personal networking that facilitates job mobility, he argues that having a large pool of casual acquaintances, each with his or her own information channels, is a decided plus: a weak connectivity that works much better than the strong connectivity of a small circle of close friends with information overlap. Indeed, weak ties of this sort are the most reliable links to out-groups, allowing for mediation across different social registers, and serving as a "macro-micro bridge"[7] between large-scale economic statistics and small-scale job prospects.

Granovetter's theory has been updated more recently by Lee Rainie and Barry Wellman to take into account the connectivity afforded by online media. In *Networked: The New Social Operating System*, Rainie and Wellman analyze the multiple weak ties developed on Facebook or Twitter in terms of "partial membership" (39): filiations that exist in the plural, that are intermittent rather than full-time, pulling in different and sometimes opposite directions, rather than institutionally given and singly designated.[8] The ties that result might seem less than spectacular, but they are difficult to stamp out, a downstream cascade interfering with any strong claim about closed-circuit domination or across-the-board policing.

To these terms proposed by Latour, Granovetter, Rainie, and Wellman, I would like to add two more. The network I will be exploring is for the most part an affective network: it has to do with forms of emotional life, what Raymond Williams in *The Country and the City* calls a "structure of feeling": not quite a philosophy or worldview but simply a "practical consciousness of a present kind, in a living and interrelating continuity."[9] Inchoate feeling of this sort, Williams goes on to say, "cannot without loss be reduced to belief-systems, institutions, or explicit general relationships, though it may include all these as lived and experienced, with or without tension."[10] And, within this affective continuum, the emotion associated with losing— finding oneself on the wrong side of history, the wrong side of any terminal event—is especially double-edged: at once traumatic and routine, sharply wounding and yet all too common. Losing is a low-bar experience known to many; it is the most ordinary of ordinary affects.[11] Could a network be built on it, a negative basis for kinship, creating a meaningful tie among those who otherwise might not have much in common? And could it be the basis for a weak form of reparation, perhaps more aspirational than actual, but nonetheless signaling an acknowledgment of the need for redress?

TRANS-PACIFIC TRAUMA

Without further ado, then, let me turn directly to Faulkner and his reparative project, linking the humiliation of the South after the Civil War to the humiliation of Japan after the Second World War. Faulkner was in Nagano, Japan, as part of the State Department's Exchange of Persons Program, the same program that sent jazz musicians all over the world as goodwill ambassadors. By the time he went, in August 1955, he was at a low point himself, a confirmed alcoholic, so shaky in his general conduct that the State Department apparently thought of cutting the tour short and sending him home. But Faulkner evidently rallied under the challenge of onsite adjustment to a foreign environment. For a period of ten days he was able to meet with members of the Nagano Seminar—fifty or so Japanese professors of American literature—every afternoon or evening, giving talks and interacting with them in Q & A sessions. Some of his remarks were quite odd, not what one would expect from someone in Japan under State Department sponsorship, such as the following, in a talk entitled "To the Youth of Japan":

> A hundred years ago, my country, the United States, was not one economy and culture, but two of them, so opposed to each other that ninety-five years ago they went to war against each other to test which one should prevail. My side, the South, lost that war, the battles of which were fought not on neutral ground in the waste of the ocean, but in our own homes, our gardens, our farms, as if Okinawa and Guadalcanal had been not islands in the distant Pacific but the precincts of Honshu and Hokkaido. Our land, our homes were invaded by a conqueror who remained after we were defeated; we were not only devastated by the battles which we lost, the conqueror spent the next ten years after our defeat and surrender despoiling us of what little war had left.[12]

As Civil War history, this was atrocious: it was one-sided, and it was reductive. Faulkner never mentioned slavery at all; the Civil War here was only a war between two incompatible regions of the United States, eternally divided by their cultural and economic differences, with one side triumphing over the other and trampling the other underfoot.

What makes this peculiar account more forgivable is the presence here of *two* regional contexts. The first was obviously Oxford, Mississippi, and the conduct of the Union army in 1863: "that night the town was occupied by Federal troops; two nights later, it was on fire (the Square, the stores and shops and the professional offices), gutted (the courthouse too), the blackened jagged topless jumbles of brick wall enclosing like a ruined jaw the blackened shell of the courthouse . . . and so in effect it was a whole year in advance of Appomattox."[13] The other context, perhaps even more present to Faulkner at that moment, was what Japan went through at the end of the Second World War. The giveaway phrase, I think, is this: "the conqueror spent the next ten years after our defeat and surrender despoiling us of what little war had left."

Why ten years? Faulkner was probably thinking less about the year 1875, ten years after Appomattox, than about the year 1955, the year of the Nagano Seminar, ten years after Japan surrendered. And he seemed to know intuitively that though Allied occupation had ended formally in April 1952, the emotional ramifications of defeat would persist long after. For the Japanese in 1955, what most struck a responsive chord from Faulkner's account of the American Civil War was no doubt this emotional lingua franca: that in every war there was going to be a losing side, an existential condition known only to those who have been subjected to it. Reaching out to his Japanese audience on just that basis, Faulkner's regionalism was now both rooted and projected: based in Oxford, Mississippi, but affiliated now thousands of miles away. Familiar names such as Appomattox now give way to four others: Okinawa, Guadalcanal, Honshu, Hokkaido. Significantly, these were not the best-known names, not the two epicenters—Hiroshima and Nagasaki—but names far more ordinary, bringing to mind no spectacular destruction, only the steady-state, weakly but persistently gnawing sense of having been brought low.

It was a deliberate choice on Faulkner's part. Regional cities were in fact the reference points for him, rather than cosmopolitan cities that towered above others, like London and Paris. In his meeting with the citizens of Nagano, while trying to map his fictional world for this Japanese audience, he came up with this comparison between two pairs of cities: "My country lies between New Orleans and Memphis. New Orleans is the big, important city that in my country is like Tokyo here. That is, Nagano would be Memphis, Tokyo would be New Orleans, because Tokyo is the larger city. My country would be between Nagano and Tokyo. They were important in my work only because they were the big cities—the life in my land, the land I know, is country, it is farmland."[14]

This, in and of itself, seems to me a regional manifesto. New Orleans is the counterpart to Tokyo only on a very special map, one that leaves out New York, Chicago, and Los Angeles. And that seemed to be the point. Even though New York had been shorthand for Faulkner elsewhere, say, in *The Sound and the Fury*, and even though he knew Los Angeles well from his stint as a screenwriter in Hollywood, for this particular audience he wanted New Orleans to set the standard for a metropolitan center. And it was with New Orleans as the standard that he could then reach out to the next level, to Memphis. But even this was too major a city for him. His country was nondescript farm country, he said, offering what seemed to be agrarianism in the most traditional sense.

And yet, even as this was being put forward, two other cities, Tokyo and Nagano, were also very much in the picture. This cross-mapping, linking the cartography of an intimately known South to that of an unknown Asia, was something that Faulkner did fairly consistently throughout his stay in Japan. Rather than settling comfortably into some tried-and-tested binaries—North versus South, city versus country—his world was now far more volatile, at once extended and ill-defined, a world in which unfamiliar names, perhaps seen together for the first time, produced fault lines as well as lines of filiation, giving us a sense of history far less predictable than the earlier, North-as-conqueror-and-South-as-victim script.

VARIETIES OF LOSING

Such a world produced new contexts for old enmities and grievances, to the point where even "winning" and "losing" began to shed their customary character, taking on new meanings. There is no better example of this than Faulkner's musings on the conduct of war—specifically, the conduct of the occupying forces—at the same meeting with the citizens of Nagano, when this question came from the floor:

> The scene of soldiers drinking liquor which appears in the beginning of the book *Soldier's* [sic] *Pay* made me recall an occurrence which arose just after the end of the Pacific war. When I was standing on one of the platforms at Nagoya, some American soldiers came along and forcibly held my neck, making me drink whisky. They then passed the bottle among themselves, drinking from the same bottle that I had drunk from. Since considerable time has elapsed since the time that *Soldier's Pay* was written of, and since things are quite peaceful now, I don't

imagine that such things happen nowadays. Could you tell me whether such scenes can be seen?[15]

The remark is interesting for at least three reasons. First, the Faulkner canon in Japan was surprisingly broad: not just on this occasion, but throughout the entire ten days, references were made not just to the standard-bearers, *The Sound and the Fury*, *Light in August*, and *Absalom, Absalom!*, but also to works such as *The Wild Palms*, *Intruder in the Dust*, and here, *Soldiers' Pay*. Second, Faulkner was right about the basis for emotional connection between postbellum South and Japan in 1955: it was exactly this shared sense of humiliation that this Japanese reader would pick up on and respond to. Finally, perhaps more interesting still was the response Faulkner came up with, the explanation that he offered for why these American soldiers would behave in that way:

> I wouldn't say that that is typical of American soldiers. If I said that was typical, I'd say that it is probably typical of all soldiers, that in this gentleman's case, these were young men who had never been this far from home before—they were in a strange country, they had been fighting in combat—suddenly combat was over, they were free of being afraid, and so they lost control temporarily. They wouldn't act like that always every time—it was the relief that anyone who has been a soldier and knows what it is to be fighting—when he gets over being in fighting, he's really not accountable for what he might do.[16]

This has to be one of the most counterintuitive accounts of the effect of war: focusing not on the out-of-control behavior of soldiers while the fighting is in process, but their out-of-control behavior once the fighting is over. According to him, this relaxing of extreme fear could have an adverse effect also not calculable. Whether or not we agree with this theory, it seems clear that, with Japan in the foreground, Faulkner was suddenly able to see military occupation in a different light, replacing the erstwhile conquerors with a vulnerable group of young men away from home for the first time, barely making it through and undone by the very burden of winning.

This was what Faulkner learned from a Mississippi-Nagano network, learned from suddenly finding himself on the winning side. That unwonted position threw into relief a psychological truth no one would have suspected: there are no victors in war. No one wins, since winning is never an option. We all lose one way or another: whether militarily, in a public surrender; or psychologically, in a mental unraveling. All of us end up being undone by war, thrown off kilter by it. This ironic twist—that supposed winners do not in fact win—makes the imagined connection between

Faulkner and his Japanese audience not just a fantasy on his part, but a fantasy perhaps with some truth. Perhaps there is indeed a low common denominator to war, in that it permits only varieties of losing. That irony also points to the possibility of a further common ground, something like a nontragic sequel to the Second World War, and perhaps all wars: a leveling-out at the absolute low point, with a hint of an upturn.

NONTRAGIC SEQUELS

That hint is all we could hope for, Faulkner said, for there is no way to deny the catastrophe of war, no way to erase the two atomic bombs: "We can't go back to a condition in which there were no wars, in which there was no bomb. We got to accept that bomb and do something about it, eliminate that bomb, eliminate the war, not retrograde to a condition before it exists."[17] History is linear in the sense that it is made up of a series of irrevocable acts, but it is not the case that each of those acts marks a dead end, a point of no return. On the contrary, it is the in-progress and updatable nature of the narrative that gives Faulkner hope. In response to an observation from a Tokyo audience, that there were new literary movements in postwar Japan, new poetry being written, Faulkner had this to say: "I think what is primarily responsible for that sort of alternation in the sound, the style, the shape of work, is disaster. I think I said before that it's hard to believe, but disaster seems to be good for people. If they are too successful too long, something dies, it dries up, and then they have to collapse with their own weight, which has happened with so many empires"[18]

Defeat as a spur to experimentation: this is the low-bar starting point for a nontragic sequel to the Second World War. The example of Japan suggests that a similar narrative might be unfolding in the United States as well. Could it be that, here too, some glimmer of the nontraumatic could come out of the trauma of slavery, the trauma of the Civil War? Faulkner would like to think so. This is what he offers in *Absalom, Absalom!*, a low point where things bottom out, also marking a point where a utopian counternarrative might begin. Here it takes the form of a bare-bones connectivity among three women—two white and one black—trying their best to survive, and succeeding because they have managed to eke out an aggregate life, not a real partnership, but enough of one to keep them going:

> not as two white women and a negress, not as three negroes or three white, not
> even as three women, but merely as three creatures who still possessed the need
> to eat but took no pleasure in it, the need to sleep but from no joy in weariness

or regeneration. . . . We grew and tended and harvested with our own hands the food we ate, made and worked that garden just as we cooked and ate the food which came out of it: with no distinction among the three of us of age or color. . . . It was as though we were one being, interchangeable and indiscriminate.[19]

This is the regionalism that rises from the ashes of defeat to give us a glimpse of the world as it could be, a desolate world, it is true, but one where blacks and whites could commingle, interchangeable and indiscriminate. This is the utopian counternarrative Faulkner had imagined back in 1936. Japan seemed to offer an affirmation, an actualization.

A cautionary word from historians is helpful here. Cooperation between black and white women based on shared economic hardship was indeed one outcome of the Civil War; however, as Drew Gilpin Faust and Thavolia Glymph have noted, such partnership was relatively rare, since the uneasy coexistence between black and white women was driven less by common need than by fear, with many mistresses reverting to or perhaps even developing new ways of managing their slaves.[20] The harsh treatment of blacks after Reconstruction was not an unprecedented turn of events but a continuation of racial oppression before, during, and after the Civil War, practiced by white women no less than white men. However tempting it is to imagine an interracial peace based on scarcity and flourishing on the axis of gender, the practice was limited. Faulkner's utopian hope might have been just that: a utopian hope.

MAKING UP INDIANS

Still, the example of the Japanese, defeated not so long ago but already on the mend, must have come as an invitation to Faulkner to imagine a parallel story, applicable not only to slavery and the Civil War but equally to the other trauma: the banishment of indigenous peoples, especially the Choctaw and Chickasaw in Mississippi. Asked about the origin of the word *Yoknapatawpha*, Faulkner said:

Yes, it's a Chickasaw Indian word. They were the Indians that we dispossessed in my country. That word means "water flowing slow through the flatland," which to me was a pleasant image, though the word in Chickasaw might be pleasanter to a Chickasaw ear than to our ear, but that's the meaning of it.[21]

The dispossession of Indians need not have come up at all for a question on etymology. Faulkner seemed to have gone out of his way to bring it up, perhaps to show that *this* catastrophe could also now be looked in the eye. Perhaps his novels and stories, in giving this word extended life, scarcely imaginable when it was only a Chickasaw word, could be a form of reparation? Encompassing the whole of his fictional world, the Chickasaw word is as good a candidate as any for a utopian interracial story, a nontragic sequel to New World genocide, as peaceful and steadfast as "water flowing slow through the flatland."

Oddly, even as Faulkner lay out this theory, some doubt seemed already to have occurred to him, giving him pause and making him add the odd qualification that the sound of *Yoknapatawpha* might be pleasanter to a Chickasaw ear than to his own. Peace might not translate easily between Anglos and Indians, just as it does not between blacks and whites. The alienness of the word *Yoknapatawpha* is only the most obvious sign of the often insurmountable barriers among humans. And nowhere are those barriers harder to ignore than in Japan. Indeed, simply being there, and needing to explain both the word *Yoknapatawpha* and what happened to the Chickasaw, and who they were to begin with, seemed to have brought home to Faulkner the sharp reality of cultural differences. Was he ever any closer to the Chickasaw than he was to the Japanese, and how steadfast was his dedication to them?

The self-conscious gesture in Japan, in 1955, a tribute to a defeated but honored people, was in fact a relatively recent development in Faulkner, the endpoint of a long process whose earlier iterations he might not have been eager to recall. Native Americans in late Faulkner, say in *Requiem for a Nun* (1951), were indeed much like those invoked and mourned in Japan. *Requiem* begins by observing that "the settlement had the records; even the simple dispossession of Indians begot in time a minuscule of archive."[22] It repeats that word, "dispossess," in a long-drawn-out parenthetical aside as it recounts the bickering over whether the town should be called "Jefferson" or "Habersham"—the latter name, from the old doctor, founder of the town, and "friend of old Issetibbeha, the Chickasaw chief (the motherless Habersham boy, now a man of twenty-five, married one of Issetibbeha's grand-daughters and in the thirties emigrated to Oklahoma with his wife's dispossessed people)."[23] The sentence is lopsided, like the equally lopsided fight between the Chickasaw and the US government: "Habersham" loses out in more senses than one. What the name signifies—friendship with Native Americans and continued landholding by them—was the road not taken by a nation with an official policy of Indian Removal, a nation whose Founding Fathers numbered Thomas Jefferson but not Indians.

Requiem for a Nun is in many ways the high-water mark for this sense of Native Americans as "dispossessed," despoiled of what was rightfully theirs. And yet, even here, Faulkner's sympathies cannot be said to be entirely on their side. In act three, "The Jail," he recounts the fateful day when Mohataha, the Chickasaw matriarch, came "to set her capital X on the paper which ratified the dispossession of her people forever," doing so while "seated in a rocking chair beneath a French parasol held by a Negro slave girl," a figure "grotesque and regal, bizarre and moribund, like obsolescence's self riding off the stage enthroned on its own obsolete catafalque."[24] This is not the first time those two words, "dispossessed" and "obsolete," are intertwined to suggest a doomed people, slave-owning, with inflated egos, destined to die out in their effete ignorance. This is the refrain throughout *Requiem for a Nun*: "the obsolete and the dispossessed, dispossessed by those who were dispossessed in turn because they were obsolete."[25]

These two are also the operative words in *Go Down, Moses* (1942), especially in "The Bear," although in that earlier work Faulkner is much less interested in dispossession as a historical fact than as a spiritual malaise, afflicting anyone who gets it into his head that he can own the land, buy or sell or bequeath it. The big woods, we are told as soon as the story opens, are "bigger and older than any recorded document:—of white man fatuous enough to believe he had bought any fragment of it, of Indian ruthless enough to pretend that any fragment of it had been his to convey."[26]

"Fatuous" whites and "ruthless" Indians are almost equal partners here, with Ikkemotubbe, the Chickasaw chief, and Ike's grandfather, L. Q. C. McCaslin, being equally culpable and equally deluded: "because it was never old Ikkemotubbe's to sell to Grandfather for bequeathment and repudiation. Because it was never Ikkemotubbe's fathers' fathers' to bequeath Ikkemotubbe to sell to Grandfather or any man because on the instant when Ikkemotubbe discovered, realised, that he could sell it for money, on that instant it ceased ever to have been his forever."[27] Dispossession in "The Bear" is simply a providential judgment, a curse incurred by Anglos and Indians both. Rather than being the outcome of a federal policy, written in a legal document and signing away the right to vast tracts of Native lands, it operates here by an entirely different syntax—"Dispossessed of Eden. Dispossessed of Canaan"—a syntax that judges those who sell even more harshly than those who buy.[28] L. Q. C. McCaslin is merely "fatuous"; it is Ikkemotubbe who is "ruthless."

That startling adjective, "ruthless," out of the blue here, seems to have been carried over from an early phase of Faulkner, especially from stories such as "Red Leaves" and "A Justice," where it would have been entirely fitting. In "A Justice," Ikkemotubbe—"not born to be the Man [the chief], because [his] mother's brother was the Man, and the Man had a son of his own, as well as a brother"—takes to calling himself "Doom," from the expression, "Du homme" [*sic*] that he has picked up in New Orleans from his French companion.[29] Armed with a little "gold box of New Orleans salt"[30] on his return, he does indeed spell doom: beginning with a puppy brought along for demonstration, then making quick work of the Man and his son, sparing the brother only because the latter, seeing what happens, has covered his head with a blanket and taken himself out of the line of succession.

That succession is just about to take place in "Red Leaves." Like "A Justice," this story also features ruthlessness of a sort, though manifest here not in Moketubbe, Issetibbeha's son and heir, who is obese and lethargic, "diseased with flesh," and not much of a schemer.[31] Ruthlessness inheres, rather, in the tribe as a whole, in their low-energy but unrelenting pursuit and capture of a black slave, who has run away to escape being buried alive with Issetibbeha, his old master.

How credible is this portrait of Native Americans? "Red Leaves" has been challenged on multiple fronts, not least about the burial practices of Native Americans in Mississippi.[32] Faulkner, when asked by a contemporary local historian "where he got his Indians," had famously replied, "I made them up."[33] In a letter to Scribner's accompanying the submission of "Red Leaves," he had also said: "So here is another story. Few people know that Miss. Indians owned slaves; that's why I suggest you all buy it. Not because it is a good story; you can find lots of good stories. It's because I need the money."[34] Faulkner's financial needs might indeed have been dire, since he had just bought a wreck of a house (later named Rowan Oak). And the muckraking impulse, to show that whites were not the only slave-owners, might indeed have been irresistible.[35] Whatever the reason, historical accuracy could not be said to be his top priority, which is why the names and identities of individuals and even of whole tribes could be switched from story to story. Native Americans, identified as Chickasaws in *Requiem for a Nun*, had started out in the early stories as Choctaws. As Robert Dale Parker and Robert Woods Sayre have pointed out, Native Americans in early Faulkner were figments of his imagination, grotesque "projections and introjections" of the slave-owning South: archaic, degenerate, and doomed.[36] With the effete Moketubbe setting the tone, the other two Indians in "Red Leaves" are also "burgherlike" and "paunchy," one wearing an "enameled snuff box" in his ear, and both receding into "a certain blurred serenity like carved heads on a ruined wall in Siam or Sumatra, looming out of a mist."[37] These fictional Indians have nothing to do with the Native populations who had stayed on in Mississippi after the Treaty of the Dancing Rabbit Creek in 1830, after even the Second Choctaw Removal of 1903, struggling to safeguard their communal holdings against land frauds and the influx of white settlers, protecting the livelihood of small subsistence farmers, while debating citizenship rights.[38]

GERALD VIZENOR, JIM BARNES, LUCIEN STRYK: REPAIR TEAM

What to do with this lacuna in Faulkner, this substitution of actual Native Americans with ones of his own making? As it turns out, a weak network—extending perilously but with some regularity across the Pacific—does offer reparative mediation of sorts. For historical reasons that warrant a full-length study in itself, many Native authors have felt specially drawn to Japan, much like Faulkner. Gerald Vizenor, posted there in 1953 with the occupation forces, was so taken with the haiku form that he wrote haiku for the rest of his life.[39] The overlapping traumas of the atomic bomb and New World genocide also resulted in a novel, *Hiroshima Bugi* (2003), featuring a character, Ronin, a composite ghost from the past haunting the present: "I am dead, the one who shatters nuclear peace. Some of my deaths have been reported in obituaries around the world. Dead Amerika indian, hafu peace boy out to sea, was the report of my second death at the orphanage. I am forever an orphan, a tatari of the ruins."[40] Is peace ever possible for such a ghost, peace that is not a travesty, an insult to the memory of the dead? Vizenor writes, "peace is untrue by nature, a counterfeit of nations" (16). And there "is no more treacherous a peace than the nuclear commerce of the Peace Memorial Museum in Hiroshima" (16), with feel-good messages emblazoned on every souvenir T-shirt: "No More Hiroshima, August 6, 1945" (17), and "Hiroshima Loves Peace"(17). Against such phony merchandise, the only truth is the tatari, "spirits of retribution and vengeance, a curse of kami" (25). This is what the Japanese believe in: "the tatari of the dead, that is, the vengeance of people who had been killed, or killed themselves, after being falsely accused or unfairly treated" (25). The tatari will "persecute its enemies, strike at the innocent in passing," and stop at nothing (25).

Here is a rejoinder of sorts, not specifically aimed at Faulkner, but devastating all the same. And yet, such is the nature of networks that it is not the last word either. I'd like to temper its verdict with two poems, by the Choctaw-Welsh poet Jim Barnes: one, a direct response to Faulkner, carefully staged, and the other, not unintended as a response at all, but, in its many accidental echoes, as good a response as any.

In "The Only Photograph of Quentin at Harvard," Barnes begins and ends with two pairs of hands and a book:

> On the far left, at the edge,
> a pair of hands holds
> an open book.
>
> At the right-hand bottom corner
> a pair of shoes hangs
> pegged to the wall,
>
> the soles outward and soiled.
> At the end of a word Shreve laces
> his hands in his laps.
>
> Central, across the checkered table,
> Quentin counts the silence in his throat
> below a half-
>
> curtained bookcase. A mirror
> reflects pictures pyramided
> up a wall.
>
> The one window is draped in white
> gauze. Time is stilled
> forever
>
> in a hushed tone of sand.
> The hands are about
> to turn a page.[41]

The photo is of course apocryphal—there could be no photo of a fictional character—though the scene here could easily have come from either *The Sound and the Fury* or *Absalom, Absalom!*; more likely the latter, given the tenor of the composition. Everything is in pairs here: the shoes; the pictures (thanks to the mirror); and the two friends, one lapsing into silence and the other about to speak, with their hands cross-stitched in their gesture of expectancy. This is a Quentin not alone, not in despair, a Quentin literally and metaphorically turning a page.

Out of the blue, Jim Barnes has come up with a nontragic sequel to Faulkner's two most iconic works, a vicarious mending all the more notable for being uninvited. Vicarious mending is also what Barnes offers in a poem featuring a postcard rather than a letter as the mediating agent: "After a Postcard from Styrk in Japan," in the very back and forth between two friends, enacts the "additive and accretive" ritual that Eve Sedgwick sees as the wellspring of reparation:

> Lucien, all
> the green river,
> falling
> green beneath
> the green bridge,
>
> all
> the green houses,
> their windows
> opening light
> onto the river
>
> falling
> now beyond
> the green bridge
> into the green sky,
>
> and now
>   all
>   quiet
> the green night blossoms[42]

The "Lucien" in question is Lucien Stryk, poet and translator of Zen poetry, born in Poland, with a lifelong attachment to the haiku of Issa and Bashō, and visiting Japan often to teach at Niigata University and Yamaguchi University.[43] In this postcard, there is no hint of the atomic bombs, and no hint of catastrophe anywhere in the world (though elsewhere, notably in the poem "Choctaw Cemetery," Barnes has been emphatic about the infant mortality and decimated populations among Native peoples: "Familiar glyphs: / *ushi holitopa* / The dates: / short years").[44] Instead, the postcard, like the apocryphal photo of Quentin, celebrates a world restored to plenitude thanks to the reciprocity extending across different experiential registers: the green bridge mirroring the green river, the houses and the sky mirroring both, making even the night green.

This is what Faulkner was hoping to find in the word *Yoknapatawpha*—"water flowing slow through the flatland"—a reciprocity doubling as a reparative gesture, no doubt illusory coming only from Faulkner, but coming now, obliquely and accidentally, from Jim Barnes and Lucien Stryk, at least standing a chance of being the real thing, framed by the forgivingly low threshold of a weak network.

NOTES

1. Eve Kosofsky Sedgwick, "Paranoid Reading and Reparative Reading, or, You're so Paranoid, You Probably Think This Essay is About You," in *Touching Feeling: Affect, Pedagogy, Performativity* (Durham, NC: Duke University Press, 2003), 123–152, quotation from 144.
2. Ibid., 149.
3. Office of National Drug Control Policy, "Alternatives to incarceration," www.whitehouse.gov/ondcp/alternatives-to-incarceration.
4. Rachel Porter, Sophia Lee, and Mary Lutz, *Balancing Punishment and Treatment: Alternatives to Incarceration in New York City* (New York: Vera Institute of Justice).
5. Bruno Latour, *Reassembling the Social: An Introduction to Actor-Network Theory* (New York: Oxford University Press, 2005), 37–42.
6. Mark S. Granovetter, "The Strength of Weak Ties," *American Journal of Sociology* 78 (1973): 1360–80; Granovetter, *Getting a Job: A Study of Contacts and Careers* (Cambridge, MA: Harvard University Press, 1974), 4.
7. Granovetter, "Strength of Weak Ties," 1360.
8. Lee Rainie and Barry Wellman, *Networked: The New Social Operating System* (Cambridge, MA: MIT Press, 2012).
9. Raymond Williams, *The Country and the City* (London: Chatto and Windus, 1973), 132.
10. Ibid.
11. I am drawing inspiration here from Kathleen Stewart, *Ordinary Affects* (Durham, NC: Duke University Press, 2007).
12. Robert A. Jelliffe, ed., *Faulkner at Nagano* (Tokyo: Kenkyusha, 1956), 185.
13. William Faulkner, *Requiem for a Nun* (New York: Random House, 1951), 232–33.
14. Jelliffe, *Faulkner at Nagano*, 139–40.
15. Ibid., 141.
16. Ibid., 141–42.
17. Ibid., 78.
18. Ibid., 37–38.
19. William Faulkner, *Absalom, Absalom!* (New York: Vintage, 1972), 155.
20. Drew Gilpin Faust, *Mothers of Invention: Women of the Slaveholding South during the Civil War* (Chapel Hill: University of North Carolina Press, 1996); Thavolia Glymph, *Out of the House of Bondage: The Transformation of the Plantation Household* (Cambridge: Cambridge University Press, 2008).
21. Jelliffe, *Faulkner at Nagano*, 82.
22. Faulkner, *Requiem for a Nun*, 3.

23. Ibid., 8.

24. Ibid., 216–17.

25. Ibid., 101. Here Faulkner invokes not only the Chickasaw but also the "nameless though recorded predecessors" they had in turn displaced: "the wild Algonquian, Chickasaw and Choctaw and Natchez and Pascagoula" (ibid.).

26. William Faulkner, *Go Down, Moses* (New York: Random House, 1942), 191.

27. Ibid., 256–57.

28. Ibid., 258.

29. William Faulkner, "A Justice," in *Collected Stories of William Faulkner* (New York: Vintage, 1995), 346.

30. Ibid., 345.

31. Faulkner, "Red Leaves," in *Collected Stories*, 321.

32. For a good summary of the controversies, see Gene M. Moore, "Faulkner's Incorrect 'Indians?'" *Faulkner Journal* 18 (Fall 2002–Spring 2003): 3–8. For a detailed critique, see Howard Horsford, "Faulkner's (Mostly) Unreal Indians in Early Mississippi History," *American Literature* 64 (1992): 311–30.

33. Lewis M. Dabney, *The Indians of Yoknapatawpha: A Study in History and Literature* (Baton Rouge: Louisiana State University Press, 1974), 11.

34. Joseph Blotner, ed., *Selected Letters of William Faulkner* (New York: Random House, 1977), 46–47.

35. Faulkner was on solid historical ground here: slaveholding was a common practice among Native Americans: "The Cherokees had the most slaves, with 1,600 before removal and about 2,500 in 1860. The Choctaw planters had the next highest number of slaves, with about 500 before removal and 2,350 in 1860. The Creek held 902 slaves in 1832 and 1,532 in 1860, while the Chickasaw had the fewest slaves—several hundred near removal and about 1,000 in 1860. The free Chickasaw population, however, was less than one-fourth the size of the Cherokee population, so the per capita slaveholding among the Chickasaw was relatively higher." See Duane Champagne, *Social Order and Political Change: Constitutional Governments among the Cherokee, the Choctaw, the Chickasaw, and the Creek* (Stanford, CA: Stanford University Press, 1992), 176–77.

36. Robert Dale Parker, "Red Slippers and Cottonmouth Moccasins: White Anxieties in Faulkner's Indian Stories," *Faulkner Journal* 18 (Fall 2002–Spring 2003): 81–100; Robert Woods Sayre, "Faulkner's Indians and the Romantic Vision," *Faulkner Journal* 18 (Fall 2002–Spring 2003): 33–49.

37. Faulkner, "Red Leaves," 313.

38. Daniel H. Usner Jr., "American Indians on the Cotton Frontier: Changing Economic Relations with Citizens and Slaves in the Mississippi Territory," *Journal of American History* 72 (1985): 297–317; and Samuel J. Wells and Roseanna Tubby, eds., *After Removal: The Choctaw in Mississippi* (Jackson: University of Mississippi Press, 1986).

39. Vizenor's haiku poems are collected in *Raising the Moon Vines* (Minneapolis, MN: Nodin, 1964); *Empty Swings* (Minneapolis, MN: Nodin, 1967); *Matsushima: Pine Islands Collected Haiku* (Minneapolis, MN: Nodin, 1984); and *Favor of Crows: New and Collected Haiku* (Middletown, CT: Wesleyan University Press, 2014).

40. Gerald Vizenor, *Hiroshima Bugi: Atomu 57* (Lincoln: University of Nebraska Press, 2003), 16–17. Hereafter cited parenthetically.

41. Jim Barnes, *On a Wing of the Sun: Three Volumes of Poetry* (Urbana: University of Illinois Press, 2001), 45.

42. Ibid., 56.

43. As editor and translator, Stryk published *World of the Buddha: An Introduction to Buddhist Literature* (Garden City, NY: Doubleday, 1968), *Zen Poems of China and Japan: The Crane's Bill* (with Takashi Ikemoto; Garden City, NY: Grove, 1973), and *The Penguin Book of Zen Poetry* (with Ikemoto; Chicago: Swallow, 1977), which won the Islands and Continents Translation Award and the Society of Midland Authors Poetry Award. His other translations include *Bird of Time: Haiku of Basho* (Vermilion, SD: Flatlands, 1983), *Triumph of the Sparrow: Zen Poems of Shinkichi Takahashi* (with Ikemoto; Urbana: University of Illinois Press, 1986), and *The Dumpling Field: Haiku of Issa* (with Noboru Fujiwara; Athens: Ohio University Press, 1991).

44. Barnes, *On a Wing of the Sun*, 123.

ACKNOWLEDGMENTS

We are very thankful for the many friends, colleagues, and organizations that have supported and enriched this project. Above all, we have benefited enormously from the chance to collaborate with our amazing group of contributors, and we want to extend our heartfelt thanks to these authors for allowing us to showcase their brilliant scholarship in this essay collection. We have also learned a great deal from the many friends and colleagues with whom we have shared or discussed work related to this volume over the years. At risk of excluding far too many people, we would like to convey our gratitude to the following interlocutors: Amanda Claybaugh, Bradin Cormack, Rita Felski, Jason Frank, Rayna Kalas, Amalia Kessler, Anna Kornbluh, Mitchel Lasser, Philip Lorenz, Tracy McNulty, Martha Nussbaum, Aziz Rana, Annelise Riles, Paul Saint-Amour, Hilary Schor, Joseph Slaughter, Eric Slauter, Matthew Smith, Chantal Thomas, Gerald Torres, and Henry Turner.

A few students and assistants also played key roles in the creation of this book. Daniel Reichert was instrumental in bringing the volume to its final form. At earlier stages, both William Evans and Mary Rock assisted with the intellectual project of thinking through the contributions and their organization. Michaela Brangan was essential to the early vision and genesis of the project. Eun Sze also labored tirelessly on the details of permissions. The many amazing students at Cornell and Stanford Universities whom we have had the pleasure of teaching in law and literature and law and humanities courses have helped shape many of our ideas. In such a spirit, we would be remiss if we failed to acknowledge our own former professors and mentors, mentors who inspired—and continue to inspire—our investment in law and literature. This volume would not exist but for Liz's opportunities to study with first Martha Nussbaum at the University of Chicago Law School and then Peter Brooks and Rita Felski in the English Department at the University of Virginia, and for Bernie's encounters with Julia Lupton, Victoria Kahn, and Brook Thomas at UC, Irvine, Martin Stone at the School of Criticism and Theory at Cornell, Janet Halley and Robert Weisberg at Stanford Law School, and Peter Brooks at Princeton.

In many ways, *New Directions* emerged out of a conference on law and literature at Cornell University in the spring of 2013, at which a number of the contributors to this volume presented early versions of their chapters. This event would never have come together without the crucial and always gracious assistance of Bonnie Jo Coughlin in all organizational matters. Mary Ahl was similarly helpful in planning the events at the Cornell Society for the Humanities, as was Karen Kudej in the Department of English. The conference was also lucky to benefit from a wide range of institutional support. In particular, we are extremely appreciative of the Cornell Law School and former Dean Stewart Schwab as well as current Dean Eduardo Peñalver; the Cornell Society for the Humanities and its former director Timothy Murray; and the Department of English, including former and current chairs Andy Galloway and Roger Gilbert. Other programs at Cornell that helped to enable this formative event include the Department of Comparative Literature, the Africana Studies and Research Center, the Department of History, the Department of Near Eastern Studies, the Department of Performing and Media Arts, the Department of Romance Studies, the Department of Science and Technology Studies, the Feminist Gender and Sexuality Studies Program, the Institute for German Cultural Studies, the Law and Society Program, the Population and Development Program, the Rose Goldsen Lecture Series, and the Sage School of Philosophy.

By no means last, this collection would not exist but for the help and patience of our families, to whom we dedicate the volume with love. Liz's parents Roy and Ellen Anker have and continue to model to her engaged and committed intellectual life, and her family, Mitchel, Sacha, and Zoe Lasser, provide joy and support every day. Inspiring Bernie's work in law and literature from the beginning, Joan Meyler supported it through every moment until her death; the encouragement of John Meyler, Matt Smith, and Calliope and Minerva Smith continues through today.

BIBLIOGRAPHY

Abel, Richard. "Redirecting Social Studies of Law." *Law and Society Review* 14 (1980): 805–29.

Ablavsky, Gregory. "Beyond the Indian Commerce Clause." *Yale Law Journal* 124 (2015): 1012–91.

Ablavsky, Gregory. "The Savage Constitution." *Duke Law Journal* 63 (2014): 999–1089.

Abrams, Kathryn, and Hila Keren. "Who's Afraid of Law and the Emotions?" *Minnesota Law Review* 94 (2010): 1997–2074.

Achebe, Chinua. *Things Fall Apart*. New York: Anchor, 1994.

Agamben, Giorgio. *Homo Sacer: Sovereign Power and Bare Life*. Translated by Daniel Heller-Roazen. Stanford, CA: Stanford University Press, 1998.

Agamben, Giorgio. *Opus Dei: An Archaeology of Duty*. Translated by Adam Kotsko. Stanford, CA: Stanford University Press, 2013.

Agamben, Giorgio. *Remnants of Auschwitz: The Witness and the Archive*. Translated by Daniel Heller-Roazen. New York: Zone, 1999.

Agamben, Giorgio. *State of Exception*. Translated by Kevin Attell. Chicago: University of Chicago Press, 2005.

Ahmed, Sara. *Strange Encounters: Embodied Others in Post-Coloniality*. New York: Routledge, 2000.

Alber, Jan. "Impossible Storyworlds—and What to Do with Them." *Storyworlds: A Journal of Narrative Studies* 1 (2009): 79–96.

Alber, Jan. "Unnatural Narratives, Unnatural Narratology: Beyond Mimetic Models." *Narrative* 18 (2010): 113–36.

Allewaert, Monique. *Ariel's Ecology: Plantations, Personhood, and Colonialism in the American Tropics*. Minneapolis: University of Minnesota Press, 2013.

Allington, Daniel, Sarah Brouillete, and David Golumbia. "Neoliberal Tools (and Archives): A Political History of Digital Humanities." *LA Review of Books*, May 1, 2016. https://lareviewofbooks.org/article/neoliberal-tools-archives-political-history-digital-humanities/.

Althusser, Louis. "Ideology and Ideological State Apparatuses." In *Lenin and Philosophy and Other Essays*. Translated by Ben Brewster, 127–186. New York: Monthly Review Press, 2001.

American Bar Association. "Section of Legal Education and Admissions to the Bar: Explanation of Changes." http://www.americanbar.org/content/dam/aba/administrative/legal_education_and_admissions_to_the_bar/council_reports_and_resolutions/201408_explanation_changes.authcheckdam.pdf.

Amnesty International. *Maze of Injustice: The Failure to Protect Indigenous Women from Sexual Violence in the USA*. New York: Amnesty International, 2007. http://www.amnestyusa.org/pdfs/MazeOfInjustice.pdf.

Amnesty International. *Stolen Sisters: A Human Rights Response to Discrimination and Violence against Indigenous Women in Canada*. New York: Amnesty International, 2004.

Amsterdam, Anthony G., and Jerome Bruner. *Minding the Law*. Cambridge, MA: Harvard University Press, 2000.

Anker, Elizabeth. *Fictions of Dignity: Embodying Human Rights in World Literature*. Ithaca, NY: Cornell University Press, 2012.

Anker, Elizabeth. "Teaching the Legal Imperialism Debate." In *Teaching Literature and Human Rights*, edited by Elizabeth Swanson Goldberg and Alexandra Schultheis. MLA Options for Teaching Series, 2015.

Anscombe, G. E. M. *Intention*. Cambridge, MA: Harvard University Press, 2000.

Arendt, Hannah. *The Human Condition*. Chicago: University of Chicago Press, 1958.

Aristophanes. *The Comedies of Aristophanes*. Vol. 4, *Wasps*. Edited and translated by Alan H. Sommerstein. Warminster, UK: Aris and Philips, 1983.

Aristotle. *De Anima*.

Aristotle. *Metaphysics*.

Aristotle. *Nicomachean Ethics*.

Aristotle. *Physics*.

Arnold, Oliver. *The Third Citizen: Shakespeare's Theater and the Early Modern House of Commons*. Baltimore, MD: Johns Hopkins University Press, 2007.

Asad, Talal. *Formations of the Secular: Christianity, Islam, Modernity*. Stanford, CA: Stanford University Press, 2003.

Ashar, Sameer M. "Deep Critique and Democratic Lawyering in Clinical Practice." *California Law Review* 104 (2016): 193–232.

Aslam, Nadeem. *Maps for Lost Lovers*. London: Faber and Faber, 2004.

Attridge, Derek. *J. M. Coetzee and the Ethics of Reading: Literature in the Event*. Chicago: University of Chicago Press, 2004.

Attridge, Derek. *The Singularity of Literature*. New York: Routledge, 2004.

Auerbach, Erich. *Mimesis: The Representation of Reality in Western Literature*. Translated by Willard Trusk. Princeton, NJ: Princeton University Press, 1953.

Ayres, Ian. "Menus Matter." *University of Chicago Law Review* 73 (2006): 3–15.

Baldwin, Peter. *Copyright's Wars: Three Centuries of Trans-Atlantic Battle*. Princeton, NJ: Princeton University Press, 2014.

Baldwin, T. W. *William Shakspere's Small Latine & Lesse Greeke*. 2 vols. Urbana: University of Illinois Press, 1944.

Balkin, Jack M. "Deconstructive Practice and Legal Theory." *Yale Law Journal* 96 (1987): 743–86.

Balkin, Jack M., and Sanford Levinson. "Interpreting Law and Music: Performance Notes on 'The Banjo Serenader' and 'The Lying Crowd of Jews.'" *Cardozo Law Review* 20 (1999): 1513–72.

Balkin, Jack M., and Reva B. Siegel. "Principles, Practices, and Social Movements." *University of Pennsylvania Law Review* 154 (2006): 927–50.

Ball, Milner S. *Lying Down Together: Law, Metaphor, and Theology*. Madison: University of Wisconsin Press, 1985.

Ball, Milner S. *The Promise of American Law: A Theological, Humanistic View of Legal Process*. Athens: University of Georgia Press, 1981.

Bandes, Susan. "Empathy, Narrative, and Victim Impact Statements." *University of Chicago Law Review* 63 (1996): 361–412.

Bandes, Susan, ed. *The Passions of Law*. New York and London: New York University Press, 1999.

Banner, Stuart. "Legal History and Legal Scholarship." *Washington University Law Quarterly* 76 (1998): 37–44.

Baptista, J., Cardinal de Luca. *Theatrum veritatis et iustitiae*. Cologne: Lit. Soc., 1685.

Barnes, Jim. *On a Wing of the Sun: Three Volumes of Poetry*. Urbana: University of Illinois Press, 2001.

Barnes, Julian. "Letter from Paris," *Times Literary Supplement*, December 21, 2001, 13.

Barnes, Mario L. "Taking a Stand? An Initial Assessment of the Social and Racial Effects of Recent Innovations in Self-Defense Laws." *Fordham Law Review* 83 (2015): 3179–3210.

Baron, Jane B. "Law, Literature and the Problems of Interdisciplinarity." *Yale Law Journal* 108 (1999): 1059–85.

Baron, Jane B. "The Rhetoric of Law and Literature: A Skeptical View." *Cardozo Law Review* 26 (2005): 2273–82.

Barthes, Roland. *Image, Music, Text*. Translated by Stephen Heath. New York: Hill and Wang, 1977.

Barthes, Roland. "Introduction to the Structural Analysis of Narrative" (1966). In *The Barthes Reader*, edited by Susan Sontag, 251–95. New York: Hill and Wang, 1982.

Barton, Anne [Anne Righter]. *Shakespeare and the Idea of the Play*. Westport, CT: Greenwood, 1977. First published in 1962.

Barton, Dunbar Plunket. *Links between Shakespeare and the Law*. London: Faber and Gwyer, 1929.

Bath, Michael. *Speaking Pictures: English Emblem Books and Renaissance Culture*. New York: Longman, 1994.

Baucom, Ian. *Specters of the Atlantic: Finance Capital, Slavery, and the Philosophy of History*. Durham, NC: Duke University Press, 2005.

Bauman, Zygmunt. *Liquid Modernity*. Cambridge: Polity, 2000.

Beauvoir, Simone de. *She Came to Stay*. Translated by Yvonne Moyse and Roger Senhouse. Cleveland, OH: World, 1954.

Becker, Gary S. *A Treatise on the Family*. Cambridge, MA: Harvard University Press, 1991.

Beckwith, Sarah. *Signifying God: Social Relation and Symbolic Act in the York Corpus Christi Plays*. Chicago: University of Chicago Press, 2001.

Ben-Yishai, Ayelet. *Common Precedents: The Presentness of the Past in Victorian Law and Fiction*. New York: Oxford University Press, 2013.

Benjamin, Walter. *The Arcades Project*. Translated by Howard Eiland and Kevin McLaughlin. Cambridge, MA: Belknap Press of Harvard University Press, 2009.

Benjamin, Walter. "Theses on the Philosophy of History." In *Illuminations: Essays and Reflections*, edited by Hannah Arendt, translated by Harry Zohn, 253–64. New York: Schocken, 1969.

Benjamin, Walter. *Walter Benjamin: Selected Writings*. Edited by Marcus Bullock and Michael W. Jennings. Cambridge, MA: Belknap Press, 1996.

Benjamin, Walter. "The Work of Art in the Age of Mechanical Reproduction." In *Illuminations: Essays and Reflections*, edited by Hannah Arendt, translated by Harry Zohn, 219–53. New York: Schocken, 1969.

Bentham, Jeremy. *Works*. Edited by John Bowring. Edinburgh: Tait, 1838–43.

Benton, Lauren. *A Search for Sovereignty: Law and Geography in European Empires, 1400–1900*. New York: Cambridge University Press, 2010.

Benvenisti, Eyal. "Margin of Appreciation, Consensus, and Universal Standards." *NYU Journal of International Law and Politics* 31 (1998): 843–54.

Berlant, Lauren. *Cruel Optimism*. Durham, NC, and London: Duke University Press, 2011.

Bernstein, Elizabeth. "The Sexual Politics of the 'New Abolitionism.'" *differences* 18, no. 3 (2007): 128–51.

Best, Stephen. *The Fugitive's Properties: Law and the Poetics of Possession*. Chicago: University of Chicago Press, 2004.

Best, Stephen, and Sharon Marcus. "Surface Reading: An Introduction." *Representations* 108 (2009): 1–21.

Bilder, Mary Sarah. *The Transatlantic Constitution: Colonial Legal Culture and the Empire*. Cambridge, MA: Harvard University Press, 2004.

Binder, Guyora, and Robert Weisberg. *Literary Criticisms of Law*. Princeton, NJ: Princeton University Press, 2000.

Blackstone, William. *Commentaries on the Laws of England*, 1st edition, edited by David Lemmings. Oxford: Oxford University Press, 2016.

Blackwell, Mark, ed. *The Secret Life of Things: Animals, Objects, and It-Narratives in Eighteenth-Century England*. Cranbury, NJ: Associated University Presses, 2007.

Blake, William. *Tiriel. The Complete Poetry and Prose of William Blake*. Edited by David V. Erdman, 276–85. Newly revised edition. New York: Anchor Books, 1988.

Blasi, Gary, and John T. Jost. "System Justification Theory and Research: Implications for Law, Legal Advocacy, and Social Justice." *California Law Review* 94 (2006): 1119–68.

Blotner, Joseph, ed. *Selected Letters of William Faulkner*. New York: Random House, 1977.

Blumenthal, Susanna L. "Of Mandarins, Legal Consciousness, and the Cultural Turn in US Legal History: Robert W. Gordon. 1984. Critical Legal Histories." *Law and Social Inquiry* 37 (2012): 167–86.

Boas, George, ed. *Horapollo's Hieroglyphica*. Princeton, NJ: Princeton University Press, 1968.

Borrows, John. "Indigenous Legal Traditions in Canada." *Washington University Journal of Law and Policy* 19, no. 13 (2005): 167–223.

Bourdieu, Pierre. *The Logic Practice*. Translated by Richard Nice. Stanford, CA: Stanford University Press, 1990.

Bouvé, Pauline Carrington. "An Aboriginal Author." *Boston Evening Transcript*, August 23, 1899, 16.

Boyer, Abel. *The Royal Dictionary Abridged*. London: Bathurst, et al., 1767.

Boyle, James D. A. *Shamans, Software, and Spleens: Law and the Construction of the Information Society*. Cambridge, MA: Harvard University Press, 1996.

Boyte, Alina Ng. "The Conceits of Our Legal Imagination: Legal Fictions and the Concept of Deemed Authorship." *New York University Journal of Legislation and Public Policy* 17 (2014): 707–62.

Brennan, Theresa. *The Transmission of Affect*. Ithaca, NY, and London: Cornell University Press, 2004.

Brest, Paul, Sanford Levinson, Jack M. Balkin, Akhil Reed Amar, and Reva B. Siegel. *Processes of Constitutional Decisionmaking: Cases and Materials*. 5th ed. New York: Aspen, 2006.

Britt, Robert Roy. "Laughter Soothes the Wounded Heart." *Flatrock*. http://flatrock. org.nz/topics/humour/no_joke.htm.

Brooks, Peter. *Enigmas of Identity*. Princeton, NJ: Princeton University Press, 2011.

Brooks, Peter. "'Inevitable Discovery': Law, Narrative, Retrospectivity." *Yale Journal of Law and the Humanities* 15 (2003): 71–102.

Brooks, Peter. "Law and Humanities: Two Attempts." *Boston University Law Review* 93 (2013): 1437–68.

Brooks, Peter. "Literature as Law's Other." *Yale Journal of Law and the Humanities* 22 (2010): 349–68.

Brooks, Peter. "Narrative Transactions: Does the Law Need a Narratology?" *Yale Journal of Law and the Humanities* 18 (2006): 1–28.

Brooks, Peter. "Narrativity of the Law." *Law and Literature* 14 (2002): 1–10.

Brooks, Peter. *Troubling Confessions: Speaking Guilt in Law and Literature*. Chicago: University of Chicago Press, 2000.

Brooks, Peter, and Paul Gewirtz. *Law's Stories: Narrative and Rhetoric in the Law*. New Haven, CT: Yale University Press, 1996.

Brophy, Alfred L. "'Over and above . . . There Broods a Portentous Shadow—The Shadow of Law': Harriet Beecher Stowe's Critique of Slave Law in *Uncle Tom's Cabin*." *Journal of Law and Religion* 12 (1996): 457–506.

Brophy, Alfred L. "Humanity, Utility, and Logic in Southern Legal Thought: Harriet Beecher Stowe's Vision in *Dred: A Tale of the Great Dismal Swamp*." *Boston University Law Review* 78 (1998): 1113–61.

Brown, Homer Obed. "*Tom Jones*: The 'Bastard' of History." *boundary 2* 7 (1979): 201–34.

Brown, Wendy. *Undoing the Demos: Neoliberalism's Stealth Revolution*. New York: Zone, 2015.

Brown, Wendy, and Janet Halley, eds. *Left Legalism/Left Critique*. Durham, NC: Duke University Press, 2002.

Browne, Anthony. "Denmark Faces International Boycott over Muslim Cartoons." *Times Online*, January 31, 2006.

Bruner, Jerome. "The Narrative Construction of Reality." *Critical Inquiry* 18 (1991): 1–21.

Brzezinski, Max. "The New Modernist Studies: What's Left of Political Formalism?" *Minnesota Review* 76 (2011): 109–25.

Burke, Edmund. "Reflections on the Revolution in France." In *The Portable Edmund Burke*, edited by Isaac Kramnick, 416–73. New York: Penguin, 1999.

Burt, Richard. *Licensed by Authority: Ben Jonson and the Discourses of Censorship*. Ithaca, NY: Cornell University Press, 1993.

Butler, Judith. *Antigone's Claim: Kinship between Life and Death*. New York: Columbia University Press, 2002.

Butler, Judith. *Bodies That Matter: On the Discursive Limits of Sex*. New York: Routledge, 2011.

Butler, Judith. *Gender Trouble: Feminism and the Subversion of Identity*. New York: Routledge, 1990.

Butler, Judith. *Giving an Account of Oneself*. New York: Fordham University Press, 2005.

Butler, Judith. *Undoing Gender*. New York: Routledge, 2004.

Butler, Michael R., and Robert F. Garnett. "Teaching the Coase Theorem: Are We Getting It Right?" *Atlantic Economics Journal* 31 (2003): 133–45.

Cacho, Lisa Marie. *Social Death: Racialized Rightlessness and the Criminalization of the Unprotected*. New York: New York University Press, 2012.

Cain, Patricia A. "Imagine There's No Marriage." *Quinnipiac Law Review* 16 (1996): 27–60.

Calabresi, Guido. "Introductory Letter." *Yale Journal of Law and the Humanities* 1 (1988): vii.

Canaday, Margot. *The Straight State: Sexuality and Citizenship in Twentieth-Century America*. Princeton, NJ: Princeton University Press, 2009.

Cardozo, Benjamin. "Law and Literature." In *Law and Literature and Other Essays and Addresses*. New York: Harcourt, Brace, 1931.

Carpi, Daniela. *The Concept of Equity in Law and Literature*. Verona: University of Verona Press, 2005.

Cave, Terence. *Recognitions: A Study in Poetics*. Oxford: Clarendon Press, 1988.

Cavell, Stanley. *Philosophy the Day after Tomorrow*. Cambridge, MA: Belknap Press of Harvard University Press, 2005.

Chakrabarty, Dipesh. *Provincializing Europe: Postcolonial Thought and Historical Difference*. 2nd ed. Princeton, NJ: Princeton University Press, 2007.

Chambers-Letson, Joshua Takano. *A Race So Different: Performance and Law in Asian America*. New York: New York University Press, 2013.

Champagne, Duane. *Social Order and Political Change: Constitutional Governments among the Cherokee, the Choctaw, the Chickasaw, and the Creek*. Stanford, CA: Stanford University Press, 1992.

Chan, Sucheng. "The Exclusion of Chinese Women, 1870–1943." In *Entry Denied: Exclusion and the Chinese Community in America, 1882–1943*, edited by Sucheng Chan, 94–164. Philadelphia, PA: Temple University Press, 1991.

Chargaff, Erwin. "On the Dangers of Genetic Meddling." Letter to *Science* 192, no. 4243 (1976): 938–39.

Chauncey, George. *Gay New York: Gender, Urban Culture, and the Making of the Gay Male World, 1890–1940*. New York: Basic Books, 1995.

Cheah, Pheng. *Inhuman Conditions: On Cosmopolitanism and Human Rights*. Cambridge, MA: Harvard University Press, 2007.

Cheah, Pheng. *What is a World? On Postcolonial Literature as World Literature*. Durham, NC: Duke University Press, 2016.

Cheng, Anne Anlin. *Second Skin: Josephine Baker and the Modern Surface*. New York: Oxford University Press, 2011.

Chesnutt, Charles W. "The Future American." *Boston Evening Transcript*, August 18, 1900. http://www.online-literature.com/charles-chesnutt/wife-of-his-youth/11.

Cheyfitz, Eric. *The Poetics of Imperialism: Translation and Colonization from "The Tempest" to "Tarzan"*. Expanded ed. Philadelphia: University of Pennsylvania Press, 1997.

Cheyfitz, Eric. "The (Post)Colonial Construction of Indian Country: U.S. American Indian Literatures and Federal Indian Law." In *The Columbia Guide to American Indian Literatures of the United States Since 1945*, edited by Eric Cheyfitz, 1–124. New York: Columbia University Press, 2006.

Cheyfitz, Eric. "Savage Law: The Plot against American Indians in *Johnson and Graham's Lessee v. M'Intosh* and *The Pioneers*." In *The Cultures of United States Imperialism*, edited by Amy Kaplan and Donald E. Pease, 109–28. Durham, NC: Duke University Press, 1993.

Choy, Philip P., Lorraine Dong, and Marlon K. Hom, eds. *Coming Man: 19th Century American Perceptions of the Chinese.* Seattle: University of Washington Press, 1994.

Clark, Sherman. "Law School as Liberal Education." *Journal of Legal Education* 63 (2013): 235–46.

Clarke, James Stanier, et al., eds. *The Naval Chronicle.* Vol. 1. London: Burney, 1799.

Coase, Ronald. "The Problem of Social Cost." *Journal of Law and Economics* 3 (1960): 1–69.

Coetzee, J. M. *Waiting for the Barbarians.* Reprint ed. New York: Penguin, 2010.

Cohen, Joshua, and Deborah Chasman, eds. *Just Marriage.* New York: Oxford University Press, 2004.

Cohn, D'Vera. "The States of Marriage and Divorce." *Pew Research Center*, October 15, 2009. http://pewsocialtrends.org/pubs/746/states-of-marriage-and-divorce.

Cole, Catherine M. *Performing South Africa's Truth Commission: Stages of Transition.* Bloomington: Indiana University Press, 2010.

Cole, David. "Agon at Agora: Creative Misreadings in the First Amendment Tradition." *Yale Law Journal* 95 (1986): 857–905.

Cole, Simon A. *Suspect Identities.* Cambridge, MA: Harvard University Press, 1986.

Cole, Simon A., and Rachel Dios-Villa. "Investigating the 'CSI Effect' Effect: Media and Litigation Crisis in Criminal Law." *Stanford Law Review* 61 (2009): 1335–74.

Coleridge, Samuel Taylor. *Biographia Literaria.* Edited by George Watson. London: Dent, 1965.

Collins, Wilkie. *The Law and the Lady.* London: Chatto and Windus, 1903.

Comaroff, Jean, and John Comaroff, eds. *Law and Disorder in the Postcolony.* Chicago: Chicago University Press, 2006.

Conant, James, and Andrea Kern, eds. *Varieties of Skepticism: Essays after Kant, Wittgenstein, and Cavell.* Berlin: De Gruyter, 2014.

Connolly, William E. "Pluralism and Faith." *Political Theologies: Public Religions in a Post-Secular World*, ed. Hent de Vries and Lawrence E. Sullivan, 278–97. New York: Fordham University Press, 2006.

Conrad, Joseph. *The Nigger of the Narcissus.* New York: Doubleday Page, 1897.

Convention for the Protection of Human Rights and Fundamental Freedoms, opened for signature Nov. 4, 1950, 213 U.N.T.S. 221, Europ. T.S. No. 5.

Conway, John A. "Safe Houses for Strange Life." *Newsweek*, June 28, 1976.

Coombe, Rosemary J. "Contingent Articulations: A Critical Cultural Studies of Law." In *Law in the Domains of Culture*, edited by Austin Sarat and Thomas R. Kearns, 21–64. Ann Arbor: University of Michigan Press, 1998.

Coombe, Rosemary J. *The Cultural Life of Intellectual Properties: Authorship, Appropriation, and the Law.* Durham, NC: Duke University Press, 1998.

Corcos, Christine. *An International Guide to Law and Literature Studies.* Buffalo, NY: W. S. Hein, 2000.

Cormack, Bradin. *A Power to Do Justice: Jurisdiction, English Literature, and the Rise of Common Law, 1509–1625.* Chicago: University of Chicago Press, 2007.

Cornell, Drucilla. *The Philosophy of the Limit.* New York: Routledge, 1992.

Cornell, Drucilla. "Post-Structuralism, the Ethical Relation, and the Law." *Cardozo Law Review* 9 (1988): 1587–628.

Cover, Robert M. *Narrative, Violence, and the Law: The Essays of Robert Cover*. Edited by Martha Minow, Austin Sarat, and Aviam Soifer. Ann Arbor: University of Michigan Press, 1996.

Cover, Robert M. "The Supreme Court, 1982 Term. Foreword: *Nomos* and Narrative." *Harvard Law Review* 97 (1982): 4–68.

Cover, Robert M. "Violence and the Word." *Yale Law Journal* 95 (1986): 1601–29.

Crane, Gregg D. *Race, Citizenship, and Law in American Literature*. Cambridge: Cambridge University Press, 2002.

Crary, Alice, and Rupert Read, eds. *The New Wittgenstein*. New York: Routledge, 2000.

Crawley, Ashon T. *Blackpentecostal Breath: The Aesthetics of Possibility*. New York: Fordham University Press, 2016.

Crenshaw, Kimberlé, Neil Gotanda, Garry Peller, and Kendall Thomas, eds. *Critical Race Theory: The Key Writings That Formed the Movement*. New York: New Press, 1996.

Critchley, Simon. "It's Time to Make Shakespeare Dangerous." *The Guardian*, September 20, 2013.

Culler, Jonathan. *On Deconstruction: Theory and Criticism after Structuralism*. Ithaca, NY: Cornell University Press, 1982.

Currie, Gregory. *The Nature of Fiction*. Cambridge: Cambridge University Press, 1990.

Cushman, Barry. *Rethinking the New Deal Court: The Structure of a Constitutional Revolution*. New York: Oxford University Press, 1998.

Cvetkovitch, Ann. *Depression: A Public Feeling*. Durham, NC: Duke University Press, 2012.

Dabney, Lewis M. *The Indians of Yoknapatawpha: A Study in History and Literature*. Baton Rouge: Louisiana State University Press, 1974.

Davis, Thadious M. *Games of Property: Law, Race, Gender and Faulkner's "Go Down, Moses."* Durham, NC: Duke University Press, 2003.

Dawes, Jason. *That the World May Know: Bearing Witness to Atrocity*. Cambridge, MA: Harvard University Press, 2007.

Dayan, Colin. *The Law Is a White Dog: How Legal Rituals Make and Unmake Persons*. Princeton, NJ: Princeton University Press, 2011.

Dayan, Colin. *With Dogs at the Edge of Life*. New York: Columbia University Press, 2016.

De Grazia, Edward. *Girls Lean Back Everywhere: The Law of Obscenity and the Assault on Genius*. New York: Random House, 1992.

Delaney, Enda. *The Irish in Postwar Britain*. Oxford: Oxford University Press, 2007.

Delgado, Richard. "Storytelling for Oppositionalists and Others: A Plea for Narrative," *Michigan Law Review* 87 (1989): 2411–41.

Delgado, Richard, and Jean Stefancic. *Critical Race Theory: The Cutting Edge*. Philadelphia, PA: Temple University Press, 1995.

DeLombard, Jeannine. *In the Shadow of the Gallows: Race, Crime, and American Civic Identity*. Philadelphia: University of Pennsylvania Press, 2012.

DeLombard, Jeannine. *Slavery on Trial: Law, Abolitionism, and Print Culture*. Chapel Hill, NC: University of North Carolina Press, 2007.

De Luca, Giovanni Battista. *Theatrum veritatis, et iustitiae*, 21 vols. Rome: Corbelletti, 1669–81.

De Man, Paul. *Blindness and Insight: Essays in the Rhetoric of Contemporary Criticism*. 2nd ed. Minneapolis: University of Minnesota Press, 1983.

De Man, Paul. *The Resistance to Theory*. Minneapolis: University of Minnesota Press, 1986.

De Man, Paul. "Semiology and Rhetoric." *Diacritics* 3, no. 3 (1973): 27–33.

De Nebrija, Antonio. *Aenigmata iuris* [1506]. Republished as *Vocabularium utrisuque iuris*. Venice: Zalterium, 1612.

De Ville, Jacques. "Mythology and the Images of Justice." *Law and Literature* 23 (2011): 324–64.

Del Mar, Maksymilian, and William Twining, eds. *Legal Fictions in Theory and Practice*. Cham: Springer International, 2015.

Derrida, Jacques. "Force of Law: The 'Mystical Foundation of Authority.'" In *Deconstruction and the Possibility of Justice*, edited by Drucilla Cornell, Michel Rosenfeld, and David Gray Carlson, 3–67. New York: Routledge, 1992.

Derrida, Jacques. *Limited Inc*. Edited by Gerald Graff, translated by Jeffrey Mehlman and Samuel Weber. Evanston, IL: Northwestern University Press, 1988.

Derrida, Jacques. "Signature Event Context." *Glyph* 1 (1977): 172–97.

Derrida, Jacques. *Sovereignties in Question: The Poetics of Paul Celan*. New York: Fordham University Press, 2005.

Dershowitz, Alan. "Life Is Not a Dramatic Narrative." In *Law's Stories: Narrative and Rhetoric in the Law*, edited by Peter Brooks and Paul Gewirtz, 99–105. New Haven, CT: Yale University Press, 1996.

Dick, Philip K. *Do Androids Dream of Electric Sheep?* New York: Doubleday, 1968.

Diène, Doudou (Special Rapporteur on Contemporary Forms of Racism, Racial Discrimination, Xenophobia, and Related Intolerance). *Racism, Racial Discrimination, Xenophobia and Related Forms of Intolerance: Follow-Up to and Implementation of the Durban Declaration and Programme of Action*, 11, A/HRC/6/6. Human Rights Council, August 21, 2007. https://documents-dds-ny.un.org/doc/UNDOC/GEN/G07/137/32/PDF/G0713732.pdf?OpenElement.

Dimock, Wai Chee. *Residues of Justice: Literature, Law, Philosophy*. Berkeley and Los Angeles: University of California Press, 1996.

Dolin, Kieran. *Fiction and the Law: Legal Discourse in Victorian and Modernist Literature*. Cambridge: Cambridge University Press, 1999.

Donohue, John J., III, "Opting for the British Rule, or if Posner and Shavell Can't Remember the Coase Theorem, Who Will?" *Harvard Law Review* 104 (1991): 1093–1119.

Douglas-Scott, Sionaidh. *Law after Modernity*. Oxford: Hart, 2013.

Douzinas, Costas, and Lynda Nead, eds. *Law and the Image: The Authority of Art and the Aesthetics of Law*. Chicago: Chicago University Press, 1999.

Doyle, Arthur Conan. *The Complete Sherlock Holmes*. New York: Gramercy, 2002.

Doyle, Arthur Conan. *Sherlock Holmes: The Complete Novels and Tales*. New York: Bantam Dell, 1986.

Dubber, Markus Dirk. "Policing Possession: The War on Crime and the End of Criminal Law." *Journal of Criminal Law and Criminology* 91 (2001): 829–996.

Dunlop, C. R. B. "Literature Studies in Law School." *Cardozo Studies in Law and Literature* 3 (1991): 63–110.

During, Simon. "Completing Secularism: The Mundane in the Neoliberal Era." In *Varieties of Secularism in a Secular Age*, edited by Michael Warner, Jonathan Vanantwerpen, and Craig Calhoun, 105–25. Cambridge, MA: Harvard University Press, 2010.

Duthu, N. Bruce. "Broken Justice in Indian Country." *New York Times*, August 11, 2008, A17.

Dworkin, Ronald. *Law's Empire*. Cambridge, MA: Harvard University Press, 1986.

Easterling, Keller. *Extrastatecraft: The Power of Infrastructure Space*. New York: Verso, 2014.

Eco, Umberto, and Thomas A. Sebeok, eds. *The Sign of Three: Dupin, Holmes, Peirce*. Bloomington: Indiana University Press, 1984.

Eden, Kathy. *Poetic and Legal Fiction in the Aristotelian Tradition*. Princeton, NJ: Princeton University Press, 1986.

Edwards, Laura F. "The History in 'Critical Legal Histories': Robert W. Gordon. 1984. Critical Legal Histories." *Law and Social Inquiry* 37 (2012): 187–99.

Eilenberg, Susan. "Mortal Pages: Wordsworth and the Reform of Copyright." *English Literary History* 56 (1989): 351–74.

Elam, Keir. *The Semiotics of Theatre and Drama*. London: Routledge, 1994.

Ellickson, Robert C. "The Case for Coase and Against 'Coaseanism.'" *Yale Law Journal* 99 (1989): 611–30.

Eliot, T. S. "Tradition and the Individual Talent." *Perspecta* 19 (1982): 36–42.

Emens, Elizabeth F. "Monogamy's Law: Compulsory Monogamy and Polyamorous Existence." *New York University Review of Law and Social Change* 29 (2004): 277–376.

Emens, Elizabeth F. "Regulatory Fictions: On Marriage and Countermarriage." *California Law Review* 99 (2011): 235–72.

Erasmus. *D. Erasmi Roterdami de Duplici Copia Verborum ac Rerum*. London, 1573.

Erasmus. *On Copia of Words and Ideas*. Translated by Donald B. King and H. David Rix. Milwaukee, WI: Marquette University Press, 1999.

Erdrich, Louise. "Rape on the Reservation." *New York Times*, February 26, 2013. http://www.nytimes.com/2013/02/27/opinion/native-americans-and-the-violence-against-women-act.html?hp

Erdrich, Louise. *The Round House*. New York: Harper Perennial, 2012.

Faizer, Akram. "Chief Justice John 'Marshall' Roberts—How the Chief's Majority Opinion Upholding the Federal Patient Protection and Affordable Care Act of 2010 Evokes Justice Marshall's Decision in *Marbury v. Madison*." *University of New Hampshire Law Review* 11 (2013): 1–26.

Faulkner, William. *Absalom, Absalom!* New York: Vintage, 1972. First published in 1936.

Faulkner, William. *Collected Stories of William Faulkner*. New York: Vintage, 1995. First published in 1950.

Faulkner, William. *Requiem for a Nun*. New York: Random House, 1951.

Faust, Drew Gilpin. *Mothers of Invention: Women of the Slaveholding South during the Civil War*. Chapel Hill: University of North Carolina Press, 1996.

Fausto-Sterling, Anne. *Sexing the Body: Gender Politics and the Construction of Sexuality*. New York: Basic Books, 2000.

Federal Law Enforcement Training Centers. Podcast transcript, https://www.fletc.gov/sites/default/files/PartIGrahamvConnor.pdf.

Felski, Rita. *The Limits of Critique*. Chicago: University of Chicago Press, 2015.

Ferguson, Frances. *Pornography, the Theory: What Utilitarianism Did to Action*. Chicago: University of Chicago Press, 2004.

Ferguson, Robert A. *Law and Letters in American Culture*. Cambridge, MA: Harvard University Press, 1984.

Finchett-Maddock, Lucy. *Protest, Property and the Commons: Performances of Law and Resistance*. New York: Routledge, 2016.

Fineman, Martha Albertson. *The Autonomy Myth: A Theory of Dependency*. New York: New Press, 2004.

Fineman, Martha Albertson. *The Neutered Mother, the Sexual Family, and Other Twentieth Century Tragedies.* New York: Routledge, 1995.

Fiss, Owen. "The Challenge Ahead." *Yale Journal of Law and the Humanities* 1 (1988): viii–xii.

Finn, Margot. "Victorian Law, Literature and History: Three Ships Passing in the Night." *Journal of Victorian Culture* 7 (2002): 134–46.

Fish, Stanley. *Doing What Comes Naturally: Change, Rhetoric, and the Practice of Theory in Literary and Legal Studies.* Durham, NC: Duke University Press, 1989.

Fish, Stanley. "Intention Is All There Is: A Critical Analysis of Aharon Barak's Purposive Interpretation in Law." *Cardozo Law Review* 29 (2008): 1109–46.

Fleming, Charles. *Royal Dictionary English and French and French and English.* Paris: Firmin Didot frères, 1846–60.

Fludernik, Monika. "A Narratology of the Law? Narratives in Legal Discourse." *Critical Analysis of Law* 1 (2014): 87–109.

Forbes, Jessica. "The Inevitable Discovery Exception, Primary Evidence, and the Emasculation of the Fourth Amendment." *Fordham Law Review* 55 (1987): 1221–38.

Ford, Richard Thompson. *Racial Culture: A Critique.* Princeton, NJ: Princeton University Press, 2005.

Ford, Richard Thompson. *Rights Gone Wrong: How Law Corrupts the Struggle for Equality.* New York: Farrar, Straus and Giroux, 2011.

Forster, E. M. *A Passage to India.* New York: Mariner, 1965.

Foucault, Michel. *Discipline and Punish: The Birth of the Prison.* Translated by Alan Sheridan. New York: Vintage, 1995.

Foucault, Michel. *The History of Sexuality.* Vol. 1, *An Introduction.* Translated by Robert Hurley. New York: Pantheon, 1978.

Foucault, Michel. *The History of Sexuality.* Vol. 3, *The Care of the Self.* Translated by Robert Hurley. New York: Pantheon, 1986.

Foucault, Michel. *Security, Territory, Population: Lectures at the Collège de France, 1977–1978.* Edited by Michel Senellart, translated by Graham Burchell. New York: Palgrave Macmillan, 2004.

Foucault, Michel. *"Society Must Be Defended": Lectures at the Collège de France, 1975–1976.* Edited by Mauro Bertani and Alessandro Fontana, translated by David Macey. New York: Picador, 2003.

Foucault, Michel. "What Is an Author?" In *Textual Strategies: Perspectives in Post-Structuralist Criticism.* Edited by Josué V. Harari, translated by Josué V. Harari, 141–60. Ithaca, NY: Cornell University Press, 1979.

Franke, Katherine M. "Longing for Loving." *Fordham Law Review* 76 (2008): 2685–707.

Fraunce, Abraham. *Insignium armorum, emblematum, hierogliphicorum, symbolorum.* London: Orwin, 1588.

Fraunce, Abraham. *Philosophiae symbolicae liber quartus* [1590]. New York: AMS Press, 1991.

Freud, Sigmund. *The Interpretation of Dreams.* Translated by James Strachey. New York: Avon Books, 1965.

Friedman, Lawrence M. "The Law and Society Movement." *Stanford Law Review* 38 (1986): 763–80.

Fuller, Lon L. *Legal Fictions.* Stanford, CA: Stanford University Press, 1967.

Gaakeer, Jeanne. *Hope Springs Eternal: An Introduction to the Work of James Boyd White.* Amsterdam: Amsterdam University Press, 1998.

Gagnier, Regenia. "Methodology and New Historicism." *Journal of Victorian Culture* 4 (1999): 116–22.

Gans, Herbert. *Popular Culture and High Culture: An Analysis and Evaluation of Taste.* New York: Basic Books, 1974.

"Gay Marriage around the World," *Pew Research Center*, June 26, 2015. http://www.pewforum.org/2015/06/26/gay-marriage-around-the-world-2013/.

Geczy, Adam. *Fashion and Orientalism: Dress, Textiles and Culture from the 17th to the 21st Century.* London: Bloomsbury Academic, 2013.

Gede, Thomas F. "Criminal Jurisdiction of Indian Tribes: Should Non-Indians Be Subject to Tribal Criminal Authority Under VAWA?" *Engage* 13, no. 2 (2012): 40–44. http://www.fed-soc.org/publications/detail/criminal-jurisdiction-of-indian-tribes-should-non-indians-be-subject-to-tribal-criminal-authority-under-vawa.

Geertz, Clifford. "Thick Description: Toward an Interpretive Theory of Culture." In *The Interpretation of Cultures: Selected Essays*, 3–30. New York: Basic Books, 1973.

Gemmette, Elizabeth Villiers. "Law and Literature: An Unnecessarily Suspect Class in the Liberal Arts Component of the Law School Curriculum." *Valparaiso University Law Review* 23 (1989): 267–340.

Gemmette, Elizabeth Villiers. *Law in Literature: An Annotated Bibliography of Law-Related Works.* Troy, NY: Whitston, 1998.

Gendler, Tamar Szabó. "The Puzzle of Imaginative Resistance." *Journal of Philosophy* 97 (2000): 55–81.

Geroulanos, Stefanos, Zvi Ben-Dor Benite, and Nicole Jerr, eds. *The Scaffold of Sovereignty: Global and Aesthetic Perspectives on the History of a Concept.* New York: Columbia University Press, forthcoming.

Gerrig, Richard J. *Experiencing Narrative Worlds.* New Haven, CT: Yale University Press, 1993.

Getches, David, Charles Wilkinson, and Robert A. Williams Jr. *Cases and Materials on Federal Indian Law.* St. Paul, MN: West Group, 1998.

Gilroy, Paul. *There Ain't No Black in the Union Jack.* Chicago: University of Chicago Press, 1987.

Ginzburg, Carlo. "Clues: Roots of an Evidential Paradigm." In *Myths, Emblems, Clues*, translated by John Tedeschi and Anne C. Tedeschi, 96–125. London: Hutchinson Radius, 1990.

Ginzburg, Carlo. "Spie. Radici di un paradigma indizario." In *Miti Emblemi Spie*, 158–209. Torino: Einaudi, 1986.

Glymph, Thavolia. *Out of the House of Bondage: The Transformation of the Plantation Household.* Cambridge: Cambridge University Press, 2008.

Goethe, Johann Wolfgang von. "Elective Affinities." In *Goethe: The Collected Works*, vol. 11, edited by David E. Wellbery, translated by Judith Ryan. Princeton, NJ: Princeton University Press, 1995.

Goffman, Erving. *The Presentation of Self in Everyday Life.* Garden City, NY: Doubleday 1959.

Goldberg, Jonathan. *James I and the Politics of Literature.* Stanford, CA: Stanford University Press, 1989.

Goldberg, Jonathan. *Willa Cather and Others.* Durham, NC: Duke University Press, 2001.

Goleman, Daniel. *Emotional Intelligence: Why It Can Matter More than IQ.* New York: Random House, 1995.

Goodfield, June. *Playing God.* New York: Harper Colophon, 1977.

Goodman, Nan. *Shifting the Blame: Literature, Law, and the Theory of Accidents in Nineteenth-Century America*. New York: Routledge, 1998.

Goodrich, Peter. *Law in the Courts of Love: Literature and Other Minor Jurisprudences*. New York: Routledge, 1996.

Goodrich, Peter. *Legal Emblems and the Art of Law: Obiter Depicta as the Vision of Governance*. New York: Cambridge University Press, 2014.

Goodrich, Peter. "Legal Enigmas: Antonio de Nebrija, *The Da Vinci Code*, and the Emendation of Law." *Oxford Journal of Legal Studies* 30 (2010): 71–99.

Goodrich, Peter. *Oedipus Lex: Psychoanalysis, History, Law*. Berkeley: University of California Press, 1995.

Goodrich, Peter. "Screening Law." *Law and Literature* 21 (2009): 1–23.

Goodrich, Peter. "Specters of Law: Why the History of the Legal Spectacle Has Not Been Written." *UC Irvine Law Review* 1 (2011): 773–812.

Goodrich, Peter. "The Theatre of Emblems." *Law, Culture and the Humanities* 11 (2012): 47–67.

Goodrich, Peter. "The Visial Line: On the Prehistory of Law and Film." *Parallax* 14, no. 4 (2008): 55–76.

Goodrich, Peter. "Visiocracy: On the Futures of the Fingerpost." *Critical Inquiry* 39 (2013): 498–531.

Gordon, Robert W. "Critical Legal Histories." *Stanford Law Review* 36 (1984): 57–126.

Gordon, Robert W. "'Critical Legal Histories' Revisited: A Response." *Law and Social Inquiry* 37 (2012): 200–215.

Granovetter, Mark S. *Getting a Job: A Study of Contacts and Careers*. Cambridge, MA: Harvard University Press, 1974.

Granovetter, Mark S. "The Strength of Weak Ties." *American Journal of Sociology* 78 (1973): 1360–80.

Greenhouse, Linda. "Science May Patent New Forms of Life, Justices Rule, 5 to 4: Dispute on Bacteria: Decision Assists Industry in Bioengineering in a Variety of Projects." *New York Times*, June 17, 1980 (late edition), A1.

Gregg, Melissa, and Gregory J. Seigworth, eds. *The Affect Theory Reader*. Durham, NC: Duke University Press, 2010.

Greenblatt, Stephen. "Invisible Bullets: Renaissance Authority and Its Subversion, *Henry IV* and *Henry V*." In *Political Shakespeare: Essays in Cultural Materialism*, edited by Jonathan Dollimore and Alan Sinfield, 18–47. 2nd ed. Ithaca, NY: Cornell University Press, 1994.

Greenblatt, Stephen J. *Learning to Curse: Essays in Modern Culture*. New York: Routledge, 1990.

Grewal, Inderpal. *Transnational America: Feminisms, Diasporas, Neoliberalisms*. Durham, NC: Duke University Press, 2005.

Gutiérrez-Jones, Carl. *Critical Race Narratives: A Study of Race, Rhetoric, and Injury*. New York: New York University Press, 2001.

Gwynne, Peter. "Genetic Watchdogs." *Newsweek*, July 4, 1976.

Haag, Pamela. *Consent: Sexual Rights and the Transformation of American Liberalism*. Ithaca, NY: Cornell University Press, 1999.

Haldeman, Joe. *The Forever War*. New York: St. Martin's, 1974.

Halley, Janet. "Rape at Rome: Feminist Interventions in the Criminalization of Sex-Related Violence in Positive International Criminal Law." *Michigan Journal of International Law* 30 (2008): 1–123.

Halley, Janet. *Split Decisions: How and Why to Take a Break from Feminism*. Princeton, NJ: Princeton University Press, 2008.

Halley, Janet, Katherine M. Franke, Clare Huntington, Susan R. Schmeiser, Philomena Tsoukala, and Darren Rosenblum. "A Tribute from Legal Studies to Eve Kosofsky Sedgwick." Special issue, *Harvard Journal of Law and Gender* 33, no. 1 (2010): 309–56.

Halley, Janet, Prabha Kotiswaran, Rachel Rebouché, and Hila Shamir. *Governance Feminism: A Handbook*. Minneapolis: University of Minnesota Press, forthcoming.

Halley, Janet, Prabha Kotiswaran, Rachel Rebouché, and Hila Shamir. *Governance Feminism: An Introduction*. Minneapolis: University of Minnesota Press, forthcoming.

Halley, Janet, Prabha Kotiswaran, Hila Shamir, and Chantal Thomas. "From the International to the Local in Feminist Legal Responses to Rape, Prostitution/ Sex Work, and Sex Trafficking: Four Studies in Contemporary Governance Feminism." *Harvard Journal of Law and Gender* 29 (2006): 335–423.

Halley, Janet, and Andrew Parker, eds. *After Sex? On Writing since Queer Theory*. Durham, NC: Duke University Press, 2011.

Hansen, Randall. *Citizenship and Immigration in Postwar Britain*. Oxford: Oxford University Press, 2000.

Harley, Alexis. "'America, a Prophecy': When Blake Meets *Blade Runner*." *Sydney Studies in English* 31 (2005): 62–76.

Hampshire, Stuart. "Types of Interpretation." In *Art and Philosophy: A Symposium*, edited by Sidney Hook, 101–08. New York: New York University Press, 1966.

Harmon, Louise. "Falling Off the Vine: Legal Fictions and the Doctrine of Substituted Judgment." *Yale Law Journal* 100 (1990): 1–71.

Harney, Stefano, and Fred Moten. *The Undercommons: Fugitive Planning and Black Study*. New York: Autonomedia, 2013.

Harring, Sidney L. *Crow Dog's Case: American Indian Sovereignty, Tribal Law, and United States Law in the Nineteenth Century*. New York: Cambridge University Press, 1994.

Hart, H. L. A. *The Concept of Law*. Oxford: Clarendon Press, 1961.

Hartman, Saidiya V. *Lose Your Mother: A Journey along the Atlantic Slave Route*. New York: Farrar, Strauss and Giroux, 2007.

Hartman, Saidiya V. *Scenes of Subjection: Terror, Slavery, and Self-Making in Nineteenth-Century America*. New York: Oxford University Press, 1997.

Hartog, Hendrik. "Introduction to Symposium on 'Critical Legal Histories': Robert W. Gordon. 1984. Critical Legal Histories." *Law and Social Inquiry* 37 (2012): 147–54.

Haverkamp, Anselm, ed. *Gewalt und Gerechtigkeit: Derrida—Benjamin*. Frankfurt: Suhrkamp, 1994.

Hayaert, Valérie. "*Calumnia: De femaosis libellis* et ripostes aux attaques injurieuses: La verve satirique de l'emblème." *Textimage* 7, no. 2 (2010): 1–19.

Hayaert, Valérie. "*Serio-ludere* et humanisme juridique: Les Gloses de Benoît Le Court aux *Arrêts d'Amour* de Martial d'Auvergne." In *Des"Arrests Parlans": Les Arrêts notables à la Renaissance entre droit et littérature*, edited by Géraldine Cazals and Stéphan Geonget, 103–26. Geneva: Droz, 2014.

HBO. "A Woman's Right to Shoes." *Sex and the City*, August 17, 2003.

Heald, Paul J. "How Copyright Keeps Works Disappeared." *Journal of Empirical Legal Studies* 11 (2014): 829–66.

Heidegger, Martin. *Basic Writings*. Edited by David Farrell Krell. London: Routledge, 1993.

Heilbrun, Carolyn, and Judith Resnik. "Convergences: Law, Literature, and Feminism." *Yale Law Journal* 99 (1990): 1913–56.

Heinlein, Robert. *The Moon Is a Harsh Mistress*. New York: Orb, 1997.

Heinlein, Robert. *Stranger in a Strange Land*. New York: Ace, 1987.

Heinzelman, Susan Sage, and Zipporah Batshaw Wiseman, eds. *Representing Women: Law, Literature, and Feminism*. Durham, NC: Duke University Press, 1994.

Helmholz, Richard H. "Support Orders, Church Courts, and the Rule of *Filius Nullius*: A Reassessment of the Common Law." *Virginia Law Review* 63 (1977): 431–48.

Ho, Daniel E., and Kevin M. Quinn. "Did a Switch in Time Save Nine?" *Journal of Legal Analysis* 2 (2010): 69–114.

Hohendahl, Peter Uwe. "A Return to History? The New Historicism and Its Agenda." *New German Critique* 55 (1992): 87–104.

Holland, Norman. "Hermia's Dream." In *New Casebooks: A Midsummer Night's Dream*, edited by Richard Dutton, 61–83. London: Macmillan, 1996.

Holmes, Oliver Wendell, Jr. "Law in Science and Science in Law." *Harvard Law Review* 12 (1899): 443–63.

Holmes, Oliver Wendell, Jr. "The Path of Law." *Harvard Law Review* 10 (1897): 457–78.

Hong, Terry. "An Interview with Nadeem Aslam." *Bookslut*, July 2013. http://www. bookslut.com/features/2013_07_020162.php.

Hong, Terry. "Mystery Is All There Is: Michael E. Halmshaw Interviews Nadeem Aslam." *Guernica*, August 15, 2015. https://www.guernicamag.com/interviews/ mystery-is-all-there-is/.

Hook, Sidney, ed. *Art and Philosophy: A Symposium*. New York: New York University Press, 1966.

Horsford, Howard C. "Faulkner's (Mostly) Unreal Indians in Early Mississippi History." *American Literature* 64 (1992): 311–30.

Howells, Richard. "'Sorting the Sheep from the Sheep': Value, Worth, and the Creative Industries." In *The Public Value of the Humanities*, edited by Jonathan Bate, 232–46. London: Bloomsbury, 2011.

Howland, Joan Sidney. "A History of Legal History Courses Offered in American Law Schools." *American Journal of Legal History* 53 (2013): 363–78.

Hunt, Lynn. *Inventing Human Rights: A History*. New York: Norton, 2007.

Hurst, James Willard. *The Growth of American Law: The Law Makers*. Union, NJ: Lawbook Exchange, 2007.

Hutson, Lorna. *Circumstantial Shakespeare*. Oxford: Oxford University Press, 2015.

Hutson, Lorna. *The Invention of Suspicion: Law and Mimesis in Shakespeare and Renaissance Drama*. Oxford: Oxford University Press, 2007.

Hutson, Lorna, ed. *The Oxford Handbook of Early Modern Law and Literature*. Oxford: Oxford University Press, forthcoming.

Imwinkelreid, Edward J. "The Second Coming of Res Gestae: A Procedural Approach to Untangling the 'Inextricably Intertwined' Theory for Admitting Evidence of an Accused's Uncharged Misconduct." *Catholic University Law Review* 59 (2010): 719–46.

Irr, Caren. *Pink Pirates: Contemporary American Women Writers and Copyright*. Iowa City: University of Iowa Press, 2010.

Ishiguro, Kazuo. *Never Let Me Go*. New York: Knopf, 2005.

Ishiguro, Kazuo. *The Remains of the Day*. New York: Random House, 1993. First published in 1989.

Jacobson, Linda A., and Mark Mather. "U.S. Economic and Social Trends since 2000." *Population Bulletin* 65 (2010): 1–16.

Jameson, Fredric. *The Political Unconscious: Narrative as a Socially Symbolic Act*. Ithaca, NY: Cornell University Press, 1981.

Jameson, Fredric. *Postmodernism: The Cultural Logic of Late Capitalism*. Durham, NC: Duke University Press, 1991.

Jardine, Lisa. "The Place of Dialectic Teaching in Sixteenth-Century Cambridge." *Studies in the Renaissance* 21 (1974): 31–62.

Jaszi, Peter. "On the Author Effect: Contemporary Copyright and Collective Creativity." In *The Construction of Authorship: Textual Appropriation in Law and Literature*, edited by Martha Woodmansee and Peter Jaszi, 29–56. Durham, NC: Duke University Press, 1994.

Jaszi, Peter. "Toward a Theory of Copyright: The Metamorphoses of 'Authorship.'" *Duke Law Journal* (1991): 455–502.

Jefferson, Thomas. *The Writings of Thomas Jefferson: Memorial Edition*. Vol. 1. Washington, DC: Thomas Jefferson Memorial Association of the United States, 1903.

Jelliffe, Robert A., ed. *Faulkner at Nagano*. Tokyo: Kenkyusha, 1956.

Jensen, Brent J. "Live, Human-Made Bacteria as Patentable Subject Matter under 35 U.S.C. §101: *Diamond v. Chakrabarty*." *Brigham Young University Law Review* 1980, no. 3 (1980): 705–19.

Johnson, Barbara. *Persons and Things*. Cambridge, MA: Harvard University Press, 2008.

Johnson, Richard. "What Is Cultural Studies Anyway?" *Social Text* 16 (1986): 38–80.

Johnson, Samuel. *A Dictionary of the English Language*. Vol. 2. London: J. and P. Knapton, et al., 1755.

Jones, Edward P. *The Known World*. New York: Amistad, 2003.

Joondeph, Bradley W. "The Affordable Care Act and the Commerce Power: Much Ado About (Nearly) Nothing." *Journal of Health and Life Sciences Law* 6 (2013).

Jordan, Constance. *Shakespeare's Monarchies: Ruler and Subject in the Romances*. Ithaca, NY: Cornell University Press, 1997.

Joyce, James. *Finnegans Wake*. London: Faber and Faber, 1939.

Juhl, P. D. *Interpretation: An Essay in the Philosophy of Literary Criticism*. Princeton, NJ: Princeton University Press, 1980.

Kahn, Paul W. *The Cultural Study of Law: Reconstructing Legal Scholarship*. Chicago and London: University of Chicago Press, 1999.

Kahn, Paul W. *Law and Love: The Trials of King Lear*. New Haven, CT: Yale University Press, 2000.

Kahn, Victoria. *Machiavellian Rhetoric: From the Counter-Reformation to Milton*. Princeton, NJ: Princeton University Press, 1994.

Kahn, Victoria. "Rhetoric and the Law." *Diacritics* 19, no. 2 (1989): 21–34.

Kahn, Victoria. *Wayward Contracts: The Crisis of Political Obligation in England, 1640–1674*. Princeton, NJ: Princeton University Press, 2004.

Kahn, Victoria, and Lorna Hutson, eds. *Rhetoric and Law in Early Modern Europe*. New Haven, CT: Yale University Press, 2001.

Kant, Immanuel. *The Critique of Pure Reason*. Edited and translated by Paul Guyer and Allen W. Wood. Cambridge: Cambridge University Press, 1998.

Kantor, Jodi. "Lawsuits' Lurid Details Draw an Online Crowd." *New York Times*, February 23, 2015. http://nyti.ms/17L2Lgn.

Kaplan, Benjamin. *An Unhurried View of Copyright*. New York: Columbia University Press, 1967.

Karp, Laurence E. "Immortal Life in the Test Tube." *Washington Post*, April 18, 1976, B1, B4.

Karsten, Peter. "Explaining the Fight over the Attractive Nuisance Doctrine: A Kinder, Gentler Instrumentalism in the 'Age of Formalism.'" *Law and History Review* 10 (1992): 45–92.

Kayman, Martin. "The Reader and the Jury: Legal Fictions and the Making of Commercial Law in the Eighteenth Century." *Eighteenth-Century Fiction* 9 (1997): 373–94.

Kennedy, David. *A World of Struggle: How Power, Law, and Expertise Shape Global Political Economy.* Princeton, NJ: Princeton University Press, 2016.

Kennedy, Duncan. *Sexy Dressing, Etc.* Cambridge, MA: Harvard University Press, 1993.

Kennedy, Duncan. "The Structure of Blackstone's *Commentaries*." *Buffalo Law Review* 28 (1979): 209–382.

Kerr, Orin. "The Rise of the Ph.D. Law Professor." *Washington Post*, October 22, 2015.

Kevles, Daniel J. "Ananda Chakrabarty Wins a Patent: Biotechnology, Law, and Society, 1972–1980." *Historical Studies in the Physical and Biological Sciences* 25, no. 1 (1994): 111–35.

Kincaid, Jamaica. *At The Bottom of the River.* New York: Farrar, Strauss and Giroux, 1978.

Kirschenbaum, Matthew. "Am I a Digital Humanist? Confessions of a Neoliberal Tool." https://medium.com/@mkirschenbaum/am-i-a-digital-humanist-confessions-of-a-neoliberal-tool-1bc64caaa984#.m43nryfc8.

Kisilevsky, Sari, and Martin Stone, eds. *Freedom and Force: Essays on Kant's Legal Philosophy.* Oxford: Hart, 2016.

Klausen, Jytte. *The Cartoons that Shook the World.* New Haven, CT: Yale University Press, 2009.

Kmiec, Douglas W., and Shelley Ross Saxer. "Equality in Substance and in Name." *San Francisco Chronicle*, March 2, 2009.

Knapp, Stephen, and Walter Benn Michaels. "Against Theory." *Critical Inquiry* 8 (1982): 723–42.

Kobayashi, Issa. *The Dumpling Field: Haiku of Issa.* Translated by Lucien Stryk and Noboru Fujiwara. Athens: Ohio University Press, 1991.

Kornstein, Daniel. *Kill All the Lawyers? Shakespeare's Legal Appeal.* Princeton, NJ: Princeton University Press, 1994.

Korobkin, Laura Hanft. *Criminal Conversations: Sentimentality and Nineteenth-Century Legal Stories of Adultery.* New York: Columbia University Press, 1998.

Korobkin, Russell. "The Endowment Effect and Legal Analysis." *Northwestern University Law Review* 97 (2003): 1228–91.

Kramer, Larry D. "Generating Constitutional Meaning." *California Law Review* 94 (2006): 1439–54.

Kramer, Larry D. *The People Themselves: Popular Constitutionalism and Judicial Review.* New York: Oxford University Press, 2004.

Kramer, Paul A. "The Case of the 22 Lewd Chinese Women: A Crazy 19th-Century Case Shows How the Supreme Court Should Deal with Arizona's Immigration Law." *Slate.com*, April 23, 2012. http://www.slate.com/articles/news_and_politics/jurisprudence/2012/04/arizona_s_immigration_law_at_the_supreme_court_lessons_for_s_b_1070_via_the_case_of_the_22_lewd_chinese_women.html.

Kramer, Paul A. "Imperial Opening: Civilization, Exemption, and the Geopolitics of Mobility in the History of Chinese Exclusion, 1868–1910." *Journal of the Gilded Age and Progressive Era* 14 (2015): 317–47.

Ku, Raymond Shih Ray, Jiayang Sun, and Yiyang Fan. "Does Copyright Law Promote Creativity? An Empirical Analysis of Copyright's Bounty." *Vanderbilt Law Review* 62 (2009): 1669–746.

LaCroix, Alison L. "Temporal Imperialism." *University of Pennsylvania Law Review* 158 (2010): 1329–73.

Lamb, Mary Ellen. "Taken by the Fairies: Fairy Practices and the Production of Popular Culture in *A Midsummer Night's Dream.*" *Shakespeare Quarterly* 51, no. 3 (2000): 277–312.

Landes, Elisabeth M., and Richard A. Posner. "The Economics of the Baby Shortage." *Journal of Legal Studies* 7 (1978): 323–48.

Latour, Bruno. *Reassembling the Social: An Introduction to Actor-Network Theory.* New York: Oxford University Press, 2005.

Latour, Bruno. "Why has Critique Run out of Steam? From Matters of Fact to Matters of Concern." *Critical Inquiry* 30 (2004): 225–48.

Legg, Andrew. *The Margin of Appreciation in International Human Rights Law: Deference and Proportionality.* Oxford: Oxford University Press, 2012.

Lévi-Strauss, Claude. *Myth and Meaning.* New York: Schocken, 1978.

Levine, Caroline. *Forms: Whole, Rhythm, Hierarchy, Network.* Princeton, NJ: Princeton University Press, 2015.

Levinson, Marjorie. "What Is New Formalism?" *PMLA* 122 (2007): 558–69.

Levinson, Sanford, and Steven Mailloux, eds. *Interpreting Law and Literature: A Hermeneutic Reader.* Evanston, IL: Northwestern University Press, 1988.

Li, David. *Imagining the Nation: Asian American Literature and Cultural Consent.* Stanford, CA: Stanford University Press, 1998.

Lindsay, Sir David. *Ane Satyre of the Thrie Estaitis.* Edited by Roderick Lyal. Edinburgh: Canongate Classics, 1989.

Llewellyn, Karl N. "Some Realism about Realism." *Harvard Law Review* 44 (1931): 1222–64.

Lobb, Theophilus. *Rational Methods of Curing Fevers . . . Together with a Particular Account of the Effects of Artificial Evacuations by Bleeding, Vomiting, etc.* London: John Oswald, 1734.

Lobban, Michael. "The Varieties of Legal History." *Clio@Thémis* 5 (2012): 1–29. http://www.cliothemis.com/IMG/pdf/TP_Lobban.pdf.

LoPucki, Lynn M. "Dawn of the Discipline-Based Law Faculty." *Journal of Legal Education* 65 (2016): 506–42.

Lorenz, Philip. *The Tears of Sovereignty: Perspectives of Power in Renaissance Drama.* New York: Fordham University Press, 2013.

Love, Heather. "Close Reading and Thin Description." *Public Culture* 25 (2013): 401–34.

Lowe, Lisa. *Immigrant Acts.* Durham, NC: Duke University Press, 1996.

Luhmann, Niklas. *Law as a Social System.* Edited by Fatima Kastner, Richard Nobles, David Schiff, and Rosamund Ziegert, translated by Klaus A. Ziegert. New York: Oxford University Press, 2004.

Lui, Mary Ting Yi. *The Chinatown Trunk Mystery: Murder, Miscegenation, and Other Dangerous Encounters in Turn-of-the-Century New York City.* Princeton, NJ: Princeton University Press, 2007.

Lupton, Julia Reinhard. *Citizen-Saints: Shakespeare and Political Theology*. Chicago: Chicago University Press, 2005.

Lussier, Mark, and Caitlin Gowan. "The Romantic Roots of *Blade Runner*." *Wordsworth Circle* 43 (2012): 165–72.

Lyotard, Jean-François. *Discourse, Figure*. Translated by Antony Hudek and Mary Lydon. Minneapolis: University of Minnesota Press, 2011.

Mack, Peter. *Renaissance Argument: Valla and Agricola in the Traditions of Rhetoric and Dialectic*. Leiden: Brill, 1993.

Macpherson, Sandra. *Harm's Way: Tragic Responsibility and the Novel Form*. Baltimore, MD: Johns Hopkins University Press, 2010.

Mahar, Heather. "Why Are There So Few Prenuptial Agreements?" *Harvard Law School John M. Olin Center for Law, Economics and Business Discussion Paper Series*, Paper 436, 2003. http://lsr.nellco.org/cgi/viewcontent.cgi?article=1224&context=harvard_olin.

Mahler, Jonathan. "Irresistible TV, but Durst Film Tests Ethics Too." *New York Times*, March 16, 2015.

Mahmood, Saba. "Feminist Theory, Embodiment, and the Docile Agent: Some Reflections on the Egyptian Islamic Revival." *Cultural Anthopology* 16 (2001): 202–36.

Mahmood, Saba. *Religious Difference in a Secular Age*. Princeton, NJ: Princeton University Press, 2015.

Maine, Henry Sumner. *Ancient Law: Its Connection with the Early History of Society, and Its Relation to Modern Ideals*. London: John Murray, 1861.

Maitland, Frederick William. "The Corporation Sole." In *The Collected Papers of Frederic William Maitland*, vol. 3, edited by H. A. L. Fisher, 210–43. Cambridge: Cambridge University Press, 1911.

The Making of Modern Law: U.S. Supreme Court Records and Briefs, 1823–1978. 5th ed. Detroit: Gale, 2005.

Mancini, Susanna. "The Power of Symbols and the Symbols of Power: Secularism and Religion as Guarantors of Cultural Convergence," *Cardozo Law Review* 30 (2009): 2629–68.

Manderson, Desmond. *Just in Time: Law in the Visual Arts*. Cambridge: Cambridge University Press, forthcoming.

Manderson, Desmond. "The Metastases of Myth: Legal Images as Transitional Phenomena." *Law and Critique* 26 (2015): 207–23.

Manning, John. *The Emblem*. London: Reaktion, 2002.

March, Andrew F. "Are Secularism and Neutrality Attractive to Religious Minorities? Islamic Discussions of Western Secularism in the 'Jurisprudence of Muslim Minorities' (*Fiqh Al-Aqalliyyat*) Discourse." *Cardozo Law Review* 30 (2009): 2821–54.

Marcus, Sharon. *Between Women: Friendship, Desire, and Marriage in Victorian England*. Princeton, NJ: Princeton University Press, 2007.

Marmor, Andrei, ed. *Law and Interpretation: Essays in Legal Philosophy*. Oxford: Clarendon Press, 1995.

Maroney, Terry A. "Law and Emotion: A Proposed Taxonomy of an Emerging Field." *Law and Human Behavior* 30 (2006): 119–42.

Mason, Emma. "Religion, the Bible, and Literature in the Victorian Age." In *The Oxford Handbook of Victorian Literary Culture*, edited by Juliet John, 331–49. Oxford: Oxford University Press, 2016.

Massumi, Brian. *Parables for the Virtual: Movement, Affect, Sensation*. Durham, NC, and London: Duke University Press, 2002.

Mathis, Ayana. *The Twelve Tribes of Hattie*. New York: Alfred A. Knopf, 2012.

Mazzeo, Tilar J. *Plagiarism and Literary Property in the Romantic Period*. Philadelphia: University of Pennsylvania Press, 2006.

Mbembe, Achille. "Necropolitics." *Public Culture* 15, no. 1 (2003): 11–40.

McClain, Charles J. *In Search of Equality: The Chinese Struggle against Discrimination in Nineteenth-Century America*. Berkeley: University of California Press, 1994.

McCloskey, Donald N. "The Essential Rhetoric of Law, Literature, and Liberty." *Critical Review* 5, no. 2 (1991): 203–23.

McCluskey, Martha. "Thinking with Wolves: Left Legal Theory after the Right's Rise." *Buffalo Law Review* 54 (2007): 1191–297.

McCune, Jeffrey Q., Jr. *Sexual Discretion: Black Masculinity and the Politics of Passing*. Chicago: University of Chicago Press, 2014.

McGill, Meredith L. "Copyright and Intellectual Property: The State of the Discipline." *Book History* 16 (2013): 387–427.

McGurl, Mark. *The Program Era: Postwar Fiction and the Rise of Creative Writing*. Cambridge, MA: Harvard University Press, 2009.

McKenzie, Jon. *Perform or Else: From Discipline to Performance*. New York: Routledge, 2001.

McSweeney, Tom. "English Judges and Roman Jurists: The Civilian Learning behind England's First Case Law." *Temple Law Review* 84 (2012): 827–62.

McVeigh, Shaun, and Shaunnagh Dorsett, "Just So: The Law Which Governs Australia Is Australian Law." *Law and Critique* 13 (2002): 289–309.

Menestrier, François. *La Philosophie des images*. Paris: Robert de la Caille, 1683.

Meyer, Linda Ross. *The Justice of Mercy*. Ann Arbor: University of Michigan Press, 2010.

Meyer, Philip. *Storytelling for Lawyers*. Oxford: Oxford University Press, 2014.

Meyler, Bernadette. "Defoe and the Written Constitution." *Cornell Law Review* 94 (2008): 73–132.

Meyler, Bernadette. "Law, Literature, and History: The Love Triangle." *UC Irvine Law Review* 5 (2015): 365–91.

Meyler, Bernadette. "The Limits of Group Rights: Religious Institutions and Religious Minorities in International Law." *St. John's Journal of Legal Commentary* 22 (2007): 535–58.

Meyler, Bernadette. "'Our Cities Institutions' and the Institution of the Common Law." *Yale Journal of Law and the Humanities* 22 (2010): 441–66.

Meyler, Bernadette. "Towards a Common Law Originalism." *Stanford Law Review* 59 (2006): 551–600.

Mezey, Naomi. "Law as Culture." *Yale Journal of Law and the Humanities* 13 (2001): 35–68.

Miller, J. Hillis. *Topographies*. Stanford, CA: Stanford University Press, 1995.

Miller, William Ian. *The Anatomy of Disgust*. Cambridge, MA: Harvard University Press, 1997.

Mills, Charles. *The Racial Contract*. Ithaca, NY: Cornell University Press, 1997.

Minda, Gary. "Reflections." *Cardozo Law Review* 26 (2005): 2397–400.

Mnookin, Jennifer L., et al. "The Need for a Research Culture in the Forensic Sciences." *UCLA Law Review* 58 (2011): 725–80.

Moddelmog, William. *Reconstituting Authority: American Fiction in the Province of the Law, 1880–1920*. Iowa City: University of Iowa Press, 2000.

Modern Poland Foundation. *The Future of Copyright*. Warsaw: Modern Poland Foundation, 2012.

Modern Poland Foundation. *The Future of Copyright 2.0*. Warsaw: Modern Poland Foundation, 2013.

Moon, Michael. *A Small Boy and Others: Imitation and Initiation in American Culture from Henry James to Andy Warhol*. Durham, NC: Duke University Press, 1998.

Moore, Gene M. "Faulkner's Incorrect 'Indians'?" *Faulkner Journal* 18 (Fall 2002–Spring 2003): 3–8.

Morawetz, Thomas. "Empathy and Judgment." *Yale Journal of Law and the Humanities* 8 (1996): 517–31.

Moretti, Franco. *Distant Reading*. London: Verso, 2013.

Morowitz, Harold. "Is High Court Blind to Life?" *Chicago Tribune*, June 27, 1980, d3.

Morowitz, Harold. "Reducing Life to Physics." *New York Times*, June 23, 1980, A23.

Morrison, Toni. *Beloved: A Novel*. New York: Knopf, 1987.

Morrison, Toni. *Song of Solomon*. New York: Vintage, 2004.

Mouffe, Chantal. "Religion, Liberal Democracy, and Citizenship." In *Political Theologies: Public Religions in a Post-Secular World*, edited by Hent de Vries and Lawrence E. Sullivan, 318–26. New York: Fordham University Press, 2006.

Mosher, Donald L., and Silvan S. Tomkins. "Scripting the Macho Man: Hypermasculine Socialization and Enculturation." *Journal of Sex Research* 25, no. 1 (Feb. 1988): 60–84.

Moy, James S. *Marginal Sights: Staging the Chinese in America*. Iowa City: University of Iowa Press, 1993.

Mumford, Kevin. *Interzones: Black/White Sex Districts in Chicago and New York in the Early Twentieth Century*. New York: Columbia University Press, 1997.

Muñoz, José Esteban. *Cruising Utopia: The Then and There of Queer Futurity*. New York: New York University Press, 2009.

Neill, Michael. "'In Everything Illegitimate': Imagining the Bastard in Renaissance Drama." *Yearbook of English Studies* 23 (1993): 270–92.

Nelson, Deborah. *Pursuing Privacy in Cold War America*. New York: Columbia University Press, 2002.

Neuman, Justin. *Fiction beyond Secularism*. Evanston, IL: Northwestern University Press, 2014.

Newes from Scotland. London: William Wright, 1591?.

Newhoff, David. "Don't Blame Disposability on Copyright: Part II." *The Illusion of More: Dissecting the Digital Utopia*, November 13, 2015. http://illusionofmore.com/dont-blame-disposability-on-copyright-part-ii.

Ngai, Mae M. *Impossible Subjects: Illegal Aliens and the Making of Modern America*. Princeton, NJ: Princeton University Press, 2014.

Ngai, Sianne. *Ugly Feelings*. Cambridge, MA, and London: Harvard University Press, 2005.

Nichols, John Bowyer. *Illustrations of the Literary History of the Eighteenth Century*. Vol. 7. London: J. G. Nichols and Son, 1848.

Nietzsche, Friedrich. *Writings from the Late Notebooks*. Edited by Rudiger Bittner. Cambridge: Cambridge University Press, 1982.

Noonan, John T., Jr. *Persons and Masks of the Law: Cardozo, Holmes, Jefferson, and Wythe as Makers of the Masks*. Berkeley: University of California Press, 2002.

Normand, Lawrence, and Gareth Roberts, eds. "News from Scotland." In *Witchcraft in Early Modern Scotland: James VI's Demonology and the North Berwick Witches*. Exeter: University of Exeter Press, 2000.

Nugent, Tom. "Engineering Life: Boon or Nightmare?" *Baltimore Sun*, July 13, 1980, K1.

Nussbaum, Martha C. *Cultivating Humanity: A Classical Defense of Reform in Liberal Education*. Cambridge, MA: Harvard University Press, 1997.

Nussbaum, Martha C. *From Disgust to Humanity: Sexual Orientation and Constitutional Law*. New York: Oxford University Press, 2010.

Nussbaum, Martha C. *Hiding from Humanity: Disgust, Shame, and the Law*. Princeton, NJ, and Oxford: Princeton University Press, 2004.

Nussbaum, Martha C. *Love's Knowledge: Essays on Philosophy and Literature*. New York: Oxford University Press, 1990.

Nussbaum, Martha C. "Narratives of Hierarchy: *Loving v. Virginia* and the Literary Imagination." *Quinnipiac Law Review* 17 (1997): 337–55.

Nussbaum, Martha C. *Poetic Justice: The Literary Imagination and Public Life*. Boston: Beacon, 1995.

Nussbaum, Martha C. *Upheavals of Thought: The Intelligence of the Emotions*. Cambridge: Cambridge University Press, 2001.

Nussbaum, Martha C., and Alison L. LaCroix. "Introduction." In *Subversion and Sympathy: Gender, Law and the British Novel*, edited by Martha C. Nussbaum and Alison L. Lacroix, 3–26. New York: Oxford University Press, 2013.

NYU Tisch School of the Arts. *Institute of Performing Arts Performance Studies B.A. M.A. Ph.D. Programs*. http://www.flipsnack.com/NYUPerformanceStudies/department-of-performance-studies-brochure.html.

Office of National Drug Control Policy. "Alternatives to Incarceration." https://www.whitehouse.gov/ondcp/alternatives-to-incarceration.

Ogden, C. K. *Bentham's Theory of Fictions*. Paterson, NJ: Littlefield, Adams, 1959.

Olivares, Kathleen M., Velmer S. Burton Jr., and Francis T. Cullen. "The Collateral Consequences of a Felony Conviction: A National Study of State Legal Codes 10 Years Later." *Federal Probation* 60, no. 3 (1996): 10–17.

Olivier, Piere J. J. *Legal Fictions in Practice and Legal Science*. Rotterdam: Rotterdam University Press, 1975.

Olson, Greta. "De-Americanizing Law and Literature Narratives: Opening up the Story." *Law and Literature* 22 (2010): 338–64.

Olson, Greta. "Narration and Narrative in Legal Discourse." In *The Living Handbook of Narratology*, edited by Peter Hühn, et al., 371–83. Hamburg: Hamburg University Press, 2014.

Orford, Anne. *International Authority and the Responsibility to Protect*. Cambridge: Cambridge University Press, 2011.

Palmer, Alan. *Fictional Minds*. Lincoln: University of Nebraska Press, 2004.

Panciroli, Guido. *Notitia utraque dignitatum iuris*. Gabiano, 1618.

Papke, David R. "Law and Literature: A Comment and Bibliography of Secondary Works." *Law Library Journal* 73 (1980): 421–37.

Pardo, Michael S. "Juridical Proof, Evidence, and Pragmatic Meaning: Toward Evidentiary Holism." *Northwestern University Law Review* 95 (2000): 399–442.

Parker, Robert Dale. "Red Slippers and Cottonmouth Moccasins: White Anxieties in Faulkner's Indian Stories." *Faulkner Journal* 18 (Fall 2002–Spring 2003): 81–100.

Pateman, Carole. *The Sexual Contract*. Stanford, CA: Stanford University Press, 1988.

Patterson, Orlando. *Slavery and Social Death: A Comparative Study*. Cambridge, MA: Harvard University Press, 1982.

Paul, Kathleen. *Whitewashing Britain: Race and Citizenship in the Postwar Era*. Ithaca, NY: Cornell University Press, 2014.

Payne, Alina. *From Ornament to Object: Genealogies of Architectural Modernism*. New Haven, CT: Yale University Press, 2012.

Peacham, Henry. *Embelemata varia* [ca. 1621]. Ilkley: Scolar, 1976.

Peirce, Charles Sanders. "Three Types of Reasoning." In *Collected Papers of Charles Sanders Peirce*, edited by Charles Hartshone and Paul Weiss, vols. 5–6, 94–111. Cambridge, MA: Harvard University Press, 1965.

Peiss, Kathy, and Christina Simmons, eds. *Passion and Power: Sexuality in History*. Philadelphia, PA: Temple University Press, 1989.

Pennington, Nancy, and Reid Hastie, "A Cognitive Model of Juror Decision Making: The Story Model." *Cardozo Law Review* 13 (1991): 519–58.

Perlmutt, David. "Stamp Honors Black Author with N.C. Roots." *News & Observer* (Raleigh, NC), October 7, 2007, B3.

Persily, Nathaniel, Gillian E. Metzger, and Trevor Morrison, eds. *The Health Care Case: The Supreme Court's Decision and Its Implications*. Oxford: Oxford University Press, 2013.

Peters, Julie Stone. "Law, Literature, and the Vanishing Real: On the Future of an Interdisciplinary Illusion." *PMLA* 120 (2005): 442–53.

Peters, Julie Stone. "Legal Performance Good and Bad." *Law, Culture and the Humanities* 4 (2008): 179–200.

Peters, Julie Stone. "'Literature,' the 'Rights of Man,' and Narratives of Atrocity: Historical Backgrounds to the Culture of Testimony." *Yale Journal of Law and the Humanities* 17, no. 2 (2005): 253–83.

Pether, Penelope. Review of *Law and Literature*, by Richard A. Posner. *Comparative Critical Studies* 7 (2010): 418–22.

Pevar, Stephen L. *The Rights of Indians and Tribes*. 3rd ed. Carbondale: Southern Illinois University Press, 2002.

Phelan, Peggy. *Unmarked: The Politics of Performance*. New York: Routledge, 1993.

Phelps, Teresa Godwin. "'Reading As If for Life': Law and Literature is More Important than Ever." In "Law and Literature Reconsidered," edited by Austin Sarat. Special issue, *Studies in Law, Politics and Society* 43 (2008): 133–52.

Philip, M. NourbeSe. *Zong!* Middletown, CT: Wesleyan University Press, 2008.

Plutarch. *Plutarch's Lives*. Edited by Arthur Hugh Clough, translated by John Dryden. 2 vols. New York: Random House, 2001.

Plutarch. *Plutarch's Lives of the Noble Grecians and Romans, Englished by Sir Thomas North* [1579]. London: David Nutt, 1895.

Pocock, J. G. A. *The Ancient Constitution and the Feudal Law: A Study of English Historical Thought in the Seventeenth Century*. New York: Cambridge University Press, 1987.

Pocock, J. G. A. *The Machiavellian Moment: Florentine Political Thought and the Atlantic Republican Tradition*. Princeton, NJ: Princeton University Press, 2003.

Polikoff, Nancy D. "Why Lesbians and Gay Men Should Read Martha Fineman." *American University Journal of Gender, Social Policy, and the Law* 8 (2000): 167–76.

Pollock, Frederick, and Frederic William Maitland. *The History of English Law before the Time of Edward I*. 2nd ed. London: Cambridge University Press, 1911.

Polloczek, Dieter Paul. *Literature and Legal Discourse: Equity and Ethics from Sterne to Conrad*. Cambridge: Cambridge University Press, 1999.

Poovey, Mary. *Making a Social Body: British Cultural Formation, 1830–1864.* Chicago: University of Chicago Press, 1995.

Pope, Alexander. *Essay on Man*, 6th edition, edited by Mark Pattison. London: Oxford Clarendon Press, 1881. First published in 1734.

Porsdam, Helle. *Legally Speaking: Contemporary American Culture and the Law.* Amherst: University of Massachusetts Press, 1999.

Post, Robert, and Reva Siegel. "Democratic Constitutionalism." In *The Constitution in 2020*, edited by Jack M. Balkin and Reva B. Siegel, 25–35. New York: Oxford University Press, 2009.

Porter, Carolyn. "History and Literature: 'After the New Historicism.'" *New Literary History* 21 (1990): 253–72.

Porter, Elizabeth. "Taking Images Seriously." *Columbia Law Review* 114 (2014): 1687–1782.

Porter, Rachel, Sophia Lee, and Mary Lutz. *Balancing Punishment and Treatment: Alternatives to Incarceration in New York City.* New York: Vera Institute of Justice, 2002.

Posner, Richard A. "Against Ethical Criticism." *Philosophy and Literature* 21 (1997): 1–27.

Posner, Richard A. "Judicial Opinions and Appellate Advocacy in Federal Courts: One Judge's Views." *Duquesne Law Review* 51 (2013): 3–40.

Posner, Richard A. *Law and Literature.* 3rd ed. Cambridge, MA: Harvard University Press, 2009.

Posner, Richard A. *Law and Literature: A Misunderstood Relation.* Cambridge, MA: Harvard University Press, 1998.

Posner, Richard A. "Law and Literature: A Relation Reargued." *Virginia Law Review* 72 (1986): 1351–92.

Prendergast, Christopher. *The Order of Mimesis: Balzac, Stendhal, Nerval, Flaubert.* Cambridge: Cambridge University Press, 1986.

Prentice, Deborah A., Richard J. Gerrig, and Daniel S. Bailis. "What Readers Bring to the Processing of Fictional Texts." *Psychonomic Bulletin and Review* 4 (1997): 416–420.

Prucha, Francis Paul, ed. *Documents of United States Indian Policy.* 3rd ed. Lincoln: University of Nebraska Press, 2000.

Quintilian. *Institutio oratoria.* Translated by Donald A. Russell. Cambridge, MA: Harvard University Press, 2001.

Rainie, Lee, and Barry Wellman. *Networked: The New Social Operating System.* Cambridge, MA: MIT Press, 2012.

Rancière, Jacques. *The Emancipated Spectator.* New York: Verso, 2009.

Rasmussen, Bridget Brander. *Queequeg's Coffin: Indigenous Literacies and Early American Literature.* Durham, NC: Duke University Press, 2012.

Raz, Joseph. *Between Authority and Interpretation: On the Theory of Law and Practical Reason.* Oxford: Oxford University Press, 2009.

Reichman, Ravit. *The Affective Life of Law: Legal Modernism and the Literary Imagination.* Stanford, CA: Stanford University Press, 2009.

Read, Alan. *Theatre and Law.* London: Palgrave Macmillan, 2015

Reid, John Phillip. *The Ancient Constitution and the Origins of Anglo-American Liberty.* DeKalb: Northern Illinois University Press, 2005.

Reid, John Phillip. "Law and History." *Loyola of Los Angeles Law Review* 27 (1993): 193–224.

Reiss, Timothy J. *The Meaning of Literature.* Ithaca, NY: Cornell University Press, 1992.

Resnik, Judith, and Dennis Curtis. *Representing Justice: Invention, Controversy, and Rights in City-States and Democratic Courtrooms*. New Haven, CT: Yale University Press, 2011.

Ricoeur, Paul. *Freud and Philosophy: An Essay on Interpretation*. Translated by Denis Savage. New Haven, CT: Yale University Press, 1970.

Riles, Annelise. "Is the Law Hopeful?" In *The Economy of Hope*, edited by Hiro Miyazaki and Richard Swedberg, 126–46. Philadelphia: University of Pennsylvania Press, 2017.

Rilke, Rainer Maria. *On Love and Other Difficulties*. Translated by John J. L. Mood. New York: Norton, 1975.

Ripa, Cesar. "To the Reader." In *Iconologia: or, Moral Emblems*, edited by P. Tempest. London: Motte, 1709.

Ripken, Susanna K. "Corporations Are People Too: A Multi-Dimensional Approach to the Corporate Personhood Puzzle." *Fordham Journal of Corporate and Financial Law* 15 (2009): 97–177.

Roach, Joseph. "Celebrity Erotics: Pepys, Performance, and Painted Ladies." *Yale Journal of Criticism* 16 (2003): 211–30.

Roach, Joseph. *Cities of the Dead: Circum-Atlantic Performance*. New York: Columbia University Press, 1996.

Robertson, Lindsay G. *Conquest by Law: How the Discovery of America Dispossessed Indigenous Peoples of Their Lands*. New York: Oxford University Press, 2005.

Robinson, Spider. "Melancholy Elephants" (1982). Reprinted in *Melancholy Elephants*. New York: Tor, 1985.

Rodensky, Lisa. *The Crime in Mind: Criminal Responsibility and the Victorian Novel*. Oxford: Oxford University Press, 2003.

Rogers, Michael. "The Double-Edged Helix." *Rolling Stone*, March 21, 1976, 48–51.

Rorty, Richard. *Contingency, Irony, and Solidarity*. Cambridge: Cambridge University Press, 1989.

Rose, Mark. *Authors and Owners: The Invention of Copyright*. Cambridge, MA: Harvard University Press, 1993.

Rosen, Rebecca J. "The Hole in Our Collective Memory: How Copyright Made Mid-Century Books Vanish." *Atlantic Monthly*, July 30, 2013.

Rowley, Hazel. *Tête-à-Tête: Simone de Beauvoir and Jean-Paul Sartre*. New York: HarperCollins, 2005.

Ryan, Marie-Laure. "Cheap Plot Tricks, Plot Holes, and Narrative Design." *Narrative* 17 (2009): 56–75.

Sackville, Thomas, and Thomas Norton. *Gorboduc, or Ferrex and Porrex*. In *Drama of the English Renaissance*, vol. 1, edited by Russell A. Fraser and Norman Rabkin, 81–100. Upper Saddle River, NJ: Prentice Hall, 1976.

Saint-Amour, Paul K. *The Copywrights: Intellectual Property and the Literary Imagination*. Ithaca, NY: Cornell University Press, 2003.

Saint-Amour, Paul K., ed. *Modernism and Copyright*. New York: Oxford University Press, 2011.

Samuel, Geoffrey. "Is Law a Fiction?" In *Legal Fictions in Theory and Practice*, edited by Maksymilian Del Mar and William Twining, 31–54. Cham: Springer International, 2015.

Sanger, Carol. "A Case for Civil Marriage." *Cardozo Law Review* 27 (2006): 1311–23.

Sarat, Austin, ed. *The Blackwell Companion to Law and Society*. Oxford: Blackwell, 2004.

Sarat, Austin. *Gruesome Spectacles: Botched Executions and America's Death Penalty*. Stanford, CA: Stanford University Press, 2014.

Sarat, Austin, Matthew Anderson, and Cathrine O. Frank, eds. *Law and the Humanities: An Introduction.* Cambridge: Cambridge: University Press, 2010.

Sarat, Austin, Cathrine O. Frank, and Matthew Anderson, eds. *Teaching Law and Literature.* New York: Modern Language Association, 2011.

Sartre, Jean-Paul. *La Nausée.* Paris: Gallimard, 1947.

Sayre, Robert Woods. "Faulkner's Indians and the Romantic Vision." *Faulker Journal* 18 (Fall 2002–Spring 2003): 33–49.

Scalia, Antonin. *A Matter of Interpretation: Federal Courts and the Law.* Princeton, NJ: Princeton University Press, 1998.

Schaffer, Kay, and Sidonie Smith. *Human Rights and Narrated Lives: The Ethics of Recognition.* New York: Palgrave Macmillan, 2004.

Schechner, Richard. *Performance Studies: An Introduction.* 3rd ed. New York: Routledge, 2013.

Schechner, Richard. "Restoration of Behavior." In *Between Theater and Anthropology,* 35–116. Philadelphia: University of Pennsylvania Press, 1985.

Schlag, Pierre. *The Enchantment of Reason.* Durham, NC, and London: Duke University Press, 1998.

Schleiermacher, Frierich. *Hermeneutics and Criticism and Other Writings.* Edited and translated by Andrew Bowie. Cambridge: Cambridge University Press, 1998.

Schmidgen, Wolfram. *Eighteenth-Century Fiction and the Law of Property.* Cambridge: Cambridge University Press, 2002.

Schneck, Peter. "*Wieland*'s Testimony: Charles Brockden Brown and the Rhetoric of Evidence." In *Law and Literature,* edited by Brook Thomas, 167–213. REAL Yearbook 18. Tübingen: Gunter Narr, 2002.

Schor, Hilary M. "Show-Trials, Character, Conviction, and the Law in Victorian Fiction." *Cardozo Studies in Law and Literature* 11 (1999): 179–95.

Schor, Naomi. *Reading in Detail: Aesthetic and the Feminine.* New York: Routledge, 2007.

Scott, Elizabeth S. "A World without Marriage." *Family Law Quarterly* 41 (2007): 537–66.

Scott, Joan Wallach. *The Politics of the Veil.* Princeton, NJ: Princeton University Press, 2007.

Scott, Ridley, director. *Blade Runner.* Burbank, CA: Warner Home Video, 2007. DVD.

Seaton, James. "Law and Literature: Works, Criticism, and Theory." *Yale Journal of Law and the Humanities* 11 (1999): 479–508.

Sedgwick, Eve Kosofsky. *Epistemology of the Closet.* Berkeley: University of California Press, 2008.

Sedgwick, Eve Kosofsky. *Novel Gazing: Queer Readings in Fiction.* Durham, NC: Duke University Press, 1997.

Sedgwick, Eve Kosofsky. *Tendencies.* Durham, NC: Duke University Press, 1993.

Sedgwick, Eve Kosofsky. "Thinking through Queer Theory." In *The Weather in Proust,* edited by Jonathan Goldberg, 190–205. Durham, NC: Duke University Press, 2011.

Sedgwick, Eve Kosofsky. *Touching Feeling: Affect, Pedagogy, Performativity.* Durham, NC: Duke University Press, 2003.

Sedgwick, Eve Kosofsky. *The Weather in Proust,* edited by Jonathan Goldberg. Durham, NC: Duke University Press, 2011.

Sedgwick, Eve Kosofsky, and Adam Frank, eds. *Shame and Its Sisters: A Silvan Tomkins Reader.* Durham, NC: Duke University Press, 1995.

Sedgwick, Eve Kosofsky, and Adam Frank. "Shame in the Cybernetic Fold: Reading Silvan Tomkins." *Critical Inquiry* 21 (1995): 496–522.

Segal, David. "Law School Economics: Ka-Ching!" *New York Times*, July 16, 2011: BU 1.

Selbourne, David. *The Making of "A Midsummer Night's Dream."* London: Faber and Faber, 2010.

Shakespeare, William. *Hamlet*. Edited by Harold Jenkins. London: Arden, 1982.

Shakespeare, William. *Henry V*. Edited by T. W. Craik. London: Bloomsbury Arden, 1995.

Shakespeare, William. *A Midsummer Night's Dream*. Edited by Peter Holland. Oxford: Oxford University Press, 1994.

Shakespeare, William. *The Winter's Tale*. Edited by J. H. P. Pafford. London: Arden, 2006.

Shanley, Mary Lyndon. "Afterword." In *Just Marriage*, edited by Joshua Cohen and Deborah Chasman, 109–16. New York: Oxford University Press, 2004.

Sherman, Brad, and Lionel Bently. "Balance and Harmony in the Duration of Copyright: The European Directive and Its Consequences." In *Textual Monopolies: Literary Copyright and the Public Domain*, edited by Patrick Parrinder and Warren Chernaik, 15–37. London: Office for Humanities Publication, 1997.

Sherwin, Richard K. *Visualizing Law in the Age of the Digital Baroque: Arabesques and Entanglements*. London: Routledge, 2011.

Sidney, Philip. *An Apology for Poetry (or the Defence of Poesy)*. Edited by Geoffrey Shepherd, revised by R. W. Maslen. Manchester: Manchester University Press, 2002.

Siegel, Reva B. "Text in Contest: Gender and the Constitution from a Social Movement Perspective." *University of Pennsylvania Law Review* 150 (2001): 297–352.

Silbey, Susan. "Making a Place for a Cultural Analysis of Law." *Law and Social Inquiry* 17 (1992): 39–48.

Siraganian, Lisa. "Theorizing Corporate Intentionality in Contemporary American Fiction." *Law and Literature* 27 (2015): 99–123.

Sir Clyomon and Sir Clamydes (1599), edited by W. W. Greg. London: Malone Society Reprints, 1913.

Skinner, Quentin. *Forensic Shakespeare*. Oxford: Oxford University Press, 2014.

Slaughter, Joseph R. *Human Rights, Inc.: The World Novel, Narrative Form, and International Law*. New York: Fordham University Press, 2007.

Slaughter, Joseph R. "'It's Good to Be Primitive': African Allusion and the Modernist Fetish of Authenticity." In *Modernism and Copyright*, edited by Paul K. Saint-Amour, 275–301. New York: Oxford University Press, 2011.

Slaughter, Joseph R. "World Literature as Property." *Alif: Journal of Comparative Poetics* 34 (2014): 39–73.

Slauter, Eric. "History, Literature, and the Atlantic World." *Early American Literature* 43 (2008): 153–86.

Slauter, Eric. "History, Literature, and the Atlantic World." *William and Mary Quarterly* 65 (2008): 135–66.

Slauter, Eric. *The State as a Work of Art: The Cultural Origins of the Constitution*. Chicago: University of Chicago Press, 2011.

Slovic, Paul. "What's Fear Got to Do with It—It's Affect We Need to Worry About." *Missouri Law Review* 69 (2004): 971–90.

Smith, Caleb. "Detention without Subjects: Prisons and the Poetics of Living Death." *Texas Studies in Literature and Language* 50 (2008): 243–67.

Smith, Caleb. *The Oracle and the Curse: A Poetics of Justice from the Revolution to the Civil War*. Cambridge, MA: Harvard University Press, 2013.

Smith, Peter J. "New Legal Fictions." *Georgetown Law Journal* 95 (2007): 1435–95.

Soifer, Aviam. *Law and the Company We Keep*. Cambridge, MA: Harvard University Press, 1995.

Spillers, Hortense J. "Mama's Baby, Papa's Maybe: An American Grammar Book." In "Culture and Countermemory: The 'American' Connection," *Diacritics* 17, no. 2 (1987): 64–81.

Spivak, Gayatri Chakravorty. *An Aesthetic Education in the Era of Globalization*. Cambridge, MA: Harvard University Press, 2012.

Spivak, Gayatri Chakravorty. "Righting Wrongs." *South Atlantic Quarterly* 103, nos. 2–3 (2004): 523–81.

Spoo, Robert. "Ezra Pound's Copyright Statute: Perpetual Rights and the Problem of Heirs." *UCLA Law Review* 56 (2009): 1775–1834.

Spoo, Robert. "Three Myths for Aging Copyrights: Tithonus, Dorian Gray, Ulysses." *Cardozo Arts and Entertainment Law Journal* 31 (2012): 77–111.

Spoo, Robert. *Without Copyrights: Piracy, Publishing, and the Public Domain*. New York: Oxford University Press, 2013.

Stacey, Robin Chapman. *Dark Speech: The Performance of Law in Early Ireland*. Philadelphia: University of Pennsylvania Press, 2007.

Stanley, Amy Dru. *From Bondage to Contract: Wage Labor, Marriage, and the Market in the Age of Slave Emancipation*. Cambridge: Cambridge University Press, 1998.

Staves, Susan. *Married Women's Separate Property in England, 1660–1833*. Cambridge, MA: Harvard University Press, 1990.

Steiner, Emily, and Candace Barrington, eds. *The Letter of the Law: Legal Practice and Literary Production in Medieval England*. Ithaca, NY: Cornell University Press, 2002.

Stern, Simon. "From Author's Right to Property Right." *University of Toronto Law Journal* 62 (2012): 29–91.

Stern, Simon. "Legal Fictions and Exclusionary Rules." In *Legal Fictions in Theory and Practice*, edited by Maksymilian Del Mar and William Twining, 157–73. Cham: Springer International, 2015.

Stern, Simon. "The Third-Party Doctrine and the Third Person." *New Criminal Law Review* 16 (2013): 364–412.

Stewart, George. *Earth Abides*. New York: Random House, 1949.

Stewart, Kathleen. *Ordinary Affects*. Durham, NC: Duke University Press, 2007.

Stock, Kathleen. "Resisting Imaginative Resistance." *Philosophical Quarterly* 55 (2005): 607–24.

Stone, Geoffrey R. "If America Only Had One Mixed Race." *Chicago Tribune*, March 30, 1999.

Story, Joseph. "Value and Importance of Legal Studies." In *The Miscellaneous Writings of Joseph Story*, edited by William W. Story, 503–48. Boston: Little, Brown, 1852.

Stowe, Harriet Beecher. *Uncle Tom's Cabin*. Edited by Elizabeth Ammons. New York: Norton Critical, 1994.

Stryk, Lucien, ed. *Bird of Time: Haiku of Basho*. Translated by Lucien Stryk. Vermilion, SD: Flatlands, 1983.

Stryk, Lucien, ed. *World of the Buddha: An Introduction to Buddhist Literature*. Garden City, NY: Doubleday, 1968.

Stryk, Lucien, and Takashi Ikemoto, eds. *The Penguin Book of Zen Poetry*. Chicago: Swallow, 1977.

Stryk, Lucien, and Takashi Ikemoto, eds. *Zen Poems of China and Japan: The Crane's Bill*. Garden City, NY: Grove, 1973.

Suggs, Jon-Christian. *Whispered Consolations: Law and Narrative in African American Life*. Ann Arbor: University of Michigan Press, 2000.

Suk, Jeannie. *At Home in the Law: How the Domestic Violence Revolution Is Transforming Privacy*. New Haven, CT: Yale University Press, 2009.

Suk, Jeannie. "The Look in His Eyes." In *Criminal Law Stories*, edited by Donna K. Coker and Robert Weisberg, 171–211. New York: Foundation Press, 2012.

Sullivan, Kathleen, and Noah Feldman. *Constitutional Law*. 18th ed. St. Paul, MN: Foundation Press, 2013.

Sullivan, Kathleen, and Gerald Gunther. *Constitutional Law*. 17th ed. New York: Foundation Press, 2010

Sunstein, Cass R. "The Right to Marry." *Cardozo Law Review* 26 (2005): 2081–120.

Sunstein, Cass R., and Richard H. Thaler. "Libertarian Paternalism Is Not an Oxymoron." *University of Chicago Law Review* 70 (2003): 1159–202.

Sutton, Jeffrey S. "The Role of History in Judging Disputes About the Meaning of the Constitution." *Texas Tech Law Review* 41 (2009): 1173–92.

Syme, Holger Schott. "(Mis)representing Justice on the Early Modern Stage." *Studies in Philology* 109, no. 1 (2012): 63–85.

Takahashi, Shinkichi. *Triumph of the Sparrow: Zen Poems of Shinkichi Takahashi*. Translated by Lucien Stryk and Takashi Ikemoto. Urbana: University of Illinois Press, 1986.

Takaki, Ronald. *Strangers from a Different Shore: A History of Asian Americans*. Revised and updated ed. New York: Little, Brown, 1989.

Taylor, Diana. *The Archive and the Repertoire: Performing Cultural Memory in the Americas*. Durham, NC: Duke University Press, 2007.

Taylor, John. *Mad Fashions, Od Fashions, All out of Fashions, or, the Emblems of These Distracted Times*. London: John Hammond, 1642.

Tchen, John Kuo Wei, and Dylan Yeats, eds. *Yellow Peril! An Archive of Anti-Asian Fear*. New York: Verso, 2014.

Thomas, Brook. *American Literary Realism and the Failed Promise of Contract*. Berkeley: University of California Press, 1997.

Thomas, Brook. *Civic Myths: A Law-and-Literature Approach to Citizenship*. Chapel Hill: University of North Carolina Press, 2007.

Thomas, Brook. *Cross-Examinations of Law and Literature: Cooper, Hawthorne, Stowe, and Melville*. Cambridge: Cambridge University Press, 1987.

Thomas, Brook. "Reflections on the Law and Literature Revival." *Critical Inquiry* 17 (1991): 510–39.

Thomas, Yan. "*Fictio Legis*: L'empire de la fiction romaine et ses limites médiévales." *Droits* 21 (1995): 17–63.

Toffler, Alvin. "What is Human Now?" *Christian Science Monitor*, June 4, 1987, 20–22.

Tomlins, Christopher L. "After Critical Legal History: Scope, Scale, Structure." *Annual Review of Law and Social Sciences* 8 (2012): 31–68.

Tomlins, Christopher L. "What Is Left of the Law and Society Paradigm after Critique? Revisiting Gordon's 'Critical Legal Histories.'" *Law and Social Inquiry* 37 (2012): 155–66.

Tomlins, Christopher L., and John Comaroff. "'Law As . . .': Theory and Practice in Legal History." *UC Irvine Law Review* 1 (2011): 1039–80.

Tomlins, Christopher L., and Bruce H. Mann eds., *The Many Legalities of Early America*. Chapel Hill: University of North Carolina Press, 2001.

Turner, Henry. *The Corporate Commonwealth: Pluralism and Political Fictions in England, 1516–1651*. Chicago: University of Chicago Press, 2016.

Tushnet, Rebecca. "Worth a Thousand Words: The Images of Copyright." *Harvard Law Review* 125 (2012): 683–759.

Tversky, Amos, and Daniel Kahneman. "The Framing of Decisions and the Psychology of Choice." *Science* 211 (1981): 453–58.

Tyler, Tom R. "Viewing *CSI* and the Threshold of Guilt: Managing Truth and Justice in Reality and Fiction." *Yale Law Journal* 115 (2006): 1050–85.

US Central Intelligence Agency. *The World Factbook: 2013–14*. Washington, DC: US Central Intelligence Agency, 2014.

Usner, Daniel H., Jr. "American Indians on the Cotton Frontier: Changing Economic Relations with Citizens and Slaves in the Mississippi Territory." *Journal of American History* 72 (1985): 297–317.

Vaidhyanathan, Siva. *Copyrights and Copywrongs: The Rise of Intellectual Property and How It Threatens Creativity*. New York: New York University Press, 2001.

Vaihinger, Hans. *Die Philosophie des Als Ob*. 4th ed. Leipzig: F. Meiner, 1920.

Valeriano, Piero. *Hieroglyphica sive de sacris Aegyptiorum literis commentarii*. Basel: n.p., 1556.

Vanderham, Paul. *James Joyce and Censorship: The Trials of Ulysses*. Houndsmills: Macmillan, 1998.

Vardoulakis, Dmitris. "The Subject of History." In *Walter Benjamin and History*, edited by Andrew Benjamin. New York: Continuum, 2005.

Vaughn, Diane. "The Dark Side of Organizations: Mistake, Misconduct, and Disaster." *Annual Review of Sociology* 25 (1999): 271–305.

Visconsi, Elliott. *Lines of Equity: Literature and the Origins of Law in Later Stuart England*. Ithaca, NY: Cornell University Press, 2008.

Vizenor, Gerald, *Empty Swings*. Minneapolis, MN: Nodin, 1967.

Vizenor, Gerald. *Favor of Crows: New and Collected Haiku*. Middletown, CT: Wesleyan University Press, 2014.

Vizenor, Gerald. *Hiroshima Bugi: Atomu 57*. Lincoln: University of Nebraska Press, 2003.

Vizenor, Gerald. *Matsushima: Pine Islands Collected Haiku*. Minneapolis, MN: Nodin, 1984.

Vizenor, Gerald. *Raising the Moon Vines*. Minneapolis, MN: Nodin, 1964.

Vizenor, Gerald. *Survivance: Narratives of Native Presence*. Lincoln: University of Nebraska Press, 2008.

Wald, Priscilla. "Cells, Genes, and Stories: HeLa's Journey from Labs to Literature." In *Genetics and the Unsettled Past: The Collision f Race, DNA and History*, edited by Keith Wailoo, Alondra Nelson, and Catherine Lee, 247–65. New Brunswick, NJ: Rutgers University Press, 2012.

Wald, Priscilla. "What's in a Cell? John Moore's Spleen and the Language of Bioslavery." In "Essays Probing the Boundaries of the Human in Science and Science Fiction." Special issue, *New Literary History* 36, no. 2 (2005): 205–25.

Walkowitz, Rebecca L. *Born Translated: The Contemporary Novel in the Age of World Literature*. New York: Columbia University Press, 2015.

Ward, Ian. *Law and Literature: Possibilities and Perspectives*. Cambridge: Cambridge University Press, 1995.

Warner, William B. *Licensing Entertainment: The Elevation of Novel Reading in Britain, 1684–1750*. Berkeley: University of California Press, 1998.

Watt, Gary. *Dress, Law and Naked Truth: A Cultural Study of Fashion and Form.* London: Bloomsbury Academy, 2013.

Webster, Noah. *An American Dictionary of the English Language.* Vol. 2. New York: S. Converse, 1828.

Weheliye, Alexander G. *Habeas Viscus: Racializing Assemblages, Biopolitics, and Black Feminist Theories of the Human.* Durham, NC: Duke University Press, 2014.

Weil, Patrick. "Why the French Laïcité Is Liberal." *Cardozo Law Review* 30 (2009): 2699–2714.

Weimann, Robert. *Shakespeare and the Popular Tradition in the Theater: Studies in the Social Dimension of Dramatic Form and Function.* Translated by Robert Schwartz. Baltimore, MD: Johns Hopkins University Press, 1987.

Weisberg, Richard. *The Failure of the Word: The Protagonist as Lawyer in Modern Fiction.* New Haven, CT: Yale University Press, 1984.

Weisberg, Richard. *Poethics: And Other Strategies of Law and Literature.* New York: Columbia University Press, 1992.

Weisberg, Richard. "Wigmore and the Law and Literature Movement." *Law and Literature* 21 (2009): 129–45.

Weisberg, Richard. "Wigmore's 'Legal Novels' Revisited: New Resources for the Expansive Lawyer." *Northwestern Law Review* 71 (1976): 17–28.

Weisberg, Richard, and Jean-Pierre Barricelli. "Literature and Law." In *Interrelations of Literature,* edited by Jean-Pierre Barricelli and Joseph Gibaldi, 150–75. New York: Modern Language Association of America, 1982.

Weisberg, Robert. "Law, Literature, and Cultural Unity: Between Celebration and Lament." In *Teaching Law and Literature,* edited by Austin Sarat, Cathrine O. Frank, and Matthew Anderson, 86–97. New York: Modern Language Association, 2011.

Weisberg, Robert. "The Law-Literature Enterprise." *Yale Journal of Law and the Humanities* 1 (1988): 1–67.

Wells, Samuel J., and Roseanna Tubby, eds. *After Removal: The Choctaw in Mississippi.* Jackson: University of Mississippi Press, 1986.

Welsh, Alexander. *Strong Representations: Narrative and Circumstantial Evidence.* Baltimore, MD: Johns Hopkins University Press, 1991.

West, Robin. *Caring for Justice.* New York: New York University Press, 1999.

West, Robin. "Literature, Culture, and Law at Duke University." Georgetown Law Faculty Working Paper No. 75, 2008. http://scholarship.law.georgetown.edu/fwps-papers/75.

White, James Boyd. "The Cultural Background of *The Legal Imagination.*" In *Teaching Law and Literature,* edited by Austin Sarat, Cathrine O. Frank, and Matthew Anderson, 29–39. New York: Modern Language Association, 2011.

White, James Boyd. *Heracles' Bow: Essays on the Rhetoric and Poetics of the Law.* Madison: University of Wisconsin Press, 1985.

White, James Boyd. "Imagining the Law." In *The Rhetoric of Law,* edited by Austin Sarat and Thomas R. Kearns. Ann Arbor: University of Michigan Press, 1994.

White, James Boyd. *The Legal Imagination: Studies in the Nature of Legal Thought and Expression.* Boston: Little, Brown, 1973.

White, James Boyd. *When Words Lose Their Meaning: Constitutions and Reconstitutions of Language, Character, and Community.* Chicago: University of Chicago Press, 1984.

Wiegman, Robyn. "The Times We're in: Queer Feminist Criticism and the Reparative 'Turn.'" *Feminist Theory* 15 (2014): 4–25.

Wigley, Mark. *White Walls, Designer Dresses: The Fashioning of Modern Architecture.* Cambridge, MA: MIT Press, 2001.

Wilf, Steven, "Law/Text/Past." *UC Irvine Law Review* (2011): 543–64.

Wilkins, David E. *American Indian Sovereignty and the U.S. Supreme Court: The Masking of Justice.* Austin: University of Texas Press, 1997.

Williams, Gary Jay. "Madame Vestris' *A Midsummer Night's Dream* and the Web of Victorian Tradition." *Theatre Survey* 18, no. 2 (1977): 1–22.

Williams, Jeffrey J. "The New Modesty in Literary Criticism." *Chronicle of Higher Education Review*, January 5, 2015.

Williams, Patricia J. *The Alchemy of Race and Rights: Diary of a Law Professor.* Cambridge, MA: Harvard University Press, 1991.

Williams, Raymond. *The Country and the City.* London: Chatto and Windus, 1973.

Williams, Raymond. *Problems in Materialism and Culture: Selected Essays.* London: Verso, 1980.

Williams, Rowan. "Civil and Religious Law in England: A Religious Perspective." *Ecclesiastical Law Journal* 10 (2008): 262–82.

Williams, Rowan. "Faith in the Public Sphere." Lecture at Leicester Cathedral, March 22, 2009. http://rowanwilliams.archbishopofcanterbury.org/articles.php/817/faith-in-the-public-square-lecture-at-leicester-cathedral.

Williams, Timothy. "Washington Steps Back from Policing Indian Lands, Even as Crime Rises." *New York Times*, November 12, 2012. http://www.amren.com/news/2012/11/washington-steps-back-from-policing-indian-lands-even-as-crime-rises/.

Wilson, Luke. *Theaters of Intention: Drama and the Law in Early Modern England.* Stanford, CA: Stanford University Press, 2000.

Wimsatt, William K. *The Verbal Icon: Studies in the Meaning of Poetry.* Lexington: University of Kentucky Press, 1954.

The Wire. "The Detail." Directed by Clark Johnson. Written by David Simon. HBO, June 9, 2002.

Witt, John Fabian. *The Accidental Republic: Crippled Workingmen, Destitute Widows, and the Remaking of American Law.* Cambridge, MA: Harvard University Press, 2004.

Wittgenstein, Ludwig. *Philosophical Investigations.* Translated by G. E. M. Anscombe. Oxford: Blackwell, 1958.

Wittgenstein, Ludwig. "Some Remarks on Logical Form." Supplementary volume, *Proceedings of the Aristotelian Society* 9 (1929): 162–71.

Wolfe, Tom. *I Am Charlotte Simmons.* New York: Farrar, Strauss and Giroux, 2004.

Wolin, Sheldon S. *Democracy Incorporated: Managed Democracy and the Specter of Inverted Totalitarianism.* Princeton, NJ: Princeton University Press, 2008.

Woloch, Alex. *The One vs. the Many: Minor Characters and the Space of the Protagonist in the Novel.* Princeton, NJ: Princeton University Press, 2003.

Wong, Edlie. *Neither Fugitive nor Free: Atlantic Slavery, Freedom Suits, and the Legal Culture of Travel.* New York: New York University Press, 2009.

Woodmansee, Martha. *The Author, Art, and the Market: Rereading the History of Aesthetics.* New York: Columbia University Press, 1994.

Woodmansee, Martha. "The Genius and the Copyright: Economic and Legal Conditions of the Emergence of the Author." *Eighteenth Century Studies* 17 (1984): 425–48.

Woolf, Virginia. *A Room of One's Own and Three Guineas.* Oxford: Oxford University Press, 1992.

Wynter, Sylvia. "Unsettling the Coloniality of Being/Power/Truth/Freedom: Toward the Human, after Man, Its Overrepresentation—An Argument." *New Centennial Review* 3 (2003): 257–337.

Wu, Jingxiong. *Cases and Materials on Jurisprudence*. St. Paul, MN: West, 1958.

Yoshino, Kenji. "The City and the Poet." *Yale Law Journal* 114 (2005): 1835–96.

Yoshino, Kenji. *Covering: The Hidden Assault on Our Civil Rights*. New York: Random House, 2006.

Yoshino, Kenji. "Miranda's Fall?" *Michigan Law Review* 98 (2000): 1399–1415.

Yoshino, Kenji. *Speak Now: Marriage Equality on Trial*. New York: Crown, 2015.

Young, Alan R. ed. *The English Emblem Tradition*, vol. 3, *Emblematic Flags of the English Civil War, 1642–1660*. Toronto: University of Toronto Press, 1995.

Yuan, Elizabeth. "'22 Chinese Women' and Other Courtroom Drama," *The Atlantic*, September 4, 2013.

Ziolkowski, Theodore. *The Mirror of Justice: Literary Reflections of Legal Crises*. Princeton, NJ: Princeton University Press, 1997.

CASES

Abad v. Bayer Corp., 563 F.3d 663 (7th Cir. 2009).

Adams v. New Jersey Steamboat Co., 45 N.E. 369 (N.Y. 1896).

Brown v. Bd. of Educ., 349 U.S. 294 (1955).

Chae Chan Ping v. United States, 130 U.S. 581 (1889).

Cherokee Nation v. Georgia, 30 U.S. 1 (1831).

Chy Lung v. Freeman, 92 U.S. 275 (1875).

Daubert v. Merrell Dow Pharmaceuticals, Inc., 509 U.S. 579 (1993).

Diamond, Commissioner of Patents and Trademarks v. Chakrabarty, 447 U.S. 303 (1980).

Dickerson v. United States, 530 U.S. 428 (2000).

District of Columbia v. Heller, 554 U.S. 570 (2008).

Duro v. Reina, 495 U.S. 676 (1990).

Estes v. Texas, 381 U.S. 532 (1965).

Ex parte Ah Fook, 49 Cal. 102 (1874).

Gonzales v. Raich, 545 U.S. 1 (2005).

Gonzalez-Servin v. Ford Motor Co., 662 F.3d 931 (7th Cir. 2011).

Graham v. Connor, 490 U.S. 386 (1989).

Hardwick v. Bowers, 478 U.S. 186 (1986).

Johnson and Graham's Lessee v. M'Intosh, 21 U.S. 543 (1823).

Lakeside v. Oregon, 435 U.S. 333 (1978).

Lawrence v. Texas, 539 U.S. 558 (2003).

Lone Wolf v. Hitchcock, 187 U.S. 553 (1903).

McQuire v. Western Morning News, 2 K.B. 100 (1903).

Mickens v. Taylor, 535 U.S. 162 (2002).

Mirehouse v. Rennell, 6 Eng. Rep. 1015, 1023; 1 Cl. & Fin. 527, 546.

Moore v. Regents of the University of California, 249 Cal. Rptr. 494, *aff'd in part*, *rev'd in part*, 51 Cal. 3d 120 (Cal. 1990).

Morris v. Pugh, 3 Burr. 1241, 1243; 97 Eng. Rep. 811 (K.B.) (1761).

Morton Salt Co. v. G. S. Suppiger Co., 314 U.S. 488 (1942).

Mullenix v. Luna, 136 S. Ct. 305 (2015).

Muller v. Oregon, 208 U.S. 412 (1908).

National Federation of Independent Business v. Sebelius, 132 S. Ct. 2566 (2012).

New York v. United States, 505, U.S. 144 (1992).

Nix v. Williams, 467 U.S. 431(1984).

Obergefell v. Hodges, 135 S. Ct. 2584 (2015).

Old Chief v. United States, 519 U.S. 173 (1997).

Oliphant v. The Suquamish Indian Tribe, 435 U.S. 191 (1978).

Ozawa v. United States, 260 U.S. 178 (1922).

Plessy v. Ferguson, 163 U.S. 537 (1896).

Practice Mgmt. Info. Corp. v. Am. Med. Ass'n, 121 F.3d 516, 521 (9th Cir. 1997),
    amended by 133 F.3d 1140 (9th Cir. 1998).

Printz v. United States, 521 U.S. 898 (1997).

Roberts v. City of Boston, 59 Mass. (5 Cush.) 198 (1849).

Sheppard v. Maxwell, 384 U.S. 333 (1966).

Spicer v. Spicer, 79 Eng. Rep. 451 (1620).

State v. Butler, 676 S.W.2d 809 (Mo. 1984).

State v. Kemp, 948 A.2d 636 (N.J. 2008).

State v. Nelson, 791 N.W.2d 414 (Iowa 2010).

Stephens v. Miller, 13 F.2d 998 (7th Cir. 1994).

Tee-Hit-Ton Indians v. United States, 348 U.S. 272, 228–29 (1955).

United States v. Andrade, 784 F.2d 1431 (9th Cir. 1986).

United States v. Feldhacker, 849 F.2d 293 (8th Cir. 1988).

United States v. Fortenberry, 971 F.2d 717 (11th Cir. 1992).

United States v. Gartmon, 146 F.3d 1015 (D.C. Cir. 1998).

United States v. Heath, 455 F.3d 52 (2d Cir. 2006).

United States v. Hill, 249 F.3d 707 (8th Cir. 2001).

United States v. Inserra, 34 F.3d 83 (2d Cir. 1994).

United States v. Kagama, 118 U.S. 375 (1886).

United States v. Levasseur, 620 F. Supp. 623 (E.D.N.Y. 1985).

United States v. Llera Plaza, 179 F. Supp. 2d 494 (E.D. Pa. 2002).

United States v. McBratney, 104 U.S. 621 (1882).

United States v. O'Brien, 391 U.S. 367 (1968).

United States v. Pepin, 514 F.3d 193 (2d Cir. 2008).

United States v. Rezaq, 134 F.3d 1121 (D.C. Cir. 1998).

United States v. Saunders, 209 F. App'x 778 (10th Cir. 2006).

United States v. Storm, 915 F. Supp. 2d 1196 (D. Or. 2012).

United States v. Thind, 261 U.S. 204 (1923).

United States v. Wheeler, 435 U.S. 313 (1978).

Utah v. Strieff, 136 S. Ct. 2056 (2016).

Worcester v. Georgia, 31 U.S. 515 (1832).

CONTRIBUTORS

Elizabeth S. Anker is Associate Professor of English and Associate Member of the Faculty of Law at Cornell University. Her books are *Fictions of Dignity: Embodying Human Rights in World Literature* (Cornell University Press, 2012), and the edited collection *Critique and Postcritique* (with Rita Felski, Duke University Press, 2017). She is completing two books, one on the role of paradox in theory and the other on constitutional metaphors. She is also editor of the series Corpus Juris: The Humanities in Politics and Law (Cornell University Press).

Peter Brooks is Sterling Professor of Comparative Literature Emeritus at Yale University, where he was the Founding Director of the Whitney Humanities Center, and is currently Andrew W. Mellon Foundation Scholar in the University Center for Human Values and the Department of Comparative Literature, Princeton University. He is the author of several books, including *Reading for the Plot* (1984) and *Troubling Confessions: Speaking Guilt in Law and Literature* (2001). His *Flaubert in the Ruins of Paris* will be published in 2017.

Anne Anlin Cheng is Professor of English and Director for the Program in American Studies at Princeton University. An interdisciplinary scholar working at the intersection of literature, law, aesthetics, and psychoanalysis, she is the author of *The Melancholy of Race: Assimilation, Psychoanalysis, and Hidden Grief* (Oxford University Press, 2000) and *Second Skin: Josephine Baker and the Modern Surface* (Oxford University Press, 2011). Her current research includes a manuscript on rethinking the ontology of feminism for the Asiatic woman through the critical labor of "ornaments"; and a second project on Race Studies at the intersection of Food and Animal Studies.

Eric Cheyfitz is the Ernest I. White Professor of American Studies and Humane Letters at Cornell University, where he has served as director of the American Indian Program, the faculty coordinator of the Mellon-Mays

Undergraduate Fellowship Program, and the director of the Mellon Post-doctoral Diversity Seminar. He teaches American literatures, American Indian literatures, and US federal Indian law, and has published three books: *The Transparent: Sexual Politics in the Language of Emerson* (1981); *The Poetics of Imperialism: Translation and Colonization from "The Tempest" to "Tarzan"* (1991, 1997), which was named by *Choice* as one of the outstanding academic books of 1991; and *The (Post)Colonial Construction of Indian Country: U.S. American Indian Literatures and Federal Indian Law*, which appears as Part I of his edited volume *The Columbia Guide to American Indian Literatures of the United States since 1945* (2006). He is the co-editor of *Sovereignty, Indigeneity, and the Law*, a special issue of *South Atlantic Quarterly*, which won the award for the best special issue of an academic journal in 2011 given by the Council of Editors of Learned Journals and was acknowledged for "Outstanding Indigenous Scholarship" in the same year by the American Indian and Alaska Native Professors Association. His most recent publications are "The Force of Exceptionalist Narratives in the Israeli-Palestinian Conflict," which appeared in the *Journal of the Native American and Indigenous Studies Association* in 2014; "Disinformation: The Limits of Capitalism's Imagination and the End of Ideology," which appeared in *boundary 2* in the same year; and "Native American Literature and the UN Declaration on the Rights of Indigenous Peoples," in *The Routledge Companion to Native American Literature*, ed. Deborah Lea Madison (2015). His fourth book, *The Disinformation Age: The Collapse of Liberal Democracy in the United States*, is being published by Routledge in 2017.

Wai Chee Dimock is William Lampson Professor of English and American Studies at Yale University. She has published widely on American literature of every period, and is best known for *Through Other Continents: American Literature Across Deep Time* (2007). Editor of *PMLA*, and film critic for the *Los Angeles Review of Books*, her essays have also appeared in *Critical Inquiry*, the *Chronicle of Higher Education*, the *New York Times*, and the *New Yorker*.

Elizabeth F. Emens, Isidor and Seville Sulzbacher Professor of Law at Columbia University, teaches and researches in the areas of antidiscrimination law, contracts, and law and sexuality. She earned her BA and JD from Yale and her PhD in English from King's College, Cambridge. Her publications include "Compulsory Sexuality" (*Stanford Law Review*, 2014); "Intimate Discrimination: The State's Role in the Accidents of Sex and Love" (*Harvard Law Review*, 2009); "Disabling Attitudes" (*American Journal of Comparative Law*, 2012; reprinted in the *Disability Studies Reader*, 4th ed., 2013); "Shape Stops Story" (*Narrative*, 2007); and "Monogamy's Law: Compulsory Monogamy and Polyamorous Existence" (*NYU Journal of Law and Social*

Change, 2004; and partially reprinted in various collections). She edited a volume, with Michael A. Stein, on *Disability and Equality Law* (Ashgate, 2013), and she is currently working on a book about the office work of life—or what she calls *Admin*.

Peter Goodrich is Professor of Law and Director of the Program in Law and Humanities at Cardozo Law School, New York. By inclination a legal semionaut, recent works include *Legal Emblems and the Art of Law* (2014) and a forthcoming study of Judge Daniel Paul Schreber, arguing that the nervous late nineteenth-century judge's *Denkwüridgkeiten* or *Remarkable Thoughts* are an important and much neglected work of jurisprudence or at the least an impressive exercise *in fictione juris*.

Janet Halley is Royall Professor of Law at Harvard Law School. She is the author of a number of essays on family law, and of *Split Decisions: How and Why to Take a Break from Feminism* and *Don't: A Reader's Guide to the Military's Anti-Gay Policy*, and is the co-editor (with Wendy Brown) of *Left Legalism/Left Critique* and (with Andrew Parker) *After Sex? New Writing Since Queer Theory*.

Shari M. Huhndorf received her PhD in Comparative Literature from New York University, and she is currently Professor of Native American Studies and Chair of the Department of Ethnic Studies at University of California Berkeley. She is the author of two books, *Going Native: Indians in the American Cultural Imagination* (Cornell University Press, 2001) and *Mapping the Americas: The Transnational Politics of Contemporary Native Culture* (Cornell University Press, 2009), and a co-editor of three volumes, including *Indigenous Women and Feminism: Politics, Activism, Culture* (University of British Columbia Press, 2010), winner of the Canadian Women's Studies Association prize for Outstanding Scholarship. Currently, she is working on a manuscript tentatively titled "Indigeneity and the Politics of Space: Gender, Geography, Culture."

Lorna Hutson is Merton Professor of English Literature at Oxford. Her interests are in the rhetorical bases of Renaissance literature, emphasizing fiction's affinities with forensic rhetoric. Her publications include *The Usurer's Daughter* (Routledge, 1994) and, with Victoria Kahn, *Rhetoric and Law in Early Modern Europe* (Yale University Press, 2000). Her most recent book, *Circumstantial Shakespeare* (2015), is based on the Oxford Wells Shakespeare Lectures delivered in 2012 and her *Oxford Handbook of English Law and Literature, 1500–1700* is forthcoming. She currently holds a Leverhulme Major Research Fellowship for research on sixteenth-century Anglo-Scots literary relations.

Bernadette Meyler is the Carl and Sheila Spaeth Professor of Law at Stanford University, where she teaches and researches on Anglo-American constitutional law and law and the humanities. She was previously Professor of Law and English at Cornell University. Her publications have appeared in many law reviews and peer-reviewed journals, including the *Cornell, Southern California*, and *Stanford Law Reviews*, as well as *Diacritics* and *Theory and Event*. She is completing two book projects—*Theaters of Pardoning* and *Common Law Originalism*. She is also co-editing the *Oxford Handbook of Law and Humanities*, with Simon Stern and Maksymilian Del Mar.

Imani Perry is the Hughes-Rogers Professor of African American Studies at Princeton University, where she also holds an affiliation with the program in Law and Public Affairs and the program in Gender and Sexuality Studies. Perry is the author of *Prophets of the Hood: Politics and Poetics in Hip Hop* (Duke University Press, 2004) and *More Beautiful and More Terrible: The Embrace and Transcendence of Racial Inequality in the United States* (New York University Press, 2011). Perry has written numerous articles in the fields of law, literary, and cultural studies. She holds a PhD in American Studies and a JD, both from Harvard University.

Julie Stone Peters is the H. Gordon Garbedian Professor of English and Comparative Literature at Columbia University, where she was founding director of the Columbia College Human Rights Program and has taught in the law school. She teaches and writes on a range of topics in the humanities, from drama, film, and media to law and culture. Her books include *Theatre of the Book: Print, Text, and Performance in Europe, 1480–1880* (Oxford, 2000) and *Women's Rights, Human Rights: International Feminist Perspectives* (co-edited with Andrea Wolper; Routledge, 1995). She is currently working on a historical study of legal performance.

Ravit Reichman is Associate Professor of English at Brown University, and the author of *The Affective Life of Law: Legal Modernism and the Literary Imagination* (Stanford University Press, 2009). She is working on a study of the relationship between property, ethics, and culture, *Lost Properties of the Twentieth Century*.

Paul K. Saint-Amour is Professor of English at the University of Pennsylvania. He wrote *The Copywrights: Intellectual Property and the Literary Imagination* (2003), which won the MLA Prize for a First Book, and edited the collection *Modernism and Copyright* (2011). Saint-Amour has been a fellow at the Stanford Humanities Center, the Society for the Humanities at Cornell, and the National Humanities Center. He co-edits, with Jessica Berman, the Modernist Latitudes series at Columbia University Press and has served as President of the Modernist Studies Association. His latest book, *Tense Future: Modernism, Total War, Encyclopedic Form* (2015), won the Modernist Studies Association Book Prize.

Austin Sarat is Associate Dean of the Faculty and William Nelson Cromwell Professor of Jurisprudence and Political Science at Amherst College and Hugo L. Black Visiting Senior Scholar at the University of Alabama School of Law. Professor Sarat is past president of the Association for the Study of Law, Culture, and the Humanities and has also served as President of the Law and Society Association and of the Consortium of Undergraduate Law and Justice Programs. He is author or editor of more than ninety books, including *Gruesome Spectacles: Botched Executions and America's Death Penalty, The Road to Abolition? The Future of Capital Punishment in the United States, The Killing State: Capital Punishment in Law, Politics, and Culture, When the State Kills: Capital Punishment and the American Condition, The Cultural Lives of Capital Punishment: Comparative Perspectives*, and *Mercy on Trial: What It Means to Stop an Execution*. Professor Sarat has received numerous prizes and awards, including, among others, the Harry Kalven Award of the Law Society Association, the James Boyd White Award of the Association for the Study of Law, Culture, and the Humanities, and the Hugo Adam Bedau Award, given to honor significant contributions to death penalty scholarship by the Massachusetts Coalition Against the Death Penalty.

Caleb Smith is professor of English and American Studies at Yale University. He is the author of two books on American literature and the history of the penal system, *The Prison and the American Imagination* (Yale University Press, 2009) and *The Oracle and the Curse* (Harvard University Press, 2013), and the editor of Austin Reed's 1858 prison memoir, *The Life and the Adventures of a Haunted Convict* (Random House, 2016). As a contributing editor at the *Los Angeles Review of Books*, Smith helped to produce *No Crisis*, a series of essays on the state of criticism in the twenty-first century. He has written about contemporary media and the arts for *Avidly, Bomb, Paper Monument*, and other venues.

Simon Stern teaches law and English at the University of Toronto. He has published articles on various aspects of Anglo-American legal and literary history, in areas such as copyright, fraud, obscenity, privacy, and search and seizure. With Robert Spoo, he edits the book series Law and Literature (Oxford University Press). He has also edited or co-edited scholarly editions of Henry Fielding's *Tom Jones*, Aphra Behn's *Oroonoko*, and William Blackstone's *Commentaries on the Laws of England*, and he is co-editor, with Nan Goodman, of *The Routledge Research Companion to Law and Humanities in Nineteenth-Century America* (2017), and of the *Oxford Handbook of Law and Humanities*, with Bernadette Meyler and Maksymilian Del Mar. His current research involves a book-length study of the history and theory of legal fictions in the Anglo-American tradition from the early modern period to the present.

Martin Jay Stone is Professor of Law at Benjamin N. Cardozo School of Law and Adjunct Professor of Philosophy at the New School. He was previously Professor of Law and Philosophy at Duke University, and he has also taught at Cornell University, Harvard University, Princeton University, University of Michigan, and University of Chicago. His main areas of interest include torts, private law theory, philosophy of law, philosophy of action, and Wittgenstein. His most recent publication is *Freedom and Force: Essays in Kant's Legal Philosophy*, Sari Kiselevsy and Martin Stone, eds. (Hart Publishing, 2017). He also likes to play the piano.

Brook Thomas is Chancellor's Professor of Law and Literature at the University of California, Irvine. He has been awarded fellowships from the Alexander von Humboldt Foundation, the Woodrow Wilson Center, the ACLS, the DAAD, and the National Endowment for the Humanities. Starting in 1984, he has produced numerous publications cross-examining law and literature that produce stories about different aspects of US culture not available if we were to confine ourselves to only one of the two disciplines. His most recent book is *The Literature of Reconstruction: Not in Plain Black and White* (2016).

Elliott Visconsi teaches at the University of Notre Dame, where he is Associate Professor of English, Concurrent Associate Professor of Law, and serves as the university's Chief Academic Digital Officer in the Provost's Office. Visconsi works on literature, law, and political thought in the early modern English world (including the Americas and India), First Amendment law, and freedom of expression in the digital age. Visconsi is the creator of software for learning in the humanities that has led to the publication of eight innovative Shakespeare editions for the iPad; he is also cofounder of the spinout company Luminary Digital Media. Currently finishing a book entitled *The Struggle for Civil Religion: Church and State in the 17th Century English World*, Visconsi is also author of *Lines of Equity: Literature and the Origins of Law in Later Stuart England* (Cornell University Press, 2008). Representative articles include: "The Literatures of Toleration and Civil Religion in Post-Revolutionary England" (2015), "The Invention of

Criminal Blasphemy: *Rex v. Taylor* (1676)" (2009), and "Vinculum Fidei: *The Tempest* and the Law of Allegiance" (2008).

Priscilla Wald teaches English and directs the program in Gender, Sexuality, and Feminist Studies at Duke University. She is the author of *Contagious: Cultures, Carriers, and the Outbreak Narrative* (Duke University Press, 2008) and *Constituting Americans: Cultural Anxiety and Narrative Form* (Duke University Press, 1995), and co-editor of *American Literature* and of the America in the Long 19th Century book series at New York University Press. Wald is currently at work on a book-length study entitled *Human Being after Genocide* that chronicles how scientific advances and geopolitical transformations reconfigured accounts of the human and of humanity in the decades following the Second World War.

INDEX

Abad v. Bayer Corp., 177
abduction, 94, 105n9
Abel, Richard, 59
Abrams, Kathryn, 110
Acker, Kathy, 331
actor-network theory, 23, 361
affect, 109–20
    defining, 111
    emotion in relation to, 23, 111
    reasonableness and, 23–24, 112–20
    role of, in law, 109–10
    scholarly analysis grounded in, 30n63
African Americans
    law and literature and, 39–40
    and personhood, 53–54
    See also Black women's literature
Agamben, Giorgio, 19, 39, 57n18,
        163, 179
Agricola, Rudolph, 150, 151
Alito, Samuel, 170
Allewaert, Monique, 239
Alternative to Incarceration
        (ATI), 360–61
American Bar Association, 4, 26n6
Amherst College, 47
Amnesty International, 270–71
Amsterdam, Anthony, 103–4, 108n35
"... and others" sensibility, 128–31,
        135, 140–41
Anker, Elizabeth S., 14, 22–23, 50, 52
Anscombe, G. E. M., 87
anxiety of influence, 43
Apess, William, 266
Aphthonius, 150
Apuleius, *The Golden Ass*, 198
Aquinas, Thomas, 87

Arabian, Armand, 350
arguments, 150–52
Aristotle, 85, 179, 184, 206
Arnold, Oliver, 164
Asad, Talal, 283
Asian Americans, 40
Aslam, Nadeem, 279, 284–91
    The Blind Man's Garden, 284
    Maps for Lost Lovers, 22, 285–91
    The Wasted Vigil, 284
Association for the Study of Law,
        Culture, and the Humanities, 36
attractive nuisance, 316, 320, 321
Aubid, Charles, 264–65
Auerbach, Erich, 145–46
Austin, J. L. (John), 109, 258–59
authenticity, 242–45
authorial intention, 77–80
authority
    in interpretation, 80–81, 87
    in jurisprudence, 171
autonomy, of art works, 78–79

Balkin, Jack, 37, 64
Ball, Milner, 38
Bandes, Susan, 110
bardos, 134–35
Barnes, Jim, 23, 372–75
    "After a Postcard from Styrk in
        Japan," 374
    "Choctaw Cemetery," 374
    "The Only Photograph of Quentin at
        Harvard," 373
Baron, Jane, 6–7, 10, 12, 15
Barrett, Andrea, 331
Barricelli, Jean-Pierre, 37–38

Barrington, Candace, 41
Barthes, Roland, 99, 145
Barton, Anne, 146–49
Bauman, Zygmunt, 241
Beauvoir, Simone de, 161–62, 168
    She Came to Stay, 161–62,
        172–73, 252–53
Beckwith, Sarah, 146–48
belief
    arguments meant to evoke, 150–52
    role of, in literary/theatrical
        imagination, 146–49, 152–55, 318
Bell, Derrick, 40
Bell, Tom W., 335
Bellini-Sharp, Carol, 127
Benjamin, Walter, 9, 37, 43, 75, 185,
        345–46, 351, 353–55, 357
Bentham, Jeremy, 55, 61, 313
Berlant, Lauren, 111
Berlinger, Joe, 106n21
Bernstein, Elizabeth, 126
Bertillonage, 96
Best, Stephen, 40, 239
Betteridge, Jesse, "The Brick in Room
        207," 340
Binder, Guyora, 7–8, 12–14, 22,
        34, 39, 49
biopolitics, 254, 331–41
biopower, 19, 30n57
bioproperty, 332
biotechnology, 344–57
    Blade Runner and, 351–57
    definitional issues in, 344–46
    legal issues involving, 347–50
Birbeck College, Department
        of Law, 42
Black, Hugo, 60
Black Lives Matter movement, 5
Blackstone, William, 239
Black women's literature, 257–62
Blade Runner (film), 20, 347, 351–57
Blake, William, 353
Bloom, Harold, 43
the body
    in *Chy Lung v. Freeman*,
        237–42, 245–46
    ornament and, 245
    personhood and, 239–41
    race and, 240
    unconventional character of, 260–61

Bono Act, 335
Borrows, John, 276
Bourdieu, Pierre, 203
Bowers v. Hardwick, 123, 124
Boyer, Abel, 201
Boyle, James, 329
Branagh, Kenneth, 73, 76, 82, 86
Brandeis, Louis, 35
Brennan, William J., 348–49
Brooks, Peter, 21, 37, 145
Brophy, Alfred L., 40
Brown, Wendy, 27n10
Brown v. Board of Education, 36
Bruner, Jerome, 100–101
Brzezinski, Max, 164
Buddhism, 134
Bureau of Indian Affairs, 268
Burke, Edmund, 308
Burlingame Treaty, 234
Burt, Richard, 41
Butler, Judith, 10, 53, 132, 200, 202, 263

Calabresi, Guido, 60, 61
California, Chinese immigration
        in, 231–39
camp, 132–33
cancer, 135
Carpi, Daniela, 43
case method, 97–98
Castile, Philando, 120
causality, narrative and, 92–104, 320–21.
        See also motives
Cave, Terence, 96
Cavell, Stanley, 73, 258, 262
cell lines, 349–50
censorship, 41–42, 334
Chabon, Michael, *The Adventures of
        Kavalier and Clay*, 339
Chakrabarty, Ananda Mohan, 347–48
Chambers-Letson, Joshua Takano, 204
Cheng, Anne Anlin, 19, 22, 53
Cherokee Nation v. Georgia, 266, 272
Chesnutt, Charles W., 40,
        300–301, 311n24
Cheyfitz, Eric, 22
Chinese Exclusion Act, 234, 241,
        248n10
Chinese immigrants, 230–42, 245–46,
        248n9, 249n18
Chinese Police Tax, 234

Chy Lung v. Freeman, 19, 233–34, 237, 241–42, 245
Cicero, 37, 150
circumstances, rhetorical, 150–52, 155–56
circumstantial evidence, 42
civil death, 315
Civil War, 363–64
close reading, 338
clothing. *See* ornament and clothing
CLS. *See* critical legal studies
clues, 94–96
Coase theorem, 308
Coetzee, J. M., *Waiting for the Barbarians*, 113, 214–15
Coke, Edward, 167
Cole, Catherine, 204
Cole, David, 43
Coleridge, Samuel Taylor, 148, 152, 318
colonialism, 214–15, 266–76. *See also* imperialism; postcolonialism
Comaroff, Jean, 219, 220
Comaroff, John L., 219, 220
Condit, Ira M., 236
Cone, Richard, 349
Congressional Plant Patent Acts, 348–49
conjectural paradigm, 97
connectivity, 362
Connolly, Bill, 283, 290
Conrad, Joseph, 104
constitutive rhetoric, 345–46
continental theory, 4, 19, 37
Coombe, Rosemary, 63, 329
Copyleft, 335
copyright, 19, 42, 327–41
    and accessibility of works, 336–37
    biologization of property by, 332, 340
    biopolitics and, 331–41
    censorship compared to, 334
    and death, 332–35
    distant reading and, 338–39
    duration of, 332–33, 335–38
    in global context, 337–38
    individualist perspective on, 331
    patent abuse applied to, 318
    principles and ideas pertaining to, 328–29
    and the public domain, 334–37
    significance of, for literature, 327–31

    thematized in literature, 330–31, 339
    See also intellectual property
Copyright Act, 332
Cormack, Bradin, 52, 164
corporate personhood, 315–17, 319, 323
countermarrige, 295–309
Cover, Robert, 63, 148, 167
    "*Nomos* and Narrative," 37, 285
    "Violence and the Word," 61, 109, 146, 276
Crane, Gregg, 39–40
Crawley, Ashon, 257
Crenshaw, Kimberlé, 40
critical legal history, 11, 166
critical legal studies (CLS), 4–5, 19, 27n10, 130–31
critical race studies, 5, 7, 40
critical theory, 4–5
cruel and unusual punishment, 117
culture, 24, 62–64. *See also* law, culture, and the humanities
Curtis, Dennis, 188

Daubert v. Merrill Dow Pharmaceuticals, 96
Davis, Angela, 256
Davis, Thadious, 257
Dawes, James, 29n37
Dayan, Colin, 52, 111, 253, 256
    The Law Is a White Dog, 19
death and dying
    biopolitics and, 332
    copyright and, 332–35
    experience of, 134–35
    law linked to, 135–36
deconstruction, 9, 37, 60
deeming provisions, 321
de Grazia, Edward, 41
Deleuze, Gilles, 39
Delgado, Richard, 27n20, 40
DeLombard, Jeannine, 53–54, 324n5
de Luca, Giovanni Battista, 196
de Man, Paul, 82–83
depressive position, 136–37
Derrida, Jacques, 9, 37, 39, 43, 70, 200
Dershowitz, Alan, 106n21
detective fiction, 93–94, 97–98
dialectic, 150–52
Diamond v. Chakrabarty, 345, 347–49, 357

Dichterjuristen (authors trained in the law), 42
Dick, Philip K., *Do Androids Dream of Electric Sheep?*, 351
Dimock, Wai Chee, 13, 23, 39, 48
distant reading, 338–39
Dolin, Kieran, 42–43
dominance feminism, 126–27, 130, 134, 140
Douglass, Frederick, 260
Douzinas, Costas, 42
Doyle, Arthur Conan, 93–98
   The Adventure of the Abbey Grange, 97–98
   The Adventure of the Speckled Band, 93–94
   The Naval Treaty, 94
   Silver Blaze, 94
Duchamp, Marcel, *Fountain*, 322–23
Duncan, Geillis, 193–94
During, Simon, 284–85
Duro fix, 277n10
Durst, Robert A., 106n21
Duthu, N. Bruce, 270
Dworkin, Ronald, 7
dying. *See* death and dying

Easterling, Keller, 219–20, 223
ECHR. *See* European Court of Human Rights
economics, 36
Eddie, "In Session," 340
Eden, Kathy, 38
Eighth Amendment, 117
Einstein, Albert, 76
Eliot, T. S., 77, 81
Ellison, Ralph, *Invisible Man*, 51, 52
Emens, Elizabeth, 5, 25
emotion. *See* affect; law and emotions
Erasmus, *De copia*, 150, 151
Erdrich, Louise, 40
   The Round House, 22, 266–67, 269–76
European Court of Human Rights (ECHR), 22, 281–82, 284
European Union Commission, 333
evidence
   imagery and, 179
   in literature, 151–52
   narrative and, 92, 102
   res gestae and, 107n24

excessive force, 117
Exchange of Persons Program, 363
explanation, interpretation and, 85–88
exploding marriage, 295, 296–98, 301
extralegal domains, 219–20
extrastatecraft, 219–20

falsifiability, 96–97
Fanon, Frantz, 53
Farah, Nuruddin, *Gifts*, 22, 213, 220–24
Faulkner, William, 23, 40, 362–75
   Absalom, Absalom!, 367–68, 373
   Go Down, Moses, 370
   "A Justice," 370–71
   "Red Leaves," 370–71
   Requiem for a Nun, 369–70, 371
   Soldiers' Pay, 365–66
   The Sound and the Fury, 373
Faust, Drew Gilpin, 368
federal Indian law, 22, 266–76
Felski, Rita, 13
feme covert, 317–18
feminism
   divisions within, 126–27
   dominance, 126–27, 130, 134, 140
   in law, 125–27
   liberal, 127
feminist legal studies, 5, 7, 40–41
Ferguson, Frances, 55
Ferguson, Robert, 38, 39
Ferris, Joshua, *Then We Came to the End*, 113
Fian, John, 193, 195
Field, Stephen, 232–33
filius nullius, 316, 320, 321
Finchett-Maddock, Lucy, 204
fingerprinting, 96–97
Fish, Stanley, 38
Fiss, Owen, 36, 38, 60, 65
Foreign Miners Tax, 234
forensic history, 166, 169
Forster, E. M., *A Passage to India*, 214
Foucault, Michel, 9, 19, 53, 55, 136–39, 331–34
   "Qu'est-ce qu'un auteur?," 328–29, 331
Fourth Amendment, 21, 94, 102–3, 117, 118–19
Fraunce, Abraham, 182

freedom of thought and expression, 279–83, 290–91

Freeman, John, 232, 246

Freud, Sigmund, 53, 95, 97, 136–38, 182, 187

Fugard, Athol, 61

Fuller, Lon, 316, 321, 321–22

Future of Copyright (anthologies), 330, 340–41

Gaakeer, Jeanne, 43

Gaddis, William, *A Frolic of One's Own*, 339

gap spaces, 256

Gede, Thomas F., 269

Geertz, Clifford, 197

Gemmette, Elizabeth Villiers, 40

gender inequality, 254–55

Genette, Gérard, 99

genocide, of Native Americans, 266, 269

Genthe, Arnold, *Dressed for the Feast, Chinatown, San Francisco*, 229

Georgetown Law School, 36

Gewirtz, Paul, 37

GF. *See* Governance Feminism

Gibson, Otis, 229, 235–38, 249n13

Ginsburg, Ruth Bader, 170–72

Ginzburg, Carlo, "Clues," 94–97

Giordano, Luca, *Allegoria della Giustizia oppressa*, 190

globalization of law and literature
    factors contributing to, 210–11
    Farah's *Gifts* and, 220–24
    and law in the postcolony, 213–24

global South, 22, 211, 212–13, 222

glosses, 81

Glymph, Thavolia, 368

Goethe, Johann Wolfgang von, *Elective Affinities*, 295, 296–98, 301, 307

Goffman, Erving, 200

Gonzalez-Servin v. Ford Motor Company, 177–78, 180–81, 190

Goodfield, June, 345, 351

Goodman, Nan, 39

Goodrich, Peter, 20, 42

Google Books, 337

Gordon, Robert, 166, 170–71

Gould, Glenn, 73

Gould, Stephen Jay, 339

Governance Feminism (GF), 125–27, 140

Graham v. Connor, 117

Granovetter, Mark, 362

Gregson v. Gilbert, 215–17

guilt, 53–54

Gutiérrez-Jones, Carl, 40

habeas corpus, 231, 237, 240, 242, 250n24

Hall, Radclyffe, *The Well of Loneliness*, 41–42

Halley, Janet, 13, 23, 27n10, 48

Hamilton College, 127–28, 133, 140

Harring, Sidney, 268

Hartman, Saidiya, 53–54
    Scenes of Subjection, 215

Harvard University, 165

Haverkamp, Anselm, 43

Heald, Paul J., 336–37

Heidegger, Martin, 85

Heilbrun, Carolyn, 41

Heinlein, Robert
    The Moon Is a Harsh Mistress, 299
    Stranger in a Strange Land, 300

Heinzelman, Susan Sage, 41

HeLa cell line, 348, 358n9

hermeneutics, 7, 36–38, 72.
    See also interpretation; legal hermeneutics

hermeneutics of suspicion, 13, 18, 30n63, 131–32, 359

historical materialism, 346, 353

historicism
    in law and literature, 49–56
    new vs. old, 163
    progressive narrative of, 346

historiography
    and law and literature, 49, 160–73
    law in relation to, 162, 165–67
    literary studies in relation to, 164–65

Hobbes, Thomas, 239

Hogan, Linda, 40

Hohendahl, Peter, 163

Holmes, Oliver Wendell, Jr., 35, 309

Holmes, Richard, 28n33

Holmes, Sherlock. *See* Doyle, Arthur Conan

Hopkins, Pauline, 40

Horapollo, *Hieroglyphica*, 181–82

Huhndorf, Shari M., 22

humanism, 6–7, 36–38

humanities, 3, 10. *See also* law and the humanities
human nature, 344–45, 351–53, 356–57
huntsman's paradigm, 95–98
Hurst, J. Willard, 165–66
Hutson, Lorna, 18–19, 25, 41
    The Invention of Suspicion, 18
Huxley, Aldous, 349

identity formation, 204, 242–45
ideology, reasonableness as, 113
imagery. *See* visual imagery
imagination, 24–25, 144–57
    and literary mimesis, 145–57
    role of, in legal practice, 144–45
    role of belief in literary/theatrical, 146–49, 152–55
imago decidendi, 179, 180, 185, 187, 189
immigration policy, 232, 239, 247n5, 248n10
imperialism, 211, 215–18. *See also* colonialism
Indian Child Welfare Act, 273, 278n36
Indian Country, 266
inevitable discovery, 94, 98, 100, 103, 105n7
Inns of Court, 18
insurance, and the slave trade, 215–16
intellectual property, 19–20, 331, 332, 339–40. *See also* copyright
intention. *See* authorial intention
interdisciplinarity
    lack and desire as motivation for, 168–69, 172
    in law and literature, 47–48
    in legal education, 4, 61–62, 123
    significance of, 1
    in the university setting, 3
International Criminal Court, 126
interpretation, 69–89
    as application of law, 72–73
    and authorial intention, 77–80
    authority and, 80–81, 87
    creativity in, 75–77, 81, 86–87, 90n22
    as criticism, 73
    decisions in, 82–83
    explanation in relation to, 85–88
    incompatibility of, 74–75
    indeterminacy in, 81–85

legal, 69, 72–73, 79–81, 83–85, 88, 148
literary, 69, 73, 77–89, 148
meanings of, 69–72, 86
as performance, 73, 76–77
philosophical sense of, 70
pluralism in, 74–77, 81, 86–87
science in relation to, 76
settings for, 71–72
success in, 76, 79, 83, 90n22
types and aims of, 72–74, 80, 88, 90n22
of visual imagery, 179–91
See also hermeneutics
interpretation-in-general, 69
Irr, Caren, 331
Iser, Wolfgang, 145
Ishiguro, Kazuo
    Never Let Me Go, 305–6
    The Remains of the Day, 24, 113–16
Italian Association of Law and Literature, 43
it-narratives, 315, 324n5
ius imaginum, 180

Jacobs, Harriet, *Incidents in the Life of a Slave Girl*, 53
James, Henry, "An Animated Conversation," 330
Jameson, Fredric, 9, 56n2
James VI, king of Scotland, 194–99
    Daemonologie, 197
SS Japan, 231–32
Japan
    Faulkner and, 363–69
    Native Americans and, 372
Jardine, Lisa, 150
Jaszi, Peter, 329
Jefferson, Thomas, 332–33, 369
Jhering, Rudolf von, 41
The Jinx (television documentary), 106n21
John Jay College, 34, 59
Johnson, Richard, 63
Johnson, Samuel, 201, 312n50
Johnson and Graham's Lessee v. M'Intosh, 266
Johnson Reed Act, 240
Jonson, Ben, 41
Jordan, Constance, 41

Joyce, James
  Finnegans Wake, 330
  Ulysses, 41, 330
judgment
  in legal matters, 148–49
  in literary matters, 148–49
  narrative's effect on passing of, 102–
    4, 106n21, 106n23
justice
  blindness of, 190
  reparative, 23, 48, 360–61
  strong vs. weak versions of, 360

Kafka, Franz, 38
  The Trial, 42
Kahn, Paul, 41, 111
Kahn, Victoria, 41
Kant, Immanuel, 39, 61, 85–86
Kaplan, Benjamin, *An Unhurried View of
    Copyright*, 328
Kayman, Martin, 42
Keats, John, "The Fall of
    Hyperion," 82–83
Kennedy, Anthony, 170
Kennedy, Duncan, 131
Keren, Hila, 110
Kincaid, Jamaica, 257
  "In the Night," 257
Kirkland College, 127–28
Klein, Melanie, 131, 135–37, 139
Kohler, Joseph, 41
Kokkinakis v. Greece, 282
Kornstein, Daniel, 41
Korobkin, Laura Hanft, 39
Kosakiewicz, Olga, 161, 168
Kosakiewicz, Wanda, 161
Kotiswaran, Prabha, 125
Kramer, Paul, 239

Lacan, Jacques, 75, 244
Lacks, Henrietta, 348
LaCroix, Alison, 47
Lakeside v. Oregon, 106n23
Lamb, Mary Ellen, 156
Langdell, C. C., 97
language. *See* legal language
Latino/a culture, 40
Latour, Bruno, 3, 23, 361
law
  as art vs. science, 35

authority and, 171
death linked to, 135–36
and dress, 237, 239–42,
    245–46, 250n26
historiography in relation to,
    162, 165–67
in indigenous communities,
    264–66, 274–76
innovation arising from, 309
literature as corrective/supplement
    to, 12–13, 51–52, 60–61,
    211–12, 218–19
negative views of, 12–13, 22–23,
    211–19 (*see also* suspicion: of law)
non-performative conceptions of,
    196–200
as performance, 24, 64–65, 179, 180,
    193–200, 204–7
in performance, 204–5
of performance, 204–5
and personhood, 50–56
politics in relation to, 163
and the real, 14, 34, 46–48, 144–46,
    160, 168
Sedgwick's view of, 124–25, 135–38
suspicion of, 23
law, culture, and the humanities, 14, 34,
    36, 63, 160
Law, Jurisprudence, and Social
    Thought, 47
law and economics, 36
law and emotions, 110–11
Law and Humanities Institute, 36, 42
law and literature
  Anglo-American emphasis in, 14
  audiences for, 10–11
  conceptions of personhood in
    recent, 49–56
  critiques of, 6, 12–14
  educational mission of, 11
  globalization of, 210–24
  hermeneutic strand of, 7, 36–38
  historical approach to, 6–7, 18–20, 39
  historiography and, 49, 160–73
  humanist strand of, 6–7, 36–38
  institutional reform as aim of, 11–12
  institutional setting of, 2–5, 34, 35,
    38, 43, 48–49, 61–62
  interdisciplinarity in, 47–48
  international participation in, 42–43

law and literature *(Cont.)*
  and mimesis, 146
  narrative strand of, 7, 27n20, 36–38
  new directions in, 17–25, 163–
      64 (*see also* present state of;
      reconceptions of)
  New Historicism as influence
      on, 163–64
  normalization of, 24, 59–60, 62
  objects of study in, 7–8
  obstacles and problems for field of, 4,
      34, 46–47, 61–62
  origins of, 24, 33–34, 60, 162
  overviews of, 1–2, 33–43,
      59–61, 162–63
  pedagogy in, 169–72
  performance-oriented perspective
      in, 197
  persistence of, 34–35
  practical applications of, 4
  present state of, 47–49 (*see also* new
      directions in)
  reconceptions of, 14–17, 62–65 (*see
      also* new directions in)
  reformative mission of, 10
  relationship of disciplines in, 8–10,
      36, 88–89, 146–48, 160, 169, 197–
      98, 220–24, 295
  revival of, 34, 39
  selective assimilation of, 62–63
  sentimentalizing tendencies in,
      12, 29n45
  skepticism in, 13
  taxonomies of, 5–12, 15
  unacknowledged influence of, 5
Law and Literature (journal), 38, 59
law and performance studies, 204
law and society, 35–36, 59, 144, 160
Law and Society Association, 35, 36, 59
law and the humanities, 160–61,
      168, 173
law as literature, 7–8, 34, 62, 73, 164,
      197–98, 265, 295
law in literature, 7–8, 34, 164, 197–98,
      295, 327, 330
lawlessness, 219
law of literature, 8, 205, 295
Lawrence, D. H., *Lady Chatterley's
      Lover*, 41
Lawrence v. Texas, 124

law schools. *See* legal education
legal discourse. *See* legal language
legal education
  interdisciplinarity in, 4, 61–62, 123
  specialization in, 4
legal fictions, 21, 313–23
  artificial limits of, 320–21
  criticisms of, 313–14
  defined, 315
  and falsity, 316, 320, 321–22
  function of, 265
  language of, 321–23
  narrative and other literary
      characteristics of, 315–20, 323
  reasonable person as, 112
  self-consciousness in, 322–23
legal formalism, 35
legal hermeneutics, 20–21
legal history, 165–67, 197
legal imaginaries, 24
legal language
  as constitutive rhetoric, 345–46
  criticisms of, 109, 112, 121n4, 216–17
legal realism, 35, 123–24, 131
legal storytelling movement, 1, 10
LeGuin, Ursula, 331
Leija, Israel, Jr., 118
Levine, Caroline, 16
Levinson, Sanford, 38, 64
Lévi-Strauss, Claude, 85
Leyla Şahin v. Turkey, 282
Li, David, 40
Das Liebeskonzil (film), 282
life, definition of, 349
Lindsay, David, 149
line marriage, 299–300
literary studies
  actor-network theory and, 361
  historiography in relation to, 164–65
  law as field of interest for, 19
  theory in, 3
literature
  and argument construction, 150–52
  authorial intention and meaning
      in, 77–80
  autonomy of, 78–79
  Black women's, 257–62
  copyright's significance for, 327–31
  as corrective/supplement to law, 12–13,
      51–52, 60–61, 211–12, 218–19

defining, 8
high culture conception of, 61
in indigenous communities, 264–66
innovation arising from, 309
law's effect on production of, 41–42
mimesis in, 145–57
and personhood, 51–56
and the real, 14, 34, 46–48, 144–46,
     155, 160, 168
real effects of, 148–49, 155–57, 291
role of belief in, 146–49, 152–55, 318
self-sufficient world of, 145–55
thematization of copyright in,
     330–31, 339
US American Indian, 266–67
See also literary studies
Literature and Law conferences, 59
literature as law, 295, 309
Lobban, Michael, 165–66
Locke, John, 239
Lone Wolf v. Hitchcock, 272
love triangles, 161–62, 166
Lowe, Lisa, 40
Luhmann, Niklas, 168
Lupton, Julia, 41
Lyotard, Jean-François, 187

Mabo case, 43
Macpherson, Sandra, 55–56
Mahmood, Saba, 283
Mailloux, Steven, 38
Maitland, F. W., 165, 230
Major Crimes Act, 267, 268
Mali, Joseph, 346
MaLossi, Leo I., 347–48
Mancini, Susanna, 282
Manji, Ambreena, 43
man on the Clapham omnibus. See
     reasonable person standard
Mansfield, William Murray, first Earl
     of, 318
margin of appreciation, 282
marriage, 294–309
     continuity of, 302–3
     end of, 306–7
     exclusivity in, 299–300
     exculpatory, 305–6
     numerosity in, 299–300
     permanence of, 296–98
     race and, 300

self-, 304–5
     value of, 294–96
Marshall, John, 266, 272
Marx, Karl, 33
Marxism, 9
Maryland v. Rusk, 103
Mason, Emma, 30n63
Massumi, Brian, 111
Mathis, Ayana, 257
     The Twelve Tribes of Hattie, 261
McCluskey, Martha, 27n10
McLuhan, Marshall, 328
McNeill, William, 346
McVeigh, Shaun, 43
meaning, narrative as disclosure
     of, 92–104
Melin, Alf, "Remote Kill," 340–41
Melville, Herman
     "Bartleby, the Scrivener," 39
     Billy Budd, 38–39
Mencken, H. L., 312n50
Mesopotamian jurisprudence, 97
Meyler, Bernadette, 18, 49, 50
Michaels, Walter Benn, 38
Mickens, Walter, 103–4
Mickens v. Taylor, 103–4
Miller, D. A., 132
Miller, Samuel, 238–39
mimesis, 206
MLA. See Modern Language Association
Moddelmog, William, 40
Modern Language Association
     (MLA), 34, 38
Modern Poland Foundation, 340
Monette, Paul, Love Alone, 42
Moore, John, 349–50, 351
Moore v. Regents of the University of
     California, 345–46, 347, 349–50,
     356, 357
morality
     and Chinese female
         immigrants, 232–38
     CLS and, 131
     narrative linked to, 102–3
     ornament and clothing linked
         to, 249n19
Morawetz, Thomas, 29n38
Morelli, Giovanni, 95
Moretti, Franco, 339
Morowitz, Harold, 349

Morrison, Robert F., 232
Morrison, Toni, 257
    Song of Solomon, 259–61
    Tar Baby, 258
motives, 149–55
Mullenix, Chadrin, 118–19
Mullenix v. Luna, 24, 118–20
Muller v. Oregon, 35
Muslim Britons, 286–91
mythistories, 346, 347, 357

Nagano Seminar, 363–64
narrative
    causality and, 92–104
    as construction, 104
    critical race studies and, 7
    in detective stories, 93–94
    as emphasis in law and literature, 7,
        27n20, 36–38
    and evidence, 92, 102
    feminist legal studies and, 7
    legal fictions and, 315–21, 323
    legal role of, 21, 92–104, 145, 265,
        285, 315–20, 346–47
    morality linked to, 102–3
    overvaluation of, 12
    and passing of judgment, 102–4,
        106n21, 106n23
    role of clues in, 94–96
    unnatural, 321, 323
    usefulness of, 96
    See also narrative integrity
narrative integrity, 93, 101,
    106n23, 107n24
National Federation of Independent
    Business (NFIB) v. Sebelius, 170–72
Native Americans, 22, 264–76
    crime on reservations of, 268, 277n15
    Faulkner and, 368–72
    and Japan, 372
    law and literature and, 40
    status of, in United States, 272
    violence against Native women,
        269–72, 278n24
Negri, Antonio, 39
Nelson, Deborah, 42
neoliberalism, 211, 219–20
networks, weak, 361–63, 372, 375
New Criticism, 1
New Historicism, 39, 41, 163–65

News from Scotland (pamphlet),
    193–95, 198–99
New York University (NYU), 202
New York v. United States, 171
Ngai, Mae, 240
Ngai, Sianne, 112–13
Nietzsche, Friedrich, 53, 70, 75
Nix v. Williams, 94, 98, 100
nonpersons, 253–54, 256
normativity, legal history and, 166–67
Northwestern University, 35
Norton, Thomas, and Thomas Sackville,
    Gorboduc, 152–55
Nuland, Sherwin, 134–35
Nussbaum, Martha, 7, 39, 47, 51, 52

Obama, Barack, 360
Obergefell v. Hodges, 123
obiter depicta, 179
obiter dicta, 176
obscenity, 41–42, 327, 330
Old Chief, Johnny Lynn, 101–2
Old Chief v. United States, 101–2, 106n23
Oliphant v. The Suquamish Indian
    Tribe, 267–69
Olivier, Laurence, 75, 82
Olson, Greta, 14
Oncale v. Sundowner Services, 133–34
originality, 328
ornament and clothing
    and the body, 245
    of Chinese female immigrants,
        234–42, 245–46
    law and, 237, 239–42,
        245–46, 250n26
    meanings of, 230–31
    moral decay linked to, 249n19
    personhood and, 230–31, 237–46
    race and, 230
Orphan Black (television series), 340
ostriches, 177, 180–85, 189–90
Ouologuem, Yambo, *Le Devoir de*
    violence, 331
Overhage, Carl, 328
Ovid, 187

Pacific Mail Ship Company, 232
Page Act, 234, 248n10
paranoid reading, 131–34, 136, 359
paranoid/schizoid position, 131, 136–40

Parke, James, 176
Parker, Robert Dale, 371
passionate utterance, 258–59, 261–62
patent abuse, 318
patents, biological, 332, 340, 345–50
paternalism, 272–73, 275
Patient Protection and Affordable Care
    Act, 170–72
patriarchy, 253–55
Peacham, Henry, 182
Peirce, C. S., 94, 105n9
People's Business Commission, 349
performance
    attitude of law toward, 206–7
    defining, 200–204
    identity formation and, 204
    interpretation as, 73, 76–77
    law as, 24, 64–65, 180,
        193–200, 204–7
    law in, 204–5
    law of, 205
    and personhood, 243–44
    as reproduction of past
        events, 205–6
    sources for scholarship on, 208n9
    substitution involved in, 206
    trials as, 199, 205–7
    of witchcraft, 194–95
performance studies, 200–202
performativity, 200, 203, 258–59
Perry, Imani, 21, 52–53
personhood, 19, 21, 229–46
    African Americans and, 53–54
    the body and, 239–41
    categories of, 241–42
    corporate, 315–17, 319, 323
    historicist renderings of, 49–56
    law and, 50–56
    legal, 230–31, 239, 241–42, 253
    literature and, 51–56
    natural, 230–31, 239, 243–45
    negative aspects of, 53
    and nonpersons, 253–54, 256
    ornament and, 230–31, 237–46
    patriarchy and, 254
    performance and, 243–44
    race and, 253–54
    reasonableness and, 52–53
    slavery and, 52–55, 239, 253
    women and, 230, 230–31

Peter of Spain, 150
Peters, Julie Stone, 6–7, 10, 14, 20, 155
    "Law, Literature, and the Vanishing
        Real," 33–34, 36, 46–49, 144–45,
        160, 168, 196–97
Phelan, Peggy, 200
Phelps, Teresa Godwin, 51–52
Philip, M. NourbeSe, *Zong!*, 216–18
Piotrowski, Rudolph, 231–32
plagiarism detection software, 339
Plautus, 149–50
plenary power, 267, 268, 272, 277n10
Plessy, Albion Homer, 40
Plessy v. Ferguson, 240
pluralism
    Aslam's *Maps for Lost Lovers*
        and, 285–91
    in interpretation, 74–77, 81, 86–87
    political, 280
    religious, 280–81
Plutarch, 157
Pocock, J. G. A., 162
political theory, 19, 163
Pollak, Louis, 96–97
Polloczek, Dieter, 43
polygamy, 299–300
polygyny, 300
Porsdam, Helle, 43
Posner, Richard, 36, 38, 61, 164, 177,
        181, 185–86
postcolonialism, 22–23, 43, 213–24
postcolonial studies, 210–11
    and the nature of law in global South,
        212–13, 219
    negative views of law in, 211–19
    positive views of law in, 212–14
postconviction petitions, 103
postcritique, 48–49
poststructuralism, 9, 19, 60, 200, 203
power
    gender and, 252–53
    varieties of, 130
    visual, 180
precedent
    pedagogical exercise in, 171
    visual imagery and, 176–81,
        184, 188–89
presentism, 167
presumptions of law, 321
Printz v. United States, 171

privacy, 42
probability, 150–55
probable cause, 98
proof, 150–51
property rights, 331, 349–50
prostitution, 126, 231, 235–36,
    247n5, 249n18

qualified immunity, 118
quantitative formalism, 338–39
queer legal studies, 123–41
    ". . . and others" sensibility in,
        128–31, 140–41
    Governance Feminism and, 140
    obstacles to, 123–24
    and paranoid reading, 131–34
    Sedgwick's influence on, 125–41
Quint, Leander, 233
Quintilian, 150–51

race
    the body and, 240
    Chinese and, 234–35
    law and literature and, 39–40
    and marriage, 300
    ornament and, 230
    personhood and, 253–54
    profiling based on, 239
    visibility of, 246
    See also critical race studies
Rainie, Lee, 362
Rancière, Jacques, 16
rape, 53, 103, 126, 269–73,
    275–76, 278n24
ratio decidendi, 176
Rawls, John, 290
Raz, Joseph, 69, 76, 86, 90n22
Read, Alan, 204
the real, 14, 34, 46–48, 144–46, 155–57,
    160, 168
realism, 42
reasonable fear, 117–20
reasonable force, 117–20
reasonableness
    affect and, 23–24, 112–20
    force and fear in relation to, 117–20
    as ideology, 113
    Ishiguro's *Remains of the Day*
        and, 113–16
    The Wire and, 116–18

reasonable person standard, 252–63
    Black women's literature as counter
        to, 257–62
    critique of, 253
    in economic perspective, 253–54
    features of, 252
    as legal fiction, 112
    legal personhood and, 253
    patriarchy and, 253–54
    unreasonableness associated
        with, 52–53
Rebouché, Rachel, 125
Rehnquist, William, 166, 267–68
Reichman, Ravit, 23–24
Reid, John, 169
Reiss, Timothy, 8
religion
    free expression of, 279–83, 290–91
    pluralism in, 280–81
renewable marriage, 301–3, 311n34
reparative action, 359, 362–75
reparative justice, 23, 48, 360–61
reparative reading, 48–49, 132–33
res gestae, 107n24
Resnik, Judith, 41, 188
retrospective prophecy, 97–104
Reynolds, Diamond, 120
rhetoric
    and argument construction, 150–52
    constitutive, 345–46
    and imagery, 179
    law and, 19, 34–35, 37, 92–93, 347
Rice Lake National Wildlife
    Refuge, 264–65
Ricoeur, Paul, 13, 131–32, 359
Riles, Annelise, 21
Rilke, Rainer Maria, 304
Ripa, Cesare, *Iconologia*, 184
Roach, Joseph, 204, 206
Roberts, John, 170–72
Roberts v. City of Boston, 240, 250n25
Robinson, Spider, "Melancholy
    Elephants," 330
Rodensky, Lisa, 42
Roe v. Wade, 345, 348
Romano, Giulio, *Iustitia*, 182–83, 184
Romanticism, 328–29, 331
Rome Statute, 126
Rorty, Richard, 258
Rose, Mark, 42, 329

Rosen, Rebecca J., 337
Rothman, David M., 350
Rushdie, Salman, *Midnight's Children*, 221
Rusk v. Maryland, 103
Russell Sage Foundation, 35
Russian Formalism, 100

Sade, Marquis de, 55
Şahin, Leyla, 282
Saint-Amour, Paul, 19–20
Sampson, Agnes, 193–95
Sarat, Austin, 14, 24, 34, 36, 47, 100
Sartre, Jean-Paul, 99, 161, 168
Sayre, Robert Woods, 371
Scalia, Antonin, 170
Schechner, Richard, 200, 201, 206
Schleiermacher, Friedrich, 72
Schmidgen, Wolfram, 42
Schmitt, Carl, 41, 43
Schneck, Peter, 43
Schor, Hilary, 42
Scott, Joan, 282
Scott, Ridley, 347, 351
search and seizure, 94, 98, 102
secularism, 282–83
Sedgwick, Eve, 13, 23, 48, 124–41, 359, 374
self-marriage, 304–5
Seneca, 149–50
"separate but equal" doctrine, 240
serio-ludere tradition, 179, 181
settler colonialism, 5, 21–22
Sex and the City (television series), 304–5
sexuality
    censorship and, 41–42
    ostriches and, 182–83
    pluralism in, 128–29
    Supreme Court decisions on sodomy and, 124–25
    in visual imagery used for judicial decision, 182–85
Shaftesbury, Anthony Ashley Cooper, third earl of, 208n20
Shakespeare, William, 19, 41, 147, 155–57
    Hamlet, 73, 75–77, 82, 295, 306–7
    Henry V, 147
    Macbeth, 197
    A Midsummer Night's Dream, 155–57

The Winter's Tale, 301–4
Shamir, Hila, 125
sharia, 286
Shaw, Lemuel, 240
Sidney, Philip, 152
Siegel, Reva, 171
Silbey, Susan, 63
Silko, Leslie Marmon, 40, 331
Sir Cloymon and Sir Clamydes (romance), 152–53
Slaughter, Joseph, 331
Slauter, Eric, 165
slavery
    imperialism and, 215–18
    personhood and, 52–55, 239, 253
    property issues involving, 349–50
Smith, Caleb, 13, 19, 21
Smith, Sidonie, and Kay Schaffer, *Human Rights and Narrated Lives*, 11
social sciences, 35–36
Socrates, 52
Soifer, Aviam, 40
Sotomayor, Sonia, 118–20, 121n4
Souter, David, 93, 101–2, 106n23, 107n24
sovereignty, 19, 163, 180, 267
Spillers, Hortense, 254, 256
Spivak, Gayatri Chakravorty, 10
Spoo, Robert, 330
Stacey, Robin Chapman, 204
"stand your ground" cases, 119
state, queer theory's view of, 123–24
statistics, 35
Staves, Susan, 42
Stefancic, Jean, 40
Steiner, Emily, 41
Sterling, Anne Fausto, 260
Stern, Simon, 5
Stevens, John Paul, 104
Stone, Geoffrey, 300–301
Stone, Martin Jay, 21
Story, Joseph, 35
Stowe, Harriet Beecher, 40, 51, 52
structures of feeling, 362
Stryk, Lucien, 374–75
Suggs, Jon-Christian, 39
Suk, Jeannie, 103, 311n34
    At Home in the Law, 5
Supreme Holy Council of the Muslim Community v. Bulgaria, 282, 284

suspicion
  hermeneutics of, 13, 18,
    30n63, 131–32
  of law, 13, 23
Syme, Holger Schott, 147–49, 155
symptomatic reading, 46–47, 56n2

Tacitus, 60, 61
Taylor, John, *Mad Fashions*, 186
Tee-Hit-Ton Indians v. United States, 272
Terence, 149–50
theater, as figure in legal discourse, 196
theatricality, 202, 203–4, 206–7
Thomas, Brook, 12, 18, 19, 28n26, 126
Thomas, Chantal, 125
three-strikes marriage, 297–98
Toffler, Alvin, 344–45, 351, 356
Tomkins, Silvan, 111, 136, 137
tone, as expression of self, 112–13
Tourgée, Albion W., 40
Trade and Intercourse Acts, 267
trafficking, 126–27, 249n18
trials, as performances, 199, 205–7
Trust for Civil Society in Central and
    Eastern Europe, 340
Turner, Henry, *The Corporate
    Commonwealth*, 11
Twain, Mark
  "The Great Republic's Peanut
    Stand," 330
  Puddn'head Wilson, 40

United Kingdom, politics and religion in,
    279–81, 283–91
United States v. Heath, 105n7
United States v. Llera Plaza, 96–97
universities, present status of, 2–3,
    48–49, 56
University of California, Berkeley, 35
University of Denver, 35
University of Wisconsin, 35
unnatural narrative, 321, 323
U.S. State Department, 363
U.S. v. Wheeler, 269
Utah v. Strieff, 121n4

Valeriano, Pierno, *Hieroglyphica*, 182, 183
Vanderham, Paul, 41
veil, 22, 243
vestibularity, 256

victim impact statements, 12, 29n43
Violence Against Women
    Reauthorization Act, 269
Visconsi, Elliott, 22
visiocracy, 180
visual imagery, 20, 176–91
  ad apparentiam, 179, 182–83,
    185–86, 188–89
  of Chinese female immigrants,
    234–42, 245–46
  flags, 180–82
  in *Gonzales-Servin*, 177, 180–81
  interpretation of, 179–91
  in judicial decisions, 178–81,
    184–86, 188–89
  legal doctrine and, 179
  legal norms and, 180
  legal power of, 180
  moral and religious valence of, 187
  of world gone mad, 185–86
Vizenor, Gerald, 372
  Hiroshima Bugi, 372
  Survivance, 264–65

Wald, Priscilla, 20
Walker, Alice, 257
Walter E. Meyer Foundation, 35
Ward, Ian, 11
Warner, William B., 41
Watt, Gary, 250n26
Webster, Noah, 201
Weisberg, Richard, 6, 36–38
Weisberg, Robert, 7–8, 12–14, 22, 34, 39,
    49, 164
Wellman, Barry, 362
Welsh, Alexander, 42
West, Robin, 27n20, 38, 167
White, James Boyd, 345–47
  The Legal Imagination, 6, 24, 33–37,
    60–61, 62, 144, 162
  When Words Lose Their Meaning, 38
Wiegman, Robyn, 49
Wigmore, John, 1, 37
Wilde, Oscar, 42, 50, 307
  The Picture of Dorian Gray, 330–31
Wilf, Steven, 165, 167
Wilkins, David, 267
Williams, Jeffrey J., 49
Williams, Patricia, 40, 112
Williams, Raymond, 362

Williams, Robert A., Jr., 266
Williams, Rowan, 280, 283
Williams, Timothy, 268
Wilson, Luke, 41, 164
The Wire (television series), 24, 116–18
Wiseman, Zipporah Batshaw, 41
witchcraft, 193–95, 197–98
Witt, John, 166
Wittgenstein, Ludwig, 69, 70, 86
Wolfe, Tom, *Charlotte Simmons*, 167
Woloch, Alex, 315, 317
Wong, Edlie, 54–55
Woodmansee, Martha, 42, 329
Woolf, Virginia, *A Room of One's Own*, 256–57

Worcester v. Georgia, 267
Wordsworth, William
    "A Plea for Authors, May 1838," 330
    "A Poet to His Grandchild," 330
"world gone mad" imagery, 185–86
Wynter, Sylvia, 262

Yale Journal of Law and the Humanities, 38
Yoshino, Kenji, 8, 12, 29n43, 62, 122n19, 146
    Covering, 242–45

Ziolkowski, Theodore, 42
Žižek, Slavoj, 39